AF522190

R. Gupta's®

POPULAR MASTER GUIDE

HTET

HARYANA TEACHER ELIGIBILITY TEST

LEVEL–3

Post Graduate Teacher (PGT)

COMMERCE

by

RPH Editorial Board

2026
EDITION

RAMESH PUBLISHING HOUSE, NEW DELHI

USEFUL BOOK FOR THIS EXAM

Haryana Teacher Eligibility Test (HTET)

(LEVEL-3) PGT–COMMERCE

Previous Years' Papers & Practice MCQs

(With Answers)

Book Code : R-2179 ○ Price : ₹ 210 ○ ISBN : 978-81-929420-2-5

Email : order@rameshpublishinghouse.com

Published by
O.P. Gupta *for* Ramesh Publishing House

Admin. Office
12-H, New Daryaganj Road, Opp. Officers' Mess,
New Delhi-110002 ✆ 23275224, 23245124

E-mail: info@rameshpublishinghouse.com
For Online Shopping: www.rameshpublishinghouse.com

Showroom
• Balaji Market, Nai Sarak, Delhi-110006 ✆ 23282525 📱 9354373464
• 4457, Nai Sarak, Delhi-110006

© Reserved with the Publisher

No Part of this book may be reproduced or transmitted in any form or by any means, electronic or mechanical including photocopying, recording or by any transformation storage and retrieval system without written permission from the Publisher.

Indemnification Clause: This book is being sold/distributed subject to the exclusive condition that neither the author nor the publishers, individually or collectively, shall be responsible to indemnify the buyer/user/possessor of this book beyond the selling price of this book for any reason under any circumstances. If you do not agree to it, please do not buy/accept/use/possess this book.

Book Code: R-1938

ISBN: 978-93-86845-75-7

Price: ₹ 480

Printed at: B.K. Offset, Delhi

CONTENTS

Scheme of Exam

Level-3: Post Graduate Teacher (PGT) Commerce.

S.No.	Subjects	No. of Questions	Marks
1.	Child Development and Pedagogy	30	30
2.	**Languages** (Hindi 15 MCQs and English 15 MCQs)	30	30
3.	**General Studies** (Quantitative Aptitude 10 MCQs, Reasoning Ability 10 MCQs and Haryana G.K. and Awareness 10 MCQs)	30	30
4.	Subject Specific (Commerce)	60	60
	Total	**150**	**150**

NATURE AND STANDARD OF QUESTIONS

- The test items on Child Development and Pedagogy will focus on educational psychology of teaching and learning relevant to the age group of 14-17 years. They will focus on understanding the characteristics, needs psychology of diverse learners, interaction with learners and the attributes and qualities of a good facilitator of learning.
- The test items for Languages (Hindi & English) will focus on the proficiencies related to the medium of instruction relevant to the age group of 14-17 years.
- The test items for Quantitative Aptitude, Reasoning Ability and Haryana G.K. and Awareness Language will focus on the elements of Mental and Reasoning ability and General Knowledge regarding Haryana State.
- The test items in subject specific will focus on the concepts, problem solving abilities and pedagogical understanding of these subjects.

NEGATIVE MARKING

- There shall be no negative marking.

LANGUAGE OF QUESTION PAPERS

- All questions except those concerning language subjects, will be bilingual *i.e.* Hindi and English.

Previous Years' Paper

Haryana Teacher Eligibility Test (HTET)

PGT Commerce (Level-3), Exam 2024

(Exam held on 30-07-2025)

PART-I : CHILD DEVELOPMENT AND PEDAGOGY

1. Which statement is ***incorrect*** about the development and its relationship with learning?
1. Deprivation of learning opportunities limits development.
2. Children can not learn until they are developmentally ready to learn.
3. Development is the product of maturation and learning.
4. Despite the limits of maturation the development can go beyond a certain point, when learning is encouraged.

2. Which one of the following is ***not*** a component of progressive education?
1. Discussion 2. Memorization
3. Experimentation 4. Interaction

3. Which of the following types of questions is **not** suitable for testing student's expression of feelings and logical thinking?
1. Analytical type
2. Critical type
3. Discussion type
4. Multiple option type

4. 'A disorder of writing ability in which a learner has difficulty with letter formation, spelling, fine motor co-ordination etc.' This disorder is called as:
1. Dyslexia 2. Dysgraphia
3. Dyspraxia 4. Dyscalculia

5. Which option is ***correct*** regarding emotions in early adolescence?
1. Intense and rational
2. Uncontrolled and rational
3. Uncontrolled and irrational
4. Controlled and intense

6. Select the ***correct*** sequence (top to bottom) of hierarchical intelligence theory of Vernon:
1. General factor → Specific factor → Major factor → Minor factor
2. Specific factor → General factor → Minor factor → Major factor
3. General factor → Major factor → Minor factor → Specific factor
4. Major factor → General factor → Specific factor → Minor factor

7. Arrange the steps of Bandura's social learning theory in sequence:

(*a*) Perception of behaviour
(*b*) Reinforcement of behaviour
(*c*) Remember of behaviour
(*d*) Convert the memory into action

Choose the ***correct*** code:
1. (*a*), (*c*), (*d*), (*b*) 2. (*b*), (*a*), (*c*), (*d*)
3. (*c*), (*d*), (*a*), (*b*) 4. (*b*), (*c*), (*d*), (*a*)

8. Which of the following is ***not*** an environmental factor affecting teaching-learning?
1. Learning material 2. Physical conditions
3. Recreational facilities 4. Maturation

9. Which of the following is ***not*** influenced by heredity?
1. Aptitude 2. Attitude
3. Emotions 4. Interest

10. When the assessment is designed to evaluate student's overall achievements and proficiency at the end of a learning period is known as:
1. Assessment of learning
2. Assessment for diagnosing
3. Assessment for learning
4. Assessment for remedy

1. 4	**2.** 2	**3.** 4	**4.** 2	**5.** 3	**6.** 3	**7.** 1	**8.** 4	**9.** 2	**10.** 1

11. According to McDougall, the emotion of 'disgust' is associated with which basic instinct?

1. Repulsion 2. Escape
3. Combat 4. Curiosity

12. Which of the following should ***not*** be a need of children with impairment from the point of view of inclusive education?

1. Need for coping with own's impairment
2. Need for proper guidance & counselling
3. Need for being dependent on others
4. Need for assistive equipments

13. Which constitutional right of children with special needs does inclusive education protect?

1. Right to Education 2. Right to Respect
3. Right to Acceptance 4. Right to Integration

14. Which of the following is ***not*** an acquired motive?

1. Affiliation 2. Achievement
3. Approval 4. Pain avoidance

15. Which of the following ways of instruction is suitable for hearing impaired children?

(*a*) Sign language (*b*) Finger spelling
(*c*) Lip reading (*d*) Cued speech

Choose the ***correct*** code:

1. (*a*) and (*c*) 2. (*a*), (*b*) and (*c*)
3. (*a*), (*c*) and (*d*) 4. (*a*), (*b*), (*c*) and (*d*)

16. According to Freud's psycho-sexual development theory, the stage in which adolescent attracts towards opposite sex, is known as:

1. Phallic stage 2. Anal stage
3. Genital stage 4. Latency stage

17. According to Piaget's cognitive development theory, when the learner maintaining a proper balance between himself/herself and his/her environment, this mechanism is called as:

1. Accommodation 2. Assimilation
3. Equilibration 4. Integration

18. Which of the following is ***not*** a characteristic of inclusive education?

1. It supports special educational needs
2. It says to celebrate diversity
3. This ensures the participation of teacher, parents, child and society
4. It is limited to the special education of disabled children

19. Which tests can be administered by the teacher to identify creative children?

(*a*) Figure construction test
(*b*) Product improvement test
(*c*) Usual uses test
(*d*) Picture completion test

Choose the ***correct*** code:

1. (*a*) and (*d*) 2. (*b*) and (*c*)
3. (*a*), (*b*) and (*d*) 4. (*a*), (*b*), (*c*) and (*d*)

20. Which of the following is ***not*** a helpful action of teacher in promoting socialization among children?

1. Giving the individual project work
2. Assigning social responsibilities
3. Organizing co-curricular activities
4. Motivating for social participation

21. Which of the following is ***not*** a child centered method of learning?

1. Demonstration
2. Field Trip
3. Programmed Instruction
4. Project

22. Which strategies of learning is **not** appropriate for the learner of senior secondary level?

1. Learning tasks at memory level
2. Allowing self-discovery of knowledge
3. Giving appropriate space to classroom interaction
4. Student centered teaching-learning

23. Which of the following statements regarding intelligence are ***not*** true?

(*a*) Intellectual development is influenced by genetics, not environment.
(*b*) Gender differences do not causes intellectual differences.
(*c*) Sharp intelligence is a sign of sharp memory.
(*d*) Intelligence gives the ability to adjust in new situations.

Choose the ***correct*** code:

1. (*a*) and (*b*) 2. (*a*) and (*c*)
3. (*b*) and (*d*) 4. (*c*) and (*d*)

24. Which of the following is **not** a feature of continuous and comprehensive evaluation?

1. Regularity of assessment
2. Frequency of unit tests
3. Diagnosis of learning gaps
4. Measuring only scholastic achievement

11. 1	**12.** 3	**13.** 1	**14.** 4	**15.** 4	**16.** 3	**17.** 3
18. 4	**19.** 4	**20.** 1	**21.** 1	**22.** 1	**23.** 2	**24.** 4

25. Which of the following is ***not*** an example of developmental changes under acquisition of new features?

1. Permanent teeth
2. Primary sex characteristics
3. Secondary sex characteristics
4. Thymus gland

26. Match the following stages of Kohlberg's moral development theory with their characteristics:

Moral Stages	**Characteristics**
(*a*) Conforming to obtain reward	(*i*) Getting the approval of others
(*b*) Maintaining social order	(*ii*) State based on self-interest
(*c*) Good interpersonal relationships	(*iii*) Eternal value accepted by conscience
(*d*) Universal ethical principles	(*iv*) Importance of justice and law

Choose the ***correct*** code:

	(*a*)	(*b*)	(*c*)	(*d*)
1.	(*ii*)	(*iv*)	(*i*)	(*iii*)
2.	(*iii*)	(*i*)	(*ii*)	(*iv*)
3.	(*iv*)	(*iii*)	(*i*)	(*ii*)
4.	(*i*)	(*ii*)	(*iv*)	(*iii*)

27. Which of the following statements is ***not*** correct regarding individual differences?

1. Individual differences exists in both cognitive and psychomotor domain.
2. Species characteristics influence individual differences.
3. The cause of individual differences is the social environment, not the physical environment.
4. Age also has an effect on individual differences.

28. In a learning situation presenting relevant facts separately from non-relevant facts, is indicative of which principle of learning?

1. Principle of multiple response
2. Principle of analogy
3. Principle of prepotency of elements
4. Principle of associative shifting

29. Which of the following is ***not*** a common characteristics of deprived children?

1. They look physically challenged
2. They are socially disadvantaged
3. They are economically deprived
4. They feel emotionally inferior

30. Which of the following gender biased actions are ***not*** to be involved in educational practices?

(*a*) Homogeneous grouping
(*b*) Gender neutral content
(*c*) Stereotyped occupation guidance
(*d*) Teacher's prejudiced attitude

Choose the ***correct*** code:

1. (*a*) and (*b*)
2. (*a*), (*c*) and (*d*)
3. (*c*) and (*d*)
4. (*a*), (*b*) and (*c*)

PART-II : भाषा - हिन्दी

निर्देश (प्रश्न संख्या 31-34): *निम्नलिखित गद्यांश को ध्यानपूर्वक पढ़कर नीचे दिये गये प्रश्नों के उत्तर दीजिए :*

नया निश्चय ही एक मूल्य है। पर निरंतरता भी एक मूल्य है। साहित्य दोनों में से एक को चुनने की हिमाकत सौभाग्य से नहीं करता है, क्योंकि वह जानता है कि एक के बिना दूसरा संभव नहीं है। परंपरा अपने को पुनर्नवा किए बिना सजीव नहीं रह सकती। मनुष्य दोनों आयामों में रहता है : इतिहास में और अनन्त में। वह बदलता है और फिर भी बना रहता है। दोनों आयाम मनुष्य के यहाँ अंतर्भुक्त हैं - वे अलग-थलग या विविक्ति नहीं होते। बहुत कुछ बदलता है : समाज, परिस्थितियाँ, आर्थिक व्यापार, मानव संबंध और उनके संगुंफन आदि पर प्रेम, ईर्ष्या, मोह-मत्सर, रोग-विराग, हर्ष-विषाद आदि वही बने रहते हैं। नयी दृष्टि होती है, तो अपने लिए अनवार्यतः नया शिल्प भी खोजती है। विश्लेषन के लिए भले हम कथ्य और शिल्प को अलग-थलग कर लेते हैं, पर रचना में वे अद्वैत हैं। नया अंततः निरंतरता में समाहित होकर अपनी वैधता पता है, पर वह निरंतरता में समाहित होकर अपनी वैधता पाता है, पर वह निरंतरता को कहीं न कहीं बदल भी देता है। निरंतरता नए के हस्तक्षेप और उसके समाहार के बाद वही नहीं रह जाती, जो पहले थी। हम यह भूल जाते हैं कि आज जो पुराना लगता है, वह कभी नया था। बिना समाकालीनता के कालातीत नहीं हुआ जा सकता, लेकिन सिर्फ समाकालीनता के बाड़े में बँचे रहकर भी कालाजीत नहीं हुआ जा सकता। नया समय को सीधे और उसके बदले हुए ब्योरों में पकड़ने के साहस से उपजता है, पर अगर वह समय के पार में देख पाये, तो टिकाऊ नहीं हो सकता। जो कालातीत है, वही हर समय नया होता चलता है।

31. साहित्य का अभीष्ट है:

1. मात्र नए को चुनना
2. मात्र निरंतरता को चुनना
3. नयेपन एवं निरंतरता दोनों को चुनना
4. मात्र समकालीन को चुनना

25. 4	**26.** 1	**27.** 3	**28.** 3	**29.** 1	**30.** 2	**31.** 3

32. निम्नलिखित में से कौन-सा कथन **सत्य** है?
1. मनुष्य की मूल प्रवृत्तियाँ समय के साथ परिवर्तनशील हैं।
2. मनुष्य का समाज समय के साथ परिवर्तनशील है।
3. मनुष्य मात्र इतिहास में जीता है।
4. निरंतरता सदैव अपरिवर्तनीय होती है।

33. कौन-सा कथन **असत्य** है?
1. साहित्य में दृष्टि का अवबोधन कथ्य से होता है।
2. नवीन कथ्य अपने लिए नवीन शिल्प भी लाता है।
3. कथ्य और शिल्प दोनों एक-दूसरे से स्वायत्त होते हैं।
4. साहित्यिक रचना में कथ्य और शिल्प परस्पर अनूस्यूत होते हैं।

34. नयापन टिकाऊ होता है:
1. जब वह समकालीन हो।
2. जब वह समकालीन भी हो और कालातीत भी।
3. जब उसमें चमत्कार हो।
4. जब वह परंपरा को बदलता हो।

35. समास की दृष्टि से **संगत** विकल्प चुनिए:
1. चक्षुश्रवा - इतरेतर द्वन्द्व
2. आपादमस्तक - बहुव्रीहि
3. जातिगत - अधिकरण तत्पुरुष
4. श्रमसाध्य - करण तत्पुरुष

36. वाक्य में प्रयुक्त क्रिया की दृष्टि से **असंगत** विकल्प का चयन कीजिए:
1. अध्यापिका छात्राओं को भूगोल पढ़ा रही है - द्विकर्मकक्रिया
2. निशीथ जोर-जोर-से हँस रहा है - अकर्मक क्रिया
3. मदारी अनेक करतब दिखलाकर बच्चों को ललचाता है - अकर्मक क्रिया
4. लड़-झगड़कर वह अपना हिस्सा ले ही मरा - रंजक क्रिया

37. निम्न में से **अशुद्ध** शब्द समूह का चयन कीजिए:
1. सीधा साधा, अठोतर, उहापोह
2. दाशरथि, स्थायित्य, विद्यार्थिपरिषद्
3. सुधीजन, प्रेयसी, निजीकरण
4. वेश्या, शशिभूषण, शक्तिीकरण

38. संधि की दृष्टि से **अनुपयुक्त** विकल्प चुनिए:
1. दैत्यारि, गत्यानुसार, अगन्याशय - यण् संधि
2. मिताहार, विकलांग, भूर्ध्व - दीर्घ संधि
3. दिग्विजय, अब्ज, वृहन्नेत्र - व्यंजन संधि
4. वयोवृद्ध, पुरोधा, प्रादुर्भूत - विसर्ग संधि

39. विलोम की दृष्टि से **असंगत** विकल्प चुनिए:
1. आकृष्ट - विकृष्ट
2. आह्वान - अनाह्वान
3. कलंकित - निष्कलंक
4. ऐहिक - पारलौकिक

40. वर्णों की ध्वनिगत विशेषताओं के संदर्भ में **असंगत** चुनिए:
1. उ - पश्च, संवृत, वृत्तमुखी
2. ऋ - अग्र, संवृत, वृत्तमुखी
3. अ - मध्य, ह्रस्व, उदासीन
4. आ - पश्च, विवृत, अवृत्तमुखी

41. प्रत्यय की दृष्टि से **संगत** विभाजन चुनिए:
1. मैथुन, शौच, राघव - 'अ' प्रत्यय
2. फिकैत, डकैत, लड़ैत - 'एत' प्रत्यय
3. नारदीय, स्थानीय, मानवीय - 'अनीय' प्रत्यय
4. कौशेय, सौजन्य, कौमार्य - 'एय' प्रत्यय

42. हिंदी अध्यापक की विशिष्ट विशेषताओं में सम्मिलित **नहीं** है:
1. साहित्य का ज्ञान
2. भाषा शिक्षण की विधियों का ज्ञान
3. हिंदी भाषा पर विशिष्ट अधिकार
4. शिक्षा तथा उपाधियाँ

43. किस विकल्प में उपसर्ग - विभाजन नियामानुसार है?
1. अपरिग्रह, अपरोक्ष, अपर्ण - 'अप' उपसर्ग
2. आरण्यक, आवश्यक, आधुनिक - 'आ' उपसर्ग
3. निःशुल्क, निष्पक्ष, निस्स्वार्थ - 'निस्' उपसर्ग
4. व्याधि, वीक्षण, व्यतिरेक - 'वी' उपसर्ग

44. किस विकल्प में सार्वनामिक विशेषण का प्रयोग **नहीं** हुआ है?
1. जिसने परिश्रम किया, वह सफल हो गया।
2. यह पुस्तक किससे मँगवाऊँ।
3. ऐसे व्यक्ति पर कभी विश्वास मत करो।
4. आपके घर से कल कोई नौकर आया था।

45. निम्नलिखित में से मौन वाचन का उद्देश्य **नहीं** है:
1. उचित लय और गति प्रदान करना।
2. स्वाध्याय की आदत विकसित करना।
3. तीव्र गति से पढ़ने का अभ्यास करना।
4. अर्थ ग्रहण कर उसका केन्द्रीय भाव समझना।

32. 2	**33.** 3	**34.** 2	**35.** 4	**36.** 3	**37.** 1	**38.** 1
39. 2	**40.** 2	**41.** 1	**42.** 4	**43.** 3	**44.** 1	**45.** 1

PART-II : LANGUAGE – ENGLISH

46. Choose the *correct* option:

Assertion A*:* The disadvantage of print material is that it lacks interaction and the use of audio-visual elements.

Assertion B*:* Print materials are not portable, not easily available and are not cost effective.

1. A is true; B is false
2. B is true; A is false
3. Both A & B are true
4. Both A & B are false

Direction: (Q. 47 to 56): *Read the following poem and answer the questions that follow:*

Mother, I am the one
you sent away
when the doctor told you
I would be
a girl – In the end they had to
give me an injection to kill me.
Before I died I heard
the traffic rushing outside, the monsoon
slush, the wind sulking through
your beloved Mumbai –
I could have clutched the neon blue
no one wanted –
No one wanted
To touch me – except later in the autopsy room
when they knew my mouth would not search
for anything – and my head could be measured
and bent cut apart.
I looked like a sliced pomegranate.
The fruit you never touched.
Mother, I am the one you sent away
When the doctor told you
I would be a girl – your second girl.
Afterwards, as soon as you could
you put on your grass – green sari –
the orange stems of the parijatak blossoms
glistened in your hair –
Afterwards
everyone smiled.
But now I ask you
to look for me, mother,
look for me because
I won't come to you in your dreams,
Look for me, mother, look
because I won't become a flower
I won't turn into a butterfly
And I am not a part of anyone's song.
Look, mother,
look for the place where you have sent me.
Look for the unspeakable.
for the place that can never be described.
Look for me, mother, because
this is what you have done.
Look for me, mother, because
this is not 'God's will'.
Look for me, mother
because I smell of formaldehyde –
I smell of formaldehyde
and still, I wish you would look
for me, mother.

47. Who does the girl address?

1. the doctor
2. the society
3. the father
4. the mother

48. In which city does the foeticide take place?

1. Delhi
2. Chennai
3. Mumbai
4. Pune

49. What does the killed infant smell of?

1. formaldehyde
2. parijatak
3. chlorine
4. slush

50. Who is "I" in the opening line?

1. the poet
2. the killed infant girl
3. mother
4. the doctor

51. Fill in the blank with the ***correct*** option:

According to the speaker the mother disliked ______.

1. oranges
2. parijatak blossoms
3. pomegranates
4. the grass-green sari

52. Find a word from the poem which means "post mortem":

1. formaldehyde
2. injection to kill
3. neon blue
4. autopsy

53. Why was the infant in the womb killed?

1. because it was defective
2. because the mother didn't want a second girl child
3. doctor's mistake
4. it was ugly

54. Which one of the following is used as a literary device in the poem for effectiveness?

1. repetition
2. climax
3. irony
4. metaphor

46. 1	**47.** 4	**48.** 3	**49.** 1	**50.** 2	**51.** 3	**52.** 4	**53.** 2	**54.** 1

55. Fill in the blank with the *correct* option:

"I looked like a sliced pomegranate" is an example of ______.

1. metaphor 2. an implied simile
3. irony 4. simile

56. Find the word in the poem which means "shone due to being wet".

1. glistened 2. sulking
3. clutched 4. blossom

57. Fill in the blank with the *correct* option:

Nesfield's grammar is an instance of ______ grammar.

1. universal 2. cognitive
3. descriptive 4. prescriptive

58. Fill in the blank with the *correct* option:

______ skill involves training the learner to listen for the English speech sounds including stress and intonation patterns.

1. listening
2. aural-oral
3. reading
4. writing

59. Fill in the blank with the **correct** option:

Teaching learners to discuss a poem in English in their native language is an instance of the use of ______.

1. evaluative comprehension
2. multilingual resources
3. pre-reading skills
4. first language acquisition

60. Fill in the blank with the *correct* option:

The two kinds of listening are ______.

1. active and passive
2. skimming and scanning
3. intensive and extensive
4. referential and inferential

PART-III : GENERAL STUDIES

Quantitative Aptitude, Reasoning Ability and GK & Awareness

61. A square and an equilateral triangle are inscribed in a cricle. If *a* and *b* denote the lengths of their sides respectively, then which of the following is **true**?

1. $2a^2 = 3b^2$
2. $3a^2 = 2b^2$
3. $a^2 = 3b^2$
4. $b^2 = 2a^2$

62. The surface areas of the two spheres are in the ratio 1 : 2. The ratio of their volumes is:

1. 1 : 2 2. $1 : \sqrt{2}$
3. $1 : 2\sqrt{2}$ 4. 1 : 4

63. Find the missing term in the following number series:

2, 9, 28, ?, 126, 217, 344

1. 37 2. 65
3. 91 4. 115

64. The volume of the metallic cylindrical pipe is 748 cm^3. Its length is 14 cm and its external radius is 9 cm. The thickness of pipe is equal to:

1. 0.25 cm 2. 0.5 cm
3. 1.0 cm 4. 1.5 cm

65. Line : Square :: Arc : ?

1. Ring 2. Sphere
3. Circle 4. Ball

66. Rekha walks 10 km straight and then turns right and walks 10 km. Then every time turning to her left, she walks 5, 15 and 15 km respectively. How far is she now from her starting point?

1. 20 km 2. 15 km
3. 10 km 4. 5 km

67. Next term of the following series is:

$\left(\frac{AG}{d}\right)^{6}, \left(\frac{GK}{g}\right)^{21}, \left(\frac{EO}{j}\right)^{45}, \left(\frac{GS}{n}\right)^{78}, ?$

1. $\left(\frac{IX}{p}\right)^{127}$ 2. $\left(\frac{IV}{q}\right)^{133}$
3. $\left(\frac{IW}{p}\right)^{120}$ 4. $\left(\frac{IX}{q}\right)^{127}$

68. A is father of C and D is son of B. E is brother of A. C is sister of D. How is B related to E?

1. Daughter 2. Sister-in-law
3. Mother 4. Husband

55. 4	**56.** 1	**57.** 4	**58.** 2	**59.** 2	**60.** 3	**61.** 2
62. 3	**63.** 2	**64.** 3	**65.** 3	**66.** 4	**67.** 3	**68.** 2

69. Five men P, Q, R, S and T read a newspaper. The one who reads first, gives it to R. The one who reads last, had taken from P. T was not the first or last to read. There were two readers between P and Q. Who reads the newspaper last?

1. Q 2. R
3. S 4. T

70. A, P, R, X, Y and Z are sitting in a row. Y and Z are in the centre and A and P are at the ends. R is sitting on the immediate left of A. Who is sitting on the immediate right of P?

1. X 2. Y
3. Z 4. R

71. If it was Saturday on 10th December, 2022, what will be the day on 8th December, 2024?

1. Saturday
2. Sunday
3. Monday
4. Tuesday

72. Find the next term of the following letter series: MONRO, JSKTL, GUHVI, DWEXF, ?

1. AYBZC 2. AZCYC
3. BYBYD 4. BZCZD

73. If $\tan\theta + \sec\theta = 4$, then the value of $\cos\theta$ is equal to:

1. $\frac{17}{8}$ 2. $\frac{8}{17}$
3. $\frac{15}{17}$ 4. $\frac{17}{15}$

74. What is the smallest number by which 2880 must be divided in order to make it a perfect square?

1. 2 2. 3
3. 4 4. 5

75. P began a business with ₹ 45,000 and Q joined with ₹ 30,000 after some time. If the profit at the end of the year were divided among them in the ratio 2 : 1, when did Q join?

1. after 3 months 2. after 4 months
3. after 5 months 4. after 6 months

76. If three numbers are in the ratio 3 : 2 : 5 such that the sum of their squares is equal to 1862, the middle number is equal to:

1. 7 2. 14
3. 21 4. 35

77. A, B and C together completed a work for ₹ 5,290. A and B together did $\frac{19}{23}$ of the whole work. Amount received by C in ₹ is equal to:

1. 920 2. 900
3. 880 4. 850

78. The difference between the compound interest and simple interest on a certain amount at 5% per annum for 2 years is ₹ 15. The principal amount is equal to:

1. 2,000 2. 4,000
3. 6,000 4. 8,000

79. The radius of a circular field, whose areas is equal to the sum of the area of the three circular fields having radii 8 m, 9 m and 12 m respectively, is equal to:

1. 16 m 2. 17 m
3. 18 m 4. 19 m

80. In a certain code language "sun shines brightly" is written as "ba lo sul", "houses are brightly lit" as "kado ula ari ba" and "light comes from sun" as "dopi kup lo nro". What code words are written for "sun" and "brightly" respectively?

1. sul, ba 2. sul, lo
3. ba, lo 4. lo, ba

81. Which of the following wild life sanctuaries is located in Shivalik hights?

1. Khaparwas Sanctuary
2. Bhindawas Sanctuary
3. Khol Hi-Raitan Sanctuary
4. Nahar Sanctuary

82. Which of the following was the theme State for the 37th Surajkund International Crafts Fair?

1. Madhya Pradesh
2. Rajasthan
3. Manipur
4. Gujarat

83. Who was the First Chairman of Haryana Public Service Commission?

1. Dalbir Singh 2. Darbari Lal Gupta
3. Bhim Singh 4. Manoj Pandey

84. Where the Indian Institute of Information Technology is being set-up?

1. Kilohad 2. Baraut
3. Pipali Khera 4. Rasulpura

69. 3	**70.** 1	**71.** 2	**72.** 1	**73.** 2	**74.** 4	**75.** 1	**76.** 2
77. 1	**78.** 3	**79.** 2	**80.** 4	**81.** 3	**82.** 4	**83.** 2	**84.** 1

85. Which of the following districts is ***not*** part of Rohtak division?

1. Jhajjar 2. Sonipat
3. Bhiwani 4. Rewari

86. The woman wrestler of Haryana who received the Arjuna Award of 2023?

1. Antim Panghal 2. Anshu Malik
3. Geetika Jakhar 4. Sakshi Malik

87. Read the following statements about Pehowa Inscription:

(*i*) The inscription was issued by a ruler of Gurjar Pratihar dynasty.

(*ii*) As per the inscription, Pehowa was a famous market of horse dealers.

Choose the **correct** code:

1. Only statement (*i*) is true.
2. Only statement (*ii*) is true.
3. Neither statement (*i*) nor statement (*ii*) is true.
4. Both the statements are true.

88. Who among the following did **not** serve as the Chief Secretary during the Chief Ministership of Manohar Lal Khattar?

1. S.C. Chaudhary 2. P.K. Gupta
3. Shakuntala Jakhu 4. Vijay Vardhan

89. Which of the following statements about Sir Chhotu Ram are ***correct***?

(*a*) He began his career as a Congress man.

(*b*) Later be joined Unionist Party.

(*c*) He was a Minister in the government of Undivided Punjab.

Choose the ***correct*** code:

1. Only statement (*b*) & (*c*) are correct.
2. Only statement (*a*) & (*c*) are correct.
3. Only statement (*a*) is correct.
4. Statement (*a*), (*b*) & (*c*) are correct.

90. Which of the following are **correctly** matched?

(*a*) Gujari Mahal – Hisar

(*b*) Aram-e-Kausar – Narnaul

(*c*) Tomb of Sheikh Tayyab – Jind

Choose the ***correct*** code:

1. (*a*) and (*c*) 2. (*a*) and (*b*)
3. (*b*) and (*c*) 4. (*a*), (*b*) and (*c*)

PART-IV : SUBJECT KNOWLEDGE—COMMERCE

Direction: *Answer the following questions by selecting* ***the most appropriate*** *option.*

91. According to R.N. Carter, "_____ is the science and art of recording correctly in the books of account all those business transactions that result in the transfer of money or money's worth."

1. Financial accounting 2. Book-keeping
3. Accounting 4. Accountancy

92. In sinking fund method of depreciation, the amount of depreciation:

1. Remains constant over years
2. Goes on increasing every year
3. Goes on decreasing every year
4. Fluctuates every year

93. What chart is used to identify the changes or the trend that exist in a series of data?

1. Line or Arithmetic chart
2. Pictograph
3. Pie chart
4. Bar graph

94. The difference in both balances (bank balance as per cash book and pass book) may not arise due to which of the following reasons?

1. Timings 2. Like and dislikes
3. Errors 4. Transactions

95. From the following particulars, calculate balance as per pass book for Verma Offset Ltd. :

(*i*) Balance as per cash book is ₹ 2,40,000.

(*ii*) Cheques issued but not presented in the bank amounts to ₹ 1,36,000.

(*iii*) Cheques deposited in bank but not yet cleared amounts to ₹ 90,000.

(*iv*) Bank charges amount of ₹ 300.

(*v*) Interest credited by bank amounts of ₹ 1,250.

1. ₹ 2,86,950 2. ₹ 3,77,250
3. ₹ 2,40,000 4. ₹ 3,52,500

96. The details pertaining to a company for the year 2022 are:

Current Ratio = 2.5 : 1; Liquid Ratio = 1.25 : 1; Inventory as on December 31, 2022 = ₹ 21 Lakh: and each of bank overdraft and pre-paid expenses is equal to zero.

Using these details find out the current liabilities of the company as on December 31, 2022:

1. ₹ 16,08,000 2. ₹ 16,80,000
3. ₹ 18,60,000 4. ₹ 28,88,000

85. 4	**86.** 1	**87.** 4	**88.** 1	**89.** 4	**90.** 2
91. 2	**92.** 1	**93.** 1	**94.** 2	**95.** 1	**96.** 2

97. How is interest on debentures typically treated in the financial statement of a company?

1. As on operating expenses
2. As a liability
3. As an asset
4. As a charge against the profits of the company

98. Which of the following is not exempted from GST?

1. Interest
2. Travelling expenses claimed by staff
3. Inter-State sale
4. Supply of sources to the government

99. Accounting for retirement benefits in the financial statement of employers comes under which Indian Accounting Standard?

1. AS-29 2. AS-25
3. AS-15 4. AS-12

100. The original cost of the asset is ₹ 2,50,000. The useful life of the asset is 10 years and net residual value is estimated to be ₹ 50,000.

Calculate the amount of depreciation to be charged every year:

1. ₹ 20,000 2. ₹ 25,000
3. ₹ 30,000 4. ₹ 18,000

101. A company has net profit margin of 5%, total assets of ₹ 90,00,000 and return on assets of 9%. Its total assets turnover ratio would be:

1. 1.6 2. 1.8
3. 1.7 4. 1.9

102. _____ is the amount received or receivable by the enterprise from its operating activities.

1. Profit 2. Income
3. Gain 4. Revenue

103. Proposed Dividend for the current year is shown under which heading?

1. Fictitious assets 2. Contingent liabilities
3. Long term liabilities 4. None of the above

104. Which source document is issued if a customer returns goods previously invoiced or the customer is allowed further discount?

1. Debit Note 2. Cash Voucher
3. Credit Voucher 4. Credit Note

105. Prince Ltd. wants to prepare its cash flow statement It sold equipment of book value of ₹ 60,000 at a gain of ₹ 8,000. The amount to be reported in its cash flow statements under activities is:

1. ₹ 8,000 2. Nil
3. ₹ 68,000 4. ₹ 60,000

106. Rama Ltd. forfeited 40 shares of ₹ 10 on which ₹ 7 were called and the shareholder had pair ₹ 5 of these, 30 shares were reissued @ ₹ 6 per share. The amount transferred to capital accumulation account will be:

1. ₹ 100 2. ₹ 30
3. ₹ 120 4. ₹ 170

107. Which of the following is *not* correct for provisions?

1. It is created for a known liability or expense pertaining to current accounting period, the amount of which is not certain.
2. It reduce taxable profits.
3. It is made for strengthening the financial position of the business. Some are also mandatory under law.
4. Charge against profit.

108. Reserve Capital is a part of which Capital in the event of winding up of a company?

1. Issued Capital 2. Authorized Capital
3. Paid-up Capital 4. Subscribed Capital

109. _____ are the customs, usage or practices followed by accountants as a guide in the preparation of financial statements.

1. Accounting principles 2. Accounting standards
3. Accounting concepts 4. Accounting conventions

110. A _____ gross profit ratio achieved by an organization compared to that of the industry's average, indicates the organization's successful attempt to produce at relatively lower costs.

1. low 2. moderate
3. high 4. positive

111. Which among the following is called the Principal Book of Accounts?

1. Cash-book 2. Ledger
3. Sales-books 4. Passbook

112. Old parents A, B and C's old profit sharing ratio is 3 : 2 : 1. D is admitted as new partner. It is agreed among the partners that new ratio between C and D will be same as between A and B. Further, relative ratio of A, B, and C will remain unchanged. What will be the new profit sharing ratio between A, B, C and D?

1. 3 : 2 : 1 : 1 2. 4 : 3 : 2 : 1
3. 9 : 6 : 3 : 2 4. 12 : 6 : 4 : 2

97. 4	**98.** 3	**99.** 3	**100.** 1	**101.** 2	**102.** 4	**103.** 2	**104.** 4
105. 3	**106.** 3	**107.** 3	**108.** 4	**109.** 4	**110.** 3	**111.** 2	**112.** 3

113. In case of dishonor of cheque, discount received, discount allowed, and cancellation of discount received or discount allowed are recorded through _____.

1. Journal Proper
2. Cash Book
3. Bank Account
4. None of the above

114. Which among the following accurately describes the role of Memorandum of Association in company formation?

1. It outlines the company's internal rules and regulations governing its management.
2. It acts as a charter of the company, defining its relationship with the external world and the scope of its activities.
3. It certifies the incorporation of the company, giving it legal existence.
4. It is a mandatory document required for acquiring a business license from local authorities.

115. A, B and C are the partners sharing profits in the ratio 7 : 5 : 4. C died on 30 June, 2022 and profits for the accounting year 2021-22 were ₹ 24,000. How much share in profit for the period 1 April, 2022 to 30 June, 2022 will be created to C's account?

1. ₹ 1,500
2. ₹ 6,000
3. ₹ 2,000
4. ₹ 2,500

116. Which of the following is ***not*** an objectives of Ratio Analysis?

1. Effective direction
2. Expressing trends
3. Showing changes
4. Inter-firm comparison

117. If any person furnishes any false or incorrect particulars of any information or suppresses any material information, of which he is aware in any of the documents filed with the Registrar in relation to the registration of a company, he shall be punishable for fraud under which Section?

1. Section 447 [Section 7(5)]
2. Section 457 [Section 7(5)]
3. Section 447 [Section 6(4)]
4. Section 457 [Section 6(4)]

118. Which of the following is ***not*** a key feature of a Computerized Accounting system?

1. Automated recording and classification of transactions
2. Real-time processing and reporting of financial data
3. Elimination of the need for internal control mechanism
4. Integration with other business processor like inventory

119. International Accounting Standard-29 is laid down for:

1. Financial reporting in hyper inflationary economics
2. Accounting for government grants and disclosure of environment assistance
3. Information reflecting the effect of changing prices
4. Interim financial reporting

120. Which ratio indicates proportion of owner's fund to total fund invested in the business?

1. Debt Equity Ratio
2. Equity Ratio
3. Debt Ratio
4. Net Profit Ratio

121. Which of the following statements is ***false*** regarding 'Partnership'?

1. It is not limited to a specific venture.
2. It is limited to a specific venture.
3. It is carried on under firm's name.
4. It is a continuing profit seeking enterprise.

122. Which one of the following is ***not*** a 'Single-Use Plan'?

1. Program
2. Projects
3. Budgets
4. Policy

123. The pricing strategy in which the company charges the same price plus freight to all customers, regardless of their location, is known as:

1. Homogenous basing-point pricing
2. Constant zone pricing
3. Dynamic pricing
4. Uniform-delivered pricing

124. Under Companies Act, 2013 which Section the Central Government empowered to direct a company, at any point of time to rectify its name if by inadvertence it has been registered with name which is identical to or too nearly resembles the name of an existing company whether registered under this Act or the previous company law?

1. Section 16
2. Section 18
3. Section 4
4. Section 1

125. A market-coverage strategy in which a firm goes after a larger share of one or a few segments is known as:

1. Differentiated marketing
2. Undifferentiated marketing
3. Niche marketing
4. Unconcentrated marketing

113. 1	**114.** 2	**115.** 1	**116.** 1	**117.** 1	**118.** 3	**119.** 1
120. 2	**121.** 2	**122.** 4	**123.** 4	**124.** 1	**125.** 3	

126. A sender's manipulation of information so that it will be seen more favourable by the receiver is known as:
1. Lying
2. Communication Apprehension
3. Information Overload
4. Filtering

127. As per expectancy theory 'the probability perceived by the individual that exerting a given amount of effort will lead to performance is called:
1. Effort-performance relationship
2. Performance-reward relationship
3. Rewards-personal goals relationship
4. Effort-reward relationship

128. An entrepreneur who likes innovation and enjoys working on something new or creative is known as:
1. Optimizers 2. Idealist
3. Analyst 4. Fire-ball

129. A runner-up firm that is fighting hard to increase its market share in an industry is called:
1. Market challenger 2. Market follower
3. Market leader 4. Market nicher

130. Which of the following is ***not*** an internal recruiting source?
1. Employee Referrals
2. Promotions
3. Employee Recommendations
4. Executive Search Firms

131. In the model of business buyer behaviour 'Product and service choice', comes under:
1. Buyer response 2. The buying organization
3. The environment 4. The situation

132. Henry Fayol was:
1. German Industrialist 2. French Industrialist
3. German Sociologist 4. Indian Sociologist

133. A leadership style marked by going beyond the leader's own self-interest and instead focusing on opportunities to help followers grow and develop is known as:
1. Servant leadership 2. Charismatic leadership
3. Socialized leadership 4. Situational leadership

134. In which business ethos principle practiced by Indian companies an individual is trained in such a way that avoids conflicts and friction?
1. Principle of 'Peace'
2. Principle of 'Non-violence'
3. Principle of 'Sacrifice'
4. Principle of 'Harmony'

135. In ADDIE model, 'A' stands for:
1. Appointment 2. Alertness
3. Analyze 4. Alternative

136. Which of the following is a 'Consumer' under Consumer Protection Act, 2019?
1. Who avails services for any commercial purposes.
2. Who avails services free of charges.
3. Who avail services under contract of service.
4. Who hire any service for a consideration which has been partly paid.

137. Face to face conversation is an example of:
1. Low channel richness
2. Medium channel richness
3. High channel richness
4. Facilitate power feedback

138. As per the Companies Act, 2013, public company may be formed for any lawful purpose by:
1. 7 or more persons 2. 5 or more persons
3. 3 or more persons 4. 2 or more persons

139. The interview in which candidates are asked to describe how they actually handle a given situation is known as:
1. Structured interview 2. Unstructured interview
3. Behavioural interview 4. Stress interview

140. The set of all product line and items that a particular seller offers for sale is known as:
1. Marketing Mix 2. Market Portfolio
3. Product Length 4. Product Mix

141. 'Capital budgeting' is which type of financial decision?
1. Investment Decision 2. Financing Decision
3. Dividend Decision 4. Marketing Decision

142. Under Consumer Protection Act, 2019 which Section empowers the Central Government to establish a Central Consumer Protection Authority to be known as the Central Authority to regulate matters relating to violation of rights of consumer?
1. Section 10 2. Section 11
3. Section 13 4. Section 16

143. The view that we can learn through both observation and direct experience is known as:
1. Equity-learning theory
2. Social-learning theory
3. Galatea effect of learning
4. Self-efficacy learning theory

126. 4	**127.** 1	**128.** 2	**129.** 1	**130.** 4	**131.** 1	**132.** 2	**133.** 1	**134.** 4
135. 3	**136.** 4	**137.** 3	**138.** 1	**139.** 3	**140.** 4	**141.** 1	**142.** 1	**143.** 2

144. The Paris Convention for the protection of Industrial Property was signed on:
1. 20 March, 2023 2. 20 March, 1883
3. 10 April, 1883 4. 10 April, 2023

145. Which one of the following is ***not*** a feature of Max Weber ideal bureaucracy?
1. Job specialization 2. Stability of Tenure
3. Formal Selection 4. Impersonality

146. Which one of the following is first step of selection process?
1. Initial screening
2. Completed application
3. Employment test
4. Background examination

147. Which international trade theory is usually formulated in terms of two-factor model?
1. Mercantilism
2. Theory of absolute advantage
3. Theory of comparative advantage
4. Hecksher-Ohlin theory

148. According to the Computerized Accounting System, which one of likes and dislikes these is ***not*** an example of non-master data?
1. Age 2. Like
3. Weight 4. Blood group

149. Which one of the following is ***not*** a characteristic of transactional leader?
1. Contingent Reward
2. Laissez-Faire
3. Inspirational Motivation
4. Management by Exception

150. A different approach determining the effectiveness of training is called:
1. Kirkpatrick's model
2. Centralized Training model
3. Brinkerhoff model
4. Karl Pearson model

EXPLANATORY ANSWERS

1. Development is always shaped by both maturation (biological readiness) and learning. While learning enriches and optimizes development, it cannot surpass the natural limits of maturation. For example, a child cannot learn abstract reasoning before the brain reaches the necessary stage of maturity. The statement suggests that learning can push development beyond these limits, which is incorrect. Maturation sets the boundaries, and learning works within those boundaries to actualize potential.

2. Progressive education, inspired by thinkers such as John Dewey, stresses experiential learning, problem-solving, interaction, and active participation. It values creativity, exploration, and critical thinking rather than passive recall. Memorization, which depends on rote learning, directly contradicts the spirit of progressive education because it focuses on repetition rather than true understanding.

3. Multiple option type questions (such as MCQs) are limited to recognition and recall of fixed choices. They do not allow students to freely express feelings, present complex reasoning, or construct arguments. In contrast, analytical, critical, and discussion-type questions give space for creativity, logical thinking, and personal expression. Therefore, multiple option type questions are unsuitable for testing these higher-order abilities.

4. Dysgraphia is a specific learning disorder related to writing ability. Learners with dysgraphia face problems in letter formation, poor spelling, and fine motor coordination. It is different from dyslexia (difficulty in reading), dyspraxia (difficulty in motor planning and coordination), and dyscalculia (difficulty in mathematical abilities).

5. In early adolescence, emotions are typically intense, unstable, and often expressed without rational control. Due to hormonal changes and ongoing brain development, adolescents may struggle with regulating emotions, leading to emotional volatility and irrational responses.

6. In Vernon's hierarchical theory of intelligence, at the top is the general factor (g), followed by two broad major group factors (verbal-educational and practical-mechanical), then narrower minor group factors, and finally specific factors at the bottom. This hierarchy shows the structured nature of intelligence from broadest to most specific.

7. According to Bandura's social learning theory, the correct order is—first, the learner perceives or observes the behaviour (*a*), then retains or remembers it (*c*), later converts this memory into action through imitation (*d*), and finally the behaviour is reinforced through rewards or consequences (*b*). This sequence shows how observation, memory, action, and reinforcement together shape learning.

8. Environmental factors influencing teaching-learning include learning materials, classroom conditions, and recreational facilities. Maturation, however, is a biological and hereditary factor, not an environmental one. It refers to the natural growth and readiness of the learner, independent of external surroundings.

9. Heredity strongly influences aptitude, emotional tendencies, and even certain interests through genetic predispositions. Attitude, however, is shaped by environment, culture, social interactions, and experiences rather than heredity. It reflects personal outlooks and values, which develop primarily through learning and socialization.

144. 2	**145.** 2	**146.** 1	**147.** 4	**148.** 4	**149.** 3	**150.** 1

10. This type of assessment is carried out at the end of a course or learning period to evaluate the learner's overall achievement, mastery of skills, and proficiency. It is summative in nature, aiming to measure learning outcomes against predefined standards or objectives.

11. According to William McDougall's theory of instincts and emotions, the emotion of disgust is directly linked to the instinct of repulsion. This instinct drives avoidance of harmful, unpleasant, or undesirable stimuli, ensuring protection and survival.

12. Inclusive education emphasizes empowering children with impairments by providing coping strategies, counselling, and assistive devices to support independence. Promoting dependency on others is contrary to inclusive principles, as the goal is to build self-reliance and equal participation in learning.

13. Inclusive education ensures that children with special needs enjoy the same constitutional right to education as other children. It guarantees access to schooling, equal opportunities, and participation in mainstream classrooms, thereby protecting their fundamental educational rights.

14. Acquired motives are learned through social interaction and experience, such as affiliation, achievement, and approval. Pain avoidance, however, is an innate or primary motive, biologically rooted in survival instincts, not acquired through learning.

15. For hearing-impaired children, multiple instructional methods are effective. These include sign language for full communication, finger spelling for letters and words, lip reading to interpret spoken language, and cued speech to clarify sounds. Using all these methods together best supports comprehensive learning and communication.

16. In Freud's psycho-sexual stages, the genital stage begins from adolescence onwards. At this stage, sexual interests are directed toward others, and adolescents experience attraction to the opposite sex. It signifies maturity of sexual instincts and development of adult relationships.

17. According to Piaget, equilibration is the process of maintaining balance between assimilation (fitting new information into existing schemas) and accommodation (modifying schemas to incorporate new information). It helps the learner achieve harmony between self and environment, driving cognitive growth.

18. Inclusive education is not confined only to children with disabilities. Instead, it embraces all learners by celebrating diversity, supporting special educational needs, and ensuring active participation of teachers, parents, peers, and the community. Limiting it to disability alone misrepresents its true scope.

19. All four tests—figure construction, product improvement, unusual uses, and picture completion—are widely recognized as effective measures of creativity. They form part of creative thinking assessments like the Torrance Tests of Creative Thinking (TTCT). These tests evaluate fluency of ideas, flexibility in thinking, originality in responses, and elaboration of concepts, making them suitable for teachers to identify creative children.

20. Socialization thrives on group interaction, cooperation, and shared responsibilities. Assigning individual project work emphasizes independence and self-reliance, which reduces opportunities for collaboration. By contrast, assigning social responsibilities, organizing co-curricular activities, and motivating children for social participation directly enhance peer bonding and group problem-solving, thus fostering socialization.

21. Demonstration is largely teacher-centered, as students watch while the teacher performs an activity. This restricts active engagement and exploration by learners. In contrast, child-centered methods like field trips, programmed instruction (which supports self-paced exploration), and project work actively involve learners, allowing them to construct knowledge through participation and experience.

22. At the senior secondary stage, learners are expected to engage in higher-order thinking, such as analysis, synthesis, critical evaluation, and application of concepts. Pure memory-level tasks are inadequate at this stage, as they do not challenge intellectual abilities or promote deeper understanding. Therefore, strategies focusing solely on rote memorization are not appropriate.

23. Statement (*a*) is not true because intellectual development is influenced by both genetics and environment; environment plays a significant role in shaping intellectual growth. Statement (*c*) is also incorrect since sharp intelligence does not necessarily indicate sharp memory—intelligence relates to reasoning, problem-solving, and adaptability, while memory is only one aspect of cognitive functioning. Statements (*b*) and (*d*) are true: gender does not create intellectual differences, and intelligence indeed helps in adjustment to new situations.

24. Continuous and Comprehensive Evaluation (CCE) emphasizes both scholastic (academic) and co-scholastic (skills, attitudes, values, creativity, participation) aspects. It involves regular and diagnostic assessment of overall growth. Limiting it only to scholastic achievement contradicts its comprehensive nature, making this option not a feature of CCE.

25. Developmental changes under acquisition of new features include permanent teeth (physical maturity), primary sex characteristics (organs directly related to reproduction), and secondary sex characteristics (features like facial hair, voice change, breast development). The thymus gland, however, does not represent acquisition of a new feature; it is an existing gland that gradually diminishes with age (involution), so it does not fall under this category.

26. • (*a*) Conforming to obtain reward → (*ii*) State based on self-interest: At this stage, children obey rules mainly for personal benefit or to gain rewards.
- (*b*) Maintaining social order → (*iv*) Importance of justice and law: At this stage, morality is guided by law, duty, and maintaining social system.
- (*c*) Good interpersonal relationships → (*i*) Getting the approval of others: Individuals seek acceptance and approval from peers and authority figures.
- (*d*) Universal ethical principles → (*iii*) Eternal value accepted by conscience: Moral reasoning is guided by universal principles of justice, equality, and human rights.

27. This is incorrect because individual differences arise due to both social and physical environments along with hereditary factors. Climate, nutrition, living conditions (physical environment), as well as family, culture, and peer

influences (social environment), all contribute. Limiting it to only social environment is therefore wrong.

28. This principle states that learners can focus on the significant elements of a task or situation while ignoring irrelevant details. Presenting relevant facts separately from non-relevant ones helps students concentrate on essential aspects, thereby improving understanding and learning efficiency.

29. Deprived children typically suffer from social disadvantage, economic deprivation, and emotional inferiority due to lack of resources, opportunities, or support. However, being physically challenged is not a common characteristic of deprivation—it relates to disability, not deprivation.

30. Gender-biased actions in education include homogeneous grouping (separating by gender), stereotyped occupational guidance (directing boys and girls into traditional roles), and teacher's prejudiced attitude. These practices reinforce inequality. On the other hand, gender-neutral content promotes equality, so it should be included in educational practices, not avoided.

31. गद्यांश में कहा गया है कि साहित्य केवल नया या केवल निरंतरता नहीं चुनता, बल्कि दोनों को साथ लेकर चलता है। परंपरा बिना नवीनता के जीवित नहीं रह सकती और नवीनता निरंतरता में समाहित होकर ही वैधता पाती है। अतः साहित्य का अभीष्ट नयेपन और निरंतरता दोनों का चयन करना है।

32. गद्यांश में स्पष्ट कहा गया है कि समाज, परिस्थितियाँ, आर्थिक व्यापार और मानव संबंध समय के साथ बदलते रहते हैं। जबकि मनुष्य की मूल प्रवृत्तियाँ (जैसे प्रेम, ईर्ष्या, मोह आदि) स्थिर रहती हैं। इसलिए सही कथन यही है कि समाज समय के साथ परिवर्तनशील है।

33. यह असत्य है क्योंकि गद्यांश में कहा गया है कि विश्लेषण के लिए कथ्य और शिल्प को अलग किया जा सकता है, लेकिन साहित्यिक रचना में वे अद्वैत और परस्पर अनुस्यूत रहते हैं। इसलिए कथ्य और शिल्प का स्वायत्त होना असत्य है।

34. गद्यांश में कहा गया है कि बिना समकालीनता के कालातीत नहीं हुआ जा सकता और केवल समकालीनता तक सीमित रहकर भी कालातीत नहीं हुआ जा सकता। नयापन तभी टिकाऊ होता है जब वह समय की वास्तविकता से जुड़ते हुए कालातीत दृष्टि भी प्रदान करे।

35. 'श्रमसाध्य' का विग्रह है - *श्रम से साध्य* (मेहनत से प्राप्त होने वाला)। यहाँ 'से' करण कारक है जिसका लोप हुआ है। यह करण तत्पुरुष समास की स्पष्ट पहचान है। अन्य विकल्पों में त्रुटि है - 'चक्षुश्रवा' करण तत्पुरुष/बहुव्रीहि है, 'आपादमस्तक' अव्ययीभाव है, और 'जातिगत' करण तत्पुरुष अधिक उपयुक्त है।

36. यह असंगत है क्योंकि 'ललचाता है' क्रिया सकर्मक है। इसका प्रभाव कर्म 'बच्चों को' पर पड़ता है। अन्य वाक्य संगत हैं - 'पढ़ा रही है' द्विकर्मक है, 'हँस रहा है' अकर्मक है, और 'मरना' रंजक क्रिया है।

37. 1. सीधा साधा, अठोतर, उहापोह : यहाँ ''अठोतर'' अशुद्ध है। सही शब्द ''अठहत्तर'' (78) या ''अठहत्तरवाँ'' होता है। बाकी शब्द ''सीधा साधा'' और ''उहापोह'' (दुविधा) शुद्ध हैं।

38. यह विकल्प अनुपयुक्त है। 'दैत्यारि' में *दीर्घ संधि* है (अ + अ = आ), 'गत्यानुसार' और 'अगन्याशय' में *यण् संधि* है। इसलिए पूरे समूह को 'यण् संधि' मानना गलत है। अन्य विकल्प सही हैं - 2 में दीर्घ संधि, 3 में व्यंजन संधि, और 4 में विसर्ग संधि है।

39. यह असंगत है क्योंकि 'आह्वान' (बुलाना) का मानक विलोम 'प्रत्याह्वान' या 'विसर्जन' माना जाता है। 'अनाह्वान' का अर्थ है 'न बुलाया गया', जो विरोधार्थी न होकर केवल निषेधार्थी है। अन्य युग्म -'आकृष्ट-विकृष्ट', 'कलंकित-निष्कलंक', और 'ऐहिक-पारलौकिक' - सही विलोम हैं।

40. यह असंगत है क्योंकि 'ऋ' स्वर *अग्र* और *संवृत* तो है, पर यह वृत्तमुखी (गोल होंठों से) नहीं है। गोल होंठों वाले स्वर केवल 'उ', 'ऊ', 'ओ', 'औ' आदि हैं। इसलिए 'ऋ' को वृत्तमुखी बताना गलत है। शेष विवरण - 'उ' (पश्च, संवृत, वृत्तमुखी), 'अ' (मध्य, ह्रस्व, उदासीन), 'आ' (पश्च, विवृत, अवृत्तमुखी)-सही हैं।

41. यह संगत है क्योंकि इन शब्दों में 'अ' (या मूल 'अण्') प्रत्यय का प्रयोग है। 'मैथुन' = मिथुना + अ, 'शौच' = शुचि + अ, 'राघव' = रघु + अ। ये भाववाचक या अपत्यवाचक संज्ञाएँ बनाते हैं। अन्य विभाजन गलत हैं - 'फिकैत, डकैत, लड़ैत' में 'ऐत' नहीं; 'नारदीय, स्थानीय, मानवीय' में 'ईय' प्रत्यय है, 'अनीय' नहीं; 'कौशेय, सौजन्य, कौमार्य' .में 'य' प्रत्यय है, 'एय' नहीं।

42. एक हिंदी अध्यापक की विशिष्ट विशेषताओं में साहित्य का गहरा ज्ञान, भाषा-शिक्षण की विधियों की समझ, और हिंदी भाषा पर विशेष अधिकार आते हैं। शिक्षा और उपाधियाँ केवल योग्यता का प्रमाण हैं, पर ये अध्यापक की विशिष्ट पेशेवर विशेषताओं में नहीं गिनी जातीं।

43. यहाँ उपसर्ग 'निस्' का प्रयोग नियमानुसार है। 'निः' + शुल्क = निःशुल्क, 'निः'+ पक्ष = निष्पक्ष, 'निस्' + स्वार्थ = निस्स्वार्थ। ध्वन्यात्मक नियमों के अनुसार 'निस्' उपसर्ग 'श' के पहले 'निः', 'प' के पहले 'नि', और 'स' के पहले 'निस्' रूप लेता है। अतः यह विकल्प सही है।

44. इस वाक्य में सार्वनामिक विशेषण का प्रयोग नहीं हुआ है। यहाँ 'जिसने' संबंधवाचक सर्वनाम और 'वह' निश्चयवाचक सर्वनाम हैं, जो संज्ञा के स्थान पर प्रयुक्त हुए हैं। वे किसी संज्ञा की विशेषता नहीं बता रहे। सार्वनामिक विशेषण तब होता है जब कोई सर्वनाम संज्ञा के पहले आकर उसे विशेषित करता है -

- यह पुस्तक - 'यह' पुस्तक की ओर संकेत करता है।
- ऐसे व्यक्ति - 'ऐसे' व्यक्ति की विशेषता बताता है।
- कोई नौकर - 'कोई' अनिश्चयवाचक सार्वनामिक विशेषण है।

अतः सही उत्तर विकल्प 1 है।

45. मौन वाचन का उद्देश्य अर्थ ग्रहण करना, केंद्रीय भाव समझना, और स्वाध्याय की आदत डालना है। परंतु इसमें उच्च स्वर से पढ़ने जैसी लय और गति प्रदान करना उद्देश्य नहीं होता। यह उद्देश्य मुखर वाचन का होता है।

46. Assertion A is correct because the limitation of print material is indeed that it lacks interactivity and cannot incorporate audio-visual elements, making it less engaging compared to digital resources. Assertion B is false because print materials *are* portable, widely available, and generally cost-effective compared to other instructional media. Therefore, only A is true.

47. The speaker directly addresses her mother throughout the poem, repeatedly saying "Look for me, mother."

48. The poem mentions "your beloved Mumbai," showing the foeticide occurs in Mumbai.

49. The infant explicitly says "I smell of formaldehyde," referring to the chemical used for preserving dead bodies.

50. The "I" is the unborn female child, who narrates her own killing through female foeticide.

51. The line "I looked like a sliced pomegranate. The fruit you never touched" shows the mother disliked pomegranates.

52. The word "autopsy room" in the poem directly refers to post-mortem examination.

53. The doctor told the mother it would be a girl, and since she was already the second girl child, the foetus was killed.

54. The poem repeatedly uses phrases like "Look for me, mother" for emphasis and emotional impact.

55. The line *"I looked like a sliced pomegranate"* is a simile because it directly compares the killed infant's body to a pomegranate using the word "like," which is the clear marker of a simile.

56. The line "the orange stems of the parijatak blossoms glistened in your hair" shows "glistened" means "shone due to being wet."

57. Nesfield's grammar belongs to the traditional prescriptive school, which sets rules of correctness and dictates how language should be used rather than how it is actually used.

58. The aural-oral skill trains learners to recognize English sounds, stress, rhythm, and intonation, forming the foundation for correct pronunciation and speech.

59. Allowing learners to discuss a poem in English using their native language utilizes multilingual resources, making comprehension easier and supporting language learning.

60. In language teaching, listening is mainly classified into intensive and extensive types. Intensive listening focuses on close, detailed listening for accuracy, pronunciation, or specific information, often in classroom practice. Extensive listening involves listening to longer or larger amounts of material, such as stories, songs, or lectures, to develop overall comprehension and fluency, usually outside the classroom or for enjoyment.

61. Square: $a = \sqrt{2}R \Rightarrow a^2 = 2R^2$
Equilateral triangle: $b = \sqrt{3}R \Rightarrow b^2 = 3R^2$
Thus, $3a^2 = 2b^2$.

62. Surface area ratio $= 1 : 2 \Rightarrow r_1 : r_2 = 1 : \sqrt{2}$
Volume ratio $= r_1^3 : r_2^3 = 1 : \sqrt{(2)^3} = 1 : 2\sqrt{2}$.

63. Series follows $n^3 + 1$:
$1^3 + 1 = 2,\ 2^3 + 1 = 9,$
$3^3 + 1 = 28,\ 4^3 + 1 = 65,$
$5^3 + 1 = 126.$
Missing term = 65.

64. Volume $V = \pi(R^2 - r^2)L,$
$R = 9,\ r = 9 - t,\ L = 14$
$\pi \cdot 14(81-(9-t)^2) = 748$
$\Rightarrow \pi \cdot 14(18t - t^2) = 748$
Using $\pi = 22/7$:
$44(18t - t^2) = 748 \Rightarrow 18t - t^2 = 17$
$t^2 - 18t + 17 = 0$

$$\Rightarrow t = \frac{18 \pm 16}{2} = 17,\ 1 \Rightarrow t = 1 \text{ cm.}$$

65. Line : Square (completed form) :: Arc : Circle (completed curve).

66. Path (take North as $+y$):
$(0, 0) \xrightarrow{10N} (0, 10) \xrightarrow{\text{right } 10E} (10, 10)$
Left turns: $+5N \to (10, 15),\ +15W \to (-5, 15),\ +15S \to (-5, 0)$
Distance from start: $\sqrt{(-5)^2 + 0^2} = 5$ km.

67. Second letter: G(7), K(11), O(15), S(19), W(23) $\Rightarrow$ +4 each $\to$ needs W.
First letter: A(1), G(7), E(5), G(7), I(9) $\to$ fits option IW.
Middle letter: *d, g, j, m, p* $\Rightarrow$ +3 each.
Numbers: 6, 21, 45, 78, 120 (diffs +15, +24, +33, +42).

68. A is father of C; C is sister of D $\Rightarrow$ A and B are parents of C & D.
E is A's brother $\Rightarrow$ B is E's sister-in-law.

69. Order: First $\to$ gives to R $\Rightarrow$ R is 2nd. Last took from P $\Rightarrow$ P is 4th.
Two between P and Q $\Rightarrow$ Q is 1st. Remaining {S, T} at {3, 5}; T not first/last $\Rightarrow$ T = 3, S = 5 (last).

70. Seats: Y, Z in centers (3, 4); A, P at ends $\to$ A at 6 (since R is left of A) $\Rightarrow$ R at 5, P at 1, remaining X at 2 $\Rightarrow$ right of P is X.

71. 10-Dec-2022 (Sat) $\to$ +365 days = 10-Dec-2023 (Sun) $\to$ +364 days = 8-Dec-2024 (Sun).

72. AYBZC : By position:
1st: M $\to$ J $\to$ G $\to$ D (−3) $\Rightarrow$ A;
2nd: O $\to$ S(+4) $\to$ U(+2) $\to$ W(+2) $\to$ Y(+2);
3rd: N $\to$ K $\to$ H $\to$ E (−3) $\Rightarrow$ B;
4th: R $\to$ T $\to$ V $\to$ X(+2) $\Rightarrow$ Z;
5th: O $\to$ L $\to$ I $\to$ F (−3) $\Rightarrow$ C.

73. Given $\tan\theta + \sec\theta = 4$. Then $\sec\theta - \tan\theta = 1/4$.
Add: $2\sec\theta = 4 + 1/4 = 17/4$
$\Rightarrow \sec\theta = 17/8 \Rightarrow \cos\theta = 8/17$.

74. $2880 = 2^6 \cdot 3^2 \cdot 5$. For a perfect square, exponents must be even $\Rightarrow$ remove the lone 5.
Smallest divisor = 5.

75. P : 45000 × 12, Q : 30000 × t, ratio 2 : 1.

$$\frac{45000 \cdot 12}{3000 \cdot t} = \frac{2}{1} \Rightarrow \frac{18}{t} = 2 \Rightarrow t = 9 \text{ months invested}$$

$\Rightarrow$ joined after 12 − 9 = 3 months.

76. Let numbers $= 3k, 2k, 5k$.
$(3k)^2 + (2k)^2 + (5k)^2 = 1862$
$\Rightarrow 9k^2 + 4k^2 + 25k^2 = 38k^2 = 1862$

$$\Rightarrow k^2 = \frac{1862}{38} = 49 \Rightarrow k = 7.$$

Middle number $= 2k = 14$.

77. A + B = 19/23 of work $\Rightarrow$ C = 4/23.
Share of C = 4/23 × 5290 = 4 × 230 = 920.

78. For 2 years, $CI - SI = P\left(\frac{r}{100}\right)^2$

$$\text{Given: } 15 = P\left(\frac{5}{100}\right)^2 = P \cdot \frac{25}{10000} = \frac{P}{400}$$

$\Rightarrow P = 15 \times 400 = 6000$.

79. We need the radius of a circular field whose area equals the combined areas of three smaller circular fields (radii 8 m, 9 m, and 12 m).

Formula: $\pi R^2 = \pi(r_1^2 + r_2^2 + r_3^2)$
Cancelling π: $R^2 = r_1^2 + r_2^2 + r_3^2$
Substitute values: $R^2 = 8^2 + 9^2 + 12^2$
$= 64 + 81 + 144 = 289$
$R = \sqrt{289} = 17$ m

So, the radius of the larger field is 17 m.

80. We must decode the words from the code language:
1. sun shines brightly → ba lo sul
2. houses are brightly lit → kado ula ari ba
3. light comes from sun → dopi kup lo nro

Step 1: Find brightly
- Common word in (1) & (2) = brightly
- Common code in (1) & (2) = ba

brightly = ba

Step 2: Find sun
- Common word in (1) & (3) = sun
- Common code in (1) & (3) = lo

sun = lo

Thus, the code for sun = lo and brightly = ba.

81. The question asks which sanctuary is in the Shivalik hills (outer Himalayas).
- **Khol Hi-Raitan Sanctuary** → Panchkula district, Haryana; located in the Shivalik range ✓
- **Khaparwas Sanctuary** → Jhajjar district, Haryana; a wetland, not in Shivaliks ✗
- **Bhindawas Sanctuary** → Jhajjar district, Haryana; a bird sanctuary in plains ✗
- **Nahar Sanctuary** → Rewari district, Haryana plains ✗

Therefore, the correct answer is Khol Hi-Raitan Sanctuary.

82. The theme state for the 37th Surajkund International Crafts Fair (February 2024) was Gujarat. The state displayed its handicrafts, folk music, tribal art, and rich heritage. Such fairs give artisans a platform to present regional culture at an international level. Gujarat's stalls attracted wide attention for their embroidery, beadwork, and traditional dance forms.

83. After Haryana was carved out from Punjab on 1st November 1966, the Haryana Public Service Commission (HPSC) was established. The very first chairman of the HPSC was Darbari Lal Gupta. He played a key role in setting up the administrative structure for recruitment in the new state. His appointment ensured smooth functioning of the state's selection process.

84. The Indian Institute of Information Technology (IIIT), Sonepat is being set up at Kilohad village in the Sonepat district of Haryana. This institution is established under the Public-Private Partnership (PPP) model. It has been declared an Institute of National Importance by the Government of India. Its aim is to promote excellence in information technology and allied studies.

85. The Rohtak Division of Haryana comprises five districts: Rohtak, Jhajjar, Sonipat, Charkhi Dadri, and Bhiwani. These districts are grouped for better administrative management. Rewari, however, is not included in Rohtak Division. Instead, Rewari falls under the Gurugram Division of Haryana.

86. The woman wrestler from Haryana who received the Arjuna Award for 2023 is Antim Panghal. She was honoured in January 2024 for her historic sporting achievements. Antim became the first Indian woman to win two consecutive U-20 World Wrestling Championship gold medals. Her award highlights Haryana's dominance in the field of wrestling.

87. The Pehowa Inscription belongs to the reign of the Gurjar-Pratihara king Mahendrapala I (c. 885–910 CE). It clearly confirms that it was issued under the Gurjar-Pratihar dynasty, making statement (*i*) true. The inscription also mentions Prithudaka (ancient Pehowa) as a bustling horse market, where dealers from different places gathered and made donations to the temple. Hence, statement (*ii*) is also true.

88. Manohar Lal Khattar became CM of Haryana in October 2014. At that time, Shakuntala Jakhu was Chief Secretary (July–Nov 2014), followed by P.K. Gupta (Nov–Dec 2014) and later Vijay Vardhan (2020–2021). S.C. Chaudhary's tenure (2013–July 2014) ended before Khattar assumed office, so he never served as Chief Secretary under Khattar.

89. Sir Chhotu Ram began his career in the Congress Party in 1916, later resigning in 1920. He co-founded and joined the Unionist Party in 1923–24, which became his primary political base. He also served as a minister in the Government of Undivided Punjab, handling Agriculture, Education, and Development portfolios. Therefore, all three statements are correct.

90.
- **Gujari Mahal – Hisar:** Built by Firoz Shah Tughlaq in Hisar for his beloved Gujari, this is correct.
- **Aram-e-Kausar – Narnaul:** A Mughal-era garden palace complex in Narnaul, also correct.
- **Tomb of Sheikh Tayyab – Jind:** Incorrect, since it is located in Kaithal, not Jind.

Thus, only (*a*) and (*b*) are correctly matched.

91. According to R.N. Carter, book-keeping is defined as "the science and art of recording correctly in the books of account all those business transactions that result in the transfer of money or money's worth." It focuses primarily on the systematic and chronological recording of monetary transactions, forming the foundation of accounting.

92. In the sinking fund method, a fixed amount is charged as depreciation every year throughout the asset's useful life. This fixed annual charge is invested outside the business to accumulate a fund (with interest) sufficient to replace the asset at the end of its useful life. Although the total fund value increases due to the interest earned, the depreciation expense recorded in the books remains uniform each year.

93. A line or arithmetic chart is used to depict trends and changes over time in a data series. By connecting plotted data points with straight lines, it clearly shows upward or downward movements, making it ideal for analyzing patterns or tendencies over a period.

94. Differences between balances as per the cash book and passbook usually arise due to timing differences (e.g., cheques not cleared), errors, or unrecorded transactions—not because of subjective reasons like "likes and dislikes." Hence, this option is not a valid cause.

95. To find the balance as per Pass Book, the following adjustments are made to the Cash Book balance:

Given data: Balance as per Cash Book = ₹ 2,40,000
Cheques issued but not presented = ₹ 1,36,000
Cheques deposited but not yet cleared = ₹ 90,000

Bank charges = ₹ 300; Interest credited by bank = ₹ 1,250
Calculation: Balance as per Cash Book = ₹ 2,40,000
Add: Cheques issued but not presented = +₹ 1,36,000
Add: Interest credited by bank = +₹ 1,250
Less: Cheques deposited but not yet cleared = –₹ 90,000
Less: Bank charges = –₹ 300
Balance as per Pass Book = ₹ 2,86,950
Therefore, Balance as per Pass Book = ₹ 2,86,950.

96. Current Ratio = CA/CL = 2.5 : 1
⇒ CA = 2.5 × CL
Liquid Ratio = (CA – Inventory)/CL
= 1.25 : 1
Inventory = ₹ 21,00,000;
Bank overdraft = 0; Prepaid = 0
Calculation:
(CA – Inventory)/CL = 1.25
⇒ (2.5CL – 21,00,000)/CL = 1.25
2.5 – 21,00,000/CL = 1.25
⇒ 1.25 = 21,00,000/CL
⇒ CL = ₹ 21,00,000/1.25 = ₹ 16,80,000.

97. Debenture interest is a finance cost debited to the Profit & Loss Account; it's a prior charge on profits (accrued unpaid portion also shown as a liability).

98. Interest on loans is exempt; staff travel reimbursements (in course of employment) are outside GST; certain services to government can be exempt. Inter-State sales are taxable (IGST), hence not exempt.

99. Employee/retirement benefits are accounted for as per AS-15 (Employee Benefits).

100. Straight-line depreciation = (Cost – Residual)/Life
= (₹ 2,50,000 – ₹ 50,000)/10
= ₹ 2,00,000/10 = ₹ 20,000 per year.

101. Return on Assets (ROA) = Net Profit Margin × Total Assets Turnover Ratio
⇒ 9% = 5% × Total Assets Turnover
Total Assets Turnover = 9 ÷ 5 = 1.8 times

102. Revenue refers to the total amount received or receivable by an enterprise from its operating activities like sale of goods or services before deducting any expenses.

103. A Proposed Dividend for the current year is only a recommendation by the Board of Directors and becomes a binding liability only after it is approved by shareholders at the Annual General Meeting (AGM). Until that approval, the company has no present obligation to pay; hence, it is not recognized as a liability in the balance sheet.

According to Ind AS 10 (Events after the Reporting Period) and the Companies Act, 2013 (Schedule III), such proposed dividends are disclosed in the Notes to Accounts under Contingent Liabilities and Commitments, as their payment depends on shareholder approval.

104. A Credit Note is issued by the seller to a customer when the latter returns goods previously sold or when an additional discount or correction of an overcharge is allowed. It signifies that the customer's account is being credited (reduced) by the seller because the amount receivable from the customer has decreased.

Common scenarios include:

- **Sales returns (return inwards):** Goods returned by the customer.
- **Allowance or correction:** When a discount or billing correction is made post-invoice.

Conversely, the buyer issues a Debit Note when returning goods to the seller.

105. Sale proceeds reported under Investing Activities
= Book value + Gain = ₹ 60,000 + ₹ 8,000 = ₹ 68,000.
(Note: The ₹ 8,000 gain is deducted from profit in Operating Activities under the indirect method, but the cash inflow shown under Investing is the full ₹ 68,000.)

106. Given: 40 shares forfeited (₹ 10 each), ₹ 7 called, ₹ 5 paid; 30 of these reissued @ ₹ 6.
Total forfeiture (40 shares) = 40 × ₹ 5 = ₹ 200
Forfeiture related to 30 reissued shares = ₹ 200 × 30/40 = ₹ 150
Discount on reissue = 30 × (₹ 7 – ₹ 6) = ₹ 30
Transfer to Capital Accumulation (Capital Reserve)
= ₹ 150 – ₹ 30 = ₹ 120.

107. This statement is incorrect for provisions because it actually describes reserves. Provisions are created to meet known liabilities or anticipated losses, the amount or timing of which is uncertain—for example, Provision for Tax, Provision for Doubtful Debts, or Provision for Depreciation. They are a charge against profit (reduce profits and taxable income) and are made to ensure a true and fair view of financial statements under the prudence principle. In contrast, reserves are appropriations of profit created after profit determination (do not reduce taxable profit) to strengthen the financial position of a business, meet future contingencies, or comply with statutory requirements (like Statutory Reserve). Hence, this option is not correct for provisions.

108. Reserve Capital is that part of the uncalled capital of a company which can be called up only in the event of winding up. It is created by passing a special resolution under Section 65 of the Companies Act, 2013. It forms part of the subscribed capital, since it is subscribed by shareholders but remains uncalled during the company's normal existence. Thus, Reserve Capital is a portion of Subscribed Capital, not issued or paid-up capital.

109. Accounting conventions are the customs, usages, and practices traditionally followed by accountants while preparing financial statements—e.g., consistency, conservatism, full disclosure, and materiality.

110. A high gross profit ratio compared to the industry average shows that the organization is producing goods at relatively lower costs, demonstrating efficiency in production and cost control.

111. The Ledger is known as the Principal Book of Accounts because it serves as the central record into which all transactions from the subsidiary books (like the cash book, sales book, purchase book, etc.) are ultimately posted. Each account—such as assets, liabilities, income, and expenses—has a separate ledger page. The ledger provides a complete summary of all financial transactions of the business and is the foundation for preparing the trial balance and final accounts (Trading, Profit & Loss Account, and Balance Sheet).

112. Old ratio of A, B, and C = 3 : 2 : 1.
It is given that the new ratio between C and D will be the same as that between A and B, i.e., 3 : 2. The relative ratio among A, B, and C will remain unchanged.

Let D's share = x.

Then, according to the ratio, C's share = $(3/2)x$.

Since A : B : C = 3 : 2 : 1,

we can multiply each term by C's equivalent (1 part = $(3/2)x$):

$$A = 3 \times (3/2)x = (9/2)x$$
$$B = 2 \times (3/2)x = 3x$$
$$C = (3/2)x;\ D = x$$

Multiply the entire ratio by 2 to remove fractions:

A : B : C : D = 9 : 6 : 3 : 2.

Thus, the new profit-sharing ratio is 9 : 6 : 3 : 2.

113. The Journal Proper (also called the General Journal) is used to record those transactions that do not find a place in any other subsidiary book. Entries such as dishonour of cheques, discount allowed or received, and cancellations of such discounts are adjustment entries that are not part of the day-to-day cash or credit records. Therefore, these are passed through the Journal Proper to ensure proper accounting treatment and accuracy in the ledger posting.

114. The Memorandum of Association (MOA) is the foundation document for the incorporation of a company. It defines the scope of the company's operations, its objectives, and its relationship with the external world. It serves as the company's charter, beyond which it cannot act; any act done outside the powers defined in the memorandum is considered ultra vires (beyond authority) and hence void. The MOA contains essential clauses like the Name Clause, Registered Office Clause, Object Clause, Liability Clause, Capital Clause, and Association Clause, all of which collectively determine the company's legal identity and authority.

115. A, B, and C share profits in the ratio 7 : 5 : 4.

C dies on 30 June 2022. The profit for the year ending 31 March 2022 is ₹ 24,000.

The share of profit for C up to the date of death (1 April to 30 June = 3 months) is calculated on a time basis assuming profits accrue evenly throughout the year.

$$\text{Profit for 3 months} = 24,000 \times \frac{3}{12} = ₹\ 6,000$$

$$\text{C's share} = \frac{4}{(7+5+4)} \times 6,000$$

$$= \frac{4}{16} \times 6,000 = ₹\ 1,500$$

Hence, the share of profit credited to C's account up to the date of death is ₹ 1,500.

116. The objective of Ratio Analysis is to interpret financial data by establishing meaningful relationships among various accounting figures. It helps in expressing trends, showing changes in financial position, and making inter-firm comparisons to assess efficiency and performance. However, effective direction is not an objective of ratio analysis—it is a function of management, not an analytical purpose. Ratio analysis aids management decisions but does not itself provide direction.

117. According to the Companies Act, 2013, if any person furnishes false or incorrect particulars or suppresses material information in documents filed with the Registrar for company registration, it is treated as fraud under Section 447, as referenced in Section 7(5). Section 447 defines punishment for fraud — imprisonment ranging from six months to ten years, and fine which may extend to three times the amount involved in the fraud. Section 7(5) specifically applies this provision to false or misleading filings made during company incorporation.

118. A Computerized Accounting System (CAS) automates the process of recording, classifying, summarizing, and reporting financial transactions. It provides real-time processing, data accuracy, and integration with other business processes such as inventory and payroll. However, it does not eliminate the need for internal control. On the contrary, internal controls become even more essential in a computerized environment to prevent data manipulation, unauthorized access, and fraud. Therefore, this option is not a feature of CAS.

119. IAS 29 (International Accounting Standard 29) deals with Financial Reporting in Hyperinflationary Economies. It provides guidelines for restating financial statements to reflect the impact of hyperinflation where the general price level changes drastically and rapidly. The standard ensures that the financial information presented remains useful and comparable by adjusting non-monetary items, equity, and income statements to reflect current purchasing power.

120. The Equity Ratio indicates the proportion of owner's funds (shareholders' equity) to the total funds (total assets or total capital employed) of the business.

$$\text{Equity Ratio} = \frac{\text{Shareholders' Funds}}{\text{Total Assets or Total Capital}}$$

A higher equity ratio signifies greater financial stability, as it reflects that a larger portion of assets is financed by owners rather than borrowed funds. Hence, it shows the proportion of owner's fund to total fund invested in the business.

121. This statement is false regarding a general partnership. A partnership is an ongoing business relationship formed by two or more persons agreeing to share profits from a business carried on by all or any of them acting for all (as per Section 4 of the Indian Partnership Act, 1932). It is a continuing profit-seeking enterprise conducted under a firm's name, not restricted to a single project. A partnership limited to a specific venture is a particular partnership, which is only one form—not the general nature—of partnership.

122. A policy is a standing plan, not a single-use plan. Standing plans guide recurring or repetitive actions (e.g., credit policy, HR policy). In contrast, single-use plans such as programs, projects, and budgets are developed for one-time situations or specific objectives and are discontinued after use. Hence, policy does not fall under the category of single-use plans.

123. In uniform-delivered pricing, the seller charges the same price including freight to all customers regardless of their geographical location. It means that customers near the factory pay the same total price as those far away, though actual shipping costs differ. The company averages freight costs and adds them uniformly to the base price, making pricing simple and competitive nationwide.

124. Under Section 16 of the Companies Act, 2013, the Central Government has the power to direct a company to rectify its name if it has been registered by inadvertence or mistake with a name identical or too nearly resembling that of an existing company. The company must then change its name within three months from the direction issued. This provision ensures avoidance of confusion and protection of existing company identities.

125. Niche marketing is a market-coverage strategy in which a firm focuses on serving a specific segment or sub-segment of the market and aims to capture a larger share within that narrowly defined niche. Instead of spreading resources across multiple segments, the firm specializes in understanding the unique needs of this smaller customer group and provides tailored products or services, gaining strong brand loyalty and profitability within that niche.

126. Filtering refers to the deliberate modification or manipulation of information by the sender so that it appears more favourable or acceptable to the receiver. It occurs when an individual distorts, omits, or adjusts information to influence perception or outcome. For instance, a subordinate might present only positive aspects of a report to a manager to maintain a good image. This selective communication reduces transparency and can lead to poor decision-making within organizations.

127. According to Vroom's Expectancy Theory of Motivation, the effort–performance relationship is the perceived probability that putting in a specific amount of effort will result in achieving a particular level of performance. This expectation depends on factors such as self-confidence, skills, training, and past experiences. If an employee believes that higher effort will yield better performance, motivation increases. Thus, this link forms the first stage in the expectancy model, connecting effort → performance → reward → satisfaction.

128. An idealist entrepreneur is one who is driven by creativity, innovation, and the desire to develop something new or original. Such individuals derive satisfaction from the process of creating rather than merely from financial gain. They are visionary, imaginative, and motivated by personal fulfilment, social contribution, or the pursuit of excellence in their work. These entrepreneurs often introduce novel ideas, products, or artistic ventures that stand out for their uniqueness.

129. A market challenger is the second-ranking or runner-up firm in an industry that competes aggressively to increase its market share and challenge the dominance of the market leader. Unlike followers, challengers take proactive steps—such as price reductions, product innovations, improved distribution, and promotional campaigns—to attract customers. For example, Pepsi often acts as a market challenger to Coca-Cola in the beverage industry. Their objective is not just survival but leadership displacement or significant share capture.

130. Executive search firms (or headhunters) are external recruiting agencies, not internal sources. They specialize in finding and recruiting highly qualified candidates for senior-level or specialized positions. Internal recruiting sources, by contrast, include employee referrals, promotions, and internal recommendations, all of which fill vacancies from within the organization. Therefore, executive search firms represent an external source of recruitment rather than an internal one.

131. In the Model of Business Buyer Behaviour, as proposed by Philip Kotler, the buying process is influenced by environmental factors, organizational characteristics, and buyer-specific elements. The model culminates in buyer responses, which include product and service choice, supplier selection, purchase timing, and purchase quantity. Thus, "Product and Service Choice" is classified as a buyer response, representing the final decision outcomes made after evaluating internal and external factors.

132. Henri Fayol (1841–1925) was a French industrialist and management theorist, often called the Father of Modern Management Theory. As a mining engineer and later managing director of a large French mining company, he developed 14 Principles of Management and identified five key managerial functions—Planning, Organizing, Commanding, Coordinating, and Controlling. His systematic approach laid the foundation for classical management theory and remains influential in modern organizational practices.

133. Servant Leadership, a concept popularized by Robert K. Greenleaf, emphasizes serving others first—particularly employees—before personal or organizational goals. A servant leader prioritizes the growth, development, and well-being of followers, helping them reach their potential. This leadership style transcends self-interest, focusing instead on empathy, humility, stewardship, and community building. The result is a positive organizational culture marked by trust, collaboration, and high morale.

134. In Indian business ethos, the Principle of Harmony teaches individuals to work cooperatively and avoid unnecessary conflicts or friction in organizational relationships. It promotes balance among personal goals, social responsibility, and organizational objectives. Rooted in Indian philosophical thought, it emphasizes unity in diversity, peaceful coexistence, and collective welfare. By following this principle, businesses foster long-term sustainability, mutual respect, and ethical decision-making.

135. In the ADDIE Model of Instructional Design, the letter A stands for Analyze. The ADDIE model consists of five sequential phases—Analyze, Design, Develop, Implement, and Evaluate. In the Analyze phase, learning needs, audience characteristics, goals, and performance gaps are assessed.

This step ensures that training or instructional content is aligned with organizational objectives and learner requirements, forming the foundation for all subsequent stages of course or training development.

136. Under the Consumer Protection Act, 2019, a consumer is a person who buys goods or hires/avails any service for a consideration—whether such consideration is paid, partly paid, or promised to be paid. The consideration may be in the form of cash, cheque, credit, or deferred payment. However, individuals availing services for commercial purposes, free of charge, or under a contract of service are not considered consumers. Therefore, a person who hires any service for a consideration that has been partly paid qualifies as a consumer under the Act.

137. Face-to-face communication is considered as the best form of communication channel because it allows for the exchange of multiple cues simultaneously—such as words, tone, facial expressions, and body language. It also enables instant feedback and clarification, reducing chances of misunderstanding. This makes it ideal for complex, emotional, or sensitive conversations requiring high levels of interaction and empathy.

138. As per Section 3(1)(a) of the Companies Act, 2013, a public company may be formed by seven or more persons for any lawful purpose by subscribing their names to a memorandum of association and complying with registration requirements. The Act further defines that there is no maximum limit on the number of members in a public company, unlike a private company which requires only two members and restricts its maximum to 200.

139. A Behavioural Interview focuses on how candidates have handled real-life situations in the past as an indicator of their future performance. Candidates are asked to describe specific incidents, challenges, or decisions from their experience—for example, "Tell me about a time when you resolved a workplace conflict." This technique is based on the belief that past behaviour is the best predictor of future behaviour, making it highly effective for evaluating competencies, attitude, and problem-solving skills.

140. The Product Mix (also known as the Product Assortment) refers to the entire range of product lines and items that a seller offers for sale. It includes four dimensions—width (number of product lines), length (total number of items), depth (varieties within each line), and consistency (how closely related the product lines are). For example, a company like Hindustan Unilever Limited (HUL) has a wide product mix covering soaps, detergents, food products, and cosmetics.

141. Capital Budgeting refers to the long-term investment decision process where a company evaluates and selects projects or assets expected to generate returns over multiple years. It involves assessing potential investments such as new machinery, expansion, product development, or acquisitions. The goal is to allocate financial resources efficiently to maximize shareholder wealth. Tools like Net Present Value (NPV), Internal Rate of Return (IRR), and Payback Period are commonly used in capital budgeting analysis.

142. Under the Consumer Protection Act, 2019, Section 10 empowers the Central Government to establish the Central Consumer Protection Authority (CCPA), known as the Central Authority. This body regulates matters relating to violation of consumer rights, unfair trade practices, and false or misleading advertisements. The CCPA has the authority to investigate complaints, recall unsafe goods, impose penalties, and ensure the protection, promotion, and enforcement of consumers' rights across India.

143. The Social Learning Theory, developed by Albert Bandura, states that individuals learn not only through direct experience but also by observing others' behaviour and its consequences. This theory integrates both cognitive and behavioural learning principles, emphasizing the importance of modeling, imitation, and reinforcement. People acquire new skills or behaviours by watching role models (such as leaders, peers, or mentors) and reproducing their actions when those behaviours are rewarded or socially accepted.

144. The Paris Convention for the Protection of Industrial Property was signed on 20 March 1883. It was one of the first international treaties aimed at protecting intellectual property rights such as patents, trademarks, industrial designs, and trade names. The convention established principles like national treatment and right of priority, promoting cooperation among member countries. It is administered today by the World Intellectual Property Organization (WIPO).

145. In Max Weber's Ideal Bureaucracy, the key features include job specialization, formal selection, hierarchy of authority, rules and procedures, and impersonality. The concept of stability of tenure (associated with Henri Fayol's management principles, not Weber's bureaucracy) is therefore not a feature of Weber's model. Weber's focus was on efficiency through structure, authority, and rational-legal systems rather than employee retention or tenure security.

146. The selection process begins with initial screening, where applicants' basic qualifications, experience, and suitability for the job are reviewed. This stage filters out candidates who do not meet the minimum eligibility criteria or essential requirements. It ensures that only those who match the fundamental specifications proceed to further steps such as completing applications, tests, and interviews, saving both time and resources for the organization.

147. The Heckscher–Ohlin Theory of international trade, developed by Eli Heckscher and Bertil Ohlin, is formulated in terms of a two-factor model—labour and capital. It explains that countries export goods that intensively use their abundant factor of production and import goods requiring factors that are relatively scarce domestically. For instance, a labour-abundant country exports labour-intensive goods, while a capital-abundant country exports capital-intensive goods, emphasizing comparative advantage based on factor endowments.

148. In a Computerized Accounting System (CAS), data is categorized as master data or non-master (transactional) data.

- Master Data refers to relatively permanent information that rarely changes, such as an employee's name, date of birth, or blood group. It forms the foundation for reference across multiple transactions.
- Non-Master Data (or transactional data) changes frequently and includes details like age, weight, and likes/dislikes, which vary over time or with activity.

Since a blood group is a fixed biological characteristic that remains constant throughout life, it is classified as master data, not non-master data.

Hence, Blood Group is not an example of non-master data.

149. A transactional leader focuses on maintaining normal operations through rewards and punishments, emphasizing structure, performance standards, and short-term tasks. Its key characteristics include Contingent Reward, Management by Exception, and occasionally Laissez-Faire elements. In contrast, Inspirational Motivation is a feature of transformational leadership, where leaders inspire and motivate employees with a compelling vision, enthusiasm, and shared goals. Thus, it does not belong to transactional leadership.

150. The Kirkpatrick Model is a globally recognized framework for evaluating the effectiveness of training programs. Developed by Donald Kirkpatrick, it assesses training across four sequential levels, each offering deeper insights into the impact of learning interventions:

1. Reaction – Measures participants' satisfaction and engagement with the training (how they felt about it).
2. Learning – Evaluates the knowledge, skills, or attitudes participants have gained as a result of the training.
3. Behaviour – Assesses how effectively participants apply the newly learned skills or knowledge in their actual work environment.
4. Results – Examines the final outcomes or business impact, such as improved productivity, quality, or profitability.

This model provides a comprehensive and systematic approach to determining training effectiveness, making it one of the most widely used methods in both corporate and educational settings.

Previous Years' Paper

Haryana Teacher Eligibility Test (HTET)

PGT Commerce (Level-3), Exam 2023

(Exam held on 02-12-2023)

PART-I : CHILD DEVELOPMENT AND PEDAGOGY

1. Which type of education would be appropriate for socially deprived children?
A. Informal education
B. Special education
C. Inclusive education
D. Religious education

2. Which of the following statement is **correct** regarding adolescence, under Erikson's Psycho-social development theory?
A. Ego-identity is a positive psycho-social aspect.
B. Ego-identity is a negative psycho-social aspect.
C. Ego-identity is a neutral psycho-social aspect.
D. Ego-identity is not just a psycho-social aspect.

3. Which of the following characteristic is **not** seen in a creative child?
A. Divergent thinking
B. Extreme curiosity
C. High imaginations
D. Conventional thoughts

4. Which of the following characteristics does **not** have a positive effect on the process of socialisation?
A. Socially approved behaviour
B. Playing approved social roles
C. Development of social attitude
D. Development of social prejudices

5. Vygotsky's 'Zone of Proximal Development' refers to:
A. What the child can do independently
B. What the child can't do independently
C. What the child can do with guidance of knowledgeable person
D. What the child can't do even under guidance of knowledgeable person

6. If a learner does **not** achieved the expected performance, what type of testing is done to find out the reason?
A. Formative
B. Diagnostic
C. Remedial
D. Summative

7. "Inclusion is not confined to the disabled but it also mean no exclusion of any child".

This meaning of inclusion in education has been clarified by:
A. NCF 2005
B. NCERT
C. UNESCO
D. UNICEF

8. Which type of changes occur in growth and development?
(*a*) Change in body size
(*b*) Change in body proportion
(*c*) Disappearance of old features
(*d*) Acquisition of new features

Choose the **correct** code:
Code:
A. (*a*), (*b*) & (*c*)
B. (*a*), (*b*) & (*d*)
C. (*a*), (*c*) & (*d*)
D. (*a*), (*b*), (*c*) & (*d*)

9. Which of the following statements does **not** explain the positive impact of motivation on learning?
A. Motivation impairs learning behaviour
B. Motivation provide definite direction to learning behaviour
C. Motivation energizes learning behaviour
D. Motivation makes learning

1. C **2.** A **3.** D **4.** D **5.** C **6.** B **7.** A **8.** D **9.** A

10. Match the stages of morality with their level, under the Moral Development theory of Kohlberg:

Stages of Morality	Level of Morality
(*a*) Good interpersonal relations	I
(*b*) Individualism and exchange	II
(*c*) Social contracts and individual rights	III
(*d*) Universal principles	

Choose the **correct** code:

Code:

	(*a*)	(*b*)	(*c*)	(*d*)
A.	I	III	II	I
B.	III	II	III	I
C.	II	III	I	II
D.	II	I	III	III

11. When the learner learns a task automatically, without any desire or purpose, then it is called:

A. Massed learning B. Whole learning
C. Part learning D. Incidental learning

12. Which of the following statement is **not** true regarding biological motives?

A. They are universal
B. They are inborn
C. They are essential to survival
D. They are not related to the homeostasis of the individual

13. Which of the following examinations are the basis of continuous and comprehensive evaluation?

(*a*) Written
(*b*) Oral
(*c*) Behavioural
(*d*) Practical

Choose the **correct** code:

Code:

A. (*a*), (*b*) & (*d*)
B. (*a*), (*b*) & (*c*)
C. (*a*), (*c*) & (*d*)
D. (*a*), (*b*), (*c*) & (*d*)

14. Which of the following statement is **not** correct in reference to intelligence tests?

A. Alexander's Pass along test is a performance test.
B. Verbal test can be either individual or group.
C. Illiterate people cannot do performance test.
D. In non-verbal tests intelligence is measured through pictures and figures.

15. Which of the following pair is not correct regarding elements of intelligence and their dimensional under the Three Dimensional Intelligence theory of Guilford?

Elements of Intelligence	Dimension
A. Unit	Product
B. Cognition	Operation
C. Evaluation	Operation
D. Relations	Content

16. Which one of the following is **not** a key feature of child centred learning approach?

A. Meaningful learning opportunities
B. Single learning pathway
C. Continuous assessment
D. Accessible learning settings

17. According to Bandura, which is **not** the interrelated processes of observational learning?

A. Attentional Processes
B. Retentional Processes
C. Motivational Processes
D. Combinational Processes

18. According to Bandura's Social Learning theory, what is it called when a person learns the same behaviour by observing and repeating the behaviour of others?

A. Adaptation B. Self-observation
C. Modeling D. Efficacy expectation

19. Which sub-component is **not** included in componential intelligence under the Sternberg Triarchic Theory?

A. Meta component
B. Experimental component
C. Performance component
D. Knowledge acquisition component

20. A learning disability that affects the acquisition of arithmetical skill is:

A. Dyscalculia B. Dysgraphia
C. Dyslexia D. Dysmagnisia

21. Choose the **correct** sequence of the five stages of Freud's Psychosexual development theory:

A. Oral stage → Phallic stage → Latency stage → Anal stage → Genital stage
B. Anal stage → Latency stage → Phallic stage → Genital stage → Oral stage
C. Oral stage → Anal stage → Phallic stage → Latency stage → Genital stage
D. Latency stage → Anal stage → Oral stage → Genital stage → Phallic stage

10. D **11.** D **12.** D **13.** D **14.** C **15.** D **16.** B **17.** D **18.** C **19.** B
20. A **21.** C

22. According to Pavlov's Classical Conditioning theory of learning, which temporal sequence presentation of natural and conditioned stimuli will most affect learning?
A. Simultaneous B. Delay
C. Trace D. Backward

23. In which stage of Piaget's Cognitive Development theory does the ability of abstract thinking and generalization develop?
A. Sensory motor
B. Pre-operational
C. Concrete-operational
D. Formal operational

24. Which of the following educational arrangements shouldn't be made for talented students?
A. Opportunities for independent project work
B. Acceleration
C. Remedial teaching
D. Enrichment program

25. Which one of the following is **not** a principle of inclusive education?
A. Principle of segregation
B. Principle of cooperation
C. Principle of celebrating diversity
D. Principle of right to education

26. Which of the following way does **not** support the teaching according to individual differences?
A. Large group of students
B. Individualized instruction
C. Curriculum adaptation
D. Knowledge of student's abilities

27. Which is **not** a role of educational institutions in addressing the needs of children with special need?
A. Admission to school without discrimination
B. Provide accessible infrastructural facilities
C. Identify their special needs and exclude them from mainstreaming
D. Provide necessary support services

28. Which of the following statement is **not** correct in context of development?
A. Development is the product of maturation and learning.
B. Later development is more critical than early development.
C. Development proceeds from head to foot.
D. Development proceeds from central axis to extremities.

29. The three dimensional model of the inclusive education propounded by whom?
A. Griffith, Cooper and Ringlaben
B. Gartuer and Lipsky
C. Kauffman and Hallahan
D. Levenski, Davis and Hooper

30. "Socialization means attaining of maturity in social relationships". This definition of socialization is given by whom?
A. John Dewey B. Garret
C. Sorenson D. Hurlock

PART-II : भाषा - हिन्दी

31. विशेषण के संबंध में कौन-सा सही सुमेलित **नहीं** है?
A. भारतीय - संज्ञा से निर्मित विशेषण
B. पवित्रतम - विशेषण की उत्तरावस्था
C. गरिश्मी - गुणवाचक विशेषण
D. आलस्य - विशेषण से निर्मित भाववाचक संज्ञा

32. किस विकल्प में शब्द-युग्म का सही अर्थ भेद **नहीं** है?
A. बाजी - दाव, वाजी - घोड़ा
B. मेध - हवन, मेघ - बादल
C. माणिक्य - चर्बी, माणिक्या - मछली
D. मुक्ता - मोती, मुक्ति - मोक्ष

33. कौन-सा युग्म संगत **नहीं** है?
A. भिक्षुक - तत्सम शब्द
B. मस्तक - तद्भव शब्द
C. खिचड़ी - देशज शब्द
D. अमानत - विदेशज शब्द

34. निम्नलिखित में से किस विकल्प का शब्द संधि-विच्छेद की दृष्टि से **संगत** है?
A. कुशासन = कुश + असन
B. वार्तालाप = वार्ता + अलाप
C. ज्ञानकीश = जनक + ईश
D. लघूर्मि = लघु + ऊर्मि

22. B	**23.** D	**24.** C	**25.** A	**26.** A	**27.** C	**28.** B	**29.** A	**30.** D	**31.** B
32. C	**33.** B	**34.** D							

35. किस विकल्प के समस्त पद में बहुव्रीहि समास का उदाहरण **नहीं** है?

A. शेषशायी, क्षपानाथ B. दीर्घश्वास, पाषाणहृदय

C. आशुतोष, मंदोदरी D. पंचशर, पशुपति

36. किस विकल्प का शब्द 'अन्' उपसर्ग से निर्मित **नहीं** है?

A. अनंतर B. अनीति

C. अनिष्ट D. अनाचार

37. निम्न में से किस विकल्प के शब्द विदेशज प्रत्ययों से निर्मित हैं?

A. पल्लवित, नीलिमा B. अड़ियल, कसावट

C. रिश्वतखोर, रोजगार D. झगड़ालू, हठीला

38. पर्यायवाची शब्दों के संबंध में कौन-सा विकल्प **अनुचित** है?

A. चन्द्रमा - हिमकर, अमृतांशु, महताब

B. गरुड़ - खगनाथ, वृषभी, भद्रा

C. चन्दन - गोरोचन, मलयज, सर्पावास

D. गंगा - अमरतटिनी, अद्रिजा, सुरसरि

39. वार्तनिक दृष्टि से किस विकल्प के सभी शब्द **शुद्ध** हैं?

A. अभ्यार्थी, त्योहार B. याज्ञवल्क्य, हस्तक्षेप

C. मैथली, अहिल्या D. वैदेहि, वापिस

40. 'महात्मा <u>गाँधी</u> ने <u>भारत</u> को आजाद कराया।' उक्त वाक्य में रेखांकित शब्द क्रमशः हैं :

A. व्यक्तिवाचक संज्ञा तथा जातिवाचक संज्ञा

B. जातिवाचक संज्ञा तथा भाववाचक संज्ञा

C. व्यक्तिवाचक संज्ञा तथा व्यक्तिवाचक संज्ञा

D. भाववाचक संज्ञा तथा व्यक्तिवाचक संज्ञा

41. निम्न में से किस मुहावरे का अर्थ संगत **नहीं** है?

A. अपने पैरों पर खड़ा होना - आत्मनिर्भर होना।

B. अंधे के हाथ बटेर लगना - बिना प्रयास के कोई चीज प्राप्त कर लेना।

C. एक घाट पानी पीना - एकता और सहिष्णुता होना।

D. कमान से तीर निकल जाना - किसी का भेद खुलना।

42. क्रिया के संबंध में **अनुचित** विकल्प चुनिए :

A. कर्म के आधार पर क्रिया के 'सकर्मक' एवं 'अकर्मक' दो भेद माने जाते हैं।

B. सभी प्रेरणार्थक क्रियाएँ अकर्मक होती हैं।

C. 'पिता पुत्र से पत्र <u>लिखवाता</u> है।' उक्त वाक्य में प्रेरणार्थक क्रिया प्रयुक्त हुई है।

D. 'बतियाना', 'लठियाना' एवं 'अपनाना' नामधातु क्रिया के उदाहरण हैं।

43. सर्वनाम के संबंध में कौन-सा कथन **असत्य** है?

A. प्रयोग के आधार पर सर्वनाम के छह भेद हैं।

B. 'कोई' तथा 'कुछ' अनिश्चयवाचक सर्वनाम शब्द हैं।

C. 'पुरुषवाचक' सर्वनाम के चार भेद माने जाते हैं।

D. जिस सर्वनाम से वक्ता के पास अथवा दूर की किसी वस्तु का बोध होता है, उसे निश्चयवाचक सर्वनाम कहते हैं।

44. किस विकल्प में विपरीतार्थक युग्म **असंगत** है?

A. नूतन - पुरातन B. दुराशय - सदाशय

C. दनुज - दानव D. जंगम - स्थावर

45. वाक्यांश के लिए एकल शब्द के संबंध में अनुचित युग्म है :

A. जो कानून की दृष्टि से उचित न हो - अवैध

B. जिसमें कोई छिद्र न हो - नीरन्ध्र

C. समुद्र में लगने वाली आग - दावानल

D. जो भोजन रोगी के लिए उचित है : पथ्य

PART-II : LANGUAGE – ENGLISH

46. Fill in the blank with the **correct** option:

Note it down ______ you should forget it.

A. that B. because of

C. till D. lest

47. Choose the **correct** option that gives the meaning of the given idiom:

Spill the beans

A. increase work

B. face a great loss

C. to leak a secret

D. segregate

48. Fill in the blank with the **correct** option:

The Pak army turned hostile ______ ISIS.

A. to B. for

C. at D. with

49. Choose the **correct** passive of the given sentence:

Please give me some more time.

A. Some more time might please be given to me.

B. Some more time may please be given to me.

C. Some more time could please be given to him.

D. Some more time should please be given to him.

35. B	**36.** B	**37.** C	**38.** B	**39.** B	**40.** C	**41.** D	**42.** B	**43.** C	**44.** C
45. C	**46.** D	**47.** C	**48.** A	**49.** B					

50. Which of the following options express the **correct** meaning of the sentence given below?

No sooner did I reach the college than the bell rang.

A. The sooner I reached the college the earlier the bell rings.
B. I reached the college and the bell was rang after.
C. Although I reached the college the bell began to ring.
D. As soon as I reached the college, the bell rang.

51. Change the narration:

He said, "What a charming sight!"

A. He exclaimed with joy that it was a very charming sight.
B. He exclaimed with joy that what a charming sight it is!
C. He told with joy that is a charming sight.
D. He said to me what a charming sight it is!

52. Fill in the blank with the **correct** form of the verb:

I ______ a lot of calls today.

A. had have B. has had
C. have had D. had had

53. Which of the following sentences is the **correct** option to express a probable condition?

A. If I were a bird, I would fly to you.
B. If you touch a live wire, you will get a shock.
C. If you will read this book, you will learn grammar.
D. If I had reached in time, I could have saved her.

54. Choose the part of the sentence that is grammatically **incorrect**:

He thought *(a)* / he will be able to do *(b)* / whatever he wanted *(c)* / with his job. *(d)*

A. *(a)* B. *(b)*
C. *(c)* D. *(d)*

55. Choose the part of the sentence that is grammatically **incorrect**:

The Jews were *(a)* / most reluctant *(b)* / to contribute *(c)* / in the Palestinian cause. *(d)*

A. *(a)* B. *(b)*
C. *(c)* D. *(d)*

56. The word 'slither' means:

A. lick B. venomous
C. hinder D. slide

57. Fill in the blank with the **correct** form of the verb:

When I last ______ her, she was deeply involved in debt.

A. have met B. met
C. has met D. did met

58. Fill in the blank with the **correct** option:

How did the thief ______ the padlock.

A. open B. opened
C. had opened D. had been opening

59. Fill in the blank with the **correct** 'Modal Auxiliary':

______ you mind lending me your pen? (Request)

A. Should B. Ought
C. Would D. Must

60. Arrange the following jumbled options in the correct order and then choose the **correct** option:

(a) is heartening *(b)* is going abroad
(c) the news *(d)* that she

A. *(c)*, *(d)*, *(b)*, *(a)* B. *(d)*, *(a)*, *(c)*, *(b)*
C. *(d)*, *(c)*, *(b)*, *(a)* D. *(d)*, *(c)*, *(a)*, *(b)*

PART-III : GENERAL STUDIES

Quantitative Aptitude, Reasoning Ability and GK & Awareness

61. If A stands on his head with his face towards North, in which direction will his left hand point?

A. North-East B. West
C. East D. North-West

62. A boat goes 20 km downstream in one hour and the same distance upstream in two hours. The speed of the boat in still water is:

A. 10 km/h B. 12 km/h
C. 13 km/h D. 15 km/h

63. In a group of 15 people, 7 read Hindi, 8 read English, while 3 of them read none of these two. How many of them read Hindi and English both?

A. 0 B. 3
C. 4 D. 5

50. D	**51.** A	**52.** C	**53.** B	**54.** B	**55.** D	**56.** D	**57.** B	**58.** A	**59.** C
60. A	**61.** C	**62.** D	**63.** B						

64. In a class of 35 students, A is placed 7th from the bottom whereas B is placed 9th from the top and C is placed exactly between these two. What is A's position from C?

A. 9th B. 10th
C. 11th D. 12th

65. In a certain code language 'CEG' is written as 'TSR' and 'FHJ' is written as 'QPO', then in the same code language 'IKM' is written as:

A. NOP B. NOL
C. NMK D. NML

66. How many meaningful words can be formed with the letter EAML?

A. 1 B. 2
C. 3 D. 4

67. The ratio of an interior angle to the exterior angle of a regular polygon is 7 : 2. The number of sides of the polygon is:

A. 7 B. 8
C. 9 D. 11

68. Find the next term of the following number series:

2, 3, 10, 15, 26, ?

A. 33 B. 34
C. 35 D. 36

69. Pipe A alone can fill a tank in 8 hours. Pipe B alone can fill it in 6 hours. If both the pipes are opened and after 2 hours pipe A is closed, then pipe B will fill the tank in:

A. 2 hours B. 2½ hours
C. 3 hours D. 3½ hours

70. In a certain pattern, if 38 * 15 = 32, 62 * 91 = 7 and 74 * 81 = 29, then in the same pattern the value of 47 * 33 is:

A. 40 B. 41
C. 38 D. 53

71. If it was Saturday on 17th December, 2002, what was the day on 22nd December, 2004?

A. Sunday B. Saturday
C. Monday D. Tuesday

72. The next of the series is:

Z1A, X2D, V6G, T21J, ?

A. R87M B. R87N
C. R88P D. R88M

73. In English alphabet, the number of letters skipped in between adjacent letters in the series is decreased by one. Which of the following series observes the rule?

A. DJOTV B. DJOSV
C. DJOSW D. DIOSU

74. The radius of the circumcircle of the triangle made by x-axis, y-axis and $4x + 3y = 12$ is:

A. 2 unit B. 2.5 unit
C. 3 unit D. 4 unit

75. Find the least number which must be added to 15463 so that the resulting number is exactly divisible by 107:

A. 52 B. 55
C. 71 D. 76

76. What proportion of water must be added to milk to gain 20% by selling it at the cost price?

A. 1 : 5 B. 2 : 5
C. 3 : 5 D. 4 : 5

77. The ratio of compound interest and simple interest on a certain sum at the rate of 4% per annum for 2 years is:

A. 52 : 51 B. 52 : 50
C. 51 : 50 D. 53 : 50

78. If A, B and C enter into a partnership with shares in the ratio $\frac{7}{2}:\frac{4}{3}:\frac{6}{5}$. After 4 months, A increase his share by 50%. If the total profit at the end of one year be ₹ 21,600, then B's share in the profit is:

A. ₹ 2,400 B. ₹ 3,600
C. ₹ 4,000 D. ₹ 4,200

79. A man sold an article at a loss of 20%. If he sells the article for ₹ 12 more, he would have gained 10%. The cost price of an article is:

A. ₹ 22 B. ₹ 30
C. ₹ 36 D. ₹ 40

80. $\frac{a^{1/2}+a^{-1/2}}{1-a}+\frac{1-a^{-1/2}}{1+\sqrt{a}}$ is equal to:

A. $\frac{a}{a-1}$ B. $\frac{a-1}{2}$
C. $\frac{2}{a-1}$ D. $\frac{2}{1-a}$

64. B	**65.** D	**66.** C	**67.** C	**68.** C	**69.** B	**70.** B	**71.** A	**72.** D	**73.** B
74. B	**75.** A	**76.** A	**77.** C	**78.** C	**79.** D	**80.** D			

81. Historical village Sugh is located in:
A. Ambala district
B. Kurukshetra district
C. Yamunanagar district
D. Panchkula district

82. Which Haryanvi conquered Mount Elbrus in August, 2023?
A. Sandeep Bishnoi B. Rohtash Bishnoi
C. Ajay Khichad D. Mohit

83. Who among the following Governors of Haryana was an ICS officer?
A. Shri Dharma Vir
B. Shri Muzaffar Hussain Burney
C. Shri Hari Anand Barari
D. Shri Surjit Singh Sandhawalia

84. The evidence of Stupa of Mauryan period is found at:
A. Topara B. Bhiwani
C. Thanesar D. Rohtak

85. Geeta Jayanti Samaroh is celebrated in the month of:
A. Kartik B. Margshirsh
C. Ashvin D. Shravana

86. Who is the Chief Commissioner of Haryana Right to Service Commission?
A. Shri T.C. Gupta
B. Shri Vijay Vardhan
C. Shri Rajesh Khullar
D. Shri Vikas Gupta

87. Read the following statements about Sadhu Nischal Das:
(*i*) He was a Dadu's disciple.
(*ii*) He compiled a book 'Vichar Sagar' which is in form of dialogue.
Choose the **correct** code:
A. Only statement (*i*) is correct.
B. Only statement (*ii*) is correct.
C. Neither statement (*i*) nor statement (*ii*) are correct.
D. Both the statements (*i*) and (*ii*) are correct

88. In Haryana, where the Chinkara Breeding Centre is located?
A. Pinjore B. Panipat
C. Jhajjar D. Bhiwani

89. When the Haryana State Cooperative Agriculture and Rural Development Board Ltd. was established?
A. January, 1967 B. November, 1966
C. March, 1980 D. January, 1996

90. Where in Haryana, the Indian Institute of Information Technology is located?
A. Sonipat B. Panipat
C. Ambala D. Kurukshetra

PART-IV : SUBJECT KNOWLEDGE—COMMERCE

91. A condition in which information inflow exceeds an individual's processing capacity:
A. Informal communication
B. Formal communication
C. Accurate information
D. Information overload

92. The product life cycle stage in which a product's sales start climbing quickly is:
A. Introduction stage B. Growth stage
C. Maturity stage D. Saturation stage

93. Which one of the following is **not** an off-the-job training method?
A. Job Rotation B. Classroom Lectures
C. Simulations D. Vestibule Training

94. To make others behave in way in which they would **not** have behaved otherwise:
A. Need of affiliation B. Need of achievement
C. Need of power D. Need of association

95. The process of monitoring and evaluating the nature and direction of change in the business environment is:
A. Environmental analysis
B. Environmental scanning
C. Both (A) and (B)
D. None of these

96. For creating a company we use:
A. Alt + F1 B. Alt + F3
C. Alt + F2 D. ESC key

81. C	**82.** B	**83.** A	**84.** A, C	**85.** B	**86.** A	**87.** B	**88.** D	**89.** *	**90.** A
91. D	**92.** B	**93.** A	**94.** C	**95.** C	**96.** B				

97. The idea that consumers will not buy enough of the firm's products unless it undertakes a large scale selling and promotion efforts:
A. Selling concept
B. Product concept
C. Promotion concept
D. Societal marketing concept

98. X, Y and Z are partners sharing profits in equal ratio. Capital balances of 1st April, 2023 are X ₹ 50,000, Y ₹ 40,000, Z ₹ 30,000. Their private assets are: X ₹ 20,000, Y ₹ 2,000 and Z ₹ 5,000. What is the extent of their liability in the firm?
A. X ₹ 50,000, Y ₹ 40,000, Z ₹ 30,000
B. X ₹ 20,000, Y ₹ 2,000, Z ₹ 5,000
C. X ₹ 70,000, Y ₹ 42,000, Z ₹ 35,000
D. None of these

99. X and Y sharing profits in the ratio of 7 : 3 admit Z for 3/7 shares in the new firm which he takes 2/7 from X and 1/7 from Y. The new ratio of X, Y and Z will be:
A. 7 : 3 : 3 B. 14 : 6 : 8
C. 29 : 11 : 30 D. 14 : 6 : 15

100. Consider the following statements:

Assertion (A): If a shareholder fails to pay the amount of one or more calls on his shares, the company may forfeit his shares.

Reason (R): Even after the forfeiture of shares, that shareholders is responsible to pay the amount due from him until the company receives full amount on those shares.

Now select your answer according to the coding scheme given below:
A. Both (A) and (R) are true and (R) is the correct explanation of (A).
B. Both (A) and (R) are true, but (R) is not the correct explanation of (A)
C. (A) is true, but (R) is false.
D. (A) is false, but (R) is true.

101. Current ratio is 4 : 5 and quick ratio is 5 : 7. If current liabilities are ₹ 3,50,000, the amount of inventory is:
A. ₹ 35,000 B. ₹ 30,000
C. ₹ 3,000 D. ₹ 3,50,000

102. ₹ 5,000 received from sub-tenant for rent and entered correctly in the cash book is posted to the debit of the rent account. In the trial balance:
A. The debit total will be greater by ₹ 10,000 than the credit total.
B. The debit total will be greater by ₹ 5,000 than the credit total.
C. Subject to other entries being correct the total will agree.
D. None of these

103. Obsolescence of a depreciable assets may be caused by:
(*a*) Technological changes
(*b*) Improvement in Production method
(*c*) Legal or other restrictions
(*d*) Change in market demand for the product or service output
A. Only (*a*) above
B. Both (*a*) and (*b*) above
C. (*a*), (*b*) and (*c*)
D. All (*a*), (*b*), (*c*) and (*d*)

104. Money received against share warrants is shown as:
A. Shareholders funds
B. Long term provisions
C. Other long term liabilities
D. Other current liabilities

105. Provision for Discount on Debtors:
A. An appropriation of profit
B. A charge on the revenue
C. An income of the business
D. None of these

106. Which one of the following is **not** a characteristic of charismatic leader?
A. Vision and articulation
B. Personal risk
C. Sensitivity to follower needs
D. Conventional behaviour

107. A small, core organization that outsources major business functions is:
A. Boundary less organisation
B. Virtual organization
C. Learner organization
D. Simple organization

108. An organisation structure that creates dual lines of authority and combines functional and product departmentalization is:
A. Complex structure
B. Function structure
C. Matrix structure
D. Production structure

97. A **98.** C **99.** C **100.** B **101.** B **102.** A **103.** D **104.** A **105.** B **106.** D
107. B **108.** C

109. Which one of the following is **not** a barrier of effective communication?
A. Filtering B. Selective perception
C. Interest level D. Emotions

110. What right does a consumer have against unfair trade practices and exploitation?
A. Right to Information
B. Right to Equality
C. Right to Seek Redressal
D. None of these

111. The drive to become what a person is capable of becoming is called:
A. Self-actualization B. Self-esteem
C. Self-realization D. Self-motivating

112. Which of the following statement is **incorrect** according to the Consumer Protection Act?
A. District Forum shall consist of a lady social worker.
B. State Commission shall consist of a person who is or has been a judge of a High Court.
C. District Forum shall consist of four members.
D. National Consumer Disputes Redressal Commission shall consist of a person who is or has been a judge of the Supreme Court.

113. Depreciation is the process of:
A. Valuation of Assets B. Allocation of Cost
C. Both (A) and (B) D. None of these

114. Dividend received by other than financial enterprise is shown in cash flow statement under:
A. Operating Activities B. Investing Activities
C. Financing Activities D. General Activities

115. Match List-I with List-II and select the **correct** answer using codes given below the lists:

List-I (Accounting Standards)	**List-II (Objects)**
(*a*) AS 9	(*i*) Revenue Recognition
(*b*) AS 10	(*ii*) Property, Plant and Equipment
(*c*) AS 16	(*iii*) Segment Reporting
(*d*) AS 17	(*iv*) Borrowing Costs

Codes:

	(*a*)	(*b*)	(*c*)	(*d*)
A.	(*i*)	(*ii*)	(*iii*)	(*iv*)
B.	(*i*)	(*iii*)	(*ii*)	(*iv*)
C.	(*i*)	(*ii*)	(*iv*)	(*iii*)
D.	(*i*)	(*iii*)	(*iv*)	(*ii*)

116. Which of the following statement is **incorrect**?
A. Depreciation is an amortised expenditure.
B. Stock at the end if appears in the Trial Balance, is taken only to the Balance Sheet.
C. Fixed costs remain relatively unaffected in a defined period of time.
D. Fixed assets are stated in the Balance Sheet at their market value

117. Which of the following statement is **true**?
A. Rent paid to landlord of the proprietors house, must be debited to Rent Account.
B. On purchases of furniture the amount spent on repairs should be debited to repairs account.
C. When errors are detected after preparation of trial balance, suspense account is opened.
D. If the errors are detected after preparing trial balance, then all the errors are rectified through suspense account.

118. Which of the following statement is **true**?
A. Accrual concept implies accounting on Cash basis.
B. Bank Account is Real Account.
C. Ledger is a set of Accounts.
D. Accounting is concerned with monetary and non-monetary transaction.

119. Contingent liability is shown a note below the balance sheet. This arises out of:
A. Convention of disclosure
B. Convention of materiality
C. Convention of observance of law
D. Convention of consistency

120. Partnership accounts of X and Y were closed for the current year. Subsequently, it was discovered that interest on drawings was not charged. For rectifying the error, which of the following account will be opened?
A. Profit & Loss Account
B. Profit & Loss Appropriation Account
C. Profit & Loss Adjustment Account
D. None of these

121. Leader who guide or motivates their followers in the direction of established goals by clarifying role and task requirements:
A. Transformational leader
B. Transactional leader
C. Situational leader
D. Authentic leader

109. C **110.** C **111.** A **112.** C **113.** B **114.** B **115.** C **116.** D **117.** C **118.** C
119. A **120.** C **121.** B

122. The mental ability to analyse and diagnose complex situation is known as:
A. Human skill B. Technical skill
C. Complex skill D. Conceptual skill

123. Intellectual property rights include:
A. Patents B. Trade Mark
C. Copyrights D. All options are right

124. Who can check the price fluctuations in the market by holding back the goods when prices fall and releasing the goods when prices rise?
A. Wholesaler B. Agent
C. Retailer D. Mercantile Agent

125. In which year Taylor wrote the book 'The Principles of Scientific Management'?
A. 1909 B. 1911
C. 1920 D. 1901

126. The idea that a subordinate should have only one supervisor to whom he or she is directly responsible:
A. Unity of command
B. Unity of direction
C. Readiness of followers
D. Supervision

127. Which one of the following is **not** a limitation of computerized accounting system?
A. Security problem
B. System failure
C. High cost of training
D. Flexible reporting

128. When debentures are issued as collateral security, interest is paid on:
A. Nominal value of debentures
B. Face value of debentures
C. Discounted value of debentures
D. No interest is paid

129. In absence of any agreement, partners are liable to receive interest on loan at the rate of:
A. .50% per month simple interest
B. 12% simple interest
C. 6% p.a. simple interest
D. None of these

130. Joint Life Policy Account of the partners is:
A. Nominal Account B. Memorandum Account
C. Assets Account D. None of these

131. Favourable balance as per Pass Book means:
A. Debit Balance in Cash Book
B. Debit Balance in Passbook
C. Credit Balance in Cash Book
D. Credit Balance in Passbook

132. At the time of dissolution a liability takes over by partner is to be debited to:
A. In Revaluation Account
B. In Partners Capital Account
C. In Realisation Account
D. In Cash or Bank Account

133. Which of the following statement is **correct**?
A. As per Table F rate of interest on calls in arrear is 12%.
B. As per Table F rate of interest on calls in advance is 10%.
C. Loss on reissue should exceed the forfeited amount.
D. Sweat equity shares are those which are issued to employees and directors at a discount.

134. The securities premium amount may be utilized by a company for:
A. Writing off any loss on sale of fixed asset
B. Writing off any loss of revenue nature
C. Writing off the expenses/discount on issue of debentures
D. All options are right

135. The appropriate sequence of the formation of a company are in the following order:
A. Promotion, commencement of business and incorporation
B. Promotion, incorporation, capital subscription and commencement of business
C. Capital subscription, promotion, incorporation and commencement of business
D. Incorporation, capital subscription, commencement of business and promotion

136. A selection device used to obtain in-depth information about a candidate is:
A. Comprehensive interview
B. Stress interview
C. Behavioural interview
D. Personal interview

137. The socialization stage where individuals confront the possible dichotomy between their organizational expectations and reality is:
A. metamorphosis stage
B. encounter stage
C. pre-arrival stage
D. orientation

122. D	**123.** D	**124.** A	**125.** B	**126.** A	**127.** D	**128.** D	**129.** C	**130.** C	**131.** D
132. C	**133.** D	**134.** C	**135.** B	**136.** A	**137.** B				

138. Which one of the following is **not** a principle of Henri Fayol?
A. Discipline
B. Remuneration
C. Centralization
D. Decentralization

139. Software and management practices designed to serve the customer from order through delivery and after sales service:
A. eCRM B. ERP
C. E-commerce D. EDI

140. With reference to the Micro, Small, and Medium Enterprises (MSMEs) consider the following statements:
(*a*) This sector is the largest employer of human resources in India.
(*b*) It generates more employment opportunities per unit of capital invested compared to large industries.
(*c*) These industries in India account for 45% of the Industrial units in the country.

How many of the above statements are **correct**?
A. Only (*a*) B. Both (*a*) & (*b*)
C. Both (*a*) & (*c*) D. All (*a*), (*b*) & (*c*)

141. Ogives can be helpful in locating graphically the:
A. Mean B. Mode
C. Median D. None of these

142. The number of subordinates manager can efficiently and effectively direct, is called:
A. Management
B. Centralization
C. Span of control
D. Decentralization

143. X Ltd. purchased a machine worth ₹ 2,88,000 and in lieu issued debentures of ₹ 100 at a discount of 4%. The number of debenture issued will be:
A. 2880 B. 3000
C. 2770 D. None of these

144. Which of the following transactions will result into Flow of Cash?
A. Deposited ₹ 20,000 into bank.
B. Sale of furniture of the book value of ₹ 7,400 at a loss of ₹ 900.
C. Converted ₹ 1,00,000 9% debentures into equity shares.
D. Withdrew cash from bank ₹ 25,000.

145. Nature of goodwill, whose value is the highest:
A. Rat nature B. Cat nature
C. Dog nature D. Elephant nature

146. Consider the following statements:

Assertion (A): In double account system, the final accounts of a company fail to disclose the true condition of its assets.

Reason (R): Because the assets of the company are shown at their cost price even when they are completely worn out.

Now select your answer according to the coding scheme given below:
A. Both (A) and (R) are correct and (R) is the correct explanation of (A)
B. Both (A) and (R) are correct, but (R) is not the correct explanation of (A)
C. (A) is true, but (R) is false.
D. (A) is false, but (R) is true.

147. When one party grants the right to use the asset to the other party in return for a periodic payment. It is known as:
A. Lease financing
B. Factoring
C. Public deposits
D. Debts

148. On retirement or death of a partner, assets and liabilities are to be shown at old values for which account to be opened is:
A. Profit & Loss Account
B. Revaluation Account
C. Memorandum Revaluation Account
D. Realisation Account

149. The total of the sales book is posted to the credit of the
A. In debtors account
B. In sales return account
C. In purchases return account
D. None of these

150. A transaction involving a decrease in debt equity ratio and increase in current ratio is:
A. Issue of debentures against the purchases of fixed assets
B. Issue of equity shares for cash
C. Issue of debentures for cash
D. Redemption of preference shares for cash

138. D **139.** A **140.** B **141.** C **142.** C **143.** B **144.** B **145.** B **146.** A **147.** A
148. C **149.** D **150.** B

EXPLANATORY ANSWERS

1. **(C):** Inclusive education is the most suitable type for socially deprived children as it ensures they learn alongside their peers from different backgrounds. This approach promotes equality, diversity, and respect, fostering a sense of belonging and reducing social barriers.

2. **(A):** According to Erik Erikson's theory, adolescence involves the crisis of identity vs. role confusion. Ego-identity, a sense of self and personal identity, is a positive psycho-social aspect of adolescence as it leads to stronger self-awareness and independence.

3. **(D):** Creative children typically exhibit qualities like divergent thinking, extreme curiosity, and high imagination. Conventional thoughts, which involve adherence to traditional or standard ways of thinking, are generally not characteristic of a creative child.

4. **(D):** Development of social prejudices does not have a positive effect on the process of socialization. Such prejudices can lead to discrimination and social conflict, which are detrimental to societal harmony and individual development.

5. **(C):** Vygotsky's 'Zone of Proximal Development' (ZPD) describes the difference between what a child can achieve independently and what they can achieve with guidance from a more knowledgeable individual. This concept underscores the importance of supportive learning environments.

6. **(B):** Diagnostic testing is used to identify the reasons why a learner has not achieved the expected performance. This type of testing analyzes specific areas of difficulty and identifies underlying causes, such as gaps in knowledge or misconceptions, allowing for targeted interventions and support.

7. **(A):** The National Curriculum Framework (NCF) 2005 in India emphasizes that inclusion in education should not be confined to children with disabilities but should ensure that no child is excluded. This broader perspective on inclusion aims to create a learning environment that is accessible and equitable for all students.

8. **(D):** Growth and development involve multiple types of changes: changes in body size (height and weight), changes in body proportions (such as limb length), disappearance of old features (like baby fat), and acquisition of new features (such as secondary sexual characteristics during puberty). All these aspects are integral to the physical and developmental changes that occur over time.

9. **(A):** Motivation impairs learning behaviour is incorrect as motivation generally has a positive impact on learning. It provides definite direction to learning behaviour, energizes learning behaviour, and makes learning more engaging and purposeful. Motivated learners are more likely to set goals, persist through challenges, and achieve higher levels of success.

10. **(D):** Under Kohlberg's Moral Development theory, the stages of morality match their levels as follows:
    (*a*) Good interpersonal relations (Stage 3) correspond to Level II (Conventional)
    (*b*) Individualism and exchange (Stage 2) correspond to Level I (Pre-conventional)
    (*c*) Social contracts and individual rights (Stage 5) correspond to Level III (Post-conventional)
    (*d*) Universal principles (Stage 6) correspond to Level III (Post-conventional)

    This classification reflects the progression from self-interest to adherence to social norms and finally to abstract principles of justice.

11. **(D):** Incidental learning occurs when a learner acquires knowledge or skills unintentionally and without a specific desire or purpose. It often happens through exposure to different environments or activities, where learning is a byproduct of the experience rather than a focused effort.

12. **(D):** Biological motives, such as hunger, thirst, and sleep, are universal, inborn, and essential for survival. They are directly related to homeostasis, which is the body's ability to maintain a stable internal environment. Therefore, the statement that they are not related to homeostasis is incorrect.

13. **(D):** Continuous and comprehensive evaluation (CCE) uses various methods to assess students, including written exams, oral tests, behavioural assessments, and practical examinations. CCE aims to provide a holistic evaluation of a student's performance across different domains, ensuring a more rounded understanding of their abilities and progress.

14. **(C):** The statement that illiterate people cannot do performance tests is incorrect. Performance tests are designed to assess intelligence through tasks that do not rely on verbal skills, making them accessible to individuals regardless of their literacy level. These tests often involve problem-solving with objects, patterns, or figures.

15. (D): In Guilford's Three-Dimensional Structure of Intellect, the elements of intelligence are categorized into operations, contents, and products. "Relations" refers to the operation dimension rather than the content dimension. Operations involve the mental processes used, such as cognition and evaluation, while contents and products describe the material and outcomes of these processes.

16. (B): Single learning pathway is not a key feature of child-centered learning. Child-centered learning emphasizes providing meaningful learning opportunities, continuous assessment, and accessible learning settings. It involves multiple learning pathways to cater to individual differences, interests, and needs, ensuring that each child can learn in a way that suits them best.

17. (D): Combinational processes are not one of the interrelated processes of observational learning according to Bandura. The key processes are attentional processes (focusing on the model's behaviour), retentional processes (remembering the behaviour), motor reproduction processes (ability to reproduce the behaviour), and motivational processes (having the desire to perform the behaviour).

18. (C): According to Bandura's Social Learning Theory, when a person learns the same behaviour by observing and repeating the behaviour of others, it is called modeling. This process involves observing the actions of a model, retaining the information, and then imitating the observed behaviour.

19. (B): The experimental component is not included in componential intelligence under Sternberg's Triarchic Theory. The three sub-components of componential intelligence are the meta component (executive processes for planning and decision-making), the performance component (processes for executing tasks), and the knowledge acquisition component (processes for learning and acquiring new information).

20. (A): Dyscalculia is a learning disability that affects the acquisition of arithmetic skills. It involves difficulties in understanding numbers, learning how to manipulate numbers, and performing mathematical calculations. This condition impacts a person's ability to perform basic arithmetic operations and understand mathematical concepts.

21. (C): Freud's Psychosexual Development Theory outlines five stages in the following sequence: Oral stage → Anal stage → Phallic stage → Latency stage → Genital stage. Each stage represents the focus of the libido on different areas of the body and significant psychological developments.

22. (B): According to Pavlov's Classical Conditioning theory, the delay conditioning, where the conditioned stimulus (CS) precedes and overlaps with the unconditioned stimulus (US), is the most effective for learning. This sequence allows the subject to associate the CS with the US strongly.

23. (D): The formal operational stage, which occurs from approximately age 12 onwards in Piaget's Cognitive Development theory, is when the ability for abstract thinking and generalization develops. Children can think logically about abstract propositions and test hypotheses systematically.

24. (C): Remedial teaching is not suitable for talented students as it is designed to help students who are struggling with their studies. Talented students benefit more from opportunities for independent project work, acceleration, and enrichment programs that challenge and extend their abilities.

25. (A): The principle of segregation is not a principle of inclusive education. Inclusive education is based on principles such as cooperation, celebrating diversity, and ensuring the right to education for all children. Segregation, on the other hand, isolates children with disabilities or differences, which is contrary to the inclusive education approach.

26. (A): Large groups of students do not support teaching according to individual differences. To address individual needs effectively, smaller groups or individualized instruction, curriculum adaptation, and understanding each student's abilities are essential. Large groups make it difficult to cater to the unique learning styles and needs of each student.

27. (C): Identifying special needs and excluding children from mainstreaming is not a role of educational institutions in addressing the needs of children with special needs. Schools should aim for inclusive education by admitting students without discrimination, providing accessible facilities, and offering necessary support services.

28. (B): The statement that later development is more critical than early development is incorrect. Early development is often considered more critical because it lays the foundation for future growth and development. Early experiences and learning are crucial in shaping a child's cognitive, social, and emotional development.

29. (A): The three-dimensional model of inclusive education was propounded by Griffith, Cooper, and Ringlaben. This model emphasizes the inclusion of all students in the educational process, considering multiple dimensions such as physical, instructional, and social inclusion.

30. (D): "Socialization means attaining of maturity in social relationships". This definition of socialization is given by Hurlock. Socialization is the process by which individuals learn and adopt the norms, values, behaviours, and social skills necessary to function effectively in society. It involves the development of mature social relationships through interaction with family, peers, and other social agents.

31. (B): 'पवित्रतम - विशेषण की उत्तरावस्था' सही सुमेलित नहीं है। सही उदाहरण 'पवित्रतम' है, जो विशेषण की उच्चतम अवस्था को दर्शाता है।

32. (C): 'माणिक्य - चर्बी, माणिक्या - मछली' सही अर्थ भेद नहीं है। 'माणिक्य' का अर्थ होता है रत्न (माणिक), जबकि 'माणिक्या' शब्द का उपयोग सामान्यतः नहीं होता है। सही युग्म 'माणिक्य - रत्न, मणिका - मछली' होता है।

33. (B): 'मस्तक - तद्‌भव शब्द' संगत नहीं है। 'मस्तक' तत्सम शब्द है, जो संस्कृत से सीधे लिया गया है। तद्‌भव शब्द वे होते हैं जो संस्कृत के शब्दों से परिवर्तित होकर हिंदी में आए हैं, जैसे 'सिर' तद्‌भव शब्द है।

34. (D): 'लघूर्मि = लघु + ऊर्मि' संगत है। यह सही संधि विच्छेद है जिसमें 'लघु' और 'ऊर्मि' शब्दों के मिलकर बनने वाला शब्द 'लघूर्मि' है।

35. (B): 'दीर्घश्वास, पाषाणहृदय' में बहुव्रीहि समास का उदाहरण नहीं है। बहुव्रीहि समास वह समास होता है जिसमें दोनों पद मिलकर किसी तीसरे पद का बोध कराते हैं, जैसे 'शेषशायी' (विष्णु जो शेषनाग पर शयन करते हैं)। 'दीर्घश्वास' और 'पाषाणहृदय' तत्पुरुष समास के उदाहरण हैं।

36. (B): 'अनीति' शब्द 'अन' उपसर्ग से निर्मित नहीं है। 'अनीति' का निर्माण 'अ-' उपसर्ग से हुआ है जो 'न' का समानार्थी है। 'अंतर', 'अनिष्ट', और 'अनाचार' सभी में 'अन' उपसर्ग का प्रयोग हुआ है।

37. (C): 'रिश्वतखोर, रोजगार' विदेशज प्रत्ययों से निर्मित शब्द हैं। 'खोर' और 'गार' प्रत्यय उर्दू और फारसी भाषा से आए हैं और हिंदी में इस्तेमाल होते हैं। अन्य विकल्पों में देशज और तद्‌भव प्रत्ययों का प्रयोग है।

38. (B): 'गरुड़ - खगनाथ, वृषभी, भद्रा' अनुचित है। गरुड़ के पर्यायवाची 'खगनाथ' और 'भद्र' हैं, लेकिन 'वृषभी' (वृषभ) और 'भद्रा' अन्य शब्दों के पर्यायवाची हैं। गरुड़ के अन्य पर्यायवाची शब्द जैसे 'वैनतेय' और 'पक्षिराज' हैं।

39. (B): 'याज्ञवल्क्य, हस्तक्षेप' वार्तनिक दृष्टि से शुद्ध शब्द हैं। याज्ञवल्क्य (एक ऋषि) और हस्तक्षेप (intervention) दोनों ही शब्द शुद्ध हैं। अन्य विकल्पों में त्रुटियाँ हैं, जैसे 'मैथली' की बजाय 'मैथिली' और 'वापिस' की बजाय 'वापस'।

40. (C): 'महात्मा गाँधी ने भारत को आजाद कराया।' इस वाक्य में 'महात्मा गाँधी' व्यक्तिवाचक संज्ञा हैं, जबकि 'भारत' भी व्यक्तिवाचक संज्ञा है। व्यक्तिवाचक संज्ञा विशेष व्यक्तियों या स्थानों के नाम होते हैं।

41. (D): 'कमान से तीर निकल जाना - किसी का भेद खुलना' का अर्थ संगत नहीं है। सही अर्थ 'घटना घट जाना या अवसर हाथ से निकल जाना' है। मुहावरे का अर्थ है कि एक बार तीर कमान से निकल गया तो वापस नहीं आ सकता, जैसे समय या अवसर चला जाना।

42. (B): 'सभी प्रेरणार्थक क्रियाएं अकर्मक होती हैं' असत्य है। प्रेरणार्थक क्रियाएं सकर्मक भी हो सकती हैं, जैसे 'लिखवाना' और 'पढ़वाना'। उदाहरण के लिए, 'पिता पुत्र से पत्र लिखवाता है' वाक्य में प्रेरणार्थक सकर्मक क्रिया 'लिखवाता' प्रयुक्त हुई है।

43. (C): 'पुरुषवाचक सर्वनाम के चार भेद माने जाते हैं' असत्य है। पुरुषवाचक सर्वनाम के केवल तीन भेद होते हैं : उत्तम पुरुष, मध्यम पुरुष, और अन्यतमा पुरुष। यह भेद वक्ता, श्रोता और अन्य व्यक्ति का बोध कराते हैं।

44. (C): 'दनुज - दानव' विपरीतार्थक युग्म असंगत है। दोनों शब्दों का अर्थ 'राक्षस' है और ये पर्यायवाची शब्द हैं। सही विपरीतार्थक युग्म 'दनुज - देवता' होता है।

45. (C): 'समुद्र में लगने वाली आग - दावानल' अनुचित युग्म है। दावानल का अर्थ 'जंगल की आग' होता है। 'बड़वानल' समुद्र में लगने वाली आग के लिए एक शब्द होगा।

46. (D): "Note it down lest you should forget it". The word "lest" means 'for fear that' and is used to introduce a clause expressing the reason for the prevention of something undesirable. Here, it implies that you should note it down to avoid forgetting it.

47. (C): Spill the beans means to leak a secret. This idiom is used when someone reveals confidential or sensitive information, often unexpectedly or prematurely.

48. (A): "The Pak army turned hostile to ISIS". The correct preposition to use here is "to", which indicates direction or orientation toward something.

49. (B): "Some more time may please be given to me". This is the correct passive form of the sentence. It retains the polite request structure and appropriately places the focus on the time being given.

50. (D): "As soon as I reached the college, the bell rang". This option correctly conveys the meaning of the sentence, indicating that the bell rang immediately after reaching the college.

51. (A): "He exclaimed with joy that it was a very charming sight". This option correctly changes the narration from direct to indirect speech and retains the exclamatory nature and joy expressed.

52. (C): "I have had a lot of calls today". The present perfect tense ("have had") is appropriate here because it refers to actions that occurred at an unspecified time before now, relevant to the present context.

53. (B): "If you touch a live wire, you will get a shock". This sentence expresses a probable condition in the present or future and follows the correct structure for a first conditional sentence, which is used to express real and possible situations.

54. (B): The error is in part (*b*). The correct tense should be "would be able to" instead of "will be able to" because the sentence is in past tense. The corrected sentence is: "He thought he would be able to do whatever he wanted with his job".

55. (D): The error is in part (*d*). The correct preposition should be "to" instead of "in". The corrected sentence is: "The Jews were most reluctant to contribute to the Palestinian cause".

56. (D): The word 'slither' means: "slide". "Slither" means to move smoothly over a surface with a twisting or oscillating motion, typically like a snake. It does not mean "lick", "venomous", or "hinder".

57. (B): "When I last met her, she was deeply involved in debt". The correct form of the verb is "met" because it is the simple past tense, which is used to indicate an action completed in the past. "Have met", "has met", and "did met" are incorrect forms in this context.

58. (A): "How did the thief open the padlock". The correct option is "open" because the sentence is in past tense, and "open" is the base form of the verb used after "did" in questions. "Opened", "had opened", and "had been opening" are incorrect forms in this context.

59. (C): "Would you mind lending me your pen? (Request)" The correct modal auxiliary for making a polite request is "would". "Should", "ought", and "must" are not typically used for making polite requests in this context.

60. (A): "The news that she is going abroad is heartening". The correct order of the jumbled options is (*c*), (*d*), (*b*), (*a*). This arrangement forms a coherent and grammatically correct sentence.

61. (C): A stand with his face towards North

$\Rightarrow$ His left hand will point in West direction.

Similarly, A stand on his head with his face towards North

$\Rightarrow$ His left hand will point in East direction.

62. (D): Let the speed of boat in still water be x km/h and the speed of current be y km/h

Then, Speed downstream $= x + y = \frac{20}{1}$

$\Rightarrow \quad x + y = 20$ km/h ...(*i*)

and speed upstream $= x - y = \frac{20}{2}$

$\Rightarrow \quad x - y = 10$ km/h ...(*ii*)

From adding (*i*) and (*ii*), we get,

$$2x = 30 \Rightarrow x = 15$$

Hence, The speed of the boat in still water is 15 km/h.

63. (B): In group of 15 people, 7 read Hindi, 8 read English and 3 read none of these languages.

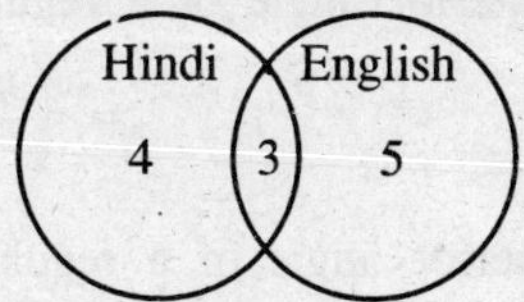

Number of people who speak at least one language $= (15 - 3) = 12$

Number of people who can speak both Hindi and English $= (7 + 8) - 12 = 15 - 12 = 3$.

64. (B):

Top

B — 9th

9

C

9

A — 7th

Bottom

Given, the number of students in a class $= 35$

A = 7th from bottom,

B = 9th from top

$\therefore$ The number of students between A and B

$= 35 - (7 + 9) = 19$

Given, C is placed exactly between A and B

$\therefore$ The number of students between A and C = B and C = 9

Hence, A's position from C = 9 + 1 = 10th.

65. (D): Given, 'CEG' is written as 'TSR'

Reverse positional letter

$C \xrightarrow[+2]{} E \xrightarrow[+2]{} G \quad T \xrightarrow[-1]{} S \xrightarrow[-1]{} R$

And FHI is written as 'QPO'

Reverse positional letter

$F \xrightarrow[+2]{} H \xrightarrow[+2]{} J \quad Q \xrightarrow[-1]{} P \xrightarrow[-1]{} O$

Similarly, IKM is written as,

Reverse positional letter

$I \xrightarrow[+2]{} K \xrightarrow[+2]{} M \quad N \xrightarrow[-1]{} M \xrightarrow[-1]{} L$

Hence, IKM is written as NML.

66. (C): Given, EAML

Meaningful words: MALE, LAME, MEAL

Hence, 3 meaningful words can be formed with the letter EAML.

67. (C): An interior angle of a regular polygon

$$= \left(\frac{n-2}{n}\right)\pi$$

and an exterior angle of a regular polygon

$$= \frac{2\pi}{n}$$

Therefore, $\left(\frac{n-2}{n}\right)\pi : \frac{2\pi}{n} = 7 : 2$

$\Rightarrow \quad \left(\frac{n-2}{n}\right)\pi \times 2 = \frac{2\pi}{n} \times 7$

$\Rightarrow \quad n - 2 = 7$

$\Rightarrow \quad n = 2 + 7$

$\Rightarrow \quad n = 9$

Hence, the number of sides of the polygon is 9.

68. (C): 2, 3, 10, 15, 26, $\boxed{35}$

Here, $1^2 + 1 = 2$

$2^2 - 1 = 3$

$3^2 + 1 = 10$

$4^2 - 1 = 15$

$5^2 + 1 = 26$

$6^2 - 1 = 35$

Hence, ? = the next term of the number series = 35.

69. (B): Part filled by pipe A in 1 hour = $\frac{1}{8}$,

and part filled by pipe B in 1 hour = $\frac{1}{6}$

$\because$ After 2 hours pipe A is closed

$\therefore$ Part filled by pipe (A + B) in 2 hours

$$= 2\left(\frac{1}{8}+\frac{1}{6}\right)$$

$$= 2\left(\frac{3+4}{24}\right) = \frac{7}{12}$$

$\therefore$ Remaining part = $1 - \frac{7}{12} = \frac{5}{12}$

Now, remaining part filled by pipe B in $\dfrac{\frac{5}{12}}{\frac{1}{6}}$ hours

$$= \frac{5}{12} \times \frac{6}{1} = \frac{5}{2}$$

Hence, remaining part of tank will be filled by pipe B in $2\frac{1}{2}$ hours.

70. (B): Given, 38 * 15 = 32

$\Rightarrow$ 83 – 51 = 32

62 * 91 = 7

$\Rightarrow$ 26 – 19 = 7

Reverse digit and subtract

Similarly, 47 * 33 = ?

$\Rightarrow$ 74 – 33 = $\boxed{41}$ which is required answer.

71. (A): The year 2004 is a leap year and hence there would be 29 days in February.

17th December 2002 to 16th December 2003 = 365 days

17th December 2003 to 16th December 2004 = 366 days (leap year)

17th December 2004 to 22nd December 2004 = 6 days

Total number of days = 365 + 366 + 5 = 737 days

737 ÷ 7 = 105 weeks 2 days

The 105th week would end on Friday. Thus, the next two days would be Saturday and Sunday. Hence, the day on 22nd December 2004 would be Sunday.

72. (D):

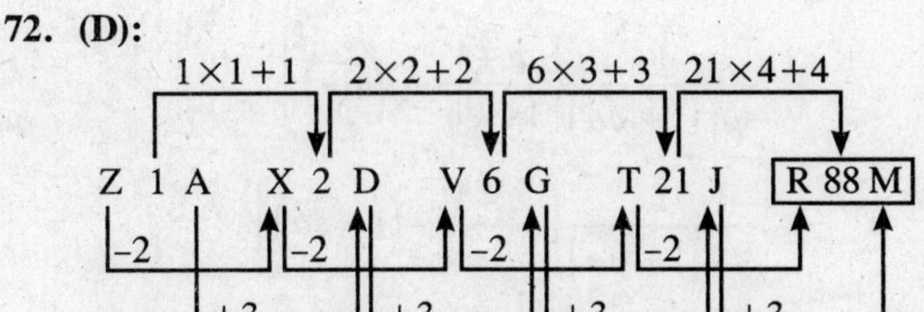

Hence, ? = the next term = R88M.

73. (B):

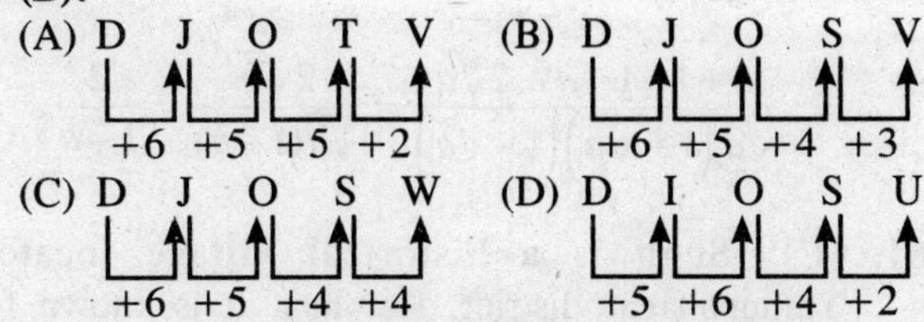

Here, option (B) observes the rule.

74. (B): The radius of the circumcircle of the triangle made by x-axis, y-axis and $4x + 3y = 12$

$\because \quad 4x + 3y = 12 \quad \ldots(i)$

$\therefore \quad \frac{4x}{12} + \frac{3y}{12} = 1$

$\Rightarrow \quad \frac{x}{3} + \frac{y}{4} = 1$

The Intercept form: The equation of line (i) which cuts x-axis at B(3, 0) and y-axis at A(0, 4).

Now, ΔAOB is right-angle triangle.

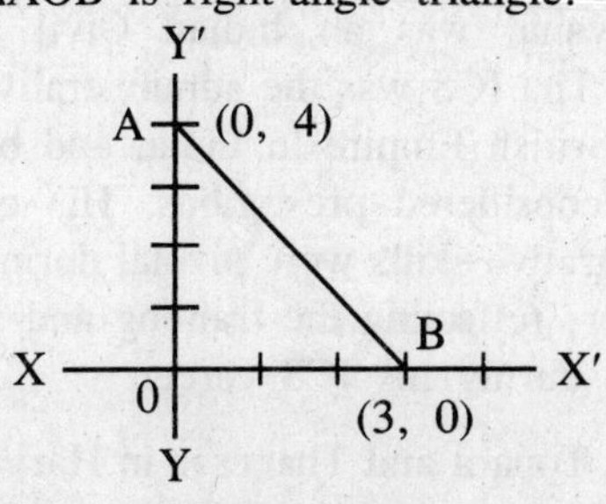

$\Rightarrow \quad \angle AOB = 90°$

We know, circum-center of right angled Δ is the mid-point of hypotenous

Here, Mid-point of AB

$\because \quad AB = \sqrt{AO^2 + OB^2}$

$= \sqrt{4^2 + 3^2}$

$= \sqrt{16 + 9} = \sqrt{25} = 5$

Hence, $\quad \text{Radius} = \frac{\text{Diameter}}{2} = \frac{5}{2}$

$= 2.5$ units.

75. (A): $\because \quad 15463 + x = 107 \times 145$

$\therefore \quad 15463 + x = 15515$

$\Rightarrow \quad x = 15515 - 15463$

$\Rightarrow \quad x = 52$

Hence, Required least number which must be added = 52.

76. (A): Let C.P. of 100 unit Milk = ₹ 100

Then, C.P. of 120 unit milk = ₹ 120

and C.P. of 20 unit water + 100 unit milk = ₹ 100

$\therefore$ S.P. of 20 unit water + 100 unit milk = ₹ 120

$\therefore \quad$ Profit = ₹ 120 – 100 = ₹ 20

= 20%

Hence, proportion of water must be added to milk = 20 : 100 = 1 : 5.

77. (C): Compound Interest

$$= P\left[\left(1+\frac{r}{100}\right)^n - 1\right] = P\left[\left(1+\frac{4}{100}\right)^2 - 1\right]$$

$$= P\left[\left(\frac{26}{25}\right)^2 - 1\right] = P\left[\frac{676}{625} - 1\right] = P\left[\frac{51}{625}\right]$$

And simple interest $= \frac{P\,r\,t}{100}$

$$= \frac{P \times 4 \times 2}{100} = \frac{8P}{100}$$

Hence, required ratio $= \frac{51P}{625} : \frac{8P}{100}$

$$= \frac{51}{25} : \frac{8}{4} = \frac{51}{25} : 2$$

= 51 : 50.

78. (C): Ratio of partnership

$$A : B : C = \frac{7}{2} : \frac{4}{3} : \frac{6}{5}$$

= 105 : 40 : 36

After 4 months:

Ratio of Share in the profit,

A : B : C

$$= 105 \times 4 + 105 \times \frac{150}{100} \times 8 : 40 \times 12 : 36 \times 12$$

$$= 420 + 105 \times \frac{3}{2} \times 8 : 480 : 432$$

= 420 + 105 × 12 : 480 : 432

= 420 + 1260 : 480 : 432

= 1680 : 480 : 432

= 35 : 10 : 9

Given, the total profit at the end of one year = ₹ 21,600

Hence, B's share in the profit

$$= 21600 \times \frac{10}{35+10+9}$$

$$= 21600 \times \frac{10}{54}$$

$$= \frac{216000}{54}$$

$$= ₹\ 4000.$$

79. (D): Let the C.P. of an article = ₹ x

Then, the S.P. of an article = ₹ $x \times \frac{100-20}{100} = \frac{4}{5}x$

Now, For profit 10%

The S.P. of the article = ₹ $\left(\frac{4}{5}x + 12\right)$

$\therefore$ Profit = S.P. – C.P.

$$= \frac{4}{5}x + 12 - x = \left(12 - \frac{1}{5}x\right)$$

$$\therefore \quad \text{Profit\%} = \frac{\text{Profit} \times 100}{\text{C.P.}}$$

$$\Rightarrow \quad 10 = \frac{\left(12 - \frac{1}{5}x\right) \times 100}{x}$$

$$\Rightarrow \quad 10x = \left(12 - \frac{1}{5}x\right) \times 100$$

$$\Rightarrow \quad x = 10\left(12 - \frac{1}{5}x\right)$$

$$\Rightarrow \quad x = 120 - 2x$$

$$\Rightarrow \quad x + 2x = 120$$

$$\Rightarrow \quad 3x = 120$$

$$\Rightarrow \quad x = 40$$

Hence, the cost price of an article = ₹ 40.

80. (D): $\dfrac{a^{1/2} + a^{-1/2}}{1-a} + \dfrac{1 - a^{-1/2}}{1+\sqrt{a}}$

$$= \frac{a^{1/2} + \frac{1}{a^{1/2}}}{1-a} + \frac{1 - \frac{1}{a^{1/2}}}{1+\sqrt{a}}$$

$$= \frac{\frac{a+1}{a^{1/2}}}{1-a} + \frac{\frac{a^{1/2}-1}{a^{1/2}}}{1+\sqrt{a}}$$

$$= \frac{1}{a^{1/2}}\left[\frac{a+1}{1-a} + \frac{a^{1/2}-1}{1+\sqrt{a}}\right]$$

$$= \frac{1}{\sqrt{a}}\left[\frac{a+1}{(1-\sqrt{a})(1+\sqrt{a})} + \frac{\sqrt{a}-1}{(1+\sqrt{a})}\right]$$

$$= \frac{1}{\sqrt{a}(1+\sqrt{a})}\left[\frac{a+1}{1-\sqrt{a}} + \sqrt{a} - 1\right]$$

$$= \frac{1}{\sqrt{a}(1+\sqrt{a})}\left[\frac{a+1}{1-\sqrt{a}} - (1-\sqrt{a})\right]$$

$$= \frac{1}{\sqrt{a}(1+\sqrt{a})}\left[\frac{a+1-(1-\sqrt{a})^2}{1-\sqrt{a}}\right]$$

$$= \frac{a+1-1-a+2\sqrt{a}}{\sqrt{a}(1+\sqrt{a})(1-\sqrt{a})} = \frac{2\sqrt{a}}{\sqrt{a}(1-a)} = \frac{2}{1-a}.$$

81. (C): Sugh is a historical village located in Yamunanagar district, Haryana. It is known for its ancient archaeological significance, with remains dating back to the Harappan civilization. This district encompasses the area where Sugh village is situated, contributing to its historical and cultural heritage.

82. (B): Rohtash Bishnoi, a Haryanvi mountaineer, successfully conquered Mount Elbrus in August 2023. Mount Elbrus is the highest peak in Europe, and conquering it is a significant achievement in mountaineering. Rohtash's feat showcases the spirit and capabilities of adventurers from Haryana in challenging international terrains.

83. (A): Shri Dharma Vir, who served as the Governor of Haryana, was an Indian Civil Service (ICS) officer. The ICS was the administrative civil service of the British Empire in India, and being a part of it was considered prestigious. His experience and administrative skills were pivotal during his tenure as governor, reflecting the training and responsibilities handled during his ICS career.

84. (A, C): Topara and Thanesar in Haryana are known for their historical importance with evidence of Buddhist structures such as stupas from the Mauryan period. Topara is especially significant due to the Topara Kalan pillar, originally erected by Emperor Ashoka, which supports the presence of Buddhist monuments like stupas. Thanesar, being an ancient site associated with both Hindu and Buddhist history, also shows signs of such ancient structures, suggesting a rich history of religious and cultural amalgamation during the Mauryan era.

85. (B): Geeta Jayanti Samaroh is celebrated in the month of Margshirsh according to the Hindu lunar calendar. This festival marks the anniversary of the Bhagavad Gita, which is believed to have been delivered by Lord Krishna to Arjuna on the battlefield of Kurukshetra on this day.

86. (A): Shri T.C. Gupta serves as the Chief Commissioner of the Haryana Right to Service Commission. This commission is tasked with ensuring that public services in Haryana are delivered in a timely, efficient, and transparent manner, with Gupta leading these efforts.

87. (B): Statement (*ii*) about Sadhu Nischal Das is correct; he compiled 'Vichar Sagar,' a book presented in the form of a dialogue, which delves into philosophical discussions. However, he was not a disciple of Dadu Dayal, making statement (*i*) incorrect.

88. (D): The Chinkara Breeding Centre in Haryana is located in Bhiwani. This center is crucial for the conservation of the Chinkara, focusing on breeding and caring for this species to support its population growth and ensure ecological balance.

90. (A): The Indian Institute of Information Technology (IIIT) is located in Sonipat, Haryana. This institution is part of the group of IIITs in India established to foster specialized education in information technology and related disciplines, aimed at enhancing technical education and research in the region.

91. (D): Information overload refers to a condition where the amount of input to a system exceeds its processing capacity. This phenomenon is commonly experienced by individuals when they receive more information than can be processed, leading to difficulties in understanding issues and making decisions.

92. (B): The growth stage of the product life cycle is characterized by a rapid climb in sales. This phase follows the introduction stage and features significant increases in market acceptance, leading to improvements in profitability and further investments in marketing and production.

93. (A): Job rotation is not an off-the-job training method; it is an on-the-job technique. Off-the-job training methods, such as classroom lectures, simulations, and vestibule training, are conducted away from the actual work environment and are structured to train employees without the pressures of ongoing operations.

94. (C): The need for power is a psychological drive that reflects a person's desire to make others behave in ways they would not have otherwise. This concept is a part of McClelland's theory of needs, which identifies different motivational drivers, including power, achievement, and affiliation.

95. (C): Both environmental analysis and environmental scanning are processes involved in monitoring and evaluating the nature and direction of change in the business environment. They are used interchangeably to describe the systematic examination of external influences on an organization's performance and strategy.

96. (B): To create a company in the accounting software Tally, the shortcut used is "Alt + F3". This allows users to access the company creation menu directly, facilitating the setup of new company data within the software environment.

97. (A): The Selling Concept in marketing posits that consumers will not purchase enough of the company's products unless there is a significant effort in selling and promotion. This concept emphasizes aggressive marketing to generate sales, reflecting an outbound marketing strategy.

98. (C): Given the unlimited liability in a partnership, the partners X, Y, and Z are responsible not only for their capital contributions but also potentially their private assets. The total extent of their liability would be the sum of their capital contributions and private assets. Therefore, for X, the liability would be ₹ 50,000 (capital) + ₹ 20,000 (private assets) = ₹ 70,000; for Y, it would be ₹ 40,000 (capital) + ₹ 2,000 (private assets) = ₹ 42,000; for Z, it would be ₹ 30,000 (capital) + ₹ 5,000 (private assets) = ₹ 35,000. This illustrates the principle of unlimited liability where all personal assets can be considered in the event of the firm's financial distress.

99. (C): Old Ratio = 7 : 3

Z's Share = 3/7

X's Sacrifice in favour of Z = 2/7

X's Sacrifice Ratio = Old Ratio – New Ratio

2/7 = 7/10 – New Ratio

New Ratio = 7/10 – 2/7

X's New Ratio = 29/70

Y's Sacrifice in favour of Z = 1/7

Y's Sacrifice Ratio = Old Ratio – New Ratio

1/7 = 3/10 – New Ratio

New Ratio = 3/10 – 1/7

Y's New Ratio = 11/70

New Ratio = X : Y : Z

New Ratio = 29/70 : 11/70 : 3/7

= 29 : 11 : 30

Therefore, if X and Y sharing profits in the ratio of 7 : 3, admit Z for 3/7 share in the new firm in which he takes 2/7 from X and 1/7 from Y. The new ratio of X, Y and Z will be 29 : 11 : 30.

100. (B): Both the assertion (A) and the reason (R) are true. A company can indeed forfeit shares if a shareholder fails to pay call amounts, but the reason given (R) that the shareholder remains responsible for the unpaid amount until fully paid by new transactions is not the explanation of the forfeiture policy. Forfeiture typically eliminates the defaulter's liability for future payments.

101. (B): To find the amount of inventory, we use the given financial ratios and the amount of current liabilities.

Given Data:

- Current Ratio = 4 : 5. This implies for every 5 units of current liabilities, there are 4 units of current assets.
- Quick Ratio = 5 : 7. This implies for every 7 units of current liabilities, there are 5 units of quick assets.
- Current Liabilities = ₹ 3,50,000.

Calculations:

1. Calculate Current Assets using the current ratio:

$$\text{Current Assets} = \frac{4}{5} \times 3,50,000 = 2,80,000$$

2. Calculate Quick Assets using the quick ratio:

$$\text{Quick Assets} = \frac{5}{7} \times 3,50,000 = 2,50,000$$

3. Determine Inventory by subtracting quick assets from current assets:

Inventory = Current Assets − Quick Assets

= 2,80,000 − 2,50,000 = 30,000

102. (A): To assess the impact on the trial balance from incorrectly posting a rent received transaction:

Given Data:

- ₹ 5,000 received for rent and entered correctly in the cash book.
- Incorrectly posted to the debit side of the rent account in the ledger.

Analysis:

- Correct Treatment: The ₹ 5,000 received should be credited to the rent account because it reduces the rental expense (or records rent income, depending on the context).
- Incorrect Posting: By debiting the rent account instead, you've effectively doubled the error amount. This is because the cash account correctly increases (debit), and the rent account incorrectly increases (debit) instead of decreasing (credit).

Effect on Trial Balance:

- Both the debit and credit sides of the rent account are affected:
- The correct credit entry is missing, and an incorrect debit entry is added.
- This results in an overstatement of the debit total by the amount of the error, doubled (once for the missing credit and once for the erroneous debit):

Overstatement = 2 × 5,000 = 10,000

Conclusion: Due to the error, the debit side of the trial balance will be greater by ₹ 10,000 than the credit total. This error misrepresents the financial records, requiring correction to ensure the trial balance's accuracy.

103. (D): Obsolescence of a depreciable asset can be caused by technological changes, improvements in production methods, legal or other restrictions, and changes in market demand. These factors collectively contribute to reducing the utility or value of an asset, hence all options (*a*), (*b*), (*c*), and (*d*) are correct.

104. (A): Money received against share warrants is shown as shareholders' funds. This is because share warrants, which allow the holder to buy company shares in the future at a pre-set price, represent potential equity and are thus considered part of the equity funding of a company until exercised.

105. (B): The provision for Discount on Debtors is a charge on the revenue. This accounting practice recognizes potential losses from trade receivables that might not be collected fully, impacting the profit and loss statement by reducing the revenue recorded from sales.

106. (D): Charismatic leaders are known for their ability to inspire and motivate followers through their vision, personal risk-taking, and sensitivity to follower needs. They typically exhibit unconventional behaviour, breaking away from traditional or estabiished norms to invoke change and innovation. This makes conventional behaviour not a characteristic of charismatic leadership, as it contradicts the very essence of what makes a leader charismatic—being extraordinary and transformational.

107. (B): A virtual organization is a small, core organization that extensively outsources major business functions. This organizational structure allows the company to remain flexible and adaptable, focusing on core competencies while leveraging external resources for other functions, effectively reducing traditional organizational boundaries and often operating with a significant online presence.

108. (C): A matrix structure in an organization creates dual lines of authority by combining functional and product departmentalization. This structure allows for more dynamic and flexible handling of projects and facilitates efficient resource use by pooling employees from different departments to work collaboratively on specific projects under dual command.

109. (C): Interest level is not typically considered a barrier to effective communication. Common barriers include filtering (altering messages to make them more favorable to the receiver), selective perception (interpreting messages based on one's interests or expectations), and emotions (how feelings can color the interpretation of messages). Interest level, if anything, can enhance the effectiveness of communication by engaging and motivating the listener.

110. (C): The Right to Seek Redressal is a consumer right against unfair trade practices and exploitation. This right allows consumers to seek a legal remedy through various forms of redress, such as compensation, refund, repair, or replacement, for any harm caused by defective goods or deficient services. This is part of broader consumer rights designed to protect against unfairness and exploitation in the marketplace.

111. (A): Self-actualization refers to the drive to become what one is capable of becoming. This concept, central to Abraham Maslow's hierarchy of needs, represents the highest level where an individual realizes their potential, seeks personal growth, self-fulfillment, and peak experiences, becoming everything they are capable of.

112. (C): According to the Consumer Protection Act, the statement that the District Forum shall consist of four members is incorrect. Typically, a District Forum consists of a president and at least two members, one of whom should be a woman. Therefore, the correct composition is not four members but rather three.

113. (B): Depreciation is the accounting process of allocating the cost of a tangible asset over its useful life. It represents the cost consumption of the asset used in earning revenues for the business. Depreciation is not about valuing assets, but rather about cost allocation to ensure accurate financial reporting.

114. (B): Dividend income received by entities other than financial enterprises is typically shown under investing activities in the cash flow statement. This classification is because dividends are returns on investments in other companies, and managing investment returns is categorized under investing activities.

115. (C): Matching the Accounting Standards (AS) with their respective objects:

(*a*) AS 9 deals with Revenue Recognition, correctly matched to (*i*).

(*b*) AS 10 pertains to Property, Plant, and Equipment, matched to (*ii*).

(*c*) AS 16 is related to Borrowing Costs, matched to (*iv*).

(*d*) AS 17 covers Segment Reporting, matched to (*iii*). This alignment correctly categorizes each standard with its specific accounting focus.

116. (D): The statement that fixed assets are stated in the Balance Sheet at their market value is incorrect. Generally, fixed assets are recorded at their historical cost and then depreciated over their useful life. The historical cost principle does not allow for the adjustment of fixed assets to their market value in regular financial reporting under most accounting frameworks.

117. (C): When errors are detected after the preparation of the trial balance, a suspense account is opened to temporarily hold unbalanced amounts until the errors are corrected. This account is used to ensure the trial balance balances while the specific errors are identified and rectified.

118. (C): The statement that a ledger is a set of accounts is true. A ledger is a collection of accounts where all the transactions of a business are categorized and recorded. Each account within the ledger records transactions related to a specific asset, liability, equity, revenue, or expense.

119. (A): The convention of disclosure supports the presentation of contingent liabilities in the notes below the balance sheet. This accounting convention mandates that all significant information that affects the decision-making process of users of the financial statements should be disclosed, including potential obligations that may arise in the future, like contingent liabilities.

120. (C): To rectify the error of not charging interest on the drawings after the partnership accounts have been closed, the appropriate account to open is the Profit & Loss Adjustment Account. This account is used to adjust the profits of the firm after the initial accounts closure, specifically addressing post-closure corrections like uncharged interest on drawings.

121. **(B):** A transactional leader is one who guides or motivates their followers towards established goals by clarifying role and task requirements. This leadership style is focused on routine, structured processes and uses rewards and punishments as motivational tools. It emphasizes clear structures and operating procedures, with the leader overseeing that followers fulfill their roles as required.

122. **(D):** The mental ability to analyze and diagnose complex situations is known as conceptual skill. This skill is crucial for senior management roles, as it involves understanding and maneuvering complex abstract ideas and integrating them into the strategy and problem-solving processes. Leaders with strong conceptual skills are able to see the big picture and make decisions that align with the overall goals of the organization.

123. **(D):** Intellectual property rights include patents, trademarks, and copyrights. These legal rights collectively provide protection to creators over their inventions, brands, and original works. Patents protect inventions, trademarks protect brand identifiers, and copyrights protect original artistic or literary works. Together, these rights are crucial for fostering innovation and creativity, allowing rights holders to benefit from their intellectual efforts.

124. **(A):** Wholesalers can check price fluctuations in the market by holding back goods when prices fall and releasing them when prices rise. This ability to manage large quantities of goods provides wholesalers with the leverage to influence market supply and demand to some extent, which can stabilize prices or maximize profits based on market conditions.

125. **(B):** Frederick W. Taylor wrote the book 'The Principles of Scientific Management' in 1911. This book lays the foundation for modern organization and decision theory and introduces principles of systematic management. Taylor's work emphasized efficiency and productivity through scientific analysis of labor processes, which significantly influenced the development of industrial engineering and management practices.

126. **(A):** Unity of command is the principle that a subordinate should have only one supervisor to whom they are directly responsible. This principle ensures clarity in direction and communication within an organization. It helps prevent confusion and conflict by establishing clear lines of authority and accountability, which are essential for efficient and effective management.

127. **(D):** Flexible reporting is not a limitation of a computerized accounting system; rather, it is one of its advantages. Computerized systems allow for more flexible, accurate, and timely reporting compared to manual systems. They can quickly generate a variety of reports tailored to different management needs, enhancing decision-making capabilities within the organization.

128. **(D):** When debentures are issued as collateral security, no interest is paid on them. These debentures are issued to secure a loan and represent a contingent liability, which only becomes an actual liability if the condition of default occurs. As such, they do not accrue interest like regular debentures issued for capital.

129. **(C):** The following rules must be followed in the absence of a partnership dead:

- The partners are entitled to an equal share of the profits and losses.
- Partners are not entitled to interest on their capital.
- For any extra work done for the firm, no partner will be paid a salary or any other reward.
- No interest will be charged on partners' drawings.
- Partners will be permitted to charge interest of 6% per year on any loans and advances they make to the firm.

130. **(C):** The Joint Life Policy Account of the partners is treated as an asset account in the accounting records. This account records the life insurance policy taken jointly by partners, which often aims to assist in funding partnership obligations or providing for the continuation of the business upon the death of a partner. This type of account is considered an asset because it represents a future economic benefit controlled by the partnership.

131. **(D):** A favourable balance as per Pass Book means it is showing a credit balance. This indicates that the bank account has more deposits than withdrawals, reflecting more funds available than have been spent. This is essentially the opposite of how balances would be represented in the Cash Book, where a credit balance indicates a negative or overdraft situation.

132. **(C):** When a liability is taken over by a partner at the time of dissolution of the partnership, the entry to record this action is a debit to the Realisation Account. The Realisation Account is used to consolidate all the adjustments related to the winding up of the business, including the disposal of assets and settlement of liabilities. The partner taking over the liability will be credited in their capital account, indicating their assumption of this obligation.

133. (D): Sweat equity shares are indeed shares issued to employees or directors at a discount or for other than cash consideration, typically in recognition of their hard work or contribution to the company. This practice is aimed at rewarding those who contribute to the development and enhancement of the company's value over time.

134. (C): The securities premium amount, according to legal regulations, may be utilized by a company for specific purposes including writing off the expenses or discounts on the issue of debentures. This use is permissible as it involves capital financing operations. Securities premium cannot be used for writing off revenue losses or the loss on the sale of fixed assets, which are not related to the issue or redemption of shares or debentures.

135. (B): The correct sequence of the formation of a company is: Promotion, Incorporation, Capital Subscription, and Commencement of Business. This sequence reflects the typical phases of a company's establishment:

- Promotion involves conceptualizing the business and planning the initial steps.
- Incorporation is the legal registration of the company, making it a distinct legal entity.
- Capital Subscription deals with securing the necessary capital for the company through issue of shares.
- Commencement of Business is the final step where the company starts its operations officially after meeting all legal and financial prerequisites.

136. (A): A comprehensive interview is a selection device used to obtain in-depth information about a candidate. This type of interview typically covers a wide range of topics, including detailed questions about the candidate's background, work experience, skills, and competencies, as well as situational and behavioural questions. It is designed to provide a thorough understanding of the candidate's capabilities and fit for the role.

137. (B): The encounter stage in the socialization process is where new employees confront the possible dichotomy between their expectations of the organization and the actual reality. This stage is crucial as individuals begin to learn what the organization is truly like and how they fit into that structure, which may differ significantly from their initial perceptions or expectations formed during the recruitment process.

138. (D): Decentralization is not a principle of Henri Fayol. Fayol's principles of management include centralization, which refers to the concentration of decision-making authority at the top of the organizational hierarchy. Fayol discussed both centralization and decentralization, but he did not list decentralization as a separate principle. His emphasis was more on finding an effective balance between the two.

139. (A): The correct software and management practices designed specifically to serve the customer from order through delivery and after-sales service is eCRM (electronic Customer Relationship Management). eCRM extends beyond traditional CRM by incorporating web-based interactions, focusing on enhancing customer interactions, personalizing services, and efficiently managing relationships across various digital platforms. This approach is tailored to improve the overall customer experience, tracking and fulfilling their needs from initial contact through the entire service lifecycle, including post-sale support. ERP systems, while they integrate various business functions, are broader in scope and not solely focused on customer service processes from order to delivery.

140. (B): Both statements (*a*) and (*b*) are correct regarding Micro, Small, and Medium Enterprises (MSMEs) in India:

(*a*) MSMEs are indeed one of the largest employers in India, providing numerous job opportunities across various sectors.

(*b*) MSMEs generate more employment opportunities per unit of capital invested compared to large industries, making them crucial for employment generation in India.

(*c*) is not correct; MSMEs do not account for 45% of the industrial units. They represent a significant portion, but the exact percentage varies and is not consistently documented at 45%.

Thus, only statements (*a*) and (*b*) are accurate.

141. (C): Ogives are useful for locating the median graphically. An ogive is a graph that represents the cumulative frequency of a dataset. By finding the point where the ogive crosses half of the total frequency, you can determine the median value of the data set. This is particularly useful in statistics for understanding the distribution and central tendency of the data.

142. (C): The term "span of control" refers to the number of subordinates a manager can efficiently and effectively direct. This concept is crucial in organizational design and affects decision-making, communication, and overall management effectiveness. A wider span of control might lead to more autonomy for subordinates, while a narrower span might ensure closer supervision and more detailed guidance.

143. (B): To calculate the number of debentures issued when purchasing a machine worth ₹ 2,88,000 with debentures of ₹ 100 each issued at a 4% discount:

- Each debenture is issued at ₹ 100 - 4% of ₹ 100 = ₹ 96.
- Therefore, the number of debentures
  = Total cost / Price per debenture
  = ₹ 2,88,000 / ₹ 96 = 3,000 debentures.

144. (B): The sale of furniture where cash is involved results in a flow of cash. In this case, the furniture with a book value of ₹ 7,400 is sold at a loss of ₹ 900. The cash received from this sale (₹ 7,400 – ₹ 900 = ₹ 6,500) represents a cash inflow, which is a flow of cash activity in financial terms.

145. (B): The term "Cat nature" refers to the type of goodwill that is personal to the owner and likely to disappear or diminish when the business changes hands. This type of goodwill is tied closely to the individual characteristics of the current owner, such as personal relationships with customers, making it less likely to transfer upon the sale or alteration of business ownership.

146. (A): Both the assertion (A) that in a double account system, the final accounts of a company fail to disclose the true condition of its assets, and the reason (R) that assets are shown at their cost price even when they are completely worn out, are correct. The double account system typically used in utility companies and railways tends to show fixed assets at historical cost, which can lead to a discrepancy between book values and actual economic values if assets are significantly depreciated or obsolete.

147. (A): Lease financing refers to an arrangement where one party grants another party the right to use an asset in return for periodic payments. This is commonly used in acquiring vehicles, machinery, and other equipment, where the lessee pays the lessor for the usage rights without acquiring ownership.

148. (C): On the retirement or death of a partner, the Memorandum Revaluation Account is used if assets and liabilities are to be shown at their old values but adjustments are needed to reflect any unrealized gains or losses. This account is not part of the double-entry system but serves to note changes in asset values for internal purposes without affecting the main accounts until realized.

149. (D): The total of the sales book is posted to the credit of the Sales Account. The sales book records all credit sales transactions, and the total represents the total sales made on credit during a period. This total is then credited to the Sales Account, which tracks all sales revenues. Therefore, the correct answer is "None of these" as "Sales Account" is not listed among the options.

150. (B): The issue of equity shares for cash involves an increase in equity (raising capital) and an increase in current assets (cash), which would decrease the debt-to-equity ratio and increase the current ratio. This strengthens the company's financial position both in terms of leverage and liquidity.

Previous Paper (Solved)

Haryana Teacher Eligibility Test (HTET)

PGT Commerce (Level-3), Exam 2022

(Exam held on 03 December, 2022)

PART-I

Child Development and Pedagogy

Directions: *Answer the following questions by selecting the **most appropriate** option.*

1. Which of the following is ***not*** a symptom of good mental health of students?
A. Living in fantasy world
B. Balance in Life
C. Knowledge of our potentials and limitations
D. Free from undesirable worries

2. Which of the following is ***not*** a level of teaching?
A. Basic Level B. Memory Level
C. Understanding Level D. Reflective Level

3. Which of the following task is ***not*** related to Baqer Mehdi's test of Creativity?
A. Unusual uses related task
B. New relation between pairs related task
C. Product improvement related task
D. Ask and guess related task

4. Which way is the most appropriate for social development of adolescents?
A. Discussion on socialization
B. Essay competition on social values
C. Organizing group activities
D. Documentary on social relations

5. Which pair is ***not*** correct with reference to emotions and basic instincts?

	Emotion		**Basic Instinct**
A.	Anger	–	Repulsion
B.	Ownership	–	Collection
C.	Wonder	–	Curiosity
D.	Fear	–	Escape

6. According to Triarchic Theory, which of the following is ***not*** a type of intelligence?
A. Analytical B. Creative
C. Theoretical D. Practical

7. Which of the following factors positively affects learning?
A. Meaningless content B. Lack of maturation
C. Lack of motivation D. Informational feedback

8. Rohit helps others to get praise. This is an example of:
A. Intrinsic Motivation B. Extrinsic Motivation
C. Innate Motivation D. None of these

9. What will be the intelligence quotient of a 15 year old boy, when his mental age is 12?
A. 80 B. 90
C. 100 D. 110

10. What type of reinforcement schedule is it, when reinforcement is provided to the learner only after a certain number of responses?
A. Fixed ratio B. Variable Ratio
C. Fixed interval D. Variable interval

11. Who developed the Thematic Apperception Test for personality assessment?
A. Murray and Morgan B. Bellack
C. Eysenck D. Allport and Cattell

12. Spranger's classification of personality is related to which approach of personality assessment?
A. Trait Approach B. Type Approach
C. Instinct Approach D. Psychoanalytic Approach

13. Development which proceeds from 'centre to the periphery', is known as:
A. Cephalic Caudal B. Proximodistal
C. Spiral D. Circular

14. Who is called the father of Trait Theory for study of personality?
A. Allport B. Woodworth
C. McDougall D. Eysenck

15. Which of the following statement is ***not*** correct with reference to individual differences?
A. No two persons can be exactly alike.
B. Individual differences may belong to different areas.
C. Individual differences affects different dimensions of development.
D. Individual differences arises only due to heredity.

16. A type of intelligence test in which the difficulty level of questions gradually increases and the time factor is secondary:
A. Verbal Test B. Power Test
C. Speed Test D. Performance Test

17. According to Kohlberg's theory, what level of morality is it, when morality includes self-accepted moral principles?
A. Pre-conventional B. Conventional
C. Post-conventional D. None of these

18. Which one of the following is ***not*** a direct method for measurement of attitude?
A. Interview B. Projection
C. Questionnaire D. Observation

19. As a teacher which of the following work would ***not*** be done by you to develop the creativity of the students?
A. Encouragement of originality
B. Removal of fear
C. Freedom to respond
D. Avoidance of divergent thinking

20. According to Piaget's Cognitive Development Theory, 'The basic unit of the cognitive structure that helps in the implementation of cognitive behaviour', is termed as:
A. Reflexes B. Basic Instincts
C. Schema D. Conservation

21. Hunger and Thirst is which type of motive?
A. Extrinsic B. Acquired
C. Intrinsic D. Social

22. 'When an adolescent is unable to show anger to his parents, then he shows his anger to his younger brother.' This is an example of which type of defence mechanism?
A. Repression B. Regression
C. Projection D. Displacement

23. Which of the following is ***not*** a general characteristic of adolescence period?
A. It is a transitional period.
B. It is period of unrealism.
C. It is time for search of identity.
D. It is the threshold of puberty.

24. Which one of the following is ***not*** a part of Bronfenbrenner's Ecological System theory?
A. Micro system B. Macro system
C. Minor system D. Meso system

25. Which of the following pairs of communication skills is ***correct*** for receiving the information?
A. Listening and Writing
B. Speaking and Reading
C. Listening and Reading
D. Speaking and Writing

26. According to Maslow's Need Hierarchical theory, 'Esteem Needs' are which type of need?
A. Personal B. Social
C. Intellectual D. Emotional

27. According to the moral development theory of Piaget, adolescence period is:
A. Stage of moral realism
B. Stage of morality constraint
C. Stage of heteronomous morality
D. Stage of autonomous morality

28. 'A horse can be brought near water, but cannot be forced to drink'. This statement reveals the truth of Thorndike's which law of learning?
A. Law of Readiness B. Law of Exercise
C. Law of Effect D. Law of Multi Responses

29. "Emotional Intelligence may be defined as the capacity to reason with emotion in four areas–to perceive emotion, to integrate it in thought, to understand it and to manage it".

Who gave this definition of emotional intelligence?
A. Daniel Goleman
B. Mayer and Peter Salovey
C. Peter and Michael
D. Halverson

30. A teaching-learning strategy in which small groups of students with different level of ability use a variety of learning activities to improve their understanding of a subject:
A. Multi-sensory learning
B. Team teaching
C. Co-operative learning
D. Programmed learning

PART-II

भाषा-I : हिन्दी

निर्देश : *निम्नलिखित प्रश्नों के उत्तर देने के लिए **सबसे उचित** विकल्प चुनिए।*

31. विलोम की दृष्टि से **असंगत** विकल्प चुनिए :
A. उपत्यका — अधित्यका
B. उन्मुख — अभिमुख
C. कल्पना — यथार्थ
D. कुत्सा — प्रशंसा

32. इनमें से कौन-सा वाक्य **अशुद्ध** है?
A. तुम्हारा व्यवहार सर्वश्रेष्ठ है।
B. हम सभी में मनुष्यी दुर्बलताएँ हैं।

C. वह पाँव से जूता उतार रहा है।
D. शीला को अपनी योग्यता पर गर्व है।

33. किस विकल्प में निजवाचक सर्वनाम का प्रयोग हुआ है?
A. हमें अपना काम स्वयं करना चाहिए।
B. तेते पाँव पसारिये, जेती लाँबी सौर।
C. हम किसी का कुछ नहीं बिगाड़ सकते।
D. जैसा करोगे, वैसा ही भरोगे।

34. ''आनन्दा चुपके-से चली गई।'' वाक्य में किस प्रकार के क्रिया-विशेषण का प्रयोग हुआ है?
A. कालवाचक B. रीतिवाचक
C. परिमाणवाचक D. स्थानवाचक

35. शब्दकोश में वर्णानुक्रम की दृष्टि से 'श्रद्धा' शब्द इनमें से किस शब्द के पहले आएगा?
A. शौर्य B. श्याम
C. शृंगार D. श्रमिक

36. 'पशु' शब्द से निर्मित विशेषण है :
A. पाशविक B. पशुपति
C. पशुता D. पशुत्व

37. समास की दृष्टि से **असंगत** विकल्प चुनिए :
A. कनकलता – कर्मधारय
B. सचिवालय – तत्पुरुष
C. चौराहा – द्विगु
D. आकंठ – बहुव्रीहि

38. उसने मुझे सदैव धोखा दिया। वाक्य में प्रयुक्त 'धोखा' शब्द कौन-सी संज्ञा का उदाहरण होगा?
A. समुदायवाचक संज्ञा
B. जातिवाचक संज्ञा
C. भाववाचक संज्ञा
D. व्यक्तिवाचक संज्ञा

39. 'तत्सम-तद्भव' की दृष्टि से **असंगत** विकल्प चुनिए :
A. लोमशा – लोमड़ी
B. रज्जु – रस्सी
C. पाषाण – पत्थर
D. मस्तक – माथा

40. इनमें से किस शब्द में 'आवट' प्रत्यय का प्रयोग **नहीं** हुआ है?
A. गुर्राहट B. सजावट
C. बुनावट D. तरावट

41. किस शब्द में एक से अधिक उपसर्गों का प्रयोग हुआ है?
A. अध्यापक B. अन्वेषण
C. अनुष्ठान D. व्याधि

42. उच्चारण की दृष्टि से 'ल' वर्ण का उच्चारण स्थान होगा :
A. ओष्ठ B. मूर्धा
C. तालु D. दन्त

43. समश्रुत भिन्नार्थक शब्दों का अर्थ भेद की दृष्टि से **बेमेल** विकल्प हैं :
A. सदेह – देह सहित; सन्देह – संशय
B. सुअन – पुत्र; सुमन – फूल
C. सुकृती – सत्कर्म; सुकृति – पुण्यवान्
D. स्वजन – बन्धु; श्वजन – कुत्ता

44. किस विकल्प में विसर्ग सन्धि का प्रयोग हुआ है?
A. युधिष्ठिर
B. वयोवृद्ध
C. परोपदेश
D. निष्ठुर

45. पर्यायवाची की दृष्टि से **असंगत** विकल्प चुनिए :
A. गधा – लंबकर्ण, वैशाखनन्दन, गर्दभ
B. गरुड़ – वैनतेय, कामारि, काक
C. गणिका – सर्ववल्लभा, वारांगना, पतुरिया
D. ग्वाला – आभीर, अहीर, गोप

Language-II : English

Direction: *Answer the following questions by selecting the* ***most appropriate*** *option.*

46. Which of the following sentences is the ***correct*** option to express present perfect continuous tense?
A. Mr. Mehta has been waking for 2 O'clock in the morning.
B. Mr. Mehta has been waking since 2 O'clock in the morning.
C. Mr. Mehta has been waked since 2 O'clock in the morning.
D. Mr. Mehta has been waking from 2 O'clock in the morning.

47. Fill in the blank with the ***correct*** option that completes the idiom:
A rolling stone ______
A. carries rough winds B. kills no one
C. gathers no sauce D. gathers no moss

48. Choose the part of the sentence that is grammatically ***incorrect***:
The thief took towards/his heels/on seeing/the Police-van arrive.
A. The thief took towards B. his heels
C. on seeing D. the Police-van arrive.

49. Change the narration:

Kavin said to Mr. Cowper, "Please, be kind to me."

A. Kavin requested Mr. Cowper to be kind to him.
B. Kavin requested Mr. Cowper to be kind to me.
C. Kavin asked Mr. Cowper to be please kind to me.
D. Kavin asked Mr. Cowper that he must be kind to him.

50. Fill in the blank with the ***correct*** form of verb:

You had better ______ your hands before you eat.

A. been washing B. washing
C. washed D. wash

51. The word 'garrulous' means:

A. talkative B. abusive
C. violent D. abundant

52. Arrange the following jumbled options in the correct order and then choose the ***correct*** option:

(*i*) too many (*ii*) spoil
(*iii*) the broth (*iv*) cooks

A. (*i*), (*iv*), (*iii*), (*ii*) B. (*i*), (*iv*), (*ii*), (*iii*)
C. (*iii*), (*iv*), (*ii*), (*i*) D. (*iv*), (*ii*), (*i*), (*iii*)

53. Fill in the blank with the ***correct*** option:

When Monisha reached the bus stand, the bus ______.

A. was already left B. had already left
C. already left D. has been already left

54. Choose the part of the sentence that is grammatically ***incorrect***:

He has committed/a blunder/mistake/today morning.

A. He has committed B. a blunder
C. mistake D. today morning

55. Which of the following options express the ***correct*** meaning of the sentence given below?

He is too cute to overlook.

A. He is too cute and he can be overlooked.
B. He is too cute but he can be overlooked.
C. He is so cute that he cannot be overlooked.
D. Although he is not cute, but he cannot be overlooked.

56. Fill in the blank with the ***correct*** form of verb:

Neither you nor she ________ made the mistake.

A. have B. has
C. had D. did

57. Fill in the blank with ***correct*** 'Modal Auxiliary':

Passengers ________ not walk across the railway line. (Prohibition)

A. should B. can
C. need D. must

58. Fill in the blank with the ***correct*** option:

Mr. Sudhir Soni is ______ R.A.S. Officer.

A. an B. a
C. the D. ×

59. Choose the ***correct*** passive of the given sentence:

Did he kill a lion?

A. Did a lion killed by him?
B. Was a lion killed by you?
C. Was a lion killed by him?
D. Had a lion been killed by you?

60. Fill in the blank with the ***correct*** option:

Let us stay here, while it ______.

A. is raining B. was raining
C. has been raining D. had been raining

PART-III

General Studies : Quantitative Aptitude, Reasoning Ability and GK & Awareness

Direction: *Answer the following questions by selecting the* ***most appropriate*** *option.*

61. If the amount is $3\frac{3}{8}$ times the sum after 3 years at compound interest compounded annually, then the rate of interest per annum is:

A. $16\frac{2}{3}\%$ B. $33\frac{1}{3}\%$
C. 33% D. 50%

62. A reduction of 20% in the price of rice enables a customer to purchase 12.5 kg more for ₹ 800. The original price of rice per kg is:

A. ₹ 12 B. ₹ 14
C. ₹ 15 D. ₹ 16

63. In a division sum, the divisor is 12 times the quotient and 5 times the remainder. If the remainder is 36, then the dividend is:

A. 2726 B. 2736
C. 2796 D. 2826

64. Find the next term of the following series:

Z1A, X2D, V6G, T21J, R88M, P445P, ?

A. N2676T B. T2670N
C. N2676S D. M2670S

65. A number when divided by 5, 9, 13 leaves remainder 2, 6 and 10 respectively. The least such number is:

A. 602 B. 592
C. 572 D. 582

66. In a certain code language "PARTICLE" is written as "USBQFMDJ" and "GENERATE" is written as "FOFHFUBS", then in same code language "DOCUMENT" will be written as:

A. VDEPUOSF
B. VDPENFUQ
C. VDPEUOFN
D. VDPEUOSF

67. A tank is filled in 5 hours by three pipes P, Q and R. The pipe R is twice as fast as Q and Q is twice as fast as P. How much time will pipe P alone take to fill the tank?

A. 22 hours B. 25 hours
C. 30 hours D. 35 hours

68. If $x=\dfrac{\sqrt{3}+1}{\sqrt{3}-1}$ and $y=\dfrac{\sqrt{3}-1}{\sqrt{3}+1}$, then the value of $(x^2 + y^2)$ is:

A. 14 B. 12
C. 13 D. 16

69. In a row of girls, A is 10th from the left and B is 14th from the right. If they interchange their positions, A becomes 24th from the left. How many girls are there in a row?

A. 31 B. 33
C. 37 D. 39

70. Out of 1865 people, 660 can speak English and 1305 can speak Hindi, but 120 persons cannot speak either language, then how many persons can speak both languages?

A. 220 B. 440
C. 120 D. 1085

71. The population of a town is 9000. If the males increase by 5% and females by 8%, the population would be 9600 in a year. The number of males is:

A. 3000 B. 4000
C. 5000 D. 5600

72. D is taller than C and E. A is not as tall as E. C is taller than A. D is not as tall as B. Who is the tallest among of them?

A. A B. B
C. C D. D

73. Pointing to a girl in photograph, X said "She is the daughter of my grandfather's only son". How is the girl related to X?

A. Father B. Brother
C. Sister D. Mother

74. A steam engine train runs from East to West and wind is blowing from North to South, then the smoke from the train would blow in which direction?

A. N-W B. N-E
C. S-E D. S-W

75. The next term of the following number series is:

3, 13, 22, 32, 59, 69, 120, 130, ?

A. 201 B. 211
C. 227 D. 232

76. The average of nine consecutive numbers is *n*. If the next two numbers are also included, the new average is:

A. remain the same B. increase by 1
C. increase by 1.5 D. increase by 2

77. A shopkeeper sells an article at 15% gain. Had he sold it for ₹ 18 more, he would have gained 18%. The cost price (in ₹) of the article is:

A. 360 B. 540
C. 600 D. 640

78. A boat covers a certain distance downstream in 3 hours, while it comes back in 4.5 hours. If the speed of the stream be 3 kmph, then the speed of the boat in still water is:

A. 10 kmph B. 12 kmph
C. 13 kmph D. 15 kmph

79. A metallic sphere of radius 10.5 cm is melted and then recast into small cones each of radius 3.5 cm and height 3 cm, then the number of cones thus formed is:

A. 112 B. 126
C. 132 D. 138

80. X and Y are facing each other at sunrise. The shadow of Y is falling towards right of X, then Y is facing in which direction?

A. North B. South
C. East D. West

81. Which of the following monuments of Haryana have the status of State protected monuments?

(*i*) Sheikh Tayyab's Tomb
(*ii*) Shobha Sagar Pond
(*iii*) Bhimadevi Temple Complex

Choose the ***correct*** code:

A. (*i*) and (*ii*) B. (*ii*) and (*iii*)
C. (*i*) and (*iii*) D. (*i*), (*ii*) and (*iii*)

82. Which of the following institute is responsible for the development of infrastructure facilities in industrial areas of Haryana?

A. HARTRON B. HUDA
C. HSIIDC D. District Industries Centre

83. Consider the following statements:

(*i*) The institution of Lokayukta was established in Haryana in the year 2002.
(*ii*) Justice Pritam Pal was the first Lokayukta in the State of Haryana.

A. Only (*i*) is correct.
B. Only (*ii*) is correct.
C. Both (*i*) and (*ii*) are correct
D. Both (*i*) and (*ii*) are incorrect

84. Who among the following is ***not*** appointed by the Governor of Haryana?
A. Chief Minister of Haryana
B. A Judge of Punjab and Haryana High Court
C. A Member of Haryana Public Service Commission
D. A Member of Haryana Human Right Commission

85. Who among the following Governors of Haryana was a civil servant?
A. Muzaffar Hussain Burney
B. Jaisukh Lal Hathi
C. Dhanik Lal Mandal
D. Babu Parmanand

86. Read the following statements about 'Parivar Pehchan Patra Yojna':
(*i*) This scheme identifies family as a unit and is creating a reliable socio-economic database of all the families in Haryana.
(*ii*) An eight digit unique family ID is being issued for every family and the ID will be linked to birth, death and marriage records.
(*iii*) The data available in family ID database will be utilized to determine automatic verification for various welfare schemes and families will not be required to apply themselves for benefits.

Choose the ***correct*** code:
A. Only (*ii*) is correct.
B. (*i*) and (*ii*) are correct.
C. (*ii*) and (*iii*) are correct.
D. (*i*), (*ii*) and (*iii*) are correct.

87. Which places of Haryana have been notified as Ramsar site under Ramsar convention of UNESCO?
A. Sultanpur National Park & Bhindawas Wildlife Sanctuary
B. Kalesar National Park & Khaparwas Wildlife Sanctuary
C. Nahar Wildlife Sanctuary & Bir Shikargarh Wildlife Sanctuary
D. Abushahar Wildlife Sanctuary & Khol-Hi-Raitan Wildlife Sanctuary

88. The Lok Sabha and Rajya Sabha seats in Haryana are:
A. 7 and 4 B. 10 and 4
C. 10 and 5 D. 12 and 5

89. Which of the city of Haryana is known as the 'City of War Heroes'?
A. Gurugram B. Sonipat
C. Panipat D. Bhiwani

90. Consider the following statements regarding the Governor of Haryana:
(*i*) He is the Chancellor of Central University of Haryana.
(*ii*) He can hold any office of the profit in the State.
(*iii*) He is the President of Indian Red Cross Society, Haryana State Branch.
(*iv*) He does not have any discretionary power granted under the Constitution.

Which of the above statement(s) is/are ***correct***?
A. (*i*), (*ii*), (*iii*) and (*iv*) B. (*ii*), (*iii*) and (*iv*)
C. Only (*iii*) D. Both (*ii*) and (*iii*)

PART-IV

Commerce

Directions: *Answer the following questions by selecting the* ***most appropriate*** *option.*

91. In which activity all profits of a company are not distributed amongst the shareholders as dividend, but a part of the profits is retained or re-invested in the business?
A. Capital Distribution
B. Ploughing back of profits
C. Liquidity Distribution
D. Profitability Distribution

92. Which ratio indicates the firm's capacity to pay long-term debts and procure additional loans and informs whether the firm is following the policy of trading on equity?
A. Proprietary ratio
B. Debt-equity ratio
C. Returns on Shareholders Funds
D. Debt-Service ratio

93. 'A' does not keep proper accounting records of his business. He gives the following information, what will be profit or loss for the year?

Opening Capital	:	₹ 2,00,000
Closing Capital	:	₹ 2,50,000
Drawings made during the year	:	₹ 60,000
Capital added during the year	:	₹ 75,000

A. ₹ 85,000 B. ₹ 1,85,000
C. ₹ 35,000 D. ₹ 3,15,000

94. Working capital of a company is ₹ 21,28,000 and total debts are ₹ 42,50,000. If the company's long term debts are ₹ 27,30,000, then current ratio will be:
A. 0.78 : 1 B. 1.4 : 1
C. 1.14 : 1 D. 2.4 : 1

95. The current liabilities of XYZ Co. Ltd. are ₹ 1,50,000. Its current ratio is 3 : 1 and liquid ratio is 1 : 1. The value of stock will be:

A. ₹ 4,50,000 B. ₹ 1,50,000
C. ₹ 3,00,000 D. Can not be computed

96. The ability of the business to pay the amount due to stakeholders as and when it is due is known as:
A. Solvency
B. Liquidity
C. Profitability
D. Liquidity Profitability Equilibrium

97. While preparing cash flow statement of financial enterprise, interest and dividend received should be classified as ______ .
A. Operating activity B. Financing activity
C. Investing activity D. Business activity

98. Representation of various factors affecting net profit and capital employed by a chart known as:
A. Standard and Poor Chart
B. NYSE Chart
C. Break-even Chart
D. Du-pont Chart

99. Which 'Hundi' is similar to 'Demand Bill'?
A. Darshani Hundi B. Shahjog Hundi
C. Muddati Hundi D. Jawabee Hundi

100. State Bank of India desires to redeem 5,000. 10% debentures of ₹ 1,000 each at par out of available sufficient divisible profits. In this case, how much amount should be transferred to debentures redemption reserve A/c as per requirement under Section 71(4) of Indian Companies Act, read with rule 18(7) of a banking company?
A. ₹ 50,00,000 B. ₹ 7,50,000
C. ₹ 12,50,000 D. Zero

101. From the following, which statement is ***not*** true for bill of exchange?
A. It is drawn by the debtor.
B. It is drawn by the creditor.
C. It contains an order to make payment.
D. It requires acceptance by the drawee or someone else on his behalf.

102. Kaushal and Gulab are partners in a firm sharing profits in the ratio of 5 : 3. They admit Raju as a new partner for 1/7 share in the profit. The new profit sharing ratio will be 4 : 2 : 1. The sacrificing ratio of Kaushal and Gulab will be:
A. 3 : 5 B. 5 : 3
C. 4 : 2 D. 1 : 7

103. On dissolution of a firm liabilities are transferred to:
A. Bank Account
B. Reserve and Surplus Account
C. Cash Account
D. Realization Account

104. The ratio in which the continuing partners have acquired the share from the retiring or deceased partner, is called:
A. Debt-equity Ratio B. Liquidity Ratio
C. Current Ratio D. Gaining Ratio

105. Which statement is ***true*** for Receipt and Payment Account?
A. It includes depreciation.
B. It does not includes depreciation.
C. It has no opening balance.
D. It include income and expenditure items related only to the current period.

106. When a partner has agreed to undertake the dissolution work for an agreed remuneration bear the realization expenses, then what will be the journal entry if payment of realization expenses is made by the firm?
A. Bank A/c Dr.
To Realization A/c
B. Partners Capital A/c Dr.
To Bank A/c
C. Realization A/c Dr.
To Bank A/c
D. Bank A/c Dr.
To Partner's Capital A/c

107. A limited has agreed to pay purchase price of building ₹ 2,20,000, half the payment was made in cash and remaining half by issue of 9% debentures of ₹ 100 each at a premium of 10%. How much debentures will be issued for paying purchase amount?
A. 1000 B. 1100
C. 2000 D. 2200

108. In which system, the monitory effect of a transaction is taken into account in the period in which they are earned rather than in the period in which cash is actually received or paid by the enterprise?
A. Cash Basis System
B. Accrual Basis System
C. Economic Basis System
D. Circular flow of Money System

109. The recurring grants in the form of maintenance grant is treated as:
A. Capital Receipts B. Donations
C. Revenue Receipts D. Endowment Fund

110. In the benefit of expenditure extends upto only for one accounting period, it is called:
A. Capital Expenditure B. Revenue Expenditure
C. Noting Charges D. Underwriting

111. Read the statements carefully and choose a ***correct*** option given below:
Statement I: Capital Expenditures and Revenue Expenditures both are non-recurring by Nature.
Statement II: Capital Expenditures increase earning capacity of business whereas Revenue Expenditures are incurred to maintain earning capacity.
A. Only statement I is correct.

B. Only statement II is correct.
C. Both statements are correct.
D. Both statements are incorrect.

112. The expenses that are incurred in connection with the formation of a company are called:
A. Capital Expenditure
B. Preliminary Expenses
C. Expenses on Issue of Shares and Debentures
D. Revenue Expenditure

113. The study of mutual relationship between different components or their totals of the financial statements for a definite period of time is called:
A. Horizontal or Dynamic analysis
B. Vertical or Static analysis
C. Internal analysis
D. External analysis

114. Petty cash book is maintained for recording ______.
A. Petty incomes only
B. Petty expenses paid in cash
C. Petty incomes received in cash only
D. Petty incomes and petty expenses

115. A company issues 1000 debentures of ₹ 100 each at a discount of 6% and the debenture are to be repaid by equal installments of ₹ 20,000 at the end of each year, starting from first year, which amount of discount is written off at the end of first year?
A. ₹ 6,000 B. ₹ 2,000
C. ₹ 1,200 D. ₹ 1,600

116. Read the statements carefully and choose a ***correct*** option given below:
Statement I: Depreciation must be charged so as to ascertain true profit or loss of the business.
Statement II: When market value of an asset is higher than book value, depreciation is not charged.
A. Only statement I is correct.
B. Only statement II is correct.
C. Both statements are correct.
D. Both statements are incorrect.

117. A company forfeited 200 shares of ₹ 100 each, ₹ 70 called-up per share, on which the shareholder paid ₹ 50 per share. These shares were reissued at ₹ 80 fully paid-up per share. The share forfeited account will be debited in the reissue entry with:
A. ₹ 6,000 B. ₹ 4,000
C. ₹ 10,000 D. ₹ 16,000

118. The entire life of the firm is divided into time intervals for the measurement of the profit of the business, is called as:
A. Cost concept
B. Going concern concept
C. Accounting period concept
D. Realization concept

119. Leverage or capital structure ratios are also known as:
A. Long-term solvency ratios
B. Short-term solvency ratios
C. Return on capital employed
D. Current ratio

120. Read the statements carefully and choose a ***correct*** option given below:
Statement I: Passbook is the statement of account of the customer maintained by the bank.
Statement II: A business firm periodically prepares a bank reconciliation statement to reconcile the bank balance as per the cash book with the passbook as these to show different balances for various reasons.
A. Only statement I is correct.
B. Only statement II is correct.
C. Both statements are correct.
D. Both statements are incorrect.

121. A principle of enlightened marketing that requires that a company seek real product and marketing improvements:
A. Customer-value marketing
B. Innovative marketing
C. Sense of mission marketing
D. Consumer-oriented marketing

122. Banking and Insurance are which type of industries?
A. Genetic industries
B. Secondary industries
C. Tertiary industries
D. Manufacturing industries

123. A partnership deed generally do ***not*** include which of the following?
A. Name of firm
B. List of employees of firm
C. Duration of business
D. Procedure for dissolution of the firm

124. The organizational structure, most suitable for large organizations having diversified activities, is:
A. Divisional structure B. Functional structure
C. Managerial structure D. Formal structure

125. Interest rate and inflation rate are included under which factor of business environment:
A. Economic environment
B. Social environment
C. Legal environment
D. Technological environment

126. What type of a bank is Import-Export bank?
A. Commercial Bank B. Cooperative Bank
C. Central Bank D. Specialized Bank

127. _______ is the extra profit the firm earns from producing and selling an additional unit of output.
A. Marginal profit B. Managerial profit
C. Marginal cost D. Total profit

128. The secretariat of the Association of SAARC is situated at:
A. New Delhi, India B. Mumbai, India
C. Kathmandu, Nepal D. Geneva, Switzerland

129. A desire to satisfy one's interests, regardless of the impact on the other party to the conflict:
A. Collaborating B. Avoiding
C. Competing D. Compromising

130. "Money is what money does" this definition of money was given by:
A. Walker B. Hawtrey
C. Crowther D. Keynes

131. A temporary pricing in which company sells products below the list price, and sometimes even below cost to increase shortrun sales:
A. Promotional pricing B. Temporary pricing
C. FOB-origin pricing D. Geographical pricing

132. Which one of the following is ***not*** an element of communication process?
A. Encoding B. Channel
C. Receiver D. Measurement

133. The present value of an investment's cash inflows (benefits) minus the present value of its cash outflow (costs) is known as:
A. Net Present Value (NPV)
B. Net Future Value (NFV)
C. Gross Present Value (GPV)
D. Gross Future Value (GFV)

134. An organized movement of citizens and government agencies to improve the rights and power of buyers in relation of sellers:
A. Consumerism B. Environmentalism
C. Sustainability D. Citizenship

135. Staff authority works as:
A. a chain of command
B. a channel of communication
C. a carrier of responsibility
D. Advice of certain matters

136. Internal elements that may interfere with the company's ability to achieve its objectives is:
A. Strength B. Weakness
C. Opportunity D. Threats

137. Which of the following is included in Fayol's principles of management?
A. Harmony, not discord
B. Cooperation, not individualism
C. Development of each and every person
D. Unity of command

138. The Foreign Trade (Development and Regulation) Act, 1992 replaced which of the following Acts?
A. Import and Export (Control) Act, 1947
B. Export Regulation Act, 1962
C. Import Development Act, 1952
D. Both (B) and (C)

139. Who determines the Cash Reserve Ratio?
A. Central bank B. Market taxes
C. Commercial banks D. Government

140. Which one of the following is the characteristics of transactional leader?
A. Inspirational motivation
B. Management by exception
C. Idealized influence
D. Intellectual stimulation

141. Process of organizing include:
A. Developing premises B. Setting objectives
C. Assignment of duties D. Selecting an alternative

142. "Efficiency through work simplification and standardization", is focused by:
A. Taylor B. Fayol
C. Simon D. Bernard

143. The opinion and belief segment of an attitude is:
A. Affective component B. Behavioural component
C. Feeling component D. Cognitive component

144. When was GATT established?
A. 1947 B. 1948
C. 1995 D. 1903

145. Which one of these can be delegated?
A. Power B. Authority
C. Responsibility D. Accountability

146. "Invisible" in the balance of payments account refer to:
A. Goods transaction B. Service transaction
C. Capital transaction D. Export promotion

147. Who has given the concept of 'POSDCORB'?
A. Ralph Davis B. E.F.L. Brech
C. Koontz D. Luther Gulick

148. Among the following sources, which one is an internal recruitment source?
A Direct recruitment
B. Recommendations of employees
C. Advertisement
D. Transfers

149. ______ occurs if a given percentage increase in all inputs results in a smaller percentage increase in output.
A. Decreasing returns to scale
B. Increasing returns to scale
C. Constant returns to scale
D. Output elasticity

150. Who has proposed the 'Need of Achievement Thoery'?
A. A.H. Maslow B. Clayton Alderfer
C. David McClelland D. Frederick Herzberg

Answers

1. (A)	**2. (A)**	**3. (D)**
4. (C)	**5. (A)**	**6. (C)**
7. (D)	**8. (B)**	**9. (A)**
10. (A)	**11. (A)**	**12. (B)**
13. (B)	**14. (A)**	**15. (D)**
16. (B)	**17. (C)**	**18. (B)**
19. (D)	**20. (C)**	**21. (C)**
22. (D)	**23. (*)**	**24. (C)**
25. (C)	**26. (B)**	**27. (D)**
28. (A)	**29. (B)**	**30. (C)**
31. (B)	**32. (B)**	**33. (A)**
34. (B)	**35. (D)**	**36. (A)**
37. (D)	**38. (C)**	**39. (C)**
40. (A)	**41. (D)**	**42. (D)**
43. (C)	**44. (B)**	**45. (B)**
46. (*)	**47. (D)**	**48. (A)**
49. (A)	**50. (D)**	**51. (A)**
52. (B)	**53. (B)**	**54. (C)**
55. (C)	**56. (B)**	**57. (D)**
58. (A)	**59. (C)**	**60. (A)**

61. (D): At compound interest compounded annually

$$\therefore \quad A = P\left(1+\frac{r}{100}\right)^n$$

$$\Rightarrow \quad 3\frac{3}{8}P = P\left(1+\frac{r}{100}\right)^3$$

$$\Rightarrow \quad 3\frac{3}{8} = \left(1+\frac{r}{100}\right)^3$$

$$\Rightarrow \quad \frac{27}{8} = \left(1+\frac{r}{100}\right)^3$$

$$\Rightarrow \quad \left(\frac{3}{2}\right)^3 = \left(1+\frac{r}{100}\right)^3$$

$$\Rightarrow \quad \frac{3}{2} = 1+\frac{r}{100} \Rightarrow \frac{3}{2}-1 = \frac{r}{100}$$

$$\Rightarrow \quad \frac{1}{2} = \frac{r}{100} \Rightarrow r = 50$$

$\therefore$ The rate of interest per annum, r = 50%.

62. (D): Let the original price of rice per kg is ₹ x

Then, new price per kg = $\dfrac{x \times 100 - 20}{100}$

$$= x \times \frac{80}{100} = ₹\ \frac{4}{5}x$$

According to question,

$$\frac{800}{\frac{4}{5}x} - \frac{800}{x} = 12.5$$

$$\Rightarrow \quad \frac{1000}{x} - \frac{800}{x} = \frac{25}{2}$$

$$\Rightarrow \quad \frac{1}{x}(1000-800) = \frac{25}{2}$$

$$\Rightarrow \quad \frac{200}{x} = \frac{25}{2}$$

$$\Rightarrow \quad 25x = 400 \Rightarrow x = 16$$

$\therefore$ The original price of rice per kg is ₹ 16.

63. (B): Let quotient = x

then, Divisor = $12x = 5 \times 36$

$$\Rightarrow \quad x = \frac{5 \times 36}{12} = 15$$

$\because$ Dividend = Divisor × Quotient + Remainder

$\therefore$ Dividend = $12x \times x + 36$

= 12 × 15 × 15 + 36

= 12 × 225 + 36

= 2700 + 36 = 2736.

64. (C)

65. (D): Here, 5 − 2 = 9 − 6 = 13 − 10 = 3

the difference of all the divisors with their corresponding remainder in each case is same as 10

So, Required number = (LCM of 5, 9, 13) − 3

= 585 − 3 = 582.

66. (C): Given,

and

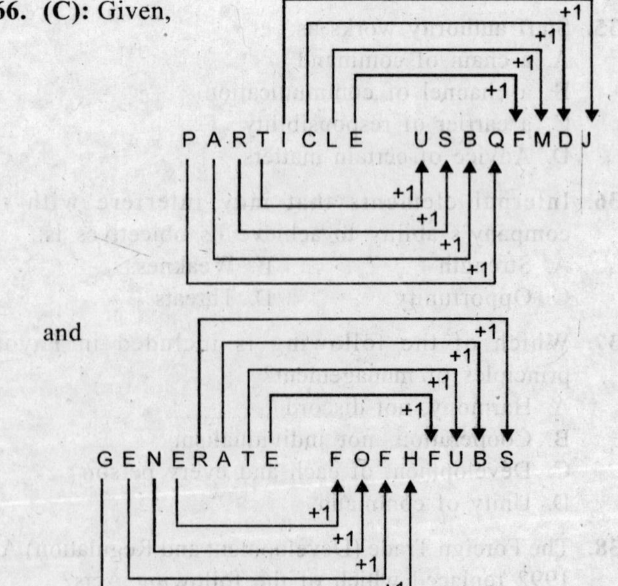

Similarly,

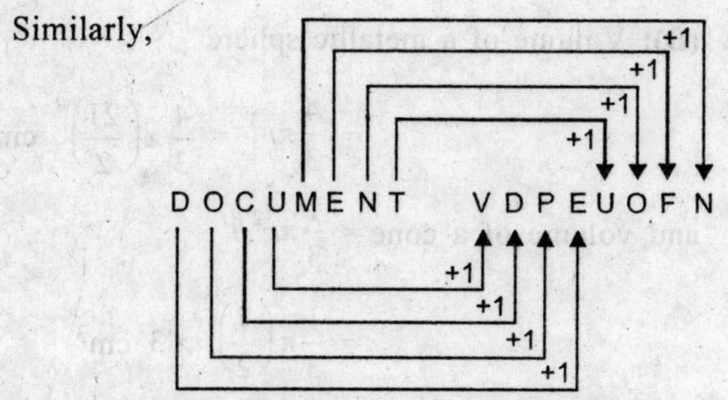

$\therefore$ In same code language 'DOCUMENT' will be written as 'VDPEUOFN'.

67. (D): Ratio of Efficiency of pipes

$$R : Q = 2 : 1$$
$$Q : P = 2 : 1$$
$$\Rightarrow \quad P : Q = 1 : 2$$
and $$Q : R = 1 : 2$$
$$\Rightarrow \quad Q : R = 2 : 4$$
$$\therefore \quad P : Q : R = 1 : 2 : 4$$

Ratio of time,

$$P : Q : R = 1 : \frac{1}{2} : \frac{1}{4} = 4 : 2 : 1$$

By question, (P + Q + R)'s 1 hour's work:

$$\frac{1}{4x} + \frac{1}{2x} + \frac{1}{x} = \frac{1}{5}$$
$$\Rightarrow \quad \frac{1+2+4}{4x} = \frac{1}{5}$$
$$\Rightarrow \quad \frac{7}{4x} = \frac{1}{5} \Rightarrow x = \frac{35}{4}$$
$$\therefore \quad \text{P's 1 hour's work} = \frac{1}{4x} = \frac{1}{4 \times \frac{35}{4}} = \frac{1}{35}$$

$\therefore$ Pipe P alone will take 35 hours to fill the tank.

68. (A): Given, $x = \frac{\sqrt{3}+1}{\sqrt{3}-1} = \frac{\sqrt{3}+1}{\sqrt{3}-1} \times \frac{\sqrt{3}+1}{\sqrt{3}+1} = \frac{(\sqrt{3}+1)^2}{3-1}$

$$= \frac{3+1+2\sqrt{3}}{2} = \frac{4+2\sqrt{3}}{2} = 2+\sqrt{3}$$

and $y = \frac{\sqrt{3}-1}{\sqrt{3}+1} = \frac{\sqrt{3}-1}{\sqrt{3}+1} \times \frac{\sqrt{3}-1}{\sqrt{3}-1}$

$$= \frac{(\sqrt{3}-1)^2}{3-1} = \frac{3+1-2\sqrt{3}}{2} = 2-\sqrt{3}$$

$$\therefore \quad x^2 + y^2 = (2+\sqrt{3})^2 + (2-\sqrt{3})^2$$
$$= 4+3+4\sqrt{3}+(4+3-4\sqrt{3})$$
$$= 7+4\sqrt{3}+7-4\sqrt{3} = 7 + 7 = 14$$
$$\Rightarrow \quad x^2 + y^2 = 14.$$

69. (C): Left 10th 14th (13 girls) Right; A, B

Again, Left 24th Right; A

$\therefore$ The number of girls in this row

$$= 24 + 13 = 37.$$

70. (A): Given, Total number of people = 1865

Number of people speak English = 660

Number of people speak Hindi = 1305

Number of persons can not speak either language = 120

$\therefore$ Number of persons can speak both language

$$= (660 + 1305 + 120) - 1865$$
$$= 2085 - 1865 = 220.$$

71. (B): Let the number of males is x

then, the number of females is $(9000 - x)$

$$\therefore \quad x \times \frac{105}{100} + (9000-x) \times \frac{108}{100} = 9600$$
$$\Rightarrow \quad \frac{105x}{100} + \frac{972000}{100} - \frac{108x}{100} = 9600$$
$$\Rightarrow \quad \frac{972000}{100} - \frac{3x}{100} = 9600$$
$$\Rightarrow \quad 9720 - 9600 = \frac{3x}{100} \Rightarrow 120 = \frac{3x}{100}$$
$$\Rightarrow \quad 3x = 12000 \Rightarrow x = 4000$$

$\therefore$ The number of males = x = 4000.

72. (B): B > D > C > E > A

Here, B is the tallest among them.

73. (C): Here, the girl is the sister of X.

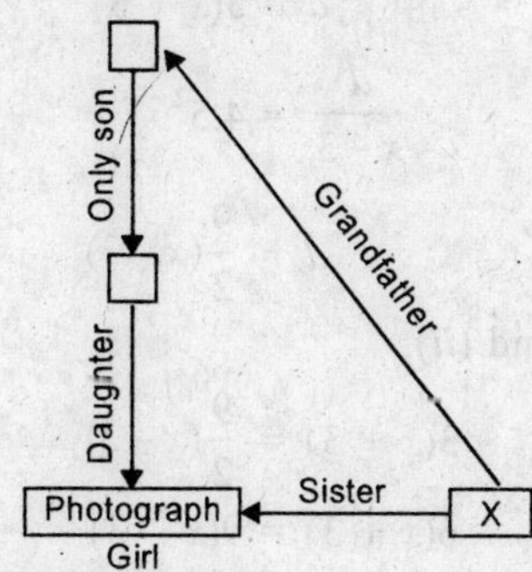

74. (C)

75. (B):

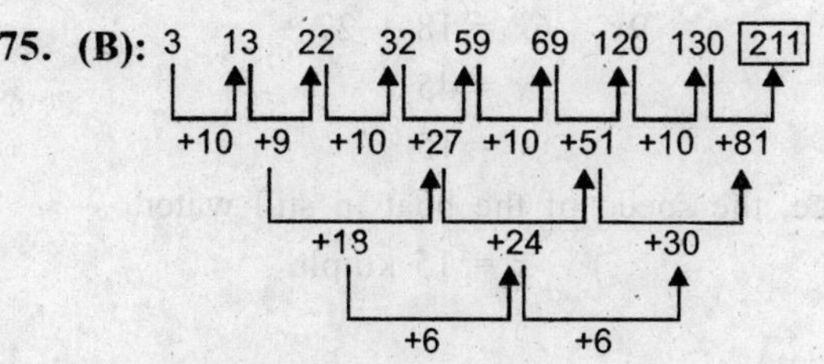

$\therefore$? = The next term = 211.

76. (B): $n = \frac{1+2+3+....+9}{9}$

$= \frac{9(9+1)}{9\times2} = \frac{10}{2} = 5$

The new average $= \frac{1+2+3+...+11}{11}$

$= \frac{11(11+1)}{11\times2} = \frac{12}{2} = 6$

Hence, the new average is increased by 1.

77. (C): Let the cost price of the article is ₹ x

Then, S.P. $= x\times\frac{115}{100}+18 = x\times\frac{118}{100}$

$\Rightarrow \frac{115}{100}x+18 = \frac{118}{100}x$

$\Rightarrow \frac{118}{100}x-\frac{115}{100}x = 18$

$\Rightarrow \frac{3x}{100} = 18$

$\Rightarrow \frac{x}{100} = 6$

$\Rightarrow x = 600$

$\therefore$ The cost price of the article = ₹ 600.

78. (D): Let the speed of the boat in still water is x kmph then, speed of boat in downstream = $(x + 3)$ kmph and speed of boat in upstream = $(x - 3)$ kmph

Let certain distance = d km

Then, $\frac{d}{x+3} = 3$

$\Rightarrow d = 3(x + 3)$ ...(*i*)

and $\frac{d}{x-3} = 4.5$

$\Rightarrow d = \frac{9}{2}(x-3)$ ...(*ii*)

From (*i*) and (*ii*),

$3(x + 3) = \frac{9}{2}(x-3)$

$\Rightarrow 6(x + 3) = 9(x - 3)$

$\Rightarrow 6x + 18 = 9x - 27$

$\Rightarrow 9x - 6x = 18 + 27$

$\Rightarrow 3x = 45$

$\Rightarrow x = 15$

Hence, the speed of the boat in still water $x = 15$ kmph.

79. (B): Volume of a metallic sphere

$= \frac{4}{3}\pi r^3 = \frac{4}{3}\pi\left(\frac{21}{2}\right)^3$ cm³

and volume of a cone $= \frac{1}{3}\pi r^2 h$

$= \frac{1}{3}\pi\left(\frac{7}{2}\right)^2 \times 3$ cm³

$\therefore$ The number of cones thus formed is

$\frac{\frac{4}{3}\pi\left(\frac{21}{2}\right)^3}{\frac{1}{3}\pi\left(\frac{7}{2}\right)^2\times3} = \frac{4\times\frac{21}{2}\times\frac{21}{2}\times\frac{21}{2}}{\frac{7}{2}\times\frac{7}{2}\times3}$

$= \frac{4}{3}\times\frac{21}{2}\times\frac{21}{2}\times\frac{21}{2}\times\frac{2}{7}\times\frac{2}{7}$

$= 3 \times 21 \times 2 = 6 \times 21 = 126.$

80. (A)	**81. (D)**	**82. (C)**
83. (C)	**84. (B)**	**85. (A)**
86. (D)	**87. (A)**	**88. (C)**
89. (D)	**90. (C)**	**91. (B)**
92. (B)	**93. (C)**	**94. (D)**
95. (C)	**96. (B)**	**97. (A)**
98. (D)	**99. (A)**	**100. (D)**
101. (A)	**102. (A)**	**103. (D)**
104. (D)	**105. (B)**	**106. (B)**
107. (A)	**108. (B)**	**109. (C)**
110. (B)	**111. (B)**	**112. (B)**
113. (B)	**114. (B)**	**115. (B)**
116. (A)	**117. (B)**	**118. (C)**
119. (A)	**120. (C)**	**121. (B)**
122. (C)	**123. (B)**	**124. (A & B)**
125. (A)	**126. (D)**	**127. (A)**
128. (C)	**129. (C)**	**130. (A)**
131. (A)	**132. (D)**	**133. (A)**
134. (A)	**135. (D)**	**136. (B)**
137. (D)	**138. (A)**	**139. (A)**
140. (B)	**141. (C)**	**142. (A)**
143. (D)	**144. (A & B)**	**145. (B)**
146. (B)	**147. (D)**	**148. (D)**
149. (A)	**150. (C)**	

Previous Paper (Solved)

Haryana Teacher Eligibility Test (HTET)

PGT Commerce (Level-3), Exam 2022

(Exam held on 03 December, 2022)

PART-I

Child Development and Pedagogy

Directions: *Answer the following questions by selecting the **most appropriate** option.*

1. Which of the following is ***not*** a symptom of good mental health of students?
A. Living in fantasy world
B. Balance in Life
C. Knowledge of our potentials and limitations
D. Free from undesirable worries

2. Which of the following is ***not*** a level of teaching?
A. Basic Level B. Memory Level
C. Understanding Level D. Reflective Level

3. Which of the following task is ***not*** related to Baqer Mehdi's test of Creativity?
A. Unusual uses related task
B. New relation between pairs related task
C. Product improvement related task
D. Ask and guess related task

4. Which way is the most appropriate for social development of adolescents?
A. Discussion on socialization
B. Essay competition on social values
C. Organizing group activities
D. Documentary on social relations

5. Which pair is ***not*** correct with reference to emotions and basic instincts?

	Emotion		**Basic Instinct**
A.	Anger	–	Repulsion
B.	Ownership	–	Collection
C.	Wonder	–	Curiosity
D.	Fear	–	Escape

6. According to Triarchic Theory, which of the following is ***not*** a type of intelligence?
A. Analytical B. Creative
C. Theoretical D. Practical

7. Which of the following factors positively affects learning?
A. Meaningless content B. Lack of maturation
C. Lack of motivation D. Informational feedback

8. Rohit helps others to get praise. This is an example of:
A. Intrinsic Motivation B. Extrinsic Motivation
C. Innate Motivation D. None of these

9. What will be the intelligence quotient of a 15 year old boy, when his mental age is 12?
A. 80 B. 90
C. 100 D. 110

10. What type of reinforcement schedule is it, when reinforcement is provided to the learner only after a certain number of responses?
A. Fixed ratio B. Variable Ratio
C. Fixed interval D. Variable interval

11. Who developed the Thematic Apperception Test for personality assessment?
A. Murray and Morgan B. Bellack
C. Eysenck D. Allport and Cattell

12. Spranger's classification of personality is related to which approach of personality assessment?
A. Trait Approach B. Type Approach
C. Instinct Approach D. Psychoanalytic Approach

13. Development which proceeds from 'centre to the periphery', is known as:
A. Cephalic Caudal B. Proximodistal
C. Spiral D. Circular

14. Who is called the father of Trait Theory for study of personality?
A. Allport B. Woodworth
C. McDougall D. Eysenck

15. Which of the following statement is ***not*** correct with reference to individual differences?
A. No two persons can be exactly alike.
B. Individual differences may belong to different areas.
C. Individual differences affects different dimensions of development.
D. Individual differences arises only due to heredity.

16. A type of intelligence test in which the difficulty level of questions gradually increases and the time factor is secondary:
A. Verbal Test B. Power Test
C. Speed Test D. Performance Test

17. According to Kohlberg's theory, what level of morality is it, when morality includes self-accepted moral principles?
A. Pre-conventional B. Conventional
C. Post-conventional D. None of these

18. Which one of the following is ***not*** a direct method for measurement of attitude?
A. Interview B. Projection
C. Questionnaire D. Observation

19. As a teacher which of the following work would ***not*** be done by you to develop the creativity of the students?
A. Encouragement of originality
B. Removal of fear
C. Freedom to respond
D. Avoidance of divergent thinking

20. According to Piaget's Cognitive Development Theory, 'The basic unit of the cognitive structure that helps in the implementation of cognitive behaviour', is termed as:
A. Reflexes B. Basic Instincts
C. Schema D. Conservation

21. Hunger and Thirst is which type of motive?
A. Extrinsic B. Acquired
C. Intrinsic D. Social

22. 'When an adolescent is unable to show anger to his parents, then he shows his anger to his younger brother.' This is an example of which type of defence mechanism?
A. Repression B. Regression
C. Projection D. Displacement

23. Which of the following is ***not*** a general characteristic of adolescence period?
A. It is a transitional period.
B. It is period of unrealism.
C. It is time for search of identity.
D. It is the threshold of puberty.

24. Which one of the following is ***not*** a part of Bronfenbrenner's Ecological System theory?
A. Micro system B. Macro system
C. Minor system D. Meso system

25. Which of the following pairs of communication skills is ***correct*** for receiving the information?
A. Listening and Writing
B. Speaking and Reading
C. Listening and Reading
D. Speaking and Writing

26. According to Maslow's Need Hierarchical theory, 'Esteem Needs' are which type of need?
A. Personal B. Social
C. Intellectual D. Emotional

27. According to the moral development theory of Piaget, adolescence period is:
A. Stage of moral realism
B. Stage of morality constraint
C. Stage of heteronomous morality
D. Stage of autonomous morality

28. 'A horse can be brought near water, but cannot be forced to drink'. This statement reveals the truth of Thorndike's which law of learning?
A. Law of Readiness B. Law of Exercise
C. Law of Effect D. Law of Multi Responses

29. "Emotional Intelligence may be defined as the capacity to reason with emotion in four areas–to perceive emotion, to integrate it in thought, to understand it and to manage it".
Who gave this definition of emotional intelligence?
A. Daniel Goleman
B. Mayer and Peter Salovey
C. Peter and Michael
D. Halverson

30. A teaching-learning strategy in which small groups of students with different level of ability use a variety of learning activities to improve their understanding of a subject:
A. Multi-sensory learning
B. Team teaching
C. Co-operative learning
D. Programmed learning

PART-II

भाषा-I : हिन्दी

निर्देश : *निम्नलिखित प्रश्नों के उत्तर देने के लिए* ***सबसे उचित*** *विकल्प चुनिए।*

31. विलोम की दृष्टि से **असंगत** विकल्प चुनिए :
A. उपत्यका — अधित्यका
B. उन्मुख — अभिमुख
C. कल्पना — यथार्थ
D. कुत्सा — प्रशंसा

32. इनमें से कौन-सा वाक्य **अशुद्ध** है?
A. तुम्हारा व्यवहार सर्वश्रेष्ठ है।
B. हम सभी में मनुष्यी दुर्बलताएँ हैं।

C. वह पाँव से जूता उतार रहा है।
D. शीला को अपनी योग्यता पर गर्व है।

33. किस विकल्प में निजवाचक सर्वनाम का प्रयोग हुआ है?
A. हमें अपना काम स्वयं करना चाहिए।
B. तेते पाँव पसारिये, जेती लाँबी सौर।
C. हम किसी का कुछ नहीं बिगाड़ सकते।
D. जैसा करोगे, वैसा ही भरोगे।

34. ''आनन्दा चुपके-से चली गई।'' वाक्य में किस प्रकार के क्रिया-विशेषण का प्रयोग हुआ है?
A. कालवाचक B. रीतिवाचक
C. परिमाणवाचक D. स्थानवाचक

35. शब्दकोश में वर्णानुक्रम की दृष्टि से 'श्रद्धा' शब्द इनमें से किस शब्द के पहले आएगा?
A. शौर्य B. श्याम
C. शृंगार D. श्रमिक

36. 'पशु' शब्द से निर्मित विशेषण है :
A. पाशविक B. पशुपति
C. पशुता D. पशुत्व

37. समास की दृष्टि से **असंगत** विकल्प चुनिए :
A. कनकलता – कर्मधारय
B. सचिवालय – तत्पुरुष
C. चौराहा – द्विगु
D. आकंठ – बहुव्रीहि

38. उसने मुझे सदैव धोखा दिया। वाक्य में प्रयुक्त 'धोखा' शब्द कौन-सी संज्ञा का उदाहरण होगा?
A. समुदायवाचक संज्ञा
B. जातिवाचक संज्ञा
C. भाववाचक संज्ञा
D. व्यक्तिवाचक संज्ञा

39. 'तत्सम-तद्भव' की दृष्टि से **असंगत** विकल्प चुनिए :
A. लोमशा – लोमड़ी
B. रज्जु – रस्सी
C. पाषाण – पत्थर
D. मस्तक – माथा

40. इनमें से किस शब्द में 'आवट' प्रत्यय का प्रयोग **नहीं** हुआ है?
A. गुर्राहट B. सजावट
C. बुनावट D. तरावट

41. किस शब्द में एक से अधिक उपसर्गों का प्रयोग हुआ है?
A. अध्यापक B. अन्वेषण
C. अनुष्ठान D. व्याधि

42. उच्चारण की दृष्टि से 'ल' वर्ण का उच्चारण स्थान होगा :
A. ओष्ठ B. मूर्धा
C. तालु D. दन्त

43. समश्रुत भिन्नार्थक शब्दों का अर्थ भेद की दृष्टि से **बेमेल** विकल्प हैं :
A. सदेह – देह सहित; सन्देह – संशय
B. सुअन – पुत्र; सुमन – फूल
C. सुकृती – सत्कर्म; सुकृति – पुण्यवान्
D. स्वजन – बन्धु; श्वजन – कुत्ता

44. किस विकल्प में विसर्ग सन्धि का प्रयोग हुआ है?
A. युधिष्ठिर
B. वयोवृद्ध
C. परोपदेश
D. निष्ठुर

45. पर्यायवाची की दृष्टि से **असंगत** विकल्प चुनिए :
A. गधा – लंबकर्ण, वैशाखनन्दन, गर्दभ
B. गरुड़ – वैनतेय, कामारि, काक
C. गणिका – सर्ववल्लभा, वारांगना, पतुरिया
D. ग्वाला – आभीर, अहीर, गोप

Language-II : English

Direction: *Answer the following questions by selecting the* ***most appropriate*** *option.*

46. Which of the following sentences is the ***correct*** option to express present perfect continuous tense?
A. Mr. Mehta has been waking for 2 O'clock in the morning.
B. Mr. Mehta has been waking since 2 O'clock in the morning.
C. Mr. Mehta has been waked since 2 O'clock in the morning.
D. Mr. Mehta has been waking from 2 O'clock in the morning.

47. Fill in the blank with the ***correct*** option that completes the idiom:
A rolling stone ______.
A. carries rough winds B. kills no one
C. gathers no sauce D. gathers no moss

48. Choose the part of the sentence that is grammatically ***incorrect***:
The thief took towards/his heels/on seeing/the Police-van arrive.
A. The thief took towards B. his heels
C. on seeing D. the Police-van arrive.

49. Change the narration:

Kavin said to Mr. Cowper, "Please, be kind to me."

A. Kavin requested Mr. Cowper to be kind to him.
B. Kavin requested Mr. Cowper to be kind to me.
C. Kavin asked Mr. Cowper to be please kind to me.
D. Kavin asked Mr. Cowper that he must be kind to him.

50. Fill in the blank with the ***correct*** form of verb:

You had better ______ your hands before you eat.

A. been washing B. washing
C. washed D. wash

51. The word 'garrulous' means:

A. talkative B. abusive
C. violent D. abundant

52. Arrange the following jumbled options in the correct order and then choose the ***correct*** option:

(*i*) too many (*ii*) spoil
(*iii*) the broth (*iv*) cooks

A. (*i*), (*iv*), (*iii*), (*ii*) B. (*i*), (*iv*), (*ii*), (*iii*)
C. (*iii*), (*iv*), (*ii*), (*i*) D. (*iv*), (*ii*), (*i*), (*iii*)

53. Fill in the blank with the ***correct*** option:

When Monisha reached the bus stand, the bus ______.

A. was already left B. had already left
C. already left D. has been already left

54. Choose the part of the sentence that is grammatically ***incorrect***:

He has committed/a blunder/mistake/today morning.

A. He has committed B. a blunder
C. mistake D. today morning

55. Which of the following options express the ***correct*** meaning of the sentence given below?

He is too cute to overlook.

A. He is too cute and he can be overlooked.
B. He is too cute but he can be overlooked.
C. He is so cute that he cannot be overlooked.
D. Although he is not cute, but he cannot be overlooked.

56. Fill in the blank with the ***correct*** form of verb:

Neither you nor she ______ made the mistake.

A. have B. has
C. had D. did

57. Fill in the blank with ***correct*** 'Modal Auxiliary':

Passengers ______ not walk across the railway line. (Prohibition)

A. should B. can
C. need D. must

58. Fill in the blank with the ***correct*** option:

Mr. Sudhir Soni is ______ R.A.S. Officer.

A. an B. a
C. the D. ×

59. Choose the ***correct*** passive of the given sentence:

Did he kill a lion?

A. Did a lion killed by him?
B. Was a lion killed by you?
C. Was a lion killed by him?
D. Had a lion been killed by you?

60. Fill in the blank with the ***correct*** option:

Let us stay here, while it ______.

A. is raining B. was raining
C. has been raining D. had been raining

PART-III

General Studies : Quantitative Aptitude, Reasoning Ability and GK & Awareness

Direction: *Answer the following questions by selecting the* ***most appropriate*** *option.*

61. If the amount is $3\frac{3}{8}$ times the sum after 3 years at compound interest compounded annually, then the rate of interest per annum is:

A. $16\frac{2}{3}\%$ B. $33\frac{1}{3}\%$
C. 33% D. 50%

62. A reduction of 20% in the price of rice enables a customer to purchase 12.5 kg more for ₹ 800. The original price of rice per kg is:

A. ₹ 12 B. ₹ 14
C. ₹ 15 D. ₹ 16

63. In a division sum, the divisor is 12 times the quotient and 5 times the remainder. If the remainder is 36, then the dividend is:

A. 2726 B. 2736
C. 2796 D. 2826

64. Find the next term of the following series:

Z1A, X2D, V6G, T21J, R88M, P445P, ?

A. N2676T B. T2670N
C. N2676S D. M2670S

65. A number when divided by 5, 9, 13 leaves remainder 2, 6 and 10 respectively. The least such number is:

A. 602 B. 592
C. 572 D. 582

66. In a certain code language "PARTICLE" is written as "USBQFMDJ" and "GENERATE" is written as "FOFHFUBS", then in same code language "DOCUMENT" will be written as:

A. VDEPUOSF
B. VDPENFUQ
C. VDPEUOFN
D. VDPEUOSF

67. A tank is filled in 5 hours by three pipes P, Q and R. The pipe R is twice as fast as Q and Q is twice as fast as P. How much time will pipe P alone take to fill the tank?

A. 22 hours B. 25 hours
C. 30 hours D. 35 hours

68. If $x=\frac{\sqrt{3}+1}{\sqrt{3}-1}$ and $y=\frac{\sqrt{3}-1}{\sqrt{3}+1}$, then the value of (x^2+y^2) is:

A. 14 B. 12
C. 13 D. 16

69. In a row of girls, A is 10th from the left and B is 14th from the right. If they interchange their positions, A becomes 24th from the left. How many girls are there in a row?

A. 31 B. 33
C. 37 D. 39

70. Out of 1865 people, 660 can speak English and 1305 can speak Hindi, but 120 persons cannot speak either language, then how many persons can speak both languages?

A. 220 B. 440
C. 120 D. 1085

71. The population of a town is 9000. If the males increase by 5% and females by 8%, the population would be 9600 in a year. The number of males is:

A. 3000 B. 4000
C. 5000 D. 5600

72. D is taller than C and E. A is not as tall as E. C is taller than A. D is not as tall as B. Who is the tallest among of them?

A. A B. B
C. C D. D

73. Pointing to a girl in photograph, X said "She is the daughter of my grandfather's only son". How is the girl related to X?

A. Father B. Brother
C. Sister D. Mother

74. A steam engine train runs from East to West and wind is blowing from North to South, then the smoke from the train would blow in which direction?

A. N-W B. N-E
C. S-E D. S-W

75. The next term of the following number series is:

3, 13, 22, 32, 59, 69, 120, 130, ?

A. 201 B. 211
C. 227 D. 232

76. The average of nine consecutive numbers is *n*. If the next two numbers are also included, the new average is:

A. remain the same B. increase by 1
C. increase by 1.5 D. increase by 2

77. A shopkeeper sells an article at 15% gain. Had he sold it for ₹ 18 more, he would have gained 18%. The cost price (in ₹) of the article is:

A. 360 B. 540
C. 600 D. 640

78. A boat covers a certain distance downstream in 3 hours, while it comes back in 4.5 hours. If the speed of the stream be 3 kmph, then the speed of the boat in still water is:

A. 10 kmph B. 12 kmph
C. 13 kmph D. 15 kmph

79. A metallic sphere of radius 10.5 cm is melted and then recast into small cones each of radius 3.5 cm and height 3 cm, then the number of cones thus formed is:

A. 112 B. 126
C. 132 D. 138

80. X and Y are facing each other at sunrise. The shadow of Y is falling towards right of X, then Y is facing in which direction?

A. North B. South
C. East D. West

81. Which of the following monuments of Haryana have the status of State protected monuments?

(*i*) Sheikh Tayyab's Tomb
(*ii*) Shobha Sagar Pond
(*iii*) Bhimadevi Temple Complex

Choose the ***correct*** code:

A. (*i*) and (*ii*) B. (*ii*) and (*iii*)
C. (*i*) and (*iii*) D. (*i*), (*ii*) and (*iii*)

82. Which of the following institute is responsible for the development of infrastructure facilities in industrial areas of Haryana?

A. HARTRON B. HUDA
C. HSIIDC D. District Industries Centre

83. Consider the following statements:

(*i*) The institution of Lokayukta was established in Haryana in the year 2002.
(*ii*) Justice Pritam Pal was the first Lokayukta in the State of Haryana.

A. Only (*i*) is correct.
B. Only (*ii*) is correct.
C. Both (*i*) and (*ii*) are correct
D. Both (*i*) and (*ii*) are incorrect

84. Who among the following is ***not*** appointed by the Governor of Haryana?
A. Chief Minister of Haryana
B. A Judge of Punjab and Haryana High Court
C. A Member of Haryana Public Service Commission
D. A Member of Haryana Human Right Commission

85. Who among the following Governors of Haryana was a civil servant?
A. Muzaffar Hussain Burney
B. Jaisukh Lal Hathi
C. Dhanik Lal Mandal
D. Babu Parmanand

86. Read the following statements about 'Parivar Pehchan Patra Yojna':
(*i*) This scheme identifies family as a unit and is creating a reliable socio-economic database of all the families in Haryana.
(*ii*) An eight digit unique family ID is being issued for every family and the ID will be linked to birth, death and marriage records.
(*iii*) The data available in family ID database will be utilized to determine automatic verification for various welfare schemes and families will not be required to apply themselves for benefits.

Choose the ***correct*** code:
A. Only (*ii*) is correct.
B. (*i*) and (*ii*) are correct.
C. (*ii*) and (*iii*) are correct.
D. (*i*), (*ii*) and (*iii*) are correct.

87. Which places of Haryana have been notified as Ramsar site under Ramsar convention of UNESCO?
A. Sultanpur National Park & Bhindawas Wildlife Sanctuary
B. Kalesar National Park & Khaparwas Wildlife Sanctuary
C. Nahar Wildlife Sanctuary & Bir Shikargarh Wildlife Sanctuary
D. Abushahar Wildlife Sanctuary & Khol-Hi-Raitan Wildlife Sanctuary

88. The Lok Sabha and Rajya Sabha seats in Haryana are:
A. 7 and 4
B. 10 and 4
C. 10 and 5
D. 12 and 5

89. Which of the city of Haryana is known as the 'City of War Heroes'?
A. Gurugram
B. Sonipat
C. Panipat
D. Bhiwani

90. Consider the following statements regarding the Governor of Haryana:
(*i*) He is the Chancellor of Central University of Haryana.
(*ii*) He can hold any office of the profit in the State.
(*iii*) He is the President of Indian Red Cross Society, Haryana State Branch.
(*iv*) He does not have any discretionary power granted under the Constitution.

Which of the above statement(s) is/are ***correct***?
A. (*i*), (*ii*), (*iii*) and (*iv*)
B. (*ii*), (*iii*) and (*iv*)
C. Only (*iii*)
D. Both (*ii*) and (*iii*)

PART-IV

Commerce

Directions: *Answer the following questions by selecting the **most appropriate** option.*

91. In which activity all profits of a company are not distributed amongst the shareholders as dividend, but a part of the profits is retained or re-invested in the business?
A. Capital Distribution
B. Ploughing back of profits
C. Liquidity Distribution
D. Profitability Distribution

92. Which ratio indicates the firm's capacity to pay long-term debts and procure additional loans and informs whether the firm is following the policy of trading on equity?
A. Proprietary ratio
B. Debt-equity ratio
C. Returns on Shareholders Funds
D. Debt-Service ratio

93. 'A' does not keep proper accounting records of his business. He gives the following information, what will be profit or loss for the year?

Opening Capital	:	₹ 2,00,000
Closing Capital	:	₹ 2,50,000
Drawings made during the year	:	₹ 60,000
Capital added during the year	:	₹ 75,000

A. ₹ 85,000
B. ₹ 1,85,000
C. ₹ 35,000
D. ₹ 3,15,000

94. Working capital of a company is ₹ 21,28,000 and total debts are ₹ 42,50,000. If the company's long term debts are ₹ 27,30,000, then current ratio will be:
A. 0.78 : 1
B. 1.4 : 1
C. 1.14 : 1
D. 2.4 : 1

95. The current liabilities of XYZ Co. Ltd. are ₹ 1,50,000. Its current ratio is 3 : 1 and liquid ratio is 1 : 1. The value of stock will be:

A. ₹ 4,50,000 B. ₹ 1,50,000
C. ₹ 3,00,000 D. Can not be computed

96. The ability of the business to pay the amount due to stakeholders as and when it is due is known as:
A. Solvency
B. Liquidity
C. Profitability
D. Liquidity Profitability Equilibrium

97. While preparing cash flow statement of financial enterprise, interest and dividend received should be classified as ______.
A. Operating activity B. Financing activity
C. Investing activity D. Business activity

98. Representation of various factors affecting net profit and capital employed by a chart known as:
A. Standard and Poor Chart
B. NYSE Chart
C. Break-even Chart
D. Du-pont Chart

99. Which 'Hundi' is similar to 'Demand Bill'?
A. Darshani Hundi B. Shahjog Hundi
C. Muddati Hundi D. Jawabee Hundi

100. State Bank of India desires to redeem 5,000. 10% debentures of ₹ 1,000 each at par out of available sufficient divisible profits. In this case, how much amount should be transferred to debentures redemption reserve A/c as per requirement under Section 71(4) of Indian Companies Act, read with rule 18(7) of a banking company?
A. ₹ 50,00,000 B. ₹ 7,50,000
C. ₹ 12,50,000 D. Zero

101. From the following, which statement is ***not*** true for bill of exchange?
A. It is drawn by the debtor.
B. It is drawn by the creditor.
C. It contains an order to make payment.
D. It requires acceptance by the drawee or someone else on his behalf.

102. Kaushal and Gulab are partners in a firm sharing profits in the ratio of 5 : 3. They admit Raju as a new partner for 1/7 share in the profit. The new profit sharing ratio will be 4 : 2 : 1. The sacrificing ratio of Kaushal and Gulab will be:
A. 3 : 5 B. 5 : 3
C. 4 : 2 D. 1 : 7

103. On dissolution of a firm liabilities are transferred to:
A. Bank Account
B. Reserve and Surplus Account
C. Cash Account
D. Realization Account

104. The ratio in which the continuing partners have acquired the share from the retiring or deceased partner, is called:
A. Debt-equity Ratio B. Liquidity Ratio
C. Current Ratio. D. Gaining Ratio

105. Which statement is ***true*** for Receipt and Payment Account?
A. It includes depreciation.
B. It does not includes depreciation.
C. It has no opening balance.
D. It include income and expenditure items related only to the current period.

106. When a partner has agreed to undertake the dissolution work for an agreed remuneration bear the realization expenses, then what will be the journal entry if payment of realization expenses is made by the firm?
A. Bank A/c Dr.
To Realization A/c
B. Partners Capital A/c Dr.
To Bank A/c
C. Realization A/c Dr.
To Bank A/c
D. Bank A/c Dr.
To Partner's Capital A/c

107. A limited has agreed to pay purchase price of building ₹ 2,20,000, half the payment was made in cash and remaining half by issue of 9% debentures of ₹ 100 each at a premium of 10%. How much debentures will be issued for paying purchase amount?
A. 1000 B. 1100
C. 2000 D. 2200

108. In which system, the monitory effect of a transaction is taken into account in the period in which they are earned rather than in the period in which cash is actually received or paid by the enterprise?
A. Cash Basis System
B. Accrual Basis System
C. Economic Basis System
D. Circular flow of Money System

109. The recurring grants in the form of maintenance grant is treated as:
A. Capital Receipts B. Donations
C. Revenue Receipts D. Endowment Fund

110. In the benefit of expenditure extends upto only for one accounting period, it is called:
A. Capital Expenditure B. Revenue Expenditure
C. Noting Charges D. Underwriting

111. Read the statements carefully and choose a ***correct*** option given below:

Statement I: Capital Expenditures and Revenue Expenditures both are non-recurring by Nature.

Statement II: Capital Expenditures increase earning capacity of business whereas Revenue Expenditures are incurred to maintain earning capacity.
A. Only statement I is correct.

B. Only statement II is correct.
C. Both statements are correct.
D. Both statements are incorrect.

112. The expenses that are incurred in connection with the formation of a company are called:
A. Capital Expenditure
B. Preliminary Expenses
C. Expenses on Issue of Shares and Debentures
D. Revenue Expenditure

113. The study of mutual relationship between different components or their totals of the financial statements for a definite period of time is called:
A. Horizontal or Dynamic analysis
B. Vertical or Static analysis
C. Internal analysis
D. External analysis

114. Petty cash book is maintained for recording ______ .
A. Petty incomes only
B. Petty expenses paid in cash
C. Petty incomes received in cash only
D. Petty incomes and petty expenses

115. A company issues 1000 debentures of ₹ 100 each at a discount of 6% and the debenture are to be repaid by equal installments of ₹ 20,000 at the end of each year, starting from first year, which amount of discount is written off at the end of first year?
A. ₹ 6,000 B. ₹ 2,000
C. ₹ 1,200 D. ₹ 1,600

116. Read the statements carefully and choose a ***correct*** option given below:
Statement I: Depreciation must be charged so as to ascertain true profit or loss of the business.
Statement II: When market value of an asset is higher than book value, depreciation is not charged.
A. Only statement I is correct.
B. Only statement II is correct.
C. Both statements are correct.
D. Both statements are incorrect.

117. A company forfeited 200 shares of ₹ 100 each, ₹ 70 called-up per share, on which the shareholder paid ₹ 50 per share. These shares were reissued at ₹ 80 fully paid-up per share. The share forfeited account will be debited in the reissue entry with:
A. ₹ 6,000 B. ₹ 4,000
C. ₹ 10,000 D. ₹ 16,000

118. The entire life of the firm is divided into time intervals for the measurement of the profit of the business, is called as:
A. Cost concept
B. Going concern concept
C. Accounting period concept
D. Realization concept

119. Leverage or capital structure ratios are also known as:
A. Long-term solvency ratios
B. Short-term solvency ratios
C. Return on capital employed
D. Current ratio

120. Read the statements carefully and choose a ***correct*** option given below:
Statement I: Passbook is the statement of account of the customer maintained by the bank.
Statement II: A business firm periodically prepares a bank reconciliation statement to reconcile the bank balance as per the cash book with the passbook as these to show different balances for various reasons.
A. Only statement I is correct.
B. Only statement II is correct.
C. Both statements are correct.
D. Both statements are incorrect.

121. A principle of enlightened marketing that requires that a company seek real product and marketing improvements:
A. Customer-value marketing
B. Innovative marketing
C. Sense of mission marketing
D. Consumer-oriented marketing

122. Banking and Insurance are which type of industries?
A. Genetic industries
B. Secondary industries
C. Tertiary industries
D. Manufacturing industries

123. A partnership deed generally do ***not*** include which of the following?
A. Name of firm
B. List of employees of firm
C. Duration of business
D. Procedure for dissolution of the firm

124. The organizational structure, most suitable for large organizations having diversified activities, is:
A. Divisional structure B. Functional structure
C. Managerial structure D. Formal structure

125. Interest rate and inflation rate are included under which factor of business environment:
A. Economic environment
B. Social environment
C. Legal environment
D. Technological environment

126. What type of a bank is Import-Export bank?
A. Commercial Bank B. Cooperative Bank
C. Central Bank D. Specialized Bank

127. ______ is the extra profit the firm earns from producing and selling an additional unit of output.
A. Marginal profit B. Managerial profit
C. Marginal cost D. Total profit

128. The secretariat of the Association of SAARC is situated at:
A. New Delhi, India B. Mumbai, India
C. Kathmandu, Nepal D. Geneva, Switzerland

129. A desire to satisfy one's interests, regardless of the impact on the other party to the conflict:
A. Collaborating B. Avoiding
C. Competing D. Compromising

130. "Money is what money does" this definition of money was given by:
A. Walker B. Hawtrey
C. Crowther D. Keynes

131. A temporary pricing in which company sells products below the list price, and sometimes even below cost to increase shortrun sales:
A. Promotional pricing B. Temporary pricing
C. FOB-origin pricing D. Geographical pricing

132. Which one of the following is ***not*** an element of communication process?
A. Encoding B. Channel
C. Receiver D. Measurement

133. The present value of an investment's cash inflows (benefits) minus the present value of its cash outflow (costs) is known as:
A. Net Present Value (NPV)
B. Net Future Value (NFV)
C. Gross Present Value (GPV)
D. Gross Future Value (GFV)

134. An organized movement of citizens and government agencies to improve the rights and power of buyers in relation of sellers:
A. Consumerism B. Environmentalism
C. Sustainability D. Citizenship

135. Staff authority works as:
A. a chain of command
B. a channel of communication
C. a carrier of responsibility
D. Advice of certain matters

136. Internal elements that may interfere with the company's ability to achieve its objectives is:
A. Strength B. Weakness
C. Opportunity D. Threats

137. Which of the following is included in Fayol's principles of management?
A. Harmony, not discord
B. Cooperation, not individualism
C. Development of each and every person
D. Unity of command

138. The Foreign Trade (Development and Regulation) Act, 1992 replaced which of the following Acts?
A. Import and Export (Control) Act, 1947
B. Export Regulation Act, 1962
C. Import Development Act, 1952
D. Both (B) and (C)

139. Who determines the Cash Reserve Ratio?
A. Central bank B. Market taxes
C. Commercial banks D. Government

140. Which one of the following is the characteristics of transactional leader?
A. Inspirational motivation
B. Management by exception
C. Idealized influence
D. Intellectual stimulation

141. Process of organizing include:
A. Developing premises B. Setting objectives
C. Assignment of duties D. Selecting an alternative

142. "Efficiency through work simplification and standardization", is focused by:
A. Taylor B. Fayol
C. Simon D. Bernard

143. The opinion and belief segment of an attitude is:
A. Affective component B. Behavioural component
C. Feeling component D. Cognitive component

144. When was GATT established?
A. 1947 B. 1948
C. 1995 D. 1903

145. Which one of these can be delegated?
A. Power B. Authority
C. Responsibility D. Accountability

146. "Invisible" in the balance of payments account refer to:
A. Goods transaction B. Service transaction
C. Capital transaction D. Export promotion

147. Who has given the concept of 'POSDCORB'?
A. Ralph Davis B. E.F.L. Brech
C. Koontz D. Luther Gulick

148. Among the following sources, which one is an internal recruitment source?
A. Direct recruitment
B. Recommendations of employees
C. Advertisement
D. Transfers

149. ______ occurs if a given percentage increase in all inputs results in a smaller percentage increase in output.
A. Decreasing returns to scale
B. Increasing returns to scale
C. Constant returns to scale
D. Output elasticity

150. Who has proposed the 'Need of Achievement Thoery'?
A. A.H. Maslow B. Clayton Alderfer
C. David McClelland D. Frederick Herzberg

Answers

1. (A)	**2. (A)**	**3. (D)**
4. (C)	**5. (A)**	**6. (C)**
7. (D)	**8. (B)**	**9. (A)**
10. (A)	**11. (A)**	**12. (B)**
13. (B)	**14. (A)**	**15. (D)**
16. (B)	**17. (C)**	**18. (B)**
19. (D)	**20. (C)**	**21. (C)**
22. (D)	**23. (*)**	**24. (C)**
25. (C)	**26. (B)**	**27. (D)**
28. (A)	**29. (B)**	**30. (C)**
31. (B)	**32. (B)**	**33. (A)**
34. (B)	**35. (D)**	**36. (A)**
37. (D)	**38. (C)**	**39. (C)**
40. (A)	**41. (D)**	**42. (D)**
43. (C)	**44. (B)**	**45. (B)**
46. (*)	**47. (D)**	**48. (A)**
49. (A)	**50. (D)**	**51. (A)**
52. (B)	**53. (B)**	**54. (C)**
55. (C)	**56. (B)**	**57. (D)**
58. (A)	**59. (C)**	**60. (A)**

61. (D): At compound interest compounded annually

$$\therefore \quad A = P\left(1+\frac{r}{100}\right)^n$$

$$\Rightarrow \quad 3\frac{3}{8}P = P\left(1+\frac{r}{100}\right)^3$$

$$\Rightarrow \quad 3\frac{3}{8} = \left(1+\frac{r}{100}\right)^3$$

$$\Rightarrow \quad \frac{27}{8} = \left(1+\frac{r}{100}\right)^3$$

$$\Rightarrow \quad \left(\frac{3}{2}\right)^3 = \left(1+\frac{r}{100}\right)^3$$

$$\Rightarrow \quad \frac{3}{2} = 1+\frac{r}{100} \Rightarrow \frac{3}{2}-1 = \frac{r}{100}$$

$$\Rightarrow \quad \frac{1}{2} = \frac{r}{100} \Rightarrow r = 50$$

$\therefore$ The rate of interest per annum, r = 50%.

62. (D): Let the original price of rice per kg is ₹ x

Then, new price per kg $= \dfrac{x \times 100 - 20}{100}$

$$= x \times \frac{80}{100} = ₹\ \frac{4}{5}x$$

According to question,

$$\frac{800}{\frac{4}{5}x} - \frac{800}{x} = 12.5$$

$$\Rightarrow \quad \frac{1000}{x} - \frac{800}{x} = \frac{25}{2}$$

$$\Rightarrow \quad \frac{1}{x}(1000-800) = \frac{25}{2}$$

$$\Rightarrow \quad \frac{200}{x} = \frac{25}{2}$$

$$\Rightarrow \quad 25x = 400 \Rightarrow x = 16$$

$\therefore$ The original price of rice per kg is ₹ 16.

63. (B): Let quotient $= x$

then, Divisor $= 12x = 5 \times 36$

$$\Rightarrow \quad x = \frac{5 \times 36}{12} = 15$$

$\because$ Dividend = Divisor × Quotient + Remainder

$\therefore$ Dividend $= 12x \times x + 36$

$= 12 \times 15 \times 15 + 36$

$= 12 \times 225 + 36$

$= 2700 + 36 = 2736.$

64. (C)

65. (D): Here, $5 - 2 = 9 - 6 = 13 - 10 = 3$

the difference of all the divisors with their corresponding remainder in each case is same as 10

So, Required number = (LCM of 5, 9, 13) − 3

$= 585 - 3 = 582.$

66. (C): Given,

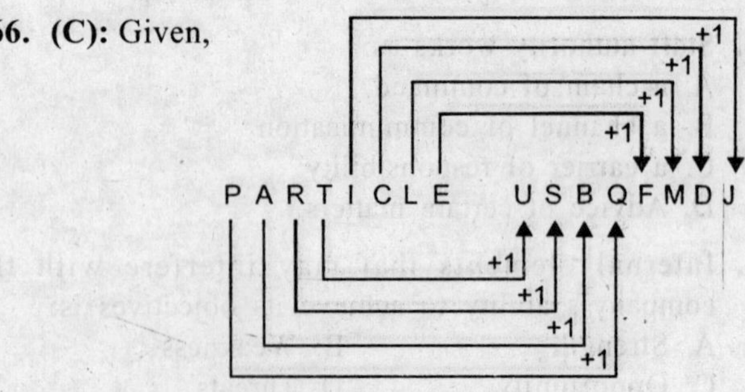

and

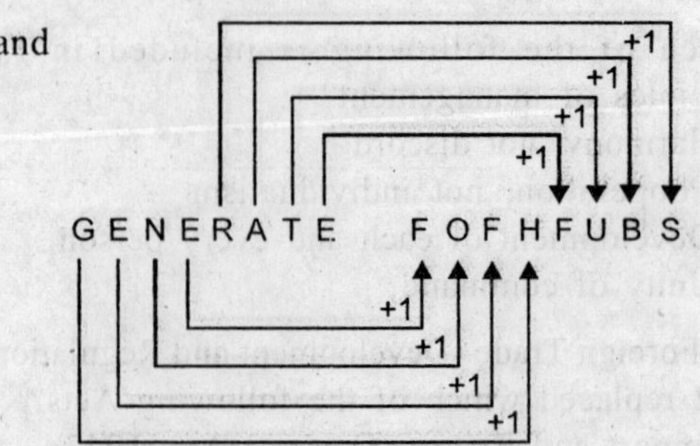

Similarly,.

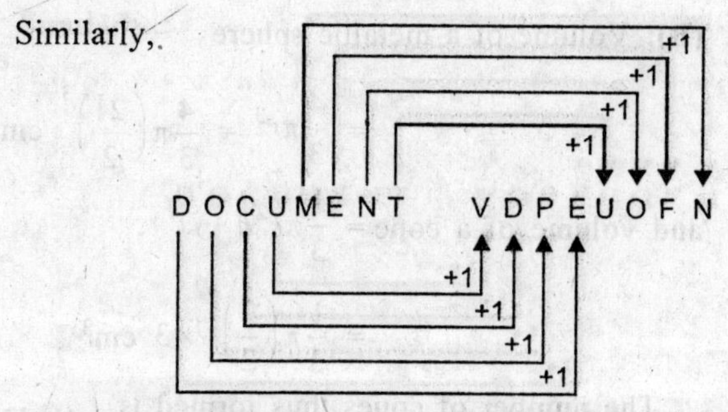

∴ In same code language 'DOCUMENT' will be written as 'VDPEUOFN'.

67. (D): Ratio of Efficiency of pipes

$$R : Q = 2 : 1$$
$$Q : P = 2 : 1$$
$$\Rightarrow \quad P : Q = 1 : 2$$
and $$Q : R = 1 : 2$$
$$\Rightarrow \quad Q : R = 2 : 4$$
$$\therefore \quad P : Q : R = 1 : 2 : 4$$

Ratio of time,

$$P : Q : R = 1 : \frac{1}{2} : \frac{1}{4} = 4 : 2 : 1$$

By question, (P + Q + R)'s 1 hour's work:

$$\frac{1}{4x} + \frac{1}{2x} + \frac{1}{x} = \frac{1}{5}$$
$$\Rightarrow \quad \frac{1+2+4}{4x} = \frac{1}{5}$$
$$\Rightarrow \quad \frac{7}{4x} = \frac{1}{5} \Rightarrow x = \frac{35}{4}$$
$$\therefore \quad \text{P's 1 hour's work} = \frac{1}{4x} = \frac{1}{4 \times \frac{35}{4}} = \frac{1}{35}$$

∴ Pipe P alone will take 35 hours to fill the tank.

68. (A): Given, $x = \frac{\sqrt{3}+1}{\sqrt{3}-1} = \frac{\sqrt{3}+1}{\sqrt{3}-1} \times \frac{\sqrt{3}+1}{\sqrt{3}+1} = \frac{(\sqrt{3}+1)^2}{3-1}$

$$= \frac{3+1+2\sqrt{3}}{2} = \frac{4+2\sqrt{3}}{2} = 2+\sqrt{3}$$

and $y = \frac{\sqrt{3}-1}{\sqrt{3}+1} = \frac{\sqrt{3}-1}{\sqrt{3}+1} \times \frac{\sqrt{3}-1}{\sqrt{3}-1}$

$$= \frac{(\sqrt{3}-1)^2}{3-1} = \frac{3+1-2\sqrt{3}}{2} = 2-\sqrt{3}$$

$$\therefore \quad x^2 + y^2 = (2+\sqrt{3})^2 + (2-\sqrt{3})^2$$
$$= 4+3+4\sqrt{3}+(4+3-4\sqrt{3})$$
$$= 7+4\sqrt{3}+7-4\sqrt{3} = 7+7 = 14$$
$$\Rightarrow \quad x^2 + y^2 = 14.$$

69. (C): Left 10th 14th (13 girls) Right

A B

Again, Left 24th Right

A

∴ The number of girls in this row

$$= 24 + 13 = 37.$$

70. (A): Given, Total number of people = 1865

Number of people speak English = 660

Number of people speak Hindi = 1305

Number of persons can not speak either language = 120

∴ Number of persons can speak both language

$$= (660 + 1305 + 120) - 1865$$
$$= 2085 - 1865 = 220.$$

71. (B): Let the number of males is x

then, the number of females is $(9000 - x)$

$$\therefore \quad x \times \frac{105}{100} + (9000 - x) \times \frac{108}{100} = 9600$$
$$\Rightarrow \quad \frac{105x}{100} + \frac{972000}{100} - \frac{108x}{100} = 9600$$
$$\Rightarrow \quad \frac{972000}{100} - \frac{3x}{100} = 9600$$
$$\Rightarrow \quad 9720 - 9600 = \frac{3x}{100} \Rightarrow 120 = \frac{3x}{100}$$
$$\Rightarrow \quad 3x = 12000 \Rightarrow x = 4000$$

∴ The number of males = x = 4000.

72. (B): B > D > C > E > A

Here, B is the tallest among them.

73. (C): Here, the girl is the sister of X.

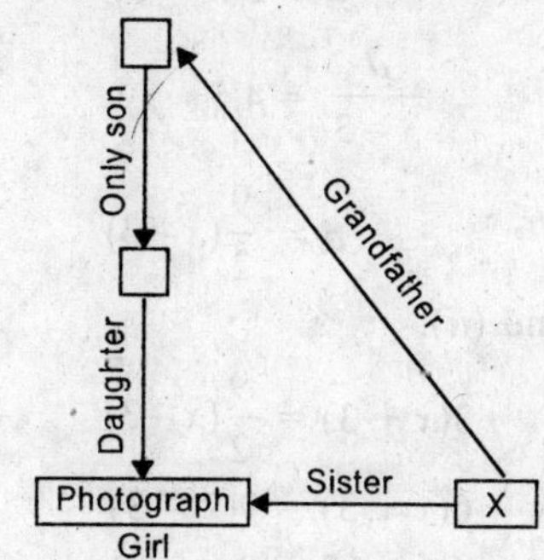

74. (C)

75. (B): 3 13 22 32 59 69 120 130 211

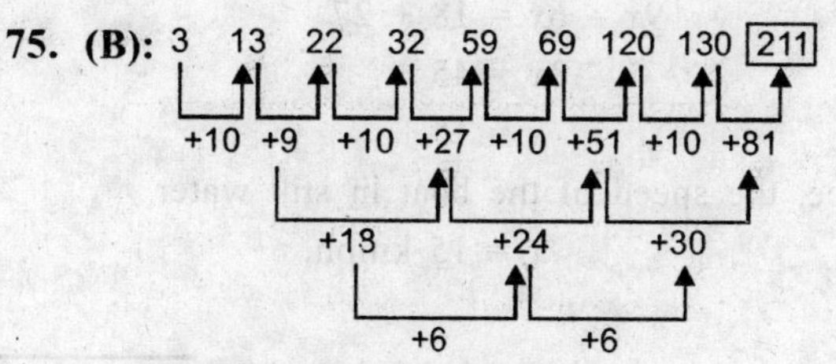

∴ ? = The next term = 211.

76. (B): $n = \frac{1+2+3+....+9}{9}$

$= \frac{9(9+1)}{9\times 2} = \frac{10}{2} = 5$

The new average = $\frac{1+2+3+...+11}{11}$

$= \frac{11(11+1)}{11\times 2} = \frac{12}{2} = 6$

Hence, the new average is increased by 1.

77. (C): Let the cost price of the article is ₹ x

Then, S.P. = $x\times\frac{115}{100}+18 = x\times\frac{118}{100}$

$\Rightarrow \frac{115}{100}x+18 = \frac{118}{100}x$

$\Rightarrow \frac{118}{100}x - \frac{115}{100}x = 18$

$\Rightarrow \frac{3x}{100} = 18$

$\Rightarrow \frac{x}{100} = 6$

$\Rightarrow x = 600$

∴ The cost price of the article = ₹ 600.

78. (D): Let the speed of the boat in still water is x kmph then, speed of boat in downstream = $(x + 3)$ kmph and speed of boat in upstream = $(x - 3)$ kmph

Let certain distance = d km

Then, $\frac{d}{x+3} = 3$

$\Rightarrow d = 3(x + 3)$ ...(*i*)

and $\frac{d}{x-3} = 4.5$

$\Rightarrow d = \frac{9}{2}(x-3)$ ...(*ii*)

From (*i*) and (*ii*),

$3(x + 3) = \frac{9}{2}(x-3)$

$\Rightarrow 6(x + 3) = 9(x - 3)$

$\Rightarrow 6x + 18 = 9x - 27$

$\Rightarrow 9x - 6x = 18 + 27$

$\Rightarrow 3x = 45$

$\Rightarrow x = 15$

Hence, the speed of the boat in still water

x = 15 kmph.

79. (B): Volume of a metallic sphere

$= \frac{4}{3}\pi r^3 = \frac{4}{3}\pi\left(\frac{21}{2}\right)^3$ cm³

and volume of a cone = $\frac{1}{3}\pi r^2 h$

$= \frac{1}{3}\pi\left(\frac{7}{2}\right)^2 \times 3$ cm³

∴ The number of cones thus formed is

$$\frac{\frac{4}{3}\pi\left(\frac{21}{2}\right)^3}{\frac{1}{3}\pi\left(\frac{7}{2}\right)^2\times 3} = \frac{4\times\frac{21}{2}\times\frac{21}{2}\times\frac{21}{2}}{\frac{7}{2}\times\frac{7}{2}\times 3}$$

$$= \frac{4}{3}\times\frac{21}{2}\times\frac{21}{2}\times\frac{21}{2}\times\frac{2}{7}\times\frac{2}{7}$$

$= 3 \times 21 \times 2 = 6 \times 21 = 126.$

80. (A)	**81. (D)**	**82. (C)**
83. (C)	**84. (B)**	**85. (A)**
86. (D)	**87. (A)**	**88. (C)**
89. (D)	**90. (C)**	**91. (B)**
92. (B)	**93. (C)**	**94. (D)**
95. (C)	**96. (B)**	**97. (A)**
98. (D)	**99. (A)**	**100. (D)**
101. (A)	**102. (A)**	**103. (D)**
104. (D)	**105. (B)**	**106. (B)**
107. (A)	**108. (B)**	**109. (C)**
110. (B)	**111. (B)**	**112. (B)**
113. (B)	**114. (B)**	**115. (B)**
116. (A)	**117. (B)**	**118. (C)**
119. (A)	**120. (C)**	**121. (B)**
122. (C)	**123. (B)**	**124. (A & B)**
125. (A)	**126. (D)**	**127. (A)**
128. (C)	**129. (C)**	**130. (A)**
131. (A)	**132. (D)**	**133. (A)**
134. (A)	**135. (D)**	**136. (B)**
137. (D)	**138. (A)**	**139. (A)**
140. (B)	**141. (C)**	**142. (A)**
143. (D)	**144. (A & B)**	**145. (B)**
146. (B)	**147. (D)**	**148. (D)**
149. (A)	**150. (C)**	

Previous Paper (Solved)

Haryana Teacher Eligibility Test (HTET)

PGT Commerce (Level-3), Exam 2021

(Exam held on 18 December, 2021)

PART-I

Child Development and Pedagogy

Directions: *Answer the following questions by selecting the* ***most appropriate*** *option.*

1. Which of the following is ***not*** the type of dynamic trait of personality given by Cattell?
A. Attitude B. Urge
C. Sentiment D. Conservative

2. Which one of the following stage is ***not*** prescribed by James Draver in the context of development of character?
A. The stage of crude emotion
B. The stage of sentiment
C. The self regard stage
D. Conforming conventional stage

3. Which of the following is the ***false*** characteristic of motivation?
A. In motivation, behaviour of person is goal oriented.
B. Motivated behaviour does continuity
C. Nature of motivated behaviour is rigid.
D. Motivation does energy changes in human beings.

4. Which of the following theory is ***not*** related with the theories of transfer of learning?
A. Theory of mental discipline
B. Theory of rote memory
C. Theory of identical elements
D. Theory of generalisation

5. Which of the following is ***not*** the characteristic of good mental health?
A. Emotional maturity
B. Self confidence
C. Intolerance
D. Capacity of self evaluation

6. For which age group the Children Apperception Test (CAT) is applicable?
A. 2 to 5 years B. 0 to 4 years
C. 16 to 18 years D. 3 to 10 years

7. Out of the following which one is the ***wrong*** statement in context of characteristics of instincts?
A. Intinct is innate.
B. Instinct is very powerful
C. Instinct is ephemeral.
D. Instinct is psycho-physical disposition.

8. Which of the following is ***not*** the other name of Thorndike's theory of Connectionism?
A. Stimulus response theory
B. Bond theory of learning
C. Theory of conditioned response
D. Trial and Error theory

9. Who developed the first intelligence test?
A. Lavator B. Sanguin
C. Francis Galton D. Alfred Binet and Simon

10. Which of the following concept is ***not*** introduced by Jean Piaget in his Cognitive Development theory?
A. Assimilation B. Accommodation
C. Symbolic D. Equilibration

11. Which of the following is ***not*** the innate motive?
A. Safety B. Hunger
C. Thirst D. Rest

12. Who was the founder of socio-culture theory of cognitive development?
A. Jean Piaget B. Jerom Bruner
C. Lev Vygotsky D. Kohlberg

13. Which one of the following is ***not*** correct way of releasing pent up emotional energy?
A. Substitute responses B. Displacement
C. Regression D. Self pity

14. Which of the following structure of mind directed according to Hedonistic and pleasure principle?
A. Id B. Ego
C. Super Ego D. Choleric

15. Which of the following is the ***correct*** logical order of elements of memory?
A. Learning → Recall → Retention → Recognition
B. Recall → Learning → Retention → Recognition
C. Learning → Recall → Recognition → Retention
D. Learning → Retention → Recall → Recognition

16. Which of the following is ***not*** the type of one of the component content under three dimensional model of intellect given by J.P. Guilford?
A. Figural B. System
C. Symbolic D. Behavioural

17. The mental activities associated with thought, decision making, language and other higher mental processes is called:
A. Visual images B. Cognition
C. Concepts D. Propositions

18. Which of the following is behavioural perspective of modern psychology?
A. Focuses on overt behaviour.
B. Focuses on cognitive processes.
C. Focuses on the biological events.
D. Focuses on critique of male bias.

19. Who was the propounder of pyschoanalytical method?
A. J.B. Watson B. Wilhelm Wundt
C. Sigmund Freud D. J.M. Cattell

20. According to Stanford-Binet IQ scale, what is the IQ range of low mentally retarded children?
A. 52 to 67 B. 36 to 51
C. 20 to 35 D. below 20

21. A branch of psychology which studies how people change physically, cognitively and socially over the entire life span is known as:
A. Clinical psychology
B. Counselling psychology
C. Developmental psychology
D. Experimental psychology

22. Which of the following is the ***false*** statement?
A. Learning is a process not a product.
B. Learning process is always purposeful.
C. Area of learning is broader.
D. Behaviour changes through instincts and reflex actions are also considered as learning.

23. Which of the following is ***not*** the type of projective technique of personality measurement?
A. Word Association Test
B. Woodworth's Personal Data Sheet
C. Sentence Completion Test
D. Thematic Apperception Test

24. Who was the propounder of Anticipatory theory of play?
A. Karl Groos B. McDougall
C. Herbert Spencer D. G. Stanley Hall

25. Who stated that "Adolescence is a period of stress, strain, storm and strife"?
A. William H. Barton
B. Stanley Hall
C. J.A. Hadfield
D. Jean Piaget

26. Which of the following is ***not*** the characteristic of Adolescence?
A. Weight of muscles is 20% of total weight of body.
B. Tendency of day dreams increased.
C. Vocabulary too increases.
D. Mental abilities reach at their highest level.

27. Which of the following is the non-projective technique of personality measurement?
A. Association technique
B. Sociometric technique
C. Construction technique
D. Completion technique

28. Which of the following is the highest level in hierarchical theory of learning given Gange?
A. Problem solving learning
B. Principle learning
C. Concept learning
D. Multiple discrimination learning

29. Who propounded Brain storming method for fostering and boosting creativity?
A. Torrance B. Myres
C. Osborn D. Gordon

30. Out of the following which one is the ***wrong*** statement in context of characteristics of habits?
A. Habit is automatic response to specific situation.
B. Habit is acquired through heredity.
C. Habit is a well learned performance.
D. Habit is performed only under similar circumstances.

PART-II

भाषा : हिन्दी

निर्देशः *निम्नलिखित प्रश्नों के उत्तर देने के लिए* ***सबसे उचित*** *विकल्प चुनिए।*

31. **अनुचित** विलोम शब्द युग्म युक्त विकल्प पहचानिए :
A. विधि – निषेध B. खल – सज्जन
C. अमर – मर्त्य D. वैर – क्रोध

32. कौन-सा वाक्य संबंधसूचक अव्यय का उदाहरण है?
A. इतना खा लिया, इसे कैसे पचाओगे।
B. शीला के समान कोई आलसी नहीं है।
C. मैंने पर्याप्त पढ़ लिया है, अब थोड़ा आराम करूँगा।
D. जरा सोच-समझकर बोलिए।

33. वाक्य के संदर्भ में कौन-सा विकल्प सुमेलित ***नहीं*** है?
A. दुष्ट! तुझे धिक्कार है। – विस्मयादिबोधक वाक्य
B. मैनें माँ का कहना नहीं माना। – निषेधबोधक वाक्य
C. हो सकता है वह आज शाम को आए। – इच्छाबोधक वाक्य
D. समय पर भोजन करोगे तो स्वस्थ रहोगे। – संकेतार्थक वाक्य

34. अर्थ की दृष्टि से कौन-सा मुहावरा संगत ***नहीं*** है?
A. खयाली पुलाव पकाना – व्यर्थ की बातें करना
B. अपना-सा मुँह लेकर रह जाना – असफल होने पर लज्जित होना
C. अँधेरे घर का उजाला – एकमात्र सहारा
D. ऊँट का सूई की नोक से निकलना – शक्तिशाली का कमजोर होना

35. निम्न में से किस विकल्प की सभी क्रियाएँ 'अकर्मक' हैं?
A. चलना, मुस्कराना, खिलना B. दौड़ना, रूठना, लिखना
C. हँसना, खाना, सोना D. रोना, उठना, काटना

36. 'दादुर, भेक, शालुर' शब्द किसके पर्यायवाची हैं?
A. हाथी B. बंदर
C. मेंढ़क D. सिंह

37. प्रत्यय की दृष्टि से ***असुमेलित*** विकल्प का चयन कीजिए :
A. भागिनेय = भगिनी + य
B. वार्धक्य = वर्धक + य
C. ऐश्वर्य = ईश्वर + य
D. वैशिष्ट्य = विशिष्ट + य

38. निम्न में से ***असंगत*** विकल्प पहचानिए :
A. सातत्य – अव्यय से निर्मित भाववाचक संज्ञा
B. निजता – सर्वनाम से निर्मित भाववाचक संज्ञा
C. रोगिणी – भाववाचक संज्ञा से निर्मित विशेषण
D. शक्तिशाली – विशेषण से निर्मित भाववाचक संज्ञा

39. निम्न में से ***सही*** संधि युक्त शब्द कौन-सा है?
A. युधि + स्थिर = युधिष्ठिर
B. गुरु + उपदेश = गुरोपदेश
C. अभि + इप्सा = अभिप्सा
D. गति + अवरोध = गत्यावरोध

40. उपसर्ग से निर्मित शब्दों के संदर्भ में कौन-सा विकल्प ***असंगत*** है?
A. परि – पर्यंक, पारिभाषिक, पर्युषण
B. अति – अत्युक्ति, अतीत, अत्यावश्यक
C. अन – अनसूया, अनधिकार, अनशन
D. प्रति – प्रत्यर्पण, प्रतीक्षा, प्रतीक

41. 'चिकना मुँह पेट खाली' लोकोक्ति का सही अर्थ है :
A. अपने हाथ से दान देना
B. देखने में सुखी भीतर से दुःखी
C. अत्यधिक प्यारा होना
D. जबरदस्ती गले पड़ना

42. समास-विग्रह की दृष्टि से कौन-सा विकल्प ***असंगत*** है?
A. शुभंकर – शुभ को करने वाला
B. रसमलाई – रस में डूबी हुई मलाई
C. नवयुवक – नौ युवकों का समूह
D. शाखामृग – शाखाओं पर रहने/दौड़ने वाला मृग

43. निम्नलिखित वर्णों के संदर्भ में कौन-सा विकल्प ***असंगत*** है?
A. य – तालव्य, अल्पप्राण, घोष
B. इ – तालव्य, ह्रस्व, अवृत्तमुखी
C. ब – ओष्ठ्य, घोष, अल्पप्राण
D. ष – मूर्धन्य, अल्पप्राण, अघोष

44. 'सचिन क्रिकेट खेलता है।' उक्त वाक्य को कर्मवाच्य में बदलिए :
A. सचिन क्रिकेट खेलेगा।
B. सचिन क्रिकेट नहीं खेलता है।
C. सचिन से क्रिकेट खेला जाता था।
D. सचिन के द्वारा क्रिकेट खेला जाता है।

45. शब्द-प्रकृति की दृष्टि से ***असंगत*** युग्म चुनिए :
A. गोस्वामी – तत्सम शब्द B. मुकद्दमा – देशज शब्द
C. पंख – तद्भव शब्द D. तहसीलदार – संकर शब्द

Language : English

Directions: *Answer the following questions by selecting the* ***most appropriate*** *option.*

46. Choose the ***correct*** meaning of the underlined idiom:

He is friendly to the minister, he jumped the queue and got promotion.
A. replace something
B. hopping
C. blame somebody
D. get something out of turn

47. Change the voice from Active to Passive. Choose the ***right*** option:

We shall discuss the question tomorrow in the meeting.
A. The question will be discussed tomorrow in the meeting.
B. We will be discussing the question tomorrow in the meeting.
C. We shall be discussing tomorrow the question in the meeting.
D. The question shall discuss tomorrow in the meeting.

48. Select the ***correct*** tense form:

The car (belong) to my mother. She (use) it today to take Tom to the dentist.
A. belonged, is using
B. belonged, using
C. belong, used
D. belongs, is using

49. Select the ***correct*** meaning of the underlined phrasal verbs:

I cannot make out the meaning of this verse.

A. discovery B. understand
C. reading D. start

50. Choose the ***correct*** form of tense given in the option:

She (play) the sitar since 6 o'clock this morning. He just (stop).

A. playing, stops
B. was played, stopping
C. has been playing, has just stopped
D. have been playing, stopped

51. Choose the option which has ***error*** in it:

(*a*) You should (*b*) tell to me
(*c*) exactly what (*d*) happened there

A. (*a*) B. (*b*)
C. (*c*) D. (*d*)

52. Select the ***correct*** preposition to fill in the blank:

They live ______ the same roof.

A. in B. before
C. after D. under

53. Select the ***correct*** preposition to fill in the blank:

He broke the jug ______ a hundred pieces.

A. in B. into
C. over D. about

54. Choose the ***correct*** option:
Transformation from Simple sentence to Complex sentence:

A lost moment is lost forever.

A. A moment which is lost is lost forever.
B. A lost moment is forever lost.
C. Forever a lost moment is lost.
D. No moment is lost forever.

55. Choose the ***correct*** option:

Transformation of sentences: Simple to Compound.

He must work hard to make up for the lost time.

A. He must work hard, cover the lost time.
B. Making up for the lost time he must work hard.
C. He must work hard and make up for the lost time.
D. Working hard will make up for the lost time.

56. Choose one word substitution for the following:

A word spelt and pronounced similar but differing in meaning.

A. Antonym B. Homonym
C. Synonym D. Pseudonym

57. Select the ***correct*** conjunctions for the blanks:

We will come ______ it rains ______ not.

A. if, and B. even, but
C. whether, or D. either, and

58. Change the following sentences into Reported Speech by choosing the ***correct*** option:

"We're waiting for the school bus," said the children, "It's late again."

A. The children told they're waiting for the school bus and it is late.
B. The children said they were waiting for the school bus and it is late.
C. The children complained that they were waiting for the school bus and it was late again.
D. The children complained that they were waiting for the school bus and it is late.

59. Change the following sentences into Reported Speech by choosing the ***correct*** option.

"If you want to smoke you'll have to go upstairs." said the landlord.

A. The landlord told him that if he wants to smoke he'll have to go upstairs.
B. The landlord told him that if he wanted to smoke he would have to go upstairs.
C. The landlord said that if he would want to smoke he would go upstairs.
D. The landlord says if you wanted to smoke you would have to go upstairs.

60. Select the ***correct*** infinitive form of the given sentence:

Seeing is believing.

A. To see is to believe. B. Seen is to believe.
C. To see is believing D. Seeing is to believe.

PART-III

General Studies : Quantitative Aptitude, Reasoning Ability and GK & Awareness

61. If the Independence Day in 1988 was celebrated on Wednesday. On what day was it celebrated in the year 1989?

A. Monday
B. Tuesday
C. Thursday
D. Friday

62. Vijay walks 10 km towards North, from there, he walks 6 km towards South, then he walks 3 km towards East. How far and in which direction is he with reference to his starting point?

A. 5 km West B. 5 km North-East
C. 7 km East D. 7 km West

63. In a row of girls, Shilpa is 8th from the left and Reena is 17th from the right, if they interchange their positions, Shilpa becomes 14th from the left. How many girls are there in a row?
A. 27 B. 29
C. 32 D. 30

64. In a certain pattern, if 9 * 3 = 36, 10 * 6 = 64, 9 * 1 = 25, then in the same pattern what is the value of 23 * 3 = ?
A. 169 B. 52
C. 32 D. 576

65. In a certain code MONKEY is written as XDJMNL. How is TIGER written in that code?
A. SDFHS B. SHFDQ
C. QDFHS D. UJHFS

66. If A means 'plus', B means 'minus', C means 'divide by', D means 'multiply'. Then what will be simplified value of

18 A 12 C 6 D 2 B 5 = ?
A. 25 B. 27
C. 15 D. 17

67. If 7 carpenters can make 7 chairs in 8 hours, how many hours will 70 carpenters take to make 70 chairs?
A. 8 hours B. 560 hours
C. 56 hours D. 70 hours

68. Which number must be added to each term of the ratio 2 : 5, so that it may equal to 5 : 6?
A. 12 B. 11
C. 13 D. 14

69. A sum of ₹ 10,000 deposited at compound interest becomes double after 5 years. After 20 years the amount will be:
A. ₹ 40,000 B. ₹ 60,000
C. ₹ 80,000 D. ₹ 1,60,000

70. A sold a watch to B at a gain of 10% and B sold it to C at a loss of 10%. If C paid ₹ 990 for it, then how much amount paid by A?
A. ₹ 900 B. ₹ 1,000
C. ₹ 1,200 D. ₹ 950

71. The price of any item is increased by 20%. Find the reduction in the consumption of the item by a consumer so that there is no increase on his expenditure:
A. $16\frac{2}{3}\%$ B. $15\frac{2}{3}\%$
C. $17\frac{2}{3}\%$ D. $16\frac{1}{3}\%$

72. What is the value of $\sqrt{2\sqrt{2\sqrt{2\sqrt{2\sqrt{2}}}}}$?
A. 0 B. 2
C. 1 D. $2^{31/32}$

73. Two trains 132 meters and 108 meters long are running in opposite direction, one at the speed of 32 km/hr and another at the speed of 40 km/hr. In what time will they cross each other?
A. 8 sec. B. 10 sec.
C. 12 sec. D. 11 sec.

74. $0.34\overline{67}+0.13\overline{33}$ is equal to:
A. 0.48 B. $0.48\overline{01}$
C. $0.\overline{48}$ D. $0.4\overline{8}$

75. What is the HCF of 11, 11.11, 0.11, 0.011?
A. 0.011 B. 1.1
C. 0.11 D. 0.111

76. The ratio of the areas of the incircle and circumcircle of a square will be:
A. 1 : 4 B. 4 : 1
C. 1 : 2 D. 2 : 1

77. Find the missing letters in the given letter series:

a_cdaab_cc_daa_bbb_ccddd
A. *bdbda* B. *bddca*
C. *dbbca* D. *bbdac*

78. The number in the following question numbers are written according to certain pattern row-wise or column-wise. Identify the pattern and find the missing character accordingly.

6	11	25
8	6	16
12	5	?

A. 18 B. 16
C. 12 D. 10

79. Find the next term of the number series:

127, 128, 136, 163, 227, ______.
A. 352 B. 350
C. 357 D. 341

80. There are five different houses A to E in a row. A is to the right of B and E is to the left of C and right of A. B is to the right of D. Which of the house is exactly in the middle?
A. A B. B
C. D D. E

81. Who among the following is the recipient of 'Padma Bhushan' in 2021?
A. Jai Bhagwan Goyal B. Virendra Singh
C. Tarlochan Singh D. Mukesh Singh

82. 'Pran Vayu Devata Pension Scheme' is aimed to:
A. Conserve older trees in Haryana State
B. Provide financial assistance to the non-government doctors in their old age
C. Provide economic relief to the non-government paramedical staff in their old age
D. Encourage plantation of Tulsi and Giloya in urban households

83. Origin of the which of the following rivers is ***not*** correctly matched?

River	Origin Site
A. Saraswati —	Dangushai
B. Indori —	Mewat hills
C. Markanda —	Sivalik hills
D. Tangdi —	Morni hills

84. Who among the following Governors of Haryana died while in the office?
A. B.N. Chakraborty
B. Ranjit Singh Narula
C. J.L. Hathi
D. Sardar H.S. Brar

85. Which of the following is ***not*** true about the proposed investment region/industrial area under Delhi-Mumbai industrial corridor in Haryana?
A. Faridabad — Palwal industrial area
B. Rewari — Hisar investment region
C. Kundli — Sonipat investment region
D. Manesar — Bawal investment region

86. Who among the following did ***not*** serve as the Chief Justice of the Punjab and Haryana High Court?
A. Justice Mukund Mudgal
B. Justice A.K. Sikri
C. Justice M.S. Jain
D. Justice Sanjay Kishan Kaul

87. The total number of medals won by the athletes of Haryana in the Tokyo Paralympics 2021 are:
A. 04 B. 06
C. 08 D. 19

88. The Haryana Public Service Commission presents its annual report of the work done by the commission to the:
A. Governor
B. President
C. Parliament
D. State Legislative Assembly

89. Identify the text/texts, in which the reference of Thanesar is found:
(*i*) Harshcharit
(*ii*) Travelogue of Yuvan Chang
(*iii*) Kadambari
(*iv*) Karpur Manjari

Choose the ***correct*** code:
A. Only (*i*) B. (*i*) and (*ii*)
C. (*i*), (*ii*) and (*iii*) D. (*i*), (*ii*) (*iii*) and (*iv*)

90. Monthly magazine 'Hariprabha' is published by:
A. Information and Public Relations Department
B. Haryana Sahitya Academy
C. Haryana Sanskrit Academy
D. Haryana Hindi Granth Academy

PART-IV

Commerce

91. A draws a bill on 25th October, 2021 for 90 days and accepted, the maturity date of the bill will be:
A. 27th January, 2022 B. 25th January, 2022
C. 26th January, 2022 D. 23rd January, 2022

92. Which of the following statement is ***true***?
A. Amount set apart to meet future losses due to known liabilities, amount of which cannot be determined properly is called provisions.
B. Amount set apart to meet future losses due to known liabilities is called reserves.
C. Amount set apart to meet future losses due to unknown liabilities is called provisions.
D. Secret reserve is shown as separate item in the Balance Sheet

93. Which method of depreciation is followed to have a uniform charge for depreciation and repairs and maintenance together?
A. Reducing balancing method
B. Fixed instalment method
C. Depletion method
D. Annuity method

94. Trade mark is a ______.
A. Tangible Real Account
B. Intangible Real Account
C. Representative Personal Account
D. Nominal Account

95. A Company can issue:
A. Zero coupon rate debentures
B. Partly convertible debentures
C. Secured debentures
D. All type of debentures as shown in (A), (B) and (C)

96. Petty Cash Book is maintained for recording ______.
A. Petty incomes
B. Petty expenses paid in cash
C. Petty incomes recerved in cash and petty expenses incurred
D. Peety incomes and petty expenses

97. Secret reserve can be prepared by:
A. Assuming capital expenditure as revenue
B. Outstanding expenses not shown in Balance Sheet and Profit & Loss account

C. Overvaluation of liabilities
D. All these reasons

98. When adjusted purchase is shown on debit column of Trial Balance, then:
A. Both opening and closing stock will be shown in the Trial Balance.
B. Only closing stock is shown in the Trial Balance.
C. Both opening and closing stock will not shown in the Trial Balance.
D. Only opening stock is shown in the Trial Balance.

99. A Supporting voucher is ______.
A. a documentary evidence of business transcations having taken place
B. secondary voucher
C. prepared by an accountant
D. a proof

100. Debit balance as per cash book as on 31st March, 2021 in ₹ 4,000. Cheques deposited but not yet cleared amounted to ₹ 300 and cheques issued but not presented yet of ₹ 200. The bank allowed interest amounting to ₹ 100 and collected divident ₹ 100 on directly, balance as per pass book should be ______ on that date.
A. ₹ 3,300 B. ₹ 3,700
C. ₹ 4,100 D. ₹ 3,900

101. The cost incurred in providing goods & services is called is ______.
A. Capital expenditure B. Expenses
C. Prime cost D. Major cost

102. Which of the following items is/are recorded in Journal profit?
A. Goods used for personal purpose
B. Opening and closing entries
C. Loss of goods by fire
D. All these items

103. Historical cost is used for recording value of purchases of an asset because ______ applies.
A. Mathcing concept
B. Convention of disclosure
C. Cost concept
D. Realisation concept

104. Interest to the allowed @ .75 per cent p.m. on partners capital of ₹ 60 lakh. Manager's commission @ 5% of net profit after charging such commission. If the net profit before charging interest on capital and manager's commission amounted to ₹ 14.85 lakh. Then manager's commission will be:
A. ₹ 74,250 B. ₹ 45,000
C. ₹ 47,250 D. ₹ 94,250

105. A company forfeited 200 shares of 100 each, ₹ 70 called up, on which the holder paid ₹ 50 per share. These shares were reissued at ₹ 80 fully paid up per share. The share forfeited account will be debited in the reissue entry with:
A. ₹ 6,000 B. ₹ 4,000
C. ₹ 10,000 D. ₹ 16,000

106. The following information is given: Opening stock ₹ 2,13,000, Purchases ₹ 16,55,000, Sales ₹ 21,32,000, Carriage inwards ₹ 32,500, Carriage outwards ₹ 38,600, return inwards ₹ 42,000.

If rate of gross profit is 25% on cost, then value of closing stock will be:
A. ₹ 2,57,800 B. ₹ 2,33,000
C. ₹ 2,36,700 D. ₹ 2,28,500

107. At the time of dissolution of the firm, following payments are due:
(i) ₹ 10,000 partners loan
(ii) Creditors for goods ₹ 12,000
(iii) ₹ 1,000 for payment of expenses incurred in selling of assets
(iv) Capital of A ₹ 5,000, B ₹ 3,000

What will be the order of payment as per section 48 u/s Partnership Act?
A. *(iii)*, *(ii)*, *(i)*, *(iv)* B. *(i)*, *(ii)*, *(iii)*, *(iv)*
C. *(ii)*, *(i)*, *(iii)*, *(iv)* D. *(ii)*, *(i)*, *(iv)*, *(iii)*

108. A, B and C are partners in a firm. In the middle of the year C retries from the firm without settling his dues. Remaining partners continues the business. C is entitled to get ______ till the final settlement.
A. Interest at the rate of 6% per annum on the unsettled amount till settlement
B. Share in profit earn by firm till settlement of his account, in the profit sharing ratio
C. Share in profit earn by the firm till settlement of his account, proportionate to his unsettled amount to total capital of the firm from the date of retirement
D. Either option (A) or (C) on his choice.

109. ₹ 1,00,000 is net sales of a concern during 2021. If inventory turnover is 4 times, calculate the inventory at the end is 1.5 times of that is the beginning:
A. ₹ 20,000 B. ₹ 30,000
C. ₹ 13,333 D. ₹ 10,000

110. A grant of ₹ 10,00,000 to a school for construction of building, cheque is received on 1st February, 2021 from the state government. While closing the accounts none of the amount is used for construction. While preparing Income and Expenditure Account and Balance Sheet at the end, where such amount will be shown?
A. Only in liabilities side of Balance Sheet as a separate item
B. Only in income side of Income to Expenditure Account
C. Only in liabilities side of Balance Sheet by adding to the Capital Fund
D. Neither in Income and Expenditure Account nor in Balance Sheet

111. The immediate recognition of losses is related to ______.
A. Conservatism convention
B. Consistency convention
C. Materiality convention
D. Disclosure convention

112. X sold goods for ₹ 20,000 in cash after allowing 10% trade discount and 5% cash discount. Give the amount which will be debited to cash and discount account in books of seller:
A. ₹ 17,100, ₹ 2,900 B. ₹ 17,100, ₹ 900
C. ₹ 17,100, ₹ 1,000 D. ₹ 19,000] ₹ 1,000

113. The gain from sale of capital assets need ***not*** to be added to revenue to ascertain the ______ of business.
A. Business Profit B. Capital Profit
C. Net Profit D. Operating Profit

114. Match List-I with List-II and select the ***correct*** answer using codes given below the lists:

List-I	List-II
(*a*) Error of Posting	(*i*) Sales book overcast
(*b*) Error of Costing	(*ii*) Goods sold to Ram but wrongly debited to Shyam
(*c*) Error of Principle	(*iii*) Goods returned by A not entered in the books
(*d*) Error of Omission	(*iv*) Wages paid for construction but debited to Wages A/c

Codes:

	(*a*)	(*b*)	(*c*)	(*d*)
A.	(*i*)	(*iii*)	(*ii*)	(*iv*)
B.	(*ii*)	(*i*)	(*iii*)	(*iv*)
C.	(*ii*)	(*i*)	(*iv*)	(*iii*)
D.	(*iii*)	(*iv*)	(*ii*)	(*i*)

115. Match List-I with List-II and select the ***correct*** answer using codes given below the lists:

List-I	List-II
(*a*) Goodwill	(*i*) Purchases consideration – Net assets
(*b*) Super profit	(*ii*) Capital employed × Normal rate of return
(*c*) Normal profit	(*iii*) Cat naure goodwill
(*d*) Institutional goodwill	(*iv*) Actual Average profit – Normal profit

Codes:

	(*a*)	(*b*)	(*c*)	(*d*)
A.	(*i*)	(*iii*)	(*iv*)	(*ii*)
B.	(*ii*)	(*iv*)	(*i*)	(*iii*)
C.	(*i*)	(*iv*)	(*ii*)	(*iii*)
D.	(*iii*)	(*iv*)	(*ii*)	(*i*)

116. A and B are partners in a firm sharing profits in the ratio of 3 : 2, C is admitted for $\frac{3}{20}$ share in profits. C acquires $\frac{1}{3}$ of his share from B and A surrenders $\frac{1}{6}$th of his share to C. What will be the new ratio of the firm?
A. 10 : 7 : 3 B. 15 : 8 : 7
C. 5 : 4 : 1 D. None of these

117. A, B and C are partners. Their capital at the beginning ₹ 50,000, ₹ 60,000 and ₹ 70,000 respectively. A introduce additional capital ₹ 20,000 after 3 months, B ₹ 25,000 after 6 months, C ₹ 30,000 after 9 months. At the end profit for the year is ₹ 25,800, which is distributed in their capital ratio. What will be the share of profit of A?
A. ₹ 7,800 B. ₹ 8,700
C. ₹ 9,300 D. ₹ 7,084

118. Which of the following is an example of Deferred Revenue expenditure?
A. Specific Research expenses
B. Special advertisement expenses
C. Heavy expenses for tranferring business at suitable place
D. All these

119. Subscription of ₹ 6,24,000 had been shown in Income & Expenditure account prepared for the year ending 31st March, 2021. Additional information is given below:

	On 31st March, 2020 (₹)	On 31st March, 2021 (₹)
Subscription outstanding	55,000	69,000
Subscription recd. in advance	31,000	35,000

The amount of subscription received during the year 2020-21 would be:
A. ₹ 6,34,000 B. ₹ 6,04,000
C. ₹ 6,14,000 D. ₹ 6,16,000

120. Patnership firm is compulsorily dissolved:
A. If the business of the firm has become illegal.
B. If number of partners in a firm has become more the 50.
C. If reorganisation of profit sharing ratio between partners is done.
D. Either (A) or (B) circumstances arise.

121. Recruitment is a:
A. Negative process
B. Positive process
C. Negative as well as positive
D. Creative process

122. Who has given 'Fourteen Principles of Management'?
A. John Fayol B. Henry Ford
C. Henry Fayol D. F.W. Taylor

123. ______ is a communication that flows from a higher level to one or more lower levels in the organization.
A. Downward communication
B. Diagonal communication

C. Horizontal communication
D. Upward communication

124. Situational Model of leadership was developed by:
A. Robert House
B. Dr. Gary Yukl
C. Robert R. Blake
D. Paul Hersey and Blanchard

125. Creating new products or services for foreign markets is known as:
A. Product adaption
B. Straight product extension
C. Product invention
D. Communication adaption

126. ______ is ***not*** one of the steps in the decision making process.
A. Identifying the problems
B. Analyzing alternative solutions
C. Implementing the decision
D. Delegating the decision

127. "Invisible" in the balance of payments account refer to:
A. Goods Transaction B. Service Transaction
C. Export Promotion D. Capital Transaction

128. Who has developed hierarchy of need motivational theory?
A. A.H. Maslow B. George Elton Mayo
C. William G. Ouchi D. L.F. Urwick

129. Which theory assumes that people generally lazy and will avoid work and responsibilities?
A. Theory Y B. Theory P
C. Theory Z D. Theory X

130. In value based pricing:
A. Customer → Value → Price → Cost → Product
B. Product → Cost → Price → Value → Customer
C. Product → Value → Cost → Price → Customer
D. Customer → Cost → Price → Value → Product

131. Ethics may be defined as:
A. A code of Material
B. A code of Conduct
C. A code of Management
D. A code of Control

132. The modern approach of Financial Management is:
A. Funds collection
B. Effective and efficient utilization of capital
C. More attention to the problems of corporate enterprises
D. More emphasis on long term problems

133. A runner-up firm that is fighting hard to increase its market share in an industry is known as:
A. Market follower B. Market challenger
C. Market developer D. Market nicher

134. Delegation of authority involves:
A. Span of control
B. Inspiring the subordinates
C. Organizational behaviour
D. Assigning of duties and authority to subordinates

135. Which of the following categories of industries are covered under oil refinery and sugar mills?
A. Analytical industries
B. Synthetical industries
C. Processing industries
D. Integrated industries

136. Registration of a cooperative society is:
A. Protected B. Compulsory
C. Optional D. Through member's

137. Factor causing unethical conduct in management is:
A. Economic Greed B. Fair Competition
C. Social Values D. Government Policies

138. Which of the following is ***not*** a feature of employment?
A. Term and Conditions
B. Agreement between employer and employee
C. Element of risk
D. Fixed wages

139. Which of the following is ***not*** an element of communication process?
A. Encoding B. Channel
C. Receiver D. Measurement

140. Internal elements that may interfere with the company's ability to achive its objectives is:
A. Strength B. Weakness
C. Opportunity D. Threats

141. Which management thinker receive the Noble Prize for Economics in 1978?
A. Herbert A. Simon B. Kurt Lewin
C. Chris Argyris D. Warren G. Bennis

142. Partnership is the result of:
A. Human Relations B. An agreement
C. Innovation D. An agency

143. What is the maximum age limit members of national commission for consumer protection?
A. 65 years B. 60 years
C. 70 years D. 75 years

144. A major characteristic of service which cannot be stored for later sale or use?
A. Service intangibility
B. Service inseparability
C. Service perishability
D. Service variability

145. Which of the following is the characteristic of transactional leader?
A. Inspirational motivation
B. Management by exception

C. Idealised influence
D. Intellectual stimulation

146. "Management is the development of people, not direction of things". Who said?
A. Lawrence Mayo B. Lawrence Appley
C. Elton Mayo D. Elton John

147. The phenomenon in which the norms for consensus overrides the realistic appraisal of alterna-tive actions:
A. Interacting group B. Nominal group
C. Group shift D. Group think

148. Which is ***not*** the element of Business Environment?
A. Legal B. Political
C. Historical D. Economic

149. Human objective of business is:
A. Labour welfare and safety
B. Development of new product
C. Adequate production
D. To create customers

150. Social Responsibilities of Business is:
A. Single Dimension B. Equal Dimension
C. Long Dimension D. Multiple Dimension

Answers

1	**2**	**3**	**4**	**5**	**6**	**7**	**8**	**9**	**10**
D	D	C	B	C	D	C	C	D	C
11	**12**	**13**	**14**	**15**	**16**	**17**	**18**	**19**	**20**
A	C	D	A	D	B	B	A	C	A
21	**22**	**23**	**24**	**25**	**26**	**27**	**28**	**29**	**30**
C	D	B	A	B	A	B	A	C	B
31	**32**	**33**	**34**	**35**	**36**	**37**	**38**	**39**	**40**
D	B	C	D	A	C	A	D	A	C
41	**42**	**43**	**44**	**45**	**46**	**47**	**48**	**49**	**50**
B	C	D	D	B	D	A	D	B	C
51	**52**	**53**	**54**	**55**	**56**	**57**	**58**	**59**	**60**
B	D	B	A	C	B	C	C	B	A
61	**62**	**63**	**64**	**65**	**66**	**67**	**68**	**69**	**70**
C	B	D	A	C	D	A	C	D	B
71	**72**	**73**	**74**	**75**	**76**	**77**	**78**	**79**	**80**
A	D	C	B	A	C	D	B	A	A
81	**82**	**83**	**84**	**85**	**86**	**87**	**88**	**89**	**90**
C	A	A	A	B	C	B	A	B	C
91	**92**	**93**	**94**	**95**	**96**	**97**	**98**	**99**	**100**
B	A	A	B	D	B	D	C	A	C
101	**102**	**103**	**104**	**105**	**106**	**107**	**108**	**109**	**110**
B	D	C	B	B	D	A	D	A	A
111	**112**	**113**	**114**	**115**	**116**	**117**	**118**	**119**	**120**
A	B	D	C	C	A	A	D	C	D
121	**122**	**123**	**124**	**125**	**126**	**127**	**128**	**129**	**130**
B	C	A	D	C	D	B	A	D	A
131	**132**	**133**	**134**	**135**	**136**	**137**	**138**	**139**	**140**
B	B	B	D	C	B	A	C	D	B
141	**142**	**143**	**144**	**145**	**146**	**147**	**148**	**149**	**150**
A	B	C	C	B	B	D	C	A	D

Explanatory Answers

61. The number of day = from 15 August, 1988 to 15 August, 1989 = 365 days

$\because$ 365 = 7 × 52 + 1

$\therefore$ Odd day = 1.

Hence, the independence day in 1989 was celebrated on Thursday (Wednesday + 1).

62. Here, Starting point = A

AB = 10 km, BC = 6 km, CD = 3 km

$$AD = \sqrt{AC^2 + CD^2} = \sqrt{4^2 + 3^2}$$

$$= \sqrt{16 + 9} = \sqrt{25}$$

$$= 5 \text{ km}$$

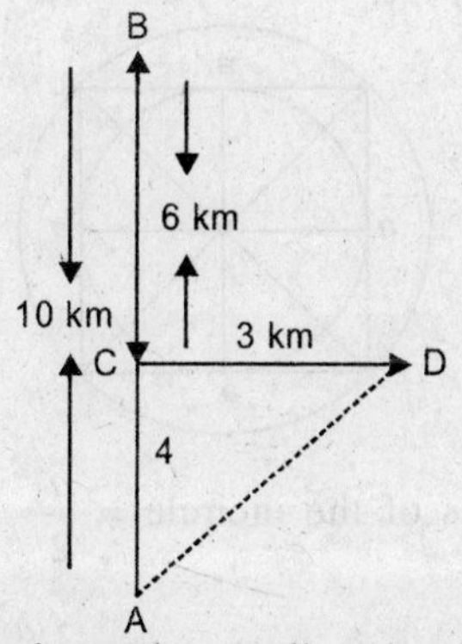

Hence, Vijay is north-east direction and 5 km far from his starting point.

63.

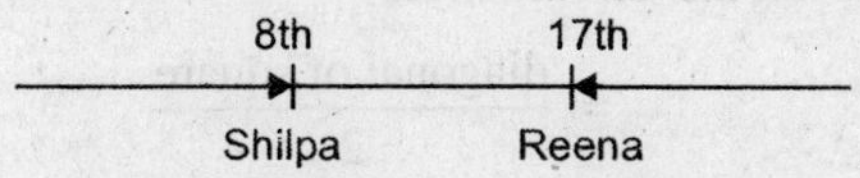

After interchange

14th

Reena Shilpa

Hence, the number of girls in row = 14 + 16 = 30.

64. Given, $\quad 9 * 3 = 36$

$$\Rightarrow \quad (9+3)\times\left(\frac{9+3}{4}\right) = 12 \times 3 = 36,$$

$$10 * 6 = 64$$

$$\Rightarrow \quad (10+6)\times\left(\frac{10+6}{4}\right) = 16 \times 4 = 64,$$

$$9 * 1 = 25$$

$$\Rightarrow \quad (9+1)\times\left(\frac{9+1}{4}\right) = 10\times\frac{5}{2} = 25$$

Similarly, $\quad 23 * 3 = (23+3)\times\left(\frac{23+3}{4}\right) = 26\times\frac{26}{4}$

$$= 13 \times 13 = 169.$$

65. Given,

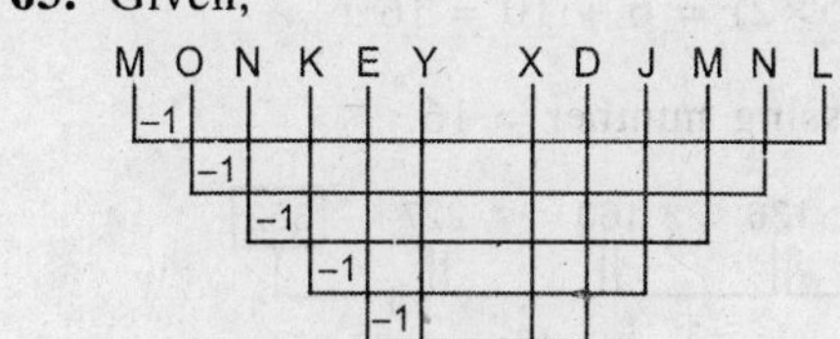

Similarly,

T I G E R Q D F H S

–1 –1 –1 –1 –1

Hence, TIGER is written as QDFHS.

66. Given, A = +, B = –, C = ÷, D = ×

$\therefore$ 18 A 12 C 6 D 2 B 5

= 18 + 12 ÷ 6 × 2 – 5

= 18 + 2 × 2 – 5

= 18 + 4 – 5 = 22 – 5 = 17.

67. Here, $\quad M_1 = 7$ carpenters,

$w_1 = 7$ chairs

$h_1 = 8$ hours

and $\quad M_2 = 70$ carpenters,

$w_2 = 70$ chairs

$\therefore \quad h_2 = ?$

$$\frac{M_1 d h_1}{w_1} = \frac{M_2 d h_2}{w_2}$$

$$\Rightarrow \quad \frac{7\times 8}{7} = \frac{70\times h_2}{70}$$

$$\Rightarrow \quad h_2 = 8 \text{ hours.}$$

68. Let x number must be added to each term.

Then, $\quad \frac{2+x}{5+x} = \frac{5}{6}$

$$\Rightarrow \quad 12 + 6x = 25 + 5x$$

$$\Rightarrow \quad 6x - 5x = 25 - 12$$

$$\Rightarrow \quad x = 13$$

Hence, the required number = x = 13.

69. Here, P = ₹ 10,000, A = ₹ 20,000, n = 5 years at compund interest.

$$A = P\left(1+\frac{r}{100}\right)^n$$

$$\Rightarrow \quad ₹\ 20{,}000 = 10{,}000\left(1+\frac{r}{100}\right)^5$$

$$\Rightarrow \quad \left(1+\frac{r}{100}\right)^5 = 2$$

$$\Rightarrow \quad \left(1+\frac{r}{100}\right)^{5\times 4} = 2^4$$

$$\Rightarrow \quad \left(1+\frac{r}{100}\right)^{20} = 16$$

$$\Rightarrow \quad 10{,}000\left(1+\frac{r}{100}\right)^{20} = 16 \times 10{,}000$$

$$\Rightarrow \quad 10{,}000\left(1+\frac{r}{100}\right)^{20} = 1{,}60{,}000$$

Hence, After 20 years the amount will be ₹ 1,60,000.

70. Let, $\quad$ C.P. for A = ₹ x,

then $\quad$ S.P. for A = $x\times\frac{110}{100}$ = ₹ $\frac{11x}{10}$

C.P. for B = ₹ $\frac{11x}{10}$,

S.P. for B = ₹ $\frac{11x}{10}\times\frac{90}{100}$ = ₹ $\frac{99}{100}x$

C.P. for C = ₹ $\frac{99}{100}x$

Therefore $\frac{99}{100}x$ = ₹ 990

$\Rightarrow$ x = ₹ 1000

Hence, Amount paid by A is ₹ 1000.

71. The required reduction $= \frac{20}{100+20}\times 100$

$= \frac{20}{120}\times 100 = \frac{1}{6}\times 100$

$= \frac{50}{3} = 16\frac{2}{3}\%.$

72. $\sqrt{2\sqrt{2\sqrt{2\sqrt{2\sqrt{2}}}}}$

$= 2^{\frac{1}{2}}.2^{\frac{1}{2}\times\frac{1}{2}}.2^{\frac{1}{2}\times\frac{1}{2}\times\frac{1}{2}}.2^{\frac{1}{2}\times\frac{1}{2}\times\frac{1}{2}\times\frac{1}{2}}.2^{\frac{1}{2}\times\frac{1}{2}\times\frac{1}{2}\times\frac{1}{2}\times\frac{1}{2}}$

$= 2^{\frac{1}{2}}\cdot 2^{\frac{1}{4}}\cdot 2^{\frac{1}{8}}\cdot 2^{\frac{1}{16}}\cdot 2^{\frac{1}{32}}$

$= 2^{\frac{1}{2}+\frac{1}{4}+\frac{1}{8}+\frac{1}{16}+\frac{1}{32}} = 2^{\frac{16+8+4+2+1}{32}} = 2^{\frac{31}{32}}.$

73. Here, Train to cover 132 + 108 = 240 m distance and trains are running in opposite direction

$\therefore$ relative speed = 32 + 40 = 72 km/hr

$= 72\times\frac{5}{18}$ m/s

= 4 × 5 = 20 m/s

Therefore, Time taken by the trains to cross each other

$= \frac{\text{distance}}{\text{speed}}$

$= \frac{240}{20} = 12$ seconds.

74. $0.34\overline{67}+0.13\overline{33}$

$= \frac{3467-34}{9900}+\frac{1333-13}{9900}$

$= \frac{3433+1320}{9900}$

$= \frac{4753}{9900} = \frac{4753}{99\times 100}$

$= \frac{48.01010101}{100} = 0.48\overline{01}.$

75. HCF of 11, 11.11, 0.11, 0.011

HCF of $11, \frac{1111}{100}, \frac{11}{100}, \frac{11}{1000}$

$= \frac{\text{HCF of } 11, 1111, 11, 11}{\text{LCM of } 1, 100, 100, 1000}$

$= \frac{11}{1000} = 0.011.$

76. Let, Side of Square = a unit

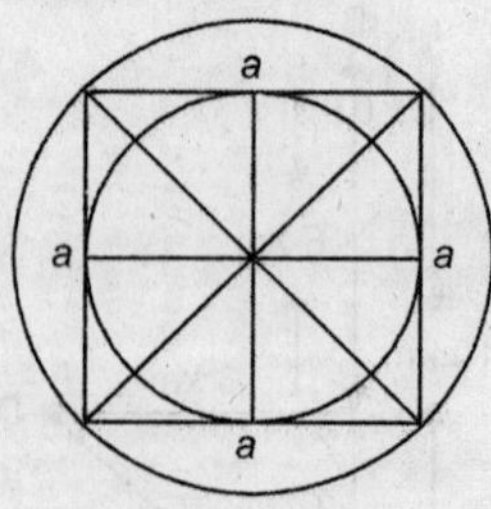

Then, radius of the incircle $= \frac{a}{2}$

$\therefore$ The area of the incircle $= \pi\left(\frac{a}{2}\right)^2 = \frac{\pi a^2}{4}$ sq. units

and radius of the circumcircle

$= \frac{\text{diagonal of square}}{2}$

$= \frac{a\sqrt{2}}{2} = \frac{a}{\sqrt{2}}$ unit

$\therefore$ The area of the circumcircle

$= \frac{\pi a^2}{2}$ sq. units

Hence, the required ratio

$= \frac{\pi a^2}{4} : \frac{\pi a^2}{2} = \frac{1}{4} : \frac{1}{2} = 1 : 2.$

78. From first row

6	11	25
8	6	16
12	5	?

$\frac{6}{2}+(11\times 2)$ = 3 + 22 = 25

From second row

$\frac{8}{2}+(6\times 2)$ = 4 + 12 = 16

From third row

$\frac{12}{2}+(5\times 2)$ = 6 + 10 = 16

Hence, the missing number = 16.

79. 127 128 136 163 227 352

$+1^3$ $+2^3$ $+3^3$ $+4^3$ $+5^3$

$\because$ 127 = First term

$\therefore$ 127 + 1^3 = 127 + 1 = 128 = Second term

128 + 2^3 = 128 + 8 = 136 = Third term

136 + 3^3 = 136 + 27 = 163 = Fourth term

163 + 4^3 = 163 + 64 = 227 = Fifth term

227 + 5^3 = 227 + 125 = 352 = Sixth term

Hence, the next term in the series = 352.

80. Given, there are five different houses in a row and their position is as follow:

DBAEC

Hence, house A is exactly in the middle.

Previous Paper (Solved)

Haryana Teacher Eligibility Test (HTET)

PGT Commerce (Level-3), Exam 2020

(Exam held on 2 January, 2021)

PART-I

Child Development and Pedagogy

Directions: *Answer the following questions by selecting the **most appropriate** option.*

1. Which of the following is ***not*** the true characteristic of Development?
A. Development involves changes
B. Early Development is more critical than later development
C. Development Patterns are unpredictable
D. There are individual differences in development

2. Which of the following is indirect method of measurement of motives?
A. Sentence completion technique
B. Questionnaire
C. Checklist
D. Interview

3. What are the basis of 'Self Concept'?
A. Social Roles
B. The Body Image
C. Above (A) and (B)
D. None of the above

4. Which of the following is ***not*** the characteristic of introverted thinking type personality as given by Jung?
A. Self Centered
B. Optimistic
C. Absorbed in his own intellectual pursuit
D. Support Theory with facts

5. What is the approximate weight of the Brain upto 16 year age?
A. 750 gm to 900 gm
B. 1200 gm to 1400 gm
C. 1000 gm to 1200 gm
D. 800 gm to 1000 gm

6. Which Psychologist presented scientific description of 'Individual differences' in his Book 'Hereditary Genius'?
A. Allport B. Biggi and Hunt
C. Jean Piaget D. Sir Fransis Galton

7. Which of the following is Direct Method of Adjustment?
A. Repression
B. Regression
C. Withdrawl and Submissiveness
D. Rationalization

8. Which of the following orientation falls under the post convention level of Moral Development Theory propounded by Kohlberg?
A. Punishment and Obedience
B. Social contract
C. Good boy/Nice girl
D. Law and Social order

9. Which of the following is ***not*** the characteristic of Adolescence?
A. Emotional Stability
B. Contrasting Mental Moods
C. Anxiety of Vocation
D. Feeling of Hero worship

10. A statement of knowledge or skills that student should master after instruction, is known as:
A. A content analysis
B. An individualized educational programme (IEP)
C. An instructional objective
D. General Aims

11. Which of the following is ***not*** the symptoms of Good Memory?
A. Rapidity
B. Average retention
C. Accuracy
D. Recall of right material at right time

12. Which of the following concept is ***not*** related with Bandura's Social Learning Theory?
A. Modelling
B. Adaptation
C. Imitation
D. Observational learning

13. What is the ranking ratio given by Sheldon for predominant endomorph person according to physique?
A. 7-1-1 B. 1-7-1
C. 1-1-7 D. 4-4-4

14. Which is the fifth stage of Personality development according to Erikson?
A. industry v/s inferiority
B. identity v/s role confusion
C. intimacy v/s isolation
D. generativity v/s stagnation

15. Which of the following is ***not*** the element of creativity as given by Guilford?
A. Fluency B. Incubation
C. Flexibility D. Originality

16. Which of the following is ***not*** the type of positive transfer of learning?
A. Lateral transfer
B. Sequential transfer
C. Horizontal transfer
D. Zero transfer

17. Which of the following is ***not*** the Freud's Psychosexual stage?
A. Phallic stage
B. Autonomy stage
C. Anal stage
D. Oral stage

18. Who stated that "Psychology is the Positive Science of conduct of living creatures"?
A. Sir William McDougall
B. Sir Francis Galton
C. Max Wertheimer
D. William James

19. Which of the following is ***not*** the type of "Psychophysical Method" of study of Educational Psychology?
A. The method of minimal changes or method of limits
B. The method of constant stimuli
C. The method of average or mean error
D. Modifying the individual attitude

20. 'Knowledge is constructed by transforming, organizing and re-organizing previous knowledge.' This best explains the idea of which of the following?
A. Piaget B. Vygotsky
C. Freud D. Bandura

21. According to the Cognitive Development Theory of Piaget, 'The basic building block of knowledge' is called:
A. Schema B. Assimilation
C. Accommodation D. Equilibration

22. An English teacher taught their students that plural of Cat is Cats, plural of House is Houses, plural of Pen is Pens, in this manner student by mistake made plural of Mouse as Mouses. This is the example of which type of transfer of learning?
A. Positive transfer
B. Negative transfer
C. Zero transfer
D. Vertical transfer

23. Which of the following is objective determinants of Attention?
A. Interest
B. Habit
C. Curiosity
D. Duration of stimulus

24. Murray's "Thematic Apperception Test" is related to which theory of personality?
A. Trait theory
B. Trait and Type theory
C. Type theory
D. Psychoanalytical theory

25. Which of the following is I.Q. Range of 'Moderate mental retarded' children?
A. 52 to 67 B. 36 to 51
C. 20 to 35 D. below 20

26. Which of the following is ***not*** the type of life styles for the development of personality given by Adler?
A. Lazy type
B. Ruling type
C. Go-getting type
D. Escaping type

27. How many cards are used in Rorschach Inkblot Test?
A. 10 B. 12
C. 15 D. 28

28. Which of the following is ***not*** a type of Personality given by Sprenger in values point of view?
A. Theoretical B. Economic
C. Asthetic D. Athletic

29. Which of the following is the subordinate law of learning given by Thorndike?
A. Law of readiness
B. Law of exercise
C. Law of mental set
D. Law of effect

30. Which of the following is ***not*** the true characteristic of Adolescence?
A. Adolescence is transitional stage between childhood and adulthood.
B. In adolescence there is a vague individual status.
C. Adolescence is the threshold of adulthood.
D. Adolescence is a time of realism.

PART-II

भाषा : हिन्दी

निर्देशः *निम्नलिखित प्रश्नों के उत्तर देने के लिए* **सबसे उचित** *विकल्प चुनिए।*

31. निजवाचक सर्वनाम युक्त वाक्य छाँटिए :

A. आप अत्यन्त आकर्षक व्यक्तित्व के स्वामी हैं।

B. लड़के आप ही चले जाएँगे।

C. आप लोग शान्त हो जाएँ।

D. आप हुज़ूर जरूर पधारें।

32. वार्तनिक दृष्टि से ***अशुद्ध*** विकल्प चुनिए :

A. मृत्योपरान्त

B. योगिराज

C. प्रोज्ज्वल

D. प्रज्वलित

33. विलोम की दृष्टि से ***असंगत*** जोड़े को छाँटिए :

A. लंबा-नाटा

B. अभिज्ञ-अनभिज्ञ

C. अनुरक्ति-विराग

D. सत्कार-तिरस्कार

34. किस विकल्प में 'इल' प्रत्यय का प्रयोग ***नहीं*** हुआ है?

A. उर्मिल B. मरियल

C. फेनिल D. जटिल

35. निम्न में से 'बकरी' का पर्याय ***नहीं*** है?

A. वृर्धकी B. छागी

C. अजा D. छेरी

36. जातिवाचक संज्ञा युक्त वाक्य ***नहीं*** है :

A. आजकल की पढ़ाइयाँ बहुत महँगी हैं।

B. ऊँचाइयाँ नापनी हैं तो पर्वतों की सैर कीजिए।

C. कभी-कभी बुराइयाँ ही अच्छाइयाँ बन जाती हैं।

D. मैंने अनुभव किया है कि उसे ऊँचाई से डर लगता है।

37. किस विकल्प में व्यंजन संधि का प्रयोग ***नहीं*** हुआ है?

A. चिदाभास

B. वागीश्वर

C. तदर्थ

D. तिरोहित

38. शुद्ध वाक्य का चयन कीजिए :

A. मैंने काम कोई वकील से ही हो सकता है।

B. मैंने उनका धन्यवाद किया।

C. कृपया दरवाजा बंद करने की कृपा करें।

D. हम सभी में मानवीय दुर्बलताएँ हैं।

39. समास की दृष्टि से ***असंगत*** विकल्प छाँटिए :

A. भयभीत - करण तत्पुरुष

B. सेठ-साहूकार - समाहार द्वन्द्व

C. विद्याहीन - अपादान तत्पुरुष

D. स्वर्गगत - कर्म तत्पुरुष

40. वाक्यांश के लिए एक शब्द की दृष्टि से ***असंगत*** विकल्प चुनिए :

A. किसी कथा के अन्तर्गत आने वाली कोई दूसरी कथा–अन्तर्कथा

B. सर्वाधिकार सम्पन्न शासक या अधिकारी–अधिनायक

C. बिना किसी प्रयास के–आयास

D. जिसे शाप दिया गया है–अभिशप्त

41. अनिश्चित संख्यावाचक विशेषण चुनिए :

A. पिछले वर्ष की तुलना में इस बार अधिक वर्षा हुई।

B. सब्जी में थोड़ा-सा नमक डालिए।

C. सारा काम मुझे ही करना होगा।

D. सारे देश आतंकवाद के खिलाफ खड़े हैं।

42. सकर्मक क्रिया युक्त वाक्य चुनिए :

A. भिखारी मंदिर के बाहर चिल्ला रहे थे।

B. मछलियाँ तालाब में तैर रही हैं।

C. धावक सड़क पर दौड़ रहे हैं।

D. बहन ने भाई को मिठाई खिलाई।

43. किस विकल्प में अव्ययीभाव समास है?

A. विरोधजनक

B. कृपापूर्वक

C. अवसरवंचित

D. स्वाधीन

44. प्रत्यय की दृष्टि से असंगत विकल्प चुनिए :

A. गृहस्थ + इक = गार्हस्थिक

B. दिष्ट + इक = दैष्टिक

C. अभिजात + त्य = आभिजात्य

D. पाणिनि + ईय = पाणिनीय

45. किस विकल्प में 'आ' उपसर्ग का प्रयोग हुआ है?

A. आधिकारिक

B. आधुनिक

C. आलम्बित

D. आरण्यक

Language : English

Directions: *Answer the following questions by selecting the* ***most appropriate*** *option.*

46. Choose the part of sentence that is grammatically ***incorrect***:

That's twice I've been forgetting to bring my diary to work this week.

A. That's twice
B. I've been forgetting
C. to bring my diary
D. to work this week

47. Fill in the blank with the ***correct*** option:

Of the two Novels, this is ....

A. interesting B. more interesting
C. interested D. much interesting

48. Change the narration:

He said, "I've been spending a lot more time with my children."

A. He told me that he had been spending a lot more time with his children.
B. He told me that he is spending a lot more time with my children.
C. He told me that he had spent a lot more time with his children.
D. He said that he spends a lot more time with his children.

49. Fill in the blank with the ***correct*** present perfect continuous tense:

Who .... was coming to see me this morning?

A. you should say B. did you say
C. you did said D. did you say that

50. Fill in the blank with the ***correct*** present perfect continuous tense:

He .... for five hours.

A. been slept B. is sleeping
C. been sleeping D. has been sleeping

51. Fill in the blanks:

The growing number of visitors .... the footpaths.

A. are damaging B. is damaging
C. were damage D. was damaged

52. Fill in the blank with the ***correct*** present perfect continuous tense:

She is one of the few people ....

A. who I look up to B. whose I look up
C. I look up to D. Both (A) and (C)

53. Choose the option and arrange the following sentence in the ***correct*** order:

I. Resigned
II. To sack him
III. Had he not
IV. We would have been forced

A. IV, III, II, I B. III, II, I, IV
C. IV, II, I, III D. III, I, IV, II

54. Change the sentence into passive:

Someone has picked my pocket.

A. My pocket is picked.
B. Somebody picked my pocket.
C. My pocket pick by somebody.
D. My pocket has been picked.

55. Choose the grammatically ***correct*** sentence:

A. No sooner we reached the station and the train arrived.
B. No sooner did we reach the station than the train arrived.
C. No sooner did we reach the station then the train arrived.
D. No sooner did we reach the station the train arrived.

56. Fill in the blank with the ***correct*** option:

............, they slept soundly.

A. Hot though was the night air
B. Hot though the night air was
C. Hot was the night air that
D. Hot although the night air was

57. Fill in the blank with the ***correct*** present perfect continuous tense:

.... thinks that Julie should be given the job.

A. neither of us
B. practically everyone
C. A no. of people
D. Both (A) and (B)

58. To have 'a bee in the bonnet' means:

A. to know perfectly
B. something you are obsessed with
C. not to take anything seriously
D. to deviate from the point

59. Choose the part of sentence that is grammatically ***incorrect***:

The world's supply of oil is soon running out.

A. The world's B. supply of oil
C. is soon running out D. Both (A) and (B)

60. The word 'juncture' means :

A. in a joyous manner
B. to put in danger
C. to sound harshly
D. point rendered critical by circumstances

PART-III

General Studies : Quantitative Aptitude, Reasoning Ability and GK & Awareness

61. In a code language, 'DISTANCE' is written as 'IDTATOEC' and 'DOCUMENT' is written as 'ODDMUFTN', then in same code language, 'THURSDAY' will be written as :

A. HTRUDSYA B. HTVSREYA
C. UHVSTEYA D. VIRUDSZB

62. Kamal walks 10 m towards North. From there, he walks 6 m towards South. Then he walks 3 m towards East. In which direction is he with reference to his starting point?

A. West B. South-West
C. North-East D. South

63. In the first year, the population of a village increased by 5% and in the next year it decreased by 5%. If at the end of the second year, the population was 79,800, what was it at the beginning of the first year?

A. 79,800 B. 80,200
C. 80,000 D. 79,600

64. Find the ***wrong*** terms of the following series: 1CV, 5FU, 9IT, 15LS, 17OR

A. 5FU B. 9IT
C. 15LS D. 17OR

65. The radii of two cylinders are in the ratio 2 : 3 and their heights are in the ratio 5 : 3. The ratio of their volumes are:

A. 27 : 20 B. 20 : 27
C. 4 : 9 D. 9 : 4

66. Mr. X said about Mrs. Y, "Mrs. Y is the wife of the grandson of my mother." How is Mr. X is related to Mrs. Y?

A. Father B. Grandfather
C. Husband D. Father-in-law

67. How many independent meaningful words can 'HEARTLESS' be divided into without changing the order of the letters and using each letter only once?

A. 1 B. 2
C. 3 D. 4

68. In an examination, 27% students failed in English and 38% failed in Science. If 19% failed in both the subjects, then the percentage of passed in both the subjects is:

A. 46% B. 54%
C. 62% D. 81%

69. Next terms of the following number series are:
20, 20, 19, 16, 17, 13, 14, 11, ?, ?

A. 10, 10 B. 10, 11
C. 13, 14 D. 10, 9

70. A man rows upstream 13 km and downstream 28 km taking 5 hours each time. What is the speed of water?

A. 1½ km/hr B. 2 km/hr
C. 2½ km/hr D. 3 km/hr

71. If Shyam writes down all the integers from 1 to 100, then how many times does he write 3 ?

A. 19 B. 11
C. 20 D. 21

72. A is elder to B while C and D are elder to E. E lies between A and C and C is elder to B, then which of the following statements is necessarily ***true***?

A. A is elder to C. B. C is elder to D.
C. D is elder to C. D. E is elder to B.

73. Among M, T, R, K and D, each having a different height, M is shorter only from T and D is taller only from K. Who will be the third tallest person among them?

A. T B. D
C. M D. R

74. The square root of $\dfrac{\left(1\frac{3}{4}\right)^4-\left(2\frac{1}{3}\right)^4}{\left(1\frac{3}{4}\right)^2-\left(2\frac{1}{3}\right)^2}$ is equal to :

A. $2\frac{11}{12}$ B. $2\frac{1}{12}$
C. $3\frac{11}{12}$ D. $3\frac{1}{12}$

75. After 5 years, father's age will be three times of his son's age. 5 years ago, father's age was 7 times of his son's age. The present age of the father is:

A. 40 years B. 30 years
C. 50 years D. 45 years

76. A man is performing yoga with his head down and legs up. His face is towards the West. In which direction will his left hand be?

A. North B. South
C. West D. East

77. Two taps A and B would fill a tank completely in 30 and 36 minutes respectively. Both taps being opened, find when the tap A must be turned off so that the tank must be just filled in 18 minutes?

A. After 15 minutes B. After 12 minutes
C. After 14 minutes D. After 16 minutes

78. In how many years will a sum of ₹ 800 become ₹ 926.10 at 10% per annum interest compound half yearly?
A. 3 years B. 1½ years
C. 4½ years D. 2 years

79. The least square number, which is divisible by 8, 15 and 24 is equal to:
A. 120 B. 1800
C. 3600 D. 6400

80. If the selling price of 6 pens is equal to the cost price of 8 pens, then profit/loss in percentage is:
A. 25% profit B. 25% loss
C. $33\frac{1}{3}$% loss D. $33\frac{1}{3}$% profit

81. Who is the Chairman of the newly constituted 6th State Finance Commission of Haryana?
A. Vikas Gupta
B. Rajesh Khullar
C. P. Raghvendra Rao
D. T.V.S.N. Prasad

82. Who is the vice-chairman of Haryana Urdu Academy?
A. Gopichand Narang B. Kumud Bansal
C. Chander Trikha D. Suraj Bhan

83. Where is the palace of Begum Samru located in Haryana?
A. Faridabad B. Sonipat
C. Gurugram D. Rohtak

84. The award is given by the Haryana Government to the gold medal winner in the Commonwealth games:
A. Three crore B. Two crore
C. Seventy Five lakh D. One & half crore

85. Who was the Collector of Rohtak during the uprising of 1857?
A. Thomas Semton B. W. Eden
C. Adam Loch D. Hudson

86. Rivulet, which is one of the tributary of Ghaggar:
A. Chautang B. Sahibi
C. Dohan D. Indori

87. In which district of Haryana 'Tikkar lake' is located?
A. Rohtak B. Panchkula
C. Karnal D. Kaithal

88. The assembly of Haryana, which has been constituted after the election of October, 2019:
A. 12th B. 13th
C. 14th D. 15th

89. Vinesh Phogat is recently honoured with which National Award?
A. Dronacharya Award
B. Arjuna Award
C. Rajiv Gandhi Khel Ratna Award
D. Dhyanchand Award

90. Which city has its ancient name as Kanaud?
A. Mahendragarh B. Ambala
C. Kaithal D. Sonipat

PART-IV

Commerce

91. The Central Consumer Protection Council is headed by:
A. A former judge of the Supreme Court
B. The Minister Incharge of the Consumer Affairs in the Central Government
C. Secretary, Ministry of Consumer Affairs
D. Prime Minister

92. The step in the selling process in which the sales person identifies qualified potential customers:
A. Proposal Solicitation
B. Promotion
C. Prospecting
D. Specification

93. Which among the following is ***not*** included in uses of funds?
A. Operating Losses
B. Payment of dividend and taxes
C. Non-trade Payments
D. Purchase of fixed asset against shares

94. The combination of inflation and recession is:
A. Stagflation B. Hyper inflation
C. Low inflation D. Stagnation

95. It is estimated that for producing one unit of product 'Y' 5 kgs of material are consumed. The standard price per kg of material is ₹ 1.50. During the month of October 7000 kgs of material @ ₹ 1.60 per kg were used for producing 1500 units of 'Y'. Calculate material cost variance, material price variance and material usage variance:
A. ₹ 70 (F), ₹ 500 (A), ₹ 550 (F)
B. ₹ 70 (A), ₹ 500 (F), ₹ 550 (A)
C. ₹ 50 (F), ₹ 700 (A), ₹ 750 (F)
D. ₹ 50 (A), ₹ 700 (F), ₹ 750 (A)

96. Adjusting prices continually to meet the characteristics and needs of individual customers and situations is:
A. Primary Pricing B. Price Elasticity
C. Dynamic Pricing D. Secondary Pricing

97. Wage rate ₹ 30 per hour; standard time 6 hours, and actual time taken 4 hours. Ascertain total amount of wages earned under Rowan Plan :

A. ₹ 180 B. ₹ 160
C. ₹ 120 D. ₹ 40

98. Which among the following is a long-term solvency ratio?

A. Earnings per share ratio
B. Proprietory ratio
C. Gross profit ratio
D. Capital turnover ratio

99. People shift their spending across food, housing, transportation, health care, and other goods and services categories as family income rises. The law known as:

A. Engel's Law B. Peter's Law
C. John's Law D. Right's Law

100. The relationship between the tax rate and the amount of tax revenue collected is:

A. Law of diminishing returns
B. Laffer curve
C. Indifference curve
D. Keynesian curve

101. A situation in which an economic gain by one country results in an economic loss by another is:

A. Zero-sum game B. Balance of payment
C. Balance of trade D. Economic balance

102. In 'FSND' classification of material 'F' stands for:

A. First B. Fast
C. Future D. Frequency

103. In a multiple choice quiz each question has 5 alternatives out of them only one answer is correct. What is the probability of 6 correct answers out of 10 questions?

A. 0.55 B. 0.055
C. 0.0055 D. 5.50

104. In how many ways can 12 cups be put in three trays in equal number?

A. 36 ways B. 5775 ways
C. 5557 ways D. 4776 ways

105. The maximum share application money can be:

A. 5% of the nominal value of shares
B. 20% of the nominal value of shares
C. 50% of the nominal value of shares
D. Full issue price of the shares

106. 'X', a minor misrepresenting that he is a major induces 'Y' to enter into a contract. 'X' is:

A. Liable on the contract.
B. Not liable on the contract.
C. Liable to pay compensation.
D. Liable on the contract on attaining majority.

107. The P/V Ratio of a firm is 50% and margin of safety is 40%. You are required to work out BEP and net profit if the sales volume is ₹ 5,00,000:

A. ₹ 2,50,000 and ₹ 1,50,000
B. ₹ 5,00,000 and ₹ 3,00,000
C. ₹ 1,50,000 and ₹ 50,000
D. ₹ 3,00,000 and ₹ 1,00,000

108. The association clause of a public company has to be signed by:

A. 10 persons B. 12 persons
C. 7 persons D. 5 persons

109. "A budget is an estimate of future needs arranged according to an orderly basis covering some or all of the activities of an enterprise for a definite period of time". Who has given this definition?

A. George R. Terry B. Brown and Howard
C. H. J. Wheldon D. Harry L. Wylie

110. A performance assessment in which co-workers provide input into employee's performance:

A. Performance-based system
B. Peer Evaluation
C. Perquisities
D. Performance program

111. The third stage of group development, characterized by close relationships and cohesiveness is known as:

A. Performing Stage B. Adjourning Stage
C. Forming Stage D. Norming Stage

112. The firm that serves small segments that the other firms in an industry overlook or ignore:

A. Market Nicher B. Market Leader
C. Market Segment D. Market Challenger

113. 'A' Limited has issued 2,000 equity shares of ₹ 100 each as fully paid. The company has earned a profit of ₹ 20,000 after tax. The market price of these shares is ₹ 160 per share. On these share dividend has been paid @ ₹ 8 per share. Find out the cost of equity capital using Earning Yield method:

A. 6.25% B. 5.25%
C. 5% D. 7%

114. Which one of the following is a quantitative technique of decision making?

A. Brain Storming B. Decision Tree
C. Delphi Technique D. Concensus Mapping

115. Firms whose future earnings are likely to withstand on economic downturn:

A. Defensive Company
B. Deferred Company
C. Independent Company
D. Diffused Company

116. A citizen of one country working in another country:

A. Folkways B. Expatriate
C. COMECON D. Communist

117. The number of units produced and sold at which the company's net income is zero, is:
A. Break-up value B. Break even point
C. Cost analysis D. Production concept

118. The error of rejecting a true null hypothesis is:
A. Type I error B. Type II error
C. Type III error D. Type IV error

119. The study of societies to learn about human beings and their activities is:
A. Anthropology B. Psychology
C. Social Psychology D. Sociology

120. Those needs that are satisfied externally, such as physiological and safety needs are:
A. Lower-order needs
B. Self-actualization needs
C. Higher-order needs
D. Middle-order needs

121. The mistake of paying more attention to the specific products a company offers than to the benefits and experiences produced by these products:
A. Marketing Myopia B. Marketing Research
C. Marketing Guide D. Marketing Audit

122. The product life cycle stage in which a product's sales start climbing quickly is:
A. Introduction Stage B. Maturity Stage
C. Decline Stage D. Growth Stage

123. Stocking the product in as many outlets as possible is:
A. Interactive distribution
B. Intensive distribution
C. Intermodal distribution
D. Internal marketing

124. Which of the following errors will cause the trial balance to be out of order?
A. ₹ 550 the total of Sales Return Book has been posted to the credit of the Purchase Returns Accounts.
B. The credit side total of Santosh's Account overcast by ₹ 100.
C. Sales Book is undercost by ₹ 50.
D. All of the three

125. Which one of the following is ***not*** a principle of Henri Fayol?
A. Division of Work B. Discipline
C. Unity of Control D. Unity of Direction

126. A and B are sharing profits in the ratio of 3 : 2. They admit C as a new partner with 1/5th share in the profits which he gets equally from A and B. Calculate the new profit sharing ratio:
A. 3 : 1 : 5 B. 5 : 3 : 2
C. 2 : 1 : 5 D. 5 : 3 : 1

127. How many arrangements can be formed with letters of word GANGAPUR?
A. 10080 B. 10800
C. 50400 D. 5400

128. At the time of retirement of a bill, the acceptor debits:
A. Bills payable account
B. Discount account
C. Bills payable account and Discount account
D. Neither of Bills payable account and nor Discount account

129. A promise to pay by the accepting party at some future date:
A. Time Draft B. Time Management
C. Promise Note D. Date Management

130. Calculate Harmonic Mean from the following data:
10, 15, 20 and 25
A. 17.5 B. 15.58
C. 1.75 D. 1.55

131. An unauthorized and illegal strike that occurs during the terms of an existing contract is:
A. Whistle Blowing B. Wildcat Strike
C. Vesting Rights D. Pen-down Strike

132. Enhancing jobs by giving employees more opportunity to plan and control their work:
A. Job enrichment B. Job evaluation
C. Job specification D. Job fairs

133. A financial protection plan for executives in case they are severed from the organization is:
A. Downsizing B. Halo error
C. Halo effect D. Golden parachute

134. A contingency theory that focuses on followers' readiness:
A. Situational Leadership Theory
B. Leader Member Exchange Theory
C. Path Goal Theory
D. Leader Participation Model

135. Which one of the following is ***not*** an assumption of monopoly market?
A. There is one seller or producer of a homogeneous product.
B. There are no close substitutes for the product.
C. There is pure competition in the factors market so that the price of each input he buys is given to him.
D. The product produced by one firm is a close substitute for the other firms.

136. A process of correcting errors using past routines and present policies is:
A. Double-loop learning
B. Single-loop learning
C. Organizational learning
D. Trial and error learning

137. The difference between gross national product and net national product equals to:
A. Indirect taxes
B. Depreciation
C. Consumer expenditure
D. Net exports

138. Which is the Central Bank of India?
A. P. N. B.
B. Central Co-operative Bank
C. S. B. I.
D. R. B. I.

139. Unsecured short-term corporate debt that is characterized by a single payment at maturity is called:
A. Commercial paper B. Corporate accounts
C. Corporate paper D. Commercial accounts

140. Which of the following is ***not*** a Big Five Factor?
A. Extraversion B. Agreeableness
C. Emotional stability D. Self-monitoring

141. Retailer that buys at less than regular wholesale prices and sells at less than retail is:
A. On-price retailer B. Off-price retailer
C. Wholeseller D. Distributors

142. The systematic search for new product ideas is:
A. Idea screening B. Idea generation
C. Product screening D. Product generation

143. The ability to apply specialized knowledge or expertise is:
A. Human Skills B. Conceptual Skills
C. Technical Skills D. Communication Skills

144. The tendency of people to associate two events when in reality there is no connection between them is known as:
A. Social Activities
B. Dual Intensity
C. Social Correlation
D. Illusory Correlation

145. A business buying situation in which the buyer wants to modify product specifications, prices, terms or suppliers:
A. Online buying B. Modified rebuy
C. Personal buying D. Personal selling

146. Perceived fairness of the amount and allocation of rewards among individuals is known as:
A. Organizational Justice
B. Distributive Justice
C. Procedural Justice
D. Interactional Justice

147. The Japanese term for an organization's commitment to continuous improvement:
A. Kirkpatrick B. Koroshi
C. Kaizen D. Offshoring

148. A currency that plays central role in the foreign exchange market:
A. Black Currency B. Vehicle Currency
C. Foreign Currency D. Domestic Currency

149. Employees are free to join the Union or not, and those who decline need not pay Union dues is:
A. Open method
B. Open shop
C. Non-exempt employees
D. Lockout

150. A trend in which the dependent variable changes at a constant rate with time:
A. Constant trend B. Linear trend
C. Log linear D. Margin trend

Answers

1	2	3	4	5	6	7	8	9	10
C	A	C	B	B	D	C	B	A	C
11	**12**	**13**	**14**	**15**	**16**	**17**	**18**	**19**	**20**
B	B	A	B	B	D	B	A	D	A
21	**22**	**23**	**24**	**25**	**26**	**27**	**28**	**29**	**30**
A	B	D	D	B	A	A	D	C	D
31	**32**	**33**	**34**	**35**	**36**	**37**	**38**	**39**	**40**
B	A	C	B	A	D	D	D	A	C
41	**42**	**43**	**44**	**45**	**46**	**47**	**48**	**49**	**50**
D	D	B	C	C	B	B	A	*	D
51	**52**	**53**	**54**	**55**	**56**	**57**	**58**	**59**	**60**
B	*	D	D	B	B	*	B	C	D
61	**62**	**63**	**64**	**65**	**66**	**67**	**68**	**69**	**70**
B	C	C	C	B	D	*	B	A	A
71	**72**	**73**	**74**	**75**	**76**	**77**	**78**	**79**	**80**
C	D	D	A	A	A	A	B	C	D

81	82	83	84	85	86	87	88	89	90
C	C	C	D	C	A	B	C	C	A
91	**92**	**93**	**94**	**95**	**96**	**97**	**98**	**99**	**100**
B	C	D	A	C	C	B	B	A	B
101	**102**	**103**	**104**	**105**	**106**	**107**	**108**	**109**	**110**
A	B	C	B	D	B	D	C	A	B
111	**112**	**113**	**114**	**115**	**116**	**117**	**118**	**119**	**120**
D	A	A	B	A	B	B	A	A	A
121	**122**	**123**	**124**	**125**	**126**	**127**	**128**	**129**	**130**
A	D	B	D	C	B	A	A	A	B
131	**132**	**133**	**134**	**135**	**136**	**137**	**138**	**139**	**140**
B	A	D	A	D	B	B	D	A	D
141	**142**	**143**	**144**	**145**	**146**	**147**	**148**	**149**	**150**
B	B	C	D	B	B	C	B	B	B

Explanatory Answers

61. Given,

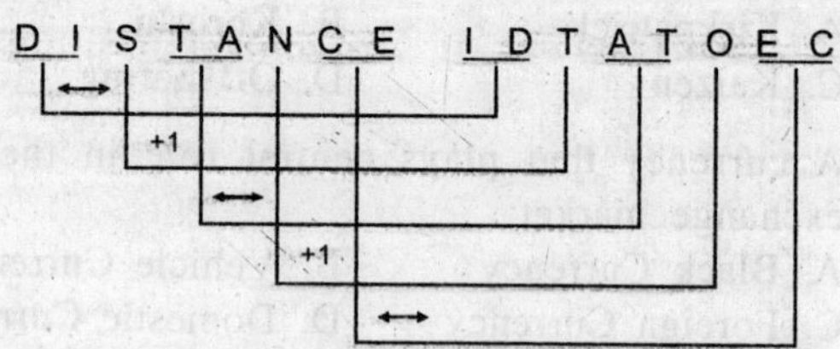

and

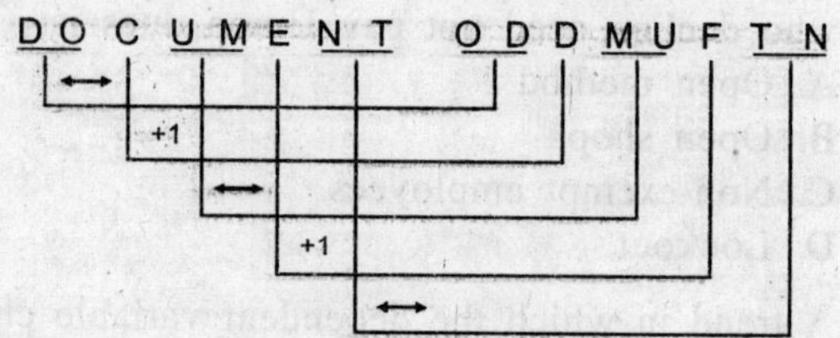

The coded pattern is as follows:

The first two and IV, V and VII, VIII letters of the word are written in the reverse order and each of the remaining letters is moved one step forward to get the code.

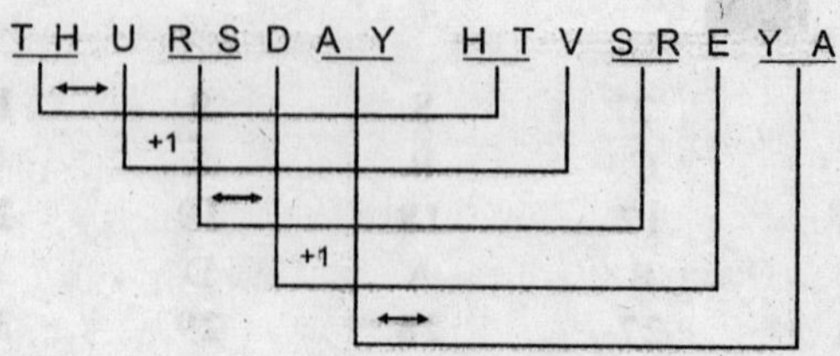

Hence, 'THURSDAY' will be written as 'HTVSREYA'.

62.

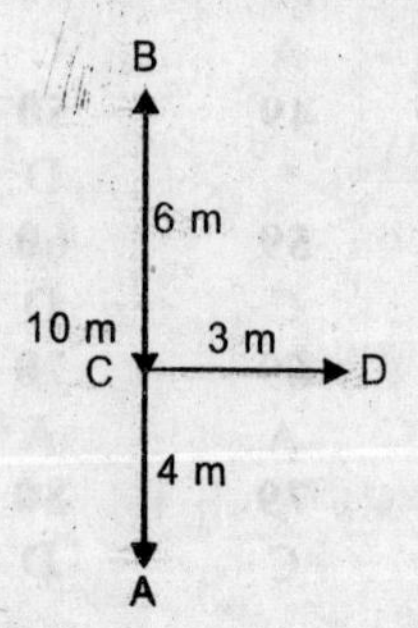

Here, starting point = A

AB = 10 m

BC = 6 m

CD = 3 m

He is in North-East direction from starting point (A).

63. Let x was the population in the beginning of the first year.

Then,

$$x\left(1+\frac{5}{100}\right)\left(1-\frac{5}{100}\right) = 79{,}800$$

$$\Rightarrow x\left(1+\frac{1}{20}\right)\left(1-\frac{1}{20}\right) = 79{,}800$$

$$\Rightarrow x\left(\frac{21}{20}\right)\left(\frac{19}{20}\right) = 79{,}800$$

$$\Rightarrow x = 79800 \times \frac{20 \times 20}{21 \times 19}$$

$$= 79800 \times \frac{400}{399}$$

$$= 200 \times 400$$

$$= 80000$$

Hence, x = 80000.

64. ICV 5FU 9IT 15LS 17OR (+3, +4, −1; 13 in place of 15)

In given series,

Place of 15LS should be 13LS

∴ Wrong term = 15LS.

65. Let the radius of two cylinders are $2r$, $3r$ and their heights are $5h$, $3h$

Then, volume = $\pi r^2 h$

$\therefore$ $V_1 = \pi(2r)^2 \times 5h$

$= \pi \times 4r^2 \times 5h$

$= 20\pi r^2 h$

and $V_2 = \pi(3r)^2 \times 3h$

$= \pi \times 9r^2 \times 3h$

$= 27\pi r^2 h$

Hence, the ratio of their volumes = $\frac{V_1}{V_2}$

$= \frac{20\pi r^2 h}{27\pi r^2 h} = \frac{20}{27} = 20 : 27.$

66. According to question,

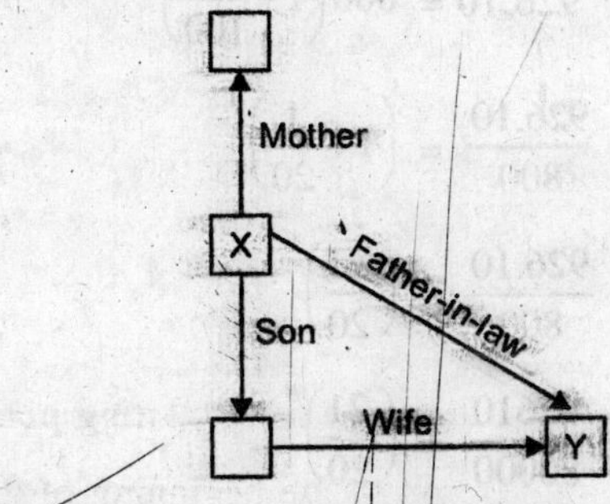

Hence, X is Father-in-law of Y.

68. $\because n(E \cup S) = n(E) + n(S) - n(E \cap S)$

$\therefore$ $n(E \cup S) = 27 + 38 - 19$

$= 65 - 19 = 46\%$

$\because$ The percentage of failed in English and Science is 46%

$\therefore$ The percentage of passed in both the subject

$= 100 - 46 = 54\%.$

69. Given, series,

20, 20, 19, 16, 17, 13, 14, 11, ?, ?

−4, −3, −2, −1

20 20 19 16 17 13 14 11 10 10

−1, −2, −3, −4

Here, the next term in the series are 10, 10.

70. Let the speed of a boat in still water is u km/hr and the speed of water is v km/hr

Then, upstream,

$u - v = \frac{13}{5}$ km/hr ...(i)

downstream, $u + v = \frac{28}{5}$ km/hr ...(ii)

From (i) + (ii), we get

$2u = \frac{13}{5} + \frac{28}{5} = \frac{41}{5}$

$\Rightarrow$ $u = \frac{41}{10} = 4.1$ km/hr

From (i),

$v = u - \frac{13}{5}$

$= \frac{41}{10} - \frac{13}{5}$

$= \frac{41 - 26}{10}$

$= \frac{15}{10}$

$= \frac{3}{2}$

$= 1\frac{1}{2}$ km/hr

Hence, the speed of water is $1\frac{1}{2}$ km/hr.

71. Clearly, from 1 to 100, there are ten numbers with 3 as the unit's digit:

3, 13, 23, 33, 43, 53, 63, 73, 83, 93

and ten numbers with 3 as the ten's digit:

30, 31, 32, 33, 34, 35, 36, 37, 38, 39.

So, required number = 10 + 10 = 20.

72. Here,

A > B, C & D > E

E is between A & C

C > B

D & C > E > A > B

Hence, it is clear that E is elder to B.

73. Given, M is shorter only from T *i.e.*, T > M

and D is taller only from K *i.e.*, D > K

Hence, T > M > R > D > K

Hence, R be the third tallest person among them.

74. Given, $\frac{\left(1\frac{3}{4}\right)^4 - \left(2\frac{1}{3}\right)^4}{\left(1\frac{3}{4}\right)^2 - \left(2\frac{1}{3}\right)^2} = \frac{\left(\frac{7}{4}\right)^4 - \left(\frac{7}{3}\right)^4}{\left(\frac{7}{4}\right)^2 - \left(\frac{7}{3}\right)^2}$

$[a^2 - b^2 = (a - b)(a + b)]$

$= \frac{\left[\left(\frac{7}{4}\right)^2 - \left(\frac{7}{3}\right)^2\right]\left[\left(\frac{7}{4}\right)^2 + \left(\frac{7}{3}\right)^2\right]}{\left(\frac{7}{4}\right)^2 - \left(\frac{7}{3}\right)^2}$

$= \left(\frac{7}{4}\right)^2 + \left(\frac{7}{3}\right)^2$ $[a^2 + b^2 = (a + b)^2 - 2ab]$

$$= \left(\frac{7}{4}+\frac{7}{3}\right)^2 - 2\times\frac{7}{4}\times\frac{7}{3} = \left(\frac{21+28}{12}\right)^2 - \frac{49}{6}$$

$$= \left(\frac{49}{12}\right)^2 - \frac{49}{6} = \frac{49}{6}\left[\frac{49}{12\times 2}-1\right]$$

$$= \frac{49}{6}\left[\frac{49-24}{24}\right] = \frac{49}{6}\times\frac{25}{24} = \frac{49\times 25}{144}$$

Hence, the required square root

$$= \sqrt{\frac{49\times 25}{144}} = \frac{7\times 5}{12} = \frac{35}{12} = 2\frac{11}{12}.$$

75. Let after 5 years, son's age = x years

then, father's age = $3x$ years

$\therefore$ son's present age = $(x - 5)$ years

and father's present age = $(3x - 5)$ years

5 years ago, son's age = $(x - 10)$ years

and father's age = $(3x - 10)$ years

According to question,

$$7(x - 10) = (3x - 10)$$

$$\Rightarrow \quad 7x - 70 = 3x - 10$$

$$\Rightarrow \quad 7x - 3x = 70 - 10 = 60$$

$$\Rightarrow \quad 4x = 60 \Rightarrow x = 15 \text{ years}$$

Hence, the present age of father

$= (3x - 5)$ years

$= (3 \times 15 - 5)$ years

$= (45 - 5)$ years = 40 years.

76.

N

Left hand

W ← → E

Right hand

S

Here, his left hand is in North direction.

77. Part filled by tap A in 1 minute = $\frac{1}{30}$

and part filled by tap B in 1 minute = $\frac{1}{36}$

Let the tap A must be turned off after x minutes

Then, $\frac{x}{30}+\frac{18}{36}=1$

$$\Rightarrow \quad \frac{x}{30}+\frac{1}{2} = 1$$

$$\Rightarrow \quad \frac{x}{30} = 1-\frac{1}{2}$$

$$\Rightarrow \quad \frac{x}{30} = \frac{1}{2}$$

$$\Rightarrow \quad x = 15 \text{ minutes}$$

Hence, the tap A must be turned off after 15 minues.

78. Given, P = ₹ 800, A = ₹ 926.10

$r = 10\%$ per annum

$\because$ Interest compounded half yearly

$\therefore \; r = \frac{10}{2} = 5\%$

$$\because \quad A = P\left(1+\frac{r}{100}\right)^n$$

$$\therefore \quad 926.10 = 800\left(1+\frac{5}{100}\right)^n$$

$$\frac{926.10}{800} = \left(1+\frac{1}{20}\right)^n$$

$$\frac{926.10}{800} = \left(\frac{21}{20}\right)^n$$

$$\frac{92610}{80000} = \left(\frac{21}{20}\right)^n$$

$$\frac{9261}{8000} = \left(\frac{21}{20}\right)^n$$

$$\left(\frac{21}{20}\right)^3 = \left(\frac{21}{20}\right)^n$$

$$n = 3$$

$\because$ Interest compounded half yearly

$\therefore$ Time = $\frac{3}{2}$ years = $1\frac{1}{2}$ years.

79. LCM of 8, 15 and 24 = 120

$\because 120 = 2^2 \times 30$

$\therefore$ The least square number $= 2^2 \times 30 \times 30$

$= 2^2 \times 30^2$

$= 4 \times 900$

$= 3600.$

80. Let the cost price of 1 pen = ₹ 1

Then, the cost price of 8 pens = ₹ 8

Given, The S.P. of 6 pens = the C.P. of 8 pens = ₹ 8

$\because$ The S.P. of 6 pens = ₹ 8

and the C.P. of 6 pens = ₹ 6

$\therefore$ Profit = S.P. – C.P.

= 8 – 6 = ₹ 2

$$\therefore \quad \text{Profit } \% = \frac{\text{Profit}\times 100}{\text{C.P.}}$$

$$= \frac{2\times 100}{6}\% = \frac{100}{3}\% = 33\frac{1}{3}\%.$$

Child Development & Pedagogy

CHILD DEVELOPMENT

CONCEPT OF DEVELOPMENT AND ITS RELATIONSHIP WITH LEARNING

The discipline of Child Development is concerned with the changes in the behaviour of children over time and explains why and how they occur. It aims to describe and explain development in the areas of physical, social, emotional, language and cognitive functioning.

Development and Growth

The term 'development' is used for changes in a person's physical and behavioural traits that emerge in orderly ways and last for a reasonable period of time. The three main characteristics of these changes are progressive, orderly and long lasting. Development refers to both quantitative as well as qualitative changes. It includes changes not only in structure but also in function.

'Growth' refers to physical increase in the size of the body. Increase in weight, height and internal organs is growth. Growth refers to a quantitative change, that is, a change that can be measured.

Growth is only one aspect of the larger process of development. Development continues even when physical changes are not visible. Physical growth slows down considerably after adolescence but development does not.

Stages of Development

The human life span has been divided into the stages of infancy, childhood, adolescence and adulthood.

The period from birth to two years of age is referred to as the period of infancy. In this period the child is totally dependent on the caregiver for the fulfilment of his needs. After birth, this is the period of most rapid growth and development. The child's skills and abilities increase. By the end of infancy he is able to walk, run, communicate his needs verbally, feed himself, identify family members, recognise himself and venture confidently in familiar surroundings.

The period of childhood is from two to twelve years of age. Development at this stage is not as rapid as during infancy. During this period the child refines the skills he has acquired during infancy and learns new skill as well. During childhood he also learns the ways of behaviour that are considered appropriate by the society. The child meets many people outside the family and forms attachments with more people. As the child grows and his thinking capacities mature, he realises that he can do many things. This gives him a feeling of confidence. During this period he becomes more independent though adult guidance is constantly needed. The period of childhood is divided into two stages : the period of early childhood (2–6 years) and middle childhood (6–12 years). The period of early childhood is also referred to as the preschool age because at this age the child is learning skills that will help him to do tasks associated with schooling. The preschooler has mastered the words to ask questions about things and people. He learns about numbers, colours, shapes and the reasons for everyday events. All these concepts develop from actually seeing things and doing various activities. The child in the age group 6–12 years has matured a great deal and is expected to behave more responsibly than the preschooler.

The next stage is referred to as the period of adolescence (12–18 years). The beginning of this period is marked by puberty. Puberty refers to the stage around 11–14 years of the age, when there is a spurt in physical growth. This results in a rapid increase in height and weight and the emergence of secondary sexual characteristics. These rapid physical changes lead to a need for emotional readjustment.

At this age the peer group becomes very important and the adolescent follows the rules and the codes of her group. Feelings of loyalty and pride for the group are very strong. At times the values of the peer group may become more important than those of the family. During adolescence thinking develops further and becomes more complex. The individual can understand and deal with varied situations. He can think of abstract problems and work out their solutions. All this helps him to prepare for the roles and responsibilities, which he will be expected to carry out as an adult.

After the age of 18 years the person is referred to as an adult. Physical changes are completed in this stage and person becomes mature.

Areas of Development

The various developments that take place during the life span of an individual can be classified thus: physical and motor development, social development, emotional development, cognitive and language development.

Physical development refers to the physical changes in the size, structure and proportion of the parts of the body that take place from the moment of conception.

Motor development means the development of control over body movements. This results in increasing coordination between various parts of the body. As a result of physical and motor development the child acquires many abilities. These developments will bring about the change from an infant who at the time of birth is capable of only lying on his back to one who learns to roll over, hold his head, sit, walk, run and climb stairs. The improving coordination between the eye and the hand movements will help him to eat food without smearing it on his face. Gradually he will learn to clothe himself, draw, skip, paint, ride a bicycle and type. As he grows he will refine the skills already acquired as well as develop new ones.

Language development refers to those changes that make it possible for an infant, who in the early months uses crying for communication, to learn words and then sentences to converse fluently. How the child learns to speak grammatically correct sentences is amazing! At first the child indicates his need for water through crying. Then he learns to say ''water''. A little later he says, ''Mummy water'' and finally he speaks a complete sentence, ''Mummy, I want to drink water''. He will be about three years by this time.

Cognitive development concerns the emergence of thinking capabilities in the individual. We can see how the child's thinking develops and changes from one age to the next. The infant is not born with the reasoning and thinking, abilities of adults. In fact, the infant acts as if an object that is removed from his sight has ceased to exist. Gradually he learns that objects and people are permanent and they exist even if he cannot see them. Around five years of age he can understand concepts such as heavy and light, fast and slow, colours and sizes which he did not comprehend earlier. Exploration of the surroundings and the questions regarding the 'why' and 'how' of things result in an increasing store of information. His thought develops but he is still unable to see a situation from another person's point of view. For example, he is unable to understand why another child cannot climb the tree when he can do so. He thinks that everybody else should be able to do what he can and feel the way he does. He believes that all things have life and feelings like him including the sun, stone, pencil and table. A ten year old has learnt to reason and analyze but this ability is limited to real life concrete situations. He cannot usually think in abstract terms or predict future event. The capacity for abstruct thinking develops fully during the period of adolescence. He can now handle complex situations. Thus at each stage of a person's life, the ability to think is qualitatively different and more developed compared to the earlier stage.

Cognitive development is the process of mental development from infancy to adulthood. Cognition refers to the process of 'coming to know', which is accomplished through the gathering and processing of information. It includes perceiving, learning, remembering, problem solving, and thinking about the world. Intelligence is a term difficult to define. Nevertheless, according to a well known definition, it refers to the individual's ability to ''act purposefully, think rationally and deal effectively with the environment''.

Social development refers to the development of those abilities that enable the individual to behave in accordance with the expectations of the society. It is concerned with the child's relationships with people and his ways of interaction with them. The infant instinctively reaches out to the person who approaches him with love and affection. Gradually he learns to recognize his mother and other caregivers and forms attachment to them.

Emotional development refers to the emergence of emotions like anger, joy, delight, happiness, fear, anxiety and sorrow and the socially acceptable ways of expressing them. As the child grows up and becomes aware of acceptable ways of behaviour, a variety of emotions also emerge. As an infant he expresses only discomfort and delight. As he grows older, expressions of joy, happiness, fear, anger and disappointment appear. He learns to express these emotions in a healthy manner. For example, initially the child hits out when angry. Gradually he learns to control this and expresses anger in other ways.

Theories of Child Development and Learning

Maturationist Theory

The maturationist theory was advanced by the work of Arnold Gessell. Maturationists believe that development is a biological process that occurs automatically in predictable, sequential stages over time. This perspective leads many educators and families to assume that young children will acquire knowledge naturally and automatically as they grow physically and become older, provided that they are healthy.

School readiness, according to maturationists, is a state at which all healthy young children arrive when they can perform tasks such as reciting the alphabet and counting; these tasks are required for learning more complex tasks such as reading and arithmetic. Because development and school readiness occur naturally and automatically, maturationists believe the best practices are for parents to teach young children to recite the alphabet and count while being patient and waiting for children to become ready for kindergarten. If a child is developmentally unready for school, maturationists might suggest referrals to transitional kindergartens, retention, or holding children out of school for an additional year. These practices are sometimes used by schools, educators, and parents when a young child developmentally lags behind his or her peers. The young child's underperformance is interpreted as the child needing more time to acquire the knowledge and skills needed to perform at the level of his or her peers.

Environmentalist Theory

Theorists such as John Watson, B.F. Skinner, and Albert Bandura contributed greatly to the environmentalist perspective of development. Environmentalists believe the child's environment shapes learning and behaviour in fact, human behaviour, development, and learning are thought of as reactions to the environment. This perspective leads many families, schools, and educators to assume that young children develop and acquire new knowledge by reacting to their surroundings.

Kindergarten readiness, according to the environmentalists, is the age or stage when young children can respond appropriately to the environment of the school and the classroom (*e.g.*, rules and regulations, curriculum activities, positive behaviour in group settings, and directions and instructions from teachers and other adults in the school). The ability to respond appropriately to this environment is necessary for young children to participate in teacher-initiated learning activities. Success is dependent on the child following instructions from the teacher or the adult in the classroom. Many environmentalist-influenced educators and parents believe that young children learn best by rote activities, such as reciting the alphabet over and over, copying letters, and tracing numbers. This viewpoint is evident in kindergarten classrooms where young children are expected to sit at desks arranged in rows and listen attentively to their teachers. At home, parents may provide their young children with workbooks containing such activities as colouring or tracing letters and numbers—activities that require little interaction between parent and child. When young children are unable to respond appropriately to the classroom and school environment, they often are labelled as having some form of learning disabilities and are tracked in classrooms with curriculum designed to control their behaviours and responses.

Constructivist Theory

The constructivist perspective of readiness and development was advanced by theorists such as Jean Piaget, Maria Montessori, and Lev Vygotsky. Although their work varies greatly, each articulates a similar context of learning and development. They are consistent in their belief that learning and development occur when young children interact with the environment and people around them. Constructivists view young children as active participants in the learning process. In addition, constructivists believe young children initiate most of the activities required for learning and development. Because active interaction with the environment and people are necessary for learning and development, constructivists believe that children are ready for school when they can initiate many of the interactions they have with the environment and people around them.

Constructivist-influenced schools and educators pay a lot of attention to the physical environment and the curriculum of the early childhood classroom. Kindergarten classrooms often are divided into different **learning centers** and are equipped with developmentally appropriate materials for young children to play with and manipulate. Teachers and adults have direct conversations with children, children move actively from one center to another, and daily activities are made meaningful through the incorporation of children's experiences into the curriculum. At home, parents engage their young children in reading and storytelling activities and encourage children's participation in daily household activities in a way that introduces such concepts as counting and language use. In addition, parents may provide young children with picture books containing very large print, and toys that stimulate interaction (such as building blocks and large puzzles). When a young child encounters difficulties in the learning process, the constructivist approach is neither to lable the child nor to retain him or her; instead, constructivists give the child some individualized attention and customize the classroom curriculum to help the child address his or her difficulties.

Today, most researchers have come to understand child development and the learning process as articulated by the constructivists. However, this view has not been widely translated into practice. Many kindergarten teachers and parents still believe that young children are not ready for school unless they can recite the alphabet, count, and have the ability to follow instructions from adults.

PRINCIPLES AND THEORIES OF CHILD DEVELOPMENT

Studying and understanding child growth and development are important parts of teaching young children. No two children are alike. Children differ in physical, cognitive, social and emotional growth patterns. Even identical twins, who have the same genetic makeup, are not exactly alike. They may differ in the way they respond to play, affection, objects and people in their environment.

Knowledge of the areas of child development is basic to guiding young children. Linked to this is the understanding of healthy brain development. These stimuli begin at birth. Therefore, it is vital for children to have loving caregivers. Young children need dependable, trusting relationships. They thrive in environments that are predictable and nurturing. Understanding theories about how people develop helps form your knowledge base in caring for young children.

Child Development

Development refers to change or growth that occurs in children. It starts with infancy and continues to adulthood. By studying child development, you will form a profile of what children can do at various ages.

Different names are used to describe young children at different ages. From birth through the first year, children are called **infants. Toddlers** are children from age one up to the third birthday (Because of an awkward style of walking, the name toddler describes this age group). The term **preschooler** is often used to describe children ages three to six years of age.

Areas of Development

The study of child development is often divided into three main areas. These include physical, cognitive and social-emotional development. Dividing development into these areas makes it easier to study.

Physical development refers to physical body changes. It occurs in a relatively stable, predictable sequence. It is orderly, not random. Changes in size and weight are also part of physical development.

Physical skills, such as crawling, walking and writing, are the result of physical development. These skills fall into two main categories:

1. **Grossmotor development :** It involves improvement of skills using the large muscles in the legs and arms. Such activities as running, skipping and bike riding fall into this category.
2. **Fine-motor development :** It involves the small muscles of the hands and fingers. Grasping, holding, cutting and drawing are some activities that require fine-motor development.

Environmental factors also affect what children can do physically. These factors include proper nutrition and appropriate toys and activities.

Cognitive development, sometimes called **intellectual development,** refers to processes people use to gain knowledge. Language, thought, reasoning and imagination are all included. Identifying colours and knowing the difference between one and many are examples of cognitive tasks.

Language and thought are a result of cognitive development. These two skills are closely related. Both are needed for planning, remembering and problem solving. As children mature and gain experience with their world, these skills develop.

The third area of development is called social-emotional development. These two areas are grouped together because they are so interrelated. Learning to relate to others is social development. Emotional development, on the other hand, involves feelings and expression of feelings. Trust, fear, confidence, pride, friendship and humor are all part of social-emotional development. Other emotional traits include timidity, interest and pleasure.

Learning to express emotions in appropriate ways begins early. Caregivers promote this learning when they positively model these skills. A person's self-concept and self-esteem are also part of this area. As children have success with all skills confidence flourishes. This leads to a healthy self-concept and sense of worth.

The physical, cognitive and social-emotional areas of development are linked to one another. Development in one area can strongly influence another area. For instance, writing words requires fine-motor skills. It also requires cognitive development. Language, a part of cognitive development, is needed to communicate with others. It is also necessary for growing socially and emotionally.

Principles of Development

Although each child is unique, the basic patterns or principles of growth and development are universal, predictable and orderly. Through careful observation and interaction with children, researchers and those who work with children understand the characteristics of the principles that follow:

1. Development tends to proceed from the head downward. This is called the **cephalocaudal principle.** According to this principle, the child first gains control of the head, then the arms, then the legs. Infants gain control of head and face movements within the first two months after birth. In the next few months, they are able to lift themselves up using their arms. By 6 to 12 months of age, infant start to gain leg control and may be able to crawl, stand or walk.
2. Development also proceeds from the center of the body outward according to the **proximodistal principle**. Accordingly, the spinal cord develops before other parts of the body. The child's arms develop before the hands and the hands and feet develop before the fingers and toes. Fingers and toes are the last to develop.
3. Development also depends on maturation. **Maturation** refers to the sequence of biological changes in children. These orderly changes give children new abilities. Much of the maturation depends on changes in the brain and the nervous system. These changes assist children to improve their thinking abilities and motor skills. A rich learning environment helps children develop to their potential.

Children must mature to a certain point before they can gain some skills. For instance, the brain of a four-month-old has not matured enough to allow the child to use words. A four-month-old will babble and coo. However, by two years of age, with the help of others, the child will be able to say and understand many words. This is an example of how cognitive development occurs from simple tasks to more complex tasks. Likewise, physical skills develop from general to specific movements. For example, think about the way an infant waves its arms and legs. In a young infant, these movements are random. In several months, the infant will likely be able to grab a block with his or her whole hand. In a little more time, the same infant will grasp a block with the thumb and fore finger.

INFLUENCE OF HEREDITY AND ENVIRONMENT

Heredity and environment greatly influence the growth, development and behaviour of a child. Each child inherits certain capacities for growth. The way in which these capacities develop is influenced by the opportunities afforded by the environment, for example, the height to which the individual is capable of growing is determined by heredity. The environment cannot change the limits imposed by heredity. Whereas a poor environment *i.e.*, lack of exposure will slow down a child who is genetically clever, a rich environment which provides and exposes a child to a lot of educational facilities will not change a child who is genetically born not clever to become clever. A good environment will enable the individual to reach these limits. The environment influences the speed with which the child develops. The environment shapes the individual's development in the sense that it promotes the growth of certain capacities and neglects the growth of others. For instance, if the child experiences more emphasis on academic and no attachment to physical education, the child's capacity to develop certain skills will be neglected.

Effects of Heredity and Environment on Development of Personality

Before discussing the contribution of hereditary factors let us see what is meant by heredity when we talk of heredity we usually have biological heredity in mind. The term 'heredity' may also be used in another sense, for example, if a child is brought up in a particular social environment say of a tribe, the value of that tribe and the norms of that tribe are inculcated in him through other members of that social group and we call it **social heredity.** In the same way, a student in a classroom situation brings with him a specific cultural heredity also. Here our discussion will be focused on the influence of only biological heredity on individual differences. Each individual has a specific set of potentials which are developed through the environment. These potentialities and characteristics possessed by the individual are the result of his biological heredity. The influence of heredity is so strong that twins brought up in drastically different environment show very much similarity in terms of their mental abilities and other traits. This shows that even drastically different environments are not capable of overcoming hereditary influences.

Hereditary, or the genetic transmission of characteristics from parents to offspring, determine personality to a certain extent. Hereditary characteristics manifest at birth such as hair and eye colour, skin colour and body type. Hereditary also includes aptitude or the capacity to learn a skill or inclination for a particular body of knowledge. It establishes the limits of one's personality traits that can be developed. This aptitude creates the desire for a person to learn something. For instance, the son of a sports hero like a boxer superstar is expected to inherit the genes of his father. His capacity for growth in the boxing arena is immense because he is born with the ability.

Behavioural geneticists, Dr. David Reiss and colleagues from George Washington University, conducted a thorough and long-term study on the effects of genetics to a person's personality. The result of their study revealed that 'it seems that genetic influences are largely responsible for how 'adjusted' kids are : how well they do in school, how they get along with their peers, whether they engage in dangerous or delinquent behaviour'.

Effect of Environment on Personality Development

Apart from heredity, environment also effects the child development. The concept of environment needs little clarification when we say the environment of the child is not good, sometimes we mean that he is living in a locality which does not have desirable people or we mean that he is living in the rural area where he does not have access to many things which an urban environment may provide. As has rightly been said, the psychological environment consists of the sum total of the stimulation the individual receives from conception till death. This is an active concept of environment *i.e.*, the physical presence of objects does not in itself constitute environment unless the objects serve as stimuli for the individual.

The role of the prenatal environment on the development of the child is well known and has been demonstrated through various experiments. The diet a mother takes at the time of pregnancy, her mental status, glandular secretions and even the thinking process influence the development of the child. Environmentalists firmly believe that, under favourable circumstances, every individual is almost infinitely improvable.

Newman, Freeman and Holzinger conducted thorough research on nineteen pairs of identical twins reared in different environments. Initially they found that the pairs reared apart show mere differences in I.Q. But Woodworth (1941) in his analysis of the results pointed out a factor called error of measurement that is always involved in intelligence testing. When this factor was taken into account and results interpreted, Woodworth concluded that environmental differences do operate to produce I.Q. differences in persons with exactly the same hereditary potentialities. But the magnitude of these differences is not as large as those found among children whose heredity is not alike.

Environment and its Interaction with Hereditary Factors

Nature refers to what a child has inherited genetically, from the parents (*e.g.* eye colour, appearance, etc). The influence of environment on the development of the child (*e.g.* liking for a type of music) is referred to as nurture. The earlier view of child development focused either entirely on nature or nurture. Many favoured heredity, and believed that we are born with certain talents and personalities. These determine who we are and what we become.

In the other view, the focus was on the role of environment. We learn to do things for which we get rewards (or praises) and do not do things for which we are punished (including disapproval from elders). Both views contained some truth but neither is complete. To understand the development of a person, we have to study the complex interaction between nature and nurture (or heredity and environment).

Let us consider an example. A child is born with a talent for music. In the child's family, this talent for music is expressed by the child at an early age, through his activities of singing and listening to music. The parents notice the child's interest in music and expose the child to more music and give him a toy musical instrument (*e.g.* ek tara or flute). The child's interest in music grows further and his talent develops and this make the parents offer even more musical experiences (*e.g.* playing music on stage, attending music concerts etc.). This has a further positive effect on the child's talent and his desire to play music.

It is thus clear that both the child's inherited talent and environment shaped his/her development. The child had the talent for music, but this led to a change in the environment by making her parents provide more musical experiences at home. Now these experiences in the environment further developed the child's talent and motivation and made the parents introduce more musical experiences to the child. The process goes on and on like this in a form of transaction. This approach to understanding development is called a transactional model (TA).

The TA model is able to explain why brothers and sisters, though physically in the same environment, always grow up in 'different' ways. This simply means that the environment of family life is always changing in the process of adjusting to the personalities of its members. A first born child grows up with very different experiences than a middle born or youngest child. A child who displays temper tantrums (getting angry easily, without sufficient cause) has a very different experience with her parents as compared to her easy going brother.

Let us take another example to make the point more clear. Suppose you as a parent (if not today, then in the future) are facing difficulty with your argumentative 12-year-old. The TA model reminds you that you must first think about the factor which has brought your child to this point. Is it a personality trait that is troubling you? Is she stubborn (does not listen to others) all the time and is thus part of her nature? Does she resist any change in her usual routine? Does she lack the ability to talk to you about what's troubling her, and could that be upsetting her? The child represents one part of the puzzle or problem which has to be solved.

The next questions you have to ask are : What is my role in all this? Am I somehow rewarding the very behaviours? Am I trying to stop by paying too much attention to them? Am I having too much expectation from a 12-year old? Am I reminded of my younger sister with whom I had faced a similar problem, and could be causing irritation in me now? The environment which includes you forms the other-part of the picture.

Finally, you need to put the two together to obtain a full picture of what is going on and how to bring about a positive change. In which way my behaviour is affecting my child? And most importantly, what do I need to change to break this pattern of behaviour (argumentation in the child) located in its transactions with nurture? How can I better understand the forces behind my child's behaviour so as to improve my response to it?

This may sound very theoretical to some of you but it's exactly the questions which many parents are always asking themselves, even if they are not aware of it. By understanding the TA-model you will be in a better position to understand the interaction between nature and nurture which is responsible for your child's behaviour and development. This will help you in deciding which role you can play for effective development and improve the child's behaviour.

In summary according to the transactional model of development, the child changes the environment which in turn changes the child. The child's development is like a complex dance in which nature and nurture both lead, and are led.

SOCIALISATION PROCESS

As a child grows up, there is a deliberate and conscious effort made through active training to make the child learn the values and expectations of the society he or she lives in. The child has to learn to adjust and accommodate her behaviour according to the rules for appropriate behaviour in the society. Parents, teachers, elders as well as the peers (same age group children) all influence and control the behaviour of a child.

According to the Indian view, a child comes to this world with certain behavioural tendencies which carry over from previous birth. The role of the family is to bring up the child in such a way that her positive capacities are developed fully and negative tendencies are controlled. Apart from the family, there are also other influences on the child from the outside environment. The important agents of socialisation include media, day-care centers, peer group, school and religion.

Parents have the most direct effect on the socialisation of the child. They are role models for children. Their responses to child behaviour, giving approval or disapproval etc. mould the personality of child and plays a very important role in acquiring rules. In addition, parents arrange the environment of a children in different ways. They take the child outside in specific settings like museum, church, temple, mosque, hill station, sea beach. The grand parents and aunts and uncles of the child also contribute in the socialisation process. Children learn manners and skills by observing parents. During the life span of a person, at different ages, specific rituals are performed. These rituals represent the changes in the child from one stage to another. They contribute in forming the identity of the child.

The influence of the **peer group** of the child, particularly during middle childhood is very important. In the interactions with the children of the same age group, a child learns the importance of team work, sharing and trust. One of the significant effects of this is that the child learns to adjust and accommodate to the view point of the others.

The school which the child attends is another very important socializing agent. The child learns different types of social, intellectual and physical skills in school. The school provides the child with a miniature society where he or she has to learnt the right values and rules and follow them. Values such as honesty, democracy and fairness etc. are learnt in the school setting.

Now-a-days, children search and know the world through TV, magazines, books, comics, radio and films. This media influences the socialisation of the child in significant ways. A positive influence can be learning the importance of family values by watching good and informative programmes. Watching aggressive programmes and programmes based on violence can influence the child negatively.

In the present way of life, when both parents are doing jobs, very young children have to be left at day-care centers. These centers, therefore, play an important role in the socialisation of the child because the child will learn many things about appropriate behaviour in the society. For children from poor background the Aganwadis under the programme of Integrated Child Developments (ICDs) help children to learn about appropriate social behaviour and the importance of community life.

Theories of Development

Psychologists continue to study human development. They are learning more about what people are like and how they develop. Over the past century, many psychologists have provided theories that are considered practical guides. A theory is a principle or idea that is proposed, researched and generally accepted as an explanation. Developmental theories provide insights into how children grow and learn. Theories are helpful for understanding and guiding developmental processes.

Theories can be useful decision-making tools. Since a variety of theories exists, teachers need to understand these different approaches for working with children. Theories will help you understand strategies for promoting children's development. Four major theories about how children learn are important. These include theories of mid-twentieth century psychologists Erik Erikson, Jean Piaget and Lev Vygotsky. The final theorist, Howard Gardner, is a twenty first century developmental psychologist. These theories are based on observation and experiences with children.

Erikson's Psychosocial Theory

Erik Erikson proposed a theory of psychosocial development. He believed development occurs throughout the life span. His theory provided new insights into the formation of a healthy personality. It emphasizes the social and emotional aspects of growth. Children's personalities develop in response to their social environment. The same is true of their skills for social interaction.

Erikson's theory includes eight stages. At each stage, a social conflict or crisis occurs. These are not generally tragic situations; however, they require solutions that are satisfying both personally and socially. Erikson believed that each stage must be resolved before children can ascend to the next stage.

Maturity and social forces help in the resolution of the crisis or conflict. Therefore, teachers and parents play a powerful role in recognizing each stage. By providing social opportunity and support, teachers and parents can help children overcome each crisis. Following table contains the first four stages of Erikson's theory. These stages occur during the early childhood years. The paragraphs that follow give a brief overview of these early stages.

Erikson's Stages of Development During Early Childhood

Stage	Approximate Age	Psychosocial Crisis
I	Birth–18 months	Trust versus mistrust
II	18 months–3 years	Autonomy versus shame and doubt
III	3–5 years	Initiative versus guilt
IV	6–12 years	Industry versus inferiority

Note : *The first four stages of Erikson's theory concern children from birth to twelve years.*

Stage 1 : Trust Versus Mistrust

During the first eighteen months of life, children learn to trust or mistrust their environment. To develop trust, they need to have warm, consistent, predictable, and attentive care. They need caregivers who will accurately read and respond to their signals. When infants are distressed, they need to be comforted. They also need loving physical contact, nourishment, cleanliness, and warmth. Then they will develop a sense of confidence and trust that the world is safe and dependable. Mistrust will occur if an infant experiences an unpredictable world and is handled harshly.

Stage 2 : Autonomy Versus Shame and Doubt

This second stage occurs between eighteen months and three years of age. During this stage, toddlers use their new motor and mental skills. They want to be independent and do things for themselves. They are in the process of discovering their own bodies and practicing their developing locomotor (physical movement) and language skills.

The objective of this stage is to gain self-control without a loss of self-esteem. Fostering independence in children is important. At this age, toddlers start to become self-sufficient. They need to learn to choose and decide for themselves. To do this, toddlers need a loving, supportive environment. Positive opportunities for self-feeding, toileting, dressing and exploration will result in *autonomy,* or independence. On the other hand, overprotection or lack of adequate activities results in self-doubt, poor achievement, and shame.

Stage 3 : Initiative Versus Guilt

Between three and five years of age, the third stage occurs. According to Erikson, it emerges as a result of the many skills children have developed. Now children have the capacity and are ready to learn constructive ways of dealing with people and things. They are learning how to take initiative without being hurtful to others. They are also busy discovering how the world works. Children begin to realize that what they do can have an effect on the world, too. Challenged by the environment, children are constantly attempting and mastering new tasks. Aided by strong initiative, they are able to move ahead energetically and quickly forget failures. This gives them a sense of accomplishment.

Children at this stage need to develop a sense of purpose. This happens when adults direct children's urges toward acceptable social practices. If children are discouraged by criticism, feelings of incompetence are likely to emerge. This can also occur if parents demand too much control.

Stage 4 : Industry Versus Inferiority

The major crisis of this stage occurs between six and twelve years of age. At this time, children enjoy planning and carrying out projects. This helps them learn society's rules and expectations. During this stage, children gain approval by developing intellectual skills such as reading, writing, and math.

The way family, neighbours, teachers, and friends respond to children affects their future development. Realistic goals and expectations enrich children's sense of self. Children can become frustrated by criticism or discouragement, or if parents demand too much control. Feelings of incompetence and insecurity will emerge.

PIAGET'S COGNITIVE DEVELOPMENT THEORY

Jean Piaget's thinking has challenged teachers to focus on the *ways* children come to know as opposed to *what* they know. His theory of cognitive development focuses on predictable cognitive (thinking) stages. Piaget believed that thinking was different during each stage of development. His theory explained mental operations. This includes how children perceive, think, understand and learn about their world.

Piaget believed that children naturally attempt to understand what they do not know. Knowledge is gathered gradually during active involvement in real-life experience. By physically handling objects, young children discover that relationships exist between them. Terms Piaget used to describe these processes were *schemata, adaptation, assimilation* and *accommodation.* These processes occur during each stage of development.

Schemata are mental representations or concepts. As children receive new information, they are constantly creating, modifying, organizing and reorganizing schemata.

Adaptation is a term Piaget used for children mentally organizing what they preceive in their environment. When new information or experiences occur, children must adapt to include this information in their thinking. If this new information does not fit with what children already know, a state of imbalance occurs. To return to balance, adaptation occurs through either assimilation or accommodation.

Assimilation is the process of taking in new information and adding it to what the child already knows.

Accommodation is adjusting what is already known to fit the new information. This process is how people organize their thoughts and develop intellectual structures.

Piaget's stages of cognitive development are the same for all children. Most children proceed through the stages in order. Each stage builds on a previous stage. However, the age at which a child progresses through these stages is variable due to differences in maturation.

Although Piaget did not apply his theory directly to education, he did strongly influence children's early education. Many teaching strategies have evolved from his work. Caregivers and teachers now know that learning is an active process. Providing children with stimulating, hands-on activities helps them build knowledge. Piaget's theory includes four stages: sensorimotor, preoperational concrete, and formal operations. The first three stages occur during early childhood and the early school-age years. The following paragraphs describe these stages.

Piaget's Stages of Development

The **sensorimotor stage** takes place between birth and two years of age. Infants use all their senses to explore and learn. In this way, sensory experiences and motor development promote cognitive development. Babies' physical actions, such as sucking, grasping and hitting, help them learn about their surroundings. Movements are random at first. Gradually they become intentional as behaviours are repeated. Children begin to learn that objects still exist even when they are out of sight. This is known as *object permanence.* Through exploration and exposure to new experiences, new concepts are learned.

The **preoperational stage** takes place between ages two and seven. Children during this stage are very *egocentric*. This means that they assume others see the world the same way they do. Children do not yet have the ability to see others' points of view. During this time, representation skills are learned. These skills include language, symbolic play, and drawing. Children learn to use symbols and internal images, but their thinking is illogical. It is very different from that of adults. Children begin to understand that changing the physical appearance of something does not change the amount of it. They are able to recognize the difference between size and volume. For example, a ball of clay can be stretched into a long rope. Even if the physical appearance changes, the amount of the object does not change. This skill is called *conservation.* At this stage, children can also classify groups of objects and put objects in a series in order.

During the ages of seven to eleven years, **concrete operations** begin. Children develop the capacity to think systematically, but only when they can refer to actual objects and use hands-on activities. Then they begin to internalize some tasks. This means they no longer need to depend on what is seen. They become capable of reversing operations. For example, they understand that 3 + 1 is the same as 1 + 3. When real situations are presented, they are beginning to understand others' points of view.

The fourth stage, *formal operations,* takes place from eleven years of age to adulthood (the age range you are in right now). According to Piaget, young people develop the capacity to think in purely abstract ways. They no longer need concrete examples. Problem solving and reasoning are key skills developed during this stage.

VYGOTSKY'S SOCIOCULTURAL THEORY

Both Jean Piaget and Lev Vygotsky believed that children build knowledge through experiences. Piaget believed this happened through exploration with hands-on activities. Vygotsky, on the other hand, believed that children learn through social and cultural experiences. Interactions with peers and adults help children in this process. While interacting with others, children learn the customs, values, beliefs, and language of their culture. For this reason, families and teachers should provide plently of social interaction for young children.

Vygotsky believed language is an important tool for thought and plays a key role in cognitive development. He introduced the term ***private speech,*** or self-talk. This refers to when children ''think out loud''. After learning language, children engage in this self-talk to help guide their activity and develop their thinking. Generally, self-talk continues until children reach school age.

One of Vygotsky's most important contributions was the *zone of* ***proximal development*** (ZPD). This concept presents learning as a scale. One end of the scale or ''zone'' includes the tasks that are within the child's current development level. The other end of the scale includes tasks too difficult for children to accomplish, even with help. In the middle are the tasks children cannot accomplish alone. These are achieved with help from another knowledgeable peer or adult. The term used for this assistance is ***scaffolding***. Just as a painter needs a structure on which to stand and point a building, scaffolding provides the structure for learning to occur. For example, a teacher could scaffold a child's learning while constructing a puzzle. The teacher might demonstrate how a piece fits or provide clues regarding colour, shape or size. The ''zone'' is constantly changing. In contrast to Piaget, Vygotsky believed that learning was not limited by stage or maturation. Children move forward in their cognitive development with the right social interaction and guided learning.

KOHLBERG'S THEORY OF DEVELOPMENT

According to him moral development of the child proceeds in sequential but distinctive stages. These stages are given below:

(a) **Stage-I :** In the early years of a child's life (from zero-four years) the physical consequences of an action determines its goodness or badness. If fire burns the child, he does not touch it. The child is ego-centric and standards of morality are external here.

(b) **Stage-II :** The child gives importance to his own point of view, (his self) and is able to take account of other's roles insofar as he can use them in his own way. This is a period of make belief. Right action is what which satisfies the needs of the child. The role of others is also important in the sense that a child does only what can bring approval of others. Thus, only that behaviour is moral which can satisfy not only self needs of the child but it must please others also.

(c) **Stage-III :** At this stage the child adopts the view pints of others on the basis of their consequences. He does not question the views of others. The child considers only that thing as right which are considered as right by others. Thus, the child is totally conformist to the standard of the society.

(d) **Stage-IV:** At this stage, the child is able to make any moral decision on his own without caring for the thinking of others. Though he considers laws and regulations set by the society as the essence of morality, yet he develops his own principles of morality on various occasions. Thus, he is a non-conformist to the norms of the society to a great extent.

(e) **Stage-V :** Standards and norms are more internalized here. The adolescents examine various view points prepared by different societies and recognize them. They think that the laws prepared by their own society are correct. Other societies may have good moral principles that must be adopted after careful appraisal.

(f) **Stage-VI :** This is the last stage of moral development according to Kohlberg. Here the universality of the view points of the individual is seen. He formulates his own universal moral principles which he thinks that all societies should adhere to it. True understanding of right and wrong is developed at this stage.

Gardner's Multiple Intelligences Theory

Howard Gardner has helped teachers rethink how they work with young children. Traditional intelligence tests mainly focus on language and math/logic skills. In contrast, Gardner's theory of **multiple intelligences** emphasizes that there are different kinds of intelligences used by the human brain. Gardner believes intelligence is the result of complex interactions between children's heredity and experiences. This theory focuses on how cultures shape human potential.

Gardner claims that children learn and express themselves in many different ways. In the process, they are using several types of intelligence. Each intelligence functions separately, but all are closely linked. According to Gardner, a potential intelligence will not develop unless it is nurtured. Learning can best be achieved by using a child's strongest intelligence. Gardner claims, however, that all children need opportunities to develop all areas of intelligence.

The multiple intelligence theory allows teachers to see the positive attributes of all children. Teachers also view Gardner's theory as a meaningful guide for making curriculum decisions. It gives them a chance to assess children's learning strengths. From this data, teachers can plan a wide variety of learning experiences. Following chart lists Gardner's eight intelligences. The paragraphs that follow explain these intelligences in detail.

(i) Bodily-Kinesthetic Intelligence

Bodily-kinesthetic intelligence involves the ability to control body movements. This includes using parts of the body to solve problems, handle objects, and express emotions. People with this type of intelligence typically enjoy sports, dance or creative drama. They are able to express themselves with their entire bodies. Children will benefit from creative-movement experiences and role-playing.

Children with this type of intelligence process knowledge through sensation. They enjoy touch and creating with their hands. Therefore, daily opportunities should be provided for hands-on activities. Clay, sand, dough, feely boxes and other sensory activities help them develop fine-motor skills. Movement is also needed for gross-motor skills and coordination. It is important for caregivers and teachers to provide activities involving physical challenges. These may include playing kickball, jumping rope, and moving to music.

(ii) Musical-Rhythmic Intelligence

Musical-rhythmic intelligence involve the ability to recognize musical patterns. It also includes the ability to produce and appreciate music. Since music evokes emotion, this is one of the earliest intelligences to emerge. Composers and musicians are examples of people with this type of intelligence.

Children with this type of intelligence love listening to music. They are drawn to the art of sound and appreciate all forms of musical expression. They have a well-developed auditory sense and can discriminate tone, pitch and rhythmic patterns. As a result, they often cannot get songs out of their minds. You will hear them repeatedly singing or humming. This helps them understand concepts and remember information.

Activities to support musical intelligence can be included throughout the day. Offer opportunities for sound exploration through listening and singing. Use songs for directions and moving children from one activity to another. Play background music during self-selected play. Include songs during large and small group activities. Record the children creating their own music while singing or chanting. Explore rhythm by moving to recorded music. Use different instruments and instruments from other cultures to add variety.

(iii) Logical-Mathematical Intelligence

Logical-mathematical intelligence is more than just the ability to use math. It is the ability to use logic and reason to solve problems. Math experts have this form of intelligence. Scientists and composers may also have it. This intelligence involves the ability to explore categories, patterns and other relationships. It includes applying the principle of cause and effect. It also involves the skill to make predictions about patterns.

Children with this type of intelligence take pleasure in finding patterns and relationships. They enjoy discovering similarities and differences. Manipulatives for matching, measuring, and counting should be provided. Blocks can encourage the children's problem-solving and reasoning skills. Storybooks that show a sequence of events hold appeal for this type of intelligence. Water and sand activities with different-size containers help teach the concept of volume.

(iv) Verbal-Linguistic Intelligence

Verbal-linguistic intelligence involves the ability to use language for expression. People with this type of intelligence have well-developed language skills. They demonstrate sensitivity to the meaning, sound and rhythm of words. Lawyers, poets, public speakers and language translators have this type of intelligence.

Young children with this intelligence learn best by talking, listening, reading and writing. These children quickly learn the words to new stories, songs and finger plays. They enjoy talking to other people and are able to speak in an interesting and engaging manner. They are also able to learn a second language with ease.

This intelligence can be nurtured by environments rich with language opportunities. Children learn language in setting where it is used. Teachers need to follow the children's interests. They can then use these interests to engage children in meaningful conversations. Children's storybooks, songs, poetry, chants, and rhymes can serve as means for learning new vocabulary words. Listening to and telling stories can also promote language development.

(v) Interpersonal Intelligence

People with *interpersonal intelligence* display excellent communication and social skills. These people have a gift for understanding the feelings, behaviours, moods and motives of others. They make friends easily. They use language to develop trust and bonds with others. They are also skilled in supporting others and empathizing with them. These skills are important for teachers, politicians, salespeople and people working in the service industry.

These skills are nurtured in young children when caring behaviours are modeled for them. Teachers should keep this in mind. They can share experiences and provide the children with chances for verbal interaction. Books focusing on emotions can be acted out.

(vi) Intrapersonal Intelligence

Intrapersonal intelligence is the ability to understand the inner self. This is also known as *self-awareness.* It involves knowing your skills, limits, and feelings. It includes understanding your desires and motives. The ability to organize groups of people is part of this strength. Communicating needs clearly is another aspect. Psychologists, social workers, religious leaders, and counsellors are examples of people with this type of intelligence.

How can you foster this type of intelligence? In the classroom, share emotions that all children experience. These include joy, sadness, regret and disappointment. Classroom examples should be shared as well as storybooks that contain emotional concepts.

(vii) Visual-Spatial Intelligence

Visual-spatial intelligence allows people to use their vision to develop mental images. People who have this type of intelligence show a preference for pictures and images. Photographers and artists are some examples. Architects, engineers, and surgeons also need this ability. They use it to see the relationship of objects in space.

Teachers can foster this intelligence by providing children with unstructured materials. Building blocks and puzzles strengthen this type of intelligence, 4-18. Make and use visual aids wherever possible. For example, classroom schedules, recipes, and stories can all be displayed on charts. Shelving units can be labelled with pictures cut from equipment catalogs.

(viii) Naturalistic Intelligence

Naturalistic intelligence is developed from the need to survive. This is the ability to classify objects in nature such as animals and plants. It depends on a type of pattern recognition. This strength also includes the ability to distinguish among types and brands of objects. Sailors, gardeners, chefs, and farmers are people who have this intelligence.

To build on this intelligence, provide cooking activities and nature walks. These help develop use of the senses to gather information. Planting and growing a garden helps the children observe cycles. Rocks, seashells, flowers, leaves, seeds, and coins can also be collected. In the classroom, they can be sorted and classified. Post picture collections and share books about natural events.

CONCEPTS OF CHILD-CENTERED AND PROGRESSIVE EDUCATION

Child-Centered Education

Child-centered education is the idea that the needs and desires of the child should take precedence in structuring the learning day. The whole idea is that learning should be fun and engaging for the child, and is most likely to be that way if the child is incharge of the learning experience, rather than the adult parent or teacher.

Child-centered education is most characterised by learning 'centers' in a classroom that promote hands-on, active participation by the child. There may be magnifying glasses and bug slides in the science center, books and puppets that could be used to re-tell the stories in the language arts center, and wood blocks and shapes in the math center. The children are free to manipulate the objects in these centers. It is the process, the activity, the experience, that is valuable, not the facts, ideas, concepts or skills.

It is a relatively new approach to education. For centuries past, adults defined what education should be and children were the ones who did the adjusting. Education was considered work, not play.

Then came the softening influences of child psychologist Jean-Jacques Rousseau, as well as Dr. Marria Montessori, John Dewey, Jean Piaget and Lev Vygotsky, who all contended that a child's self-esteem and self-concept should be built up in order to create a better learner. Soon, the colleges of education were promoting child-centered education instead of instructionally centered education.

Role of Learner in Child-Centered Education

Learners are active as opposed to passive recipients of knowledge. Learners may assume a decision-making role in the classroom. Learners often decide what is to be learned, through which activities and at what pace. Learners can also produce materials and provide activities for the classroom.

Role of Teacher in Child-Centered Education

To put this approach into practice, teachers need to help students set achievable goals; they encourage students to assess themselves and their peers; help them to work co-operatively in groups and ensure that they know how to make use of all the available resources for learning.

Progressive Education

During most of the twentieth century, the term 'progressive education' has been used to describe ideas and practices that aim to make schools more effective agencies of a democratic society. Although there are numerous differences of style and emphasis among progressive educators, they share the conviction that democracy means active participation by all citizens in social, political and economic decisions that will affect their lives. The education of engaged citizens, according to this perspective, involves two essential elements: (1) respect for diversity, meaning that each individual should be recognised for his or her own abilities, interests, ideas, needs, and cultural identity, and (2) the development of critical, socially engaged intelligence, which enables individuals to understand and participate effectively in the affairs of their community in a collaborative effort to achieve a common good. These elements of progressive education have been termed 'child-centered' and 'social reconstruction' approaches, and while in extreme forms they have sometimes been separated, in the thought of John Dewey and other major theorists they are seen as being necessarily related to each other.

The term 'progressive' arose from a period (roughly 1890–1920) during which many Americans took a more careful look at the political and social effects of vast concentrations of corporate power and private wealth. Dewey, in particular, saw that with the decline of local community life and small scale enterprise, young people were losing valuable opportunities to learn the arts of democratic participation, and he concluded that education would need to make up for this loss. In his Laboratory School at the University of Chicago, where he worked between 1896 and 1904, Dewey tested ideas he shared with leading school reformers such as Francis W. Parker and Ella Flagg Young. Between 1899 and 1916 he circulated his ideas in works such as The School and Society, The Child and the Curriculum, Schools of Tomorrow, and Democracy and Education, and through numerous lectures and articles. During these years other experimental schools were established around the country, and in 1919 the Progressive Education Association was founded, aiming at "reforming the entire school system of America".

Therefore, progressive education is a reaction against the traditional style of teaching which teaches facts largely at the expense of understanding what is being taught. According to **John French,** "The progressive school teaches the child to think for himself instead of passively accepting stereotyped ideas. It keeps always in mind that each child is different from every other, and that what makes an educated person useful in his particular walk of life, what makes him interesting, what makes him an individual, is not his resemblance to other people, but his differences".

Philosophies and Practices of Progressive Education

1. Curriculum is strongly influenced by what the children are interested in, and is child-centered rather than adult driven.
2. Learning is 'hands-on', experiential and the emphasis is on process rather than product children are 'learning to learn'.
3. Children learn through integrated, theme-based units or inquiry projects and the 'theme' often emerges from the children.
4. Assessment is authentic and holistic. Children are well known by their teachers and peers.

There are no tests or letter grades. Instead, narrative reports are written about children that cover all aspects of their development: social, emotional, personal, physical and intellectual level.

5. Classes are usually of mixed ages and no ability grouping is used. Children are able to work at their own pace and cross-age friendships are encouraged.
6. Progressive education practices a developmental approach which holds that each child is a unique being unfolding and developing at their own pace according to a specific pattern. At each stage of development there are things that can be learned and things that should not be learned. Respecting a child's development is central to progressive education.

Types of Progressive Education

1. **Humanistic :** The humanistic form of progressive education focuses on the humanities, arts and social sciences. Its emphasis is on the individual child and not the curriculum. This type of progressivism aims to build a well-rounded individual with highly developed critical thinking and reasoning skills. The children learn think for themselves instead of accepting everything teachers tell them. Social development and interaction among the students are seen as valuable learning techniques.
2. **Constructivism :** Constructivism is a type of child-centered progressivism. It focuses on the child's creativity and learning abilities. Teachers should build the curriculum around the requirements and interests of the child. It maintains that education should consider children's developmental stages. Swiss psychologist **Jean Piaget** influenced the theories of constructivist education. Experiential learning, or learning by doing, allows students to construct their own knowledge.
3. **Montessori :** Italian doctor Marria Montessori started the Montessori progressive educational system. She developed her teaching theories by clinical observation and analysis of how children learn. Her method of education focused on how children naturally learn, all by themselves, without the help of adults. Maria Montessori concluded that children teach themselves, and it's the job of teachers to facilitate this process, not dominate it. Montessori teachers provide a sensory-rich environment and hands-on activities.

CRITICAL PERSPECTIVE OF THE CONSTRUCT OF INTELLIGENCE

Introduction

The most important variable that affects schooling or performance on a job is intelligence. Psychologists have interpreted the term intelligence in different ways and there is no consensus among them on the term even so far. In psychology this term is treated as a construct whose structure is different in different individuals.

The vagueness of the term arises due to the fact that intelligence is not a concrete material. It is rather abstraction from the behaviour of the individual which is indirectly inferred and elaborated as an adjective.

The dictionary meaning of term "intelligence" is the capacity to acquire and apply knowledge. **Boring** defines intelligence as intelligence is what an intelligence test measures.

Definitions of Intelligence

Several psychologists have classified and defined intelligence in several ways. Some of them are given below:

1. Vernon's Classification of Intelligence

(a) *Biological Approach:* Man is an organism among millions living on earth. Environment works as a foe for him. Intelligence is the capacity to adapt to the environment or new situations of life at every moment.

This definition of intelligence can be criticized on the ground that there have been many intelligent and renowned persons who were ill adapted to their social and physical environment. Besides, if we want to study individual differences in a society, this definition serves no practical purpose.

(b) *Psychological Approach :* According to psychologists intelligence is the relative effects of heredity and environment both. An English psychologist, **C. Burt** defined intelligence as the innate general cognitive ability.

In support of psychological definitions of intelligence **Hebb** and **R.B. Catell** distinguished two kinds of intelligence. The first is intelligence "A" which is Fluid intelligence and which is related to genetic potentialities or innate qualities of the individual's nervous system. Second is intelligence "B" which is crystalised "intelligence" and which is related to experiences, learning and environmental factors. These two types of intelligence in normal circumstances so much overlap on each other that they are practically indistinguishable.

(c) *Operational Approach :* These definitions help us to understand the concept of intelligence in clear and definite terms. In this approach scientific terms are first of all defined operationally and then observations are conducted with reference to these terms. For example, in order to determine a child's IQ, we first administer a test of a specific kind. Then we observe his performance on the test and finally draw certain conclusions in the context of the pre-determined objectives.

2. Freeman's Classification

(a) *Ability of adjustment :* An individual is intelligent to the extent to which he is able to adjust to new situations and problems of life. The more a person is intelligent, the more he is able to adapt to his environment in antagonistic conditions. The person who is low in intelligence has less capacity to adjust to the new situations of life.

(b) *Ability of learning :* Learning ability is also an index of intelligence. The more a person is intelligent, the more he will be able to learn new things.

(c) *Ability to carry on abstract thinking :* This category of definitions of intelligence is related to the effective use of concepts and symbols in dealing with situations and solving the problems through the use of verbal and numerical symbols. According to **Terman**, an individual is intelligent to the extent he is able to carry on abstract thinking.

3. E.L. Thorndike's Classification

(a) *Concrete intelligence :* The intellectual ability in relation to concrete materials is called concrete intelligence. It is the ability of a person to comprehend the actual situations and react to them adequately. This kind of intelligence is measured by using performance tests or picture tests in which the subject manipulates the concrete materials.

(b) *Abstract intelligence :* It is the ability to respond to words, letters, numbers or symbols. This type of intelligence is required in all academic activities in schools or outside the schools. The highest level of abstract intelligence is manifested in the thoughts of philosophers or in the inventions of scientists and mathematicians.

(c) *Social intelligence :* It is the ability of an individual to react to social situations of life. It is the ability to understand others and to react to them in such a manner that they may not feel unjust attitude regarding them.

4. Intelligence as a Global Capacity

A comprehensive definitions of intelligence : **Stoddard** (1943) and **Wechsler** (1944) have defined intelligence in the following words :

"Intelligence is the aggregate or the global capacity of the individual to act purposefully, to think rationally and to deal with the environment effectively".

Stoddard further elaborated that intelligence is the capacity of a person to undertake such activities which are: (*i*) difficult (*ii*) complex (*iii*) abstract (*iv*) economical (*v*) goal directed (*vi*) valuable from social view points (*vii*) original. These activities demand concentration of energy and a resistance to emotional forces.

Characteristics of Intelligence

From the above definitions of intelligence, we can draw the following characteristics of intelligence:

(*i*) Intelligence is the composite of several intellectual skills, such as thinking, doing, reasoning, dealing, learning etc.

(*ii*) Intelligence is displayed by the behaviour of the individual as a whole and intelligent behaviour is always goal directed.

(*iii*) Intelligence is the ability to adjust to abnormal and challenging situations of life.

(*iv*) Intelligence is not related to ordinary tasks of life. It is always related to extra ordinary manipulation.

(*v*) Wechsler has included the concepts of drive and incentive which are implied in his statement. "To act purposefully" and "to deal effectively". But many psychologists are of the view that drive and incentive are non-intellectual traits of personality and if they are included in a test of mental ability, more confusions will be created thereof.

(*vi*) There are seven fundamental elements of intelligence according to **Stoddard.** Intelligent person can undertake difficult and abstract tasks with ease. He can manipulate and deal the abstract ideas and concepts efficiently. Similarly, economy refers to the rate at which a mental task is done or a problem is solved. If "A" solves a problem sooner than 'B' then 'A' will be considered more intelligent than 'B'. The term social value indicates whether a mental task performed by a person is in accordance with the socially desirable and acceptable norms or not. The last term original refers to a person's, ability to discover something new and different, *i.e.*, this term is directly related to creative potential of a person. Discovery of some new facts and principles and inventions of new concrete materials by the scientists are few examples of originality.

Stoddard's definition of intelligence has been criticized on two grounds :

(a) It includes social values in intelligence, *i.e.*, intelligent task must be socially desirable. Psychologists criticize this point by saying that social value is a subjective phenomenon, *i.e.*, what is desirable for me, may not be necessarily desirable for others. So, there is no scope of subjectivity in an objective intelligence test.

(b) He has included two conditions of intelligent behaviour in his definition. First is concentration of energy and second is resistance to emotional forces. Psychologists say that these elements are non-intellectual traits and hence they should not be included in mental abilities at any cost.

Theories of Intelligence

1. Faculty theory of intelligence:

This is the oldest theory of intelligence given during the period of pre-experimental psychology. According to this theory mind is made up of different faculties like reasoning, logic, memory, imagination and discrimination. These faculties are independent of each other and can be developed by rigorous mental exercises of the difficult subject-matter.

This theory does not take the hereditary factors of intelligence into account and thus this theory was discarded by the later psychologists who believed that we can never improve the intellectual capacity of a person if he is mentally slow by birth.

2. Unifactor theory:

According to Alfred Binet (1916) intelligence is a general intellectual ability which is made up of several discrete abilities. These abilities include

(i) to reason well with abstract material

(ii) to comprehend well

(iii) to have a clear direction of thoughts

(iv) to relate thinking with the attainment of a desirable end and

(v) to be self-critical.

All these abilities combined together is called general mental ability. Thus, intelligence is a single but complex mental process which can be measured by different kinds of materials designed for the purpose.

3. Two factors theory:

This theory was developed by an English psychologist, **Charles Spearman** in 1904. According to him, intellectual abilities consist of two factors, general ability known as 'G' factors and specific abilities known as 'S' factors.

Characteristics of G factors

(i) It is universal inborn ability.

(ii) It is general mental energy.

(iii) It is constant, *i.e.*, it remains the same in all the individuals and does not change with time.

(iv) The amount of G differs from person to person depending on his genes.

(v) It is used in every life activity.

(vi) Greater the amount of G in an individual, larger is the chance of his success in life.

Characteristics of 'S' factors

(i) It is learnt and hence acquired in the environment.

(ii) It varies from activity to activity in the same individual.

(iii) The amount of S also differs from person to person due to his accessibility to learning situations.

(iv) 'S' factors are related to the specific activity. A low correlation between two or more functions or activities indicates the presence of 'S' factor involved in the activity. A person can be expert only in one or few activities because of the specific factors involved in the activity.

According to Spearman, out of these two factors 'G' factor is more important and thus it is an important measure of intelligence. So, any intelligence test should measure only 'G' factor because it provides most important basis of predicting a person's behaviour in different situations. Raven's Progressive Matrices and Catell's Culture Fair Test both measure 'G' factor.

Spearman has explained his theory with the help of a tetrad equation which is given below :

rap × rbq – raq × rbp = 0

Here,

a = opposites
b = discrimination
p = completion
q = cancellation

Thus, rap means correlation between opposites and completions, rbq means correlation between cancellation and discrimination, raq means correlation between opposite and cancellation and rbp means correlation between discrimination and completion. This theory can also be explained with the help of a diagram given below :

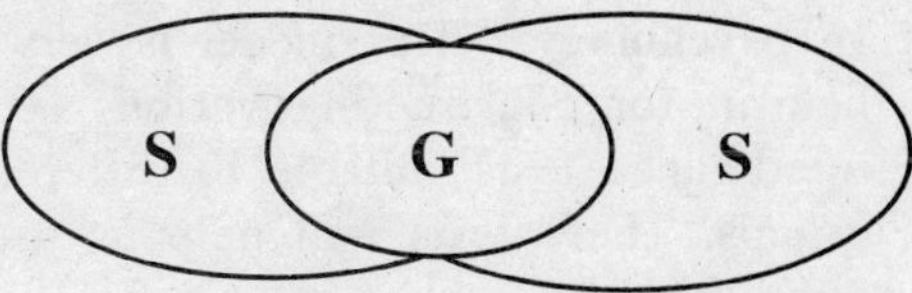

4. Multi-factors theory :

This theory was developed by an American psychologist, **E.L. Thorndike.** He opposed the theory of general intelligence by saying that there are specific stimuli and specific mental responses. Intelligence is nothing more than a potential specific connections between these stimuli and responses. Differences of intelligence among people are due to the different number of such connections in the neurological system. This theory is also called **atomistic theory** of intelligence. There are **four attributes of intelligence** according to him:

(a) *Level :* It refers to the difficulty of a task that can be removed by using intelligence. If different tasks are arranged in increasing difficulty order, then the height that a person can attain determines his level of intelligence. It is a kind of power test.

(b) *Range :* It refers to the number of tasks of the same difficulty value that a person can do in a certain period of time. Theoretically, an individual possessing a certain level of intelligence should be able to solve the whole range of tasks at a given level. It is a kind of speed test.

Range and level can not be completely isolated from each other. We can not measure range without altitude (level) and vice versa.

(c) *Area :* It refers to the total numbers of situations at each level to which the individual is able to respond. Area is the summation of all ranges at each level of intelligence. Area = Level × Range.

(d) *Speed :* It refers to the rapidity with which an individual can respond to a test items. Speed and level are positively correlated. It is different from range in the sense that no specific time is given here to complete a task.

Every intelligence test should consist of these four attributes.

5. Group factor structure of intelligence (PMA Test) :

This theory was developed by **L.L. Thurstone.** According to him, intelligence is not an expression of general factor but a combination of group of traits. They are intermediate factors, *i.e.*, they are not so universal as 'G' factor and they are not so specific as 'S' factor. This primary group of factors give the common mental abilities, a functional cohesiveness and then constitute a group. Another group of common mental abilities is said to have another primary factor and so on. In this way, there are a number of groups of mental abilities each of which has its own primary factors. On the basis of factor analysis of these groups, Thurstone identified the following seven group factors which are termed as primary mental abilities (PMA).

1. Number factor (N) : It is the ability to do numerical calculations rapidly and accurately.
2. Verbal factor (V) : They are related to the operations involving verbal comprehension.
3. Space factor (S) : It is related to the tasks in which subject manipulates an object imaginary in space.
4. Word fluency factor (W) : It is involved to the situation when the subject is asked to think of isolated words at a fast rate.
5. Reasoning factors (R) : It is used in those tasks that require the subject to discover a rule or principles involved in series or groups of letters.
6. Rote memory (M) : It is the ability to memorize a fact quickly.
7. Perceptual speed (P) : It is the ability to note perceptual (visual) details rapidly.

The point to be noted here is that these seven abilities are significantly correlated with each other.

6. Structure of intelligence (SI) model :

This model was given by **J.P. Guilford** in 1966 in the University of California on the basis of factor analysis of many tests. According to him human mind is composed of at least three dimensions—operations, contents and products, and each dimension of intellect is sufficiently distinct which can be detected by factor analysis. These three dimensions of mind are given below:

(A) Operations : Operations can be divided into five major groups of intellectual abilities.

- **Cognition :** It includes discovery, recognition of informations and new understanding of the facts.
- **Memory :** It is the ability to recognize or recall previously learnt material.
- **Divergent thinking :** This operation is closely associated with creative potential.

It refers to the ability to search out and think in a novel out of track way.

- **Convergent thinking :** It refers to the generation of information from given information and drawing conclusion from the given facts.
- **Evaluation :** It is the ability to make judgement on the basis of merits and demerits of a phenomenon. Here, value judgement on knowledge and thoughts is placed after critically examining them.

(B) Contents : Five kinds of contents are involved here. Operations are performed on these contents.

- **Figural content :** It is the concrete material perceived through the senses. Visual materials have three properties, size, form and colour.
- **Auditory content :** It includes nature and characteristics of sound perceived.
- **Symbolic content :** It includes letters, digits and other conventional signs usually organised in general pattern.
- **Semantic content :** It refers to those verbal meanings, ideas and concepts for which no examples are necessary.
- **Behavioural content :** It includes knowledge regarding other persons.

(C) Products : When five operations are applied to five types of contents, six kinds of products are made.

- **Units :** It refers to the production of a single word, definition or isolated bits of informations.
- **Classes :** It refers to the production of a concept.
- **Relations :** It refers to the production of any form of relationship, such as, analogy, opposite or similar ones.
- **System :** It refers to the production of internally consistent set of classification of various forms.
- **Transformation :** It refers to the production of changes in meaning, organisation or some other arrangement.
- **Implication :** It refers to the production of such information which is beyond the data given.

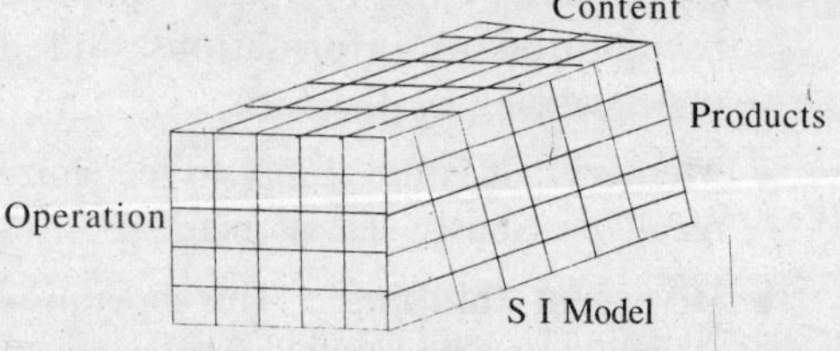

S I Model

On the basis of the model given above it can be stated that there are 5 × 5 × 6 = 150 factors involved in intelligent acts.

Educational Implication of the Model

(a) In psychology : This model is very much helpful for constructing various types of intelligence tests suitable to different age groups. These tests will help us to study individual differences in the society. This model is taxonomic in nature and has discovered many abilities which were not known before. If test maker has included items representing contents and operations, he can see whether products are same or different. Conversely, if products are shown by the subject through the test, the test maker can find out the content and operation and match them with the items given in the test.

(b) In vocational testing : This model shows that there are 150 intellectual abilities. This model predicts five kinds of mental abilities classified as content. This means that different kinds of test items are needed in vocational testing. Six types of products are also tested on the basis of items representing the products. For example, if a person is able to deal with items of figural contents, he can deal with machines, operators, engineers etc. and any or all of the six types of products can be made by him, such as, he can define a machine or any operator. He can give clear concept about how a machine is operated and so on.

(c) In the field of education : Conventionally, learner was considered to be a kind of stimulus response device. Once the stimulus is given to him, he will respond but the new conception of the learner in the light of SI model is that of electronic computer which not only stores information but uses that information to generate new information either by divergent or convergent thinking.

Thus, this model gives the idea that learning is not merely the association of informations but it is the discovery of information as well. Model suggests that in order to understand human learning and higher mental processes of thinking, some drastic modifications are to be made in our theory of curriculum construction and pedagogy of instruction. Similarly, education is no longer considered to be the training of mind. Now, main emphasis on education is given to the learning of specific skills and modification of behaviour and all these materials are not taught merely for the purpose of training the mind of humans.

7. Two Level Process Theory of Intelligence : This theory was developed by **Jensen** in 1968. According to him intelligence is a combination of two levels of processes. One is associative intelligence and the other is abstract intelligence. Associative intelligence includes those kinds of tests that depend upon memory and simple verbal association. Abstract intelligence includes those factors as concept learning, thinking, problem solving skills, multiple discrimination, principle learning etc.

8. Burt and Vernon's hierarchy theory :

Burt (1940) separated four factors of intelligence by using statistical techniques :

- General factors (common to all traits)
- Group factors (common to some of the traits)
- Specific factors (limited to few traits)
- Error factors (limited to a particular trait when it is measured)

When human mind is put at the top, there will be 5 level hierarchical model of intelligence where general factors will come next to intelligence and error factors will come in the last.

Vernon, on the other hand, suggested that intelligence tests measure an overall factor G as well as two other mental abilities. First are related to verbal, numerical and educational. Second are related to practical, mechanical, spatial and physical. These two major factors can be divided into minor group factors. These minor factors can further be divided into various specific factors and so on.

MEASUREMENT OF INTELLIGENCE

Historical development of mental testing can be divided into three periods for the purpose of convenience.

(A) Pre-Binet Period :

In the 19th century, there was a good deal of interest in the field of psychophysics in which attempts were made to develop general rule of sensory judgement. The functioning of sensory reactions of the typical individuals is actually studied in psycho-physics. Method of limits procedure was used here to measure the extent to which people were able to differentiate between stimuli. But the limitation of these experiments was that accurate generalization of the result was not possible.

Francis Galton was the first psychologist who took interest in studying whether individual characteristics are acquired or inherited. For this purpose, he studied the lives of prominent English men and in his book "Hereditary Genius" he demonstrated that personal characteristics, (mental and physical) of men are inherited. He developed a series of tests to measure these characteristics. It was the starting point of mental measurement.

The first laboratory of experimental psychology was established by **Wundt** in 1879 in Leiping. He employed two methods to test vision, hearing, reaction time and psychosomatic problems—*(i)* psycho-physical method *(ii)* Introspection method. He also developed mental tests which could measure the keenness of vision and hearing, muscular strength, reaction time and other sensory motor functions of body.

Many of **Galton's** ideas were brought to USA by an American psychologist **J.M. Catell.** Like **Galton** he also believed that intellectual functions can best be measured by the reaction time and sensory discrimination tests.

In the last quarter of the 19th century, many psychological laboratories came into existence and studies of individual differences in mental abilities started.

The word "**Mental Test**" was first used by Catell in 1890 but his tests were actually tests of sensory discrimination, speed of motor responses and the like.

Thus, upto this period mental ability was identified as sensory acuity of an individual. The correlation between mental abilities and academic achievements was not known at the time.

Drawbacks of this period:

- Psychologists were unable to identify and define the nature of intelligence. Keenness of sensory motor reactions were related to intelligence.
- They were unable to measure the complex functions of the body.
- Intelligence tests developed during this period were measuring other than intelligence.

(B) Binet Period :

An important incident led the people to think about mental measurement during this period. In the beginning of the 20th century in France, a large number of students failed in the examination. For this teachers and students blamed each other. Seeing this, superintendent of public instruction appointed a committee to device some techniques to screen out slow learners in the schools. Binet and Simon were among members of the committee. They developed a variety of paper pencil tests in their psychological laboratory established in 1889, to administer them on children of different ages. Through these tests Binet tried to measure more complex mental functions such as power of judgement and reasoning, memory, arithmetic ability, etc.

An important contribution of Binet and Simon is that they categorised their tests in terms of age levels by administering their test items to children of different ages. In this way, an age scale of intelligence was also developed. For example, if an item was correctly answered by majority of seven years old children but only few six years old children could respond it correctly, then this item was reserved for seven years old children. In this way, Binet and Simon developed separate tests for different ages.

Similarly, if an item suited to eight years old child was correctly answered by a child of 6 years and if the same trend was shown by the six years old child in most of the cases of a test, then the mental age of the child was considered to be eight years not six years, though his chronological age is six years only. Thus, the concept of mental age was also introduced by Binet and Simon for the first time in the history of mental testing and with the help of this concept we could assess the intellectual ability of a person. Some of the tests developed during this period are given below:

Binet-Simon Scale

The first scale of Binet-Simon was published in 1905. This scale consisted of 30 items arranged in increasing order of difficulty. This scale was a crude measure of intelligence of school going children.

In order to remove some of its defects they revised their scale in 1908. It was the first age based scale and it created a lot of interest among the psychologists across the world. The items in the tests were grouped according to the appropriate age levels from 3 to 13 years.

Some items for three years age

- Point to your nose, eyes and mouth.
- Repeat two digits 3, 5.
- Repeat sentences of six syllables.
- Enumerate objects in a picture.
- Give family names.

Some items of eight years age

- Read a passage and remember two lines.
- Add up the value of five coins.
- Name four colours.
- Count reverse from 20 to zero.
- Give differences between two objects.

1908 revision of Binet-Simon Scale was adopted by many psychologists of America, Switzerland and Germany and many suggestions were given by them for the improvement of the scale. Binet-Simon accepted their suggestions and revised their scale again in 1911.

Some sample items of 1911 scale are given below:

(A) Age = 8 years

- Gives difference between two objects.
- Counts reverse from 20 to zero.
- Points out omissions from unfinished pictures.
- Tells the dates correctly.
- Repeats the digits.

(B) Age = 10 years

- Arranges five blocks in order of increasing weights.
- Reproduces two geometric designs by using memory.
- Criticizes absurd statements.
- Comprehends and answers difficult questions.
- Uses three given words in two sentences.

Main Features of Binet-Simon Scale

(i) They are really scales, *i.e.*, items of the tests are arranged in the increasing difficulty order. Easiest items are put in the beginning and the most difficult item is put in the last. Thus, these scales measure the level or aptitude of an examinee and not their speed.

(ii) These tests measure the general abilities of intelligence instead of specific abilities.

(iii) They can also measure the mental growth of the subject because they are arranged according to different ages from 3 to 14 years.

(iv) They are administered on subjects individually.

(v) Their system of scoring is tied to age norms. A child's performance on the scale will be compared to that of children of his own age.

L.M. Terman's revision of Binet–Simon Scale: L.M. Terman of **Stanford** University revised this scale in 1916 to adapt to American situations. He introduced one new concept which was intelligence Quotient (IQ) in his revision. His scale consisted of 90 items ranging from 3 to 14 years of age. Some items of this scale are given below:

Age = 7 years

- Knows number of fingers on both hands.
- Describes pictures.
- Repeats five digits.
- Gives differences between paired objects.
- Ties a bowknot.

1937 Revision of Binet-Simon Scale : Terman along with his associate Merill revised 1916 scale again in 1937. This revision had two equivalent forms L and M. The number of items in the test was raised to 129 in each L M. forms. A new change was also introduced in the test which was the calculation of chronological age. Upto 13 years CA was taken to be as original but after 13 years CA was computed in the following manner.

At 14 years = 13 yrs+2/3 of 14th year = 13 2/3 years.

At 15 years = 13+2/3 of 2 years = 14 1/3 years.

At 16 years = 13+2/3 of 3 years = 15 years.

Besides, 16 years was taken to be the last age for calculation of IQ. After that, CA was taken to be constant.

LM form revision of 1960 : Binet-Simon scale was last revised in 1960 in which items of both L and M forms were included in the scale. This revision has a range of 2 years of mental age scores to 22 years and 11 months of mental age score. This form of the test measures abilities from 7 categories namely, language, memory, reasoning, social intelligence, conceptual phenomenon, numerical, reasoning and visual motor. Test items are in the form of words, objects and pictures and the responses given by the examinees are in the form of drawing, calculating, writing and speaking. Administration of the test requires one full hour. In this revision intelligence is expressed in terms of standard scores of the deviation IQ.

Wechsler Scale : This scale may be considered an improvement over Binet-Simon scale as it can measure the intelligence of adults very effectively. David Wechsler developed this scale in 1939. This scale was developed in two equivalent forms, each form consisted of ten subtests of which five tests were verbal and five were non-verbal or performance type. This scale was revised in 1955 and was renamed as Wechsler Adult Intelligence Scale (WAIS). It comprised of 11 sub tests of which six were verbal and five were non-verbal. This scale is used on persons above 16 years of age upto 64 and administration time of the scale is one hour. The detail of these 11 subtests are given below:

(a) Verbal subtests :

1. *Information* : 29 questions are given here to test the recall of knowledge concerning wide varieties of information.
2. *Comprehension* : 14 questions are given here to test understanding of knowledge concerning a particular subject or event.
3. *Arithmetic* : 14 questions are given here to test numerical ability. These questions are solved orally without using paper and pencil at all.
4. *Similarity* : 13 questions are given here to measure abstract verbal reasoning. Examinees are required here to compare two objects and find out the relationship between them.
5. *Digit span* : Memory for digits are measured here. In the first half, the examinee is asked to repeat in the same order, three to nine digits presented in the forward directions and in the second half, the digits are repeated in a backward direction.
6. *Vocabulary* : 40 words of increasing difficulty value are presented before the examinees here and they are asked to tell the meaning of these words.

(b) Non-verbal or performance subtests:

1. *Digit symbol* : Nine digits each with different digit symbols are given to the examinees here and they are asked to give the right code for each digits or symbols.
2. *Picture completion* : This subtest measures the ability of the examinees to analyse the parts from the whole. Examinees are given 21 cards containing incomplete pictures and they are asked to fill the missing part of each picture.
3. *Block design* : Its purpose is to measure the ability to analyse the complex whole. There are only 7 designs in these blocks which have red, white and red-white sides. Examinees are asked to produce a given design with the help of these blocks.
4. *Picture arrangement* : Its purpose is to measure the ability to identify the whole from the parts. Here six set of pictures are given to the examinees and they are asked to arrange them in an order which tells a meaningful story.
5. *Object assembly* : Its purpose is to measure the ability to synthesise the whole with the help of parts. Here examinees are given some puzzle pictures each representing some parts of the human body and they are asked to assemble them in the form of a complete man.

Speed and accuracy factors are also scored in Arithmetic, digit symbol, block design, picture arrangement and object assembly. Raw scores of each subject are converted into normalized standard scores with a mean of 10 and SD of 3. This makes the scores of each sub tests comparable. Separate IQ for verbal and non-verbal subtest forms is calculated by adding up the respective subtests of the two forms and if we add up scores on all the 11 subtests, we obtain total scale score. These standard scores are expressed in the form of deviation IQ with a mean of 100 and SD of 15.

Wechsler developed another scale known as Wechsler intelligence Scale for Children in 1949 to test the intelligence of children from 5 to 15 years of age. It also takes one hour to administer, though there are 12 subtests in this scale. Maze test is the only test which is extra in WISC. Maze subtest has eight mazes to be traced by the examinee with a pencil. These mazes are given in increasing order of difficulty.

The scoring system of both the tests WAIS and WISC are the same. Here also the total scores are converted into deviation IQ with a mean of 100 and SD of 15.

Advantages of Wechsler Scales

(i) Though Binet's scale and Wechsler's scale both are individual scales, yet the later can be administered on small groups of children and adults.

(ii) Wechsler's scale is easier to administer than Binet's Scale and its scoring is also less complex than the former.

(iii) Wechsler has prepared separate scales for children and adults Binet's scale does not possess this advantage.

Other differences of Wechsler Scales and Stanford Binet Scale

(i) In Wechsler scale, items are not grouped in terms of mental age as is the case of Stanford-Binet scale. Points are given here for all correct responses. Thus, WAIS or WISC is a point scale.

(ii) In Stanford-Binet scale items are interpreted in terms of different age levels of the examinees but in WAIS or WISC similar types of items are grouped together to form subtests.

(iii) WAIS has separate age norms for adults but in SB Scale all the individuals above 18 are treated in a similar manner as far as computation of IQ is concerned. Thus, people of all age levels are treated as 18 years of age after 18.

(iv) In SB tests items are varied, unrelated and upgraded but in WAIS and WISC tests, items are graded according to various range of ages.

(v) SB scale is internally standardized and rigid but WAIS is externally standardized and flexible.

(vi) SB scale refers to qualitative evaluation while WAIS refers to quantitative evaluation.

(vii) Slight chance of statistical treatment is possible in SB scale but WAIS is fully subject to all statistical analysis.

(c) Post Binet period :

This period is particularly known for testing intelligence in groups and thus group test of intelligence became popular during this periods.

A group test is one that can be given to a number of subjects at a time by a single examiner. This type of test came into being during first World War for the purpose of classifying soldiers for various jobs in accordance with their mental abilities. Army Alpha and Army Beta, two tests were developed during this period. Army Alpha is a verbal group test of intelligence meant for literate people. Army beta is a non-verbal group test of intelligence meant for illiterate persons.

We will discuss here some more group test of intelligence :

1. **Catell's Culture Fair Test :** This test was developed by RB Catell and was published by IPAT (Institute for Personality and Ability Testing) in 1961. The test has three scales and can be administered on children and adults both.

   Scale I meant for 4-8 years

   Scale II meant for 8-15 years

   Scale III meant for 15 years and above

   This test measures the general intelligence factor and takes 30-60 minutes to administer. The test has been prepared in such a manner that previously learnt skill or knowledge does not help the examinee to score more on this test. That is why, it is said to be independent of school achievement, social advantages and environmental influences.

2. **Large Thorndike's Intelligence Test :** This test is meant for primary and secondary school children graded into five different levels. The purpose of the test is to measure verbal comprehension, numerical skill and reasoning abilities. Test has verbal as well as non-verbal items. Only non-verbals items are, however, included at the lower levels. The administration of the test takes 30 minutes in all.

3. **Raven Progressive Matrices Test :** This test was developed in England. It consists of geometric figures and designs. The subjects find out the relationship between figures and select appropriate parts for completion of each pattern of relations.

Classification of Intelligence Test

(A) Classification from the point of view of administration

1. **Individual intelligence test :** An individual intelligence test is one which is administered to only one person at a time. Binet-Simon is an example.

2. **Group intelligence test :** A group intelligence test is one which can be administered to more than one persons at a time. Army Alpha and Army Beta are two examples of such tests.

Some general characteristics of group intelligence tests are as follows :

(i) They have been developed on the assumption that intelligence is a general capacity and can be measured by sampling a variety of mental activities.

(ii) In group tests the similar types of items are pooled together in different subtests.

(iii) Every group test is standardized for a special range of ages or school grades.

(iv) Construction of individual test is also very difficult and costly as compared to group tests. Their scoring and standardization is also time consuming process.

(v) It is very difficult to establish rapport between the examiner and the examinees and hence examinees can not be motivated properly in group tests of intelligence. These two limitations are not seen in individual tests.

(vi) Group tests are superior to individual tests in the sense that norms established here are more dependable than that of individual tests. It is because these norms are calculated on the basis of a very large sample.

(vii) Individual test provides qualitative performance of the individual while group tests are mostly point scale and express the performance in quantities.

(B) Classification from the point of view of nature of items of the test

1. **Verbal test :** Verbal test of intelligence is one in which instructions and items are produced before the examinees through the written language. So, examinees must be literate to take these tests. Mohsin's General intelligence Test, Joshi's General Mental Ability test and Jalota's Group General Mental Ability Test are some examples of verbal tests of intelligence of Indian origin.
2. **Non-verbal test :** A non-verbal test is one which requires the use of language only to impart instructions. The examinees are asked to manipulate the test materials in their own way. Since language is not needed to respond to items here, it can be administered to illiterate persons as well. They are also culturally free and hence they can be applied to any situation representing any culture. Test items are usually of figured relation type. Army Beta is a good example of non-language test
3. **Performance test :** A performance test is one in which a subject has to perform some thing or to manipulate some concrete materials without much use of the language ability. Non-verbal and performance tests are useful for the following groups of people:

   (a) Deaf and Dumb : Those children who cannot hear or speak can be tested with the help of performance test.

   (b) Illiterates : Verbal test of intelligence is useless for those who cannot read or write. Performance test is useful for them.

   (c) Shy children : Many withdrawn children are hesitant to express before others. Performance and non-verbal test of intelligence will suit them very much.

   (d) Educationally deficient children : Verbal test of intelligence generally measure learning along with intelligence. If children are educationally poor, they will perform poorly on intelligence test too and thus they will be wrongly declared as children of below average intelligence. Such a problem can be overcome by using performance test or non-verbal intelligence test.

   (e) Useful for children of other culture : A particular culture dominates in every verbal intelligence test and thus the test can not be adopted by other cultures. Due to free from culture, performance test is suitable for these foreign students.

Some performance tests of intelligence are given below :

(a) Pintner Paterson Scale : This is the first systematic performance test. This scale was standardized in 1917. It consists of 15 subtests.

(b) Goodenough Drawing Test : This scale was developed by Florence Goodenough in 1926. Here child is asked to draw the picture of a man as best as possible without any time limit. This is especially useful for those children who are suspected to be mentally retarted.

Weaknesses of performance test :

- Here the subject can score high due to practice effect and chance success is more frequent than verbal tests. Because of this reason, reliability coefficient is very low.
- They fail to distinguish between gifted and average children due to limited scope of these tests.
- These scales fail to test fine mental abilities such as, ability to make abstraction or concept formation or evaluation abilities of mind.

Interpretation of Intelligence Test Scores : Intelligence test scores can be interpreted in the following three ways:

1. **Mental age :** This concept was first introduced by **Afred Binet** of France in 1908. It refers to a score that is determined by comparing a child's score with the scores obtained by younger or older children in the norming group. Here a child's score is compared with the average score of his own age. For example, if a 9-year-old child scores 60 on an

intelligence test and suppose mental age norms for that scale are as follows:

Mental age of 8 years = 60

Mental age of 9 years = 70

Mental age of 10 years = 80

Then, in that case, mental age of the child will be considered as 8 years instead of 9 though his chronological age is 9 years.

Similarly, if another child of 8 years obtains a score of 80, then his mental age will be 10 years, though his chronological age is 8 years only.

Thus, we can say that the mean performance of each age level becomes the mental age for that age level.

2. **Intelligent Quotient (IQ) :** IQ is also based on the concept of mental age. It is the ratio of mental age to the chronological age multiplied by 100.

$$IQ = \frac{MA}{CA} \times 100.$$

Suppose, the mental age of a 10-year-old child is 12 years on the basis of his scores on an intelligence test, his IQ will be

$$\frac{12}{10} \times 100 = 120.$$

Similarly, if mental age of a person is nine years two months and his age is 12 years 6 months, then his IQ will be

$$\frac{110}{150} \times 100 = 73.3.$$

General classification of persons in terms of IQ

IQ	Classification
140 and above	Genius
130-140	Very superior
120-130	Superior
110-120	Bright
90-110	Average
80-90	Dull
70-80	Borderline
Below 70	Mentally retarded.

Shortcomings of IQ: Some of the main short comings of IQ are as follows:

(i) It is a well-known fact that after 18 years, the mental age of a person tends to stabilize. Thus, if IQ is calculated after this age, the result will be misleading, *i.e.*, a person will be less intelligent if he grows in age.

(ii) Variability of IQ scores from one test to another is not the same. As a result IQ scores for different tests would not be directly comparable.

(iii) It has also been found that variability in IQ scores for the different age levels on the same test is not the same. In that case IQ scores would be a misleading index because it would indicate that a person's IQ may increase or decrease as he grows in age. An example will illustrate this point.

Age	IQ	SD
9 years old child	120	12
7 years old child	120	9

Here IQ of 120 of both the children is not the same due to difference in SD.

3. **Deviation IQ :** Now-a-days IQ ratio is converted into a normalized standard score with a fixed mean of 100 and SD of 15. This is known as DIQ. This fixed mean and SD remain constant through all the age levels. It means that if a child's score is 1 SD above the mean his DIQ will be 100 + 15 = 115. Similarly, if his score is 1 SD below the mean his DIQ will be 100 – 15 = 85 and so on. Thus, with the help of these **DIQ** scores inter age comparison is also possible.

Uses of Intelligence Test

Intelligence tests can be applied in the following situations.

1. **Measurement of general learning abilities:** Intelligence and achievement in schools are highly correlated. If a person is high on an intelligence test, he is expected to score high on school achievements also. Conversely if a person scores high on an intelligence test and still his school achievement is very poor, we can find out other reasons for his educational backwardness.

2. **Assessment of individual differences and categorization :** With the help of intelligence tests we can categories a particular class into several convenient groups and plan our instructional strategies accordingly. Thus, intelligence testing is very useful for educational guidance.

3. **Exact definition of mental retardation is possible :** It is said that those who are below 70 in IQ are retarded but to what extent they are mentally retarded can further be studied with the help of higher screening. We may define the three groups of mentally retarted in the following ways.

Category	IQ level
Morons	45-69
Imbeciles	25-45
Idiots	Below 25

4. **Identification of gifted children :** Gifted children are the treasure of the society. They must be identified in the earlier stages of their lives so that they can be fully guided and helped for their better advancement which is directly related to the advancement of the society as well. Intelligence testing will help the concerned organisations to chalk out plans in the desired manner.
5. **Vocational guidance :** Some children are very forward in verbal abilities and some are superior in non-verbal abilities. This identification is possible only with the help of intelligence tests. Since academic subjects need verbal intelligence and technical subjects need non-verbal or performing abilities, hence children may be guided accordingly.
6. **Screening :** In today's age of competition and rush, screening has become a necessity. Every school has limited seats of admission and it has to select only those students who can raise the academic level of the school high and get name for it. Same is the case with appointments in jobs. For all these purposes, intelligence testing is a must.
7. **Study of mental growth :** Mental abilities develop in a sequential order onward. We can use intelligence tests for studying the trends of mental development of individuals. Intelligence tests have made it clear that mental development of children is a steady consistent process from year-to-year till the age of 25. Intelligence tests show that mind does not develop rapidly in the period of adolescence like the physical and emotional development, but in childhood, it develops rapidly.

Limitations of Intelligence Tests

1. Generally intelligence test shows what a person can do at a certain point of time. These abilities are tested on the basis of certain items included in the test. In order to make the results dependable, a proper size of the sample must be selected for standardization of the test.
2. Some people may be fatigued earlier than others when take a test. This extent of fatigue may reduce their scores and hence intelligence testing will not be accurate. So scores should be taken with caution.
3. No intelligence test is fully free from cultural influences. So, home or school background may affect the intelligence test scores of subjects.
4. Administration of the test also affects the scores of subjects. If proper rapport is there between the examiner and the examinee. IQ scores may be high. On the other hand, if children are frightened with the testing situation as is case of slow learners they will perform poorly on the test.
5. Taking intelligence scores in absolute form is misleading. Intelligence tests do not reveal all the mental abilities in most of the cases. So, intelligence test must be supplemented with clinical setting and case history method to collect detailed information about a subject as is done in clinics by physician who does not entirely believe in physical investigations. He rather takes the help of clinical diagnosis before giving remedial treatment to the patients.

THOUGHT AND LANGUAGE

In this section we examines the relationship between language and thought: that language determines thought, that thought determines language, and that thought and language have different origins. Let us examine these three viewpoints in some detail.

Language as Determinant of Thought

In Hindi and other Indian languages we use a number of different words for various kinship relationships. We have different terms for mother's brother, father's elder brother, father's younger brother, mother's sister's husband, father's sister's husband and so on. An English person uses just one word *uncle* to describe all these kinship relationships. In the English language there are dozens of words for colours whereas some tribal languages have only two to four colour terms. Do such differences matter for how we think? Does an Indian child find it easier to think about and differentiate between various kinship relationships compared to her English-speaking counterpart? Does our thinking process depend on how we describe it in our language?

Benjamin Lee Whorf was of the view that language determines the contents of thought. This view is known as **linguistic relativity hypothesis**. In its strong version, this hypothesis holds what and how individuals can possibly think is determined by the language and linguistic categories they use **(linguistic determinism).** Experimental evidence, however, maintains that it is possible to have the same level or quality of thoughts in all languages depending upon the availability of linguistic categories and structures. Some thoughts may be easier in one language compared to another.

Thought as Determinant of Language

The noted Swiss psychologist, Jean Piaget believed that thought not only determines language, but also precedes it. Piaget argued that children form an internal representation of the world through thinking. For example, when children see something and later copy it (a process called imitation), thinking does take place, which does not involve language. A child's observation of other's behaviour and imitation of the same behaviour, no doubt involves thinking but not language. Language is just one of the vehicles of thinking. As actions become internalised, language may affect children's range of symbolic thinking but is not necessary for the origins of thought. Piaget believed that though language can be taught to children, understanding of the words require knowledge of the underlying concepts (*i.e.* thinking). Thus, thought is basic, and necessary if language is to be understood.

Different Origins of Language and Thought

The Russian psychologist, Lev Vyogotsky, argued that thoughts and language develop in a child separately until about two years of age, when they merge. Before two years thought is preverbal and is experienced more in action (Piaget's sensory motor stage). The child's utterances are more automotic reflexes—crying when uncomfortable—than thought-based. Around two years of age, the child expresses thought verbally and her/his speech reflects rationality. Now children are able to manipulate thoughts using soundless speech. He believed that during this period the development of language and thinking become interdependent; the development of conceptual thinking depends upon the quality of inner speech and vice versa. Thought is used without language when the vehicle of thinking is non-verbal such as visual or movement-related. Language is used without thought when expressing feelings or exchanging pleasantries, for example ''Good morning! How are you?'' ''Very well, I am fine''. When the two functions overlap, they can be used together to produce verbal thought and rational speech.

Development of Language

Language is a complex system and unique to human beings. Psychologists have tried to teach sign language, use of symbols to chimpanzees, dolphins, parrots, etc. But it is observed that, human language is more complex, creative, and spontaneous than the system of communication other animals can learn. There is also a great deal of **regularity** with which children all over the world seem to be learning the language or languages to which they are exposed. When we compare individual children, we find that they differ a great deal in the rate of their language development as well as in how they go about it. But when we take a general view of children's acquisition of language all over the world we find some *predictable pattern* in which children proceed from almost no use of language to the point of becoming competent language users. Language develops through some of the stages discussed below.

Newborn babies and young infants make a variety of sounds, which gradually get modified to resemble words. The first sound produced by babies is crying. Initial crying is undifferentiated and similar across various situations. Gradually, the pattern of crying varies in its pitch and intensity to signify different states such as hunger, pain, and sleepiness, etc. These differentiated crying sounds gradually become more meaningful *cooing sounds* (like 'aaa', 'uuu', etc). usually to express happiness.

At around six months of age children enter the *babbling* stage. Babbling involves prolonged repetition of a variety of consonants and vowel sounds (for example, da—, aa—, ba—). By about nine months of age these sounds get elaborated to strings of some sound combinations, such as 'dadadadadada' into repetitive patterns called *echolalia.* While the early babblings are random or accidental in nature, the later babblings seem to be imitative of adult voices. Children show some understanding of a few words by the time they are six months old. Around the first birthday (the exact age varies from child-to-child) most children enter the *one-word-stage.* Their first word usually contains one syllable—*ma or da*, for instance. Gradually they move to one or more words which are combined to form whole sentences or phrases. So they are called *holophrases*. When they are 18 to 20 months of age, children enter a *two-word stage* and begin to use two words together. The two-word stage exemplifies *telegraphic speech.* Like telegrams (got admission, send money) it contains mostly nouns and verbs. Close to their third birthday, *i.e.* beyond two-and-a-half years, children's language development gets focused on rules of the language they hear.

How is language acquired? You must be wondering: ''How do we learn to speak?'' As with many other topics in psychology, the questions of whether a behaviour develops as a result of inherited characteristics (nature) or from the effects of learning (nurture) has been raised with regard to language. Most psychologists accept that both nature and nurture are important in language acquisition.

Behaviourist B.F. Skinner believed we learn language the same way as animals learn to pick keys or press bars. Language development, for the behaviourists follow the learning principles, such as association (the sight of bottle with the word 'bottle'), imitation (adults use of word ''bottle''), and reinforcement (smiles and hugs when the child says something right). There is also evidence that children produce sounds that are appropriate to a language of the parent or care-giver and are reinforced for having done so. The principle of shaping leads to successive approximation of the desired responses so that the child eventually speaks as well as the adult. Regional differences in pronunciation and phrasing illustrate how different patterns are reinforced in different areas.

Linguist Noam Chomsky put forth the innate proposition of development of language. For him the *rate at which children acquire words and grammar* without being taught can not be explained only by learning principles. Children also *create all sorts of sentences* they have never heard and, therefore, could not be imitating. Children throughout the world seem to have a *critical period*—a period when learning must occur if it is to occur successfully—for learning language. Children across the world also go through the same stages of language development. Chomsky believes language development is just like physical maturation given adequate care, it ''just happens to the child''. Children are born with ''universal grammar''. They readily learn the grammar of whatever language they hear.

Skinner's emphasis on learning explains why infants acquire the language they hear and how they add new words to their vocabularies. Chomsky's emphasis on our built-in readiness to learn grammar helps explain why children acquire language so readily without direct teaching.

GENDER AS A SOCIAL CONSTRUCT; GENDER ROLES, GENDER-BIAS AND EDUCATIONAL PRACTICE

Gender refers to the social distinctions between boys and girls and men and women that are socially constructed rather than biologically determined. These distinctions are reflected in the roles that boys and girls play in society and the status that they occupy within it. Gender roles tend to be dynamic. They vary from one culture and time period to another and are characterized by unequal power relationships.

Ending gender bias and discrimination is crucial to the empowerment of women and girls and to the achievement of gender equality in education Applying a gender perspective helps to make differences in power relations visible. It also helps us to see more clearly the needs and rights of girls and boys in particular geographical, cultural and economic contexts.

The ultimate goal is to eliminate gender biases and discriminatory practices and policies, both overt and covert. This is at the heart of gender analysis. Gender analysis should therefore be a prerequisite for identifying and understanding problems as they relate to education, and especially to the continued exclusion of girls from quality schooling. Gender analysis guides the process of finding viable and sustainable solutions to the problems of access, quality and learning achievement.

Gender analysis of what learners bring to education (including early childhood socialization, feeding and health access, cultural heritage and language), the content of education, teaching and learning processes, learning environments and learning outcomes help to highlight bad (and good) educational practices and policies. This analysis, in turn, should form the basis for educational interventions that are sensitive to both gender and human rights.

Gender Bias in Teaching

A common response from teachers when asked about gender inequity in classrooms is that they treat all their students the same. There are two problems with this statement. First, students are diverse and have different learning issues, thus treating all students in the same way means that some students will have a better learning experience than their peers. Second, teachers may be ignoring their unconscious gender biases towards their students, their schools and themselves. If ignored, these gender biases, which may have developed from cultural norms, may lead to bias in the classroom.

Gender bias occurs when people make assumptions regarding behaviours, abilities or preferences of others based upon their gender. Because there are strong gender role stereotypes for masculinity and femininity, students who do not match them can encounter problems with teachers and with their peers. For example, the expectation is that boys naturally exhibit boisterous, unruly behaviour, are academically able, rational, and socially uncommunicative, whereas girls are quiet, polite, and studious. Girls are also expected to possess better social skills than boys and to excel at reading and the language arts. So girls who present discipline problems for teachers, or quiet, studious boys, may encounter a lack of understanding from peers and teachers. Within the classroom, these biases unfold in students' practices and teachers' acceptance of certain behaviours from one student or another based upon the students' gender. Also, bias due to a person's gender is not mutually exclusive of other social categories such as race, ethnicity, class, religion, and language. For example, some teachers may perceive African American or other Black girls as loud and uncontrollable because the girls do not exhibit the feminine behaviours associated with White women, such as quiet, self-effacing and malleable.

Gender bias can occur within subject areas and school activities. For example, in subjects such as mathematics and the sciences, there are different participation patterns for girls and boys. Gender bias promulgates a myth that boys are naturally better at mathematics and science than girls. The implications are that if girls succeed in these subjects it is due to their hard work, not their intelligence, whereas boys' success is credited to their natural talent. There are some signs that gender bias in schools may be decreasing in some areas. The percentage of girls participating in science has increased and achieved parity with boys in biology, chemistry and algebra. However, subjects that are prerequisites for college majors such as engineering or physics remain dominated by men. Only 25% of high school students enrolled in physics are female. Moreover, there has been little increase in the percentage of women in engineering programs.

Males are also more likely than females to be in remedial programs and students' race also impacts these patterns. For example, African American males are more likely than White or female peers to enroll in remedial reading and mathematics courses. And non-White students have a higher representation in vocational and noncollege preparatory courses than their White peers. Teachers are critical components in challenging gender bias in schooling, but they also can be major contributors to it as well, through their pedagogical practices, curriculum choices, and assessment strategies.

Gender Bias in Teachers

Teachers' unconscious gender biases can produce stereo-typic expectations for students' success and participation in the classroom. Teachers view male students' domination of the classroom and their time as typical masculine behaviour. However, these biases have consequences for the students and the classroom climate. More than two decades ago, researchers identified and named groups of students who dominated the teacher's time and the classroom resources as "target students" (Tobin & Gallagher, 1987). Target students were typically white and male. They answered most of the teacher's questions and also asked most of the questions. This behaviour pattern was particularly insidious in mathematics and science classrooms because teachers did not expect girls to have competent knowledge in these subject areas. Classroom observations documented that target students typically called out answers to the teacher's questions, thus denying other students the opportunity to engage in dialogue with the teacher or get to grips with the subject matter. Furthermore, because boys are perceived as having natural talent in science, teachers asked boys harder and more complicated questions than girls. If girls attempted to answer more difficult questions than boys and faltered, teachers often repeated the question and asked that another student, typically a boy, provide the answer. However, if a boy failed to answer correctly, teachers reframed the question or broke it into a series of simpler questions that could help the student find the answer. Teachers' unconscious stereotyped gender bias that boys are smarter than girls, especially in mathematics and the sciences, meant they were willing to work with boys to reach the answer because they perceived boys were capable of achieving that goal but girls were not. Conversely, teachers of subjects perceived as feminine will spend more time engaged with girls.

Teachers' gendered perceptions of students' ability is also reflected in the type of praise and expectations they have of their students. Teachers often give girls less meaningful and less critical praise than boys. Boys' work is described as unique or brilliant, while girls' work is often undervalued, critically ignored and praised for its appearance. This aspect of teachers' behaviour is particularly detrimental to girls because it means they do not receive feedback on their work that could help them develop deeper understandings of concepts (Liu, 2006).

Teachers also use target students to maintain the tempo and pace of classroom instruction. For example, in a lecture or whole class discussion when a teacher is posing questions to the class, he or she may encourage target students to call out answers in order to keep the lesson moving, rather than wait for the other students to process the question and provide an answer. This short "wait time" may be detrimental to learning. More than three decades ago, researchers found that if teachers waited three to five seconds before accepting a student's answer, more students became engaged in the classroom and also improved their understanding of the content. Moreover, the longer wait time meant that teachers began to ask more cognitively challenging questions. However, the existence of target students in classes who often call out answers without direction from teachers meant that fewer students, especially girls, engaged in the lessons. In the absence of proactive teacher intervention, these patterns in which males dominate classroom interactions also occur in mixed-gender, small groups.

Target students dominate classroom interactions and exchanges at all education levels. In the early

2000s, researchers identified these same patterns of engagement in a professional development program for science teachers. When alerted to the invasive behaviours of the male teachers in the cohort, faculty began using overt breaching strategies to stop the target students calling out answers, dominating the human and materials resources of the classroom, and showing disrespect to their peers (Martin Milne & Scantlebury, 2006).

Teachers' gender bias towards students can also extend to their response to students who challenge their authority. Such risk-taking behaviour in boys is expected and at times praised, but assertiveness in girls is viewed negatively and labelled unfeminine. Similarly, boys who do not exhibit stereotypic masculine behaviours may be ridiculed (Renold, 2006).

Teachers use gender expectations as a means of maintaining classroom control. For example, teachers will seat undisciplined boys next to girls as a classroom management strategy. Further, teachers use the gendered expectation that girls' nurturing characteristics will lead them to place others' needs before their own. In other words, teachers often ask girls to assume mothering roles towards students who have fallen behind with learning because of inattentiveness, absenteeism through truancy, or in-school disciplinary procedures, and often those students are male.

Effects of Gender Bias

Gender bias can impact students' attitudes towards learning and their engagement with the subject. If affected by gender bias, girls will tend to believe that any success they have is due to hard work rather than any innate talent or intelligence. Boys may be encouraged to believe that success in science and mathematics should come easily to them because of their gender. Some males report dropping out of college science and mathematics programs because they no longer perceive these subjects as easy. Overall, teachers have lower expectations for girls' academic success compared to boys, and their attitudes are shown through the type and quality of the student-teacher interaction. The type and quality of critique teachers give their students can also have an impact. Teachers' comments on girls' work focuses on its appearance but with boys' work teachers focus on the content. Girls often do not receive substantive comments or criticism from teachers from which they could improve their ability to learn. During the many hours spent in classrooms, girls receive less time and attention from teachers than their male peers. Teachers usually ask girls easier questions than they ask boys. Typically, girls receive fewer opportunities to engage in classroom discourse, use equipment and assert their knowledge in classrooms.

Reducing Gender Bias

Gender bias in education is a series of microinequities whose impact is cumulative and often ignored. Girls are rewarded and praised for compliant behaviour. Teachers do not challenge girls with questions and rarely offer criticisms of their works. Teachers can reduce and challenge gender bias through an examination of their pedagogical practices and by posing simple questions about their practices. For example, which students do they frequently interact with? Are target students evident in their classroom? If so, how does the teacher deal with those students? What questioning techniques does the teacher use to engage students? Does the teacher ask complicated questions to girls as well as boys? Does the teacher use a variety of pedagogical and assessment practices? Which students are engaged with the curriculum?

Another way of reducing gender bias would be for teachers to videotape their classes and review their interactions with the students. Or they could invite a colleague to watch their teaching and record which students are being asked questions and what type of questions. However, teachers must also prepare for the consequences of changing their practices. Girls are conditioned to receiving less of the teacher's attention, and they do not usually cause discipline problems if they are not receiving their fair share, but boys can react negatively to losing the teacher's attention, causing disruption to lessons and becoming discipline problems. Moreover, research has also shown that boys avoid written work and often have poor communication skills when asked to work in singlesex groups.

However, the gains in reducing gender bias in education may disappear with the requirements of high-stakes testing required by No Child Left Behind (NCLB). NCLB requires that states report academic achievement data in most social categories, except gender (Kahle, 2004). This may result in less attention being placed on gender bias and less data that might reveal it. Continued monitoring of gender bias is necessary to minimize its impact on students' opportunities for learning and achievement.

INDIVIDUAL DIFFERENCES AMONG LEARNERS

It is not unusual to find a wide range of differences among students in a class or a group. These differences are invariably identified in terms of student's characteristics such as physical (appearance, height, size, sex, colour, etc.), demographic (age, caste, socio-economic status, etc.) and cognitive behaviour (thinking, remembering, problem solving, creating idea, etc.). The differences that exist among students due to physical, demographic, affective behaviour and cognitive behaviour characteristics are referred to as individual differences.

Differences due to physical and demographic characteristics are conspicuous and easy to identify. However, the differences that exist in the way they solve problem in Mathematics or in their ability to interpret and explain ideas are not easily visible but are identified through their performance. Let us examine, for instance, the answers given by Bitto and Neha, two students of the same class to the following proverb.

Interpret the saying, ''Pen is mighter than the sword''.

Bitto's Interpretation

It means that writing had always been able to influence mankind more than any amount of sheer physical strength; writing undoubtedly makes a more lasting impact in the minds of the people than any form of physical demonstration. In the case of the latter the impact might be forceful though less lasting. Great thinkers, writers and philosophers have from time immemovial been able to hold sway over the minds of the people by means of their profound knowledge through their writings. For example, Socrates won the wrath of a powerful state, because of his great ability to hold spellbound the young through his discourses. Similarly, the writing of Voltaire and Rousseau inspired the French to rise up in revolt.

Neha's Interpretation

It is a common proverb which simply means that through writing it is possible to win more victories than by using physical force and weapons. When any good book is read it is possible to retain in our memory the message it contains. On the other hand, success achieved through physical might is not for mankind.

The above illustration reflects the differences between Bitto and Neha in their interpretation of the proverb. While Bitto delves deep in her interpretation, Neha states only the meaning.

According to Skinner, individual differences in learner behaviours are the result of the organism's genetic endowment and reinforcement. Thus, Skinner believed that defective genetic endowment and/or defective reinforcement contingencies in an individual's experience result in a failure to acquire a variety of learned behaviours.

The process of an individual's mental activities such as remembering, analysing, interpreting, reasoning, problem solving and thinking are cognitive domain behaviours and are essential for learning and achievement. How we think, what and how we remember, how we solve problem and how we create ideas are cognitive domain behaviours and individuals differ by these behaviours. Such differences are often identified by psychologists in terms of intelligence, aptitude, creating and academic achievement.

Individual differences are crucial for teachers who are responsible for guiding all forms of learning. In fact, many educators would suggest that the primary role of teachers is to provide education to meet the individual differences and to develop student cognitive process.

Do Individuals Differ in Intelligence?

Well, they do differ. But how? Differences are due to the differences in the level of general intellectual ability and the underlying cognitive process among individuals.

How do we identify differences in intelligence?

Using suitable intelligence tests we can measure and identify the difference. An intelligence test may contain sub-tests (sub-sections) and each sub-test represents a different set of ability. The scores obtained in all sub-tests are added up to obtain a single score to represent the general ability of the student. Thus, the single score obtained for each individual in a test is expressed in terms of **intelligence quotient** (IQ). IQ is a measure of intelligence and is defined as the ratio of mental age (average age of children who give correct responses/ answers in an intelligence test) to the chronological age (actual age) multiplied by 100 (to avoid fraction). Thus mental age is:

$$\text{IQ} = \frac{\text{Mental age}}{\text{Chronological age}} \times 100$$

IQ scores help us estimate individual differences by categorising individuals on the basis of their IQs. These differences have important consequences for learning and performance. Let us examine the different categories of students based on their intelligence level.

Gifted : Those students who possess IQs of 130 or above are called gifted students. They are superior in intelligence and have high ability to reason. As compared to other children, they can perform academic activities grasping concepts, memorising, perceiving, seeing relationships, generalising, dealing with abstract ideas, critical thinking and solving problems more effectively and quickly. They have a broad attention span that permits concentration and the ability for a high level of academic performance. They take initiative in intellectual work and follow complex directions. Such individuals are small in number as compared to normal or average children. Normal groups have those children whose IQs range from 90 to 110 and they are able to profit from regular school programmes with varying degrees of effort.

Disabled : There are children with **disability** due to low level to intellectual functioning or specific learning deficits. Children with low level or below-average intellectual functioning are called mentally retarded. The children with inadequate level of intelligence are impaired in their ability to learn and to adapt to the demands of society. Mentally retarded children are of different categories. They can be:

- **Border line** (IQ ranges 90-70) and **educable mentally retarded** (IQ ranges 70-50) children can perform academic activities but are slow in their learning. Special instructional strategies can help them to profit from learning activities. They can take care of themselves and live independently as adults.
- **Trainable mentally retarded** (IQ ranges 50-35) are capable of learning only certain rudimentary literacy materials and simple occupational skills. They possess some ability to take care of their personal needs and can be trained in daily living skills. Such children require special classes or schools to study in.
- **Severely retarded** (IQ below 35) have quite limited adaptive behaviour and are never found in school. They are dependent on their families for their personal needs.

Children with specific learning defects are called learning disabled group. They are normal to above-average on intelligence but have difficulties in one or more psychological processes involved in understanding or in using language or numbers (written or spoken). The difficulties manifest in their ability to listen, think, speak, read, write, spell or do mathematical calculations. These difficulties are identified as **aphasia** (difficulty in grasping spoken language), **dylesia** (difficulty in reading), **hyperlexia** (little or no comprehension), **dyscalculia** (difficulty in doing arithmetic) and **dysgraphia** (difficulty in writing). Some are hyperactive in the sense that they are excessively active inattentive and behave impulsively. They follow instructions poorly and do not often complete the assigned tasks.

Instructional Strategies for Handling Individual Differences

- Organise instruction for the development of cognitive process.
- Use existing cognitive level as base.
- Strengthen memory.
- Formulate level specific instructional strategy.
- Use individual meeting.
- Provide instructions to overcome learning disability.

Do Individuals Differ in Aptitude?

Yes, they do differ. An individual may have a mechanical aptitude, another may have an aptitude for mathematics or yet another may have an aptitude for language, music or athletics. Such differences are due to the differences in the combination of abilities related to the cognitive processes, and the sensory and psychomotor components. For instance, when we talk of mechanical aptitude, we may deal with ability for spatial relations, ability to acquire information on mechanical matters and ability to comprehend mechanical relations, besides sensory and psychomotor abilities. Similarly, when we discuss aptitude in music, we may identify ability for musical memory, pitch discrimination, loudness discrimination, time discrimination and judgement of rhythm. Likewise, abilities required for science or mathematics are different and each requires a separate set of abilities.

The differences in aptitude can be identified using aptitude tests. Aptitude tests for areas such as mechanical skills, mathematics, science, language, music and graphic art can be used to identify the aptitude of students in each area of performance. You might have heard of the use of aptitude tests in medicine, engineering, business management, law or teacher training for selection of students for studies in the respective fields. The aptitude test, in fact, provides a measure of the candidates promise or teachability in a field of study, say, medicine. In other words, the test would tell whether the candidate possesses the required aptitude or readiness to profit from studies in the concerned field of study.

Instructional Strategy for Handling Individual Differences

The suggested approach for handling individual differences is **adaptive instructional system**. In this approach at least two alternative instructional treatments are needed to ensure academic success. Which is the most appropriate instructional treatment for the student depends upon his or her existing level of aptitude (learning readiness). Students with high aptitude may choose unstructured instructional strategy. With minimum guidance from teacher, they may be encouraged to learn through the discovery oriented approach. You may use the inductive process but instructional treatment is essentially learner-centered.

In contrast, highly structured instructional treatment for low aptitude learners is designed in small units through sequential steps and feedback. Frequent summary and review with simplified illustration, analogy and precise explanation of concepts and principles to be learned will facilitate progressive learning. Periodic achievement and aptitude assessments and comparison of these scores with the aptitude scores obtained at the start of instruction would tell the degree to which each learner in the specific treatment group has achieved.

However, for those who are unable to profit from either of the alternative treatments presented above, **compensatory aptitude training** is suggested. This consists of directed reading skill, study habits, self-learning skills, note taking and related activities. The main aim of compensatory aptitude training is to develop readiness for entry into structured treatment. Periodic monitoring should be formulated to identify the students who reach the required level for entry into alternative treatment.

Do Learners Differ in their Academic Achievements?

They do differ, but how? We have seen that those who possess appropriate pre-requisite knowledge learn more effectively than those who lack such knowledge. Differences in pre-requisite knowledge possessed by students create differences in the attainment of knowledge. Further, knowledge is attained progressively. Progressive differences in knowledge attainment leads to cumulative differences in knowledge attainment and this form of differences is often called **Mathew Effect.** It means that academically rich get richer and those who are poor continue to be poor. Thus, differences in pre-requisites and cumulative knowledge lead to differences in the knowledge possessed by the students likewise, they also differ in their capabilities to manipulate the knowledge in a given situation and the differences are identified in terms of the abilities to apply, analyse, synthesise and evaluate knowledge. In fact, ability is an essential condition for learning and the abilities related to intelligence, aptitude and creativity are important for academic achievement. We have seen the instructional strategies for meeting the differences in intelligence, aptitude and creativity through classroom situations. It means that differences in intelligence, aptitude and creativity do create differences in academic achievement.

The differences in academic achievement can be identified using an achievement test in the concerned subject. However, if the achievement test contains only knowledge level items (questions), it tells only knowledge level differences. On the other hand, if it contains items (questions) on knowledge and capabilities—comprehension, application, analysis, synthesis and evaluation—the various levels of differences can be identified. Besides, the total marks, each level-wise total is needed to identify the strengths and weaknesses of every student as well as the differences among students. As a teacher, if you know the strengths and weaknesses of your students in a subject, you may be able to adopt appropriate instructional strategies to suit their strenghts and weaknesses in that subject.

Apart from these achievement differences are quite often identified in terms of categories of achievers by classifying students as high, average and low achievers. Though there is no strict cut-off points, these categories can be created using marks. High achievers are those who possess higher level of knowledge and capabilities (say, with marks 66% and above) than the rest and those who possess average level of knowledge and capabilities (say, with marks 36% to 65%) are called average achievers. On the other extreme, you may find learners with low level knowledge and capabilities (with 35% and below marks). They are called low achievers. If you are interested in identifying the high, average and low achievers in a subject, say Science or language, the categories are created using the marks obtained in the concerned subject. However, categories can also be created based on the overall achievement in a class.

As a teacher, you may be curious to know the strategies for meeting the achievement differences in your classroom or the challenges posed by the strengths and weaknesses of the students in teaching-learning situations. Let us discuss important instructional strategies.

What are Instructional Strategies?

Let us discuss the major strategies to cope up with the differences in academic achievement.

- Provide appropriate pre-requisites to organise and learn new information.
- Use visual aids.
- Use analogy, example and illustration.
- Ensure learner's active involvement in learning.
- Periodic assessment.

EVALUATION AND ASSESSMENT

Evaluation

Evaluation, particularly educational evaluation is a series of activities designed to measure the effectiveness of the teaching-learning systems as a whole. According to Mary Thorpe (1980), ''Evaluation is the collection, analysis and interpretation of information about any aspect of a programme of education.'' Teaching-learning process is a continuous activity. It needs to be evaluated from beginning to end. Evaluation during the learning process (continuous assessment), often termed as ''formative evaluation'', is important for learners and teachers alike.

The bases of evaluation are learning objectives, performance standards and achievement tests on the one hand, and learners' and experts' opinions on the other. Evaluation helps to build an educational programme, assess its achievement and improve upon its effectiveness. It also provides valuable feedback on the design, development and implementation of the programme. It is, of course, an important component of the teaching-learning process. It helps in making the value judgement, determining educational status, or measuring achievement of learners.

The scope of evaluation in schools extents to almost all the areas of learner's personality development. It includes both scholastic and non-scholastic areas. It reveals the strengths and weaknesses of the learners, so that the learners have better opportunity to understand and improve themselves.

Evaluation is helpful to teachers also. It provides feedback to them to reshape their teaching strategies according to the needs of the learners. Evaluation in education in general and in distance education in particular becomes imperative to know as to what extent the goals of education have been achieved.

Thus, evaluation is not merely assigning grades to learners. It is a continuous process of acquiring and processing information in order to improve one's learning and to assess decisions made in designing an instructional system. If we analyse the above statement we easily notice that it has three important implications for the entire teaching-learning system. They are as follows:

1. Evaluation is a continuous process and not a one time performance measurement, effected at the end of a course/programme. It starts at the stage of curriculum development and continues until the instruction ends.
2. Evaluation process is goal-directed. It is aimed at finding ways and means to improve learning and thereby to achieve learning objectives more effectively and more efficiently.
3. Evaluation requires the use of accurate and appropriate measuring instructions to collect information for taking decisions about the quality and operation of education.

It is clear that in designing an effective learning system, one of the earliest steps we need to take is to prepare a comprehensive evaluation plan, which should be developed soon after the learning objectives have been formulated. This practice will help us to:

- determine whether the objectives are attainable or need revisions before we start designing the instructional system;
- collect data/information in a form that suits our purposes adequately and at a time when it is available, otherwise the opportunity to collect specific information may be lost; and
- have sufficient time to test the effectiveness of a design.

Continuous and Comprehensive Evaluation (CCE)

Continuous and Comprehensive Evaluation (CCE) refers to a system of school based evaluation of a student that covers all aspects of a student development. It is a developmental process of student which emphasizes on two fold objectives. These objectives are continuity in evaluation and assessment of broad based learning and behaviourial outcomes on the other.

The term **'continuous'** is meant to emphasise that evaluation of identified aspects of students **'growth and development'** is a continuous process rather than an event, built into the total teaching-learning process and spread over the entire span of academic session. It means regularity of assessment, frequency of unit testing, diagnosis of learning gaps, use of corrective measures, retesting and feedback of evidence to teachers and students for their self evaluation.

The second term **'comprehensive'** means that the scheme attempts to cover both the scholastic and the co-scholastic aspects of the students' growth and development. Since abilities, attitudes and aptitudes can manifest themselves in forms other than the written word, the term refers to application of variety of tools and techniques (both testing and non-testing) and aims at assessing a learner's development in areas of learning, like:

- Knowledge
- Understanding
- Applying
- Analyzing
- Evaluating
- Creating

Objectives of CCE

- To help develop cognitive, psychomotor and affective skills.
- To lay emphasis on thought process and de-emphasise memorization.
- To make evaluation an integral part of teaching-learning process.
- To use evaluation for improvement of students achievement and teaching-learning strategies

on the basis of regular diagnosis followed by remedial instructions.

- To use evaluation as a quality control device to maintain desired standard of performance.
- To determine social utility, desirability or effectiveness of a programme and take appropriate decisions about the learner, the process of learning and the learning environment.
- To make the process of teaching and learning a learner-centered activity.

Features of CCE

- The **'continuous'** aspect of CCE takes care of **'continual'** and **'periodicity'** aspect of evaluation.
- Continual means assessment of students in the beginning of instructions (placement evaluation) and assessment during the instructional process (**formative evaluation**) done informally using multiple techniques of evaluation.
- Periodicity means assessment of performance done frequently at the end of unit/term (**summative evaluation**).
- The **'comprehensive'** component of CCE takes care of assessment of all round development of the child's personality. It includes assessment in **Scholastic as well as Co-Scholastic** aspects of the pupil's growth.
- Scholastic aspects include curricular areas or subject specific areas, whereas Co-Scholastic aspects include Life Skills, Co-Curricular Activities, Attitudes and Values.
- Assessment in Scholastic areas is done informally and formally using multiple techniques of evaluation continually and periodically. The diagnostic evaluation takes place at the end of unit/term test. The causes of poor performance in some units are diagnosed using diagnostic tests. These are followed with appropriate interventions followed by retesting.
- Assessment in Co-Scholastic areas is done using multiple techniques on the basis of identified criteria, while assessment in Life Skills is done on the basis of Indicators of Assessment and Checklists.

Functions of CCE

- It helps the teacher to organize effective teaching strategies.
- Continuous evaluation helps in regular assessment to the extent and degree of Learner's progress (ability and achievement with reference to specific Scholastic and Co-Scholastic areas).
- Continuous evaluation serves to diagnose weaknesses and permits the teacher to ascertain an individual learner's strengths and weaknesses and her needs. It provides immediate feedback to the teacher, who can then decide whether a particular unit or concept needs a discussion again in the whole class or whether a few individuals are in need of remedial instruction.
- By continuous evaluation, children can know their strengths and weaknesses. It provides the child a realistic self assessment of how he/she studies. It can motivate children to develop good study habits, to correct errors, and to direct their activities towards the achievement of desired goals. It helps a learner to determine the areas of instruction in where more emphasis is required.
- Continuous and comprehensive evaluation identifies areas of aptitude and interest. It helps in identifying changes in attitudes and value systems.
- It helps in making decisions for the future, regarding choice of subjects, courses and careers.
- It provides information/reports on the progress of students in Scholastic and Co-Scholastic areas and thus helps in predicting the future success of the learner.

Continuous evaluation helps in bringing awareness of the achievement to the child, teachers and parents from time-to-time. They can look into the probable cause of the fall in performance if any, and may take remedial measures of instruction in which more emphasis is required. Many times, because of some personal reasons, family problems or adjustment problems, the children start neglecting their studies, resulting in sudden drop in their performance. If the teacher, child and parents do not notice the sudden drop in the performance of the child in academics, it could result in a permanent deficiency in the childs' learning.

The major emphasis of CCE is on the continuous growth of students ensuring their intellectual, emotional, physical, cultural and social development and therefore, it will not be merely limited to assessment of learner's scholastic attainments. CCE uses assessment as a means of motivating learners to provide feedback and follow up work to improve upon the learning in the classroom and to present a comprehensive picture of a learner's profile. It is this that has led to the emergence of the concept of **School Based Continuous and Comprehensive Evaluation.**

Scholastic and Co-Scholastic Assessment

In order to have Continuous and Comprehensive Evaluation, both Scholastic and Co-Scholastic aspects need to be given due recognition. Such a holistic assessment requires maintaining an ongoing and comprehensive profile for each learner that is honest, encouraging and discreet. While teachers frequently reflect, plan and implement remedial strategies, the child's ability to retain and articulate what has been learned over a period of time also requires periodic assessment. These assessments can take many forms but all of them should be as comprehensive and discreet as possible. **Weekly**, **fortnightly**, or **quarterly** reviews (depending on the learning area), that do not openly compare one learner with another are generally recommended. The objective is to promote and enhance not just learning and retention among children, but their soft skills as well.

Scholastic Assessment

The objectives of the Scholastic domain are:-

- Desirable behaviour related to the learner's knowledge, understanding, application, evaluation, analysis and the ability to apply it in an unfamiliar situation.
- To improve the teaching learning process.
- Assessment should be both **Formative** and **Summative**.

Summative and Formative Assessment

Assessment is often divided into formative and summative categories for the purpose of considering different objectives for assessment practices.

Summative Assessment

Summative assessment is intended to measure learning outcomes and report those outcomes to students, parents and administrators. In an educational setting, it generally occurs at the conclusion of a class, course, semester or academic year. In the context of a course summative assessments are typically used to assign students a course grade. It is also referred to in a learning context as **''assessment of learning''**. **Performance-based assessment** is similar to summative assessment, as it focuses on achievement. A well-defined task is identified and students are asked to create, produce, or do something, often in settings that involve real-world application of knowledge and skills. Proficiency is demonstrated by providing an extended response. Performance formats are further differentiated into products and performances. The performance may result in a product, such as a painting, portfolio, paper, or exhibition, or it may consist of a performance, such as a speech, athletic skill, musical recital, or reading.

Definitions of Summative Assessment

- ''Good summative assessments—tests and other graded evaluations—must be demonstrably reliable, valid, and free of bias'' (Angelo and Cross, 1993).
- '...assessment (that) has increasingly been used to sum up learning' (Black and William, 1999).
- '...looks at past achievements ... adds procedures or tests to existing work ... involves only marking and feedback grades to student ... is separated from teaching ... is carried out at intervals when achievement has to be summarized and reported.' (Harlen, 1998).

Features of Summative Assessment

- Assessment of learning.
- Generally taken by students at the end of a unit or semester to demonstrate the **''sum''** of what they have or have not learned.
- Summative assessment methods are the most traditional way of evaluating student work.

Formative Assessment

Formative assessment is generally carried out throughout a course or project. In an educational setting, formative assessment is used by teachers to consider approaches to teaching and next steps for individual learners and the class, and would not necessarily be used for grading purposes. Formative assessment, also referred to as **''educative assessment''** or **''assessment for learning''**, is used to aid learning. Assessment for learning is defined as ''all those activities undertaken by teachers and/or students, which provide information to be used as feedback to modify the teaching and learning activities in which they are engaged'' (Black and William 2004).

Definitions of Formative Assessment

- '... often means no more than that the assessment is carried out frequently and is planned at the same time as teaching'. (Black and William, 1999)
- '... provides feedback which leads to students recognizing the (learning) gap and closing it ... it is forward looking ...' (Harlen, 1998).
- '... includes both feedback and self-monitoring'. (Sadler, 1989)
- '... is used essentially to get a feedback into the teaching and learning process.' (Tunstall and Gipps, 1996)

Features of Formative Assessment

- Is diagnostic and remedial.
- Makes provision for effective feedback.

- Provides a platform for the active involvement of students in their own learning.
- Enables teachers to adjust teaching to take account of the results of assessment.
- Recognizes the profound influence assessment has on the motivation and self-esteem of students, both of which are crucial influences on learning.
- Recognizes the need for students to be able to assess themselves and understand how to improve.
- Builds on students' prior knowledge and experience in designing what is taught.
- Incorporates varied learning styles to decide how and what to teach.
- Encourages students to understand the criteria that will be used to judge their work.
- Offers an opportunity to students to improve their work after they get the feedback.
- Helps student to support their peer group and vice-versa.

A common form of formative assessment is **"diagnostic assessment"**. Diagnostic assessment measures a student's current knowledge and skills for the purpose of identifying a suitable program of learning. **"Self-assessment"** is a form of diagnostic assessment which involves students assessing themselves. **"Forward-looking assessment"** asks those being assessed to consider themselves in hypothetical future situations.

Co-Scholastic Assessment

The desirable behaviour related to learner's life skills, attitudes, interests, values, co-curricular activities and physical health are described as skills to be acquired in co-scholastic domain.

The process of assessing the students' progress in achieving objectives related to scholastic and co-scholastic domain is called comprehensive evaluation. It has been observed that usually under the scholastic domain such as knowledge and understanding of the facts, concepts, principles etc. of a subject are assessed. The Co-Scholastic elements are either altogether excluded from the evaluation process or they are not given adequate attention. For making the evaluation comprehensive, both Scholastic and Co-Scholastic aspects should be given importance. Simple and manageable means of assessment of Co-Scholastic aspects of growth must be included in the comprehensive evaluation scheme.

Comprehensive evaluation would necessitate the use of a variety of tools and techniques. This will be so because both different and specific areas of learner's growth can be evaluated through certain special techniques.

School Based CCE

School based Evaluation is held at school level unlike external examination conducted by the Boards of School Education. This is done by the teachers according to the schedule developed by the school and guidelines given by the Board. Though this evaluation has been done at school level all along, certain shortcomings have crept into this system. These shortcomings can be attributed to various factors. The basic factor is the misconception of teachers regarding the place of evaluation and its importance in the educational process. The other factor has been the imitation of the practice of external examination which is generally held at the end of the session.

In the School Based System of evaluation, the focus on the purpose of assessment has changed. Now, it includes readiness testing, screening of development, evaluation of performance in cognitive, affective and psychomotor domains more frequently, systematically and effectively.

In other words, School Based Evaluation is child-centred, school-centred and multidimensional evaluation. Hence, in its true spirit, it triggers an all round development of the learner. It encourages all kinds of learning in life both inside the school as well as outside it. It is child-centered as it attempts to consider the learner as a unique entity for its individual pattern of development. It builds on individual child's abilities, progress and development in achieving already set goals and objectives of education as an individual and not just his/her position in relation to other learners.

Further, this evaluation helps a learner to use his/her potential in a better manner and also provides insight to the teachers to discover the methods which may be helpful to the individual learner in resolving his/her problems and difficulties.

Besides being ***child-centred,*** this evaluation is ***school-centred*** as well. It means that no outside agency interferes in this evaluation process. It is entirely school based and done by the teacher. The teacher is trusted and given full responsibility of evaluating students with the brief that the teacher knows best about his/her students.

School Based Evaluation is ***multidimensional***. Its multidimensional nature is reflected in recognizing and taking care of learners' social, emotional, physical, intellectual and other areas of development which are interrelated and cannot be considered in isolation. It also calls for the use of multiple techniques and tools of evaluation.

Aim of School Based CCE

- Elimination of chance element and subjectivity (as far as possible), de-emphasis on memorization, encouraging comprehensive evaluation incorporating both Scholastic and Co-Scholastic aspects of learners development.
- Continuous evaluation spread over the total span of the instructional time as an integral built-in aspect of the total teaching-learning process.
- Functional and meaningful declaration of results for effective use by teachers, students, parents and the society.
- Wider uses of test results for purposes not merely of the assessment of levels of pupils' achievements and proficiencies, but mainly for their improvement, thorough diagnosis and remedial/enrichment programmes.
- Improvement in the mechanics of conducting examinations for realizing a number of other allied purposes.
- Introduction of concomitant changes in instructional materials and methodology.
- Introduction of the semester system.
- The use of grades in place of marks in determining and declaring the level of pupil performance and proficiency.

Its Characteristics

School Based Evaluation has the following characteristics:

- Is broader, more comprehensive and continuous than traditional system.
- Aims primarily to help learners for systematic learning and development.
- Takes care of the needs of the learner as responsible citizens of the future.
- Is more transparent, futuristic and provides more scope for association among learners, teachers and parents.

School based evaluation provides opportunities to teachers to **know the following about their learners:**

- What they learn?
- How they learn?
- What type of difficulties/limitations they face in working in tandem?
- What do the children think?
- What do the children feel?
- What are their interests and dispositions?

The focus has shifted to developing a deep learning environment. There is a paradigm shift in the pedagogy and competencies from 'controlling' to 'enriching' to 'empowering' schools.

Traditional Schooling	Enriching Schooling	Empowering Schooling
• Teacher centred	• Student centred	• Experience centred
• Subjects and classes-teacher directed	• Self directed	• Virtual authenticity
• Sorting and ranking individuals	• Continuous assessment	• Multi literacies
Competency:	**Competency:**	**Competency:**
• Memory	• Critical thinking	• Risk taking
• Competitive	• Collaborative	• Ethical
	• Creative	• Interactive

Implementing School Based Assessment would mean:

- Elimination of chance element and subjectivity (as far as possible), de-emphasis of memorization, encouraging Comprehensive evaluation incorporating both scholastic and co-scholastic aspects of learners development.
- Continuous evaluation spread over the total span of the instructional time as an integral built-in aspect of the total teaching-learning process.
- Functional and meaningful declaration of results for effective use by teachers, students, parents and the society.
- Wider uses of test results for purposes not merely of the assessment of levels of pupils' achievements and proficiencies, but mainly for its improvement, through diagnosis and remedial/enrichment programmes.
- Improvements in the mechanics of conducting examinations for realizing a number of other allied purposes.
- Introduction of concomitant changes in instructional materials and methodology.

- Introduction of the semester system from the secondary stage onwards.
- The use of grades in place of marks in determining and declaring the level of pupil performance and proficiency.

The above goals are relevant for both external examination and evaluation in schools.

Shortcoming of Traditional External Examination

- It is a one shot examination at the end of a year at the terminal stage of schooling.
- It mainly evaluates only the scholastic aspects of learning of the students.
- It does not evaluate all the abilities of the children. On the basis of marks obtained in written examination the students are declared pass or fail and further classified into predetermined divisions.
- Pass and fail system causes frustration and is inhumane because the failed candidates come to feel that they are good for nothing.
- Co-scholastic areas are almost totally ignored and have no place in the currently prevalent scheme of education and evaluation.
- The practice of testing of untaught content also reflects poor learning achievement.
- Only limited techniques of evaluation without potential for judging a student are being used.
- The aim of evaluation is to improve learner's quality which is not served by external examination.
- The current practice of awarding marks suffers from many discrepancies due to variety of errors.
- The varied ranges of obtained scores of students in different subjects create the problem in declaring reliable results.
- Analysis and interpretation of test results is not done in a scientific way.

School Based Continuous and Comprehensive Evaluation System should be Established to:

- reduce stress on children.
- make evaluation comprehensive and regular.
- provide space for the teacher for creative teaching.
- provide a tool of diagnosis and remediation.
- produce learners with greater skills.

Four Assessment Paradigms

Assessment *of* Learning

The 'assessment **of** learning' is defined as a process whereby someone attempts to describe and quantify the knowledge, attitudes or skills possessed by another. Teacher direction is paramount and the student has little involvement in the design or implementation of the assessment process in these circumstances.

- Teacher designs learning
- Teacher collects evidence
- Teacher judges what has been learnt (and what has not been learnt)

Assessment *for* Learning

The 'assessment **for** learning' involves increased level of student autonomy, but not without teacher guidance and collaboration. The assessment **for** learning is sometimes seen as being akin to 'formative assessment'. There is more emphasis towards giving useful advice to the student and less emphasis on the giving of marks and the grading function.

- Teacher designs learning
- Teacher designs assessment with feedback to student
- Teacher judges what has been learnt (student develops insight into what has not)

Assessment *as* Learning

The 'assessment **as** learning' is perhaps more connected with diagnostic assessment and can be constructed with more of an emphasis on peer learning. Assessment **as** learning generates opportunities for self assessment and peer assessment. Students take on increased responsibility to generate quality information about their learning and that of others.

- Teacher and student co-construct learning
- Teacher and student co-construct assessment
- Teacher and student co-construct learning progress map

Assessment **for** learning and assessment **as** learning activities should be deeply embedded in teaching and learning and be the source of interactive feedback, allowing students to adjust, re-think and re-learn.

Assessment *in* Learning

The 'assessment **in** learning' places the question at the centre of teaching and learning. It deflects the teaching from its focus on a 'correct answer' to a focus on 'a fertile question'. Through enquiry students engage in processes that generates feedback about their learning, which come from multiple sources and activities. It contributes to the construction of other learning activities, line of enquiry and the generation of other questions.

- Student as the centre of learning

- Student monitors, assesses and reflects on learning
- Student initiates demonstration of learning (to self and others)
- Teacher as coach and mentor.

Teachers and students need to understand the purpose of each assessment strategy. The overall assessment 'package' being used by learners and teachers should accurately capture, generate and use meaningful learning information to generate deep learning and understanding.

ASSESSING LEARNERS

Any meaningful report on the quality and extent of a child's learning needs to be comprehensive. We need a curriculum whose creativity, innovativeness, and development of the whole being, the hallmark of a good education makes uniform tests that assess memorised facts and textbook-based learning obsolete. We need to redefine and seek new parameters for and ways of evaluation and feedback. In addition to the learner's achievements in specific subject areas that lend themselves to testing easily, assessment would need to encompass attitudes to learning, interest, and the ability to learn independently.

ASSESSMENT IN THE COURSE OF TEACHING

Preparing report cards is a way for the teacher to think about each individual child and review what she/he has learnt during the term, and what she/he needs to work on and improve. To be able to write such report cards, teachers would need to think about each individual child, and hence pay attention to them during their everyday teaching and interaction. One does not need special tests for this; learning activities themselves provide the basis for such ongoing observational and qualitative assessments of children. Maintaining a daily diary based on observation helps in continuous and comprehensive evaluation. An extract from the diary of a teacher for a week notes the following: ''Kiran enjoyed his work. He took an instant liking to the books that were informative and brief. He says that he likes simple and clear language. In noting down facts, he goes for short answers. He says that it helps him understand things easily. He favours a practical approach.'' Similarly, keeping samples and notes of the child's work at different stages provides both the teacher and the learner herself or himself with a systematic record of his/her learning progress.

The belief that assessment must lead to finding learning difficulties to then be remediated is often very impractical and not founded on a sound understanding of pedagogic practice. Problems regarding conceptual development cannot and do not wait for formal tests in order to be detected. A teacher can, in the course of teaching itself, come to know of such problems by asking questions that make children think or by giving them small assignments. She can then attend to them in the process of teaching—by ensuring that her planning is flexible and responsive to the learners and their learning.

CURRICULAR AREAS THAT CANNOT BE 'TESTED FOR MARKS'

Each area of the curriculum may not lend itself to being 'tested'; it may even be antithetical to the nature of learning in the curricular area. This includes areas such as work, health, yoga, physical education, music and art. While the skill-based component of physical education and yoga could be tested, the health aspect needs continuous and qualitative assessments. Currently, this has the effect of making these subjects and activities 'less important' in the curriculum; these areas are inadequately provided for in terms of material resources and curricular planning, and marked by a lack of seriousness. Further, the time allocated for them is also frequently sacrificed to accommodate special classes. This is a serious compromise with parts of the curriculum that have deep educational significance and potential.

Even if 'marks' cannot be given, children can be assessed for their development in these areas. Participation, interest, and level of involvement, and the extent to which abilities and skills have been honed, are some markers that can help teachers to gauge the benefits of what children learn and gain through such activities. Asking children to self-report on their learning can also provide teachers with insight into children's educational progress and give them feedback on improving curriculum or pedagogy.

DESIGN AND CONDUCT OF ASSESSMENT

Assessments and examinations must be credible, and based on valid ways of gauging learning.

As long as examinations and tests assess children's ability to remember and recall textbook knowledge, all attempts to redirect the curriculum towards learning will be thwarted. First, tests in knowledge-based subject areas must be able to gauge what children have learnt, and their ability to use this knowledge for problem solving and application in the real world. In addition, they must also be able to test the processes of thinking to gauge if the learner has also learnt where to find information, how to use new information, and to analyse and evaluate the same.

The types of questions that are set for assessment need to go beyond what is given in the book. Often children's learning is restricted as teachers do not accept their answers if they are different from what is presented in the guidebooks.

Questions that are open-ended and challenging could also be used. Designing good test items and questions is an art, and teachers should spend time thinking about and devising such questions. The interest and ability of teachers to design good questions can be promoted through district—or state-level competitions. All question papers must be designed graded for difficulty in order to permit all children to experience a level of success, and to gain confidence in their ability to answer and solve problems.

Trying to devise a good and effective open-book examination can be a challenge that we must try to take up in our curricular efforts at all levels of school. This would require teachers and examination setters to emphasise the interpretation and application of learning over the arguments and facts that can be located in the book. There have been successful demonstrations that such examinations can be carried out on a large scale, and that teachers can themselves be trusted with moderating the results of such examinations. In this way, the assessment of projects and lab work can also be made credible and sound.

It is important that after receiving their corrected papers, children rewrite the answers and that these are again reviewed by teachers to ensure that children have learnt and gained something out of the ordeal.

Competition is motivating, but it is an extrinsic rather than intrinsic form of motivation. It is, of course, much easier to establish and to manipulate, and therefore frequently resorted to by teachers and school systems as a way creating and nurturing the drive for excellence. Schools begin 'ranking' children as early as their pre-primary years as a way of inculcating in them a competitive spirit. Such a competitive drive has several negative side effects on learning, often superficial learning is sufficient to create and maintain impressions, and over time students lose their ability to take initiative or do things for the fulfilment of one's own interest; hence, areas that cannot be 'marked' are neglected. This has unhealthy consequences for classroom culture, making children individualistic and unsuited to team work. There is an absurd and unnecessary importance given to term examinations, often accompanied by extreme arrangements of invigilation and secrecy. While the physical and psychological effects of this may not be readily visible until middle school, they frequently lead to high levels of stress in children, and cause early burnout. Schools and teachers need to ask themselves whether there is really much to be gained out of such practices and to what extent learning requires such systems of marking and ranking.

SELF-ASSESSMENT AND FEEDBACK

The role of assessment is to gauge the progress that both learner and teacher have made towards achieving the aims that have been set and appraising how this could be done better. Opportunity for feedback, leading to revision and improvement of performance, should constantly be available, without exams and evaluations being used as a threat to study.

Grading and correction carried out in the presence of students and providing feedback on the answers they get right and wrong, and why. Asking children about why they answered what they did assists teachers in going beyond the written answer to engage with children's thinking. Such processes also take away the frightening judgemental quality of marks obtained in a test, and enable children to understand and focus on their mistakes and learn through these mistakes. Sometimes head teachers object, claiming that correction in the presence of the child reduces 'objectivity'. This is a misplaced concern for 'objectivity', stemming from a competitive system that believes in judging children. Such a concern for 'objectivity' is misplaced in evaluation, which is consistent with educational goals.

Not only learning outcomes but also learning experiences themselves must be evaluated. Learners happily comment on the totality of their experience. Exercises, both individual and collective, can be designed to enable them to reflect on and assess their learning experiences. Such experiences also provide them with self-regulatory capabilities essential for 'learning to learn'. Such information is also valuable feedback to the teacher, and can be used to modify the learning system as a whole.

Every classroom interaction with children requires their evaluation of their own work, and a discussion with them about what should be tested and the ways of finding out whether the competencies are being developed or not. Even very young children are able to give correct assessments of what they can or cannot do well. The role of teaching is to provide an opportunity to each child to learn to the best of his or her ability and provide learning experiences that develop cognitive qualities, physical well-being and athletic qualities, as also affective and aesthetic qualities.

Report cards need to present to children and parents a comprehensive and holistic view of the child's development in many fields. Teachers must be able to say things about each child/student, that conveys to them a sense of individualised attention, reaffirms a positive self-image, and communicates personal goals for them to work towards. Whether it is marks or grades that are reported, a qualitative statement by the teacher is necessary to support the assessment. Only through such a relationship with each child can any teacher succeed in influencing him/her, and contributing to his/her learning. Along with the teacher assessing each child, each student could also assess himself or herself and include this self-assessment in the report card.

Currently, many report cards carry information on subject areas and have nothing to say about other aspects of the child's development, including health, physical fitness and abilities in games, social skills, and abilities in art and craft. Qualitative statements about these aspects of children's education and development would provide a more holistic assessment of educational concerns.

AREAS THAT REQUIRE FRESH THINKING

There are many areas of the curriculum that can be assessed but for which we still do not have reliable and efficient instruments. This includes assessing learning that is carried out in groups, and learning in areas such as theatre, work and craft where skills and competencies develop over longer time scales and require careful observation.

Continuous and comprehensive evaluation has frequently been cited as the only meaningful kind of evaluation. This also requires much more careful thinking through about when it is to be employed in a system effectively. Such evaluation places a lot of demand on teachers' time and ability to maintain meticulous records if it is to be meaningfully executed and if it is to have any reliability as an assessment. If this simply increases stress on children by reducing all their activities into items for assessment, or making them experience the teacher's 'power', then it defeats the purpose of education. Unless a system is adequately geared for such assessment, it is better for teachers to engage in more limited forms of evaluation, but incorporating into them more features that will make the assessment a meaningful record of learning.

Finally, there is a need to evolve and maintain credibility in assessment so that they perform their function of providing feedback in a meaningful way.

ASSESSMENT AT DIFFERENT STAGES

ECCE and Classes I and II of the Elementary Stage: At this stage, assessment must be purely qualitative judgements of children's activities in various domains and an assessment of the status of their health and physical development, based on observations through everyday interactions. On no account should they be made to take any form of test, oral or written.

Class III to Class VIII of the Elementary Stage: A variety of methods may be used, including oral and written tests and observations. Children should be aware that they are being assessed, but this must be seen by them as a part of the teaching process and not as a fearful constant threat. Grades or marks along with qualitative judgements of achievement and areas requiring attention are essential at this stage. Children's own self-evaluation can also be a part of the report card from Class V onwards. Rather than examinations, there could be short tests from time-to-time, which are criterion based. Term-wise examinations could be commenced from Class VII onwards when children are more psychologically ready to study large chunks of material and, to spend a few hours in an examination room, working at answering questions. Again, the progress card must indicate general observations on health and nutrition, specific observations on the overall progress of the learner, and information and advice for the parents.

Class IX to Class XII of the Secondary and Higher Secondary Stages: Assessment may be based more on tests, examinations and project reports for the knowledge-based areas of the curriculum, along with self-assessment. Other areas would be assessed through observation and also through self-evaluation.

Reports could include much more analysis about the students, various skill/knowledge areas and percentiles, etc. This would assist them by pointing out the areas of study that they need to focus on, and also help them by providing a basis for further choices that they make regarding what to study thereafter.

CONCEPT OF INCLUSIVE EDUCATION & UNDERSTANDING CHILDREN WITH SPECIAL NEEDS

INCLUSIVE EDUCATION: DEFINITION AND CONCEPT

Inclusive Education denotes that all children irrespective of their strengths and weaknesses will be part of the mainstream education. Thus, inclusive education means, "the act of ensuring that all children despite their differences, receive the opportunity of being part of the same classroom as other children of their age, and in the process get the opportunity to being exposed to the curriculum to their optimal potential."

Every child is special for his/her parent and, every child has a special need for love, acceptance and a feeling of belongingness. Here, we call **children with special needs** to those who are "different" from their cohorts. They are born equal with some limitations and with the help of inclusion be able to actively participate as equal citizens in all aspects of society and community life. Thus, children with special needs refer to "all those children who require adaptations to the normal process of education due to problems of vision, hearing, movement, learning and intellect." In other words, these children have some kind of **disability**.

Disability: Definitions

Disability refers to any limitations experienced by the disabled in comparisons to able persons of similar age, sex and culture. The UN Declaration on the Rights of Disabled Persons has defined disabled person as "any person unable to ensure by himself or herself, wholly or partly, the necessities of a normal individual and/or social life, as a result of a deficiency, either congenital or not, in his or her physical or mental capabilities".

DISTINCTIONS AMONG IMPAIRMENT, DISABILITY AND HANDICAP

The World Health Organisation (WHO) has made distinctions between the definitions of impairment, disability and handicap as follows:

- Impairment is any loss or abnormality of psychological, physiological or anatomical structure or function generally taken to be at organ level. Impairment is a damage to tissue due to disease or trauma.
- A disability is any restriction or lack of ability (resulting from an impairment) to perform an activity in the manner or within the range considered normal for a human being.
- A handicap is a disadvantage for an individual, resulting from impairment or disability that limits or prevents fulfilment of a role that is normal (depending on age, sex and social cultural factors) for that individual. Handicap is a condition or burden, which is imposed on the person confronted with the disability.

Types of Disability According to PWD Act, 1995

The PWD Act, 1995 has given the following seven types of disability as:

1. Blindness
2. Low Vision
3. Leprosy-cured
4. Hearing impairment
5. Locomotor disabilities
6. Mental retardation
7. Mental illness

EDUCATIONAL PROVISIONS FOR CHILDREN WITH SPECIAL NEEDS

The last two decades of the 19th century has witnessed the knowledge and processes of educating the disabled children through Christian Missionaries. The first school for the deaf was established in Mumbai in 1883 and the first school for the blind in Amritsar in 1887. At that time, it was believed that children with disabilities could not be educated alongwith normal children. Therefore, education to disabled children was offered through special school. This trend continued early sixties of the last century with the help of some international agencies who developed programme of integrated education. Here, children disabilities were placed in regular school so that they could study alongwith their non-disabled 'peers". The integrated education adopts various models for service deliver. Presently the emphasis is on the need to provide education for all in appropriate environment with inclusive philosophy through inclusive education.

Integrated Education for the Disabled Children (IEDC)

With the development of science and technology and improvement in Medical Services and Aggressive neo-natal intervention has ensured that a large number of babies who would earlier have not survived but often with different abilities. The number of differently abled children is on the increasing trend but it is not possible to create the required number of special schools throughout the country to meet this challenge due to the high cost and also due to the fact that the population is so scattered. The best alternative under these situations is to make use of the infrastructural facilities already present in terms of regular schools and integrate children into the mainstream of education.

Consequent on the success of international institutions in introducing differently abled children in regular schools, the planning commission, Govt. of India, in 1971 includes in its plan a programme for integrated education. In 1974, the Union Government introduced a scheme called "Integrated Schools" to do just this. This scheme was later revised and a plan of action formulated. The important aims of IEDC includes:

- Provide educational opportunity to differently abled children in regular schools.
- Facilitate retention of differently abled in the school system.
- Integrate children from special school to common schools.

The scope of the scheme of IEDC includes pre-school training, counselling for the parents, and special training in skills for all kinds of differently abled children. It provides facilities in the form of books, stationary, uniforms and allowances for transport, reader and escort etc.

Project Integrated Education for the Disabled (PIED)

This scheme was launched by MHRD Govt. of India in collaboration with UNICEF in 1987 to strengthen the integration of differently abled into regular schools. Under this scheme, a cluster instead of individual school is given importance. This scheme is an improvement over the special schools in one or many ways and provides a way towards universalisation of elementary education and Education for All including for differently abled children.

ASSUMPTION ABOUT INTEGRATED EDUCATION

Integrated education assumes a process of bringing disabled children into mainstream schools, where the system remains the same. As per the system, the child is the problem. So, it is essential to change the child where the resources are focused on the individual child. The failure is due to the child's problem; he is not able, not ready, not good enough to cope up with the system.

In integrated education; it is the children with disabilities who are seen as the problem, who must be "fixed", "changed" & "adapted" to suit the existing regular, mainstream school. It is the disabled child who is seen as a square peg in a round table. The system remains the same. The onus for successful integration therefore, is on the disabled child.

ASSUMPTION ABOUT INCLUSIVE EDUCATION

Assumptions of inclusive education is opposite to integrated education. Inclusive education assumes that changes the system to fit the child. It is essential to addresses all types of individual needs, not just disability. Teachers and schools are held responsible for children's learning. It focuses on flexibility of curriculum, teacher training and change in environmental. Failure is the problem with the system not with the child. It is quite essential to assumes that all children can learn and that all children need their learning to be supported in diverse ways.

In this model of inclusive education, it is not the child, but the education system, which is seen as a problem. Therefore, it is the system (with all its components) with should be changed, modified & made flexible enough to accommodate the diverse needs of all learners, including children with disabilities. The onus for success is therefore on the flexibility of the system. It focuses on the environment, as the "disabling" cause because it fails to provide appropriate access to equal opportunities for all persons to participate fully in social life.

Though integrated education of differently abled children has gained momentum all over the country since 1974, there are some other possibilities too for these children to get education. For example, the NIOS (National Institute of Open Schooling) offers education which have the advantage of being specially adopted to the needs of every child as well as aimed at giving the child every opportunity to progress at his/her pace. Another example is alternative schooling and community-based rehabilitation programmes.

EDUCATION FOR A COHESIVE SOCIETY

Despite more than half a century of independence, India is struggling for freedom from various kinds of biases and imbalances such as rural/urban, rich/poor, and differences on the basis of caste, religion, ideology, gender etc. Education can play a very significant role in minimising and finally eliminating these differences by providing equality of access to quality education and opportunity.

Equality of opportunity means ensuring that every individual receives suitable education at a pace and through methods suited to his/her being. Children of the disadvantaged, and socially discriminated groups and also those suffering from specific challenges must be paid special attention.

Provision for equal opportunity to all not only in access, but also in the conditions for success is a precondition for the promotion of equality. The curriculum must create an awareness of the inherent equality of all with a view to removing prejudices and complexes transmitted through the social environment and the factor of birth.

EDUCATION OF GIRLS

Equality among sexes is a fundamental right under the constitution of India. The state, however, also has the right to exercise positive protective discrimination in favour of the disadvantaged population groups including women. Emphasis in education has moved from 'Equality of Educational Opportunity' (NPE, 1968) to 'Education for Women's Equality and Empowerment' (1986). As a result, the curricular and training strategies for the education of girls now demand more attention. Besides, making education accessible to more and more girls, especially rural girls, removing all gender discrimination and gender bias in school curriculum, textbooks and the process of transaction is absolutely necessary. There is a need to develop and implement gender inclusive and gender sensitive curricular strategies to nurture a generation of girls and boys who are equally competent and are sensitive to one another, and grow up in a caring and sharing mode as equals, and not as adversaries.

EDUCATION OF LEARNERS FROM DISADVANTAGED GROUPS

For achieving a cohesive society it would be essential to respond to specific educational needs of learners from different sections of the society with special emphasis on the Scheduled Castes, the Scheduled Tribes and the other socially and economically disadvantaged groups. In order to do so, there is a need for integrating the socio-cultural perspectives partly by showing concern for their linguistic specificities and pedagogic requirements. Implications of the multilingual and multicultural environment shall have to be taken care of through specifically devised methodology. Contextualisation of curriculum shall have to be effected through curricular materials. The fundamental rights of the disadvantaged groups have to be consciously incorporated in the curriculum. Even the problem of educating the migrating population shall have to be handled through specific condensed educational programmes based on the main ingredients of the national curriculum.

EDUCATION OF THE GIFTED AND TALENTED

An educational system has the dual role of promoting equality as well as excellence. Education is increasingly called upon to liberate all the creative potentialities of human consciousness. Man essentially fulfils himself in and through creation. It is in the context of this, that education of gifted and talented children assumes great importance. A curricular programme while on the one hand should identify such children, on the other it should also nurture their diverse creative abilities by paying them special attention. It is also important that the identification and nurturance begins right from the earliest stage of education. Moreover, the task of identifying the gifted and talented must be accomplished on the basis of a broad conceptualisation of the process from multiple perspectives rather than as a search for a unitary human attribute. Not only their IQ (Intelligence Quotient) but also their EQ (Emotional Quotient) and SQ (Spiritual Quotient) ought to be assessed.

NATIONAL LEVEL POLICY AND LEGISLATION

Kothari Commission (1964-66)

The Kothari Commission first suggested that the education of handicapped children has to be organised not merely on humanitarian grounds, but also an aspects of utility. The commission emphasised that the education of children with disability should be "an inseparable part of the general education system. The commission also specifically emphasised that the education of children with disability should be "an inseparable part of the general education system. The commission also specifically emphasised. the importance of integrated education in meeting this target as it is cost effective and useful in developing mutual understanding between children with and without disabilities.

National Policy on Education (1986)

The National Policy on Education was adopted by Indian Parliament in 1986. The policy emphasized the removal of disparities, and ensuring equalisation of educational opportunity under its para education of the disabled.

National Policies for Persons with Disabilities (2006)

This recognises that persons with disabilities are valuable human resources for the country and seek to create an environment that provides them equal opportunities, protection of their rights and full participation in society.

Persons with Disabilities (Equal Opportunities, Protection of Rights & Full Participation) Act, 1995

Landmark legislation in the history of special education in India is the persons with Disabilities Act, 1995. This comprehensive Act covers seven disabilities, namely blindness, low vision, hearing impaired, loco-motor impaired, mental retardation, leprosy cured and mental illness.

The Rehabilitation Council of India (RCI) Act, 1992

This Act was passed in 1992 for the purpose of constituting the Rehabilitation Professionals and for maintenance of a Central Rehabilitation Register. It was amended by Rehabilitation Council of India (Amendment) Act, 2000 to provide for monitoring the training of rehabilitation professionals and personal, promoting research in rehabilitation and special education as additional objectives of the council.

LEARNING AND PEDAGOGY

HOW CHILDREN THINK AND LEARN

Children learn from anything and everything they see and act upon. They have learnt a lot before they join school, and they continue to learn outside the school hours. If we believe that children learn only in school, it is because of what we wrongly regard as learning. When a child spends hours on trying to solve a Jigsaw puzzle (say), he/she is often reprimanded by adults for wasting study time. Little do the grown-ups realise that it is through such interesting games that this child may be increasing his/her understanding of shapes and size. And, this learning is taking place outside the school hours, without formal instruction. A curriculum built upon assumptions about children's learning, that ignore this aspect, is also responsible for children losing interest in mathematics or in any formal learning.

From the time a child is born, his/her interaction with the world around his/her starts. He/she perceives things around his/her, and gradually makes sense of them. He/she slowly begins to recognise people and objects, relate more and more to the environment, and observe things through the senses of touch, sight, taste, smell and sound. There are **four different stages** of learning or development that each child goes through.

Sensorimotor

This is from the ages of birth to about two years old. During this time the child's primary mode of learning occurs through the five senses. He/she learns to experience environment. The child touches things, holds, looks, listens, tastes, feels, bangs, and shakes everything in sight. When the child adds motor skills such as creeping, crawling and walking, his/her environment expands by leaps and bounds. The child is now exploring their environment with both senses and the ability to get around.

Preoperational

This is the stages between ages two and seven. During this stage the child is busy gathering information or learning, and then trying to figure out ways that they can used what they have learned to begin solving problems.

During this stage of his/her life child will be thinking in specifics and will find it very difficult to get generalise anything. This is the time when a child learns by asking questions. The child generally will not want a real answer to his question at this point. When he asks why do we have grass .... He simply wants to know that it is for him to play in. No technical answers for know. The child in this age group judges everything on the 'me' basis—How does it affect me? Do I like it?

Concrete Operations Period

This is the period of time when child is between the ages of seven to ten. This is a wonderful age as this is when children begin to manipulate data mentally. They take the information at hand and begin to define, compare and contrast it. They, however, still think concretely.

The concrete operational child is capable of logical thought. This child still learns through their senses, but no longer relies on only them to teach him. He now thinks as well. A good teacher for this age group would start each lesson at a concrete level and then more toward a generalised level. The child, during this period, is very literal in their thinking.

Formal Operations Period

The period begins at about age eleven. At this time the child will break through the barrier of literalism and more on to thinking in more abstract terms. He no longer restricts thinking to time and space. This child now starts to reflect, hypothesize and theorize.

In the formal operation period, children need to develop cognitive abilities. The following is a list of six simple categories of cognitive abilities. The following is a list of six simple categories of cognitive abilities:

1. **Knowledge of facts and principals:** This is the direct recall of facts and principals. **Examples:** memorisation of dates, name, definition, vocabulary words.
2. **Comprehension:** Understanding of facts and ideas.
3. **Application:** Needs to know, rules, principles, and procedures and how to use them.
4. **Analysis:** Breaking down concepts into parts.
5. **Synthesis:** Putting together information or ideas.
6. **Evaluation:** Judging the value of information.

BASIC PROCESSES OF TEACHING AND LEARNING

Teaching-learning process is the heart of education. On it depends the fulfilment of the aims & objectives of education. It is the most powerful instrument of education to bring about desired changes in the students. Teaching learning are related terms. In teaching-learning process, the teacher, the learner, the curriculum & other variables are organised in a systematic way to attain some pre-determined goal.

Essential Aspects of the Teaching-learning Process

According to Diana Laurillard, there are four aspects of the teaching-learning process:

1. **Discussion**—between the teacher and learner.
2. **Interaction**—between the learner and some aspect of the world defined by the teacher.
3. **Adaptation**—of the world by the teacher and action by the learner.
4. **Reflection**—on the learner's performance by both teacher and learner.

According to **Burton** in the figure above

1. Teaching can become effective only by relating it to process of learning.
2. Teaching objective cannot be realised without being related to learning situation.
3. We may create and use teaching aids to create some appropriate learning situation.
4. The strategies and devices of teaching may be selected in such a manner that the optimal objectives of learning area achieved.
5. To understand principles, goals, objectives of education in right perspective.
6. Appropriate learning situation condition may be created for congenial and effective teaching.

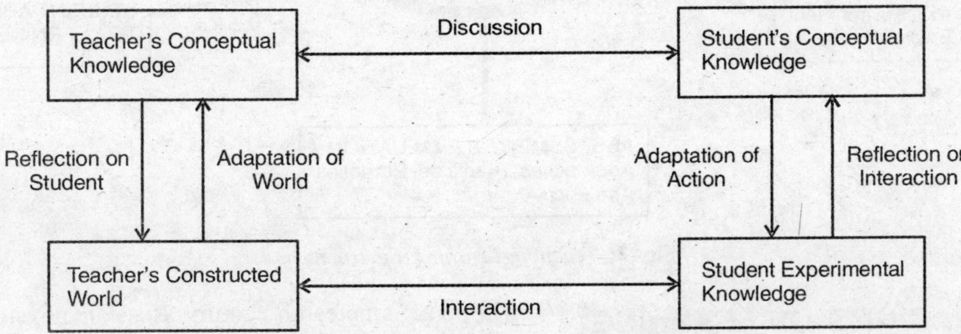

Fig. 1: *Essential aspects of the ideal teaching-learning process*

Approaches to Learning Theories

Aspect	Behaviourist	Cognitivist	Humanist
Learning theorists	Thorndike, Pavlov, Watson, Guthrie, Hull, Tolman, Skinner	Koffka, Kohler, Lewin, Piaget, Ausubel, Bruner, Gagne	Maslow, Rogers
View of the learning process	Change in behaviour	Internal mental process (including insight, information processing, memory, perception)	A personal act to fulfil potential
Locus of learning	Stimuli in external environment	Internal cognitive structuring	Affective and cognitive needs

Aspect	Behaviourist	Cognitivist	Humanist
Purpose in education	Produce behavioural change in desired direction	Develop capacity and skills to learn better	Become self-actualized autonomous
Educator's role	Arranges environment to elicit desired response	Structures content of learning activity	Facilitates development of the whole person
Manifestations in adult learning	Behavioural objectives	Cognitive development	Andragogy
	Competency-based education	Intelligence, learning and memory as function of age	Self-directed learning
	Skill development and training	Learning how to learn	

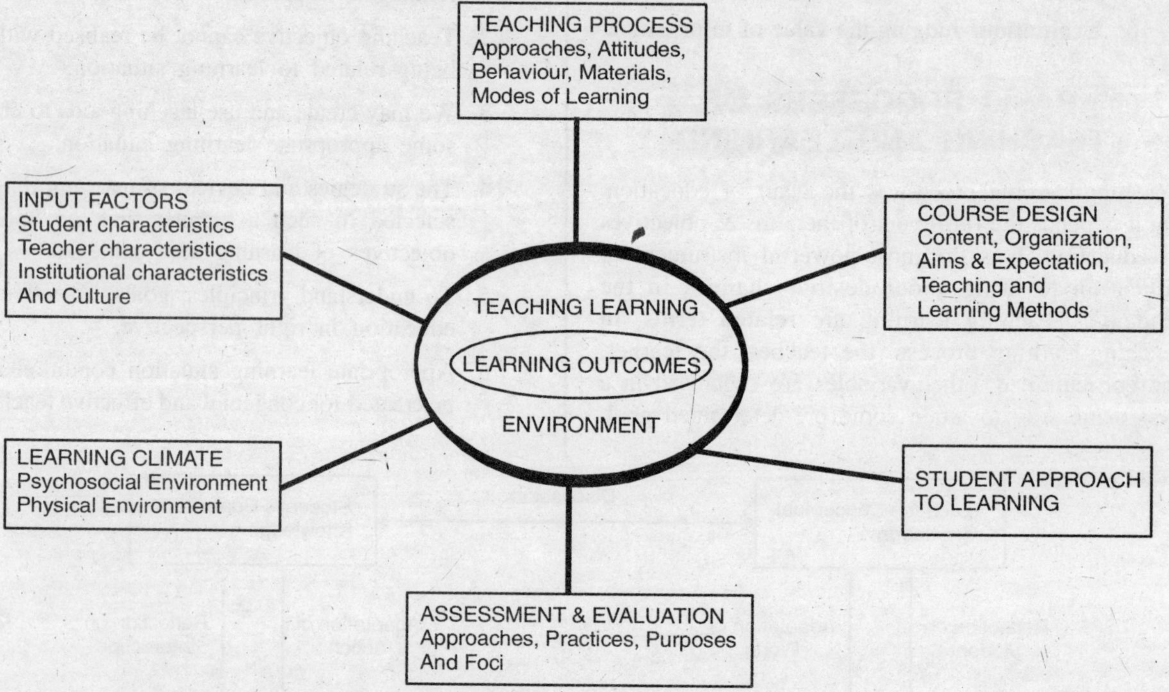

Fig. 2: *Teaching-Learning Environment*

PARADIGMS OF LEARNING

Learning takes place in many ways. There are some methods that are used in acquisition of simple responses while other methods are used in the acquisition of complex responses. The simplest kind of learning is called conditioning. Two types of conditioning have been identified. The first one is called classical conditioning and the second instrumental/operant conditioning. In addition, we have observational learning, cognitive learning, verbal learning, concept learning and skill learning.

Classical Conditioning

This type of learning was first investigated by Ivan P. Pavlov. Like many great scientific advances, classical conditioning was discovered accidentally. The nineteenth-century Russian physiologist Ivan Pavlov was looking at salivation in dogs in response to being fed, when he noticed that his dogs would begin to salivate whenever he entered the room, even when he was not bringing them food. However, when Pavlov discovered that any object or event which the dogs learnt to associate with food (such as the food bowl) would trigger the same response, he realised that he had made an important scientific discovery, and he devoted the rest of his career to studying this type of learning.

Classical conditioning is 'classical' in that it is the first systematic study of basic laws of learning. Classical conditioning involves learning to associate an unconditioned stimulus that already brings about a particular response (*i.e.* a reflex) with a new (conditioned) stimulus, so that the new stimulus brings about the same response. The unconditioned stimulus (or UCS) is the object or event that originally produces the reflexive/natural response.

Once the neutral stimulus has become associated with the unconditioned stimulus, it becomes a conditioned stimulus (CS). The conditioned response (CR) is the response to the conditioned stimulus. Thus, learning situation in classical conditioning is one of S-S learning in which one stimulus becomes a signal of another stimulus.

Determinants of Classical Conditioning

How quickly and strongly acquisition of a response occurs in classical conditioning depends on several factors. Some of the major factors influencing learning a CR are described below:

1. Time Relations between Stimuli: The classical conditioning procedures, discussed below, are basically of four types based on the time relations between the onset of conditioned stimulus (CS) and unconditioned stimulus (US). The first three are called forward conditioning procedures, and the fourth one is called backward conditioning procedure. The basic experimental arrangements of these procedures are as follows:

(*a*) When the CS and US are presented together, it is called simultaneous conditioning.

(*b*) In delayed conditioning, the onset of CS precedes the onset of US. The CS ends before the end of the US.

(*c*) In trace conditioning, the onset and end of the CS precedes the onset of US with some time gap between the two.

(*d*) In backward conditioning, the US precedes the onset of CS.

It is now well established that delayed conditioning procedure is the most effective way of acquiring a CR. Simultaneous and trace conditioning procedures do lead to acquisition of a CR, but they require greater number of acquisition trials in comparison to the delayed conditioning procedure. It may be noted that the acquisition of response under backward conditioning procedure is very rare.

2. Type of Unconditioned Stimuli: The unconditioned stimuli used in studies of classical conditioning are basically of two types, *i.e.* appetitive and aversive. Appetitive unconditioned stimuli automatically elicits approach responses, such as eating, drinking, caressing, etc. These responses give satisfaction and pleasure. On the other hand, aversive US, such as noise, bitter taste, electric shock, painful injections, etc. are painful, harmful, and elicit avoidance and escape responses. It has been found that appetitive classical conditioning is slower and requires greater number of acquisition trials, but aversive classical conditioning is established in one, two or three trials depending on the intensity of the aversive US.

3. Intensity of Conditioned Stimuli: This influences the course of both appetitive and aversive classical conditioning. More intense conditioned stimuli are more effective in accelerating the acquisition of conditioned responses. It means that the more intense the conditioned stimulus, the fewer are the number of acquisition trials needed for conditioning.

Operant/Instrumental Conditioning

B.F. Skinner is regarded as the father of operant conditioning, but his work was based on **Thorndike's law of effect.** In the late nineteenth century, psychologist Edward Thorndike proposed the law of effect. The law of effect states that any behaviour that has good consequences will tend to be repeated, and any behaviour that has bad consequences will tend to be avoided. In the 1930s, B.F. Skinner, extended this idea and began to study operant conditioning. Operant conditioning is a type of learning in which responses come to be controlled by their consequences.

Operants are those behaviours or responses, which are emitted by animals and human beings voluntarily and are under their control. The term operant is used because the organism operates on the environment. Conditioning of operant behaviour is called operant conditioning. Skinner conducted his studies on rats and pigeons in specially made boxes, called the Skinner Box.

Determinants of Operant Conditioning

The operant or instrumental conditioning is a form of learning in which behaviour is learned, maintained or changed through its consequences. Such consequences are called **reinforcers**. A reinforcer is defined as any stimulus or event, which increases the probability of the occurrence of a (desired) response. A reinforcer has numerous features, which affect the course and strength of a response. They include its type—positive or negative, number or frequency, quality—superior or inferior, and schedule—continuous or intermittent (partial).

Reinforcement may be positive or negative. Positive reinforcement involves stimuli that have pleasant consequences. They strengthen and maintain the responses that have caused them to occur. Positive reinforcers satisfy needs, which include food, water, medals, praise, money, status, information, etc. Negative reinforcers involve unpleasant and painful stimuli. Responses that lead organisms to get rid of painful stimuli or avoid and escape from them provide negative reinforcement. Thus, negative reinforcement leads to learning of avoidance and escape responses. For instance, one learns to put on woollen clothes, burn firewood or use electric heaters to avoid the unpleasant cold weather. One learns to move away from dangerous stimuli because they provide negative reinforcement. It may be noted that negative reinforcement is not punishment. Use of punishment reduces or suppresses the response while a negative reinforcer increases the probability of avoidance or escape response. For instance, drivers and co-drivers wear their seat belts to avoid getting injured in case of an accident or to avoid being fined by the traffic police.

Classical and Operant Conditioning : Differences

1. In classical conditioning, the responses are under the control of some stimulus because they are reflexes, automatically elicited by the appropriate stimuli. Such stimuli are selected as US and responses elicited by them as UR. Thus Pavlovian conditioning, in which US elicits responses, is often called respondent conditioning.

   In instrumental conditioning, responses are under the control of the organism and are voluntary responses or 'operants'. Thus, in the two forms of conditioning different types of responses are conditioned.
2. In classical conditioning, the CS and US are well-defined, but in operant conditioning CS is not defined. It can be inferred but is not directly known.
3. In classical conditioning, the experimenter controls the occurrence of US, while in operant conditioning the occurrence of the reinforcer is under the control of the organism that is learning. Thus, for US in classical conditioning the organism remains passive, while in operant conditioning the subject has to be active in order to be reinforced.
4. In the two forms of conditioning, the technical terms used to characterise the experimental proceedings are different. Moreover what is called reinforcer in operant conditioning is called US in classical conditioning. An US has two functions. In the beginning, it elicits the response and also reinforces the response to be associated and elicited later on by the CS.

OBSERVATIONAL LEARNING

The other form of learning takes place by observing others. Earlier this form of learning was called **imitation**. Bandura and his colleagues in a series of experimental studies investigated observational learning in detail. In this kind of learning, human beings learn social behaviours, therefore, it is sometimes called **social learning**. In many situations individuals do not know how to behave. They observe others and emulate their behaviour. This form of learning is called **modelling**.

Examples of observational learning abound in our social life. Fashion designers employ tall, pretty, and gracious young girls and tall, smart, and well-built young boys for popularising clothes of different designs and fabrics. People observe them on televised fashion shows and advertisements in magazines and newspapers. They imitate these models. Observing superiors and likeable persons and then emulating their behaviour in a novel social situation is a common experience.

The children observe adults' behaviours, at home and during social ceremonies and functions. They enact adults in their plays and games. For instance, young children play games of marriage ceremonies, birthday parties, thief and policeman, house keeping, etc. Actually they enact in their games what they observe in society, on television, and read in books.

Children learn most of the social behaviours by observing and emulating adults. The way to put on clothes, dress one's hair, and conduct oneself in society are learned through observing others. It has also been shown that children learn and develop various personality characteristics through observational learning. Aggressiveness, prosocial behaviour, courtesy, politeness, diligence, and indolence are acquired by this method of learning.

COGNITIVE LEARNING

Some psychologists view learning in terms of cognitive processes that underlie it. They have developed approaches that focus on such processes that occur during learning rather than concentrating solely on S-R and S-S connections. Thus, in cognitive learning, there is a change in what the learner knows rather than what he/she does. This form of learning shows up in insight learning and latent learning.

Insight Learning

Kohler demonstrated a model of learning which could not be readily explained by conditioning. He performed a series of experiments with chimpanzees that involved solving complex problems. Kohler placed chimpanzees in an enclosed play area where food was kept out of their reach. Tools such as poles and boxes were placed in the enclosure. The chimpanzees rapidly learned how to use a box to stand on or a pole to move the food in their direction. In this experiment, learning did not occur as a result of trial and error and reinforcement, but came about in sudden flashes of insight. The chimpanzees would roam about the enclosure for some time and then suddenly would stand on a box, grab a pole and strike a banana, which was out of normal reach above the enclosure. The chimpanzee exhibited what Kohler called insight learning—the process by which the solution to a problem suddenly becomes clear.

In a normal experiment on insight learning, a problem is presented, followed by a period of time when no apparent progress is made and finally a solution suddenly emerges. In insight learning, sudden solution is the rule. Once the solution has appeared, it can be repeated immediately the next time the problem is confronted. Thus, it is clear that what is learned is not a specific set of conditioned associations between stimuli and responses but a cognitive relationship between a means and an end. As a result, insight learning can be generalised to other similar problem situations.

Latent Learning

Another type of cognitive learning is known as latent learning. In latent learning, a new behaviour is learned but not demonstrated until reinforcement is provided for displaying it. Tolman made an early contribution to the concept of latent learning. To have an idea of latent learning, we may briefly understand his experiment. Tolman put two groups of rats in a maze and gave them an opportunity to explore. In one group, rats found food at the end of the maze and soon learned to make their way rapidly through the maze. On the other hand, rats in the second group were not rewarded and showed no apparent signs of learning. But later, when these rats were reinforced, they ran through the maze as efficiently as the rewarded group.

Tolman contended that the unrewarded rats had learned the layout of the maze early in their explorations. They just never displayed their latent learning until the reinforcement was provided. Instead, the rats developed a cognitive map of the maze, *i.e.* a mental representation of the spatial locations and directions, which they needed to reach their goal.

LEARNING AS A SOCIAL ACTIVITY

Learning is a social activity. Our learning is intimately associated with our connection with other human beings, our teachers, our peers, our family as well as casual acquaintances, including the people before us or next to us. We are more likely to be successful in our efforts to educate, if we recognise this principle rather than try to avoid it. Much of traditional education, as Dewey pointed out, is directed towards isolating the learner from all social interaction, and towards seeing education as a one-on-one relationship between the learner and the objective material to be learned. In contrast, progressive education (to continue to use Dewey's formulation) recognizes the social aspect of learning and uses conversations interaction with others, and the application of knowledge as an integral aspect of learning.

SOCIAL CONTEXT OF LEARNING

Social Learning theory

Social learning theory focuses on the learning that occurs within a social context. It considers that people learn from one another, including such concepts as observational learning, imitation, and modelling. Among others **Albert Bandura** is considered the leading proponent of this theory.

General Principles of Social Learning Theory Follows:

1. People can learn by observing the behaviour is of others and the outcomes of those behaviours.
2. Learning can occur without a change in behaviour. Behaviourists say that learning has to be represented by a permanent change in behaviour, in contrast social learning theorists say that because people can learn through observation alone, their learning may not necessarily be shown in their performance. Learning may or may not result in a behaviour change.
3. Cognition plays a role in learning. Over the last 40 years social learning theory has become increasingly cognitive in its interpretation of human learning. Awareness and expectations of future reinforcements or punishments can have a major effect on the behaviours that people exhibit.
4. Social learning theory can be considered a bridge or a transition between behaviourist learning theories and cognitive learning theories.

How the Environment Reinforces and Punishes Modelling:

People are often reinforced for modelling the behaviour of others. Bandura suggested that the environment also reinforces modelling. This is in several possible ways:

1. The observer is reinforced by the model. For example, a student who changes dress to fit in with a certain group of students has a strong likelihood of being accepted and thus reinforced by that group.
2. The observer is reinforced by a third person. The observer might be modelling the actions of someone else, for example, an outstanding class leader or student. The teacher notices this and compliments and praises the observer for modelling such behaviour thus reinforcing that behaviour.
3. The imitated behaviour itself leads to reinforcing consequences. Many behaviours that we learn from others produce satisfying or reinforcing results. For example, a student in my multimedia class could observe how the extra work a classmate does is fun. This student in turn would do the same extra work and also receive enjoyment.
4. Consequences of the model's behaviour affect the observers behaviour vicariously. This is known as vicarious reinforcement. This is where in the model is reinforced for a response and then the observer shows an increase in that same response. Bandura illustrated this by having students watch a film of a model hitting a inflated clown doll. One group of children saw the model being praised for such action. Without being reinforced, the group of children began to also hit the doll.

Contemporary Social Learning Perspective of Reinforcement and Punishment

1. Contemporary theory proposes that both reinforcement and punishment have indirect effects on learning. They are not the sole or main cause.
2. Reinforcement and punishment influence the extent to which an individual exhibits a behaviour that has been learned.
3. The expectation of reinforcement influences cognitive processes that promote learning. Therefore, attention pays a critical role in learning. And attention is influenced by the expectation of reinforcement. An example would be, where the teacher tells a group of students that what they will study next is not on the test. Students will not pay attention, because they do not expect to know the information for a test.

Cognitive Factors in Social Learning

Social learning theory has cognitive factors as well as behaviourist factors (actually operant factors).

1. **Learning without performance:** Bandura makes a distinction between learning through observation and the actual imitation of what has been learned.
2. **Cognitive processing during learning:** Social learning theorists contend that attention is a critical factor in learning.
3. **Expectations:** As a résult of being reinforced, people form expectations about the consequences that future behaviours are likely to bring. They expect certain behaviours to bring reinforcements and others to bring punishment. The learner needs to be aware however, of the response reinforcements and response punishment. Reinforcement increases a response only when the learner is aware of that connection.
4. **Reciprocal causation:** Bandura proposed that behaviour can influence both the environment and the person. In fact each of these three variables, the person, the behaviour, and the environment can have an influence on each other.
5. **Modelling:** There are different types of models. There is the live model, and actual person demonstrating the behaviour. There can also be a symbolic model, which can be a person or action portrayed in some other medium, such as television, videotape, computer programs.

Behaviours that can be learned through modelling:

Many behaviours can be learned, at least partly, through modelling. Examples that can be cited are, students can watch parents read, students can watch the demonstrations of mathematics problems, or seen someone acting bravely and a fearful situation. Aggression can be learned through models. Much research indicate that children become more aggressive when they observed aggressive or violent models. Moral thinking and moral behaviour are influenced by observation and modelling. This includes moral judgments regarding right and wrong which can in part, develop through modelling.

Conditions Necessary for Effective Modelling to Occur:

Bandura mentions four conditions that are necessary before an individual can successfully model the behaviour of someone else:

1. **Attention:** the person must first pay attention to the model.
2. **Retention:** the observer must be able to remember the behaviour that has been

observed. One way of increasing this is using the technique of rehearsal.

3. **Motor reproduction:** the third condition is the ability to replicate the behaviour that the model has just demonstrated. This means that the observer has to be able to replicate the action, which could be a problem with a learner who is not ready developmentally to replicate the action. For example, little children have difficulty doing complex physical motion.
4. **Motivation:** the final necessary ingredient for modelling to occur is motivation, learners must want to demonstrate what they have learned. Remember that since these four conditions vary among individuals, different people will reproduce the same behaviour differently.

Effects of Modelling on Behaviour:

Modelling teaches new behaviours.

Modelling influences the frequency of previously learned behaviours.

Modelling may encourage previously forbidden behaviours.

Modelling increases the frequency of similar behaviours. For example, a student might see a friend excel in basketball and he tries to excel in football because he is not tall enough for basketball.

Educational implications of social learning theory:

Social learning theory has numerous implications for classroom use.

1. Students often learn a great deal simply by observing other people.
2. Describing the consequences of behaviour is can effectively increase the appropriate behaviours and decrease inappropriate ones. This can involve discussing with learners about the rewards and consequences of various behaviours.
3. Modelling provides an alternative to shaping for teaching new behaviours. Instead of using shaping, which is operant conditioning, modelling can provide a faster, more efficient means for teaching new behaviour. To promote effective modelling a teacher must make sure that the four essential conditions exist; attention, retention, motor reproduction, and motivation.
4. Teachers and parents must model appropriate behaviours and take care that they do not model inappropriate behaviours.
5. Teachers should expose students to a variety of other models. This technique is especially important to break down traditional stereotypes.
6. Students must believe that they are capable of accomplishing school tasks. Thus, it is very important to develop a sense of self-efficacy for students. Teachers can promote such self-efficacy by having students receive confidence-building messages, watch others be successful, and experience success on their own.
7. Teachers should help students set realistic expectations for their academic accomplishments. In general in my class that means making sure that expectations are not set too low. I want to realistically challenge my students. However, sometimes the task is beyond a student's ability, example would be the cancer group.
8. Self-regulation techniques provide an effective method for improving student behaviour.

CHILD AS A PROBLEM SOLVER AND A SCIENTIFIC INVESTIGATOR

Problem solving is the foundation of a young child's learning. It must be valued, promoted, provided for and sustained in the early childhood classroom. Opportunities for problem solving occur in the everyday context of a child's life. By observing the child closely, teachers can use the child's social, cognitive, movement and emotional experiences to facilitate problem solving and promote strategies useful in the lifelong process of learning.

Problem solving is thinking that is goal-directed. Almost all our day-to-day activities are directed towards a goal. Here, it is important to know that problems are not always in the form of obstacles or hurdles that one faces. It could be any simple activity that you perform to reach a defined goal, for example, preparing a quick snack for your friend who has just arrived at your place. In problem solving there is an initial state (*i.e.* the problem) and there is an end state (the goal). These two anchors are connected by means of several steps or mental operations. Following table would clarify our understanding of various steps through which one solves a problem.

Table: Mental Operations Involved in Solving a Problem

Let us look at the problem of organising a play in school on the occasion of Teachers' Day. Problem solving would involve the following sequence.

Mental operation	Nature of problem
1. Identify the problem	A week is left for teachers' day and you are given the task of organising a play.
2. Represent the problem	Organising a play would involve identification of an appropriate theme, screening of actors, actresses, arranging money, etc.
3. Plan the solution: Set sub-goals	Search and survey various available themes for a play, and consult teachers and friends who have the expertise. The play to be decided, based on such considerations as cost, duration, suitability for the occasion, etc.
4. Evaluate all solutions (plays)	Collect all the information/stage rehearsal.
5. Select one solution and execute it	Compare and verify the various options to get the best solution (the play).
6. Evaluate the outcome	If the play (solution) is appreciated, think about the steps you have followed for future reference for yourself as well as for your friends.
7. Rethink and redefine problems and solutions	After this special occasion you can still think about ways to plan a better play in future.

Learning Through Problem Solving

By exploring social relationships, manipulating objects, and interacting with people, children are able to formulate ideas, try these ideas out, and accept or reject what they learn. Constructing knowledge by making mistakes is part of the natural process of problem solving. Through exploring, then experimenting, trying out a hypothesis, and finally, solving problems, children make learning personal and meaningful. Piaget states that children understand only what they discover or invent themselves. It is this discovery within the problem solving process that is the vehicle for children's learning. Children are encouraged to construct their own knowledge when the teacher plans for problem solving; bases the framework for learning in problem solving; and provides time, space, and materials.

Teacher's Role

Changing through problem solving is modelled by adults and facilitated by the teacher in the classroom environment. When teachers articulate the problems they face and discuss solutions with children, children become more aware of the significance of the problem-solving process. Being a problem solver is modelled by the teacher and emulated by the children. The teacher's role is two-fold: first, to value the process and be willing to trust the learner, and second, to establish and maintain a classroom environment that encourages problem solving. It is the attitude of the teacher that must change first in the problem-solving classroom. Values and goals must be clearly defined to include a child-centered curriculum, the development of communication skills, promotion of cooperative learning, and inclusion of diverse ideas.

The teacher must be willing to become a learner, too. By being curious, observing, listening, and questioning, the teacher shares and models the qualities that are valued and promoted by the problem-solving process.

Planning for Problem Solving

A curriculum that accommodates a variety of developmental levels as well as individual differences in young children sets the stage for problem solving. Choices, decision-making, and a curriculum framework that integrates learning, such as Katz and Chard's project method, are especially appropriate for young learners. The project approach facilitates cooperative learning and promotes diverse ideas. Donna Ogle's K-W-L (what you KNOW, what you WANT to know, and what you have LEARNED) is another method of organizing work that promotes problem solving. Themes, units, webbing, and the KWL method are all ways of organizing curriculum that can support problem solving. Beginning with the needs and interests of the children, problem solving develops from meaningful experiences important to the children. The teacher-designed curriculum provides the classroom basis for these experiences.

For example, a second grade investigation of waste materials from a classroom led one group of young children to explore the topic in an integrated way. Reading, writing, counting, measuring, interviews of community people, and science experiments were planned, initiated and reported. Solutions to many problems posed during the investigation were tried out and some were found to be successful. Through group work, individuals were able to participate and communicate as cognitive and social needs were met. Each child, at individual levels and in individual ways, was successful within the group experience. Problem solving empowers children.

Providing for Problem Solving

Problem solving is a skill that can be learned and must be practiced. It is facilitated by a classroom schedule that provides for integrated learning in large blocks of time, space for ongoing group projects, and many open-ended materials. The teacher provides the time, space, and materials necessary for in-depth learning.

1. Time: Teachers can provide for problem solving by enlarging blocks of learning time during the school day. Because making choices, discussing decisions, and evaluating mistakes takes time, large time blocks best suit the problem-solving process. It is important that children know they have time to identify and solve problems.

2. Space: Projects and group meetings may require an assessment of classroom space. Moving desks and tables together facilitates communication and cooperation in the classroom. Once the teacher has observed the patterns of traffic in the classroom, equipment can be moved or eliminated to promote problem solving.

3. Materials: The open-ended materials that are needed for the construction and concrete solving of problems should be safe, durable, and varied. Well-marked storage units should be easily accessible to children, and materials should be available for ongoing exploration and manipulation. Access to a variety of materials encourages children to use materials in new and diverse ways. This freedom promotes problem solving.

The Problem-Solving Model

Individuals or groups can solve problems. Group problem solving is important to young children because many diverse ideas are generated. Both individual and group processes should be included in the early childhood classroom. Becoming skillful at problem solving is based on the understanding and use of sequenced steps. These steps are:

1. Identifying the problem,
2. Brainstorming a variety of solutions,
3. Choosing one solution and trying it out, and
4. Evaluating what has happened.

Choosing Good Problems

Goffin provides teachers with guiding questions that will help them identify appropriate problems for young children. Some of these are:

1. Is the problem meaningful and interesting?
2. Can the problem be solved at a variety of levels?
3. Must a new decision be made?
4. Can the actions be evaluated?

Problem solving is a way to make sense of the environment and, in fact, control it. The process allows children in an increasingly diverse world to be active participants and to implement changes. By including problem solving in the early childhood classroom, we equip children with a life-long skill that is useful in all areas of learning.

Obstacles to Solving Problems

Two major obstacles to solving a problem are mental set and lack of motivation.

Mental Set

Mental set is a tendency of a person to solve problems by following already tried mental operations or steps. Prior success with a particular strategy would sometimes help in solving a new problem. However, this tendency also creates a mental rigidity that obstructs the problem solver to think of any new rules or strategies. Thus, while in some situations mental set can enhance the quality and speed of problem solving, in other situations it hinders problem solving. You might have experienced this while solving mathematical problems. After completing a couple of questions, you form an idea of the steps that are required to solve these questions and subsequently you go on following the same steps, until a point where you fail. At this point you may experience difficulty in avoiding the already used steps. Those steps would interfere in your thought for new strategies. However, in day-to-day activities we often rely on past experiences with similar or related problems.

Like mental set, **functional fixedness** in problem solving occurs when people fail to solve a problem because they are fixed on a thing's usual function. If you have ever used a hardbound book to hammer a nail, then you have overcome functional fixedness.

Lack of Motivation

People might be great at solving problems, but all their skills and talents are of no use if they are not motivated. Sometimes people give up easily when they encounter a problem or failure in implementing the first step. Therefore, there is a need to persist in their effort to find a solution.

ALTERNATIVE CONCEPTIONS OF LEARNING

When teachers provide instruction on concepts in various subjects, they are teaching students who already have some pre-instructional knowledge about the topic. Student knowledge, however, can be erroneous, illogical or misinformed. These erroneous understandings are termed alternative conceptions or misconceptions (or intuitive theories). Alternative conceptions (misconceptions) are not unusual. In fact, they are a normal part of the learning process. We quite naturally form ideas from our everyday experience, but obviously not all the ideas we develop are correct with respect to the most current evidence and scholarship in a given discipline. Moreover, some concepts in different content areas are simply very difficult to grasp. They may be very abstract, counterintuitive or quite complex. Hence, our understanding of them is flawed. In addition, things we have already learned are sometimes unhelpful in learning new concepts/theories. This occurs when the new concept or theory is inconsistent with previously learned material. Accordingly, as noted, it is very typical for students (and adults) to have misconceptions in different domains (content knowledge areas). Indeed, researchers have found that there is a common set of alternative conceptions (misconceptions) that most students typically exhibit. There is one class of alternative theories (or misconceptions) that is very deeply entrenched. These are "ontological misconceptions," which relate to ontological beliefs (*i.e.*, beliefs about the fundamental categories and properties of the world).

Alternative conceptions (misconceptions) can impede learning for several reasons. First, students generally are unaware that the knowledge they have is wrong. Moreover, misconceptions can be very entrenched in student thinking. In addition, new experiences are interpreted through these erroneous understandings, thereby interfering with being able to correctly grasp new information. Also, alternative conceptions (misconceptions) tend to be very resistant to instruction because learning entails replacing or radically reorganizing student knowledge. Hence, conceptual change has to occur for learning to happen. This puts teachers in the very challenging position of needing to bring about significant conceptual change in student knowledge. Generally, ordinary forms of instruction, such as lectures, labs, discovery learning, or simply reading texts, are not very successful at overcoming student misconceptions. For all these reasons, misconceptions can be hard nuts for teachers to crack. However, several instructional strategies have been found to be effective in achieving conceptual change and helping students leave their alternative conceptions behind and learn correct concepts or theories.

Instructional strategies that can lead to change in students' alternative conceptions (misconceptions) and to learning of new concepts and theories

1. Present new concepts or theories that you are teaching in such a way that students see as plausible, high-quality, intelligible and generative.
2. Use students' correct conceptions and build on those by creating a bridge of examples to the new concept or theory that students are having trouble learning due to misconceptions they hold.
3. Use model-ased reasoning, which helps students construct new representations that vary from their intuitive theories.
4. Use diverse instruction, wherein you present a few examples that challenge multiple assumptions, rather than a larger number of examples that challenge just one assumption.
5. Help students become aware of (raise student metacognition about) their own alternative conceptions (misconceptions).
6. Present students with experiences that cause cognitive conflict in students' minds. Experiences (as in strategy 3 above) that can cause cognitive conflict are ones that get students to consider their erroneous (misconception) knowledge side-by-side with, or at the same time as, the correct concept or theory.
7. Engage in Interactive Conceptual Instruction (ICI).
8. Develop students' epistemological thinking, which incorporates beliefs and theories about the nature of knowledge and the nature of learning, in ways that will facilitate conceptual change. The more naive students' beliefs are about knowledge and learning, the less likely they are to revise their misconceptions.
9. Help students "self-repair" their misconceptions.
10. Once students have overcome their alternative conceptions (misconceptions).

Presenting new concepts or theories

In presenting new concepts or theories, teachers should be sure to show these theories or concepts as:

1. Plausible: The new information should be shown to be consistent with other knowledge and able to explain the available data. Learners must see how the new conception (theory) is consistent with other knowledge and a good explanation of the data.

2. High quality: Of course, the theory/concept to be taught is of high quality from a scientific point of view, since it is a correct theory. However, the presented theory should take a better account of the data than what students currently have available to them. For example, the instructor should deal with the problem from the perspective of the students (*e.g.*, students for whom a "flat earth" theory provides a better account of the data available than does a "spherical earth" theory). Hence, the quality of the new theory must be considered along with the kind of data that students know about.

3. Intelligible: Teachers should do what they can to increase the intelligibility of the new theory. Learners must be able to grasp how the new conception works. To increase intelligibility, teachers can use methods such as use of:

(*a*) analogies,

(*b*) models, and

(*c*) direct exposition.

4. Generative/fruitful: Teachers should show that the new concept/theory can be extended to open up new areas of inquiry. Learners must be able to extend the new conception to new areas of inquiry. Teachers might accomplish this by illustrating the application of the new concept/theory to a range of problems. These problems can include familiar ones and new ones.

UNDERSTANDING CHILDREN'S 'ERRORS' AS SIGNIFICANT STEPS IN THE LEARNING PROCESS

The legacy of Jean Piaget to the world of early childhood education is that he fundamentally altered the view of how a child learns. And a teacher, he believed, was more than a transmitter of knowledge she was also an essential observer and guide to helping children build their own knowledge.

As a university graduate, Swiss-born Piaget got a routine job in Paris standardizing Binet-Simon IQ tests, where the emphasis was on children getting the right answers. Piaget observed that many children of the same ages gave the same kinds of incorrect answers. What could be learned from this?

Piaget interviewed many hundreds of children and concluded that children who are allowed to make mistakes often go on to discover their errors and correct them, or find new solutions. In this process, children build their own way of learning. From children's errors, teachers can obtain insights into the child's view of the world and can tell where guidance is needed. They can provide appropriate materials, ask encouraging questions, and allow the child to construct his own knowledge.

Piaget's continued interactions with young children became part of his life-long research. After reading about a child who thought that the sun and moon followed him wherever he went, Piaget wanted to find out if all young children had a similar belief. He found that many did indeed believe this. Piaget went on to explore children's countless "why" questions, such as, "Why is the sun round?" or "Why is grass green?" He concluded that children do not think like adults. Their thought processes have their own distinct order and special logic. Children are not "empty vessels to be filled with knowledge" (as traditional pedagogical theory had it). They are "active builders of knowledge-little scientists who construct their own theories of the world."

COGNITION & EMOTIONS

What is Cognition?

Cognition is the ability to preceive, memorise, reason and understand. These abilities change with age. As the child grows, her thinking becomes more mature and efficient. Therefore, cognition can simply be defined as the process of acquiring, processing, organising and using knowledge. The development of cognition means development of all these abilities. A child's thinking changes as result of both age (maturation) and increased experiences.

Major Cognitive Characteristics of Children

Infancy

It is interesting to see the number of changes that take place in the first two years. Children at this stage are very active learners. Even when it seems the child is only lying and looking at nothing (e.g. 2 month old) she is actually looking at and trying to understand the things around her.

The first two years children begin by exploring their own bodies and move to the outside objects. Children at 2/3 months discover their thumb or hand or occasionally their own foot. These fascinate them they try to play with them. For a two month old a toy is not as satisfying as her/his own thumb in her/his mouth. Gradually, by about six months, children begin to play with objects outside the body. This could be the toy, the sheet, the bottle, etc. Later, by two years they can even indulge in pretend play [example doctor-doctor, house-house, etc.].

What children also achieve by two years is the understanding of object permanance. **Object**

permanance is the understanding that things exist even if you can not see them. Let us take an example. If you show a five month old a toy she gets excited. If you hide the toy the child soon forgets that any toy even existed. This is because she thinks out of sight is out of mind. Do the same thing with a 1½ year old and you will find the child is either looking for it or asks you to find it. This is because she knows the toy exists even if she can not see it. This understanding, that things exist even if you can not see them, is called object permanance.

The other major development that happens by two years is that children begin to learn the symbols. What are symbols? A two year old can convey her thoughts and desires through language. All these are essential processes of cognition.

Early Childhood

This is a period when the childs mastery in use of symbols increases. We can observe this in the everyday behaviour and activities of the child, *i.e.* in what she plays, her language etc. Gradually her representations of objects become more flexible and less self centred. A one year old while playing does not need a toy phone to pretend speaking on the phone. She can use any object. This is indicative of flexibility in thinking. Gradually, children also start directing play between dolls, *e.g.,* one doll is the mother and the other doll the child. This is indicative of the child moving away from self to becoming less self centred.

Children at this stage also believe that all objects have feelings like human beings. That is why you will often see the child feeding her teddy bear.

Children at this stage can also focus on only one aspect of a situation and can not go back. Let us now take an example. You offer cola to a 4 yr old in a tall glass. You then change your mind and pour the coke from the tall glass to a short glass and give it to the child. You will find the child will say I want the big glass. This is because she can only focus on one aspect (height) at a time. Also, she is not able to go back mentally and realise that in the process of pouring from big to small glass, no cola was taken away.

Similarly, take two plates and put in one 6 pieces of chocolate spreadout and in the other make a tower of 6 pieces of chocolate. You will find the child thinking the spread out chocolate is more. This is because the child can only focus on one aspect at a time. This limitation seriously restricts the problem solving and logical thinking abilities of the child.

It also indicates the child's inability to understand that another point of view different from her own can exist, *e.g.,* you often find children responding to your question by nodding their heads, even if they are not in the same room as you. This is because they do not see another's point of view.

Middle Childhood

During this period, children begin to understand that another view point can exist. They are also able to focus on more than one aspect of a situation and go back and forth on their thinking. This makes their thinking more logical and efficient. However, children are only comfortable with concrete ideas/objects. It means, something that is real for them, *i.e.,* either something they have seen, *e.g.,* a house or something is in front of them, a plant or something linked to what they know, *e.g.,* blue like the sky. They are not able to think about abstract ideas, *e.g.,* what would happen if everyone could fly?

Emotion

Emotions, put simply, are feelings. In infants we can see these very clearly in the form of joy, anger and fear. These are similar to the emotions that adults have.

1. **The variety of emotions increases with age:** The basic emotions of joy, fear, anger are visible in infants. Gradually, as a sense of self develops; children begin to relate with people around them and value their opinions. Then we can see the emotion like pride, shame, sympathy, guilt also developing in them.
2. **The expression of emotion also changes with age:** Emotions are both innate and learnt. The instinctive response to a stimulus is innate but how to express that feeling is learnt, *e.g.* taking away of a toy makes the child angry (innate) but instead crying she is encouraged to ask for it back (learnt). Frustration tolerance increases with age. As children grow older, their responses change in both as well as instinctive method of expression, *e.g.,* when 2 year old falls downs she cries loudly and later forgets quickly. A 6 year old on the other hand, may not cry but forgets far less easily.
3. **The triggers or cause of emotions change with age:** The stimuli that elicit emotion also change with age, *e.g.,* an infant may cry on hearing the loud explosion of a cracker but a middle childhood child may laugh. Sucking a thumb may give great joy to an infant but provides no pleasure to a child is middle childhood.
4. **The coping techniques change with age:** Methods of coping with frustration and stress change with age. While a younger child may cry, or cling to the adult, an older child is likely to suppress the emotion.

Factors Affecting Emotional Development

If we look round in our environment, we will find that people differ in the emotions they experience and express. Some are happy, some are angry, some moody, some helpful. What then affects our emotional development?

1. **Parenting style:** Democratic parenting where induction is used as a method of disciplining allows for more mature emotional development and also for development of personal behaviour.
2. **Role model:** There are two factors which influence what a child ultimately learns:
   (i) How adults and others in the child's environment handle their emotions.
   (ii) How successful is the emotional expression in achieving their needs.
3. **Violence in the child's environment:** The kind of behaviour the child see in the community (*e.g.* during riots) or on TV will affect her expressions of emotions.
4. **Cultural norms:** Emotional expressions are learnt from the environment. It is the environment that tells us how to react in a situation (*e.g.* some people feel the emotion of fear when a black cat crosses their path). It is also the environment that tells us the acceptable way of expressing ones emotions (*e.g.* in many families it is unacceptable for boys to express their distress by crying). Therefore, our cultural beliefs and values also influence our emotional development.

MOTIVATION AND LEARNING

Motivation

Motivation is the heart of the learning process. It generates the will in an individual to do something. Adequate motivation not only engages the student in an activity which results in learning, but also sustains and directs learning. Two types of motivation are commonly recognised. These are: intrinsic and extrinsic motivation.

Intrinsic motivation arises when the resolution of tension is to be found in mastering the learning task itself; the material learned provides its own reward. For example, the student who studies the construction of model aeroplanes diligently so that he can make a model, is experiencing a kind of intrinsic motivation.

Extrinsic motivation occurs when a student pursues a learning task, but for reasons which are external. If a student engages in construction of model aeroplanes because he thinks it will please his father, who is an ex-pilot, rather than because of intrinsic motivation. We should remember that in most learning situations motivation can not be dichotomised so neatly. It is the function of the total learning situation and hinges on some blend of personal concern for the work itself and the concern for some extrinsic factors as well. As a working principle, motivation is probably a function of an interactive situation where reward to a particular action acts as an incentive. Some of the common forms of extrinsic motivation are:

- **Purposive striving, goals and ideals:** The goal and purposes of learning clearly perceived by the individual, provide strong motivation for better action and learning.
- **Knowledge of results:** Knowledge of results in terms of success and failure provides incentive for greater efforts on the part of the student. If a student practices a task without knowing the accuracy or inaccuracy of his performance, he may practise wrong task. In such a case, all learning will be futile. Therefore, if results of performance are known to the student, he learns better as compared to when he does not know about the results. Mere repetition of a task without knowledge of its results fails to bring about learning. Knowledge of results serves two purposes: (i) it enables the subject to evaluate his efficiency and to change his responses in the direction of greater accuracy, and (ii) it adds to the satisfaction in reaching a goal, one tends of repeat rewarded responses.
- **Punishment and rewards:** Punishment can be understood as an act of inflicting pain deliberately with the purpose of affecting the future conduct of an individual being punished. Punishment is based on fear of physical pain, embarrassment and loss of status. Thus, punishment of fear of being punished is one of the common and obvious methods of keeping under control and guiding the students. Punishment or fear is a very strong stimuli, a negative incentive to learning especially when errors occur. Thorndike showed that generally punishment speeds up learning and reduces the number of errors as it produces emotional excitement which tends to fix at punished response. But it does not mean that punishment under all the circumstances and with all the students is equally effective. For example, it may prove disastrous and destructive when task is very difficult.

  Contrary to punishment, rewards are certainly better and positive incentives to learning. They are responsible for initiative, energy, competition, self-expression and creative ability. According to law of effect, reward is satisfying and pleasant, thus reward strengthens learning. Rewards may in the form of gifts, prizes, money, badges, cups, certificates of merit, or other objects of some value. Motivation through such objects feeds the natural drive in all the human beings. But, when these rewards are too much strived for, they degenerate the whole learning.

- **Praise and blame:** These are also strong incentives for effective learning. Praise stimulates average and inferior children, but has less effect on those of superior intelligence. Reproof is felt most by superior children, but girls seem more susceptible to praise than do boys. Regardless of age sex, or initial ability, praise is the most effective of the incentives. Reproof seems to be less effective for all students. Chase (1932) reported praise to be less effective than blame with young children, but Hurlock (1920) generalised, still accepted by contemporary investigators, that praise is more effective stimulus in motivating both immediate and long-continued tasks.
- **Rivalry:** The rivalry between students which leads to resentment, jealousy, etc., or rivalry between groups of students which creates hatred, is the least desirable type of incentive to be encouraged in the schools. Self-rivalry or rivalry in the form of healthy competition is the most valuable type. This tendency should be developed in the student. Though experimental researchers have shown rivalry to be a powerful motivation influence, the emotional and social consequences of rivalry must be considered by the teacher.

Functions of Motivation

The major functions of motivation in learning are as follows:

- To energies the students in learning
- To direct behaviour
- To select behaviour
- To help capture the attention
- To help in acquiring knowledge
- To help in character formation
- To develop social qualities

Attention in Relation to Motivation

Attention is the basic pre-requisite of all learning in the classroom. Learning is possible only if students concentrate their attention on the object or stimuli to be learnt. Attention increases the amount and rate of learning, and also the efficiency of work.

Attention is closely related to motivation. Attention is motivated behaviour, in which the student makes a variety of efforts for achieving the goal. Thus motivation helps in capturing attention. You can help your students by motivating them to concentrate their attention on the tasks to be learnt by them.

Between the two types of motivation, intrinsic motivation should be preferred to extrinsic motivation. It produces better learning because it is related to interest. The learner pursues the activity in which he has interest without waiting for any external pressure. When the learner does not show any intrinsic motivation or interest in learning we have to resort to extrinsic motivation by the use of 'incentives'—whether financial or non-financial (monetary or non-monetary)—such as rewards, awards, prizes, competitions, praise, etc.

In-built Motivation

Another type of motivation is called in-built motivation. Whatever may be the type of motivation, it should be an in-built component of the whole programme of education/training. Right type of trainers, attractive and need-based reading materials, supportive training methodologies, constant awareness of the new dimensions of the programme will facilitate motivation in an in-built manner.

Theories of Motivation

The main theories of motivation are: (a) Psycho-analytic Theory, (b) Maslow's Theory of Self-actualisation, (c) Physiological Theory and (d) Achievement-Motivation Theory.

Psycho-Analytic Theory

According to this theory, motivation gives the vital life forces which are the prime mover of life and its activities. 'It is will power that motivates a person', *i.e.,* 'no will power—no activity'. All these versions agree on one point *i.e.,* 'building ego of man'.

Maslow's Theory of Self-Actualisation

This theory is based on human needs and their satisfaction. Maslow (1998) has arranged man's basic needs in a hierarchy, *i.e.,* some needs are strong or more important than others. According to him the five basic needs, progressing from physiological needs through safety needs, love, esteem needs and the need for self-actualisation. These basic needs are described here under:

- **Physiological needs:** Maslow states that physiological needs are undoubtedly the most powerful of all needs. Examples are the needs for food, sleep or rest. Until the biological needs are met, an individual may lack awareness of other needs. When a person is gratified he/she is released and higher needs can emerge. Some potential adult learners from low-economic background actually have unmet physiological needs, such as hunger, which prevent them from learning. An old person may not be able to see or hear well and he might not be open to satisfying other needs.

- **Safety Needs:** When physiological needs are satisfied, safety needs emerge, such as need for security, for physical safety, for stability in one's life. Safety needs are seen when a person prefers the familiar over the unfamiliar. An adult would rather go to a meeting in a building with which he is familiar than in a building new to him.
- **Love or Belongingness:** If both the physiological and safety needs are gratified, the needs for love, affection and belongingness emerge. Love needs involve both giving and receiving love. They involve the feeling of being wanted. The person who does not feel he belongs, no matter what the reason, probably will not continue with the group and discontinue his participation in adult education programme. The teacher should be affectionate towards adult learners and develop a group spirit among learners.
- **Esteem:** All people in our society have a need, a desire, for self-respect or self-esteem and for the esteem of others. There are two types: The desire for achievement and the desire for prestige or recognition from others. Satisfaction of the need for self-esteem leads to feelings of self-confidence and of being useful to the society. Thwarting of these needs produce feelings of inferiority or weakness. Fear or failure or lack of self-esteem might prevent an adult from participating in educational activities.
- **Self-Actualisation:** Even after the earlier needs are satisfied a person might still feel restless unless he becomes everything he is capable of becoming. This is called self-fulfilment or self-actualisation. The specific form of this needs varies from person-to-person. One person might desire to be an ideal mother or an ideal leader.
- **Implications for Adult Learning:** Before starting the adult education class, the basic needs of the learners should be studied. It may be possible that due to poverty and less per capita income, the basic biological needs of the learners may not be fulfilled. Then the main aim of adult education should be to provide regular income to the learners. This can be done by starting various income generating projects. The educators should also help by marketing of such products produced by the learners. The officials connected with adult education should take steps to start such programmes. This will make the classes more interesting to the learners. The teacher needs to strengthen the group spirit among learners and should identify himself/herself with the group. The learning experiences in the centres should promote the talents, attitudes capacities and potentialities of adults.

Physiological Theory of Motivation

This theory has been developed by Clifford Morgan and William James. According to this theory of the body determines attitudes and interests and explains activities and behaviour of people.

Implications for Adult Education: Participa-tion in physical activities decrease with age so also interests change as a person becomes older. Many physical limitations affect the amount of time an adult has for educational activities. After working all day at a job, some adults are too tired to participate in educational activity, such people can be motivated giving them work which gives them relaxation. Hearing and vision also decrease with age. The ages of the group members will determine the size of letters that a teacher writes on a black board, the colour of the chalk used, the size of the articles he holds for the adults to see, and how loudly and distinctly he speaks. The size, type and quality of handout material are also important.

Achievement-Motivation Theory

This theory has been developed by McClelland (1985). According to this theory all human behaviour is intended to reduce tension and reach a state of physiological and psychological equilibrium. It is a desire to do better, to achieve unique accomplishment, to compete with a standard of excellence and to involve oneself with long term achievement goals. It can be identified on the basic of individual expectation of success. It applies only when the individual knows that his/her performance will be evaluated by himself or by others in terms of excellence, and that the consequences of his action will either succeed or fail.

FACTORS CONTRIBUTING TO LEARNING

Introduction

Learning, can be considered as the process by which skills, attitudes, knowledge and concepts are acquired, understood, applied and extended. All human beings, whether grown ups or children engage in the process of learning, either consciously, sub-consciously or subliminally. It is through learning that their competence and ability to function in their environment get enhanced. It is important to understand that while we learn some ideas and concepts through instruction or teaching, we also learn through our feelings and experiences. Feelings and experiences are a tangible part of our lives and these greatly influence what we learn, how we learn and why we learn.

Learning has been considered partly a cognitive process and partly a social and affective one. It qualifies as a cognitive process because it involves the functions of attention, perception, reasoning, analysis, drawing of conclusions, making interpretations and giving meaning to the observed phenomena. All of these are mental processes which relate to the intellectual functions of the individual. Learning is a social and affective process, as the societal and cultural context in which we function and the feelings and experiences which we have, greatly influence our ideas, concepts, images and understanding of the world. These constitute inner subjective interpretations and represent our own unique, personalized constructions of the specific universe of functioning. Our knowledge, ideas, concepts, attitudes, beliefs and the skills which we acquire are a consequence of these combined processes.

CLASSIFICATION OF FACTORS: PERSONAL & ENVIRONMENT

To understand how we categorise the factors affecting learning, let us begin by considering the following examples:

- Ravi is sixteen year old and wants to please his mother by getting good results in his board examinations. He is so eager to please her, that he spends long hours of concentrated time and energy on his studies. He consciously tries to control other sources of distraction in his life and reduces the time spent on watching television, playing games and chatting with his friends.
- Rita Williams wants to be a famous tennis player. To achieve her goal, she practices tennis whenever she can, even though she gets no encouragement from her family. She makes it a point to watch tennis matches and maintain a good rapport with her sports teacher.
- Yuvraj is a good student, but lately he has been scoring very low marks at school. He is not able to concentrate or pay attention and his class work and home assignments reflect a very poor quality. Sources revealed that his parents fight a lot with each other and are about to get divorced.
- Arti and Kavita are two sisters. Arti is very good at art and craft and can sketch just about anything she sees. Kavita has a ear for music. She knows most songs and can sing them even if she has heard them only once. Both of them spend hours together pursuing their respective interest areas.
- Sayeeda is tall, attractive and has a very good figure. She wants to be a model or an air-hostess and nurtures this secretly as her dream. She is too scared to share her wishes with her family, since she belongs to an orthodox family, where girls at best can pursue teaching as a career. When she tries telling her mother what she wants, she is firmly told that she can only do her B.Ed and can go to the coaching classes for these.

The above cited examples illustrate that learning is a universal phenomenon mediated by a number of factors, both personal and environmental in nature. The dictum "everybody learns" is as true as its corollary, *i.e.*, everybody learns in accordance with his/her unique, individualized blend of personal and environmental factors. For example, in case of Ravi, the desire to please his mother, striving to do well in his board exams and managing his life situations appropriately constitute the key factors which influence him. For Rita Williams, it is her intrinsic desire to be a good tennis player which is paramount. She is not deterred by the lack of family support and continues to make efforts to promote her love for tennis on her own and fulfil her desire to be successful.

In case of Yuvraj, in spite of his innate capacity to study and perform well, his lack of achievement can be attributed to the emotional insecurity stemming from his parents' divorce. As far as Arti and Kavita are concerned, their special interests and talent in art and music respectively, seem to guide their activities.

For Sayeeda, the home environment and family culture and values determine her professional choice. Her own inner interests, desires and wishes are not to be taken into cognizance.

In all the examples cited, we can find evidence of both personal and environmental factors influencing the process of learning. Learning can thus be defined as a function of the interaction of personal and environmental factors.

$L = f(EF \times PF)$

L = learning; f = function; EF = environmental factors; PF = personal factors.

Personal factors are the intra individual factors like motivation, interests, abilities etc which predispose an individual towards learning as in the case of Rita Williams, Arti and Kavita. Environmental factors on the other hand, are those contextual factors which highlight the role of the environment in learning, such as the socio-emotional, societal and cultural factors as seen in the case of Yuvraj and Sayeeda. Although the two factors represent different categories, they operate in a common system. The environmental factors provide the context within which the personal factors, operate. The learner and the learning process can only be completely understood with reference to the interaction of both environmental and personal factors. This may be diagrammatically represented as follows:

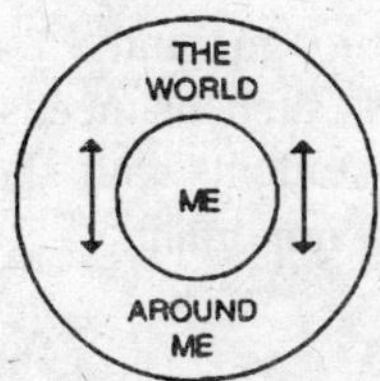

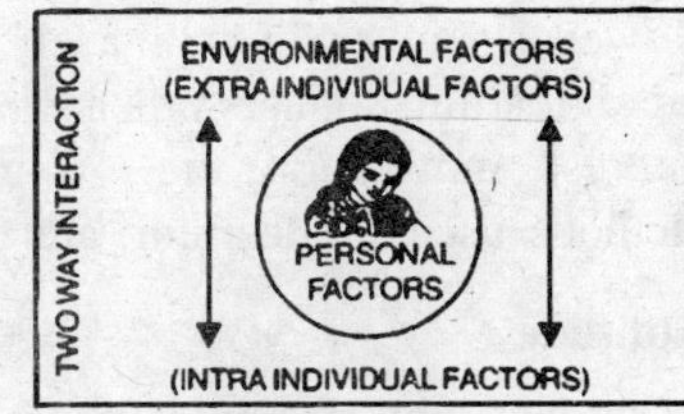

Fig: *Factors affecting learning*

Personal Factors Influencing Learning

The process of learning is influenced by a variety of personal factors. A thorough knowledge of these factors will prove very helpful for teachers and parents in understanding and guiding their children's learning. Some of the personal factors that influence the learning process may be classified as under : sensation and perception, fatigue and boredom, maturation, emotional condition, needs, interests, motivation, attention, intelligence, aptitude, attitude, etc. Let us discuss the important personal factors in the following sub-sections.

Sensation and Perception

Apart from the general health of the students, sensation and perception are the psychological factors which help in learning. Sensation is at the core of perception. There are five sense organs *i.e.*, skin, ears, tongue, eyes and nose. These sense organs are the gateways of knowledge and help in perception of various stimuli in the environment. Any defect in any of the sense organs will affect learning and hence acquisition of knowledge. For example, defects of vision such as myopia, hypermetropia, astigmatism, etc., cause headaches, nausia and general disinclination to study. A blind person depends upon the sense of touch or skin for learning and thus acquires knowledge and skills, as he can not visualise the objects. The stimuli are preceived and assimilated, and hence learnt through various sense organs. In this way we can say that sensation and perception is the bases of knowledge and learning.

Fatigue and Boredom

It is virtually boredom or lassitude rather than fatigue which bothers the students. The difference between the two is that fatigue is mental or physical tiredness which decreases in efficiency and competency to work. Boredom, on the other hand, is a lack of desire on an aversion to work. Such an aversion makes one feel fatigued without being actually fatigued. Studying seldom causes fatigue. It is mainly boredom which, besides causing the impression of fatigue, decreases student efficiency in learning.

Age and Maturation

Learning is directly dependent upon age and maturation. No learning can take place unless individual is matured enough to learn. Some children can learn better at earlier age while others take more time to learn the same content.

Mental age increases with the chronological age and ceases at about the age of sixteen years. Increase in age means intellectual maturation which helps in solving difficult problems. The principle of maturation warns us against enforcing learning on a child when he is not mature enough to learn the specific skills. Teachers should explain this principle to parents who are over ambitious or over enthusiastic in sending their children to school at the very early age.

Emotional Conditions

Desirable emotional conditions enhance the quality and speed of learning. Happiness, joy and satisfaction are always favourable for any type of learning. Adverse emotional conditons, on the other hand, hinder learning. Many studies have established the fact that emotional strain, stress, tensions, disturbances, etc., are extremely inimical to scholastic pursuits.

Needs

A need is the lack of something which, if provided, would facilitate child's usual behaviour. The lack of something is experienced by the child. The child then tries to perform that activity which culminates in the satisfaction of the need. Thus, the needs are associated with goals. Among human beings, the needs are realtively permanent tendencies which seek satisfaction in achieving certain specific goals. When these goals are achieved, the particular need is satisfied or met for the time being, but it recurs sooner or later and energises further activity. The needs in human beings can be physiological such as need for oxygen, food, water, etc. They may be social such as the need for affection, recognition, self-regard, etc. Social needs are however, quite different from physiological needs. Social needs might originate after physiological needs are satisfied. These needs have a complex structure and dominate the individual's behaviour.

There is not equal urgency in the satisfaction of all needs. Some have to be satisfied before others can manifest themselves.

In schools, children are not expected to do any intellectual thinking unless their physiological needs are satisfied. Poor, starved children may concentrate less on attainment of knowledge than on food. Similarly, very cold or hot classrooms or over-crowded seats will not be conducive to good learning. Likewise the need for safety, love and esteem, all act as powerful motives in the learning situations. If the child is afraid of the teacher or feels unsafe while in the school on account of too much beating or some other form of punishment, no learning can take place. Similarly, his needs for warmth and affection are very stimulating and hence results in effective learning.

Interests

Various types of interests of the students can be exploited to facilitate their learning. The interests during early infancy are mostly limited and short lived. As the child grows older his interests diversify and stabilize. You, a school teacher, should have thorough knowledge of children's interests. You can eliminate much drudgery, monotony and boredom from the school work if you make your instruction lively and stimulating and arouse student interest in it.

Once the students' interest is aroused in an activity you should expend more effort on it. No learning can be achieved without proper expenditure of effort on it. Students can even overcome distraction, fatigue and boredom if they feel interested in your instruction and class activities. It has often been found that, in most cases, fatigue in reality is loss of interest in the learning activity. Interest, should be exploited to yield results of greater quantity and quality learning in school.

Life is so exciting that many interesting things and activities often clamor to attract our attention. Children frequently face the dilemma of mutually conflicting interests. Immediate interests often seem to be clashing with the remoter ones. A student might be in a quandary at least for the time being when his interest in sports impels him towards the play-field and his interest in studies force him to concentrate on books.

In such cases of conflicting interests a lot of hesitancy, wastage, frustration and unhappiness is bound to follow. What is needed is education at home and school which helps/trains children to achieve a healthy balance in their interests. They should be trained to budget their time in such a manner as to pay a reasonable attention to various interests, scholastic, athletic, social etc., within the time at their disposal.

Motivation

Motivation is the heart of the learning process. It generates the will in an individual to do something. Adequate motivation not only engages the student in an activity which results in learning, but also sustains and directs learning. Two types of motivation are commonly recognised. These are: intrinsic and extrinsic motivation.

Intelligence

Intelligence as expressed by an I.Q. score on an intelligence test is positively related to learning. Generally, students with higher I.Q. learn rapidly. However, higher I.Q. in itself is no guarantee for rapid learning, since other factors such as needs, interest, motivation, etc., of the students and the methods used for learning are also important.

Aptitude

A student who possesses appropriate aptitude for a particular subject of study or skill, will learn better and retain it for a longer time. On the other hand, he will require relatively longer time to study a subject for which he lacks natural aptitude. He is liable to forget it soon besides feeling bored and unhappy all the time while learning it. Hence, it is extremely desirable to analyse the aptitude of students before prescribing courses of study for them.

Attitude

The learning process is also influenced considerably by the attitude of the student. If he is alert, attentive and interested in the material to be learnt, he is bound to have a favourable attitude towards it. Such an attitude will enable him to tackle the learning situation economically, pleasantly and effectively. Conversely, if he is inattentive and is uninterested in the material his attitude is bound to be unfavourable. This will hinder the smooth learning of the material in hand besides involving undue strain and tension in the learner.

Environmental Factors

Environmental influences begin since the time of the conception of the child in the womb of the mother. Mother's mental, physical and emotional conditions influence the development of foetus in the womb. The external environment starts from the time of birth of the child. It (external environment) refers to the surroundings which prevail in home, school and locality. At these places, the child interacts with members of the family, teachers, classmates or peers and neighbours and establishes relationship with them. The relationship with the members of the society, and the surroundings may affect the development of the child and also the way he learns. Some of the environmental factors are discussed as follows:

Surrounding : Natural, Social and Cultural

As the title of the sub-section indicates, we shall discuss here natural, social and cultural environment the child interacts with and get influenced.

Natural surrounding covers the climatic and atmospheric condition. These conditions affect learning directly. It has been found that high temperature and humidity reduces mental efficiency. For a limited time, humidity and high temperature can be tolerated but prolonged humidity and high temperature become unbearable and decrease mental efficiency. The intellectual productivity and creativeness of people living in hot regions are much low. Likewise, the morning time is always better for mastering difficult tasks. Mental efficiency decreases due to increased humidity and temperature. Studies on the academic progress of evening school students shows losses of efficiency varying from one to six per cent.

Social surrounding includes especially the environment of home, school and locality. Physical conditions at home such as large family, small family, (specific place of the study), insufficient ventilation, improper lighting, uncomfortable temperature, noisy home environment due to use of radio, TV, etc., noisy neighbourhood, constant visits by friends or relatives, etc., influence the intellectual learning of the student. The socio-emotional factors such as child rearing practices, reward and punishment, scope for freedom and independence in activities and decision making, play and study facilities, ambitions and aspirations of the parents, disorganisation and discord among birth positions such as eldest, youngest or single child have their definite influence on learning. For example, a student who comes from a very poor family and never had any intellectual stimulation at home remains dull and unresponsive in the class. In some societies there is a strong sex bias. Girls are directly or indirectly told that education is not meant for them. In the middle class families, on the other hand, parents are rather over-ambitious. They wish their children to make quick academic progress, grow-up and find a respectable vocation preferably a white collar job. Such children, therefore get sufficient incentive from their families. This, of course, is most favourable to scholastic learning, although an overdose of family emphasis on acquiring academic excellence might affect the child's mental and physical health adversely. Similarly, school activities, study facilities and teaching methods and behaviour of teachers, principals and non-teaching staff have an impact upon learning. If the school atmosphere is unconducive, it adversely affects the learning process. Locality also has an influence on a child. If the locality is bad, the learning will be ineffective to some extent.

Cultural demands and social expectations also influence learning. The spirit of culture is reflected in its social and educational institutions. Children's learning, therefore, is greatly determined by the demands and expectations of their culture. Thus, for instance, in an industrialized culture the emphasis mostly centres mechanical sciences and preparing children for highly mechanised vocations. In an agriculture based community, on the other hand, the educational process focusses on preparing its members for those skills which are suited to the needs of an agrarian community.

The philosophical elements of culture also influence the spirit of children's learning. Children in a democratic culture tend to acquire democrative and values and attitudes. A feudal, aristocratic or dictatorial culture, on the other hand, promotes autocratic modes of thought and behaviour.

Relationship with Teacher, Parents and Peers

The teacher is an important constituent in the instructional process. She/he plays an important role in shaping the behaviour of students. The way he teaches and manages the students has an affect on their learning. An authoritarian teacher will create an aggression and hostility among students while a democratic teacher will create a participatory climate for learning. The democratic environment leads students to constructive, thoughtful and cooperative behaviour. Generally, students learn better in a democratic set up because they like democratic procedures. The teacher is no more an instructor or the director of learning in a democratic set up. She/he helps his/her students in their learning. The teachers no more dominate the scene, they can get better results by decentralizing authority, increasing independence of students. They can attend to the comments and questions of the students. They can encourage students to participate in learning activities in and outside the class. There should be more emphasis on activity-centred classroom where student's active participation in the teaching-learning process is encouraged and the teacher acts as a guide to promote learning.

Relationship with parents plays a vital role in the learning process of the student. If the child-parents relationship is based on mutual respect and faith, it can provide the child a congenial atmosphere which in turn can facilitate his/her learning. A distorted and unhealthy environment, on the other hand, adversely affects the learning of the student. The upward mobility brings resistance on the part of the student to learn. Students in such families find themselves unable to cope up. A subtle but powerful influence on the growing child arises from his/her position among the children in the family. The parents of the first born expect the child to act like miniature adults and hence the first-born are found to encounter a variety of expectations and stresses. Whereas parents tend to be more relaxed in their do's and dont's with the last-born. Factors like traumatic events at home, separation or death can also precipitate learning problems in the normal child.

A healthy peer group relationship also plays an important role in learning. Student-student relationship in the classroom, school, society, etc., create a particular type of emotional climate. The climate solely depends upon their relationships. A sound relationships provides a tension free environment to the student to learn more and to compete in the class. If the relationship among peers is not good, it adversely affects their learning. Therefore, to improve the classroom learning climate, free discussion should be there. You should help your students understand each other in formal or informal meetings. They should be encouraged to meet each other and their teachers freely. If any mis-understanding is created or developed, it should be immediately clarified so as to maintain the healthy climate and cordial relationship among peers.

Media Influence on Learning

Media has been considered an important component of transmitting information. Media can be divided into two broad categories—print and non-print media. Print media refers to texts or printed materials. It is economical and has traditionally been used for pedagogical purposes.

But, it may not be the only or the perfect medium to impart education. Non-print media, also known as modern electronic media, have certain unique qualities which, in certain cases, facilitate learning much more faster than the print medium. These helps meet diverse learning objectives more efficiently than the printed matter.

Certain non-print media formats and delivery systems contribute well to student's learning actitivies, For example, audio tapes or computers can be used effectively to drill and practice in language and learning arithmatic. Electronic media can help promote the discovery approach to learning. For example, a film can be exploited for discovery teaching in the physical sciences. Students keep watching the various sections of the film until they perceive the relationships between the visuals. Then they are curious to find out the principles that explain those relationships. Likewise, in the social sciences various media can be used to present students with visual and auditory experiences that provide related inquiry. Films and stimulation are often used to present real-life or laboratory learning situations to students.

The role of the electronic media has proved effective for teaching students. These excite the student psychologically and prepare/motivate them to participate in teaching-learning activites. Non-print media perform following fuctions:

- direct attention,
- arouse motivation,
- increase student's concentration, and
- help them actively involve in the learning process.

PRACTICE PAPER

1. Mass media, cinema and library are passive agencies of education because
(*a*) learner can not react to the feedback system of these agencies directly
(*b*) they provide informal education
(*c*) they can not come closer to the educant
(*d*) all of these

2. Education of a child really begins
(*a*) Once he takes birth
(*b*) Once he attains the age of three
(*c*) Once he is admitted to post nursery schools
(*d*) Once he learns to speak

3. Family is the original social institution from which all other institutions emerged, who said this
(*a*) Brown (*b*) Ballard
(*c*) Machiver (*d*) None of them

4. Which of the following is not the primary function of schools
(*a*) reorganization and reconstruction of Human experiences
(*b*) all-round development of the child
(*c*) to make the children self reliant
(*d*) advancement of culture

5. In a democratic country, school should reflect
(*a*) National aspirations
(*b*) Community related local aspirations
(*c*) Both of these
(*d*) None of these

6. The best teacher in a village school is he who
(*a*) carries community experiences to the class room
(*b*) prepares instructional programmes in the interest of the community
(*c*) carries classroom experiences to the community
(*d*) all of these

7. Universalisation of education is the concept adopted by
(*a*) modern state (*b*) democratic state
(*c*) totalitarian state (*d*) religious state

8. Secular education in India means
(*a*) an education opposed to religion
(*b*) an education indifferent to religion
(*c*) an education emphasizing equality of religions
(*d*) none of these

9. School works as a social sub system for
(*a*) transmission of culture
(*b*) preservation of culture
(*c*) advancement of culture
(*d*) all of these

10. "Society is nothing but a process of interaction among people." Who said this?
(*a*) Lapier (*b*) Cuber
(*c*) Reuter (*d*) Payne

11. The best model of schooling is
(*a*) Close interaction between education of society
(*b*) Self reliant society by education
(*c*) Reflection of openness by schools
(*d*) All of these

12. Special provisions have been made for socially and educationally backward classes of the nation under article
(*a*) 29 (*b*) 31
(*c*) 15 (*d*) 19

13. Religious education is prohibited in government schools and colleges under Article
(*a*) 29 (*b*) 28 (1)
(*c*) 39 (2) (*d*) 15 (a)

14. Religious and linguistic minorities shall have the right to establish and administer their own educational institutions under Article
(*a*) 30(1) (*b*) 31(2)
(*c*) 40 (*d*) 41

15. Article 351 is about
(*a*) education of tribals
(*b*) promotion of Hindi
(*c*) promotion of secularism
(*d*) English as official language

16. Status of central university is given to any educational institution under union list of
(*a*) Entry 65 (*b*) Entry 63
(*c*) Entry 66 (*d*) None of these

17. Entry 25 of concurrent list states about
(*a*) vocational and technical training of labour
(*b*) the education of working class
(*c*) the education of disabled
(*d*) none of the above

18. Education in the mother tongue at primary stage to children belonging to linguistic minorities has been mentioned in Article
(*a*) 250 (*b*) 350
(*c*) 349 (*d*) 351

19. Educational and economic interests of SCs and STs have been safeguarded under Article
(*a*) 46 (*b*) 45(a)
(*c*) 351 (*d*) 52

20. Education of union territories is administered by the central government under Article
(*a*) 350 (*b*) 229
(*c*) 239 (*d*) 50

21. Education was transferred from state list of subjects to concurrent list in
(*a*) 1976 (*b*) 1972
(*c*) 1980 (*d*) 1950

22. Which of the following statements about growth and development is not correct?
(*a*) Growth generally refers to quantitative changes while development refers to qualitative changes
(*b*) Growth is a function of the environment
(*c*) Growth is not possible without development and vice versa
(*d*) Growth is determined by intrinsic and genetic factors of the organism

23. The limit of growth is fixed by
(*a*) internal factors of the organism
(*b*) nutrition and exercise
(*c*) both of these
(*d*) none of these

24. Development is
(*a*) Maturation
(*b*) Learning
(*c*) Synthesis of abilities
(*d*) All of these

25. Development takes place when
(*a*) environmental forces work on the organism
(*b*) environmental forces interact with the hereditary forces in an organism
(*c*) both of these
(*d*) none of these

26. Which of the following statements about development is correct?
(*a*) Process of development can be improved by exercise and nutrition
(*b*) Development may be positive and negative both
(*c*) Development proceeds from general to specific
(*d*) All of these

27. The son of a goldsmith becomes an expert goldsmith. It is an example of a
(*a*) biological heredity
(*b*) social heredity
(*c*) transfer of instinct
(*d*) none of these

28. All humans contain .... chromosomes.
(*a*) 26 (*b*) 36
(*c*) 46 (*d*) 42

29. DNA test helps us to know
(*a*) the genetic traits of a person
(*b*) nature of personality and its composition
(*c*) both of these
(*d*) none of these

30. The law of inheritance was discovered by Gregor Mendel in
(*a*) 1866 (*b*) 1911
(*c*) 1888 (*d*) 1920

31. Which of the following statements regarding personality traits is correct?
(*a*) Traits of personality can not be developed in isolation without taking the help of environment
(*b*) Subjective traits of the individual are determined by genetic factors
(*c*) Bad environment can surpass good inheritance but good environment is not a substitute for poor heredity
(*d*) All of these

32. Which of the following characteristics denote infancy period?
(*a*) Physical growth is curvilinear
(*b*) Physical growth is rapid
(*c*) Head grows at relatively slower rate as compared to other parts of the body
(*d*) All of these

33. Which of the following is not the characteristic of infancy period?
(*a*) From bilateral to unilateral trend in motor organs
(*b*) From general to specific trend in motor organs
(*c*) Emotional/social development is not associated with motor development
(*d*) Steady mental development

34. Which of the following illustrates conceptual development?
(*a*) Perception is the beginning of concept formation
(*b*) Concept changes with changes in experiences
(*c*) Concept changes with age
(*d*) All of these

35. There is one thing common in language and physical development what is that?
(*a*) Spurts of development at different ages
(*b*) Dependence on experience
(*c*) Dependence on training
(*d*) None of these

36. Which of the following characteristics is not associated with emotional development?
(*a*) Emotion is accompanied by physiological changes
(*b*) Emotions start immediately after birth
(*c*) Intense form of emotions are seen during early childhood period
(*d*) Emotions are unrelated to physical development

37. The child acquires about three fourth of the brain weight by the age of
(*a*) 2½ years (*b*) 2 years
(*c*) 6 years (*d*) 8 years

38. Social development of an infant depends on
(*a*) his chance of interaction with others
(*b*) love and affection shown to the child
(*c*) the extent to which he is able to attract the attention of others
(*d*) all of the above

39. In which of the following stages the child looks self centred?
(*a*) Infancy (*b*) Early childhood
(*c*) Adolescence (*d*) Adulthood

40. In the period of infancy, emotions are
(*a*) intense, frequent and unstable
(*b*) like an open book(overt)
(*c*) need based
(*d*) all of these

41. Which of the following organs of the body shows rapid growth in infancy?
(*a*) growth of hands (*b*) growth of head
(*c*) growth of legs (*d*) growth of fingers

42. In normal learning environment, forgetting is caused
(*a*) due to back of practice for a long time
(*b*) due to the interference of other learnt material
(*c*) due to lack of consolidation of memory traces
(*d*) all of these

43. Clear conception of size, weight, colour, time etc., is seen at the age of
(*a*) six (*b*) four
(*c*) four and half (*d*) five

44. Which of the following is not the characteristics of intellectual development of early childhood?
(*a*) increased span of attention
(*b*) exploration of the environment
(*c*) ability to verbalize all known concepts
(*d*) ability to distinguish past, present and future

45. Social development by the end of early childhood is marked by
(*a*) the feeling of autonomy
(*b*) the end of solitary plays
(*c*) the temperament of co-operation and friendliness
(*d*) all of these

46. Fictional world of the child starts at the age of
(*a*) 5-6 (*b*) 6-8
(*c*) 3-4 (*d*) 4-5

47. Girls are more dominating than boys in social situations in which of the following periods?
(*a*) pre-adolescent period
(*b*) early childhood period
(*c*) both of these
(*d*) none of these

48. In the period of early childhood, child is
(*a*) helpless to hide his emotions
(*b*) seen shifting his emotions very rapidly and frequently
(*c*) guided by his innate tendencies and instincts
(*d*) all of these

49. A nursery teacher should organize
(*a*) group games in the school
(*b*) those games which involve motor organs of the body
(*c*) those games which help the child to manipulate the environment
(*d*) all of these

50. Later childhood is called latency period because
(*a*) creative potentials are dormant
(*b*) sex remains dormant
(*c*) it is a period of inactivity
(*d*) all of these

51. Physical development of later childhood is marked by
(*a*) Auscification of bones
(*b*) Permanent teeth
(*c*) Excessive motor activity
(*d*) All of these

52. Girls surpass boys physically in
(*a*) infancy
(*b*) later childhood
(*c*) early childhood
(*d*) adolescence

53. The period of later childhood is marked by
(*a*) intellectual maturity
(*b*) high muscular energy
(*c*) hero worship
(*d*) all of these

54. Which of the following is not the characteristics of intellectual development of later childhood?
(*a*) High interest in science fiction
(*b*) Increased logical power
(*c*) Careful for future
(*d*) End of imaginary fears

55. Children are very much hateful or indifferent to opposite sex at the age of
(*a*) 11-12 (*b*) 13-14
(*c*) 10-11 (*d*) 15-16

56. Period of later childhood is marked by
(*a*) slow and steady physical growth
(*b*) stability in emotions
(*c*) anger against injustice
(*d*) all of these

57. At the end of later childhood period, the child
(*a*) feels himself superior to girls
(b) becomes independent of his family
(c) wants to become hero
(d) all of these

58. The best place of social development for a 12 years old child is
(*a*) neighbourhood
(*b*) family
(*c*) playground
(*d*) school

59. Group activities and group loyalties are at its peak at the age of
(*a*) 10-12 (*b*) 13-15
(*c*) 8-10 (*d*) 18-20

60. A teacher should not let a 12 years old child any time free because
(*a*) child is always interested to get involve in physical or mental activities
(*b*) spurts of creativity are seen at this age
(*c*) child is frustrated
(*d*) all of these

61. Elektra complex refers to
(*a*) daughter comes closer to the father
(*b*) son comes closer to the mother
(*c*) inferiority complex in the presence of girls
(*d*) none of these

62. According to Freud, super ego is properly developed during
(*a*) latency period (*b*) anal period
(*c*) phallic period (*d*) none of these

63. Development is a process of observable social interaction. This is the opinion of
(*a*) Erikson (*b*) Skinner
(*c*) Robert Sears (*d*) None of these

64. The secondary behaviour of the child according to Robert Sears starts with
(*a*) reinforcement (*b*) imitation
(*c*) modelling (*d*) none of these

65. The period of sensory motor adoptation of Piaget is
(*a*) 0-2 years (*b*) 1-3 years
(*c*) 3-5 years (*d*) 4-6 years

66. The child adopts the view points of others on the basis of consequences of these views in the
(*a*) third stage of Kohlberg's theory
(*b*) second stage of Kohlberg's theory
(*c*) fourth stage of Kohlberg's theory
(*d*) fifth stage of Kohlberg's theory

67. Which of the following is not the view point of cognitive theories of development?
(*a*) moral principles are acquired automatically with age
(*b*) super ego is formed during the period of adolescence
(*c*) Moral values are determined by culture
(*d*) Mural principles are universal

68. Organization of sensory experiences about a particular object is called
(*a*) percepts (*b*) reasoning
(*c*) concept (*d*) none of these

69. The concept building in a person depends on
(*a*) the age and maturity of the person
(*b*) past experiences of the learner
(*c*) intelligence of the learner
(*d*) all of these

70. Agreement on a concept is possible because
(*a*) concepts are subjective
(*b*) concepts are objective
(*c*) concepts are hierarchical
(*d*) b and c both

71. Which of the following statements about concepts is correct?
(*a*) Some concepts are more powerful than others
(*b*) All concepts are universal
(*c*) Concepts are differentiated on the basis of their attributes
(*d*) None of these

72. Which is the highest level of concept formation?
(*a*) formal level (*b*) sensory level
(*c*) concrete level (*d*) none of these

73. How many steps of problem solving has been given by Gates?
(*a*) Six (*b*) Seven
(*c*) Five (*d*) Ten

74. Freeman considers intelligence as an ability
(*a*) to adjust in an adverse situation
(*b*) to learn better and faster
(*c*) to manipulate abstract materials
(*d*) all of these

75. Single factor theory of intelligence was given by
(*a*) Alfred Binet (*b*) Thorndike
(*c*) Freeman (*d*) None of them

76. Which of the following is not the characteristics of 'S' factor according to Spearman ?
(*a*) It is the acquired capacity of the individual
(*b*) Specialization in only one trade is possible
(*c*) It varies from activity to activity in the same individual
(*d*) Individuals differ only in 'S' factor of intelligence

77. In multifactor theory, range is related to
(*a*) Number of tasks that a person can do in a limited period of time

(*b*) Difficulty level of items
(*c*) General intelligence of learners
(*d*) None of these

78. SI model of intelligence was given by J P Guilford in
(*a*) 1911 (*b*) 1904
(*c*) 1967 (*d*) 1975

79. Hierarchy theory of intelligence was given by
(*a*) Jenson
(*b*) Thorndike
(*c*) Burt and Vernon
(*d*) None of them

80. In the pre-Binet period, intelligence was considered as
(*a*) Sensory acuity of the individual
(*b*) Verbal ability of the individual
(*c*) Associative ability of the individual
(*d*) All of these

81. An age scale of intelligence was first developed by
(*a*) Spearman (*b*) Terman
(*c*) Binet-Simon (*d*) None of them

82. Binet-Simon scale of intelligence measures
(*a*) General mental abilities not specific ones.
(*b*) Mental growth of the individual over a period of time
(*c*) The aptitude or level of an examinee not their speed
(*d*) All of these

83. WAIS came into being in
(*a*) 1939 (*b*) 1955
(*c*) 1960 (*d*) 1964

84. Wechsler developed an intelligence test for children in
(*a*) 1939 (*b*) 1949
(*c*) 1955 (*d*) 1956

85. Catell's culture fair test of intelligence was developed in
(*a*) 1960 (*b*) 1961
(*c*) 1965 (*d*) 1955

86. Non-verbal test of intelligence is suitable for
(*a*) deaf and dumb
(*b*) illiterates
(*c*) backward children
(*d*) all of these

87. Intelligence testing is useful for knowing
(*a*) individual difference
(*b*) mental retardation
(*c*) educational backwardness
(*d*) all of these

88. Scores on intelligence tests can not be fully relied on because
(*a*) fatigue level can influence the performance
(*b*) cultural factors can influence the score
(*c*) they generally do not reveal all the mental abilities of a person
(*d*) all of these

89. Who among the following psychologists is of the view that a learner can be motivated by satisfying his needs?
(*a*) Henry Murray (*b*) Abraham Maslow
(*c*) Both of these (*d*) None of these

90. Permanent change in behaviour brought about by experience or training is called.
(*a*) Learning (*b*) Motivation
(*c*) Assimilation (*d*) None of these

91. The book "**A Theory of Motivation**" has been written by
(*a*) Maslow (*b*) K B Madson
(*c*) Murray (*d*) None of them

92. Motivated behaviour of a person is
(*a*) Well directed and well guided towards the goal
(*b*) Agitated until the goal is achieved
(*c*) Both of these
(*d*) None of these

93. Factors affecting motivations are
(*a*) Physiological factors only
(*b*) Psychological factors only
(*c*) Psycho-social factors
(*d*) All of these

94. Process of motivation is affected by all except
(*a*) Habits
(*b*) Mental sets and values
(*c*) Physical factors
(*d*) None of these

95. Which of the following does not come under the category of social motives?
(*a*) Prestige and Status
(*b*) Social approval
(*c*) Personal goal
(*d*) Money hoarding

96. Our action and behaviour is motivated by the desire for getting pleasure and avoiding pain. This is the opinion of
(*a*) Thomas Hobbes (*b*) Descartes
(*c*) Kant (*d*) John Locke

97. Fundamental instincts of humans are inherited rather than acquired. These instincts are the spring of human behaviour. The above opinion was held by
(*a*) Charles Darwin (*b*) Mc Dougall
(*c*) Both of these (*d*) None of these

98. Instinct theory of behaviour was rejected by psychologists on which of the following grounds?
(*a*) Adult behaviour is guided by experience and learning also. It is not always guided by instinct
(*b*) Human behaviour is affected by the cultural factors also

(*c*) Human being is a rational animal. He is not supposed to be directed by instincts only
(*d*) All of these

99. Central motive state was explained by
(*a*) Morgan
(*b*) Mc Dougall
(*c*) Murray
(*d*) None of them

100. Abraham Maslow was basically a
(*a*) Pragmatist (*b*) Humanist
(*c*) Realist (*d*) All of them

101. A self actualized person is one who
(*a*) Does not accept restrictions imposed by the society
(*b*) Always seeks perfection
(*c*) Is very good in inter personal relationship with others
(*d*) All of these

102. The theory of achievement motivation was developed by Mc Clelland of Harward University in
(*a*) 1949 (*b*) 1951
(*c*) 1965 (*d*) 1944

103. Achievement motive in a child can be developed by
(*a*) Proper guidance and high expectation from the child
(*b*) Telling the stories of great men to the child
(*c*) Setting a realistic goal for the child
(*d*) All of these

104. Which of the following is not a characteristic of learning?
(*a*) Learning is a relatively permanent change in behaviour
(*b*) Learning is a growth of the organism
(*c*) Learning is directly observed
(*d*) Learning is a goal directed process

105. In the beginning of life, the baby is guided by
(*a*) maturation
(*b*) instincts
(*c*) learning
(*d*) none of these

106. Accumulation of knowledge or facts becomes learning when
(*a*) It is applied in real life situation
(*b*) It is done by the learner himself
(*c*) It is provided by the teacher
(*d*) None of these

107. Dancing, driving, writing etc are the examples of
(*a*) Mechanical learning
(*b*) Perceptual motor learning
(*c*) Psychomotor learning
(*d*) both (*b*) and (*c*)

108. In Gagne's hierarchy, learning has been divided into
(*a*) eight parts (*b*) nine parts
(*c*) seven parts (*d*) none of the above

109. Match the following:

(A)	(B)
(*i*) Classical conditioning	1. Kohler
(*ii*) Drive reduction	2. Hull
(*iii*) Sign gestalt	3. Pavlov
(*iv*) Learning by insight	4. Tolman

	(*i*)	(*ii*)	(*iii*)	(*iv*)
(*a*)	1	2	3	4
(*b*)	3	2	4	1
(*c*)	2	1	3	4
(*d*)	4	3	2	1

110. Reflexes are of two types according to Pavlov. They are physiological and
(*a*) Psychic (*b*) Neural
(*c*) Mental (*d*) None of these

111. In classical conditioning, extinction will take place when
(*a*) Organism is poor in generalization
(*b*) CS is given without UCS for a long time
(*c*) CS > UCS
(*d*) None of these

112. Backward conditioning will take place when
(*a*) UCS is presented prior to CS
(*b*) CS is presented prior to UCS
(*c*) Reward is not given to the organism
(*d*) None of these

113. When connection is not established between a CS and CR, due to any factor, that is called
(*a*) Spontaneous recovery
(*b*) Extinction
(*c*) Inhibition
(*d*) None of these

114. When a child responds to all women who wear black suit because of the black suit of her mother, it is the example of
(*a*) internal inhibition
(*b*) generalization
(*c*) assimilation
(*d*) all of these

115. Which of the following is not a behaviourist?
(*a*) Watson
(*b*) Skinner
(*c*) Pavlov
(*d*) Lewin

116. Learning according to Watson is
(*a*) the shifting of old responses to the new stimuli
(*b*) the result of connection between S-R formed in the brain
(*c*) both of these
(*d*) none of these

117. Which of the following points differentiates the theories of Watson and Guthrie?
(*a*) law of contiguity
(*b*) law of recency
(*c*) generalization
(*d*) law of frequency

118. In operant conditioning reward works as motives but in Guthrie's theory motives are
(*a*) Stimuli given to the learner
(*b*) Actions done by the learner
(*c*) Both of these
(*d*) None of these

119. We forget something not by disuse but by other learning. This is the theory of
(*a*) contiguity
(*b*) trial and error
(*c*) learning by insight
(*d*) perception

120. Which of the following is not an essential requirement for trial and error learning?
(*a*) Drive
(*b*) Barrier
(*c*) Chance success
(*d*) Selective movement of the organism

121. According to the law of trial and error, learning occurs when
(*a*) it is satisfying for the learner
(*b*) bond between S-R is strengthened by the repeated use
(*c*) drive is there in the learner to act
(*d*) all of these

122. Which of the following facilitates learning according to Thorndike?
(*a*) Transfer of training
(*b*) Mental set of the learner
(*c*) Law of contiguity
(*d*) All of these

123. In Hull's theory, for learning to occur, the S-R connection must be associated with the
(*a*) cognitive field of the learner
(*b*) diminution of the need
(*c*) both of these
(*d*) none of these

124. Reinforcement in Skinner's theory is similar to drive reduction in which theory
(*a*) Hull's theory
(*b*) Guthrie's theory
(*c*) Lewin's theory
(*d*) None of these

125. Which of the following theories is most quantitatively measurable?
(*a*) Pavlov's
(*b*) Skinner's
(*c*) Hull's
(*d*) None of these

126. In drive reduction theory, the effective stimulus in learning is the trace. It is formed
(*a*) in the brain
(*b*) by the bond of S-R
(*c*) in the nervous system
(*d*) none of these

127. In drive reduction theory, habit formation is a function of
(*a*) stimulus potential
(*b*) stimulus generalization
(*c*) reaction potential
(*d*) all of these

128. Hull may be considered superior to other S-R Theorists in the sense that he was able to measure
(*a*) latency of response
(*b*) reinforcement potential
(*c*) both of these
(*d*) none of these

129. Which of the following points differentiates Skinner from other S-R theorists?
(*a*) His operant conditioning (type R learning)
(*b*) His schedule of reinforcement
(*c*) His way of shaping behaviour
(*d*) All of these

130. Skinner's theory is more objective in nature than the others because
(*a*) operant behaviour is external
(*b*) reflexes never have zero strength
(*c*) reinforcement is followed by responses
(*d*) all of these

131. Aversive stimuli in operant conditioning means
(*a*) individual will not do a particular act because of fear of such stimuli
(*b*) individual will not do a particular act because of the disapproval from others
(*c*) both of these
(*d*) none of these

132. In Skinner's theory, reinforcement is given to the learner when
(*a*) his response is 100% correct
(*b*) his response is closer to the correct behaviour
(*c*) both of these
(*d*) none of these

133. Which of the following statements regarding S-R theories is not correct?
(*a*) Man behaves like a machine
(*b*) Behaviour is overt and can be objectively measured
(*c*) Learning proceeds from simple to complex
(*d*) Things are perceived in the context of figure ground *i.e.*, in relation to other things

134. Which of the following statements regarding field theories are correct?
(*a*) Learning is not additive

(*b*) Molar approach of behaviour is followed here
(*c*) Interaction between organism and the environment is essential for learning
(*d*) All of these

135. Operant conditioning is different from respondent conditioning in which of the following points
(*a*) In OC reinforcement is given after the response is made
(*b*) In operant conditioning, behaviour is controlled by central nervous system
(*c*) A chain of responses is needed for shaping the behaviour (learning)
(*d*) All of these

136. Thorndike and Skinner do not differ at all in
(*a*) the law of effect
(*b*) law of readiness
(*c*) law of contiguity
(*d*) all of these

137. According to gestalt psychologists, behaviour can not be quantified because
(*a*) it is always changeable
(*b*) it is governed by the configuration produced in the mind
(*c*) it is rarely overt
(*d*) all of these

138. Law of pragnanz is the other name of the law of
(*a*) continuity
(*b*) closure
(*c*) contiguity
(*d*) none of these

139. How does the law of similarity work according to field theorists?
(*a*) Similar ideas and experiences get associated to form a whole
(*b*) Similar objects or experiences are easily learnt
(*c*) Both of these
(*d*) None of these

140. Learning by insight looks similar to some extent to which of the following theories?
(*a*) Need reduction theory
(*b*) R type of learning
(*c*) Trial and error theory
(*d*) None of the above

141. The other name of conditioned reflexes is
(*a*) psychic reflexes
(*b*) motor reflexes
(*c*) physiological reflexes
(*d*) none of the above

142. According to Renzuli, a gifted child is one
(*a*) Who possesses above average ability in almost every field
(*b*) Who is committed to task and highly motivated
(*c*) Who is definitely creative
(*d*) All of these

143. Gifted and talented children must be identified as early as possible because
(*a*) If their potentials are not developed by proper guidance of the teacher, it is a loss of the society
(*b*) They are likely to create problems for others, if they are not given work according to their ability
(*c*) Ordinary level of curriculum will not suit to these children
(*d*) All of these

144. Achievement test can be a good indicator of intellectual power if
(*a*) It is conducted immediately after the teaching is over
(*b*) A student shows good performance consistently on different achievement test
(*c*) Both of these
(*d*) None of these

145. Which of the following skills does not require high intellectual ability?
(*a*) Technical skills
(*b*) Mechanical skills
(*c*) Teaching skills
(*d*) Management skills

146. Cognitive abilities related to giftedness are all except
(*a*) High comprehensive and analytical abilities
(*b*) High level of verbal intelligence
(*c*) High retention power
(*d*) None of these

147. A superior child is advanced to a normal child by at least
(*a*) 2½ years
(*b*) Four years
(*c*) 1 years
(*d*) 1½ years

148. A gifted child is
(*a*) realistic in his approach
(*b*) highly interested in solving social problems
(*c*) more frequently chosen by his age mates and peers
(*d*) all of these

149. Which of the following enrichment programmes is suitable for gifted children in the school?
(*a*) Mathematics or Science Olympiad
(*b*) Challenging home assignments
(*c*) Map work during studies
(*d*) All of these

150. Which of the following does not come under the category of acceleration for gifted children?
(*a*) Skipping of classes

(b) Early admission
(c) Extra laboratory work
(d) Organizing summer camps

151. Under achievers are those who
(a) Score low on intelligence tests
(b) Achieve low in the class consistently despite their superior intelligence
(c) Are unable to correspond their achievement to the level of their innate abilities
(d) Both (b) and (c)

152. Which of the following conditions must be satisfied in order to designate a person mentally retarded?
(a) Sub-normal intellectual functioning
(b) Very poor adaptive ability
(c) Dependability on others
(d) All of these

153. The best measure of identifying mildly mentally retarded is
(a) Administration of standardized intelligence test
(b) Administration of behaviour test
(c) Administration of adjustment test
(d) A combination of all

154. Physical trauma during pregnancy may cause
(a) Mental retardation
(b) Blindness
(c) Deafness
(d) All of these

155. All of the following may cause mental retardation except
(a) Blood incompatibility
(b) Action of toxic agent
(c) Radio-activity
(d) None of these

156. Which of the following is an important postnatal cause of mental retardation?
(a) Brain injury
(b) Infection
(c) Severe malnutrition
(d) All of these

157. Dullers do not differ from normal children in
(a) Physical characteristics
(b) Level of social expectancy
(c) Both of these
(d) None of these

158. Which of the following things is not required for educating mildly mentally retarded children?
(a) Regular counseling
(b) Remedial teaching
(c) Modification in the curriculum
(d) Regular evaluation

159. Teaching of which of the following skills is not suitable to borderline cases?
(a) Electric fitting
(b) Repairing of electric or electronic equipments
(c) Oratory skills
(d) Activity based skills

160. IQ range of morons are in the range of
(a) 60-90 (b) 50-75
(c) 60-80 (d) 30-50

161. Morons are slow in
(a) Physical growth
(b) Thinking and planning
(c) Taking initiative
(d) All of these

162. Unsatisfactory relation of a mentally retarded child with the environment is technically called
(a) Autism
(b) Maladjustment
(c) Pseudo-dullness
(d) None of these

163. All of the following are characteristics of morons except
(a) They are restricted to unskilled or semi skilled occupations
(b) They are likely to be delinquent more easily
(c) They have stronger sex drives than the normals
(d) They are educable upto normal level but at a slower rate

164. Which of the following modifications in the curriculum is needed for morons?
(a) Activity based curriculum
(b) Skill dominated curriculum
(c) Emphasis on social training
(d) All of these

165. Which of the following things can not be taught to Imbeciles?
(a) Self help skills
(b) Unskilled job to be performed under supervision
(c) Writing skills
(d) Social skills

166. In which of the following cases divergent thinking is required?
(a) Attempting a multiple choice items
(b) Writing an essay
(c) Doing a research activity
(d) Both (a) and (c)

167. Which of the following tests is similar to Guilford's test of cognitive abilities?
(a) Word association test
(b) Things test
(c) Hidden shapes test
(d) None of these

168. In Hidden shapes test of creativity, which of the following things is used?
(a) Pictures

(*b*) Words
(*c*) Things
(*d*) None of them

169. A creative child in the class can not be satisfied unless
(*a*) He is given freedom to manipulate ideas or things
(*b*) He is allowed to ask questions in his own way
(*c*) Both of these
(*d*) None of these

170. A creative child is one who
(*a*) Is ideationally productive and unconventional
(*b*) Does not stick to social and religious norms in a hard manner
(*c*) Is all the time restless to do something uncommon and unique
(*d*) All of these

171. For the development of creative potential of a child, the teacher should
(*a*) Allow him to be critical to ideas and people
(*b*) Give them chance of problem solving
(*c*) Both of these
(*d*) None of these

172. New ideas (Eureka) suddenly comes in the minds of the creative children in the stage of
(*a*) Preparation
(*b*) Illumination
(*c*) Revision
(*d*) Incubation

173. The technique to foster creativity in children is
(*a*) Brain storming
(*b*) Problem solving
(*c*) Both of these
(*d*) None of these

174. A teacher can foster creativity in children by
(*a*) Developing confidence in them
(*b*) Giving them opportunity to express
(*c*) Both of these
(*d*) None of these

175. Learning disabled children are
(*a*) Deficient in using potentials
(*b*) Low in intelligence
(*c*) Slow in activity
(*d*) None of these

176. Learning disabled children perform very poorly in
(*a*) academic areas
(*b*) technical areas
(*c*) both of these
(*d*) none of these

177. Problem of learning disability is more complex than that of other disabilities because
(*a*) Its causes can not be easily ascertained by applying usual tests
(*b*) It is associated to behaviour problems
(*c*) Both of these
(*d*) None of these

178. Educationally, learning disabled look similar to
(*a*) dullers
(*b*) backward children
(*c*) both of these
(*d*) none of these

179. In which of the following physical characteristics learning disabled children differ from the normal ones?
(*a*) They are all the time clumsy and awkward
(*b*) Poor coordination of motor abilities
(*c*) Height, weight and health
(*d*) All of these

180. Which of the following methods is most suitable for learning disabled children?
(*a*) Behaviour guidance method
(*b*) Remedial teaching
(*c*) Brain storming
(*d*) None of them

181. In order to improve work habits of learning disabled what should be done?
(*a*) Unattending behaviour should be penalized
(*b*) Close monitoring of the behaviour is needed
(*c*) Cues and prompt should be given
(*d*) All of these

182. Those who are normal in intelligence but slow in academic achievement due to psycho-social reasons are called
(*a*) Backward children
(*b*) Gifted under achievers
(*c*) Both of these
(*d*) None of these

183. Consistent low achievement leads to low intelligence because
(*a*) 50% intellectual ability is expressed in verbal form
(*b*) Learning develops thinking and reasoning power
(*c*) Both of these
(*d*) None of these

184. Which of the following situations may lead to educational backwardness?
(*a*) Sensory impairment
(*b*) Motor disability
(*c*) Long diseases and health problems.
(*d*) All of these

185. Emotional disturbances may lead to educational backwardness because
(*a*) Proper emotional development is necessary for social interactions
(*b*) Emotions will develop intellectual power, *i.e.*, emotional intelligence

(c) Both of these
(d) None of these

186. Which of the following factors will not lead to educational backwardness?
(a) Poor socio economic status of the family
(b) Poor educational environment of the school
(c) Occupation of the family
(d) Poor emotional climate of the family

187. Which of the following is an important cause of educational backwardness at primary level of education in India?
(a) Poor school organisation
(b) Lack of accountability
(c) Attitude of the masses towards education
(d) All of these

188. Which of the following measures should be adopted by the teacher to check educational backwardness?
(a) Continuous evaluation and regular feedback
(b) Remedial teaching
(c) Adjustment and behaviour training
(d) All of these

189. Teaching by small steps and frequent short assignment techniques are useful for
(a) Slow learners
(b) Learning disabled
(c) Educationally backward children
(d) Children of all types of disabilities

190. Special schools are required for backward children when
(a) Backwardness is due to any serious physical handicap
(b) The size of population of backward children in the society is very large as is the case of Gujarat where the achievement of students in mathematics is always seen very low
(c) Both of these
(d) None of these

191. Which of the following should be considered the most important quality of a teacher at primary level?
(a) Patience and perseverance
(b) Competence in methods of teaching and knowledge of subjects
(c) Competence to teach in highly standardised language
(d) Eagerness to teach

192. A teacher, because of his/her democratic nature, allows students to sit all over the class. Some sit together and discuss or do group reading. Some sit quietly and read themselves. A parent does not like it. Which of the following may be the best way to handle the situation?
(a) Parents should request the principal to change the section of their ward
(b) Parents should show trust in the teacher and discuss the problem with the teacher
(c) Parents should take away the child from that school
(d) Parents should complain against the teacher to the principal

193. The stage in which a child begins to think logically about objects and events is known as
(a) Formal operational stage
(b) Pre-operational stage
(c) Concrete operational stage
(d) Sensori-motor stage

194. 'Mind mapping' refers to
(a) a plan of action for an adventure
(b) drawing the picture of a mind
(c) researching the functioning of the mind
(d) a technique to enhance comprehension

195. The best way, specially at primary level, to address the learning difficulties of students is to use
(a) expensive and glossy support material
(b) easy and interesting textbooks
(c) story-telling method
(d) a variety of teaching methods suited to the disability

196. Which of the following will foster creativity among learners?
(a) Providing opportunities to question and to nurture the innate talents of every learner
(b) Emphasizing achievement goals from the beginning of school life
(c) Coaching students for good marks in examination
(d) Teaching the students the practical value of good education

197. According to Piaget, at which of the following stages does a child begin to think logically about abstract propositions?
(a) Formal operational stage (11 years and up)
(b) Sensori-motor stage (Birth–02 years)
(c) Pre-operational stage (02–07 years)
(d) Concrete operational stage (07–11 years)

198. Learning can be enriched if
(a) more and more teaching aids are used in the class
(b) teachers use different types of lectures and explanation
(c) due attention is paid to periodic tests in the class
(d) situations from the real world are brought into the class in which students interact with each other and the teahcer facilitates

199. Which of the following statements ***cannot*** be considered as a feature of the process of learning?
(a) Learning is a comprehensive process
(b) Learning is goal-oriented
(c) Unlearning is also a learning process
(d) Educational institutions are the only place where learning takes place

200. A student of V-grade with 'visual deficiency' should be
(*a*) helped with his/her routine-work by parents and friends
(*b*) treated normally in the classroom and provided support through Audio CDs
(*c*) given special treatment in the classroom
(*d*) excused to do a lower level of work

201. Which of the following is ***not*** related to the socio-psychological needs of the child?
(*a*) Need for emotional security
(*b*) Regular elimination of waste products from the body
(*c*) Need for company
(*d*) Need for appreciation or social approval

202. Which is the place where the child's 'cognitive' development is defined in the best way?
(*a*) School and classroom environment
(*b*) Auditorium
(*c*) Home
(*d*) Playground

203. .... is considered a sign of motivated teaching.
(*a*) Remedial work given by the teacher
(*b*) Questioning by students
(*c*) Pin drop silence in the class
(*d*) Maximum attendance in the class

204. Which of the following is ***not*** a sign of an intelligent young child?
(*a*) One who has the ability to communicate fluently and appropriately
(*b*) One who carries on thinking in an abstract manner
(*c*) One who can adjust oneself in a new environment
(*d*) One who has the ability to cram long essays very quickly

205. "Children actively construct their understanding of the world" is a statement attributed to
(*a*) Pavlov (*b*) Kohlberg
(*c*) Skinner (*d*) Piaget

206. Kritika who does ***not*** talk much at home, talks a lot at school. It shows that
(*a*) teachers demand that children should talk a lot at school
(*b*) she does not like her home at all
(*c*) her thoughts get acknowledged at school
(*d*) the school provides opportunities to children to talk a lot

207. A teacher should make an attempt to understand the potentialities of her/his students. Which of the following fields is related to this objective?
(*a*) Social Philosophy
(*b*) Media – Psychology
(*c*) Educational Psychology
(*d*) Educational Sociology

208. Motivation, in the process of learning,
(*a*) differentiates new learning from old learning
(*b*) makes learners think unidirectionally
(*c*) creates interest for learning among young learners
(*d*) sharpens the memory of learners

209. The term 'curriculum' in the field of education refers to
(*a*) overall programme of the school which students experience on a day-to-day basis
(*b*) evaluation process
(*c*) text-material to be used in the class
(*d*) methods of teaching and the content to be taught

210. At lower classes, play-way method of teaching is based on
(*a*) principles of methods of teaching
(*b*) psychological principles of development and growth
(*c*) sociological principles of teaching
(*d*) theory of physical education programmes

211. "A young child responds to a new situation on the basis of the response made by him/her in a similar situation as in the past." This is related to
(*a*) 'Law of Effect' of learning
(*b*) 'Law of Attitude' of learning process
(*c*) 'Law of Readiness' of learning
(*d*) 'Law of Analogy' of learning

212. .... is ***not*** considered a sign of 'being gifted'.
(*a*) Fighting with others
(*b*) Novelty in expression
(*c*) Curiosity
(*d*) Creative ideas

213. Education of children with special needs should be provided
(*a*) by methods developed for special children in special schools
(*b*) in special schools
(*c*) by special teachers in special schools
(*d*) along with other normal children

214. To make assessment a 'useful and interesting' process, one should be careful about
(*a*) labelling students as intelligent or average learners
(*b*) using a variety of ways to collect information about the student's learning across the scholastic and co-scholastic boundaries
(*c*) using technical language to give feedback
(*d*) making comparisons between different students

215. 'Dyslexia' is associated with
(*a*) Mathematical disorder

(*b*) Reading disorder
(*c*) Behavioural disorder
(*d*) Mental disorder

216. Parents should play a .... role in the learning process of young children.
(*a*) proactive
(*b*) sympathetic
(*c*) neutral
(*d*) negative

217. "Development is a never ending process." This idea is associated with
(*a*) Principle of continuity
(*b*) Principle of integration
(*c*) Principle of interaction
(*d*) Principle of interrelation

218. The 'insight theory of learning' is promoted by
(*a*) Pavlov
(*b*) Jean Piaget
(*c*) Vygotsky
(*d*) 'Gestalt' theorists

219. In which of the following stages do children become active members of their peer group?
(*a*) Adulthood
(*b*) Early childhood
(*c*) Childhood
(*d*) Adolescence

220. Four distinct stages of children's intellectual development are identified by
(*a*) Erikson (*b*) Skinner
(*c*) Piaget (*d*) Kohlberg

ANSWERS

1	**2**	**3**	**4**	**5**	**6**	**7**	**8**	**9**	**10**
(*a*)	(*a*)	(*b*)	(*d*)	(*c*)	(*d*)	(*a*)	(*c*)	(*d*)	(*c*)
11	**12**	**13**	**14**	**15**	**16**	**17**	**18**	**19**	**20**
(*a*)	(*c*)	(*b*)	(*a*)	(*b*)	(*b*)	(*a*)	(*b*)	(*a*)	(*c*)
21	**22**	**23**	**24**	**25**	**26**	**27**	**28**	**29**	**30**
(*a*)	(*b*)	(*a*)	(*d*)	(*c*)	(*d*)	(*b*)	(*c*)	(*c*)	(*a*)
31	**32**	**33**	**34**	**35**	**36**	**37**	**38**	**39**	**40**
(*d*)	(*d*)	(*c*)	(*d*)	(*a*)	(*d*)	(*b*)	(*d*)	(*a*)	(*d*)
41	**42**	**43**	**44**	**45**	**46**	**47**	**48**	**49**	**50**
(*c*)	(*d*)	(*a*)	(*c*)	(*d*)	(*a*)	(*c*)	(*d*)	(*d*)	(*b*)
51	**52**	**53**	**54**	**55**	**56**	**57**	**58**	**59**	**60**
(*d*)	(*b*)	(*d*)	(*c*)	(*a*)	(*d*)	(*d*)	(*c*)	(*a*)	(*a*)
61	**62**	**63**	**64**	**65**	**66**	**67**	**68**	**69**	**70**
(*a*)	(*a*)	(*c*)	(*b*)	(*a*)	(*a*)	(*c*)	(*a*)	(*d*)	(*d*)
71	**72**	**73**	**74**	**75**	**76**	**77**	**78**	**79**	**80**
(*b*)	(*a*)	(*c*)	(*d*)	(*a*)	(*d*)	(*a*)	(*c*)	(*c*)	(*a*)
81	**82**	**83**	**84**	**85**	**86**	**87**	**88**	**89**	**90**
(*c*)	(*d*)	(*b*)	(*b*)	(*b*)	(*d*)	(*d*)	(*d*)	(*c*)	(*a*)
91	**92**	**93**	**94**	**95**	**96**	**97**	**98**	**99**	**100**
(*a*)	(*c*)	(*d*)	(*d*)	(*c*)	(*a*)	(*c*)	(*d*)	(*a*)	(*b*)
101	**102**	**103**	**104**	**105**	**106**	**107**	**108**	**109**	**110**
(*d*)	(*b*)	(*d*)	(*c*)	(*b*)	(*a*)	(*d*)	(*a*)	(*b*)	(*a*)
111	**112**	**113**	**114**	**115**	**116**	**117**	**118**	**119**	**120**
(*b*)	(*a*)	(*c*)	(*b*)	(*d*)	(*c*)	(*d*)	(*a*)	(*a*)	(*d*)
121	**122**	**123**	**124**	**125**	**126**	**127**	**128**	**129**	**130**
(*d*)	(*d*)	(*b*)	(*a*)	(*c*)	(*c*)	(*a*)	(*a*)	(*d*)	(*a*)
131	**132**	**133**	**134**	**135**	**136**	**137**	**138**	**139**	**140**
(*a*)	(*c*)	(*d*)	(*d*)	(*d*)	(*a*)	(*b*)	(*b*)	(*a*)	(*c*)
141	**142**	**143**	**144**	**145**	**146**	**147**	**148**	**149**	**150**
(*a*)	(*d*)	(*d*)	(*c*)	(*a*)	(*d*)	(*a*)	(*d*)	(*d*)	(*c*)
151	**152**	**153**	**154**	**155**	**156**	**157**	**158**	**159**	**160**
(*d*)	(*d*)	(*d*)	(*d*)	(*d*)	(*d*)	(*c*)	(*c*)	(*c*)	(*b*)

161	162	163	164	165	166	167	168	169	170
(*d*)	(*a*)	(*d*)	(*d*)	(*d*)	(*d*)	(*b*)	(*a*)	(*c*)	(*a*)
171	**172**	**173**	**174**	**175**	**176**	**177**	**178**	**179**	**180**
(*c*)	(*b*)	(*c*)	(*c*)	(*d*)	(*a*)	(*a*)	(*b*)	(*b*)	(*a*)
181	**182**	**183**	**184**	**185**	**186**	**187**	**188**	**189**	**190**
(*d*)	(*a*)	(*c*)	(*d*)	(*c*)	(*c*)	(*d*)	(*d*)	(*d*)	(*c*)
191	**192**	**193**	**194**	**195**	**196**	**197**	**198**	**199**	**200**
(*a*)	(*b*)	(*c*)	(*c*)	(*d*)	(*a*)	(*d*)	(*d*)	(*d*)	(*b*)
201	**202**	**203**	**204**	**205**	**206**	**207**	**208**	**209**	**210**
(*b*)	(*a*)	(*b*)	(*d*)	(*d*)	(*c*)	(*c*)	(*c*)	(*a*)	(*b*)
211	**212**	**213**	**214**	**215**	**216**	**217**	**218**	**219**	**220**
(*a*)	(*a*)	(*d*)	(*b*)	(*b*)	(*a*)	(*a*)	(*d*)	(*d*)	(*c*)

GLOSSARY

Accommodation : Piaget used this term for modification or reorganisation of existing cognitive structure (schemata) to deal with environmental demands. Accommodation is the adjustment the individual makes when incorporating external reality. Piaget uses this concept in conjunction with assimilation, which is the individual's response to the immediate and compelling environmental demands that have been and are being assimilated.

Advance organisers : Introductory information intended to facilitate a student's learning by providing a framework and organisation for the material to be learned.

Affective domain : One of the categories of educational objectives for students attitudes, values and emotional growth. The affective domain includes five basic categories: receiving, responding, valuing, organisation and characterisation by a value.

Assimilation : Assimilation is the process of taking within or internalising, one's environmental experience. The term is used by Piaget for the process of making sense of experiences and perceptions by fitting them into previously established cognitive structure (schemata). Assimilation is used by Piaget in conjunction with the concept of accommodation. Piaget believes that assimilation is a spontaneous process on the part of the child.

Attitudes : A learned predisposition to respond either positively or negatively to persons, situations, or things. Attitudes carry a strong emotional component and therefore can never be neutral.

Attribution theory : The term attribution refers to the explanation a person gives for his or her own or another person's actions or beliefs. An attribution based on internal factors is called a dispositional attribution, and one based on external factors is called a situational attribution.

Behaviourism : A school of thought in Psychology usually considered to have originated in the work and writings of John B. Watson in 1913. Watson argued against the use of introspection in gathering psychological data. He considered observable behaviour the only valid data in Psychology. According to Watson, any concepts, like mind or consciousness, that have mentalistic overtones must be purged from the field of psychology. The most famous current representative of this tradition is Harvard University's B.F. Skinner.

Classical conditioning : A procedure in which the conditioned stimulus after being paired with the unconditioned stimulus often enough, can then be substituted for it. It is often called ''stimulus substitution.''

Cognition : The process of faculties by which knowledge is acquired and manipulated (*e.g.*, thinking or remembering).

Cognitive domain : A part of Bloom's Taxonomy of educational objectives. Bloom divided the objectives in the cognitive domain into six categories: knowledge, comprehension, application, analysis, synthesis and evaluation.

Cognitive style : The consistent way in which an individual responds to a wide range of perceptual tasks.

Computer-assisted instruction (CAI) : The use of a computer as tutor to present information, give students opportunities to practice what they learn, evaluate student achievement, and provide additional instruction.

Concept learning : The acquisition of pattern-recognition knowledge involving the learning of a rule or rules for classifying a number of objects into mutually exclusive categories based on one or more salient characteristics of the objects.

Conditioned response : A response elicited by a conditioned stimulus. The response is similar but not identical to its associated unconditioned response.

Cognitive learning : The view that learning is based on a restructuring of perceptions and thoughts occurring within the organism is called cognitive learning. This restructuring allows the learner to perceive new relationships, solve new problems and gain understanding of a subject area. Cognitive learning theorists stress the reorganisation of one's perceptions in order to achieve understanding, as opposed to the behaviourist theorists, who stress the importance of associations formed between stimuli and responses.

Conditioned response : The term is used both in classical conditioning, and in operant conditioning. In classical conditioning, the conditioned response is the response being elicited by the conditioned stimulus. The stronger the conditioning, the greater the magnitude of the conditioned response and the shorter its latency. In Pavlov's experiment the conditioned response was the dog's salivation to the tone.

In operant conditioning, since the response must precede the reinforcer, the conditioned response is defined not in terms of magnitude or latency, but in terms of either the rate of response or its resistance to extinction. For example, a strongly conditioned operant will occur for more rapidly than one that has been only weakly conditioned. Also, a strongly conditioned operant will be far more difficult to extinguish.

Conditioned stimulus : In classical conditioning, the previously neutral stimulus takes on the power to elicit the response through association with an unconditioned stimulus. For this to occur, the conditioned stimulus must precede the unconditioned stimulus on enough occasions to cause the conditioned stimulus to serve as a signal that the unconditioned stimulus will follow. In Pavlov's experiment on conditioning the dog, the tone was used as the conditioned stimulus. The tone was consistently followed by the meat powder, until the dog began salivating to the tone alone.

Conditioning : Process of learning whereby stimuli and responses become associated through training. There are two general types of conditioning, classical and operant. In classical conditioning a conditioned stimulus is presented, followed by an unconditioned stimulus. Conditioning is exhibited when the organism learns to respond to the conditioned stimulus alone. In operant conditioning the operant is allowed to occur and then is followed by a reinforcing stimulus. Operant conditioning is exhibited when the rate of responding increases over the original, preconditioned rate.

Convergent thinking : A term used by Guilford to describe the type of thinking in which an individual produces a single response to a specific question or problem.

Creativity : The capacity of individuals to produce novel or original answers or products.

Culture : The ways in which a group of people think, feel, and react in order to solve problems of living in their environment.

Cumulative records : A file on a student that includes such information as family data, health, academic grades, standardized test scores, attendance and teacher comments.

Discovery learning : Term is used to describe a form of learning that results not from rote memorisation or conditioning but from the active exploration of alternatives on the part of the learner. This learning is largely a result of learner's own efforts. Learning attained through discovery is more meaningful and long-lasting than that from memorisation.

Divergent thinking : A term used by Guilford to describe the type of thinking wherein an individual produces multiple responses or solutions (often non-traditional) to a single question or problem. Divergent thinking is associated with creativity.

Egocentrism : Piaget's term for describing children in the preperational stage, who have difficulty in assuming the point of view of others.

Enactive : Bruner's first stage of cognitive development, in which children understand the environment through physical action on that environment.

Encoding : The short-term memory process of transforming incoming information into episodic or semantic form and associating it with old knowledge for storage in long-term memory.

Entry behaviour : The knowledge, skills, or attitudes that a learner brings into a new learning situation.

Formal-operations stage : This is a stage of cognitive development according to Jean Piaget, occurring during early adolescence. The period of formal operations (eleven to sixteen years) is the last of Piaget's stages and is characterised by the youth's ability to develop full, formal patterns of thinking based on abstract symbolism. The youth is able to reason things out logically at the abstract level, develop symbolic meanings, and generalize to other situations. This is the highest level of thinking and according to Piaget, must await the maturation of certain structures in the brain for its full development.

Equilibration : A motivation principle in Piaget's theory that identifies human beings as active and exploratory in attempting to impose order and meaningfulness on experiences. This order or balance occurs through the processes of assimilation and accommodation.

Evaluation : This is a process of obtaining information to form judgments so that educational decisions can be made.

External locus of control : A feeling that one has little control over one's and the failure to perceive a cause-and-effect relationship between actions and consequences.

Extrinsic motivation : Motivation influenced by external events such as grades, marks or money.

Gestalt psychology : A school of thought maintaining that the organised whole, configuration, or totality of psychological experience should be the proper object of study. Founded in Germany by Max Wertheimer in the early 1900s, gestalt psychology's first interest was in the field of perception. Later, under Wolfgang Kohler's direction, studies were done in the area of learning, and under Kurt Lewin's direction, in the area of motivation. Gestalt psychologists tend to emphasize cognitive processes in the study of learning. They stress that true understanding occurs only through the reorganisation of ideas and perceptions, not through memorisation or conditioning.

Information processing : Theory of learning and remembering that is based on the computer as a model. Information is seen as following into and within the organism. The sense organs respond to incoming information, and it is passed along and encoded in the memory and nervous system. The encoded information may then be stored and processed and finally retrieved and acted on. As with the computer, there is information input, storage and/or processing, and output.

Insight : A suddenly realised solution to a problem, sometimes called the ''a-ha! phenomenon''. Introduced by Wolfgang Kohler, the concept of insight is used to explain the apparently spontaneous appearance of a solution to a problem. Insight results from the reorganisation of ideas and perceptions rather than from simple trial-and-error behaviour. The concept of insight is used typically by gestalt psychologists.

Inquiry learning : A process that is similar to discovery learning. Students learn strategies to manipulate and process information, test hypothesis and apply their conclusions to new content or situations.

Intelligence : The capacity, or a set of capacities that allows an individual to learn, solve problems, and/or interact successfully with his or her environment. As hypothetical construct, intelligence has come to mean higher-level thought processes, or intellectual abilities. Statistical studies of intelligence utilise the concept of measured intelligence, which is the score received on a standardised intelligence test.

Intelligence Quotient (IQ) : Originally, a measure of intelligence calculated by dividing a student's mental age (MA) by the chronological age (CA) and multiplying by 100, that is, IQ = MA/CA × 100. This is called the ratio method of obtaining an IQ.

More recently, IQ has been computed by the deviation method. One's deviation IQ is defined by one's relative standing among peers. The deviation IQ is computed on the basis of how far one's score deviates from the mean score obtained for the entire group of individuals of the same chronological age. This technique is based on the standard, or z-score concept and assumes a normal distribution for each age group.

Law of effect : This is one of E.L. Thorndike's main laws of learning. It states that when an association between a stimulus and response is followed by a satisfying state of affairs, the association (or connection) is strengthened. When the association is followed by an annoying state of affairs, it is weakened. In brief, reward strengthens and punishment weakens any connection between stimuli and responses. In a later version of the law, Thorndike soft-pedaled the importance of punishment of a weakening agent. Thorndike's law of effect is considered by many psychologists to be the cornerstone on which B.F. Skinner built his system of operant conditioning.

Law of exercise : One of E.L. Thorndike's three main laws of learning. It states that the more frequently a stimulus response connection occurs, the stronger the resulting association and hence, the stronger the learning. The repetition of a learned response strengthens the bond between stimulus situation and the response. The law was later amended to incorporate the importance of the consequences of the action; thus, practice without knowledge of results is not nearly as effective as when the consequences become known to the learner.

Law of readiness : One of E.L. Thorndike's three main laws of learning. It states that learning occurs when the student is mentally ready to learn. The reference here is to momentary readiness rather than maturational readiness.

Learning : Learning is a very general term refering to a process that leads to a relatively permanent change in behaviour resulting from experience. Thus, such activities as acquiring physical skills, memorizing poems, acquiring attitudes, etc., are all examples of learning. Learning may be conscious or unconscious, adaptive or maladaptive, overt or covert. Although the learning process is typically measured on the basis of a change in performance, most psychologists agree that an accompanying change occurs within the nervous system. Though there are a great many theories and explanations concerning learning, there is general agreement regarding its definition.

Locus of control : The concept identifies the type of personal control used by an individual. When the locus of control is internal, individual views himself as personally in charge of his own destinies. When the locus of control is external, the person feels he is at the mercy of external circumstances.

Long-term memory (LTM) : In the information-processing system, LTM is the second of the two main storage systems. Information that is in short-term memory may, under certain conditions, be passed along for processing and consolidation into a more permanent storage site, long-term memory. Long-term memory has the potential for holding encoded information for long periods.

Mental age : Term first used by Alfred Binet as the unit for measuring intelligence. Binet defined mental age in terms of the age at which a given number of test items are passed by an average child. If, for example, the average six-year-old could correctly answer a certain number of items, then any other child correctly answering the same number of items would be assigned at least a mental age of six.

Motivation : A general psychological term used to explain behaviour initiated by needs and directed towards a goal. Motives may be biogenic (that is stemming from tissue needs within the organism) or acquired (that is, learned through interaction with the environment, especially the social environment).

Among learning theorists, Jerome Bruner makes much of the principle of motivation, assuming that almost all children have a built-in ''will to learn''.

Nature-nurture controversy : Debate over which component, nature (heredity) or nurture (environment), is more influential in determining behaviour. In Psychology the behaviourists consistently argued on behalf of nurture, and the intelligence testers favoured nature. Educational Psychology has long been the battleground on which this issue has been fought, since the psychologists primarily concerned with this issue were the learning theorists (largely behaviourists).

Need hierarchy : Theory proposed by Abraham Maslow that suggests that human beings place their needs on the following universal, order-of-importance scale: (*i*) physiological needs, (*ii*) safety needs, (*iii*) love needs, (*iv*) esteem needs, and (*v*) self-actualising needs.

Needs : The part of the motivational cycle seen as deficits that lie within the individual. These may be physiological (*e.g.*, the needs for food) or psychological (*e.g.*, the need for approval).

Non-verbal behaviour : Body language. Based largely on the theroy of Charles Galloway and some research by Robert Rosenthal, the teacher's non-verbal behaviour represents an important avenue for the transmission of teacher expectations. Galloway has shown how non-verbal behaviour can promote or reduce student learning. Rosenthal has shown how his test (Profile of Non-verbal Sensitivity) can identify the channels for communicating how teachers really feel about their students.

Operants : Responses, according to B.F. Skinner, for which the original stimuli are either unidentified or non-existent are called operants. The consequences of operant behaviour can be observed even though the stimulus is not known. For example, if a rat presses the lever in a Skinner box and this results in reinforcement, an increase in operant rate will be observed despite the fact that no stimulus could be identified as initiating the original stimulus could be identified as initiating the original lever pressing. In operant conditioning, reinforcement is contingent on the operant's first being emitted. The organism must in some way ''operate'' on the environment in order that the reinforcement will follow. Operant responding at one time was called instrumental responding by some psychologists.

Operant conditioning : A type of learning that involves an increase in the probability that a response will occur as a function of reinforcement. This is a forn of conditioning, described by B.F. Skinner, in which the free operant is allowed to occur and is followed by a reinforcing stimulus that is, in turn, followed by an increased likelihood of the operant's occurring again. For optimum conditioning the reinforcing stimulus should follow the operant immediately. The rate of responding for a conditioned operant may jump dramatically over the preconditioned rate (operant level).

Operant level : The original, or preconditioned, rate of operant responding before any reinforcing stimuli have been introduced. If a rat happens to press the lever in a Skinner box four times an hour (without being reinforced), the operant level for that response is established at four per hour. Thus, the operant level is the rate at which the free operant is typically emitted prior to conditioning.

Positive reinforcement : A procedure that maintains or increases the rate of a response by presenting a stimulus (a positive reinforcer) following the response.

Preoperational stage : The second stage in Piaget's theory of cognitive development, in which the lack of logical operations forces children to make decisions bases on their perceptions.

Primary reinforcement : The process of using a stimulus that is reinforcing in the absence of any learning. Such stimuli as food and water are primary reinforcers.

Programmed instruction (PI) : PI is an arrangement of instructional material in a step-by-step sequence designed to lead the student to a specified goal. The material being presented is broken down into small steps called frames. There are two general approaches to programming: (*i*) linear programmes, in which all students go through the entire programme and the frames gradually increase in difficulty, and (*ii*) branched programmes, in which the student skips forward or backward in the programme (the order of the frame presentation varies) as a result of the success or failure experienced in responding.

PI can be in book form, or it can be presented through the use of a teaching machine and/or computer. The concept of programmed instruction is credited to B.F. Skinner.

Psychoanalytic theory : This reveals the theory/method of studying and treating mental illness presented by Sigmund Freud. The theory attempts to give a rational explanation for irrational thoughts and responses. Psychoanalytic theory states (*i*) that all behaviour is determined by specific motives; (*ii*) that most human motives lie at the unconscious level, and therefore people are unaware of the reasons for most of their own behaviour; (*iii*) that neurotic symptoms result from an individual's inner conflicts; and (*iv*) that inner conflicts are a product of childhood trauma and anxiety. The technique is based on the therapist's revealing to the patient the source of his or her anxiety and helping the patient achieve insight and emotional release.

Puberty : The biological changes that lead to reproductive maturity. Its onset is identified by such factors as the growth of body hair, voice changes in males, and menstruation and breast development in females.

Punishment : A method for controlling behaviour through the use of aversive stimulation. In other words, punishment is a procedure in which an aversive stimulus is presented immediately following a response, resulting in a reduction in the rate of response. Punishment, though not itself causing the extinction of a conditioned response, does severely reduce the rate of responding while the punishment is in force. Punishment should not be confused with negative reinforcement.

Reinforcement : Any stimulus that increases the likelihood of a response's recurring. Reinforcement, as a Skinnerian concept, should not be confused with reward, feelings of pleasure, or any other concept with subjective of mentalistic overtones. Reinforcement may be used in either classical (respondent) or operant conditioning. In respondent condition the unconditioned stimulus serves as the reinforcement. In operant conditioning the presentation of any stimulus following the emitted response can be considered a reinforcement if it results in a higher response rate.

Schemata : Cognitive structures created through the abstraction of previous experience. Schemata function in the comprehension and recall of data and can aid learning or be responsible for many types distortion in recall.

Secondary reinforcement : A process that uses a stimulus that is not originally reinforcing but that acquires reinforcing properties when paired with a primary reinforcer. Money is a secondary reinforcer.

Self-actualization : Maslow's term for the psychological need to develop one's capabilities and potential in order to enhance personal growth. It refer to a person's constant striving to realise the potential within and to develop inherent talents and capabilities.

Self-concept : The total organisation of the perceptions individuals have of themselves.

Self-esteem : The value, or judgement, individuals place on their behaviour. Self-esteem and self-concept are often used interchangeably in educational literature.

Self-reinforcement : A procedure in which individuals reinforce their own behaviour.

Sensitive period : This is a time period when an organism is susceptible to a change in behaviour due to certain kinds of environmental stimulation. The sensitive periods typically occur early in the organism's life and tend to produce behaviour changes that are relatively long-lasting. The process of mother-infant bounding is said to occur only during the baby's first three days of life.

Short-term memory (STM) : In the information processing system, STM is the first of two main storage systems. Sometimes it is called working or active memory. Estimates of how long information may be retained in short-term memory vary from about twenty seconds to over a minute.

Social facilitation : The concept from the field of social psychology is used to explain the fact that in some circumstances individuals perform more quickly when in a group situation than when alone. Social facilitation is most pronounced in the case of fairly simple mechanical tasks. The more difficult and the more intellectual the task, the less the effect of social facilitation.

Social learning theory : Theory, proposed by Albert Bandura, suggests that a large part of what a person learns occurs through imitation or modelling. Bandura's major concern is with learning that takes place in the context of a social situation in which individuals come to modify behaviour as a result of how others in the group respond. Social learning does not require primary reinforcement.

Stimulus-response : A theory that stresses the importance of the build up of stimulus response associations in defining learning. Most behaviourists adhere to stimulus response learning theories, the major exception being E.C. Tolman. The leading stimulus response theorists are E.L. Thorndike, Ivan Pavlov, J.B. Watson, Edwin Guthrie, C.L. Hull, and B.F. Skinner. Stimulus response theorists stress the importance of nurture in the nature-nurture debate. Most theories of learning during the first half of the twentieth century were stimulus response theories. The cognitive-gestalt position, however, was not based on a stimulus-response theory.

Stimulus variety : Variation, at all sensroy modes, of stimulus inputs. Stimulus variety was seen by many early-experience theorists as the crucial ingredient in intellectual development. The more the child hears, sees, and touches, the more he or she will want to hear, see, and touch and the more intellectual growth will occur.

Teaching machine : A device used to present an instructional programme one step (or frame) at a time. The student either writes in answers or presses a button corresponding to the correct alternative. The advantages of the teaching machine are that (*i*) the student can proceed at his or her own pace; (*ii*) the student receives immediate feedback; (*iii*) for many students the machines are intrinsically motivating.

Unconditioned response : An unconditioned response is any response that can be elicited automatically by the presentation of a certain stimulus, without any training or learning. The term is used in classical conditioning and in Ivan Pavlov's original experiment the unconditioned response was salivation to the stimulus of meat powder being placed in the dog's mouth.

Unconditioned stimulus : Any stimulus that will elicit a given response automatically, without any training or learning. The term is used in classical conditioning and in the case of Ivan Pavlov's own experiment, the unconditioned stimulus was meat powder placed in the dog's mouth.

COMMERCE

Fundamental Principles and Basic Concepts of Accounting

1. Accounting standards are:
A. written policy documents issued by expert accounting body
B. set of broad accounting policies to be followed by an entity
C. set in the form of general principles
D. All of the above

2. X and Y are partners with capitals of ₹ 10,000 and ₹ 20,000 respectively and sharing profits equally. They admitted Z as their third partner with one-fourth profits of the firm on the payment of ₹ 12,000. The amount of hidden goodwill is:
A. 6,000 B. 10,000
C. 8,000 D. None of the above

3. Which account is the odd one out?
A. Office Furniture & Equipment
B. Freehold Land and Buildings
C. Stock of raw materials
D. Plant and Machinery

4. Purchases book records:
A. All cash purchases only
B. All credit purchases only
C. Credit purchases of goods in trade only
D. Both cash and credit purchases

5. Trial balance is a statement which shows the total of the ______ or the ______ balances of all the accounts.
A. Opening, Closing B. Current, Future
C. Debit, Credit D. Cash, Bank

6. Contra entries are passed only when
A. Double column cash book is prepared
B. Three-column cash book is prepared
C. Simple cash book is prepared
D. None of the above

7. Mr. Anand buys goods of ₹ 2,50,000 paying cash ₹ 2,00,000. What is the amount of expense as per the accrual concept?
A. ₹ 2,50,000 B. ₹ 2,00,000
C. ₹ 50,000 D. Nil

8. Profit or loss on revaluation at the time of admission of partner, is shared among the partners in ______ ratio.
A. Old Profit Sharing B. New Profit Sharing
C. Capital D. Equal

9. All of the following errors do not affect the trial balance, except
A. Compensating errors
B. Errors of complete omission
C. Errors of partial omission
D. Errors of principle

10. Errors are ______ mistakes.
A. Intentional B. Unintentional
C. Undetected D. None of the three

11. Which of the following is an example of capital expenditure?
A. Drawings Account
B. Outstanding Expenses Account
C. Machinery Account
D. Debtors Account

12. Interest on capital will be paid to the partners if provided for in the agreement but only from ______.
A. Profits B. Reserves
C. Accumulated Profits D. Goodwill

13. Present liability of uncertain amount, which can be measured reliably by using a substantial degree of estimation, is termed as ______.
A. Provision
B. Liability
C. Contingent liability
D. Reserve

14. If a purchase return of ₹ 94 has been wrongly posted to the debit of the sales return account, but had been correctly entered in the suppliers account, the total of the trial balance would show
A. the credit side to be ₹ 94 more than debit side
B. the debit side to be ₹ 94 more than credit side
C. the credit side to be ₹ 188 more than debit side
D. the debit side to be ₹ 188 more than credit side

15. X and Y are partners with the capital ₹ 1,50,000 and ₹ 1,40,000 respectively. They share profits and losses equally. Z is admitted on bringing ₹ 1,50,000 as capital only and nothing was bought against goodwill. Goodwill in Balance Sheet of ₹ 20,000 is revalued as ₹ 35,000. What will be value of goodwill in the books after the admission of Z?
A. ₹ 55,000 B. ₹ 35,000
C. ₹ 20,000 D. ₹ 15,000

16. The profits of last three years are ₹ 43,000; ₹ 38,000 and ₹ 45,000. Find out the goodwill if it is valued at two years purchase of average profits.
A. ₹ 42,000 B. ₹ 84,000
C. ₹ 1,26,000 D. ₹ 36,000

17. If capital employed by a partnership firm is ₹ 1,00,000 and its average profit is ₹ 20,000 normal rate of return is 15%, then find goodwill if it is valued on the basis of one year purchase of super profits.
A. ₹ 30,000 B. ₹ 5,000
C. ₹ 1,33,333 D. ₹ 33,333

18. Total capital employed by a partnership firm is ₹ 1,00,000 and its average profit is ₹ 25,000. Normal rate of return is 20% in similar firm working under similar conditions. The firms earns super profit of:
A. ₹ 3,000 B. ₹ 5,000
C. ₹ 4,000 D. ₹ 2,000

19. In the absence of any provision in the partnership agreement, profits and losses are shared
A. In the ratio of capitals
B. Equally
C. In the ratio of loans given by them to the partnership firm
D. None of the above

20. A company forfeited 2,000 shares of ₹ 10 each (which were issued at par) held by Mr. X for non-payment of first & final call money of ₹ 4 per share. The called-up value per share was ₹ 9. On forfeiture, the amount debited to share capital will be
A. ₹ 10,000 B. ₹ 8,000
C. ₹ 20,000 D. ₹ 18,000

21. Abacus Ltd. issued shares of ₹ 10 each at a discount of 10%. Mr. Mahesh purchased 30 shares and paid ₹ 2 on application but did not pay the allotment money of ₹ 3. The company forfeited his entire shares, the forfeiture account will be credited by
A. ₹ 90 B. ₹ 81
C. ₹ 60 D. ₹ 54

22. A company cannot issue redeemable preference shares for a period exceeding
A. 6 years B. 7 years
C. 8 years D. 20 years

23. ₹ 200 paid as wages for erecting a machine should be debited to
A. Repair account B. Machine account
C. Capital account D. Furniture account

24. If sales are ₹ 2,000 and the rate of gross profit on cost of goods sold is 25%, then the cost of goods sold will be
A. ₹ 2,000 B. ₹ 1,500
C. ₹ 1,600 D. None of the above

25. If Cost of goods sold is ₹ 80,700, Opening stock ₹ 5,800 and Closing stock ₹ 6,000. Then the amount of purchase will be
A. ₹ 80,500 B. ₹ 74,900
C. ₹ 74,700 D. ₹ 80,900

26. Under the straight line method of depreciation, the amount of yearly depreciation ______________.
A. Remains the same
B. Fluctuates
C. Increases year after year
D. Decreases year after year

27. A Bank Reconciliation Statement is prepared to know the causes for the difference between:
A. the balance as per cash column of Cash Book and the Pass Book
B. the balance as per bank column of Cash Book and the Pass Book
C. the balance as per bank column of Cash Book and balance as per cash column of Pass Book
D. None of the above

28. In case of redemption of preference shares out of distributable profits, an amount equal to the nominal value of preferences shares redeemed must be transferred to the:
A. development rebate reserve
B. investment allowance reserve
C. capital redemption reserve
D. premium on redemption of preference shares

29. When preparing a Bank Reconciliation Statement, if you start with a debit balance as per the Cash Book, cheques issued but not presented within the period should be:
A. Added
B. Deducted
C. Not required to be adjusted
D. None of the above

30. The assumption underlying the fixed instalment method of depreciation is that of ________ of the asset over different years of its useful life.
A. Usage B. Equal usage
C. Charge D. None of the above

31. Original cost = ₹ 1,26,000. Salvage value = 6,000. Useful Life = 6 years. Annual depreciation under Straight Line Method will be
A. ₹ 21,000 B. ₹ 20,000
C. ₹ 15,000 D. ₹ 14,000

32. Preference shares amounting to ₹ 1,00,000 are redeemed at a premium of 5% by issue of shares amounting to ₹ 50,000 at a premium of 10%. The amount to be transferred to capital redemption reserve account will be:
A. ₹ 55,000 B. ₹ 50,000
C. ₹ 45,000 D. ₹ 57,500

33. Brave Ltd. issued 60,000 shares of ₹ 10 each at a discount of ₹ 1 per share. The application money was ₹ 2, allotment money was ₹ 4, and first call was of ₹ 1. The amount of final call will be:
A. ₹ 3 B. ₹ 2
C. ₹ 1 D. ₹ 4

34. Discount on issue of debentures is shown as ______ on the assets side of balance sheet.
A. Preliminary expenses
B. Miscellaneous expenditure
C. Capital expenditure
D. None of the above

35. Which of the following expenses are debited in trading account?
A. Carriage outwards B. Salaries
C. Carriage inwards D. Rent of office premises

36. As per the accounting equation:
A. Capital + Liabilities = Assets
B. Capital + Assets = Liabilities
C. Liabilities + Assets = Capital
D. Assets = Liabilities – Capital

37. In Double Entry System of Book-keeping every business transaction affects:
A. Two accounts with equal but opposite effect.
B. Two sides of the same account
C. The same account on two different dates
D. All of the above

38. ______ is an intangible real account.
A. Land B. Building
C. Goodwill D. Cash

39. Journal entry for outstanding salary to clerk ₹ 6,000 will be:
A. Dr. Salary A/c and Cr. Cash A/c ₹ 6,000
B. Dr. Outstanding salary A/c and Cr. Salary A/c ₹ 6,000
C. Dr. Salary A/c and Cr. Outstanding salary A/c ₹ 6,000
D. Dr. Cash A/c and Cr. Salary A/c ₹ 6,000

40. What is the order in which the accounting transactions and events are recorded in the books?
A. Journal, Subsidiary books, Ledger and Trial Balance
B. Ledger, Journal, Subsiding books, and Trial Balance
C. Subsidiary books, Ledger and Trial Balance and Journal
D. Profit and loss account, Ledger, Balance sheet, Journal

41. The two amount columns in double column cash book are:
A. Cash and bank
B. Cash and discount
C. Bank and discount
D. None of the above

42. The error caused because of the failure to differentiate between capital and revenue expenditures and capital and revenue receipts is:
A. compensatory errors B. errors of commission
C. errors of omission D. errors of principle

43. ₹ 5,00,000 spent on advertising to introduce a new line of product is______.
A. Capital expenditure
B. Revenue expenditure
C. Deferred revenue expenditure
D. None of the above

44. When a trial balance does not agree, the difference can be transferred to ______.
A. Nominal account
B. Personal account
C. Real account
D. Suspense account

45. Bank pass book is also known as ______
A. Bank book B. Bank account
C. Bank column D. Bank statement

46. Machinery costing ₹ 20,00,000 was purchased on 1.4.2010. The installation charges amounting ₹ 5,00,000 were incurred. The depreciation at 10% per annum on straight line method for the year ended 31st March, 2011 will be:
A. ₹ 2,50,000 B. ₹ 2,00,000
C. ₹ 50,000 D. ₹ 1,50,000

47. Debit balance as per Cash Book of Yeti Enterprises as on 31.3.2011 is ₹ 20,000. Cheques deposited but not cleared amounts to ₹ 2,000 and Cheques issued but not presented of ₹ 4,000. Balance as per pass book should be:
A. 22,000 B. 18,000
C. 20,000 D. 24,000

48. In the books of Deepak Ltd. the machinery account shows a debit balance of ₹ 60,000 as on April 1, 2009. The machinery was sold on September 30, 2010 for ₹ 30,000. The company charges depreciation @ 20% p.a. on diminishing balance method. Profit/Loss on sale will be:
A. ₹ 13,200 profit B. ₹ 13,200 loss
C. ₹ 6,800 profit D. ₹ 6,800 loss

49. The balance sheet of Mr. Kapoor consists of Capital ₹ 7,00,000; Machinery ₹ 5,00,000 and cash ₹ 2,00,000. If he spends ₹ 5,000 to buy a car for personal use, the balance of capital account will be:
A. ₹ 7,00,000 B. ₹ 6,95,000
C. ₹ 7,05,000 D. ₹ 1,95,000

50. Withdrawal of money by the proprietor is not an expense but a reduction of ______.
A. Capital B. Liability
C. Asset D. None of the above

51. If the rate of gross profit is 25% on cost of goods sold and the sales is ₹ 5,00,000, the amount of gross profit will be ________.
A. 1,00,000 B. 1,50,000
C. 1,25,000 D. 1,20,000

52. Internally generated goodwill is:
A. shown in Trading account
B. shown in Profit and loss account
C. shown in Balance sheet
D. not recorded in the books

53. If outstanding wages appears in the trial balance it is shown in __________ .
A. Balance sheet
B. Both in balance sheet and profit and loss account
C. Profit and loss account
D. Trading account

54. Which of the financial statement represents the accounting equation?
A. Manufacturing account
B. Cash flow statement
C. Balance sheet
D. Profit and loss account

55. Capital expenditures are recorded in the ______.
A. Balance sheet
B. Profit and loss account
C. Trading account
D. Manufacturing account

56. Cost of floating a company is an example of:
A. Wasting assets B. Intangible assets
C. Fictitious assets D. Liquid assets

57. A & B are partners sharing profits and losses in the ratio 5 : 3. On admission of C, new profit sharing ratio between A, B and C is 7 : 5 : 4. Find the sacrificing ratio as A : B
A. 3 : 1 B. 4 : 7
C. 5 : 4 D. 2 : 1

58. Ram and Shyam are partners sharing profits and losses in the ratio of 3 : 2 having the capital of ₹ 180,000 and ₹ 150,000 respectively. They are entitled to 10% p.a. interest on capital before distributing the profits. During the year firm earned ₹ 7,800 after allowing interest on capital. Profits apportioned among Ram and Shyam is:
A. 4,680 and 3,120 B. 4,800 and 3,000
C. 5,000 and 2,800 D. 6,000 and 1,800

59. At the time of death of a partner, firm gets ________ from the insurance company against the Joint Life Policy taken jointly for all the partners.
A. Policy Amount
B. Surrender Value
C. Policy Value for the dead partner and Surrender Value for the rest
D. Surrender Value for all the partners

60. Preference shares amounting to ₹ 1,00,000 are redeemed at a premium of 5% from the profits of the company. The amount to be transferred to capital redemption reserve account will be:
A. ₹ 1,05,000 B. ₹ 1,00,000
C. ₹ 95,000 D. ₹ 90,000

61. In the absence of any provision in the partnership agreement, the partners have right to receive interest on loan at:
A. 12% p.a. B. 6 % p.a.
C. 20% p.a. D. Nil

62. Goods Outward Journal is meant for recording all returns of goods:
A. Sold on credit B. Purchased on credit
C. Purchased on cash D. None of the above

63. A, B and C are equal partners. D is admitted to the firm for one-fourth share. D brings ₹ 20,000 capital and ₹ 5,000 for goodwill. The value of goodwill of the firm is:
A. ₹ 10,000 B. ₹ 40,000
C. ₹ 20,000 D. ₹ 50,000

64. A company issued 5,000 10% Debentures of ₹ 100 each at 10% discount. All the debentures were subscribed and allotted by crediting 10% Debentures account with:
A. ₹ 10,00,000 B. ₹ 12,00,000
C. ₹ 5,00,000 D. ₹ 4,50,000

65. Bajaj Ltd. issued 5,000 equity shares of ₹ 10 each payable as ₹ 2 on application, ₹ 3 on allotment, ₹ 2 on first call and the balance in the final call. The amount to be debited to bank account at the time of receipt of first call money will be:
A. ₹ 30,000 B. ₹ 10,000
C. ₹ 40,000 D. ₹ 50,000

66. Mr. Verma holding 1000 equity shares of ₹ 10 each issued at a discount of 10% could not pay final call of ₹ 3.50 and his shares were forfeited. In the books of the company, shares forfeited account will be credited by:
A. ₹ 2,500 B. ₹ 5,500
C. ₹ 3,500 D. ₹ 2,000

67. Making provision for bad debts in respect of doubtful debts is based on the convention of ________.
A. Consistency B. Disclosure
C. Conservatism D. Materiality

68. Preference shares can be redeemed only if they are:
A. Partly paid up B. Fully paid up
C. Both of the above D. None of the above

69. If sales revenues are ₹ 4,00,000; cost of goods sold is ₹ 3,10,000, the gross profit is:
A. ₹ 90,000 B. ₹ 4,00,000
C. ₹ 3,10,000 D. ₹ 7,10,000

70. If Average Stock = ₹ 24,000, Closing stock is ₹ 6,000 more than opening stock then the value of closing stock will be:
A. ₹ 24,000 B. ₹ 48,000
C. ₹ 20,500 D. ₹ 27,000

71. It is essential to standardize the accounting principles and policies in order to ensure:
A. Transparency B. Consistency
C. Comparability D. All of the above

72. Which of the following is not a tangible asset for the firm?
A. Furniture B. Goodwill
C. Machinery D. Land and Building

73. The determination of the amount of bad debts is an accounting:
A. policy B. estimate
C. parameter D. None of the above

74. The transactions recorded through accounting equation are based on:
A. Going concern B. Business entity
C. Dual aspect D. None of the above

75. The debit balance of a cash account shows:
A. Amount receivable B. Amount payable
C. Cash in hand D. Liability

76. The balance of the petty cash is ________.
A. an expense B. income
C. an asset D. liability

77. Opening, closing and adjustment entries are recorded in:
A. Purchase Book B. Sales Book
C. Petty Cash Book D. Journal Proper

78. Journal entry for purchase of furniture ₹ 8,000 will be:
A. Dr. Furniture A/c and Cr. Cash A/c ₹ 8,000
B. Dr. Purchases A/c and Cr. Cash A/c ₹ 8,000
C. Dr. Cash A/c and Cr. Purchases A/c ₹ 8,000
D. Dr. Cash A/c and Cr. Furniture A/c ₹ 8,000

79. Sales Returns book records:
A. All cash sales returned by customers
B. All credit sales of the business
C. Credit sales of goods in trade returned by customers
D. Both cash and credit sales returned by customers

80. Journal entry for purchase of furniture for personal use ₹ 8,000 will be
A. Dr. Furniture A/c and Cr. Cash A/c ₹ 8,000
B. Dr. Drawings A/c and Cr. Cash A/c ₹ 8,000
C. Dr. Cash A/c and Cr. Drawings A/c ₹ 8,000
D. Dr. Cash A/c and Cr. Furniture A/c ₹ 8,000

81. Rectification in the next financial year is done through:
A. Profit and loss account
B. Profit and loss appropriation account
C. Profit and loss adjustment account
D. None of these

82. White-washing charges of ₹ 50,000 were debited to building account. It is ________.
A. Error of omission B. Error of commission
C. Error of principle D. Compensating error

83. If outstanding wages appears in the trial balance it is shown in ________
A. Balance sheet
B. Both in balance sheet and profit and loss account
C. Profit and loss account
D. Trading account

84. Rent outstanding account is an example of ________ account.
A. Real B. Nominal
C. Personal D. None of the above

85. According to the decision in Garner vs. Murray, in the absence of any agreement to the contrary, the deficiency of the insolvent partner must be borne by the solvent partners in the:
A. Capital ratio
B. Old profit sharing ratio
C. New profit sharing ratio
D. None of the above

86. Under ________ method, the charge for depreciation for an accounting period is calculated in proportion of the remaining life of the asset at the beginning of every accounting period.
A. Reducing balance method
B. Sum of year's digit method
C. Double declining balance method
D. Fixed instalment method

87. Which of the following errors are not disclosed by the trial balance?
A. Error of casting
B. Wrong balancing of an account
C. Double posting in one account
D. Compensating errors

88. A ________ is given to the customer when he returns the goods.
A. Credit note B. Debit note
C. Invoice D. None of these

89. An expense on major repairs of machinery purchased second hand has been debited to repairs account; it involves an error of ________.
A. Error of omission B. Error of commission
C. Error of principle D. Compensating error

90. A and B are partners in a firm. During the year 2010, A withdrew ₹ 1,000 p.m. and B withdrew ₹ 500 p.m. on the first day of each month for personal use. Interest on drawing is charged @ 10% p.a. What is the interest on drawings?
A. ₹ 1,800 B. ₹ 975
C. ₹ 900 D. ₹ 650

91. Unrecorded liability paid at the time of dissolution of a partnership is debited to_____ account.
A. Partners' capital account
B. Realisation account
C. Liability account
D. Revaluation account

92. A and B are partners sharing profits and losses in the ratio of 5 : 3. They admit C into partnership and the profit sharing ratio of the three partners is agreed at 7 : 5 : 4. The gaining or sacrificing ratio among A and B will be:
A. Gaining ratio of 3 : 1
B. Gaining ratio of 1 : 3
C. Sacrificing ratio of 1 : 3
D. Sacrificing ratio of 3 : 1

93. Which of the following books is used to record purchase of machinery by cash?
A. Cash book
B. Purchases book
C. Journal proper
D. Purchases returns book

94. At the time of admission of a new partner, if the value of land and building is over-stated in the books, it is written back by:
A. Debiting to revaluation account
B. Crediting to revaluation account
C. Debiting to partner's account
D. Crediting to partner's account

95. ₹ 5,000 incurred for upgradation of computer by installation of 128 MB RAM is:
A. Capital expenditure
B. Deferred revenue expenditure
C. Revenue expenditure
D. None of the above

96. Errors of commission arises when:
A. Any transaction is recorded on the wrong side of the account
B. Any transaction is omitted to be recorded partially
C. Any transaction is omitted to be recorded completely
D. Revenue expenditure is treated as capital expenditure

97. Furniture purchased for resale is an example of:
A. Capital expenditure
B. Deferred revenue expenditure
C. Revenue expenditure
D. Current liability

98. A change in accounting policy is justified:
A. To comply with accounting standard
B. To ensure more appropriate presenta-tion of the financial statement of the enterprise
C. To comply with law
D. All of the above

99. Original cost = 2,26,000. Salvage value = 26,000. Useful Life = 5 years. Annual depreciation under Straight Line Method will be:
A. ₹ 40,000 B. ₹ 20,000
C. ₹ 80,000 D. ₹ 60,000

100. If Cost of goods sold is ₹ 2,50,000, Opening stock ₹ 20,000 and Closing stock ₹ 36,000, Then, the amount of purchase will be:
A. ₹ 2,50,000 B. ₹ 2,66,000
C. ₹ 2,00,000 D. ₹ 3,00,000

101. If Average Stock = ₹ 12,000, Closing stock is ₹ 6,000 more than opening stock, then the value of closing stock will be:
A. ₹ 12,000 B. ₹ 24,000
C. ₹ 15,000 D. ₹ 18,000

102. Ganesh got a salary ₹ 10,000 per month and withdrew goods worth ₹ 2,500 for personal use and got salary ₹ 9,500 in cash. The excess payment of ₹ 2,000 will be debited to:
A. Sales account B. Goods account
C. Salary account D. Salary in advance account

103. If sales revenues are ₹ 4,00,000; cost of goods sold is ₹ 3,10,000 and operating expenses are ₹ 60,000, the gross profit is:
A. ₹ 30,000 B. ₹ 90,000
C. ₹ 3,40,000 D. ₹ 60,000

104. If sales are ₹ 2,000 and the rate of gross profit on cost of goods sold is 25%, then the cost of goods sold will be:
A. ₹ 2,000 B. ₹ 1,500
C. ₹ 1,600 D. None of the above

105. In case of retirement, accumulated profits/losses are transferred to the capital accounts in the:
A. Capital ratio
B. Old profit sharing ratio
C. New profit sharing ratio
D. None of the above

106. A, B & C are sharing profits in the ratio of 1/2 : 3/10 : 1/5. Calculate the new profit sharing ratio if A retires:
A. 2 : 3 B. 3 : 2
C. 5 : 2 D. 2 : 5

107. A, B and C are the partners sharing profits and losses in the ratio of 4 : 3 : 1. B died on June 30th 2010. What will be the share of B in goodwill of the firm if it is decided to value goodwill on the basis of two year's purchase of average profits of 4 completed years immediately preceding the year of the death of the partner. Profits for the year ended 2007 is ₹ 1,60,000, 2008 is ₹ 20,000, 2009 is ₹ 20,000 and 2010 is ₹ 80,000.
A. 1,20,000 B. 60,000
C. 52,500 D. 90,000

108. Zodiac Ltd. issued 10,000 shares of ₹ 10 each. The called up value per share was ₹ 8. The company forfeited 200 shares of Mr. A for non-payment of 1st call money of ₹ 2 per share. He paid ₹ 6 for application and allotment money. On forfeiture, the share capital account will be ______.

A. Debited by ₹ 2,000
B. Debited by ₹ 1,600
C. Credited by ₹ 1,600
D. Debited by ₹ 1,200

109. A to whom 100 shares of ₹ 10 each was allotted at par, paid ₹ 3 on application, ₹ 3 on allotment but could not pay the first and final call money of ₹ 4. His shares were forfeited by the directors. The amount to be credited to shares forfeited account will be:

A. ₹ 500 B. ₹ 400
C. ₹ 600 D. ₹ 1,000

110. Ashish Ltd. issued shares of ₹ 100 each at a premium of 25%. Manas, who has 2,000 shares of Ashish Ltd., failed to pay first and final call totalling ₹ 5. Premium was taken by Ashish Ltd. at the time of allotment. On forfeiture of Manas's shares, the amount to be debited to Share premium account will be:

A. ₹ 5,000 B. ₹ 10,000
C. ₹ 15,000 D. Nil

111. Indigo Ltd. had ₹ 9000, 10% redeemable preference shares of ₹ 10 each, fully paid up. The company decided to redeem these preference shares at par by the issue of sufficient number of equity shares of ₹ 10 each fully paid up at a discount of 10%. The number of equity shares issued should be:

A. 9,000 B. 11,000
C. 10,000 D. None of the above

112. Bank overdraft is shown on the ______ side of trial balance.

A. Debit B. Credit
C. None D. Both

113. Aditya Ltd. issued equity shares of 50,000 shares of ₹ 10 each for subscription. 40,000 shares were subscribed by the public by paying ₹ 3 as application money. Number of shares allotted to public by Aditya Ltd. will be:

A. 50,000 shares B. 40,000 shares
C. 30,000 shares D. 10,000 shares

114. Recovery of bad debt is a:

A. Revenue receipt
B. Capital receipt
C. Capital expenditure
D. Revenue expenditure

115. Depreciation is provided only on:

A. fixed assets B. current assets
C. liquid assets D. fictitious assets

116. A company issued 1,00,000 equity shares of ₹ 10 each at a premium of ₹ 2 and 5,000 10% Debentures of ₹ 100 each at 10% discount. All the shares and debentures were subscribed and allotted by crediting 10% Debentures account with:

A. ₹ 10,00,000 B. ₹ 12,00,000
C. ₹ 5,00,000 D. ₹ 4,50,000

117. Trading account is a:

A. Real account B. Personal account
C. Nominal account D. None

118. Balance sheet is a:

A. Period statement B. Point statement
C. Both D. None

119. Maximum number of partners in a banking partnership firm is:

A. 10 B. 20
C. 25 D. 30

120. Journal records the transactions of the firm in a:

A. Analytical manner
B. Chronological order
C. Periodical manner
D. Summarized manner

121. Discount allowed to Sohan ₹ 73 has been credited to his account by ₹ 37. The error will be rectified by:

A. Crediting Sohan by ₹ 36
B. Debiting Sohan by ₹ 36
C. Crediting discount by ₹ 36
D. None

122. Preference shares amounting to ₹ 1,00,000 are redeemed at a premium of 5% by issue of shares amounting to ₹ 50,000 at a premium of 10%. The amount to be transferred to capital redemption reserve account will be:

A. ₹ 55,000 B. ₹ 50,000
C. ₹ 45,000 D. ₹ 57,500

123. While finalizing the current year's profit, the company realized that there was an error in the valuation of closing stock of the previous year. In the previous year, closing stock was valued more by ₹ 50,000. As a result:

A. Previous year's profit is overstated and current year's profit is also overstated
B. Previous year's profit is understated and current year's profit is overstated
C. Previous year's profit is understated and current year's profit is also understated
D. Previous year's profit is overstated and current year's profit is understated

124. Which of the following are of capital nature?

A. Purchase of a goods
B. Cost of repair
C. Wages paid for installation of machinery
D. Rent of a factory

125. Discount on issue of debentures is a ________.
A. Revenue loss to be charged in the year of issue
B. Capital loss to be written off from capital reserve
C. Capital loss to be written off over the tenure of the debentures
D. Capital loss to be shown as goodwill

126. If the incoming partner brings any additional amount in cash other than his capital contributions, then it is termed as ______
A. Capital B. Reserves
C. Profits D. Premium for goodwill

127. Fluctuating capital account is credited with ______.
A. Interest on capital
B. Profits of the year
C. Salaries or remuneration of the partners
D. All of the above

128. On 1.1.2011, a machine costing ₹ 10,000 and a piece of furniture costing ₹ 20,000 was purchased. Depreciation is provided @ 5% on furniture and 10% per annum on machine. The depreciation for the year ended 31st March, 2011 should be:
A. ₹ 1,000 B. ₹ 300
C. ₹ 1,250 D. ₹ 500

129. Which of the following errors will affect the trial balance?
A. Repairs to building wrongly debited to Building A/c
B. Total of Purchase Journal by ₹ 1,000 short
C. Freight paid on new machinery debited to Freight A/c
D. None of the three

130. Difference of totals of both debit and credit side of the trial balance is transferred to:
A. Difference account B. Trading account
C. Miscellaneous account D. Suspense account

131. Machinery costing ₹ 20,00,000 was purchased on 1.4.2009. The installation charges amounting ₹ 5,00,000 were incurred. The depreciation at 10% per annum on diminishing balance method for the year ended 31st March, 2011 will be:
A. ₹ 2,50,000 B. ₹ 2,00,000
C. ₹ 2,25,000 D. ₹ 1,50,000

132. The petty cashier generally works on ________ system.
A. Accrual B. Balancing
C. Imprest D. None of the three

133. All expense and ________ accounts appearing in the trial balance are transferred to the trading and profit and loss account.
A. Loss B. Revenue
C. Asset D. Liability

134. ________ principle requires that the same accounting method should be used from one accounting period to the next.
A. Conservatism B. Consistency
C. Business entity D. Money measurement

135. Under straight line method, depreciation is calculated on:
A. Written down value B. Scrap value
C. Original cost D. None of the three

136. Which of the following is not a transaction?
A. Goods are purchased on cash basis for ₹ 1,000
B. Salaries paid for the month of May, 2006
C. Land is purchased for ₹ 10 lacs
D. An employee dismissed from the job

137. Unintentional omission or commission of amounts and accounts in the process of recording transactions are known as:
A. Frauds B. Misinterpretation
C. Errors D. None of the above

138. "Treating a revenue expense as a capital expenditure" is an example of:
A. Compensating errors B. Errors of principle
C. Errors of omission D. Errors of commission

139. Narrations are given at the end of:
A. Final accounts B. Trial balance
C. Each ledger account D. Each journal entry

140. Interest on capital paid to the sole-proprietor from business is debited to:
A. Interest account B. Bank account
C. Capital account D. Not to be shown books

141. When the balance as per Cash Book is the starting point, direct deposits by customers are:
A. Added
B. Subtracted
C. Not required to be adjusted
D. None of these

142. A Bank Reconciliation Statement is a:
A. Part of Cash Book
B. Part of Bank Account
C. Part of financial statements
D. None of the above

143. When balance as per Pass Book is the starting point, interest allowed by Bank is:
A. Added
B. Subtracted
C. Not required to be adjusted
D. None of the above

144. A Bank Reconciliation Statement is prepared with the help of:
A. Bank statement and bank column of the Cash Book.
B. Bank statement and cash column of the Cash Book

C. Bank column of the Cash Book and cash column of the Pass Book
D. None of the above

145. Debit balance as per Cash Book of ABC Enterprises as on 31.3.2011 is ₹ 1,500. Cheques deposited but not cleared amounts to ₹ 100 and Cheques issued but not presented of ₹ 150. The bank allowed interest amounting ₹ 50 and collected dividend ₹ 50 on behalf of ABC Enterprises. Balance as per pass book should be:
A. ₹ 1,600 B. ₹ 1,450
C. ₹ 1,850 D. ₹ 1,650

146. The cash book showed an overdraft of ₹ 1,500, but the pass book made up to the same date showed that cheques of ₹ 100, ₹ 50 and ₹ 125 respectively had not been presented for payments; and the cheque of ₹ 400 paid into account had not been cleared. The balance as per the pass book will be:
A. ₹ 1,100 B. ₹ 2,175
C. ₹ 1,625 D. ₹ 1,375

147. When drawing up a Bank Reconciliation Statement, if you start with a debit balance as per the Bank Statement, the unpresen-ted cheques should be:
A. Added
B. Deducted
C. Not required to be adjusted
D. None of these

148. A debit balance in the depositor's Cash Book will be shown as:
A. A debit balance in the Bank Statement
B. A credit balance in the Bank Statement
C. An overdrawn balance in the Bank Statement
D. None of the above

149. When preparing a Bank Reconciliation Statement, if you start with a debit balance as per the Cash Book, cheques issued but not presented within the period should be:
A. Added
B. Deducted
C. Not required to be adjusted
D. None of the above

150. When the balance as per Pass Book is the starting point, direct payment by bank are:
A. Added in the bank reconciliation statement
B. Subtracted in the bank reconciliation statement
C. Not required to be adjusted in the bank reconciliation statement
D. Neither of the above

151. When balance as per Cash Book is the starting point, uncollected cheques are:
A. Added in the bank reconciliation statement
B. Subtracted in the bank reconciliation statement
C. Not required to be adjusted in the bank reconciliation statement
D. Neither of the above

152. A debit note for ₹ 2,000 issued to Mr. F for goods returned by us is to be accounted for
A. Bills Receivable Book
B. Purchases Book
C. Journal Proper (General Journal)
D. Purchases Return

153. When the balance as per Pass Book is the starting point, uncollected cheques are:
A. Added in the bank reconciliation statement
B. Subtracted in the bank reconciliation statement
C. Not required to be adjusted in the bank reconciliation statement
D. Neither of the above

154. When balance as per Cash Book is the starting point, interest charged by Bank is:
A. Added in the bank reconciliation statement
B. Subtracted in the bank reconciliation statement
C. Not required to be adjusted in the bank reconciliation statement
D. Neither of the above

155. A Bank Reconciliation Statement is prepared by:
A. The Bank
B. The Government
C. The Bank Account holder
D. The user of financial statements

156. A Bank Statement is a copy of:
A. Cash column of the cash book
B. Bank column of the cash book
C. A Customer's account in the bank's book
D. None of the above

157. The difference in the balances of both the cash book and the pass book can be because of:
A. Errors in recording the entries either in the cash book or pass book
B. Omission of same entry in both cash book and pass book
C. Debit balance of cash book is the credit balance of pass book
D. None of the above

158. Direct payment to the third party on behalf of the account holder is entered in
A. The cash book when the amount is paid by the bank
B. The cash book when the entry is posted in the pass book
C. The pass book when the entry is posted in the pass book
D. None of the above

159. Payment done by the account holder through issuing a cheque is entered in
A. The pass book at the time of issuing the cheque
B. The cash book at the time of presenting the cheque to the bank for payment
C. The pass book at the time of presenting the cheque to the bank for payment
D. The cash book when informed by the third party

160. Which of the following is not the salient feature of bank reconciliation statement?
A. Any undue delay in the clearance of cheques will be shown up by the reconciliation
B. Reconciliation statement will help in finding the person doing any fraud
C. Reconciliation is done by the bankers
D. It helps in finding out the actual position of the bank balance

161. The main objective of providing depreciation is ____.
A. to calculate true profit
B. to calculate financial position
C. to reduce tax burden
D. to reduce profit

162. Depreciation arises because of ___.
A. fall in the market value of an asset
B. physical wear and tear
C. fall in the value of money
D. rise in the value of money

163. Under the straight line method of charging depreciation, depreciation ____.
A. increases every year B. decreases every year
C. is constant D. fluctuate every year

164. Under the diminishing balance method depreciation is calculated on ___.
A. original value B. written down value
C. scrap value D. market value

165. Depreciation is provided on ___.
A. current assets B. fixed assets
C. fictitious assets D. investment

166. Loss of usefulness occasioned by improved production methods is known as ____.
A. physical deterioration
B. obsolescence
C. disuse
D. inadequacy

167. Mines quarries oilfields and forest are example of:
A. fixed assets B. current assets
C. wasting assets D. intangible assets

168. Estimated sale value of the asset at the end of its economic life is known as____.
A. purchase value B. market value
C. written down value D. residual value

169. Provision for depreciation account appears on the _____.
A. Asset side
B. Liability side
C. P & L account debit side
D. P & L account credit side

170. Income tax authorities recognize this method ___.
A. straight line method
B. written down value method
C. annuity method
D. depreciation fund method

171. Under which method of depreciation the earlier year of the life of the asset profits are more:
A. straight line method
B. written down value method
C. annuity method
D. depreciation fund method

172. Straight line method is also called ____.
A. written down value method
B. annuity method
C. depreciation fund method
D. fixed instalment method

173. Diminishing balance method is also called ____.
A. written down value method
B. annuity method
C. depreciation fund method
D. fixed instalment method

174. Reducing instalment method is also called ____.
A. straight line method
B. written down value method
C. annuity method
D. depreciation fund method

175. Written down value method is also called ____.
A. diminishing balance method
B. annuity method
C. depreciation fund method
D. fixed instalment method

176. Straight line method is also called ____.
A. written down value method
B. annuity method
C. original cost method
D. depreciation fund method

177. Original cost method of depreciation is also called ___.
A. diminishing balance method
B. annuity method
C. depreciation fund method
D. fixed instalment method

178. Fixed instalment method of depreciation is also called ___.
A. written down value method
B. annuity method
C. original cost method
D. depreciation fund method

179. Diminishing balance method of depreciation is also called ___.
A. reducing balance method
B. annuity method
C. depreciation fund method
D. fixed instalment method

180. Under annuity method the amount of depreciation is found out from ___.
A. log tables B. sinking fund tables
C. annuity tables D. present value tables

181. Depreciation fund is also called ___.
A. reserve fund B. compensation fund
C. workers fund D. sinking fund

182. Under sinking fund method, the amount of depreciation is calculated with reference to ___.
A. log tables B. annuity tables
C. sinking fund tables D. present value tables

183. Under depreciation fund method depreciation is charged to ___.
A. profit and loss account
B. trading account
C. balance sheet
D. profit & loss appropriation account

184. Under insurance policy method the premium is paid in the ___.
A. beginning of each year
B. end of each year
C. beginning of each month
D. end of each month

185. Depletion method is also called ___.
A. annuity method
B. insurance policy method
C. output method
D. reducing balance method

186. Expenses which can be directly identified with or incurred for particular department are called ___.
A. direct expenses B. indirect expenses
C. monthly expenses D. weekly expenses

187. Expenses which cannot be identified with a particular department are called ___.
A. direct expenses B. indirect expenses
C. monthly expenses D. weekly expenses

188. Repairs to buildings, maintenance of premises should be divided among the different departments on the basis of ___.
A. light points B. H.P. of machine
C. sales ratio D. floor area

189. Lighting expenses should be divided among the different departments on the basis of ___.
A. light points B. H.P. of machine
C. sales ratio D. floor area

190. Carriage inward expenses should be divided among the different departments on the basis of ___.
A. light points B. purchase value
C. sales ratio D. floor area

191. Power expenses should be divided among the different departments on the basis of ___.
A. light points B. H.P. of machine
C. sales ratio D. floor area

192. Indirect expenses is also called ___.
A. prime cost B. common expenses
C. direct expenses D. management expenses

193. Indirect expenses is also called ___.
A. prime cost B. management expenses
C. joint expenses D. notional cost

194. Expenses which cannot be apportioned to department must be shown in the ___.
A. balance sheet
B. trading account
C. P & L account
D. P & L Appropriation account

195. When goods are transferred from one department to other department, they are called ___.
A. inter departmental transfers
B. outer departmental transfers
C. not a transfer
D. regular transfer

196. When goods are transferred from one department to other, the department transferring the goods should be ___.
A. debited B. credited
C. added D. subtracted

197. When goods are transferred from one department to other, the department transferring the goods should be credited and department receiving the goods should be ___.
A. debited B. credited
C. added D. subtracted

198. In departmental accounts expenses like director fees, interest is transferred to ___.
A. balance sheet
B. trading account
C. general P & L account
D. P & L Appropriation account

199. Branch which does not maintain its own set of books is ___.
A. dependent branch B. independent branch
C. foreign branch D. local branch

200. Branches not keeping full system of accounting are ___.
A. independent branch B. dependent branch
C. local branch D. foreign branch

201. All branch expenses such as rent, salary, are paid by the head office in case of ______.
A. independent branch B. local branch
C. regional branch D. dependent branch

202. Dependent branch makes ______.
A. only cash sales B. only credit sales
C. cash and credit sales D. instalment sales

203. Under stock and debtors system the head office opens ______.
A. branch adjustment account
B. branch debtors account
C. branch creditors account
D. branch cash account

204. In branch account, goods sent by branch X to branch Y, will be debited to ______.
A. branch K B. branch X
C. branch Z D. branch Y

205. Under branch accounts debtors system, the depreciation of an asset is ______.
A. shown in debtors account
B. shown in debit side of branch account
C. not shown in branch account
D. shown in credit side of branch account

206. Under branch accounts debtors system, opening balance of assets are recorded in ____.
A. credit side
B. debit side
C. first credit and debit side
D. first debit and credit side

207. Under branch accounts debtors system, closing balance of assets are recorded in ______.
A. credit side
B. debit side
C. first credit and debit side
D. first debit and credit side

208. Under branch accounts debtors system, opening balance of liabilities are recorded in ______.
A. first credit and debit side
B. first debit and credit side
C. credit side
D. debit side

209. Under branch accounts debtors system, loading on goods sent to branch adjusted in ______.
A. debit side B. credit side
C. asset side D. liabilities side

210. The difference between goods sent by head office and received by the branch is known as ______.
A. goods in transit
B. goods in godown
C. goods in production
D. goods in warehouse

211. Under stock and debtors system of branch account, the account prepared to record all the transactions relating to branch debtors is recorded in ______.
A. branch expenses account
B. branch adjustment account
C. branch debtors account
D. branch creditors account

212. In pure single entry which account is recorded:
A. Personal B. Real
C. Nominal D. Asset

213. All personal, real and nominal accounts are opened in:
A. single entry system B. double entry system
C. accrual system D. mercantile system

214. Only personal account and cash account are opened in:
A. single entry system B. double entry system
C. accrual system D. mercantile system

215. Trial balance cannot be prepared in______.
A. single entry system B. double entry system
C. accrual system D. mercantile system

216. Balance sheet can be prepared ______.
A. in single entry system
B. in double entry system
C. with the help of cash book
D. with the help of bank account

217. Balance sheet cannot be prepared ______ .
A. in single entry system
B. in double entry system
C. with the help of cash book
D. with the help of bank account

218. In single entry system, net worth method is also called ______.
A. double entry system
B. mercantile system
C. statement of affairs method
D. accrual system

219. Opening capital can be found by preparing ______.
A. cash book
B. bank account
C. statement of affairs
D. statement of bank pass book

220. A statement of affairs is just like a ______.
A. balance sheet B. profit and loss account
C. cash account D. trading account

221. In statement of affairs assets are shown on the ______.
A. right hand side B. left hand side
C. left hand side top D. left hand side bottom

222. In statement of affairs liabilities are shown on the ______.
A. right hand side B. left hand side
C. right hand side top D. right hand side bottom

223. Under single entry system, closing capital can be found by preparing a statement of affairs ________.
A. at the end of the year
B. at the beginning of the year
C. at the end of every month
D. at the end of every quarter

224. Under single entry system, opening capital can be found by preparing a statement of affairs ________.
A. at the end of the year
B. at the beginning of the year
C. at the end of every month
D. at the end of every quarter

225. Under single entry system in net worth method, additional capital is deducted with ________.
A. opening capital
B. closing capital
C. additional capital
D. drawings

226. Under single entry system in conversion method, a total debtors account is prepared to find out ______.
A. credit sales B. cash sales
C. credit purchases D. cash purchases

227. Under single entry system in conversion method, a total debtors account is prepared to find out ______.
A. credit purchases
B. cash purchases
C. cash sales
D. closing balance of debtors

228. Debtors account is a ________.
A. personal account B. real account
C. nominal account D. cash account

229. Total creditors account is prepared to find out ______.
A. credit sales B. cash sales
C. credit purchases D. cash purchases

230. Total creditors account is prepared to find out ______.
A. opening balance of debtors
B. closing balance of debtors
C. opening balance of creditors
D. closing balance of creditors

231. A bills receivable account is prepared to ascertain bills ________.
A. accepted B. received
C. drawn D. endorsed

232. A bills payable account is prepared to ascertain bills ________.
A. accepted B. received
C. drawn D. endorsed

233. Bills receivable dishonoured will be posted to ________ side of debtors account.
A. debit B. credit
C. outside D. inside

234. Bills receivable dishonoured will be posted in ________.
A. debit B. credit
C. outside D. inside

235. Transfer to creditors account will be posted in which side of debtors account:
A. Debit B. Credit
C. Outside D. Inside

236. Transfer to creditors account will be posted in which side of creditors account:
A. Debit B. Credit
C. Outside D. Inside

237. Bills payable dishonoured will be posted in which side of bills payable account:
A. Debit B. Credit
C. Outside D. Inside

238. Opening balance of debtors will be posted in which side of debtors account:
A. Debit B. Credit
C. Outside D. Inside

239. Closing balance of debtors will be posted in which side of debtors account:
A. Debit B. Credit
C. Outside D. Inside

240. Closing balance of creditors will be posted in which side of creditors account:
A. Debit B. Credit
C. Outside D. Inside

241. Opening balance of creditors will be posted in which side of creditors account:
A. Debit B. Credit
C. Outside D. Inside

242. Cash account opening balance will appear in ________.
A. debit B. credit
C. outside D. inside

243. Cash account closing balance will appear in ________.
A. debit B. credit
C. outside D. inside

244. Bills payable account closing balance will appear in ________.
A. debit B. credit
C. outside D. inside

245. Bills receivable account opening balance will appear in ________.
A. debit B. credit
C. outside D. inside

246. An agreement of sale is made under ________.
A. instalment system B. credit system
C. hire purchase system D. cash system

247. Under which system, ownership is transferred on payment of final instalment:
A. Instalment system B. Credit system
C. Hire purchase system D. Cash system

248. Under hire purchase system the buyer is called _____.
A. buyer B. hirer
C. hire vendor D. debtor

249. Under instalment system the relationship between the buyer and seller is that of a _____.
A. buyer and seller B. bailor and bailee
C. pawner and pawnee D. debtor and creditor

250. Under hire purchase system who has the right of sell _____.
A. buyer B. hirer
C. hire vendor D. debtor

251. Under hire purchase system, if instalment is not paid the hire vendor has right to _________.
A. sell the goods B. repossession of goods
C. repair the goods D. purchase the goods

252. Under hire purchase system, the agreement can be _________.
A. renewed B. registered
C. terminated D. endorsed

253. Instalment system is governed by _________.
A. Hire Purchase Act
B. Sale of Goods Act
C. Instalment Act
D. Properties Registration Act

254. Under hire purchase system, the retail price of the articles is called _________.
A. MRP B. wholesale price
C. retail price D. cash price

255. Cash price plus interest is _________.
A. instalment price B. hire purchase price
C. maximum retail price D. retail price

256. The advance amount under hire purchase system is called _________.
A. cash price B. retail price
C. interest D. down payment

257. Under hire purchase system, interest is calculated on _________.
A. cash price B. hire purchase price
C. MRP D. outstanding balance

258. If the hire purchaser fails to make payment of any instalment, it is called ____.
A. default B. repossession
C. sale D. purchase

259. If the hire vendor may take away all the goods on which there is default of instalment it is called _____.
A. repossession B. partial repossession
C. complete repossession D. purchase

260. The hire vendor takes away only a portion of the goods on which there is default of instalments it is called _________.
A. repossession B. partial repossession
C. complete repossession D. purchase

261. In the books of hirer, for payment of instalment hire vendor account will be _________.
A. debited B. credited
C. rectified D. reversed

262. In the books of hirer, for interest due at the end of the year hire vendor account will be _________.
A. debited B. credited
C. rectified D. reversed

263. In the books of Hirer, the interest and depreciation account will be transferred to _____.
A. Trading account
B. P & L account
C. P & L appropriation account
D. Balance sheet

264. In the books of hirer, when the asset is repossessed hire vendor account will be _____.
A. debited B. credited
C. rectified D. reversed

265. In the books of hirer, when the asset is repossessed, asset account will be _____.
A. debited B. credited
C. rectified D. reversed

266. In the books of hire vendor, when down payment is received, the hirer account will be _________.
A. debited B. credited
C. rectified D. reversed

267. The average clause in a loss of profits policy protects by _____.
A. Insured B. Insurer
C. Workers D. None of the above

268. Debtor ledger is meant for keeping _________.
A. personal A/c of trade debtors
B. real A/c
C. nominal A/c
D. impersonal A/c

269. Creditors ledger is meant for keeping _________.
A. real A/c
B. nominal A/c
C. personal A/c of creditors
D. impersonal A/c

270. Errors can be easily found out if _______ system is maintained.
A. single ledger
B. self balancing ledger
C. single entry
D. double entry

271. The amount set aside from P&L A/c is called as ________.
A. reserve B. provision
C. depreciation D. fund

272. The amount set aside for meeting future losses is ________.
A. reserve B. provision
C. depreciation D. fund

273. The amount which is appropriated out of profit is ________.
A. reserve B. provision
C. depreciation D. fund

274. Which one of the following is an example of reserve?
A. P&L A/c
B. Provision for depreciation
C. Provision for bad debts
D. Provision for income tax

275. Which one of the following is an example of provision?
A. Securities premium B. Revaluation reserve
C. Capital reserve D. Provision for bad debts

276. Which of the following item gives tax benefit?
A. Creation of secret reserve
B. Creation of capital reserve
C. Creation of general reserve
D. Creation of provision

277. Reserve is debited to ________.
A. Trading A/c
B. P&L A/c
C. P&L Appropriation A/c
D. Manufacturing A/c

278. Provision is debited to ________.
A. Trading A/c
B. P&L A/c
C. P&L Appropriation A/c
D. Manufacturing A/c

279. Which one of the following is utilized for distribution of dividend?
A. Capital Redemption Reserve
B. Securities premium
C. Revaluation reserve
D. General reserve

280. Reserve which is created out of capital profit is ________.
A. revenue reserve B. capital reserve
C. provision D. general reserve

281. Unpaid salary for ₹ 340 is to be provided for in the accounts.
A. Bills Receivable Book
B. Purchases Book
C. Journal Proper (General Journal)
D. Purchases Return

282. Which one of the following is not a specific reserve?
A. Debenture Redemption Reserve
B. Dividend Equalization Reserve
C. General reserve
D. Investment Fluctuation Fund

283. Secret reserve can be created by ________.
A. debiting P&L A/c
B. undervaluing assets
C. crediting P&L A/c
D. crediting P&L Appropriation A/c

284. Fire insurance policy can be taken for ________.
A. loss of stock
B. loss of profit
C. life of a partner
D. loss of stock or/and loss of profit

285. The stock which is rescued from fire is ________.
A. scrap B. defectives
C. salvaged stock D. claim

286. The period for which insurance policy is taken against the risk of fire is ________.
A. accounting period B. calendar period
C. indemnity period D. standard period

287. The difference between standard turnover and affected period turnover is ________.
A. short sales
B. annual turnover
C. accounting year turnover
D. saved turnover

288. In order to calculate value of closing stock, which A/c is to be prepared:
A. P&L A/c
B. P&L Appropriation A/c
C. Memorandum Trading A/c
D. Memorandum P&L A/c

289. In debtor ledger A/c, only ________ is prepared.
A. trade creditors A/c B. all creditors A/c
C. cash purchase A/c D. cash sales A/c

290. In creditor ledger A/c only ________ is prepared.
A. trade creditors A/c B. all creditors A/c
C. cash purchase A/c D. cash sales A/c

291. Creditors ledger adjustment A/c normally shows the opening balance in ________.
A. debit B. credit
C. either debit or credit D. debit and credit

292. General ledger adjustment A/c in debtor ledger shows ________ balance.
A. debit B. credit
C. either debit or credit D. debit and credit

293. General ledger adjustment A/c in creditor ledger shows ________ balance.
A. debit B. credit
C. either debit or credit D. debit and credit

294. An account which contains all the trade debtors is ________.
A. purchase ledger B. sales ledger
C. general ledger D. subordinate ledger

295. An account which contains all the trade creditors is ________.
A. purchase ledger B. sales ledger
C. general ledger D. subordinate ledger

296. The branch which does not maintain its own set of books is ________.
A. dependent branch B. independent branch
C. foreign branch D. local branch

297. Which of the following method is used to ascertain profit in single entry system?
A. net worth method B. lump sum method
C. net asset method D. double accounting system

298. Total debtors A/c reveals (as a balancing figure) ________.
A. cash collected from debtors
B. credit purchase.
C. cash paid to creditors
D. closing stock.

299. Total creditors A/c reveals (as a balancing figure) ________.
A. credit purchases B. credit sales
C. closing stock D. closing debtors

300. Bills payables A/c reveals ________ as a balancing figure.
A. opening B/P B. opening stock
C. opening debtors D. opening creditors

301. Creating a reserve is ________.
A. optional B. compulsory
C. essential D. statutory

302. Under Debtors system, the cash sales are ________.
A. debited to the branch A/c
B. credited to the branch A/c
C. debited to debtors A/c
D. credited to creditors A/c

303. Under annuity method, the amount of depreciation is ________.
A. increasing every year B. decreasing every year
C. fixed for all the years D. change every year

304. Sundry debtors means a person who purchases goods on ________.
A. cash basis B. credit basis
C. instalment basis D. cash and credit basis

305. General Ledger Adjustment A/c(s) are opened in ____.
A. debtors ledger
B. creditor ledger
C. debtors and creditors ledger
D. bills receivable ledger

306. Under hire purchase system is interest is calculated on ________.
A. outstanding balance B. hire purchase price
C. cash price D. down payment

307. The reserve which is not disclosed by the balance sheet ________.
A. general reserve B. specific reserve
C. secret reserve D. capital reserve

308. In each department, depreciation is to apportioned on the basis of ________.
A. value of machinery
B. life time of machinery
C. production capacity of machinery
D. power consumed by the machinery

309. Nature of hire purchase agreement is ________.
A. agreement of sale B. option to transfer
C. option to buy D. option to sell

310. The amount of purchase if
Cost of goods sold is ₹ 80,700
Opening stock : ₹ 5,800
Closing stock : ₹ 6,000
A. ₹ 80,500 B. ₹ 74,900
C. ₹ 74,700 D. ₹ 80,900

311. Average stock = ₹ 12,000. Closing stock is ₹ 3,000 more than opening stock. The value of closing stock = ________.
A. ₹ 12,000 B. ₹ 24,000
C. ₹ 10,500 D. ₹ 13,500

312. If the profit is 25% of the cost price, then it is:
A. 25% of the sales price
B. 33% of the sales price
C. 20% of the sales price
D. 20% of the sales price

313. Goods purchased ₹ 1,00,000. Sales ₹ 90,000. Margin 20% on cost. Closing stock = ?
A. 15,000 B. 10,000
C. 25,000 D. 28,000

314. In purchases Book the record is in respect of:
A. Cash purchase of goods
B. Credit purchase of goods dealt in,
C. All purchases of goods
D. None of these

315. If the goods purchased are in transit, then the journal entry at the end of the period will be
A. Goods-in-transit A/c Dr.
To Supplier's A/c
B. Goods-in-transit A/c Dr.
To Purchase A/c
C. Stock A/c Dr.
To Good-in-transit A/c
D. Supplier's A/c Dr.
To Goods-in-transit A/c

316. On April 07, 2005, *i.e.,* a week after the end of the accounting year 2004-05, a company undertook physical stock verification. The value of stock as per physical stock verification was found to be ₹ 35,000. The following details pertaining to the period April 01, 2005 to April 07, 2005 are given:

I. Goods costing ₹ 5,000 were sold during the week.
II. Goods received from consignor amounting to ₹ 4,000 included in the value of stock.
III. Goods earlier purchased but returned during the period amounted to ₹ 1,000.
IV. Goods earlier purchased and accounted but not received ₹ 6,000.

After considering the above, the value of stock held as on March 31, 2005 was

A. ₹ 27,000 B. ₹ 19,000
C. ₹ 43,000 D. ₹ 51,000

317. While finalizing the current year's profit, the company realized that there was an error in the valuation of closing stock of the previous year. In the previous year, closing stock was valued more by ₹ 50,000. As a result

A. Previous year's profit is overstated and current year's profit is also overstated
B. Previous year's profit is understated and current year's profit is overstated
C. Previous year's profit is understated and current year's profit is also understated
D. Previous year's profit is overstated and current year's profit is understated

318. The total cost of goods available for sale with a company during the current year is ₹ 12,00,000 and the total sales during the period are ₹ 13,00,000. If the gross profit margin of the company is $33\frac{1}{3}\%$ on cost, the closing inventory during the current year is

A. ₹ 4,00,000 B. ₹ 3,00,000
C. ₹ 2,25,000 D. ₹ 2,60,000

319. A company follows weighted average cost method for the valuation of its inventory. The details of purchase and issue of raw-materials pertaining to the company during the week April 01, 2006 to April 07, 2006 are as follows

Date	Particulars	Purchases (Units)	Issues (Units)	Rate per Unit (₹)
April 01	Opening stock	50		44
April 02		100		47
April 04			50	

The value of inventory at the end of the week under weighted average method is

A. ₹ 4,600 B. ₹ 4,550
C. ₹ 4,700 D. ₹ 4,400

320. Consider the following data pertaining to H Ltd. for the month of March 2005.

Particulars	As on March 01, 2005 (₹)	As on March 31, 2005 (₹)
Stock	1,80,000	90,000

The company made purchases amounting ₹ 3,30,000 on credit. During the month of March 2005, the company paid a sum of ₹ 3,50,000 to the suppliers. The goods are sold at 25% above the cost. The sales for the month of March 2005 were:

A. ₹ 4,12,500 B. ₹ 5,25,000
C. ₹ 90,000 D. ₹ 3,15,000

321. Consider the following data pertaining to a company for the month of March 2005:

Particulars	₹
Opening stock	22,000
Closing stock	25,000
Purchases less returns	1,10,000
Gross profit margin (on sales)	20%

The sales of the company during the month are

A. ₹ 1,41,250 B. ₹ 1,35,600
C. ₹ 1,33,750 D. ₹ 1,28,400

322. Consider the following data pertaining to R Ltd. for the month of June 2004:

Particulars	₹
Opening stock	30,000
Closing stock	40,000
Purchases	5,60,000
Returns outward	15,000
Returns inward	20,000
Carriage inward	5,000

If the gross profit is 20% of net sales, the gross sales for the month of June 2004 is:

A. ₹ 6,95,000
B. ₹ 6,75,000
C. ₹ 5,40,000
D. ₹ 6,68,750

323. Consider the following for Q Co. for the year 2005-06:

Cost of goods available for sale	₹ 1,00,000
Total sales	₹ 80,000
Opening stock of goods	₹ 20,000
Gross profit margin	25%

Closing stock of goods for the year 2005-06 was

A. ₹ 80,000
B. ₹ 60,000
C. ₹ 40,000
D. ₹ 36,000

324. Which of the following is false?

A. The value of ending inventory under simple average price method is realistic

B. Usually profit or loss will not arise out of pricing the issues on the basis of simple average price method

C. The value of stock is shown on the assets side of the balance-sheet as fixed assets

D. None of these

325. Under inflationary conditions, which of the methods will not show highest value of closing stock?

A. FIFO

B. LIFO

C. Weighted Average

D. None of the above

326. Under inflationary conditions, which of the methods will not show lowest value of closing stock?

A. FIFO B. LIFO

C. Weighted Average D. All of the above

327. Under inflationary conditions, which of the methods will not show greatest value of cost of goods sold?

A. FIFO B. LIFO

C. Weighted Average D. None of the above

328. Under inflationary conditions, which of the methods will not show lowest value of goods sold?

A. FIFO B. LIFO

C. Weighted Average D. None of the above

329. The balance of the petty cash is:

A. An expense B. An income

C. An asset D. A liability

330. Fixed assets are:

A. Kept in the business for use over a long time for earning income

B. Meant for resale

C. Meant for conversion into cash as quickly as possible

D. All of the above

331. Goodwill is:

A. A current asset B. An intangible fixed asset

C. A tangible fixed asset D. An investment.

332. Inventory is:

A. Included in the category of fixed assets

B. An investment

C. A part of current assets

D. An intangible fixed asset

333. The manufacturing account is prepared:

A. To ascertain the profit or loss on the goods produced

B. To ascertain the cost of the manufactured goods

C. To show the sale proceeds from the goods produced during the year

D. Both B and C

334. On 1.1.2011, X draws a bill on Y for ₹ 20,000 for 3 months maturity date of the bill will be:

A. 1.4.2011 B. 3.4.2011

C. 4.4.2011 D. 4.5.2011

335. On 15.8.2011, X draws a bill on Y for 3 months for ₹ 20,000. 18th Nov. was a sudden holiday, maturity date of the bill will be:

A. 17th Nov B. 18th Nov

C. 19th Nov D. 15th Nov

336. On 16.6.2011, X draws a bill on Y for ₹ 25,000 for 30 days. 19th July is a public holiday, maturity date of the bill will be:

A. 19th July B. 18th July

C. 17th July D. 16th July

337. X draws a bill on Y for ₹ 30,000 on 1.1.2011. X accepts the same on 4.1.2011 for period of 3 months after date. What will be the maturity date of the bill:

A. 4.4.2011 B. 3.4.2011

C. 7.4.2011 D. 8.4.2011

338. X draws a bill on Y. X endorsed the bill to Z. The payee of the bill will be:

A. X B. Y

C. Z D. None

339. A bill of ₹ 12,000 was discounted by A with the banker for ₹ 11,880. At maturity, the bill returned dishonoured, noting charges ₹ 20. How much amount will the bank deduct from A's bank balance at the time of such dishonour?

A. ₹ 12,000 B. ₹ 11,880

C. ₹ 12,020 D. ₹ 11,900

340. X draws a bill on Y for ₹ 20,000 on 1.1.2011 for 3 months after sight, date of acceptance is 6.1.2011. Maturity date of the bill will be:

A. 8.4.2011 B. 9.4.2011

C. 10.4.2011 D. 11.4.2011

341. X sold goods to Y for ₹ 1,00,000. Y paid cash ₹ 30,000. X will grant 2% discount on balance, and Y request X to draw a bill for balance, the amount of bill will be:

A. ₹ 98,000 B. ₹ 68,000

C. ₹ 68,600 D. ₹ 70,000

342. On 1.1.2011, X draws a bill on Y for ₹ 50,000 for 3 months. X got the bill discounted 4.1.2011 at 12% rate. The amount of discount on bill will be:

A. ₹ 1,500 B. ₹ 1,600

C. ₹ 1,800 D. ₹ 1,450

343. Mr. A draws a bill on Mr. Y for ₹ 30,000 on 1.1.2011 for 3 months. On 4.2.2011, X got the bill discounted at 12% rate. The amount of discount will be:

A. ₹ 900 B. ₹ 600

C. ₹ 300 D. ₹ 650

344. X draws a bill on Y for ₹ 20,000 for 3 months on 1.1.2011. The bill is discounted with banker at a charge of ₹ 100. At maturity the bill return dishonoured. In the books of X, for dishonour, the bank account will be credited by:

A. ₹ 19,900 B. ₹ 20,000
C. ₹ 20,100 D. ₹ 19,800

345. On 1.1.2011, X draws a bill on Y for ₹ 10,000. At maturity Y request X to renew the bill for 2 month at 12% p.a. interest. Amount of interest will be:

A. ₹ 200 B. ₹ 150
C. ₹ 180 D. ₹ 190

346. On 1.1.2011, X draws a bill on Y for ₹ 15,000 for 3 months. At maturity Y request X to accept ₹ 5,000 in cash and for balance to draw a fresh bill for 2 months together with 12% p.a. interest, amount of interest will be:

A. ₹ 200 B. ₹ 300
C. ₹ 240 D. ₹ 380

347. On 1.8.2011, X draws a bill on Y "for 30 days after sight". The date of acceptance is 8.8.2011. The maturity date of the bill will be:

A. 8.9.2011 B. 10.9.2011
C. 11.9.2011 D. 9.9.2011

348. On 1.6.2011, X draws a bill on Y for ₹ 25,000. At maturity Y request X to accept ₹ 5,000 in cash and noting charges incurred ₹ 100 and for the balance X draw a bill on Y for 2 months at 12% p.a. Interest amount will be:

A. ₹ 410 B. ₹ 420
C. ₹ 440 D. ₹ 400

349. On 1.1.2011, X draws a bill on Y for ₹ 50,000. At maturity, the bill returned dishonoured as Y become insolvent and 40 paise per rupee is recovered from his estate. The amount recovered is:

A. ₹ 20,000 B. Nil
C. ₹ 30,000 D. 40 paise

350. X draws a bill on Y for ₹ 3,000. X endorsed to Z. Y will pay the amount of the bill to:

A. X B. Z
C. To himself D. None

351. On 1.1.2011, X draws a bill on Y for 3 months for ₹ 10,000. On 4.3.2011, Y pay the bill to X at 12% p.a. discount, the amount of discount will be:

A. 100 B. 200
C. 300 D. 50

352. The purpose of accommodation bill is:

A. To finance actual purchase or sale of goods
B. To facilitate trade transmission
C. When both parties are in need of funds
D. None of the above

353. On 1.1.2011, X draws a bill on Y for ₹ 30,000. At maturity Y request X to draw a fresh bill for 2 months together with 12% p.a. interest. Noting charges ₹ 100. The amount of interest will be:

A. ₹ 600 B. ₹ 602
C. ₹ 500 D. ₹ 550

354. On 18.2.2011, A draw a bill on B for ₹ 10,000. B accepted the bill on 21.2.2011. The bill is drawn for 30 days after sight. The maturity date of the bill will be:

A. 24.3.2011 B. 22.3.2011
C. 26.3.2011 D. 21.3.2011

355. X sold goods to Y for ₹ 3,00,000. ½ of the amount will be received in cash and balance in B/R. For what amount X should draw the bill on Y.

A. ₹ 1,50,000 B. ₹ 3,00,000
C. ₹ 1,00,000 D. ₹ 1,20,000

356. A draws a bill on B for ₹ 50,000 for 3 months. At maturity, the bill returned dishonoured, noting charges ₹ 500. 40 paise in a rupee is recovered from B's estate. The amount of deficiency to be recorded on insolvency in the books of B will be:

A. ₹ 20,200 B. ₹ 30,300
C. ₹ 19,800 D. ₹ 19,000

357. A sold goods to B for ₹ 20,000. A will grant 5% discount to B. B requested A to draw a bill. The amount of the bill will be:

A. ₹ 20,000 B. ₹ 19,000
C. ₹ 19,200 D. Nil

358. Fees paid in cash to Notary Public is charged by:

A. Drawer
B. Drawee
C. Holder of the bill of exchange
D. None

359. A draws a bill on B for ₹ 50,000. A endorsed it to C in full settlement of ₹ 50,500. Noting charges of ₹ 200 as the bill returned dishonoured. A want to pay the amount to C at 2% discount. The amount to be paid by A to C will be:

A. ₹ 49,000 B. ₹ 49,490
C. ₹ 49,686 D. ₹ 50,500

360. A draws a bill on B for ₹ 1,00,000. A endorsed the bill to C. The bill return dishonoured. Noting charges ₹ 1,000. B request A to accept the amount at 2% discount by a single cheque. The cheque amount will be:

A. ₹ 98,000 B. ₹ 98,980
C. ₹ 99,000 D. ₹ 99,980

361. The promissory note should be signed by:

A. Drawer B. Drawee
C. Payee D. Promiser

362. Kuntal draws a bill on Shyam for ₹ 3,000. Kuntal endorsed it to Ram. Ram endorsed it to Rahim. The payee of the bill will be:

A. Kuntal B. Ram
C. Shyam D. Rahim

363. A bill is drawn on 29th Jan. 2011 for one month after date. The date of acceptance is 2nd Feb. 2011. The maturity date of the bill will be:

A. 28th February B. 1st March
C. 2nd March D. 3rd March

364. Mr. Rex accepted a bill drawn by Mr. Rabin. Mr. Rabin endorsed the bill to Mr. Shekhar. On the due date, the bill is dishonoured as Mr. Rex became insolvent. To record the dishonour of the bill in the books of Mr. Rabin, which of the following accounts should be credited?

A. Mr. Rex's account B. Bills Receivable account
C. Mr. Shekhar's account D. Bills Payable account

365. Which of the following statements is true?

A. A bill cannot be endorsed more than two times
B. A bill is drawn by purchaser
C. A bill contains an unconditional promise to pay
D. Noting charges are borne by the drawee in the event of dishonour of bill

366. For mutual accommodation of A and B, B accepted a bill drawn on him by A for 2 months for ₹ 6,000. The said bill is discounted at 12% p.a. and remitted 1/3rd of the proceeds to B. The amount remitted by A to B will be:

A. ₹ 2,000 B. ₹ 1,960
C. ₹ 1,920 D. ₹ 1,900

367. Lara draws an accommodation bill on Sachin. The proceeds are to be borne between Sachin and Lara in the ratio of 3 : 1. The amount of bill ₹ 6000, discounting charges ₹ 120. Discount borne by Sachin will be:

A. ₹ 90 B. ₹ 120
C. ₹ 100 D. None

368. Which of the following instrument is not a negotiable instrument?

A. Bearer cheque
B. Promissory note
C. Bill of exchange
D. Account Payee Crossed cheque

369. Neelam sold goods to Dhiman for ₹ 4,000 on 1.5.2011. On the same day, she drew on Dhiman a bill for the amount for 3 months, which Dhiman duly accepted. Neelam got the bill discounted with her bank before the due date, Dhiman became insolvent. Later, his estate could pay only 40% of the amount due. What will be the amount of deficiency in the books of Dhiman.

A. ₹ 3,200 B. ₹ 2,200
C. ₹ 2,400 D. ₹ 2,000

370. Which of the following is not a foreign bill?

A. A bill drawn in India, on a person resident outside India and made payable outside India.
B. A bill drawn outside India, on a person resident outside India
C. A bill drawn outside India, made payable in India
D. A bill drawn on a person resident in India, made payable in India

371. A drew a bill on B for ₹ 50,000 for 3 months. Proceeds are to be shared equally. A got the bill discounted at 12% p.a. and remits required proceeds to B. The amount of such remittance will be:

A. ₹ 24,250 B. ₹ 25,000
C. ₹ 16,167 D. ₹ 32,333

372. From the following information, find out who can draw the bill if Mr A sold goods to B:

A. A will draw a bill on B
B. B will draw a bill on A
C. None of these
D. Third party will draw a bill on A

373. When the bill are to be produced to notary public:

A. At the time of drawing the bill
B. At the time of acceptance of the bill
C. At the time of dishonour of the bill
D. At the time of "bill for collection"

374. Which of the following statement is false?

A. B/R is a negotiable instrument
B. B/R must be accepted by drawee
C. There can be three parties in respect of bills of exchange – drawer, drawee & payee
D. Oral bill of exchange is also valid

375. Under which circumstances drawer and payee is same person:

A. When drawer discounted the bill with banker
B. When drawer endorse the bill to the third party
C. When drawer held the bill till maturity
D. When drawee rejects to accept the bill

376. Which of the following statement is true?

A. Noting charge is an expense to be borne by drawer
B. Noting charge is an expense to be borne by drawee
C. Noting charge is an expense to be borne by payee
D. Noting charge is an expense to be borne by bank

377. Which of the following statement is true?

A. Account payables can draw a bill on Account receivables
B. Account receivables can draw a bill on Account payables
C. Bank will draw a bill on customer at the time of overdraft
D. One can draw the bill on another under any circumstances

378. X draws a bill on Y on 1.1.2011 for ₹ 20,000 for 30 days. What will be the maturity date of the bill?
A. 2.2.2011 B. 3.2.2011
C. 1.2.2011 D. 31.1.2011

379. Ram's acceptance to Din for ₹ 8,000 renewed at 3 months on the condition that ₹ 4,000 be paid in cash immediately and the remaining amount will carry interest @ 12% p.a. The amount of interest will be:
A. ₹ 120 B. ₹ 80
C. ₹ 90 D. ₹ 160

380. A draws a bill on B for ₹ 30,000. A wants to endorse it to C in settlement of ₹ 35,000 at 2% discount with the help of B's acceptance and balance in cash. How much cash A will pay to B?
A. ₹ 4,300 B. ₹ 4,000
C. ₹ 4,100 D. ₹ 5,000

381. Ram gets Ghosh's acceptance for ₹ 12,000 discounted at 2 months at 12% p.a. The amount of discount will be:
A. ₹ 240 B. ₹ 120
C. ₹ 360 D. Nil

382. If the due date is a public holiday, what will be the due date of the bill?
A. Following day B. Preceding day
C. The same day only D. One month later

383. Which of the following is not a subfield of accounting?
A. Management accounting
B. Cost accounting
C. Financial accounting
D. Book-keeping

384. Purposes of an accounting system include all the following except:
A. Interpret and record the effects of business transaction
B. Classify the effects of transactions to facilitate the preparation of reports
C. Summarize and communicate information to decision makers
D. Dictate the specific types of business enterprise transactions that the enterprises may engage in

385. Book-keeping is mainly concerned with:
A. Recording of financial data
B. Designing the systems in recording, classifying and summarising the recorded data
C. Interpreting the data for internal and external users
D. None of the above

386. All of the following are functions of Accounting except:
A. Decision making
B. Measurement
C. Forecasting
D. Ledger posting

387. Financial statements are part of:
A. Accounting
B. Book-keeping
C. All of the above
D. None of the above

388. Financial position of the business is ascertained on the basis of:
A. Records prepared under book-keeping process
B. Trial balance
C. Accounting reports
D. None of the above

389. Users of accounting information include:
A. Trade payables/Suppliers
B. Lenders
C. Customers
D. All of the above

390. Financial statements do not consider:
A. Assets expressed in monetary terms
B. Liabilities expressed in monetary terms
C. Only assets expressed in non-monetary terms
D. Assets and liabilities expressed in non-monetary terms

391. On January 1, Sohan paid rent of ₹ 5,000. This can be classified as:
A. An event
B. A transaction
C. A transaction as well as an event
D. Neither a transaction nor an event

392. On March 31, 2011 after sale of goods worth ₹ 2,000, he is left with the closing inventory of ₹ 10,000. This is:
A. An event
B. A transaction
C. A transaction as well as an event
D. Neither a transaction nor an event

393. All the following items are classified as fundamental accounting assumptions except:
A. Consistency B. Business entity
C. Going concern D. Accrual

394. Two primary qualitative characteristics of financial statements are:
A. Understandability and materiality
B. Relevance and reliability
C. Neutrality and understandability
D. Materiality and reliability

395. Kanika Enterprises follows the written down value method of depreciating machinery year after year due to:
A. Comparability
B. Convenience
C. Consistency
D. All of the above

396. A purchased a car for ₹ 5,00,000, making a down payment of ₹ 1,00,000 and signing a ₹ 4,00,000 bill payable due in 60 days. As a result of this transaction:
A. Total assets increased by ₹ 5,00,000
B. Total liabilities increased by ₹ 4,00,000
C. Total assets increased by ₹ 4,00,000
D. Total assets increased by ₹ 4,00,000 with corresponding increase in liabilities by ₹ 4,00,000

397. Mohan purchased goods for ₹ 15,00,000 and sold 4/5th of the goods amounting ₹ 18,00,000 and met expenses amounting ₹ 2,50,000 during the year, 2011. He counted net profit as ₹ 3,50,000. Which of the accounting concept was followed by him?
A. Entity B. Periodicity
C. Matching D. Conservatism

398. A businessman purchased goods for ₹ 25,00,000 and sold 80% of such goods during the accounting year ended 31st March, 2011. The market value of the remaining goods was ₹ 4,00,000. He valued the closing inventory at cost. He violated the concept of:
A. Money measurement
B. Conservatism
C. Cost
D. Periodicity

399. Capital brought in by the proprietor is an example of:
A. Increase in asset and increase in liability
B. Increase in liability and decrease in asset
C. Increase in asset and decrease in liability
D. Increase in one asset and decrease in another asset

400. Assets are held in the business for the purpose of:
A. Resale
B. Conversion into cash
C. Earning revenue
D. None of the above

401. Revenue from sale of products, is generally, realized in the period in which:
A. Cash is collected
B. Sale is made
C. Products are manufactured
D. None of the above

402. The concept of conservatism when applied to the balance sheet results in:
A. Understatement of assets
B. Overstatement of assets
C. Overstatement of capital
D. None of the above

403. Decrease in the amount of trade payables results in:
A. Increase in cash
B. Decrease in bank over draft account
C. Decrease in assets
D. No change in assets

404. The determination of expenses for an accounting period is based on the principle of:
A. Objectivity B. Materiality
C. Matching D. Periodicity

405. Economic life of an enterprise is split into the periodic interval to measure its performance is as per:
A. Entity B. Matching
C. Periodicity D. Accrual

406. If an individual asset is increased, there will be a corresponding:
A. Increase of another asset or increase of capital
B. Decrease of another asset or increase of liability
C. Decrease of specific liability or decrease of capital
D. Increase of drawings and liability

407. Purchase of machinery for cash:
A. Decreases total assets
B. Increases total assets
C. Retains total assets unchanged
D. Decreases total liabilities

408. Consider the following data pertaining to Alpha Ltd.:

Particulars	₹
Cost of machinery purchased on 1st April, 2010	10,00,000
Instalation charges	1,00,000
Market value as on 31st March, 2011	12,00,000

While finalizing the annual accounts, if the company values the machinery at ₹ 12,00,000. Which of the following concepts is violated by the Alpha Ltd.?
A. Cost B. Matching
C. Accrual D. Periodicity

409. The rent paid to landlord is credited to:
A. Landlord's account B. Rent account
C. Cash account D. None of the above

410. In case of a debt becoming bad, the amount should be credited to:
A. Trade receivables account
B. Bad debts account
C. Cash account
D. Sales account

411. Sunset Tours has a ₹ 3,500 account receivable from Mohan. On January 20, the Rotary makes a partial payment of ₹ 2100 to Sunset Tours. The journal entry made on January 20 by Sunset Tours to record this transaction includes:
A. A credit to the cash received account of ₹ 2,100.
B. A credit to the Accounts receivable account of ₹ 2,100.
C. A debit to the cash account of ₹ 1,400.
D. A debit to the Accounts receivable account of ₹ 1,400.

412. Which financial statement represents the accounting equation?
Assets = Liabilities + Owner's equity:
A. Income Statement
B. Statement of Cash flows
C. Balance Sheet
D. None of the above

413. Which account is the odd one out?
A. Office furniture & Equipment
B. Freehold land and Buildings
C. Inventory of materials
D. Plant and Machinery

414. The debts written off as bad, if recovered subsequently are:
A. Credited to Bad Debts Recovered Account
B. Credited to Trade receivables Account
C. Debited to Profit and Loss Account
D. None of the above

415. Prepaid salary account comes under:
A. Personal
B. Real
C. Nominal
D. None of the above

416. Bill payable account comes under:
A. Personal B. Real
C. Nominal D. None of the above

417. Rent account comes under:
A. Personal B. Real
C. Nominal D. None of the above

418. Proprietor's account comes under:
A. Personal B. Real
C. Nominal D. None of the above

419. Patents account comes under:
A. Personal B. Real
C. Nominal D. None of the above

420. Salaries comes under:
A. revenue (R) B. expense (E)
C. asset (A) D. liability (L)

421. Equipment comes under:
A. revenue (R) B. expense (E)
C. asset (A) D. liability (L)

422. Accounts payable comes under:
A. revenue (R) B. expense (E)
C. asset (A) D. liability (L)

423. Membership fees earned comes under:
A. revenue (R) B. expense (E)
C. asset (A) D. liability (L)

424. Inventory comes under:
A. revenue (R) B. expense (E)
C. asset (A) D. liability (L)

425. Accounts receivable comes under:
A. revenue (R) B. expense (E)
C. asset (A) D. liability (L)

426. Building comes under:
A. revenue (R) B. expense (E)
C. asset (A) D. liability (L)

427. Profits comes under:
A. revenue (R)
B. expense (E)
C. asset (A)
D. owner's capital (OC) item

428. In Double Entry System of Book-keeping every business transaction affects:
A. Two accounts
B. Two sides of the same account
C. The same account on two different dates
D. All of the above

429. A sale of goods to Ram for cash should be debited to:
A. Ram B. Cash
C. Sales D. Capital

430. A withdrawal of cash from business by the proprietor should be credited to:
A. Drawing Account
B. Capital Account
C. Cash Account
D. Purchase Account

431. The process of transferring the debit and credit items from a Journal to their respective accounts in the ledger is termed as:
A. Posting
B. Purchase
C. Balancing of an account
D. Arithmetically accuracy test

432. The technique of finding the net balance of an account after considering the totals of both debits and credits appearing in the account is known as:
A. Posting
B. Purchase
C. Balancing of an account
D. Arithmetically accuracy test

433. Journal and ledger records transactions in:
A. A chronological order and analytical order respectively
B. An analytical order and chronological order respectively
C. A chronological order only
D. An analytical order only

434. Ledger book is popularly known as:
A. Secondary book of accounts
B. Principal book of accounts
C. Subsidiary book of accounts
D. None of the above

435. At the end of the accounting year all the nominal accounts of the ledger book are:
A. Balanced but not transferred to profit and loss account
B. Not balanced and also the balance is not transferred to the profit and loss account
C. Balanced and the balance is transferred to the balance sheet
D. Not balanced and their balance is transferred to the profit and loss account

436. A trial balance will not balance if:
A. Correct journal entry is posted twice
B. The purchase on credit basis is debited to purchases and credited to cash
C. ₹ 500 cash payment to creditor is debited to Trade payables for ₹ 50 and credited to cash as ₹ 500
D. None of the above

437. ₹ 1,500 received from sub-tenant for rent and entered correctly in the cash book is posted to the debit of the rent account. In the trial balance:
A. The debit total will be greater by ₹ 3,000 than the credit total
B. The debit total will be greater by ₹ 1,500 than the credit total
C. Subject to other entries being correct the total will agree
D. None of the above

438. After the preparation of ledgers, the next step is the preparation of:
A. Trading accounts
B. Trial balance
C. Profit and loss account
D. None of the above

439. After preparing the trial balance the accountant finds that the total of debit side is short by ₹ 1,500. This difference will be:
A. Credited to suspense account
B. Debited to suspense account
C. Adjusted to any of the debit balance account
D. Adjusted to any of the credit balance account

440. The debit note issued are used to prepare:
A. Sales return book
B. Purchase return book
C. Sales book
D. Purchases book

441. An allowance of ₹ 50 was offered for an early payment of cash of ₹ 1,050.
A. Sales Book
B. Cash Book
C. Journal Proper (General Journal)
D. Purchase Book

442. A second hand motor car was purchased on credit from B Brothers for ₹ 10,000.
A. Journal Proper (General Journal)
B. Sales Book
C. Cash Book
D. Purchase Book

443. Goods were sold on credit basis to A Brothers for ₹ 1,000.
A. Cash Book
B. Journal Proper (General Journal)
C. Sales Book
D. Bills Receivable Book

444. Accounting for partial recovery from Mr. C of an amount of ₹ 2,000 earlier written off as bad debt.
A. Journal Proper (General Journal)
B. Sales Book
C. Purchase Book
D. Cash Book

445. Credit purchase of stationery worth ₹ 5,000 by a stationery dealer.
A. Purchase Book
B. Sales Book
C. Cash Book
D. Journal Proper (General Journal)

446. A bills receivable of ₹ 1,000, which was received from a debtor in full settlement for a claim of ₹ 1,100, is dishonoured.
A. Purchases Return Book
B. Bills Receivable Book
C. Purchases Book
D. Journal Proper (General Journal)

447. Purchased goods from E worth ₹ 5,000 on credit basis.
A. Bills Receivable Book
B. Purchases Book
C. Journal Proper (General Journal)
D. Purchases Return

448. The Sales Returns Book records:
A. The return of goods purchased
B. Return of anything purchased
C. Return of goods sold
D. None of these

449. The Sales Book:
A. Is a part of journal
B. Is a part of the ledger
C. Is a part of the balance sheet
D. None of these

450. The weekly or monthly total of the Purchase Book is:
A. Posted to the debit of the Purchases Account
B. Posted to the debit of the Sales Account
C. Posted to the credit of the Purchases Account
D. None of these

ANSWERS

1	2	3	4	5	6	7	8	9	10
D	A	C	C	C	B	A	A	C	B
11	12	13	14	15	16	17	18	19	20
C	A	C	D	B	B	B	B	B	D
21	22	23	24	25	26	27	28	29	30
C	D	B	C	D	A	B	C	A	B
31	32	33	34	35	36	37	38	39	40
B	B	B	B	C	A	A	C	C	A
41	42	43	44	45	46	47	48	49	50
B	D	C	D	D	A	A	B	B	A
51	52	53	54	55	56	57	58	59	60
A	D	A	C	A	C	A	A	A	B
61	62	63	64	65	66	67	68	69	70
B	B	C	C	B	B	C	B	A	D
71	72	73	74	75	76	77	78	79	80
D	B	B	C	C	C	D	A	C	B
81	82	83	84	85	86	87	88	89	90
C	C	A	B	A	B	D	A	C	A
91	92	93	94	95	96	97	98	99	100
B	D	A	A	C	A	C	D	A	B
101	102	103	104	105	106	107	108	109	110
C	D	A	C	A	B	C	B	C	D
111	112	113	114	115	116	117	118	119	120
C	B	B	A	A	C	C	B	A	B
121	122	123	124	125	126	127	128	129	130
A	B	D	C	C	D	D	D	B	D
131	132	133	134	135	136	137	138	139	140
C	C	A	B	C	D	C	B	D	A
141	142	143	144	145	146	147	148	149	150
A	D	B	A	D	C	A	B	A	A
151	152	153	154	155	156	157	158	159	160
B	D	A	B	C	C	A	B	C	C
161	162	163	164	165	166	167	168	169	170
A	B	C	B	B	B	C	D	B	B
171	172	173	174	175	176	177	178	179	180
A	D	A	B	A	C	D	C	A	C
181	182	183	184	185	186	187	188	189	190
D	C	A	A	C	A	B	D	A	B
191	192	193	194	195	196	197	198	199	200
B	B	C	C	A	B	A	C	A	B
201	202	203	204	205	206	207	208	209	210
D	C	A	D	C	A	A	C	B	A
211	212	213	214	215	216	217	218	219	220
C	A	B	A	A	A	A	C	C	A
221	222	223	224	225	226	227	228	229	230
A	B	A	B	B	A	D	A	C	D

231	232	233	234	235	236	237	238	239	240
B	A	A	B	B	A	C	C	D	A
241	242	243	244	245	246	247	248	249	250
D	A	B	C	A	A	C	B	D	C
251	252	253	254	255	256	257	258	259	260
B	C	B	C	B	D	D	A	C	B
261	262	263	264	265	266	267	268	269	270
A	B	B	A	B	B	A	A	C	B
271	272	273	274	275	276	277	278	279	280
B	B	A	A	D	D	C	B	D	A
281	282	283	284	285	286	287	288	289	290
C	C	B	D	C	C	A	C	A	B
291	292	293	294	295	296	297	298	299	300
B	B	A	B	A	A	A	A	A	A
301	302	303	304	305	306	307	308	309	310
A	B	C	B	C	C	C	A	C	D
311	312	313	314	315	316	317	318	319	320
D	D	C	A	B	C	D	C	A	B
321	322	323	324	325	326	327	328	329	330
C	A	C	D	B&C	A&C	A&C	B&C	C	A
331	332	333	334	335	336	337	338	339	340
B	C	B	C	C	B	A	C	C	B
341	342	343	344	345	346	347	348	349	350
C	A	B	B	A	A	B	D	A	B
351	352	353	354	355	356	357	358	359	360
A	C	B	C	A	B	B	C	C	B
361	362	363	364	365	366	367	368	369	370
D	D	D	C	D	B	A	D	C	D
371	372	373	374	375	376	377	378	379	380
A	A	C	D	C	B	A	B	A	A
381	382	383	384	385	386	387	388	389	390
A	B	D	D	A	D	A	C	D	D
391	392	393	394	395	396	397	398	399	400
B	A	B	B	C	D	C	B	A	C
401	402	403	404	405	406	407	408	409	410
B	A	C	C	C	B	C	A	C	A
411	412	413	414	415	416	417	418	419	420
B	C	C	A	A	A	C	A	B	B
421	422	423	424	425	426	427	428	429	430
C	D	A	C	C	C	D	A	B	C
431	432	433	434	435	436	437	438	439	440
A	C	A	B	D	C	A	B	B	B
441	442	443	444	445	446	447	448	449	450
B	A	C	D	A	D	B	C	A	A

●●●

2 Business Law

1. The Limited Liability Partnership Act, 2008 (6 of 2009) is an Act to make provisions for the
A. formulation and regulation of General Partnership Firms and Limited Liability formed under Indian Partnership Act, 1932
B. formulation and regulation of Joint Ventures with unlimited liability formed under Indian Contract Act, 1872
C. formulation and regulation of Chit Funds Organisations with unlimited liability formed under the Chit Funds Act, 1982
D. formation and regulation of Limited Liability Partnership with limited liability formed under the Limited Liability Partnership Act, 2008

2. Foreign Limited Liability Partnership (FLLP) under the Limited Liability Partnership Act, 2008 means
A. a Limited Liability Partnership formed, incorporated or registered in that country to which the partners belong
B. a Limited Liability Partnership formed, incorporated or registered under Economic Council of UNO
C. a Limited Liability Partnership formed, incorporated or registered in Indian territory
D. a Limited Liability Partnership formed, incorporated or registered outside India which establishes a place of business within India

3. Every Limited Liability Partnership as per the Limited Liability Partnership Act, 2008 shall have at least two Designated Partners (DPs) who are individuals and
A. at least one among them shall be resident in India
B. both of them shall belong to one family residing in India
C. both of them should be non-resident Indians (NRIs)
D. both of them should belong to a single country outside India

4. Prior to the Indian Partnership Act, 1932 which came into force from 1 October, 1932 except section 69 which came into force from 1 October, 1933, the law of partnership was provided in
A. Sale of Goods Act, 1930
B. Indian Contract Act, 1872
C. Transfer of Property Act, 1908
D. English Partnership Act, 1890

5. Unilateral dissolution of partnership by partner who is minority shareholder is
A. not permissible
B. permissible
C. permissible if all minority share-holders agree
D. permissible if Memorandum of Association prescribes

6. An act, to be called on 'act of a firm', within the meaning of section 2(*a*) of the Indian Partnership Act, 1932 is
A. every act of the partners
B. only such acts which give rise to a right enforceable by or against the firm
C. such acts which do not give rise to a right enforceable by or against the firm
D. either A *or* B or C

7. Any act or omission, to be an act of a firm, within the meaning of section 2(*a*) of the Indian Partnership Act, 1932 must be act or omission of
A. all the partners
B. any of the partner
C. agent of the firm
D. either A or B or C

8. Whether an act of a partner or agent can be regarded as an 'act of the firm' is a
A. question of fact
B. question of law
C. mixed question of fact & law
D. either A or C

9. The term 'business' has been defined under
A. section 2(*a*)
B. section 2(*b*)
C. section 2(*d*)
D. section 2(*e*)

10. Under section 2(*b*) of the Indian Partnership Act, business includes
A. every trade and occupation
B. every occupation and profession
C. every trade, occupation and profession
D. every trade and profession

11. The term 'partnership' has been defined under
A. section 3
B. section 4
C. section 5
D. section 6

12. Under section 4 of the Indian Partnership Act, partnership is a
A. compulsory legal relation
B. creation of the choice and voluntarily agreement between the concerned parties
C. a relation arising from status
D. either A or B or C

13. Which of the following enactments insist for a written agreement of partnership
A. the Indian Partnership Act, 1932
B. the Indian Contract Act, 1872
C. the Indian Registration Act, 1908
D. neither A nor B nor C

14. A partnership can be
A. a general partnership B. a particular partnership
C. either A or B D. only A and not B

15. Section 8 of the Indian Partnership Act, 1932 provides for
A. a pārticular partnership
B. a general partnership
C. a partnership at will
D. all the above

16. The relation of partnership arises from contract and not from status, has been prescribed under
A. section 4 B. section 5
C. section 6 D. section 7

17. Section 7 of the provides for
A. partnership in undertaking
B. general partnership
C. partnership at will
D. all the above

18. A partnership firm is
A. a distinct legal entity from its partners
B. not a distinct legal entity from its partners
C. a juristic person
D. either A or C

19. For the purposes of income-tax, a partnership firm
A. can be assessed as an entity distinct and separate from its partners
B. cannot be assessed as an entity separate and distinct from its partners
C. can be assessed as an entity distinct and separate from its partners only with the permission of the court
D. can be assessed as an entity distinct and separate from its partners only if all the partners agree for the same

20. A partnership cannot be constituted by
A. two individuals
B. two Hindu joint families
C. both A and B
D. neither A or B

21. The historic case laying down the test for determining the existence of a partnership is
A. Grace v. Smith B. Waugh v. Carver
C. Bloream v. Pell D. Cox v. Hickman

22. The mode of determining the existence of partnership has been laid down in
A. section 6 B. section 5
C. section 9 D. section 10

23. Which of the following in itself is not sufficient to constitute a partnership
A. the sharing of profits by persons having a joint or common interest
B. the receipt by a person of a share of the profits
C. the receipt by a person of a payment varying with the profits earned by business
D. all the above

24. Which of the following is a valid partnership
A. partnership between two partnership firm
B. partnership between one partnership firm and an individual
C. partnership between individual mental of one firm and the individual members oil another firm
D. neither A nor B nor C

25. A partnership firm is entitled to enter into a partnership with
A. another firm
B. Hindu undivided family
C. an individual
D. neither A nor B nor C

26. Mutual agency among the partner is
A. a test to determine the existence of a partnership
B. a legal incidence of partnership
C. both A and B
D. neither A nor B

27. A Hindu undivided family is entitled to enter into an agreement of partnership with
A. another joint Hindu family
B. another partnership firm
C. an individual
D. neither A nor B nor C

28. Which of the following is a valid partnership
A. partnership between the Karta of a joint Hindu family in his representative capacity and an individual co-parcener of the same family
B. partnership between two Hindu joint families
C. partnership between a Hindu joint family and a partnership firm
D. all the above

29. Section 5 of the Indian Partnership Act, 1932 does not apply to
A. Muslim Trading Family
B. Christian Trading Family
C. Burmese Buddhist husband and wife carrying on the business
D. all the above

30. Section 5 of the Indian Partnership Act, 1932 does not apply to
A. Muslim Trading Family
B. Christian Trading Family
C. both A and B
D. only A and not B

31. The concept of partnership commensurate with
A. principal and agent B. co-owners of property
C. joint owners of property D. all the above

32. A right to participate in profits, although strong but not a conclusive test of partnership. It was so held in
A. Tellis v. Saldanha B. Cox v. Hickman
C. Re: Stanton Iron Co. D. Grace v. Smith.

33. Which of the following is not an essential requisite for creating a partnership as per section 4
A. an agreement to carry on a business
B. sharing of profits
C. sharing of losses
D. business to be carried by all or any of them acting for all

34. A person who has lent money to a person or firm engaged in a business and has agreed to take a proportion of the profits of the business in addition to or in lieu of his interest, does not by that reason alone becomes a partner, in the business, has been laid down in
A. Badeley v. Consolidated Bank
B. Janes v. Whitbread
C. Marconis Wireless Telegraph Co. v. Newman
D. Price v. Groom.

35. The Indian Partnership Act, 1932 provides for and recognises
A. partnerships for a specified and fixed period
B. partnerships for a specified and fixed venture
C. both A and B
D. only A and not B

36. A partnership for which no period or duration is fixed, under the Indian Partnership Act, 1932 is known as
A. general partnership B. partnership at will
C. particular partnership D. co-ownership

37. Under section 7 of the Indian Partnership Act, 1932, partnership at will is subject to
A. one exception B. two exceptions
C. three exceptions D. five exceptions

38. Which of the following is an exception to the partnership at will, as provided under section 7 of the Indian Partnership Act, 1932
A. where there is a provision for the duration of the partnership
B. where there is a provision for determination of the partnership
C. both A and B
D. only A and not B

39. Where a partnership firm is constituted for a fixed period and after the expiration of that term, the firm continues to carry on business, without any new agreement,
A. the partnership stands extended till the new agreement is made
B. the partnership becomes partnership at will
C. the partnership becomes illegal
D. the partnership stands dissolved on the date of expiry of the term and no partnership can be said to be in existence

40. In a partnership at will
A. a partner of a firm can retire from the firm at any time by giving a notice of his intention to retire to his co-partners
B. a partner of a firm can dissolve the firm at any time by giving a notice of his intention to dissolve the firm to his copartners
C. either A or B
D. only B and not A

41. The test to determine whether the given partnership is a 'partnership at will' and 'whether the partnership could be dissolved by a single partner', has been laid down in
A. Crawshay v. Maule
B. Abbot v. Abbot
C. Cuffe v. Murtagh
D. Kurumuthu T. Chettiar v. EM. Mutliappa Chettiar

42. For constituting a partnership within the meaning of section 4 of the Indian Partnership Act, 1932
A. the business has to be of permanent nature
B. the business can be of temporary nature
C. it is immaterial as to whether the business is of temporary or permanent nature
D. only A and not B

43. The principles governing partners' mutual relations have been laid down in
A. Chapter II of the Indian Partnership Act
B. Chapter III of the Indian Partnership Act
C. Chapter IV of the Indian Partnership Act
D. Chapter V of the Indian Partnership Act

44. General duties of partners have been laid down in
A. section 9 of the Act B. section 10 of the Act
C. section 11 of the Act D. section 13 of the Act

45. Under section 9 of the Indian Partnership Act, 1932, in doing best for the common body
A. a partner is regarded as a kind of trustee for the other partners
B. a partner is liable to render the accounts to other partners in a fiduciary capacity
C. both A and B
D. neither A nor B

46. Under section 10 of the Indian Partnership Act, every partner is under a duty
A. to indemnify the firm for any loss caused to it by his fraud in the conduct of the business of the firm
B. to render true accounts and full information
C. not to carry on any business other than that of the firm
D. to be just and faithful to each other

47. The rights and duties of partners inter se can be regulated and varied by the consent of the partners by virtue of
A. section 14 of the Act B. section 13 of the Act
C. section 12 of the Act D. section 11 of the Act

48. Under section 11 of the Indian Partnership Act, 1932, in case of any conflict between the provision of the Act and the articles of the agreement, the articles of the agreement with it, will be
A. valid
B. invalid
C. voidable at the instance of any of the partner
D. viodable at the instance of a third party

49. An agreement in restraint of trade in a partnership under section 11 of the Act is
A. valid B. voidable
C. void D. invalid

50. Section 12 of the Indian Partnership Act, 1932 is
A. a statement of rights of the partners in reference to the conduct of business
B. a statement of duties of the partners in the conduct of the business
C. a mixed statement of rights and duties of partners in reference to the conduct of the business
D. neither A nor B

51. Section 12(*c*) of the Indian Partnership Act provides for a
A. rule of majority B. rule of unanimity
C. both A and B D. only A and not B

52. The rule of majority contained in section 12(*c*) of the Indian Partnership Act, 1932 is applicable in
A. trivial matters B. ordinary matters
C. fundamental matters D. all the above

53. The rule of unanimity contained in section 12(*c*) of the Indian Partnership Act, 1932 has a reference to
A. fundamental matters B. ordinary matters
C. trivial matters D. all the above

54. The rights and duties of a partner contained in section 12 of the Indian Partnership Act, 1932 are
A. subject to the provision of the Indian Partnership Act, 1932
B. subject to a contrary arrangement between the partners
C. subject to the provisions of the Indian Contract Act, 1872
D. subject to the provisions of the Indian Trusts Act, 1882

55. An agreement to carry on business in partnership in the future creates a partnership
A. immediately on the agreement
B. on the date mentioned in the agreement irrespective of whether the business has commenced or not on that date
C. only on the date when the business is actually commenced
D. never creates a partnership and any such agreement is void

56. Whether a partnership exists or not is a
A. question of fact
B. question of law
C. mixed question of fact and law
D. either A or C

57. The maxim 'socii mei socius meu socius non est' means
A. my partner's partner is not necessarily my partner
B. my partner's partner is necessarily my partner
C. the partnership has become illegal
D. the partnerships stands dissolved by the 'act of God'

58. The minimum number of persons required for a partnership is
A. two B. five
C. ten D. twenty

59. The maximum number of partners in a partnership, has been provided under
A. the Indian Partnership Act, 1932
B. the Indian Companies Act, 1956
C. the Indian Contract Act, 1872
D. the Indian Trusts Act, 1882

60. Under section 11 of the Indian Companies Act, 2013 for a non-banking business, the maximum number of partners for private companies can be
A. ten B. twenty
C. twenty-five D. two hundred

61. For a banking business, the maximum number of partners in a partnership, under section 11 of the Indian Companies Act, 1956, can be
A. ten B. fifteen
C. twenty D. twenty-five

62. A partnership in which the number of partners exceeds than that allowed under section 11 of the Indian Companies Act, shall be
A. valid
B. voidable at the instance of any of the partners
C. voidable at the instance of third parties
D. illegal

63. An illegal partnership
A. can sue B. can be sued
C. cannot be sued D. can sue and be sued

64. The members of an illegal partnership
A. have a remedy against each other for the partnership dealings and transactions
B. have no remedy against each other for the partnership dealings and transactions
C. have a remedy against each other for the partnership dealings and transaction only with the permission of the court
D. either A or C

65. If the partners are equally divided on a issue, the rule is: 'in re comtnuni potior est conditio prohibentis', which means
A. those who forbid a change must have their way
B. those who do not forbid *i.e.*, in favour of the change, must have their way
C. the discussion on the issue be defered for another day
D. opinion on the issue be taken from an expert

66. A partner has a right to have access to all the books of accounts etc., of the firm
A. during the subsistence of the partnership
B. during the proceedings for the dissolution of the firm
C. after the dissolution of the firm
D. all the above

67. A partner has a right to examine the account books etc., of the firm
A. himself
B. through legal representatives
C. through agent
D. either A or B or C

68. A partner can examine the books etc., of the partnership firm
A. as many number of times without any restriction
B. once a year
C. once a month
D. once a week

69. Section 13 of the Indian Partnership Act, 1932 is
A. a mixed statement of rights and duties of the partners
B. a mixed statement of duties and liabilities of the partners
C. a mixed statement of rights and liabilities of the partners
D. a mixed statement of rights, duties and liabilities of the partners

70. The rate of interest prescribed under section 13, where a partner, advances money beyond the amount of capital, for the business of the partnership, is
A. six percent B. nine percent
C. twelve percent D. fifteen percent

71. Where a partner is entitled to interest on the capital subscribed, such interest is payable
A. out of profits only B. out of capital if no profits
C. out of capital if losses D. either A or B or C

72. Section 13(*a*) of the Indian Partnership Act, 1932 provides for
A. payment of remuneration to a partner as a matter of right
B. payment of remuneration to a partner only when there is an agreement to that effect between the partners
C. non-payment of remuneration to a partner only when there is an agreement to that effect between the parties
D. both A and C

73. Under section 13(*b*) of the Indian Partnership Act, 1932 all the partners are entitled to
A. share the profits and losses in the ratio of their capital contributions
B. share the profits and losses equally irrespective of any agreement between them to the contrary
C. share the profits and losses equally in the absence of any agreement to the contrary between them
D. share the profits and losses in the ratio of their personal efforts input

74. Where a change occurs in the constitution of a firm and no new agreement is made
A. the ratio of profit sharing shall become equal for all the partners
B. the ratio of profit sharing shall remain the same to the extent to which it is consistent with the altered composition of the firm
C. the ratio of profit sharing shall change in the ratio of capital contributions
D. the ratio of profit sharing shall change in the ratio of personal efforts/labour input of the partners

75. As a general rule, by virtue of section 13 of the Indian Partnership Act, 1932
A. partner is not entitled to interest on the capital subscribed by him
B. partner is not entitled to interest on the advance made over and above the share capital
C. both A and B
D. neither A nor B

76. As regards the capital contribution in the partnership business, the status of a partner is that of
A. a creditor of the firm
B. a partner of the firm
C. an employee of the firm
D. all the above

77. The status of a partner, making advances to the firm for its business, over and above the capital subscribed, is that of
A. a partner of the firm
B. a creditor of the firm
C. an employee of the firm
D. both A and B

78. On the dissolution of the partnership
A. the interest on capital ceases run whereas interest of advances keeping running upto the date of payment
B. the interest on capital and the interest on advances cease to run
C. the interest on capital keeps running upto the date of payment whereas interest on advances cease to run
D. the interest on capital as well as on advances keeps running upto the date of payment

79. A partner has a right to indemnity for the acts done in
A. the ordinary & proper conduct of the business
B. an emergency
C. both A and B
D. only B and not A

80. The right to indemnity is lost on
A. the dissolution of the partnership
B. the death of the partner
C. the retirement of the partner
D. neither A nor B nor C

81. Section 13(*f*) of the Indian Partnership Act, 1932 provides for
A. indemnity in favour of the partner against the firm
B. indemnity in favour of the firm against a partner
C. indemnity in favour of the third parties against the firm
D. all the above

82. An action for indemnity against a partner can be brought by
A. the firm only B. an individual partner
C. either A or B D. neither A nor B

83. What constitutes the property of the firm has been dealt with in
A. section 16 B. section 15
C. section 14 D. section 13

84. Section 14 of the Indian Partnership Act, 1932 is
A. exhaustive B. inclusive
C. conclusive D. both A and C

85. Under section 14 of the Indian Partnership Act, 1932, the property thrown into the common stock at the commencement of the business
A. becomes the property of the firm
B. remains the individual property of the partners in the shares contributed by them
C. becomes the individual property of the partners in equal shares irrespective of their contributions and profit sharing ratio
D. either A or C

86. A property belonging to a partners and entering into a partnership and used for the purposes of partnership
A. becomes the property of the firm
B. remains the property of that partner
C. becomes the property of the partner having highest share of capital contribution
D. becomes the property of the partners in their profit sharing ratio

87. All the benefits and liabilities arising out of a contract made on behalf of a partnership do not
A. belong to the partnership if the contract has been performed before the dissolution of the firm
B. belong to the partnership if the contract has been performed before the retirement of the firm
C. belong to the partnership if the contract has been performed after the dissolution of the firm or retirement of a partner
D. none of the above

88. The property of the firm includes all property
A. acquired by or for the firm
B. for the purpose or in the course of business of the firm
C. property purchase with money belonging to the firm
D. all the above

89. When the property is purchased out of the partnership funds but in the name of an individual partner, it
A. becomes an estate of the partner
B. becomes a joint estate
C. is a question of fact to be determined with reference to the intention of the partners
D. is a question of law to be decided on legal principles

90. When the personal property of a partner is being used in the business of the firm, it
A. is a question of fact to be determined with reference to the partner's intention whether it has become the property of the firm
B. becomes the joint estate
C. remains an estate of the partner
D. is a question of law to be decided on legal principles.

91. Under section 14 of the Indian Partnership Act, 1932, goodwill of the business is
A. property of the firm
B. property of the managing partner
C. property of the partner having the highest share in the profits
D. property of the partner having the lowest share in the profits

92. Since the partnership property vests in all the partners and every partner has an interest in the property of the partnership, during the subsistence of partnership
A. a partner can deal with the property as his own
B. a partner can deal with a portion of the property upto his share in the partnership, as his own
C. a partner can deal with a specific item of the partnership property as his own
D. a partner cannot deal with any particular property or any portion of the property as his own

93. In a partnership property, a partner has
A. something in the nature of personal ownership
B. only certain rights
C. both A and B
D. either A or B

94. If a partner chooses to use any assets of the partnership for his own purpose, it gives rise to
A. a civil liability of that partner
B. a criminal liability of that partner
C. both A and B
D. either A or B

95. Where a partner is authorised to recover dues of the partnership & spend the same for the business of the partnership and if he does not deposit the money so collected in the bank the partner is
A. guilty of criminal breach of trust
B. accountable civilly to the other
C. both A and B
D. either A or B

96. Goodwill of the partnership business is the property of the partnership
A. under section 14 B. under section 15
C. under section 16 D. under section 17(*b*)

97. The term 'goodwill' is a thing very to describe but very difficult to define, is stated by
A. Lord Herschell B. Lord Haldane
C. Lord MacNaughten D. Lord Eldon

98. Section 15 of the Indian Partnership Act provides that
A. the property of the firm shall be held and used by the partners exclusively for the purposes of the business of the firm
B. the property of the firm can be used by the partners for any of his/their personal use
C. the property of the firm can be used by the partners for the personal use of all the partners
D. both A and C

99. Section 15 of the Indian Partnership Act is a statement of a
A. right of the partners
B. duty of the partners
C. privilege of the partners
D. liability of the partners

100. The term company is defined under which sec of the Act?
A. Sec 2 (20) B. Sec 4 (2)
C. Sec 2 (4) D. Sec 1 (3)

101. Property of the company belongs to
A. Company B. Share holders
C. Members D. Promoters

102. Which company shares can be freely transferable
A. Private Company B. Public Company
C. Both A and B D. None of the above

103. Minimum number of members in case of public company
A. 1 B. 2
C. 5 D. 7

104. Minimum number of members in case of private company is
A. 1 B. 2
C. 3 D. 4

105. Maximum no. of members in case of private company is
A. 50 B. 100
C. 150 D. 200

106. Maximum no. of members in case of public company is
A. 0 B. unlimited
C. 50 D. 100

107. Which of these section provides for restrictions on non-cash transactions involving directors?
A. Section 156 B. Section 192
C. Section 200 D. Section 366

108. Minimum subscription should be received with in _____days
A. 120 B. 125
C. 130 D. 135

109. If minimum subscription is not received application money should be refunded with in ______ days
A. 20 B. 25
C. 30 D. 10

110. Liability of a member in case of a private company is
A. Limited B. Unlimited
C. Both A or B D. None of the above

111. Maximum no. of persons in case of partnership banking business ______
A. 10 B. 20
C. 30 D. 5

112. Minimum paid up share capital in case of a private company is ______
A. 1 Lakh B. 2 Lakhs
C. 3 Lakhs D. 4 Lakhs

113. Minimum paid up share capital in case of a public company is ______
A. 1 Lakh B. 3 Lakhs
C. 5 Lakhs D. 7 Lakhs

114. Minimum no. of Directors in case of a public company is ______
A. 1 B. 2
C. 3 D. 4

115. Minimum no. of Directors in case of private company is ______
A. 1 B. 2
C. 3 D. 4

116. Age limit of Directors in case of public company is ______
A. 65 B. No limit
C. 75 D. 80

117. Age limit of Directors in case of private company is ______
A. 65 B. 70
C. 75 D. No limit

118. The company's nationality is decided by its
A. Shareholders
B. Registered office
C. Place at books of accounts are kept
D. None of the above

119. The liability of members if company is limited by guarantee.
A. Unpaid value of shares
B. Guarantee amount
C. Unlimited liability
D. None of the above

120. The liability of members if company is limited by shares
A. Unpaid value of shares
B. Guarantee amount
C. Unlimited liability
D. None of the above

121. If the company failed to refund application money with in 130 days from the date of issue of prospectus on non receipt of minimum subscription who will be personally liable.
A. Company B. Directors
C. Shareholders D. None of these

122. Transfer of shares in the company is
A. Restricted B. Freely transferable
C. Prohibited D. None of these

123. Transfer of shares in the partnership firm is
A. Restricted B. Freely transferable
C. Prohibited D. None of these

124. Generally Company liability is
A. Limited B. Unlimited
C. Situation does not arise D. none of the above

125. Generally partnership firm liability is
A. Limited B. Unlimited
C. Situation does not arise D. none of the above

126. Partners are of the firm
A. Owners B. Employers
C. Agents D. None of these

127. XYZ private company had reduced to a single member and continued business more than 6 months. The company's liability will be
A. Limited B. Unlimited
C. None of the above D. situation never arise

128. In the case of partnership firm. Audit is
A. Compulsory B. Optional
C. None of the above D. both A and B

129. In the case of Company, Audit is
A. Compulsory B. Optional
C. None of the above D. both A and B

130. Generally rights and obligations of the company are regulated in
A. A.O.A B. M.O.A
C. Partnership deed D. None of these

131. Generally rights and obligations of the Partnership firm are regulated in
A. A.O.A. B. M.O.A.
C. Partnership deed D. None of the above

132. X is a director who has experience of 20 years on this basis X Co. and taken him as a director.
Can the X Co. say that the director X experience is company's experience
A. Yes
B. No
C. Situation does not arise
D. none of the above

133. A company is named as govt. company if it is holds ______% of paid up share capital
A. more than 30 B. more than 40
C. more than 50 D. None

134. Which companies are exempted to add "Ltd" or "Pvt Ltd" at the end of their name
A. Private
B. Govt
C. Defunct
D. Association not for profits

135. If the companies does not increase their paid up capital by 1/5 lakhs with in 2 years such companies are known as
A. Private B. Public
C. Defunct D. Govt Company

136. Under which sec. a private company can voluntarily converted into public company
A. 14 B. 44
C. 54 D. 64

137. Under which sec. a private company can automatically converted into a public company
A. 18 B. 43
C. 53 D. 35

138. Central Government permission is required in case of ______ conversion
A. Private to public B. Public to private
C. Both A or B D. None of the above

139. Within how many days prospectus or statement in lieu of prospectus should file with ROC
A. 30 B. 40
C. 20 D. 50

140. ______% of shares should be held by a company in another company so as to become subsidiary
A. more than 50 B. more than 40
C. more than 30 D. more than 20

141. Liability under ______sec. may be imposed only if it is proved that the companies business has been carried on with a view to defraud the creditors
A. 447 B. 541
C. 542 D. 543

142. In case of Non-Profit making Companies notice of general meeting should be given with in ______days
A. 14 B. 15
C. 21 D. 22

143. In case of companies other than Non-Profit making Companies notice of G.M. should be given with in ______days

A. 14 B. 15
C. 21 D. 22

144. In case of Non-Profit making Companies books of accounts are required to be preserved for ______ years

A. 2 B. 4
C. 6 D. 8

145. According to which sec. name of the company should end with "Ltd" or "Pvt Ltd"

A. 8 B. 11
C. 12 D. 13

146. The companies which are formed under special charter granted by the king or queen of England are called

A. Statutory companies B. Registered companies
C. Chartered companies D. None of these

147. The companies which are formed under special Act. Those companies are called as

A. Chartered companies B. Statutory companies
C. Registered companies D. None of these

148. The companies which are formed under Companies Act., 2013. They will be called as

A. Chartered companies
B. Statutory companies
C. Registered companies
D. None of these

149. If the guarantee Co. having no share capital the liability of shareholders will be

A. To the extent of guarantee
B. Unpaid value of shares
C. Unlimited
D. None of the above

150. If the guarantee Co. having share capital the liability of shareholders will be

A. Guarantee + unpaid value of shares
B. Unpaid value of shares
C. Unlimited
D. None of the above

151. If a company which is formed with unlimited liability wants to convert to limited liability then it should pass

A. Ordinary resolution B. Special resolution
C. No need D. either A or C

152. Maximum capital of private company is

A. 50 Lakhs B. 1 Crore
C. 1.5 Crore D. Unlimited

153. Transfer of shares in case of private company is

A. Prohibited B. Restricted
C. Freely transferable D. None of these

154. Maximum members in case of private company

A. 50 B. 200
C. 75 D. None of these

155. While calculating maximum limit in case of private company which of the following will not be included

A. Employee + Member B. Member + Employee
C. Member D. None of these

156. Managing director will be counted as ______ while calculating maximum limit in case of private company.

A. Member B. Employee
C. Shareholder D. None of these

157. Where the registrar strikes off the register the name of a company as a defunct one, the court has the power to order restoration of name with in:

A. 5 years B. 7 years
C. 10 years D. 20 years

158. Accepting of deposits from public in case of private company is

A. Prohibited B. Restricted
C. Acceptable D. None of these

159. Invitation to public offering shares or debentures in case of private company

A. Prohibited B. Restricted
C. Acceptable D. None of these

160. Maximum paid up capital in case of public company.

A. 50 Lakhs B. 100 Lakhs
C. 125 Lakhs D. None of these

161. Y Pvt. Co. is subsidiary of X Co. which is a public Company? Mention Y is a

A. Private Co. B. Public Co.
C. Government Co. D. None of these

162. Transfer of shares in the case of public company is

A. Prohibited B. Restricted
C. Freely transferable D. None of these

163. XYZ Co, is having 10% share capital held by another Public Company and 35% held by Central Government and 55% held by people then that Company is

A. Government Company B. Private Company
C. Public Company D. None of these

164. XYZ Co, is having 15% share capital held by X Company and 50% held by Central Government and 10% held by State Government and 25% held by other people then that company will be

A. Government Company
B. Private Company
C. Public Company
D. None of these

165. XYZ Company is a Government Company and X Co. is a subsidiary of XYZ Co. Then X Co. will be

A. Public Company B. Private Company
C. Government Company D. None of these

166. For every special resolution passed the form attached should be

A. Form no. 32 B. MGT-14
C. Form no. 23 D. None of these

167. In the process of conversion of a private company into a public company which prospectus must be issued
A. Deemed prospectus
B. Shelf prospectus
C. Statement in lieu of prospectus
D. None of the above

168. Company should file a prospectus in case of conversion of private company into a public company within _________ from the date of resolution
A. 30 days B. 45 days
C. 60 days D. none of these

169. How many members should sign the MOA in case of public company
A. 1 B. 3
C. 5 D. 7

170. How many members should sign the MOA in case of private company
A. 1 B. 2
C. 3 D. 4

171. In case of appointment of Directors ______ form is to be filed.
A. DIR-12 B. 32
C. 18 D. 1

172. ______ is the conclusive evidence in case of company that statutory requirements have complied with
A. Certificate of Incorporation
B. Certificate of Commencement of Business
C. Both
D. None of the above

173. Private company can start its business immediately after the issue of
A. Certificate of Commencement of Business
B. Certificate of Incorporation
C. Both
D. None of the above

174. Public company should start business only after getting certificate of
A. Incorporation
B. Commencement of business
C. None of these
D. either A or B

175. Private company can start business only after getting certificate of
A. Incorporation
B. Commencement of business
C. None of these
D. both A and B

176. The doctrine of indoor management is an ______to the doctrine of constructive notice
A. Exception B. Extension
C. Alternative D. None of the above

177. The doctrine of ___ does not apply to acts void ab initio.
A. Ultra virus B. Intra virus
C. constructive notice D. Indoor management

178. A company can change its name at its own discretion by passing ________
A. Ordinary resolution B. Special resolution
C. Boards resolution D. None of the above

179. Any change in the address of the registered office must be communicated to the registrar with in:
A. 15 days B. 30 days
C. 1 month D. 12 months

180. An act ultra virus the directors can be rectified if it is not ultra vires
A. the articles B. the memorandum
C. Company Act D. None of the above

181. The lending of funds ultra vires, the company has no rights
A. under the Company's Act
B. contract Act
C. under equity
D. None of the above

182. If a new company get registered with a name which resembles the name of existing company then it should apply to whom?
A. NCLT B. SEBI
C. ROC D. None of the above

183. Companies are now allotted a ______ in addition to their name
A. PAN B. SIN
C. PIN D. CIN

184. In how many days did the company have its registered office after incorporation
A. 10 B. 20
C. 30 D. 40

185. Under which sec. if company fails to commence its main object the court may order winding up
A. 403 (f) B. 271 (f)
C. 423 (f) D. 433 (f)

186. In case of forgeries acts done in the name of the company are
A. Valid B. Void
C. Void ab initio D. None of the above

187. Signature of memorandum and articles should be done by ____ number of persons in case of public company
A. 7 B. 5
C. 4 D. None of these

188. Signature of memorandum and articles should be done by ____ number of persons in case of private company
A. 3 B. 4
C. 2 D. None of these

189. MOA should be in form ______ in case of company limited by shares.
A. Table A B. Table B
C. Table C D. Table D

190. MOA should be in form ______ in case of company limited by guarantee not having share capital.
A. Table A B. Table B
C. Table C D. Table D

191. MOA should be in form ______ in case of company limited by guarantee and having share capital.
A. Table A B. Table B
C. Table C D. Table D

192. MOA should be in form ______ in case of a unlimited liability company and not having share capital.
A. Table A B. Table B
C. Table D D. None of these

193. In the MOA there are 6 classes. We can alter all clauses expect one clause. What is that clause?
A. Objects clause B. Name clause
C. Association clause D. None of these

194. If any body wants to file a case against the company they should file at what place
A. Company B. Registered Office
C. BOD D. Books of accounts

195. Address of the registered office is situated in
A. MOA B. AOA
C. Prospectus D. None of these

196. Which of the following need not have MOA.
A. Public company B. Private company
C. Government company D. Statutory Corporation

197. A company can change its name by passing
A. Ordinary resolution
B. Special resolution
C. Either by special resolution or by ordinary resolution
D. None of the above

198. Ultra vires means
A. Beyond the power B. with in the power
C. Both D. None of the above

199. Ultra vires loans granted by the company are
A. Void B. Voidable
C. Valid D. None of the above

200. _____ is the charter of a company
A. Memorandum B. Articles
C. Both A and B D. None of the above

201. The granting of the certificate of incorporation renders the illegal objects include in the memorandum:
A. Legal B. Void
C. Voidable D. None of the above

202. Change in objects clauses can be effected
A. For any reason
B. For special reason only
C. to comply with C.G order
D. None of the above

203. The capital clause of a company can be changed with the permission of ______
A. Company law board B. Registrar
C. Court D. None of the above

204. ______ conceives the idea of the business
A. Promoters B. Directors
C. Auditors D. None of the above

205. ______ stands in the fiduciary position of the company
A. Directors B. Promoters
C. Auditors D. None of the above

206. ______ are the contracts entered into by promoters on behalf of a prospectus company.
A. Provisional contracts
B. Pre-Incorporation contracts
C. Preliminary contracts
D. Both A & B

207. Contracts made after incorporation but before the grant of Certificate of commencement of Business ______
A. Provisional contracts
B. Pre-incorporation contracts
C. Preliminary contracts
D. Both B and C

208. Pre-incorporation contract is also known as
A. Provisional B. Preliminary
C. Illegal D. Legal

209. A public company can borrow money
A. before incorporation
B. soon after incorporation
C. after issuing a proposal
D. after obtaining certificate to commerce business

210. A private company can borrow funds
A. after incorporation
B. after obtaining certificate to commerce business
C. after holding first annual general meeting
D. None of the above

211. When there is a untrue statement in a prospectus who can sue
A. Subscribed in primary market
B. Subscribed in secondary market
C. Rights issue
D. None of the above

212. Definition of prospectus was given under which section
A. 2 (70) B. 2 (32)
C. 2 (34) D. 2 (36)

213. Which of the following are not required to issue prospectus?
A. Private company B. Incase of right issue
C. Sweat equity issue D. All the above

214. ____are the prospectus issued instead of full prospectus.
A. Abridged B. Statement in lieu
C. Shelf D. Red herring

215. Which one of the following has a right to claim compensation for any loss due to misstatement in prospectus
A. Purchasing shares in Primary Market
B. Secondary Market
C. Subscribers to memo
D. All the above

216. _______ years of imprisonment will be imposed in case of issue of prospectus with untrue statements.
A. 1 B. 2
C. 3 D. 4

217. _____ includes an engineer, valuationer, accountant.
A. Expert B. Promoter
C. Auditor D. Director

218. What is the liability of an expert for misstatement
A. Fine – 3 times the amount involved or more
B. Imprison – 10 years
C. Both A and B
D. None of the above

219. What is the liability not delivering that can be imposed for statement in lieu of prospectus
A. Fine – 10,000 B. Imprisonment – 2 years
C. Both A and B D. None of the above

220. _______ are the prospectus issued by the issuing house.
A. Deemed prospectus
B. Shelf prospectus issued by the issuing house
C. Red herring
D. None of the above

221. ______ prospectus were issued in case securities were issued in stages.
A. Deemed B. Shelf
C. Red herring D. None of the above

222. _______ are required to file prior to making second and subsequent issue of securities in case shelf prospectus are filed.
A. Information memorandum
B. Information articles
C. Form 13
D. None of the above

223. Information memorandum + shelf prospectus together constitutes
A. Memorandum B. Articles
C. Prospectus D. None of the above

224. The minimum application money should be _______ of nominal value.
A. 5% B. 3%
C. 2% D. None of these

225. The minimum application money should be _______ of nominal value as per SEBI guidelines.
A. 25% B. 30%
C. 40% D. None of these

226. Can shares be allotted immediately after the issue of prospectus
A. Yes B. No
C. None of the above D. both A and B

227. The min subscription amount is reckoned with amounts payable in
A. cash only B. kind only
C. cash as well as kind D. None of the above

228. Allotment of shares or debentures must be made after getting _______ subscription against entire public issue as per SEBI guidelines.
A. 80% B. 90%
C. 100% D. None of these

229. If the refunds are delayed by more than 10 days after this period. The directors become liable to repay the money with how much interest as per SEBI Guidelines.
A. 10% B. 15%
C. 20% D. None of these

230. If the company has not received permission for listing from stock exchange and repayment of amount delayed by more than 8 days the minimum interest should be paid is
A. 4% B. 3%
C. 2% D. none of these

231. From the above how much will be maximum interest
A. 10% B. 12%
C. 15% D. None of these

232. After the expiry of how much time the company must think that the permission was not granted
A. 11 weeks B. 12 weeks
C. 10 weeks D. None of these

233. In case minimum subscription is not received and refund is delayed ______% of interest to be paid by the company.
A. 5 B. 6
C. 7 D. 8

234. As per SEBI application money should be refunded from the end of ______ day.
A. 60 B. 70
C. 80 D. 90

235. An appeal is made to whom against stock exchange for refusing the permission of listing.
A. SAI B. NCLT
C. MAT D. ROC

236. If permission from S.E is not obtained amount should be refunded within how many days.
A. 2 B. 4
C. 6 D. 8

237. A company cannot pay under writing commission unless it is authorized by its
A. Articles B. Memorandum
C. Both A and B D. None of the above

238. In case of shares under writing commission will be
A. 2% B. 3%
C. 5% D. None of these

239. In case of debentures underwriting commission will be
A. 3% B. 4%
C. 2.5% D. None of these

240. If company wants to place shares to brokers they should give a maximum of ____ as brokerage commission.
A. 3% B. 2%
C. 1.5% D. None of these

241. What is maximum period for which deposits can be issued?
A. 36 months B. 24 months
C. 12 months D. None of these

242. What is minimum period for which deposits can be issued?
A. 6 months B. 7 months
C. 8 months D. None of these

243. A company can accept or renew deposits for a period less than 6 months if they do not exceed 10% of the aggregate of
A. Paid up capital
B. Free reserves
C. Paid up capital and Free reserves
D. None of the above

244. Rate of brokerage for the deposits which have term up to 1 year
A. 1% B. 1.5%
C. 2% D. None of these

245. Rate of brokerage for the deposits which have term between 12 years
A. 1.5% B. 2%
C. 1% D. None of these

246. Rate of brokerage for the deposits which have term for more than two years
A. 1.5% B. 2%
C. 2.5% D. None of these

247. If the company failed to comply with the order of NCLT they will be punishable with fine and imprisonment up to
A. 2 years B. 3 years
C. 4 Years D. None of these

248. Public deposit matures and claimed but remains unpaid, penal interest will be
A. 17% B. 16%
C. 18% D. None of these

249. Public deposit matures and claimed but remains unpaid, penal interest will be in case of small deposits
A. 16% B. 18%
C. 20% D. None of these

250. Small deposits means a depositor who had deposits a sum not exceeding ____ in a financial year
A. 15,000 B. 20,000
C. 18,000 D. None of these

251. ____ includes any amount borrowed by a company.
A. Deposits B. Funds
C. Both A and B D. None of the above

252. What is the ceiling imposed by the government on company on any deposits
A. 10 B. 25
C. 35 D. 5

253. Advertisement given for deposits is valid for ___ months
A. 3 B. 6
C. 9 D. 12

254. Deposits should issued with in ____ weeks from the date of receipt of money.
A. 2 B. 4
C. 6 D. 8

255. Register of deposits should be maintained for ____ years.
A. 2 B. 4
C. 8 D. 16

256. Return of deposits is to be filed on or before ____ with ROC
A. 30th day of June B. 30th day of July
C. 30th day of January D. 30th day of May

257. Failure to comply with the order of NCLT is punishable with an imprisonment upto ____ years.
A. 1 B. 2
C. 3 D. 4

258. Deposit holder can file winding up petition under which sec.
A. 433 (*a*) B. 270
C. 433 (*e*) D. 433 (*f*)

259. ____ declares a company as a sick company.
A. B.I.F.R B. M.R.T.P
C. FERA D. None of the above

260. U/s 274 (f) (g) directors are disqualified for how many ____ years.
A. 1 B. 3
C. 5 D. 7

261. In case of default with regards to deposits intimation to NCLT should be made with how many days.
A. 10 B. 20
C. 30 D. 40

262. A Notice inviting deposits from the public is ____.
A. Deposit B. Fund
C. Share D. None of the above

263. When the shares are transferred to X from Y. Y will be a ____ of the company.
A. Member B. Shareholder
C. Partner D. None of these

264. The person who is holding share warrant will be a ____ of the company.
A. Member B. Shareholder
C. Partner D. None of these

265. Which of the given below members are not shareholders
A. Death of members B. Insolvent
C. Share warrant holders D. All of the above

266. Which of the following is a right of the members of a company
A. Right to have share
B. Right Appoint Auditor
C. Right Appoint Director
D. All the above

267. Which of the following is not a member of a company?
A. Partnership firm B. Foreigner
C. Government D. HUF

268. For quorum the Joint holders will be collectively counted as _______ members.
A. 1 B. 2
C. 3 D. 4

269. In the event of appointing a proxy joint holders shall sign the proxy form
A. Singularly B. Jointly
C. None of the above D. both A and B

270. A company can become a members of another company if it is so authorized by
A. MOA B. AOA
C. Both A and B D. None of the above

271. Which of the following is not true
A. Every member is a contributory
B. Every contributory is a member
C. Both A and B
D. None of the above

272. For calculating number of members in a private company joint holders will be as
A. 1 B. 2
C. 3 D. 4

273. A company must inform the registrar about redemption of preference shares with in
A. 21 days B. 15 days
C. 30 days D. None of the above

274. Share premium amount is treated as the ______ capital of a company.
A. Issued B. Reserve
C. Subscribe D. None of the above

275. A company can create 'reserve capital' by passing
A. an ordinary resolution B. a special resolution
C. a board resolution D. None of the above

276. The capital which is part of the uncalled capital of the company which can be called up only in the event of its winding up it is called
A. Issued capital B. Nominal capital
C. Authorised Capital D. Reserve capital

277. XYZ Co. is a holding of XZ Pvt. Company. XZ Co. issued deferred shares. The issue is valid or void
A. Valid
B. Void
C. Situation does not arise
D. none of the above

278. What is the maximum period for redemption in case of preference shares issued by the company
A. 10 years B. 15 years
C. 20 years D. None of these

279. Capital redemption reserve must be used for issue of
A. Fully paid bonus shares B. Fully paid equity shares
C. Preference shares D. None of the above

280. Part of the issued capital taken by public is called
A. Subscribed B. Called – up capital
C. Un called capital D. Paid up capital

281. Part of authorized capital which is offered by the company for subscription.
A. subscribed B. Issued
C. Un called D. called up

282. Stamp duty on registration of the company is payable based on ______ capital.
A. Nominal B. Authorized
C. Both A and B D. None

283. Deferred shares are also known as ______ shares.
A. Founders B. Equity
C. Preference D. None

284. _______ Preference shares carry the right to cumulate the dividends
A. Converted B. Cumulative
C. Non-converted D. None

285. The Negotiable Instruments Act, 1881 applies to
A. the whole of India
B. the whole of India except the State of Jammu and Kashmir
C. those states as notified by the Union Government from time to time in the Official Gazette
D. the whole of India except the State of Jammu and Kashmir and the North- Eastern States

286. The Negotiable Instruments Act, 1881 came into force on
A. 9th December, 1881 B. 19th December, 1881
C. 1st March, 1882 D. None of the above

287. The undertaking contained in a promissory note, to pay a certain sum of money is
A. conditional
B. unconditional
C. may be conditional or unconditional depending upon the circumstances
D. none of the above

288. A bill of exchange contains a/an
A. unconditional undertaking
B. unconditional order
C. conditional undertaking
D. conditional order.

289. Cheque is a
A. promissory note B. bill of exchange
C. both A and B above D. None of the above

290. The term "a cheque in the electronic form" is defined in the Negotiable Instruments Act, 1881, under
A. section 6(*a*)
B. section 6(l)(*a*)
C. explanation 1(*a*) of section 6
D. section 6A

291. The term 'Negotiable instrument' is defined in the Negotiable Instruments Act, 1881, under section
A. 12 B. 13
C. 13A D. 2(*d*)

292. The term 'negotiation' in section 14 of the Negotiable Instruments Act, 1881 refers to
A. the transfer of a bill of exchange, promissory note or cheque to any person, so as to constitute the person the holder thereof
B. the payment by a bank on a negotiable instrument after due verification of the instrument
C. the bargaining between the parties to a negotiable instrument
D. all of the above

293. If an instrument may be construed either as a promissory note or bill of exchange, it is
A. a valid instrument
B. an ambiguous instrument
C. a returnable instrument
D. none of the above

294. If in an instrument the amount undertaken or ordered to be paid is stated differently in figures and in words
A. the instrument is void due to uncertainty
B. the amount stated in figure shall be the amount undertaken or ordered to be paid
C. the amount stated in words shall be the amount undertaken or ordered to be paid
D. none of the above

295. Under section 16 of the Negotiable Instrument Act, 'indorsement in blank' of an instrument means
A. where the indorser does not write anything on the instrument
B. where the indorser signs his name only on the instrument
C. where the indorser writes the name of the person who is directed to pay
D. none of the above

296. 'At sight' under section 21 of the Negotiable Instrument Act, 1881, means
A. on presentation B. on demand
C. on coming into vision D. none of the above

297. A promissory note or bill of exchange which is not expressed to be payable on demand, at sight or on presentment is at maturity
A. on the 30th day after the day on which it is expressed to be payable
B. on the 3rd day after the day on which it is expressed to be payable
C. on the 5th day after the day on which it is expressed to be payable
D. on the 4th day after the day on which it is expressed to be payable

298. If a minor draws, indorses, deliver or negotiates an instrument, such instrument binds
A. all parties to the instrument including the minor
B. only the minor and not other parties to the instrument
C. all parties to the instrument except the minor
D. none of the above

299. In a promissory note, the amount of money payable
A. must be certain
B. may be certain or uncertain
C. is usually uncertain
D. none of the above

300. An authority to draw bills of exchange
A. itself import an authority to indorse
B. does not itself import an authority to indorse
C. sometime import an authority to indorse
D. none of the above

ANSWERS

1	2	3	4	5	6	7	8	9	10
A	D	A	B	D	D	D	A	B	C
11	**12**	**13**	**14**	**15**	**16**	**17**	**18**	**19**	**20**
B	A	A	C	A	B	C	B	B	B
21	**22**	**23**	**24**	**25**	**26**	**27**	**28**	**29**	**30**
A	A	D	D	D	C	D	A	C	C
31	**32**	**33**	**34**	**35**	**36**	**37**	**38**	**39**	**40**
C	C	B	A	C	B	B	C	A	C
41	**42**	**43**	**44**	**45**	**46**	**47**	**48**	**49**	**50**
B	C	B	A	C	A	B	B	C	C
51	**52**	**53**	**54**	**55**	**56**	**57**	**58**	**59**	**60**
B	B	B	A	B	A	A	A	B	D

61	62	63	64	65	66	67	68	69	70
C	D	D	D	C	D	D	A	C	A
71	**72**	**73**	**74**	**75**	**76**	**77**	**78**	**79**	**80**
A	C	B	A	C	B	B	C	C	D
81	**82**	**83**	**84**	**85**	**86**	**87**	**88**	**89**	**90**
B	C	C	D	A	A	C	D	B	A
91	**92**	**93**	**94**	**95**	**96**	**97**	**98**	**99**	**100**
A	D	C	A	A	A	C	A	C	A
101	**102**	**103**	**104**	**105**	**106**	**107**	**108**	**109**	**110**
A	A	D	B	D	B	B	A	D	C
111	**112**	**113**	**114**	**115**	**116**	**117**	**118**	**119**	**120**
A	A	C	C	B	A	D	B	D	A
121	**122**	**123**	**124**	**125**	**126**	**127**	**128**	**129**	**130**
B	B	A	A	B	C	B	B	A	B
131	**132**	**133**	**134**	**135**	**136**	**137**	**138**	**139**	**140**
C	A	C	D	C	A	A	B	A	A
141	**142**	**143**	**144**	**145**	**146**	**147**	**148**	**149**	**150**
A	A	C	B	A	C	B	C	A	A
151	**152**	**153**	**154**	**155**	**156**	**157**	**158**	**159**	**160**
B	D	A	B	A	A	C	A	A	A
161	**162**	**163**	**164**	**165**	**166**	**167**	**168**	**169**	**170**
B	C	C	A	C	B	C	A	D	B
171	**172**	**173**	**174**	**175**	**176**	**177**	**178**	**179**	**180**
A	A	B	A	A	B	D	B	C	C
181	**182**	**183**	**184**	**185**	**186**	**187**	**188**	**189**	**190**
A	A	D	C	B	C	A	C	A	B
191	**192**	**193**	**194**	**195**	**196**	**197**	**198**	**199**	**200**
C	C	C	B	B	D	C	A	A	A
201	**202**	**203**	**204**	**205**	**206**	**207**	**208**	**209**	**210**
B	B	C	A	B	D	C	B	D	A
211	**212**	**213**	**214**	**215**	**216**	**217**	**218**	**219**	**220**
A	A	D	A	A	C	A	C	A	A
221	**222**	**223**	**224**	**225**	**226**	**227**	**228**	**229**	**230**
B	A	C	A	A	B	A	B	A	A
231	**232**	**233**	**234**	**235**	**236**	**237**	**238**	**239**	**240**
C	C	B	A	A	D	A	C	C	C
241	**242**	**243**	**244**	**245**	**246**	**247**	**248**	**249**	**250**
A	A	C	A	A	B	B	C	C	B
251	**252**	**253**	**254**	**255**	**256**	**257**	**258**	**259**	**260**
A	C	B	D	C	A	C	B	A	C
261	**262**	**263**	**264**	**265**	**266**	**267**	**268**	**269**	**270**
C	A	B	B	D	D	A	A	B	A
271	**272**	**273**	**274**	**275**	**276**	**277**	**278**	**279**	**280**
B	A	C	B	B	D	B	C	A	A
281	**282**	**283**	**284**	**285**	**286**	**287**	**288**	**289**	**290**
B	C	A	B	B	C	B	B	B	C
291	**292**	**293**	**294**	**295**	**296**	**297**	**298**	**299**	**300**
B	A	B	C	B	B	B	C	A	D

●●●

3 Cost Accounting

1. .... provides information for income determination.
A. Financial accounting
B. Cost accounting
C. Management accounting
D. None of these

2. .... helps in ascertaining costs beforehand.
A. Financial accounting
B. Cost accounting
C. Management accounting
D. None of these

3. The scope of cost accounting include ...., ... and ....
A. cost ascertainment, cost presentation, cost control
B. tax planning, tax accounting, financial accounting
C. presentation of accounting information, creation of policy, day-to-day operation
D. None of the above

4. Cost accounting disclose ....
A. the financial position
B. profit/loss of a product, job or service
C. effect and impact of cost on business
D. None of these

5. .... is a post mortem of past costs.
A. Financial accounting B. Cost accounting
C. Both A & B D. None of these

6. .... aids in price fixation.
A. Financial accounting
B. Cost accounting
C. Management accounting
D. None of these

7. .... is the oldest branch of accounting.
A. Financial accounting
B. Cost accounting
C. Management accounting
D. None of these

8. .... includes financial and cost accounting, tax planning and tax accounting.
A. Financial accounting
B. Cost accounting
C. Management accounting
D. None of these

9. In automobile, ... costing is used.
A. process B. batch
C. multiple D. job

10. Service costing is used in industries producing ....
A. products B. service
C. Both A & B D. None of these

11. .... costing is applicable to printers.
A. Process B. Batch
C. Multiple D. Job

12. Process costing is also known as .... costing.
A. continuous B. batch
C. multiple D. job

13. Operating costing is also known as .... costing.
A. service B. batch
C. multiple D. job

14. .... costing is a type or technique of costing.
A. Marginal B. Batch
C. Multiple D. Job

15. .... costing is a type or technique of costing.
A. Absorption B. Batch
C. Multiple D. Job

16. .... is not the scope of Cost Accountancy.
A. Ascertaining cost B. Cost accounting
C. Cost control D. Tax planning

17. Cost Accounting has been developed because of .... of Financial Accounting.
A. limitations B. advantages
C. Both A & B D. None of these

18. Cost Accountancy is the science, art and .... of a cost accountant.
A. practice B. exercise
C. hard work D. effort

19. The ordinary trading account is a locked storehouse of most valuable information to which cost system is the ....
A. key B. lock
C. house D. None of these

20. Cost accounts deal partly with facts and figures and partly with ....
A. estimates B. costs
C. income D. revenue

21. Cost accounting provides data for managerial ....
A. decision making B. recruitment
C. retrenchment D. None of the above

22. Cost accounting is based on .... figures.
A. estimated B. historical
C. actual D. None of these

23. Cost accounting provides detailed information about .... of various products, processes, services and operations.
A. costs B. income
C. Either A or B D. None of these

24. Cost accounting records both monetary and .... units.
A. physical B. cost
C. Both A & B D. None of these

25. The method of costing used in a refinery is .... costing.
A. process B. batch
C. multiple D. job

26. .... costing is used in transport undertakings.
A. Process B. Service
C. Multiple D. Job

27. The total variable cost .... in total proportion to output.
A. increases B. does not increase
C. decreases D. None of these

28. Variable cost per unit ....
A. remains constant B. varies
C. decreases D. increases

29. Sunk costs are .... for decision-making
A. irrelevant B. relevant
C. useful D. None of these

30. Costing and cost accounting are ....
A. not the same B. one and the same
C. not related at all D. None of these

31. Fixed cost .... in the same proportion in which output changes.
A. does not change B. changes
C. increases D. None of these

32. Administration expenses are mostly ....
A. semi-variable B. variable
C. fixed D. None of these

33. Abnormal cost is ....
A. uncontrollable B. controllable
C. fixed D. None of these

34. Cost of production is equal to ....
A. works cost plus administration overheads
B. prime cost plus works cost
C. prime cost plus works overhead
D. works overhead plus administration overheads

35. Variable cost increases with .... in output.
A. increase B. decrease
C. increase or decrease D. None of these

36. .... Accounting provides information for cost control.
A. Financial B. Cost
C. Human Resource D. None of these

37. .... is one which can be conveniently identified with and charged to a particular unit of cost.
A. Direct cost B. Indirect cost
C. Overhead D. None of these

38. Cost centre and cost unit are ....
A. not the same B. the same
C. not related D. None of these

39. Fixed cost per unit .... with rise in output and .... with fall in output.
A. decreases, increases
B. increases, decreases
C. is constant, remains same
D. None of the above

40. Period costs charged to ....
A. cost of production B. products
C. period D. None of these

41. Standard costs is ....
A. predetermined cost B. budgeted cost
C. actual cost D. None of these

42. .... are costs which have been applied against revenue of particular accounting period.
A. Expenses B. Income
C. Loss D. None of these

43. .... is the smallest segment of activity or area or responsibility for which costs are accumulated.
A. Cost object B. Cost centre
C. Cost driver D. None of the above

44. The primary emphasis of .... cost is on the planning function of management.
A. budgeted B. standard
C. period D. None of these

45. .... cost is irrecoverable cost.
A. Marginal B. Out of pocket
C. Sunk D. None of these

46. .... is the value of a benefit where no actual cost is incurred.
A. Imputed B. Sunk
C. Out of pocket D. None of these

47. .... is the cost which involves payment to outsiders.
A. Out of pocket cost B. Imputed cost
C. Notional cost D. None of these

48. .... is the maximum possible alternative earning that might have been earned if the productive capacity is put to some alternative use.
A. Opportunity B. Incremental revenue
C. Alternative revenue D. None of these

49. An item of cost that is direct for one business may be .... for another business.
A. important B. direct
C. indirect D. None of the above

50. The total of all direct expenses is known as .... cost.
A. prime B. works
C. production D. Both A & B

51. .... costs are partly fixed and partly variable in relation to output.
A. Variable B. Fixed
C. Semi-variable D. Both A & B

52. An opportunity cost is ....
A. the advantage foregone
B. the cost
C. the income
D. None of the above

53. Works cost is a total of ....
A. indirect material, indirect labour
B. direct material, direct labour, direct or chargeable expenses and works expenses
C. direct material, direct labour
D. indirect material, indirect labour, indirect expenses

54. An opportunity cost does not involve ....
A. cash outlays B. direct cost
C. indirect cost D. None of the above

55. Variable costs change .... with change in output.
A. proportionately B. inversely
C. disproportionately D. sometimes

56. Fixed cost per unit .... with increase in output.
A. decreases B. increases
C. changes D. sometimes

57. Depreciation is .... expenditure.
A. fixed B. variable
C. adjustable D. semi-variable

58. Out of pocket costs involve payment to ....
A. outsiders B. self
C. employees D. None of the above

59. Added value is the change in ....
A. market value B. cost
C. income D. None of the above

60. .... Accounting is not only a positive science but also a normative science because it includes techniques of budgetary control and standard costing.
A. Financial B. Cost
C. Both A & B D. None of these

61. Material control does not cover the following stage:
A. purchase of materials B. storing of materials
C. issue of materials D. production

62. Material control aims at achieving effective ....
A. material management B. quality control
C. accounting of material D. material supply

63. Stores Ledger is maintained in the ....
A. store
B. finance department
C. cost accounting department
D. Both A & B

64. Stock verification sheets are maintained to record the results of ....
A. physical verification
B. financial control
C. financial verification
D. quality verification

65. Stock Adjustment Account is debited with .... and credited with ....
A. surplus, shortage of stock
B. shortage of stock, surplus
C. excess, loss
D. None of these

66. Bin card is a record of .... only.
A. cost B. value
C. quantity D. expense

67. Bin card is maintained by the ....
A. Cost accountant B. Clerk
C. Storekeeper D. Branch accountant

68. Material abstract is also known as ....
A. material issue analysis sheet
B. bill of materials
C. stores ledger
D. None of the above

69. Material should be issued by the store keeper against ....
A. material requisition B. bill of materials
C. Both A & B D. None of these

70. First in first out method of valuing material issues is suitable in times of ....
A. rising prices B. falling prices
C. fluctuating prices D. None of these

71. Last in first out method is suitable in times of ....
A. rising prices B. falling prices
C. fluctuating prices D. None of these

72. Average cost method of valuing material issues is suitable when ....
A. prices rise
B. prices fall
C. prices fluctuate considerably
D. None of these

73. Inflated price method of valuing material issues is suitable when ....
A. materials are subject to natural wastage
B. prices rise
C. prices fall
D. None of these

74. Specific price method of valuing material issue is used when............
A. materials are purchased for specific job or work order
B. materials are subject to natural wastage
C. prices fluctuate
D. None of these

75. Market price method is considered to be the best method when ....
A. quotations have to be sent
B. prices fluctuate
C. materials are subject to natural wastage
D. None of these

76. A bill of material serves the purpose of ....
A. material requisition
B. stores ledger
C. material issue analysis sheet
D. None of these

77. A bill of material is prepared in case of a .... job.
A. standard job B. non-standardized job
C. Both A & B D. None of these

78. Stock verification sheets are maintained to record the results of ....
A. physical verification B. financial control
C. financial verification D. quality verification

79. The quantity of material to be ordered at one time is known as ....
A. ordering quantity
B. commercial order quantity
C. economic order quantity
D. None of these

80. .... represents that quantity of material which is normally ordered when a particular material reaches re-ordering level.
A. Maximum level B. Re-order level
C. Minimum level D. Re-order quantity

81. The principle types of inventories are raw materials and, ... and finished goods.
A. processed materials B. goods-in-progress
C. stored goods D. goods for dispatch

82. Re-ordering level = Maximum consumption × ....
A. Average re-order period
B. Maximum usage
C. Maximum re-order period
D. Normal usage

83. Inventory turnover ratio = Cost of inventory consumed during the period ÷ Cost of .... held during the period
A. average inventory B. minimum inventory
C. maximum inventory D. None of these

84. Inventory turnover in days = Days during the period ÷ ....
A. inventory turnover ratio
B. material consumed during the period
C. cost of average stock during the period
D. None of these

85. .... is a technique of material cost control which leads to low carrying cost as a result of low investment in inventory.
A. ABC Analysis
B. JIT Inventory System
C. VED Analysis
D. Perpetual Inventory System

86. .... is a technique of stock control which leads to saving of time of the management because attention is required to be paid only to some of the items rather than on all the items.
A. ABC Analysis
B. JIT Inventory System
C. VED Analysis
D. Perpetual Inventory System

87. .... is used primarily for control of spare parts.
A. ABC Analysis
B. JIT Inventory System
C. VED Analysis
D. Perpetual Inventory System

88. Inventory turnover ratio = Cost of ...... during the period ÷ Cost of average inventory held during the period.
A. inventory consumed B. minimum inventory
C. maximum inventory D. None of these

89. Re-ordering level = ... × Maximum re-order period
A. Average re-order period
B. Maximum usage
C. Maximum consumption
D. Normal usage

90. .... obviates the necessity for the physical checking of all items of stores at the end of the year and thereby avoids dislocation of production.
A. ABC Analysis
B. JIT Inventory System
C. VED Analysis
D. Perpetual Inventory System

91. .... forms part of cost of production.
A. Abnormal waste B. Normal waste
C. Both A & B D. None of these

92. .... does not form part of production.
A. Abnormal waste B. Normal waste
C. Both A & B D. None of these

93. Material losses due to abnormal reasons should be transferred to ....
A. Profit and loss account
B. Costing Profit and Loss Account
C. Trading Account
D. None of these

94. Defectives are that portion of production which can be .... at some extra cost of re-operation.
A. sold B. rectified
C. purchased D. None of these

95. .... is a method of evaluating the job in terms of its money value.
A. Job analysis B. Job evaluation
C. Work measurement D. Motion study

96. The requirements of a particular job are known as ....
A. job description B. job specifications
C. job evaluation D. Both A & B

97. Qualities demanded from the job holder is technically known as ....
A. job description B. job specifications
C. job evaluation D. Both A & B

98. .... is concerned with discovery of facts concerning a job and .... is concerned with ascertaining the money value of a job.
A. Job description, job evaluation
B. Job specifications, job evaluation
C. Job analysis, job evaluation
D. None of these

99. For conducting .... workers are studied at their jobs and all their movements and motions are noted.
A. time study B. motion study
C. merit rating D. None of these

100. .... is the assessment of the relative worth of jobs within a company whereas .... is the assessment of the relative worth of man behind the job.
A. Job evaluation, merit rating
B. Job analysis, job evaluation
C. Job analysis, merit rating
D. None of these

101. .... is maintained to know how the worker's time shown by the time card is spent on various jobs.
A. Daily time sheets B. Weekly time sheets
C. Job cards D. None of the above

102. In time wage system, wages are paid according to the ....
A. production B. time
C. Both A & B D. None of these

103. Under piece rate system of wage payment, payment is made according to the ....
A. quantity of work done B. time
C. Both A & B D. None of these

104. For a work order, standard time and time taken are 20 hours and 15 hours respectively. Time rate being ₹ 2 per hour, total wages payable under Rowan Premium Plan will be:
A. 40 B. 37.50
C. 35 D. None of these

105. Taylors differential piece rate system provides for higher rate to .... workers.
A. inefficient B. efficient
C. Both A & B D. lazy

106. .... is most suitable when quality of work is of prime importance.
A. Piece rate system B. Time wage system
C. Both A & B D. None of these

107. Formula of calculation of wages under Halsey Premium System is ....
A. $\sqrt{R}$ + %(S – T)R B. T × R + % (S – T) R
C. $\frac{S-T}{S} \times T \times R$ D. R × S × T

108. Under Merrick's multiple piece rate system, 110% of the ordinary piece rate is given to workers whose level of performance is between .... of the standard output.
A. 83% and 100% B. 100% and 120%
C. 0% and 83% D. None of these

109. Under Merrick's multiple piece rate system, 120% of the ordinary piece rate is given to workers whose level of performance is between .... of the standard output.
A. 83% and 100% B. 100% and 120%
C. 0% and 83% D. None of these

110. Under Merrick's multiple piece rate system, ordinary piece rate is given to workers whose level of performance is between .... of the standard output.
A. 0% and 100% B. 0% and 120%
C. 0% and 83% D. None of these

111. In ...., two piece rates are set for each job.
A. Merrick's multiple piece rate system
B. Rowan's Premium Plan
C. Taylor's differential piece rate system
D. None of these

112. Basis of apportionment of stores service expenses is ....
A. value of materials consumed
B. units of material consumed
C. products produced
D. None of these

113. Basis of apportionment of welfare department expenses is ....
A. wages of each department
B. number of employees
C. materials consumed
D. number of machineries

114. Basis of apportionment of crèche expenses is ....
A. number of employees
B. number of female employees
C. number of male employees
D. Both B & C

115. Under step method of re-apportionment of costs of service departments, the cost of last service department is apportioned only to the ....
A. production departments
B. service departments
C. Both A & B
D. None of these

116. Machine hour rate is obtained by dividing the total running expenses of a machine during a particular period by the ....
A. number of hours
B. number of products produced
C. number of workers
D. wages

117. .... is the amount by which the absorbed overheads fall short of the actual amount of overheads incurred.
A. Over absorption of overheads
B. Under absorption of overheads
C. Overheads absorption
D. None of these

118. .... is the excess of overheads absorbed over the actual amount of overheads incurred.
A. Over absorption of overheads
B. Under absorption of overheads
C. Overheads absorption
D. None of these

119. When .... is used on the basis of budgeted overheads and the rate is applied to the actual base, the actual overhead expenses may be different from the charged overheads.
A. a predetermined rate
B. actual rate method of absorption
C. Both A & B
D. None of these

120. Expenses incurred during production other than direct materials and direct labour are called .... factory expenses; those charged to production on estimated basis are called ....
A. actual, applied B. applied, actual
C. indirect, direct D. None of these

121. The per unit expense of the .... portion factory overhead varies with the volume of production while .... portion remains the same with volume.
A. fixed, variable B. variable, fixed
C. variable, semi-variable D. None of these

122. .... expenses are excluded from cost.
A. Normal B. Abnormal
C. Both A & B D. None of these

123. Such expenses which are included (even though they are not incurred) for taking managerial decisions are called ....
A. notional expenses B. actual expenses
C. imputed D. None of these

124. .... expenses are partly fixed and partly variable.
A. All expenses B. Variable
C. Fixed D. Semi-variable

125. Unsuccessful research expenditure should be .... cost accounts.
A. excluded from B. included in
C. apportioned in D. None of these

126. Salary paid to general manager is an item of .... expenses.
A. fixed B. variable
C. semi-variable D. estimated

127. Fancy packing is an example of .... expenses.
A. selling B. distribution
C. administration D. factory

128. Telephone expense is .... expense.
A. variable B. semi-variable
C. fixed D. None of these

129. Primary packing is an item of ....
A. selling overheads
B. prime cost
C. distribution overheads
D. factory overheads

130. When factory overhead control account has an ending debit balance, factory overhead was...............
A. over applied B. under applied
C. Both A & B D. None of these

131. Under applied or over applied factory overhead should be:
A. carried forward to next year
B. shown as an extraordinary item
C. apportioned among cost of goods sold and applicable to inventory
D. written off

132. Credit and collection cost is an item of:
A. selling overhead B. office overhead
C. prime cost D. administrative overhead

133. Warehousing cost is an item of:
A. office overhead B. distribution overhead
C. material cost D. works overhead

134. In .... each job is a cost unit to which all costs are assigned.
A. Batch costing B. Job costing
C. Process costing D. Operation costing

135. Material Costs of each job are determined from ....
A. material requisition notes
B. bill of materials
C. Both A & B
D. None of these

136. Printers use .... costing.
A. Process B. Batch
C. Job D. Contract

137. Each job has a .... prepared for it that bears the job number and which is used to collect all cost data relating to job.
A. Job Time Sheet B. Job Cost Card
C. Job Ticket D. Job Account

138. An automobile service unit uses .... costing.
A. specific order B. batch
C. job D. contract

139. Where the work is undertaken to Customers' special requirements and each order is of comparatively short-duration, it is called .... costing.
A. job B. batch
C. operation D. output

140. Economic Batch Quantity is an important point to be determined in industries where .... costing is employed.
A. job B. batch
C. operation D. output

141. Economic Batch Quantity depends on .... and .... costs.
A. material, labour
B. set-up costs, carrying
C. transportation, carrying
D. warehousing, labour

142. The .... costing is applied when a quantity of similar and identical products are manufactured together as one Job.
A. job B. batch
C. operation D. output

143. The loss incurred on an incomplete contract is transferred to .... account.
A. costing profit and loss account
B. profit and loss account
C. trading account
D. deferred to next year

144. When the completion stage of the contract is more than half, the profit to be credited to Profit and Loss account will be equal to ....

A. $\frac{1}{3}$rd of Notional Profit $\times \frac{\text{Cash received}}{\text{Work certified}}$

B. $\frac{1}{2}$ of Notional Profit $\times \frac{\text{Cash received}}{\text{Work certified}}$

C. $\frac{2}{3}$rd of Notional Profit $\times \frac{\text{Cash received}}{\text{Work certified}}$

D. Full Notional Profit

145. When the completion stage of a contract is less than $\frac{1}{4}$, the total expenditure on the contract is transferred to .... account.
A. Work-in-progress B. Profit and loss account
C. Miscellaneous account D. None of these

146. If the amount of work certified is less than .... of the contract price, then no profit should be taken to Profit & Loss Account.
A. 20% B. 25%
C. $33\frac{1}{3}$% D. 40%

147. Contract costing is not used in one of the following industries:
A. Ship building B. Civil construction
C. Automobiles D. Construction of bridges

148. The sum of value of work certified and uncertified appearing in the Contract Account is called ....
A. Work in Progress B. Work in Process
C. Work Completed D. Work Done

149. .... is the most suitable method in a transport industry.
A. Operation costing B. Service costing
C. Process costing D. Job costing

150. Room/day is the cost unit used in ....
A. hotels B. hospitals
C. schools D. None of these

151. Maintenance charges are in the nature of .... expenses.
A. Fixed B. Variable
C. Semi-variable D. None of these

152. In transport costing .... charges vary more or less in direct proportion to kilometers run.
A. running B. petrol
C. drivers salary D. tax

153. Service costing is called as ....
A. Operation costing B. Operating costing
C. Multiple costing D. None of these

154. In electricity supply company uses .... as cost unit.
A. kilo watt hour B. per household
C. voltage D. None of these

155. In transportation costing a composite unit such as .... is used.
A. passenger mile/km or Ten kilometer
B. per km
C. per passenger
D. per stop

156. Boiler house costing is an example of .... costing.
A. operation B. process
C. service D. None of these

157. In service costing, fixed charges are also called as ....
A. standing charges B. variable charges
C. fixed charges D. None of these

158. Service costing is not used in one of the following:
A. Electricity B. Hospitals
C. Transport D. Electronics

159. If the present cost of the car is ₹ 1,00,000 residual value at the end of the 5th year is ₹ 20,000, the monthly depreciation is ....
A. ₹ 20,000 B. ₹ 16,000
C. ₹ 1,333 D. ₹ 17,333

160. A bus carries 25 passengers daily for 25 days and its mileage per month is 1000 kms. Its passenger miles are ....
A. 30,000 B. 12,500
C. 20,000 D. 25,000

161. In .... costing where standardized goods or services result from a sequence of repetitive and more or less continuous operations to which costs are collected and averaged over the units produced during the year:
A. Multiple B. Process
C. Operation D. Single

162. The method of costing applied in biscuit industries is .... costing and in steel industry .... costing.
A. job, process B. job, contract
C. batch, multiple D. process, operation

163. Average unit cost for each process is calculated by dividing the .... by ....
A. Total cost, number of units
B. Total process cost, number of units in process
C. Total process cost, number of finished goods
D. Total cost, number of units produced

164. Where raw material is to pass certain stages, before it is converted into finished goods, the method of costing used is ....
A. Job costing B. Operating costing
C. Process costing D. Both B and C

165. When the actual loss is more than the estimated loss, the difference between the two is considered to be ....
A. abnormal loss B. normal loss
C. loss D. None of these

166. When actual loss is less than the estimated loss, the difference between the two is considered to be ....
A. abnormal gain B. abnormal loss
C. normal loss D. income

167. When actual loss is .... than the estimated loss, the difference between the two is considered to be abnormal gain.
A. more B. less
C. higher D. None of these

168. When actual loss is .... than the estimated loss, the difference between the two is considered to be abnormal loss.
A. more B. less
C. Both A & B D. None of these

169. When 1000 units are 60% complete in a process, it is equivalent to .... completed units.
A. 60 B. 600
C. 6000 D. 1000

170. Equivalent units represent the production of a process in terms of .... units.
A. completed B. total production
C. semi-finished D. Both A & C

171. .... process loss should be transferred to costing profit & loss account.
A. abnormal B. normal
C. Both A & B D. None of these

172. The cost of .... process loss is absorbed in the cost of production of good units.
A. abnormal B. normal
C. Both A & B D. None of these

173. In inter process profits, the output of one process is transferred from one process to another not at .... but at ....
A. market price, actual cost
B. actual cost, market price
C. Both A & B
D. None of these

174. Where actual loss in a process is less than the anticipated loss, the difference between the two is considered to be ....
A. abnormal loss B. normal loss
C. abnormal gain D. normal gain

175. In process costing, the abnormal loss is treated as .... cost and written off to profit & loss account.
A. unit B. period
C. future D. process

176. The process costing is not used in one of the following:
A. chemical B. textiles
C. cement D. oil refining

177. .... arises where the actual process loss is less than the normal predetermined process loss.
A. Normal loss B. Abnormal loss
C. Abnormal gain D. None of these

178. An input of 5000 kg of material introduced into the process and the expected loss is 8% and if the actual output from the process is 4300, the abnormal loss is .... kg.
A. 400 B. 300
C. 500 D. 600

179. Budgeting system .... key managerial functions.
A. dismisses B. integrates
C. discharges D. None of these

180. .... is a budget which is updated continuously by adding a further period (a month/quarter) and deducting a corresponding earlier period.
A. Rolling budget B. Continuous budget
C. Annual budget D. Both A & B

181. The budget relating to .... must be prepared first and the other budgets should be prepared in the light of that factor.
A. limiting factor B. materials
C. labour D. production

182. .... budget is the most important budget and it forms the basis on which all the other budgets are built up.

A. Production B. Material
C. Cash budget D. Sales

183. .... budget may be classified into material cost budget, labour cost budget and overhead budget.

A. Cost of production B. Purchase
C. Sales D. Cash

184. .... budget gives an estimate of the anticipated receipts and payment of cash during the budget period.

A. Sales B. Production
C. Cash D. Master

185. .... is the consolidated summary of the various functional budgets.

A. Master budget B. Sales budget
C. Performance budget D. Cash budget

186. .... budget is designed to remain unchanged irrespective of the volume of output or turnover attained.

A. Master B. Fixed
C. Flexible D. All of these

187. .... budget gives different budgeted costs for different levels of activity.

A. Master B. Fixed
C. Flexible D. All of these

188. .... budget is the preparation of budget starting from a clean state.

A. Performance B. Zero Base
C. Cash D. None of these

189. Calendar Ratio =

A. $\frac{\text{Number of actual working days in a period}}{\text{Number of working days in the budget period}} \times 100$

B. $\frac{\text{Actual hours worked}}{\text{Budgeted hours}} \times 100$

C. $\frac{\text{Standard hours for actual production}}{\text{Actual hours worked}} \times 100$

D. $\frac{\text{Standard hours for actual production}}{\text{Budgeted standard hours}} \times 100$

190. Capacity Ratio =

A. $\frac{\text{Number of actual working days in a period}}{\text{Number of working days in the budget period}} \times 100$

B. $\frac{\text{Actual hours worked}}{\text{Budgeted hours}} \times 100$

C. $\frac{\text{Standard hours for actual production}}{\text{Actual hours worked}} \times 100$

D. $\frac{\text{Standard hours for actual production}}{\text{Budgeted standard hours}} \times 100$

191. Efficiency Ratio =

A. $\frac{\text{Number of actual working days in a period}}{\text{Number of working days in the budget period}} \times 100$

B. $\frac{\text{Actual hours worked}}{\text{Budgeted hours}} \times 100$

C. $\frac{\text{Standard hours for actual production}}{\text{Actual hours worked}} \times 100$

D. $\frac{\text{Standard hours for actual production}}{\text{Budgeted standard hours}} \times 100$

192. Activity Ratio =

A. $\frac{\text{Number of actual working days in a period}}{\text{Number of working days in the budget period}} \times 100$

B. $\frac{\text{Actual hours worked}}{\text{Budgeted hours}} \times 100$

C. $\frac{\text{Standard hours for actual production}}{\text{Actual hours worked}} \times 100$

D. $\frac{\text{Standard hours for actual production}}{\text{Budgeted standard hours}} \times 100$

193. .... is a summary of all function budgets in a Capsule form.

A. Master budget B. Sales budget
C. Performance budget D. Cash budget

194. .... determines the priorities of functional budget.

A. Principal Budget Factor B. Limiting Factor
C. Both A & B D. None of the above

195. Cash Budget is a .... budget.

A. long-term B. very long-term
C. short-term D. very short-term

196. The primary difference between a fixed budget and a variable(flexible) budget is that a fixed budget:

A. Includes only fixed costs, while a variable budget includes only variable costs.
B. Is concerned only with future acquisitions of fixed assets, while a variable budget is concerned with expenses which vary with sales.
C. Cannot be changed after the period begins, while a variable budget can be changed after the period begins.
D. Is a plan for a single level of sales (or other measure of activity), while a variable budget consists of several plans, one for each of several levels of sales (or other measure of activity)

197. Sales budget is a:

A. Functional budget B. Master budget
C. Expenditure budget D. None of these

198. In the case of plant, the limiting factor may be:

A. insufficient capacity
B. shortage of experienced salesmen
C. general shortage of power
D. shortage of materials

199. The difference between fixed and variable cost has a special significance in the preparation of:
A. flexible budget
B. master budget
C. cash budget
D. sales budget

200. The budget that is prepared first of all is ....
A. cash budget
B. master budget
C. budget for the key factor
D. sales budget

ANSWERS

1	**2**	**3**	**4**	**5**	**6**	**7**	**8**	**9**	**10**
A	B	A	B	A	B	A	C	C	B
11	**12**	**13**	**14**	**15**	**16**	**17**	**18**	**19**	**20**
D	A	A	A	A	D	A	A	A	A
21	**22**	**23**	**24**	**25**	**26**	**27**	**28**	**29**	**30**
A	A	A	A	A	B	A	A	A	A
31	**32**	**33**	**34**	**35**	**36**	**37**	**38**	**39**	**40**
A	C	A	A	A	B	A	A	A	C
41	**42**	**43**	**44**	**45**	**46**	**47**	**48**	**49**	**50**
A	A	B	A	C	A	A	A	C	A
51	**52**	**53**	**54**	**55**	**56**	**57**	**58**	**59**	**60**
C	A	B	A	A	A	D	A	A	B
61	**62**	**63**	**64**	**65**	**66**	**67**	**68**	**69**	**70**
D	A	C	A	B	C	C	A	C	B
71	**72**	**73**	**74**	**75**	**76**	**77**	**78**	**79**	**80**
A	C	A	A	A	A	B	A	A	D
81	**82**	**83**	**84**	**85**	**86**	**87**	**88**	**89**	**90**
B	C	A	B	B	A	C	A	C	D
91	**92**	**93**	**94**	**95**	**96**	**97**	**98**	**99**	**100**
B	A	B	B	B	A	B	C	B	A
101	**102**	**103**	**104**	**105**	**106**	**107**	**108**	**109**	**110**
C	B	A	B	B	B	B	A	B	C
111	**112**	**113**	**114**	**115**	**116**	**117**	**118**	**119**	**120**
C	A	B	B	A	A	B	A	B	A
121	**122**	**123**	**124**	**125**	**126**	**127**	**128**	**129**	**130**
A	B	A	D	A	A	A	B	B	B
131	**132**	**133**	**134**	**135**	**136**	**137**	**138**	**139**	**140**
C	A	B	B	C	C	B	C	A	B
141	**142**	**143**	**144**	**145**	**146**	**147**	**148**	**149**	**150**
B	B	B	C	A	B	C	A	B	A
151	**152**	**153**	**154**	**155**	**156**	**157**	**158**	**159**	**160**
C	A	B	A	A	C	A	D	C	D
161	**162**	**163**	**164**	**165**	**166**	**167**	**168**	**169**	**170**
C	A	B	C	A	A	B	A	B	A
171	**172**	**173**	**174**	**175**	**176**	**177**	**178**	**179**	**180**
A	B	B	C	B	C	C	B	B	D
181	**182**	**183**	**184**	**185**	**186**	**187**	**188**	**189**	**190**
A	D	A	C	A	B	C	B	B	B
191	**192**	**193**	**194**	**195**	**196**	**197**	**198**	**199**	**200**
C	D	A	C	C	D	A	A	A	C

●●●

4 Financial Management

1. The appropriate objective of an enterprise is:
A. Maximisation of sale
B. Maximisation of owner's wealth
C. Maximisation of profits
D. None of these

2. The job of a finance manager is confined to:
A. Raising funds
B. Management of cash
C. Raising of funds and their effective utilization
D. None of these

3. Financial decision involves:
A. Investment, financing and dividend decision
B. Investment, financing and sales decision
C. Financing, dividend and cash decision
D. None of these

4. Net Profit Ratio Signifies:
A. Operational Profitability
B. Liquidity Position
C. Solvency
D. Profit

5. Working Capital Turnover measures the relationship of Working Capital with:
A. Fixed Assets B. Sales
C. Purchases D. Stock

6. Dividend Payout Ratio is:
A. PAT Capital
B. DPS ÷ EPS
C. Pref. Dividend ÷ PAT
D. Pref. Dividend ÷ Equity Dividend

7. Inventory Turnover measures the relationship of inventory with:
A. Average Sales B. Cost of Goods Sold
C. Total Purchases D. Total Assets

8. The term 'EVA' is used for:
A. Extra Value Analysis
B. Economic Value Added
C. Expected Value Analysis
D. Engineering Value Analysis

9. Return on Investment may be improved by:
A. Increasing Turnover
B. Reducing Expenses
C. Increasing Capital Utilization
D. All of the above

10. In Current Ratio, Current Assets are compared with:
A. Current Profit B. Current Liabilities
C. Fixed Assets D. Equity Share Capital

11. There is deterioration in the management of working capital of XYZ Ltd. What does it refer to?
A. That the Capital Employed has reduced
B. That the Profitability has gone up
C. That Debtors Collection period has increased
D. That Sales has decreased

12. Debt to Total Assets Ratio can be improved by:
A. Borrowing More
B. Issue of Debentures
C. Issue of Equity Shares
D. Redemption of Debt

13. Ratio of Net Income to Number of Equity Shares known as:
A. Price Earnings Ratio B. Net Profit Ratio
C. Earnings per Share D. Dividend per Share

14. A Current Ratio of less than one means:
A. Current Liabilities < Current Assets
B. Fixed Assets > Current Assets
C. Current Assets < Current Liabilities
D. Share Capital > Current Assets

15. A firm has Capital of ₹ 10,00,000; Sales of ₹ 5,00,000; Gross Profit of ₹ 2,00,000 and Expenses of ₹ 1,00,000. What is the Net Profit Ratio?
A. 20% B. 50%
C. 10% D. 40%

16. Suppliers and Creditors of a firm are interested in:
A. Profitability Position B. Liquidity Position
C. Market Share Position D. Debt Position

17. Which of the following is a measure of Debt Service capacity of a firm?
A. Current Ratio
B. Acid Test Ratio
C. Interest Coverage Ratio
D. Debtors Turnover

18. Gross Profit Ratio for a firm remains same but the Net Profit Ratio is decreasing. The reason for such behaviour could be:
A. Increase in Costs of Goods Sold
B. If Increase in Expense
C. Increase in Dividend
D. Decrease in Sales

19. Which of the following statements is correct?
A. A Higher Receivable Turnover is not desirable
B. Interest Coverage Ratio depends upon Tax Rate
C. Increase in Net Profit Ratio means increase in Sales
D. Lower Debt-Equity Ratio means lower Financial Risk

20. Debt to Total Assets of a firm is .2. The Debt to Equity boo would be:
A. 0.80 B. 0.25
C. 1.00 D. 0.75

21. Which of the following helps analysing return to equity Shareholders?
A. Return on Assets B. Earnings per Share
C. Net Profit Ratio D. Return on Investment

22. In Inventory Turnover calculation, what is taken in the numerator?
A. Sales B. Cost of Goods Sold
C. Opening Stock D. Closing Stock

23. Financial Planning deals with:
A. Preparation of Financial Statements
B. Planning for a Capital Issue
C. Preparing Budgets
D. All of the above

24. Financial planning starts with the preparation of:
A. Master Budget B. Cash Budget
C. Balance Sheet D. None of the above

25. Process of Financial Planning ends with:
A. Preparation of projected statements
B. Preparation of actual statements
C. Comparison of actual with projected
D. Ordering the employees that projected figures come true.

26. Capital Budgeting is a part of:
A. Investment Decision
B. Working Capital Management
C. Marketing Management
D. Capital Structure

27. Capital Budgeting deals with:
A. Long-term Decisions B. Short-term Decisions
C. Both A and B D. Neither A nor B

28. Which of the following is not used in Capital Budgeting?
A. Time Value of Money B. Sensitivity Analysis
C. Net Assets Method D. Cash Flows

29. Capital Budgeting Decisions are:
A. Reversible B. Irreversible
C. Unimportant D. All of the above

30. Which of the following is not incorporated in Capital Budgeting?
A. Tax-Effect
B. Time Value of Money
C. Required Rate of Return
D. Rate of Cash Discount

31. Which of the following is not a capital budgeting decision?
A. Expansion Programme
B. Merger
C. Replacement of an Asset
D. Inventory Level

32. A Sound Capital Budgeting technique is based on:
A. Cash Flows
B. Accounting Profit
C. Interest Rate on Borrowings
D. Last Dividend Paid

33. Which of the following is not a relevant cost in Capital Budgeting?
A. Sunk Cost B. Opportunity Cost
C. Allocated Overheads D. Both A and C above

34. Capital Budgeting Decisions are based on:
A. Incremental Profit B. Incremental Cash Flows
C. Incremental Assets D. Incremental Capital

35. Which of the following does not effect cash flows proposal?
A. Salvage Value
B. Depreciation Amount
C. Tax Rate Change
D. Method of Project Financing

36. Cash Inflows from a project include:
A. Tax Shield of Depreciation
B. After-tax Operating Profits
C. Raising of Funds
D. Both A and B

37. Which of the following is not true with reference capital budgeting?
A. Capital budgeting is related to asset replacement decisions
B. Cost of capital is equal to minimum required return
C. Existing investment in a project is not treated as sunk cost
D. Timing of cash flows is relevant

38. Which of the following is not followed in capital budgeting?
A. Cash flows Principle
B. Interest Exclusion Principle
C. Accrual Principle
D. Post-tax Principle

39. Depreciation is incorporated in cash flows because it:
A. is unavoidable cost B. is a cash flow
C. reduces tax liability D. involves an outflow

40. Which of the following is not true for capital budgeting?
A. Sunk costs are ignored
B. Opportunity costs are excluded
C. Incremental cash flows are considered
D. Relevant cash flows are considered

41. Which of the following is not applied in capital budgeting?
A. Cash flows be calculated in incremental terms
B. All costs and benefits are measured on cash basis
C. All accrued costs and revenues be incorporated
D. All benefits are measured on after-tax basis

42. Evaluation of Capital Budgeting Proposals is based on Cash Flows because:
A. Cash Flows are easy to calculate
B. Cash Flows are suggested by SEBI
C. Cash is more important than profit
D. None of the above

43. Which of the following is not included in incremental A flows?
A. Opportunity costs
B. Sunk costs
C. Change in working capital
D. Inflation effect

44. A proposal is not a Capital Budgeting proposal if it:
A. is related to fixed assets
B. brings long-term benefits
C. brings short-term benefits only
D. has very large investment

45. In Capital Budgeting, Sunk cost is excluded because it is:
A. of small amount B. not incremental
C. not reversible D. All of the above

46. Savings in respect of a cost is treated in capital budgeting as:
A. An Inflow B. An Outflow
C. Nil D. None of the above

47. In capital budgeting, the term Capital Rationing implies:
A. That no retained earnings available
B. That limited funds are available for investment
C. That no external funds can be raised
D. That no fresh investment is required in current year

48. Feasibility Set Approach to Capital Rationing can be applied in:
A. Accept-reject situations
B. Divisible projects
C. Mutually exclusive projects
D. None of the above

49. In case of divisible projects, which of the following can be used to attain maximum NPV?
A. Feasibility Set Approach
B. Internal Rate of Return
C. Profitability Index Approach
D. Any of the above

50. In case of the indivisible projects, which of the following may not give the optimum result?
A. Internal Rate of Return B. Profitability Index
C. Feasibility Set Approach D. All of the above

51. Profitability Index, when applied to Divisible Projects, impliedly assumes that:
A. Project cannot be taken in parts
B. NPV is linearly proportionate to part of the project taken up
C. NPV is additive in nature
D. Both B and C

52. If there is no inflation during a period, then the Money Cashflow would be equal to:
A. Present Value
B. Real Cash flow
C. Real Cash flow + Present Value
D. Real Cash flow – Present Value

53. The Real Cashflows must be discounted to get the present value at a rate equal to:
A. Money Discount Rate
B. Inflation Rate
C. Real Discount Rate
D. Risk free rate of interest

54. Real rate of return is equal to:
A. Nominal Rate × Inflation Rate
B. Nominal Rate ÷ Inflation Rate
C. Nominal Rate – Inflation Rate
D. Nominal Rate + Inflation Rate

55. If the Real rate of return is 10% and Inflation rate is 40%, then Money Discount Rate is:
A. 14.4% B. 2.5%
C. 25% D. 14%

56. If the Money Discount Rate is 19% and Inflation Rate is 12%, then the Real Discount Rate is:
A. 7% B. 5%
C. 5.70% D. 6.25%

57. Money Discount Rate if equal to:
A. (1 + Inflation Rate) (1 + Real Rate) – 1
B. (1 + Inflation Rate) 4 – (1 + Real Rate) – 1
C. (1 + Real Rate) 4 – (1 + Inflation Rate) – 1
D. (1 + Real Rate) + (1 + Inflation Rate) – 1

58. Real Discount Rate is equal to:
A. (1 + Inf. Rate) (1 + Money D Rate) – 1
B. (1 + Money D Rate) + (1 + Inf. Rate) – 1
C. (1 + Money D Rate) 4 – (1 + Inf. Rate) – 1
D. (1 + Money D Rate) – (1 + Inf. Rate) – 1

59. Two mutually exclusive projects with different economic lives can be compared on the basis of:
A. Internal Rate of Return
B. Profitability Index
C. Net Present Value
D. Equivalent Annuity Value

60. Risk in Capital budgeting implies that the decision-maker knows .... of the cash flows.
A. Variability B. Probability
C. Certainty D. None of the above

61. In Certainty-equivalent approach, adjusted cash flows are discounted at:
A. Accounting Rate of Return
B. Internal Rate of Return
C. Hurdle Rate
D. Risk-free Rate

62. Risk in Capital budgeting is same as:
A. Uncertainty of Cash flows
B. Probability of Cash flows
C. Certainty of Cash flows
D. Variability of Cash flows

63. Which of the following is a risk factor in capital budgeting?
A. Industry specific risk factors
B. Competition risk factors
C. Project specific risk factors
D. All of the above

64. In Risk-adjusted Discount Rate method, the normal rate of discount is:
A. Increased B. Decreased
C. Unchanged D. None of the above

65. In Risk-adjusted Discount Rate method, which one is adjusted?
A. Cash flows B. Life of the proposal
C. Rate of discount D. Salvage value

66. NPV of a proposal, as calculated by RADR real CE Approach will be:
A. Same B. Unequal
C. Both A and B D. None of A and B

67. Risk of a Capital budgeting can be incorporated:
A. Adjusting the cash flows
B. Adjusting the discount rate
C. Adjusting the life
D. All of the above

68. Which element of the basic NPV equation is adjusted by the RADR?
A. Denominator B. Numerator
C. Both A and B D. None of these

69. Cost of Capital refers to:
A. Flotation Cost
B. Dividend
C. Required Rate of Return
D. None of the above

70. Which of the following sources of funds has an Implicit Cost of Capital?
A. Equity Share Capital
B. Preference Share Capital
C. Debentures
D. Retained earnings

71. Which of the following has the highest cost of capital?
A. Equity shares B. Loans
C. Bonds D. Preference shares

72. Cost of Capital for Government securities is also known as:
A. Risk-free Rate of Interest
B. Maximum Rate of Return
C. Rate of Interest on Fixed Deposits
D. None of the above

73. Cost of Capital for Bonds and Debentures is calculated on:
A. Before Tax basis
B. After Tax basis
C. Risk-free Rate of Interest basis
D. None of the above

74. Weighted Average Cost of Capital is generally denoted by:
A. k_A B. k_w
C. k_0 D. k_c

75. Which of the following cost of capital require tax adjustment?
A. Cost of Equity Shares B. Cost of Preference Shares
C. Cost of Debentures D. Cost of Retained Earnings

76. Which is the most expensive source of funds?
A. New Equity Shares B. New Preference Shares
C. New Debts D. Retained Earnings

77. Marginal cost of capital is the cost of:
A. Additional Sales B. Additional Funds
C. Additional Interests D. None of the above

78. In case the firm is all-equity financed, WACC would be equal to:
A. Cost of Debt B. Cost of Equity
C. Neither A nor B D. Both A and B

79. In case of partially debt-financed firm, k_0 is less:
A. k_d B. k_c
C. Both A and B D. None of the above

80. In order to calculate Weighted Average Cost of weights may be based on:
A. Market Values B. Target Values
C. Book Values D. All of the above

81. Firm's Cost of Capital is the average cost of:
A. All sources
B. All borrowings
C. Share capital
D. Share Bonds & Debentures

82. An implicit cost of increasing proportion of debt is:
A. Tax should would not be available on new debt
B. P.E. Ratio would increase
C. Equity shareholders would demand higher return
D. Rate of Return of the company would decrease

83. Cost of Redeemable Preference Share Capital is:
A. Rate of Dividend
B. After Tax Rate of Dividend
C. Discount Rate that equates PV of inflows and outflows relating to capital
D. None of the above

84. Which of the following is true?
A. Retained earnings are cost free
B. External Equity is cheaper than Internal Equity
C. Retained Earnings are cheaper than External Equity
D. Retained Earnings are costlier than External Equity

85. Cost of capital may be defined as:
A. Weighted Average cost of all debts
B. Rate of Return expected by Equity Shareholders
C. Average IRR of the Projects of the firm
D. Minimum Rate of Return that the firm should earn

86. Minimum Rate of Return that a firm must earn in order to satisfy its investors, is also known as:
A. Average Return on Investment
B. Weighted Average Cost of Capital
C. Net Profit Ratio
D. Average Cost of borrowing

87. Cost Capital for Equity Share Capital does not imply that:
A. Market Price is equal to Book Value of share
B. Shareholders are ready to subscribe to right issue
C. Market Price is more than Issue Price
D. AC of the three above

88. In order to calculate the proportion of equity financing used by the company, the following should be used:
A. Authorised Share Capital
B. Equity Share Capital plus Reserves and Surplus
C. Equity Share Capital plus Preference Share Capital
D. Equity Share Capital plus Long-term Debt

89. The term capital structure denotes:
A. Total of Liability side of Balance Sheet
B. Equity Funds, Preference Capital and Long-term Debt
C. Total Shareholders Equity
D. Types of Capital issued by a Company

90. Debt Financing is a cheaper source of finance because of:
A. Time Value of Money
B. Rate of Interest
C. Tax-deductibility of Interest
D. Dividends not payable to lenders

91. In order to find out cost of equity capital under CAPM, which of the following is not required?
A. Beta Factor
B. Market Rate of Return
C. Market Price of Equity Share
D. Risk-free Rate of Interest

92. Tax-rate is relevant and important for calculation of specific cost of capital of:
A. Equity Share Capital B. Preference Share Capital
C. Debentures D. Both A and B

93. Advantage of Debt financing is:
A. Interest is tax-deductible
B. It reduces WACC
C. Does not dilute owners control
D. All of the above

94. Cost of issuing new shares to the public is known as:
A. Cost of Equity B. Cost of Capital
C. Flotation Cost D. Marginal Cost of Capital

95. Cost of Equity Share Capital is more than cost of debt because:
A. Face value of debentures is more than face value of shares
B. Equity shares have higher risk than debt
C. Equity shares are easily saleable
D. All of the three above

96. Which of the following is not a generally accepted approach for Calculation of Cost of Equity?
A. CAPM
B. Dividend Discount Model
C. Rate of Pref. Dividend plus Risk
D. Price-Earnings Ratio

97. Operating leverage helps in analysis of:
A. Business Risk B. Financing Risk
C. Production Risk D. Credit Risk

98. Which of the following is studied with the help of financial leverage?
A. Marketing Risk
B. Interest Rate Risk
C. Foreign Exchange Risk
D. Financing Risk

99. Combined Leverage is obtained from OL and FL by their:
A. Addition B. Subtraction
C. Multiplication D. Any of these

100. High degree of financial leverage means:
A. High debt proportion B. Lower debt proportion
C. Equal debt and equity D. No debt

101. Operating leverage arises because of:
A. Fixed Cost of Production
B. Fixed Interest Cost
C. Variable Cost
D. None of the above

102. Financial Leverage arises because of:
A. Fixed cost of production
B. Variable cost
C. Interest cost
D. None of the above

103. Operating Leverage is calculated as:
A. Contribution ÷ EBIT B. EBIT ÷ PBT
C. EBIT ÷ Interest D. EBIT ÷ Tax

104. Financial Leverage is calculated as:
A. EBIT ÷ Contribution B. EBIT ÷ PBT
C. EBIT ÷ Sales D. EBIT ÷ Variable Cost

105. Which combination is generally good for firms?
A. High OL, High FL B. Low OL, Low FL
C. High OL, Low FL D. None of these

106. Combined leverage can be used to measure the relationship between:
A. EBIT and EPS B. PAT and EPS
C. Sales and EPS D. Sales and EBIT

107. FL is zero if:
A. EBIT = Interest B. EBIT = Zero
C. EBIT = Fixed Cost D. EBIT = Pref. Dividend

108. Business risk can be measured by:
A. Financial leverage B. Operating leverage
C. Combined leverage D. None of the above

109. Financial Leverage measures relationship between:
A. EBIT and PBT B. EBIT and EPS
C. Sales and PBT D. Sales and EPS

110. Use of Preference Share Capital in Capital structure:
A. Increases OL B. Increases FL
C. Decreases OL D. Decreases FL

111. Relationship between change in sales and change in EPS is measured by:
A. Financial leverage B. Combined leverage
C. Operating leverage D. None of the above

112. Operating leverage works when:
A. Sales increases B. Sales decreases
C. Both A and B D. None of A and B

113. Which of the following is correct?
A. CL = OL + FL B. CL = OL – FL
C. OL = OL × FL D. OL = OL ÷ FL

114. If the fixed cost of production is zero, which one of the following is correct?
A. OL is zero B. FL is zero
C. CL is zero D. None of the above

115. If a firm has no debt, which one is correct?
A. OL is one B. FL is one
C. OL is zero D. FL is zero

116. If a company issues new share capital to redeem debentures, then:
A. OL will increase B. FL will increase
C. OL will decrease D. FL will decrease

117. If a firm has a DOL of 2.8, it means:
A. If sales increase by 2.8%, the EBIT will increase by 1%
B. If EBIT increase by 2.896, the EPS will increase by 1%
C. If sales rise by 1%, EBIT will rise by 2.8%
D. None of the above

118. Higher OL is related to the use of higher:
A. Debt B. Equity
C. Fixed Cost D. Variable Cost

119. Higher FL is related the use of:
A. Higher Equity B. Higher Debt
C. Lower Debt D. None of the above

120. In order to calculate EPS, Profit after Tax and Preference Dividend is divided by:
A. MP of Equity Shares
B. Number of Equity Shares
C. Face Value of Equity Shares
D. None of the above

121. Trading on Equity is:
A. Always beneficial B. May be beneficial
C. Never beneficial D. None of the above

122. Benefit of 'Trading on Equity' is available only if:
A. Rate of Interest < Rate of Return
B. Rate of Interest > Rate of Return
C. Both A and B
D. None of A and B

123. Indifference Level of EBIT is one at which:
A. EPS is zero B. EPS is minimum
C. EPS is highest D. None of these

124. Financial Break-even level of EBIT is one at which:
A. EPS is one B. EPS is zero
C. EPS is infinite D. EPS is negative

125. Relationship between change in Sales and the Operating Profit is known as:
A. Financial Leverage B. Operating Leverage
C. Net Profit Ratio D. Gross Profit Ratio

126. If a firm has no preference share capital, financial break-even level is defined as equal to:
A. EBIT B. Interest liability
C. Equity dividend D. Tax liability

127. At Indifference level of EBIT, different capital have:
A. Same EBIT B. Same EPS
C. Same PAT D. Same PBT

128. If the intrinsic value of a share is less than the market price, which of the most reasonable?
A. That shares have lesser degree of risk
B. That market is over valuing the shares
C. That the company is high dividend paying
D. That market is undervaluing the share

129. For a constant EBIT, if the debt level is further increased then:
A. EPS will always increase
B. EPS may increase
C. EPS will never increase
D. None of the above

130. Between two capital plans, if expected EBIT is more than indifference level of EBIT, then:
A. Both plans be rejected
B. Both plans are good
C. One is better than other
D. None of the above

131. Financial break-even level of EBIT is:
A. Intercept at Y-axis B. Intercept at X-axis
C. Slope of EBIT-EPS line D. None of the above

132. Which of the following is true for Net Income Approach?
A. Higher equity is better B. Higher debt is better
C. Debt ratio is irrelevant D. None of the above

133. In case of Net Income Approach, the Cost of equity is:
A. Constant B. Increasing
C. Decreasing D. None of the above

134. In case of Net Income Approach, when the debt proportion is increased, the cost of debt:
A. Increases B. Decreases
C. Constant D. None of the above

135. Which of the following is true of Net Income Approach?
A. $V_F = V_E + V_D$ B. $V_E = V_F + V_D$
C. $V_D = V_F + V_E$ D. $V_F = V_E - V_E$

136. Net Operating Income Approach, which one of the lowing is constant?
A. Cost of Equity B. Cost of Debt
C. WACC & k_d D. k_e and k_d

137. NOI Approach advocates that the degree of debt financing is:
A. Relevant B. May be relevant
C. Irrelevant D. May be irrelevant

138. 'Judicious use of leverage' is suggested by:
A. Net Income Approach
B. Net Operating Income Approach
C. Traditional Approach
D. All of the above

139. Which one is true for Net Operating Income Approach?
A. $V_D = V_F - V_E$ B. $V_E = V_F + V_D$
C. $V_E = V_F - V_D$ D. $V_D = V_F + V_E$

140. In the Traditional Approach, which one of the following remains constant?
A. Cost of Equity B. Cost of Debt
C. WACC D. None of the above

141. In MM-Model, irrelevance of capital structure is based on:
A. Cost of Debt and Equity
B. Arbitrage Process
C. Decreasing k_0
D. All of the above

142. 'That there is no corporate tax' is assumed by:
A. Net Income Approach
B. Net Operating Income Approach
C. Traditional Approach
D. All of these

143. 'That personal leverage can replace corporate leverage' is assumed by:
A. Traditional Approach
B. MM Model
C. Net Income Approach
D. Net Operating Income Approach

144. Which of the following argues that the value of levered firm is higher than that of the unlevered firm?
A. Net Income Approach
B. Net Operating Income Approach
C. MM Model with Taxes
D. Both A and C

145. In Traditional Approach, which one is correct?
A. k_c rises constantly
B. k_d decreases constantly
C. k_0 decreases constantly
D. None of the above

146. Which of the following assumes constant k_d and k_c?
A. Net Income Approach
B. Net Operating Income Approach
C. Traditional Approach
D. MM Model

147. Which of the following is true?
A. Under Traditional Approach, overall cost of capital remains same
B. Under NI Approach, overall cost of capital remains same
C. Under NOI Approach, overall cost of capital remains same
D. None of the above

148. Risk-aversion of an investor can be measured by:
A. Market Rate of Return B. Risk-free Rate of Return
C. Portfolio Return D. None of the above

149. A firm has EBIT of ₹ 50,000. Market value of debt is ₹ 80,000 and overall capitalization rate is 20%. Market value of firm under NOI Approach is:
A. ₹ 2,50,000 B. ₹ 1,70,000
C. ₹ 30,000 D. ₹ 1,30,000

150. Which of the following is incorrect for NOI?
A. k_0 is constant B. k_d is constant
C. k_e is constant D. k_d & k_0 are constant

151. Which of the following is incorrect for value of the firm?
A. In the initial preposition, MM Model argues that value is independent of the financing mix
B. Total value of levered and unlevered firms is otherwise arbitrage will take place.
C. Total value incorporates borrowings by firm but excludes personal borrowing.
D. Total value does not change because underlying does not change with financing mix.

152. Which of the following appearing in the balance, generates tax advantage and hence affects the c, structure decision?
A. Reserves and Surplus
B. Long-term Debt
C. Preference Share Capital
D. Equity Share Capital

153. In MM Model with taxes, where 'r' is the interest rate, 'D' is the total debt and 't' is tax rate, then present valued shields would be:
A. $r \times D \times t$ B. $r \times D$
C. $D \times t$ D. $(D \times r)/(l - t)$.

154. Walter's Model suggests for 100% DP Ratio when:
A. $k_e = r$ B. $k_e < r$
C. $k_e > r$ D. $k_e = 0$

155. If a firm has $k_e > r$ the Walter's Model suggests for:
A. 0% Payout B. 100% Payout
C. 50% Payout D. 25% Payout

156. Walter's Model suggests that a firm can always increase *i.e.,* of the share by:
A. Increasing Dividend B. Decreasing Dividend
C. Constant Dividend D. None of the above

157. 'Bird in hand' argument is given by:
A. Walker's Model B. Gordon's Model
C. MM Mode D. Residuals Theory

158. Residuals Theory argues that dividend is a:
A. Relevant Decision B. Active Decision
C. Passive Decision D. Irrelevant Decision

159. Dividend irrelevance argument of MM Model is based on:
A. Issue of Debentures B. Issue of Bonus Share
C. Arbitrage D. Hedging

160. Which of the following is not true for MM Model?
A. Share price goes up if dividend is paid
B. Share price goes down if dividend is not paid
C. Market value is unaffected by Dividend policy
D. All of the above

161. Which of the following stresses on investor's preference reorient dividend than higher future capital gains?
A. Walter's Model B. Residuals Theory
C. Gordon's Model D. MM Model

162. MM Model of Dividend irrelevance uses arbitrage between:
A. Dividend and Bonus
B. Dividend and Capital Issue
C. Profit and Investment
D. None of the above

163. If $k_e = r$, then under Walter's Model, which of the following is irrelevant?
A. Earnings per share
B. Dividend per share
C. DP Ratio
D. None of the above

164. MM Model argues that dividend is irrelevant as:
A. the value of the firm depends upon earning power
B. the investors buy shares for capital gain
C. dividend is payable after deciding the retained earnings
D. dividend is a small amount

165. Which of the following represents passive dividend policy?
A. that dividend is paid as a % of EPS
B. that dividend is paid as a constant amount
C. that dividend is paid after retaining profits for reinvestment
D. All of the above

166. In case of Gordon's Model, the MP for zero payout is zero. It means that:
A. Shares are not traded
B. Shares available free of cost
C. Investors are not ready to offer any price
D. None of the above

167. Gordon's Model of dividend relevance is same as:
A. No-growth Model of equity valuation
B. Constant growth Model of equity valuation
C. Price-Earning Ratio
D. Inverse of Price Earnings Ratio

168. If 'r' = 'ke', than MP by Walter's Model and Gordon's Model for different payout ratios would be:
A. Unequal B. Zero
C. Equal D. Negative

169. Dividend Payout Ratio is:
A. PAT ÷ Capital
B. DPS ÷ EPS
C. Pref. Dividend ÷ PAT
D. Pref. Dividend ÷ Equity Dividend

170. Dividend declared by a company must be paid in:
A. 20 days B. 30 days
C. 32 days D. 42 days

171. Dividend Distribution Tax is payable by:
A. Shareholders to Government
B. Shareholders to Company
C. Company to Government
D. Holding to Subsidiary Company

172. Shares of face value of ₹ 10 are 80% paid up. The company declares a dividend of 50%. Amount of dividend per share is:
A. ₹ 5 B. ₹ 4
C. ₹ 80 D. ₹ 50

173. Which of the following generally not result in increase in total dividend liability?
A. Share-split B. Right Issue
C. Bonus Issue D. All of the above

174. Dividends are paid out of:
A. Accumulated Profit B. Gross Profit
C. Profit after Tax D. General Reserve

175. In India, Dividend Distribution Tax is paid on:
A. Equity Share
B. Preference Share
C. Debenture
D. Both A and B

176. Every company should follow:
A. High Dividend Payment
B. Low Dividend Payment
C. Stable Dividend Payment
D. Fixed Dividend Payment

177. 'Constant Dividend Per Share' Policy is considered as:
A. Increasing Dividend Policy
B. Decreasing Dividend Policy
C. Stable Dividend Policy
D. None of the above

178. Which of the following is not a type of dividend payment?
A. Bonus Issue B. Right Issue
C. Share Split D. Both B and C

179. If the following is an element of dividend policy?
A. Production capacity B. Change in management
C. Informational content D. Debt service capacity

180. Stock split is a form of:
A. Dividend payment B. Bonus issue
C. Financial restructuring D. Dividend in kind

181. In stock dividend:
A. Authorized capital always increases
B. Paid up capital always increases
C. Face value per share decreases
D. Market price for share decreases

182. Which of the following is not considered in Lintner's Model?
A. Dividend Payout Ratio B. Current EPS
C. Speed of Adjustment D. Preceding year EPS

183. Which of the following is not relevant for dividend payment for a year?
A. Cash flow position B. Profit position
C. Paid up capital D. Retained earnings

184. Cash Budget does not include:
A. Dividend Payable B. Postal Expenditure
C. Issue of Capital D. Total Sales Figure

185. Which of the following is not a motive to hold cash?
A. Transactionary Motive B. Pre-scautionary Motive
C. Captal Investment D. None of the above

186. Cheques deposited in bank may not be available for immediate use due to:
A. Payment Float B. Receipt Float
C. Net Float D. Playing the Float

187. Difference between the bank balance as per Cash Book and Pass Book may be due to:
A. Overdraft B. Float
C. Factoring D. None of the above

188. Concentration Banking helps in:
A. Reducing Idle Bank Balance
B. Increasing Collection
C. Increasing Creditors
D. Reducing Bank Transactions

189. The Transaction Motive for holding cash is for:
A. Safety Cushion B. Daily Operations
C. Purchase of Assets D. Payment of Dividends

190. Miller-Orr Model deals with
A. Optimum Cash Balance
B. Optimum Finished Goods
C. Optimum Receivables
D. All of the above

191. Float management is related to:
A. Cash Management
B. Inventory Management
C. Receivables Management
D. Raw Materials Management

192. Which of the following is not an objective of cash management?
A. Maximization of cash balance
B. Minimization of cash balance
C. Optimization of cash balance
D. Zero cash balance

193. Which of the following is not true of cash budget?
A. Cash budget indicates timings of short-term borrowing
B. Cash budget is based on accrual concept
C. Cash budget is based on cash flow concept
D. Repayment of principal amount of law is shown in cash budget

194. Baumol's Model of Cash Management attempts to:
A. Minimise the holding cost
B. Minimization of transaction cost
C. Minimization of total cost
D. Minimization of cash balance

195. Which of the following is not considered by Miller-Orr Model?
A. Variability in cash requirement
B. Cost of transaction
C. Holding cost
D. Total annual requirement of cash

196. Marketable securities are primarily:
A. Equity shares
B. Preference shares
C. Fixed deposits with companies
D. Short-term debt investments

197. 5Cs of the credit does not include:
A. Collateral B. Character
C. Conditions D. None of the above

198. Which of the following is not an element of credit policy?
A. Credit Terms
B. Collection Policy
C. Cash Discount Terms
D. Sales Price

199. Ageing schedule incorporates the relationship between:
A. Creditors and Days Outstanding
B. Debtors and Days Outstanding
C. Average Age of Directors
D. Average Age of All Employees

200. Bad debt cost is not borne by factor in case of:
A. Pure Factoring
B. Without Recourse Factoring
C. With Recourse Factoring
D. None of the above

ANSWERS

1	2	3	4	5	6	7	8	9	10
B	C	A	A	A	B	B	B	D	B
11	**12**	**13**	**14**	**15**	**16**	**17**	**18**	**19**	**20**
C	D	C	C	A	B	C	B	D	B
21	**22**	**23**	**24**	**25**	**26**	**27**	**28**	**29**	**30**
B	B	C	D	C	A	A	C	B	D
31	**32**	**33**	**34**	**35**	**36**	**37**	**38**	**39**	**40**
D	A	D	B	D	D	C	C	C	B
41	**42**	**43**	**44**	**45**	**46**	**47**	**48**	**49**	**50**
C	C	B	C	B	A	B	A	C	C
51	**52**	**53**	**54**	**55**	**56**	**57**	**58**	**59**	**60**
D	B	C	B	A	D	A	C	D	B
61	**62**	**63**	**64**	**65**	**66**	**67**	**68**	**69**	**70**
D	D	D	A	C	B	D	A	C	D
71	**72**	**73**	**74**	**75**	**76**	**77**	**78**	**79**	**80**
A	A	B	C	C	A	B	B	B	D
81	**82**	**83**	**84**	**85**	**86**	**87**	**88**	**89**	**90**
A	C	C	C	D	B	D	B	B	C
91	**92**	**93**	**94**	**95**	**96**	**97**	**98**	**99**	**100**
C	C	D	C	B	C	A	D	C	A
101	**102**	**103**	**104**	**105**	**106**	**107**	**108**	**109**	**110**
A	C	A	B	C	C	B	B	B	B
111	**112**	**113**	**114**	**115**	**116**	**117**	**118**	**119**	**120**
B	C	C	D	B	D	C	C	B	B
121	**122**	**123**	**124**	**125**	**126**	**127**	**128**	**129**	**130**
B	A	D	B	B	B	B	B	B	C
131	**132**	**133**	**134**	**135**	**136**	**137**	**138**	**139**	**140**
B	B	A	B	A	C	C	C	C	D
141	**142**	**143**	**144**	**145**	**146**	**147**	**148**	**149**	**150**
B	D	B	D	D	A	C	D	B	C
151	**152**	**153**	**154**	**155**	**156**	**157**	**158**	**159**	**160**
D	B	C	C	A	D	B	C	C	C
161	**162**	**163**	**164**	**165**	**166**	**167**	**168**	**169**	**170**
C	B	C	A	C	C	B	C	B	B
171	**172**	**173**	**174**	**175**	**176**	**177**	**178**	**179**	**180**
C	B	A	C	D	C	C	C	C	C
181	**182**	**183**	**184**	**185**	**186**	**187**	**188**	**189**	**190**
D	D	D	D	C	B	B	B	B	A
191	**192**	**193**	**194**	**195**	**196**	**197**	**198**	**199**	**200**
A	C	B	C	D	D	D	D	B	C

●●●

5 Corporate Regulations

1. The concept of DIN (Directors Identification Number) was brought into force w.e.f.:
A. 1-4-2006 B. 1-1-2006
C. 1-11-2006 D. 1-7-2006

2. Limited Liability Partnership Act came into effect in the year:
A. 2005 B. 2006
C. 2007 D. 2008

3. Section 3 of the Companies Act, 2013 allows formation of ....
A. One person Company B. Private Company
C. Public Company D. None of these

4. In case of issue of shares by a company to the public, if minimum subscription, as stated in prospectus has not been received in 30 days of issue of prospectus or such other period as specified by SEBI, then the application money shall be repaid within a period of .... days from the closure of the issue.
A. 21 B. 15
C. 12 D. 7

5. "A company remains free from the hazards of all personal misfortunes of its members" is derived from the benefit of incorporation of company being............
A. Limited liability B. Perpetual succession
C. Infinite membership D. Independent legal entity

6. The powers of a company are contained in the .... clause of memorandum of association.
A. Capital B. Object
C. Membership D. None of these

7. Restrictions on transferability of shares is relevant in case of:
A. Only private company having share capital
B. Private company incorporated as a pure guarantee company
C. Private company having either Share capital or Guarantee company
D. None of these

8. A private company is required compulsorily to limit through its articles, the number of members to ....
A. 20 B. 50
C. 200 D. 500

9. The committee to recommend formation of OPC (One Person Company) in India is ....
A. Alagh B. J.J. Irani
C. H.C. Baba D. None of these

10. Which one of the following is not a relaxation given to an OPC?
A. Need not prepare Cash Flow Statement
B. Annual report can be signed by Director
C. No need to hold AGM
D. No need to appoint Company Secretary

11. In case of public company total managerial remuneration can't exceed .... per cent of the net profits.
A. 5 B. 7
C. 11 D. 12

12. With regard to government company, identify the statement representing correct feature of Government company:
A. Govt company can't sue the government in its own name as litigant
B. Employees of government company are not employees of central/state government
C. A government company can't wound like any other company
D. A government company must use either limited or Private Limited at the end of its name

13. Which one of the following financial institutions shall not be regarded as Public financial institutions as per section 2(72) of Companies Act 2013?
A. LIC
B. IDFCL
C. Institutions notified by central government in consultation with RBI
D. KFC

14. An unregistered company can't have more than .... members.
A. 20 B. 25
C. 50 D. 100

15. Section 9 of Companies Act describes ....
A. Allotment of CIN
B. Filing of documents for registration
C. Remuneration of promoters
D. Effect of certificate of incorporation

16. The Companies (Amendment) Act, 2015 omitted section .... of Company's Act, 2013 that provides all companies whether private or public to commence business immediately after obtaining certificate of incorporation.
A. 10 B. 11
C. 12 D. 13

17. Which one of the following need permission from central government to make alteration in the memorandum of association?
A. Alteration in name clause
B. Shift registered office from one state to other
C. Alteration of object clause
D. Alteration of capital clause

18. Section 12 requires that One Person company shall mention along with its name (in brackets) ....
A. One Person Company
B. OPC
C. One Person Company Pvt Ltd or Ltd
D. None of the above

19. The clause that states the name of state where registered office of the company is situated.
A. Object B. Capital
C. Registered office D. Name

20. A company must file prescribed documents stating its registered office within .... days of its incorporation.
A. 21 B. 27
C. 30 D. 40

21. The term ultra virus means:
A. Against power B. Beyond power
C. Against authority D. Beyond authority

22. In case of a company limited by shares, a shareholder has paid full on his shares, his liability will be:
A. as decided by directors
B. an equal amount to already paid up value of share
C. Nil
D. None of these

23. As per sec 4(1) (e) of Companies Act 2013, a company having a share capital, the memorandum of association must state the amount of ....
A. Authorised/registered capital
B. Paid-up share capital
C. Called-up capital
D. Reserved capital

24. Section 13 provides that the name of company may be changed at any time by:
A. Passing special resolution at general meeting of company
B. Passing ordinary resolution at general meeting
C. Passing either ordinary or special resolution at general meeting
D. Can't be changed

25. Who among the following are not proper authority to call a meeting?
A. Board of directors B. Shareholders
C. Tribunal D. Company secretary

26. When a company changes its name or obtains a new name under sub-section(1) of section 16, it shall within a period of .... days from the date of such change, give notice of the change to the registrar.
A. 15 B. 16
C. 21 D. 7

27. Within 30 days of passing the resolution, a notice of increase in the share capital along with an altered memorandum must be filed with the ....
A. Ministry of Corporate affairs
B. SEBI
C. Board of Directors
D. Registrar of Companies

28. .... defines the company's objects and various powers it possesses.
A. Articles B. Memorandum
C. Prospectus D. Annual report

29. Which of the following is incorrect statement as to memorandum and articles of association?
A. Act done by company beyond the scope of memorandum is ultra virus
B. Memorandum may include any clause contrary to provisions of Companies Act.
C. Generally articles can be altered by the members by passing a special resolution only
D. The articles are subsidiary to Companies Act and memorandum

30. Section 14 of Companies Act, 2013 allows companies to alter:
A. Articles
B. Memorandum
C. Both articles and memorandum
D. None of these

31. Section 17, Rule 34 of company (incorporation rules) 2014 provides that a company shall on payment of prescribed fee send a copy of each of memorandum or association to a member within .... days of the request.
A. 3 B. 5
C. 7 D. 10

32. Section 33 of the Companies Act, 2013 provides that no form of application for the purchase of the securities of a company shall be issued unless it is accompanied by:
A. Draft prospectus B. Abridged prospectus
C. Redherring prospectus D. Shelf prospectus

33. No prospectus shall be issued after .... days from the date on which a copy of it was delivered to the registrar.
A. 21 B. 43
C. 75 D. 90

34. Which of the following is incorrect as to a share?
A. It has a nominal value
B. It has a distinct number
C. It may be transferred in fractions
D. All shares of a class are of equal denominations

35. No company limited by shares can issue any preference shares which are irredeemable as per section.
A. 34 B. 46
C. 55 D. 72

36. The process by which demand for the securities proposed to be issued by a body corporate is elicited and built up and the price for such securities is assessed for the determination of the quantum of such securities is called ....

A. Offer for sale B. Private placement
C. Book building D. None of these

37. The cap on the price band (in book building) shall be less than or equal to .... per cent of floor price.

A. 100 B. 120
C. 200 D. 500

38. An issue shall be opened after at least 3 working days from the date of registering the .... with the registrar of companies.

A. Draft prospectus B. Abridged prospectus
C. Redherring prospectus D. Shelf prospectus

39. Except otherwise provided in the regulations a public issue shall be kept open for atleast 3 working days but not more than .... working days including the days for which the issue is kept open in case of revision in price band.

A. 5 B. 6
C. 7 D. 10

40. In the event of non-receipt of minimum subscription, all application money received shall be refunded to the applicants forth with, not later than .... days of closure of issue in case of non-underwritten issue.

A. 10 B. 15
C. 70 D. 90

41. FPO stands for:

A. Forward Public Offer B. First Public Offer
C. Future Public Offer D. Further Public Offer

42. The basic purpose of Green shoe option is to act as stabilizing force when issue is ....

A. Under subscribed
B. Over subscribed
C. Either Under or Over subscribed
D. None of these

43. An amount payable on application shall not be less than .... per cent of the share or other percentage specified by SEBI.

A. 25 B. 20
C. 5 D. 10

44. Which of the following condition is incorrect as to buy back of shares?

A. Buy back is authorised by articles
B. Buy back is 20 per cent or less of the aggregate of paid up capital
C. Shares/securities specifies for buy back are fully paid up
D. Buy back is out of free reserves

45. To issue sweat equity shares, company shall ensure that it has elapsed at least .... year after commencement of business.

A. 5 B. 7
C. 1 D. 10

46. Right issue of shares is concerned with section:

A. 62 B. 56
C. 46 D. 54

47. A bonus share is always:

A. issued free of charge B. fully paid
C. partly paid D. Both A and B

48. Diminution of capital denotes:

A. Cancellation of unsubscribed part of issued capital
B. Reduction of capital under the maning of Act
C. Write of past losses against capita
D. None of these

49. In case of forfeiture of shares, a notice requiring payment of the amount together with any interest accured must be served mentioning a further day not less than .... from date of service of the notice

A. 7 B. 10
C. 14 D. 15

50. The company liquidator must submit a preliminary report to the tribunal within ..... days from the winding up order.

A. 16 B. 15
C. 60 D. 50

ANSWERS

1	2	3	4	5	6	7	8	9	10
C	D	A	B	D	B	A	C	B	D
11	**12**	**13**	**14**	**15**	**16**	**17**	**18**	**19**	**20**
C	B	D	C	D	B	A&B	A	C	C
21	**22**	**23**	**24**	**25**	**26**	**27**	**28**	**29**	**30**
B	C	A	A	D	A	D	B	B	A
31	**32**	**33**	**34**	**35**	**36**	**37**	**38**	**39**	**40**
C	B	D	C	C	C	B	C	D	B
41	**42**	**43**	**44**	**45**	**46**	**47**	**48**	**49**	**50**
D	B	C	B	C	A	D	A	C	C

●●●

6 Auditing

1. An auditor is like a:
A. Blood haunt
B. Watch dog
C. May both according to situation
D. None of these

2. The term 'Audit' is derived from a Latin word *"audire"* which means:
A. To inspect B. To examine
C. To hear D. To investigate

3. Process of verifying the documentary evidences of transactions are known as:
A. Auditing B. Testing
C. Vouching D. Verification

4. Auditing is compulsory for:
A. Small scale business B. Partnership firms
C. Joint stock companies D. Proprietary concerns

5. The main object of an audit is:
A. Expression of expert opinion
B. Detection and prevention of fraud and error
C. Both A and B
D. Depends on the type of audit

6. Concealment of shortage by delaying the recording of cash receipts is known as:
A. Embezzlement B. Misappropriation
C. Lapping D. None of these

7. The title of AAS2 issued by Council of ICAI is:
A. Objective and Scope of the Financial Statements
B. Objective and Scope of the Audit of Financial Statements
C. Objective and Scope of Business of an Entity
D. Objective and Scope of Financial Statements Audit

8. Lapping is also known as:
A. Teeming and lading B. Embezzlement
C. Looping D. Hacking

9. Which of the following is not true about opinion on financial statements?
A. The auditor should express an opinion on financial statements.
B. His opinion is no guarantee to future viability of business
C. He is responsible for detection and prevention of frauds and errors in financial statements
D. He should examine whether recognised accounting principle have been consistently

10. A sale of ₹ 25,000 to A was entered as a sale to B. This is an example of:
A. Error of omission B. Error of commission
C. Compensating error D. Error of principle

11. 'Goods sent on approval basis' have been recorded as 'Credit sales'. This is an example of:
A. Error of principle B. Error of commission
C. Error of omission D. Error of duplication

12. Which of the following statements is not true?
A. Management fraud is more difficult to detect than employee fraud
B. Internal control system reduces the possibility of occurrence of employee fraud and management fraud
C. The auditor's responsibility for detection and prevention of errors and frauds is similar
D. All statements are correct.

13. As per AAS4, if auditor detects an error then:
A. He should inform the management
B. He should communicate it to the management if it is material
C. The auditor should ensure financial statements are adjusted for detected errors.
D. Both B and C

14. Which of the following is not a limitation of audit as per AAS4?
A. Objectivity of auditor's judgment
B. Selective testing
C. Persuasiveness of evidence
D. Limitations of internal control system.

15. Internal audit is undertaken
A. By independent auditor
B. Statutorily appointed auditor
C. By a person appointed by the management
D. By a government auditor

16. The scope of internal audit is decided by the:
A. Shareholders B. Management
C. Government D. Law

17. Audit of banks is an example of:
A. Statutory audit
B. Balance sheet audit
C. Concurrent audit
D. All of the above

18. Concurrent audit is a part of:
A. Internal check system B. Continuous audit
C. Internal audit system D. None of these

19. In India, balance sheet audit is synonymous to:
A. Annual audit B. Continuous audit
C. Detailed audit D. Statutory audit

20. Audit in depth is synonymous for:
A. Complete audit B. Completed audit
C. Final audit D. Detailed audit

21. Institute of Chartered Accountants of India was established:
A. 1956 B. 1949
C. 1958 D. 1948

22. Which of the following statements is not true about continuous audit?
A. It is conducted at regular interval
B. It may be carried out on daily basis
C. It is needed when the organization has a good internal control system
D. It is expensive

23. Internal check is carried on by:
A. Staff specially appointed for the purpose
B. Internal auditor
C. Supervisor of the staff
D. Members of the staff

24. Errors of Omission are:
A. Technical errors
B. Errors of principle
C. Compensating errors
D. None of the above

25. Window dressing implies:
A. Curtailment of expenses
B. Checking of wastages
C. Under valuation of assets
D. Over valuation of assets

26. Test Checking refers to:
A. Testing of accounts and records
B. Checking of selected number of transactions
C. Examination of adjusting and closing entries
D. Checking of all transactions recorded

27. Which of the following statements is not correct about materiality?
A. Materiality is a relative concept
B. Materiality judgments involve both quantitative and qualitative judgments
C. Auditor's consideration of materiality is influenced by the auditor's perception of the needs of an informed decision maker who will rely on the financial statements
D. At the planning state, the auditor considers materiality at the financial statement level only

28. .... the audit risks .... the materiality and .... the audit effort.
A. Lower, higher, lower
B. Lower, lower, higher
C. Higher, lower, lower
D. Lower, higher, higher

29. When issuing unqualified opinion, the auditor who evaluates the audit findings should be satisfied that the:
A. Amount of known misstatement is documented in working papers
B. Estimates of the total likely misstatement is less than materiality level
C. Estimate of the total likely misstatement is more than materially level
D. Estimates of the total likely misstatement cannot be made

30. In determining the level of materiality for an audit, what should not be considered?
A. Prior year's errors
B. The auditor's remuneration
C. Adjusted interim financial statements
D. Prior year's financial statements

31. Analytical procedures issued in the planning stage of an audit, generally:
A. Helps to determine the nature, timing and extent of other audit procedures
B. Directs attention to potential risk areas
C. Indicates important aspects of business
D. All of the above

32. Which of the following statements is most closely associated with analytical procedure applied at substantive stage?
A. It helps to study relationship among balance sheet accounts
B. It helps to discover material misstatements in the financial statements
C. It helps to identify possible oversights
D. It helps to accumulate evidence supporting the validity of a specific account balance

33. For all audits of financial statements made in accordance with AAS14, the use of analytical procedures is at the discretion of the auditor in which stage?
A. Substantive testing B. Planning stage
C. Overall review stage D. All of the above

34. Verification refers to:
A. Examining the physical existence and valuation of assets
B. Examining the journal and ledger
C. Examination of vouchers related to assets
D. None of the above

35. Stock should be valued at:
A. Cost
B. Market price
C. Cost or Market price whichever is lower
D. Cost less depreciation

36. 'Auditor is not a valuer', was stated in:
A. Kingston Cotton Mills case
B. London Oil Storage Co. case
C. London and General Bank case
D. None of the above

37. Floating assets are valued at:
A. Cost
B. Market price
C. Cost or market price whichever is lower
D. Cost less depreciation

38. Goods sold on the basis of 'sales or return' should:
A. Be included in the stock
B. Not be included in the stock
C. Not be checked by auditor
D. None of the above

39. Of the following, which is the least persuasive type of audit evidence?
A. Bank statements obtained from the client
B. Documents obtained by auditor from third parties directly.
C. Carbon copies of sales invoices inspected by the auditor
D. Computations made by the auditor

40. Which of the following statements is, generally, correct about the reliability of audit evidence?
A. To be reliable, evidence should conclusive rather than persuasive
B. Effective internal control system provides reliable audit evidence
C. Evidence obtained from outside sources routed through the client
D. All are correct

41. In an audit of financial statements, substantive tests are audit procedures that:
A. may be eliminated for an account balance under certain conditions
B. are designed to discover significant subsequent events
C. will increase proportionately when the auditor decreases the assessed level of control risk
D. may be test of transactions, test of balance and analytical procedures

42. The nature, timing and extent of substantive procedures is related to assessed level of control risk:
A. Randomly
B. Disproportionately
C. Directly
D. Inversely

43. Which of the following factors is most important in determining the appropriations of audit evidence?
A. The reliability of audit evidence and its relevance in meeting the audit objective
B. The objectivity and integrity of the auditor
C. The quantity of audit evidence
D. The independence of the source of evidence

44. When is evidential matter, generally, considered sufficient?
A. When it constitutes entire population
B. When it is enough to provide a basis for giving reasonable assurance regarding truthfulness
C. When it is objective and relevant
D. When auditor collects and evaluates it independently

45. Which of the following is not corroborative evidence?
A. Minutes of meetings
B. Confirmations from debtors
C. Information gathered by auditor through observation
D. Worksheet supporting consolidated financial statements

46. Which of the following statements is not true with respect to management representations obtained as per AAS11?
A. Authenticated copy of relevant minutes of meetings may be regarded as management representation
B. It should always be in working
C. It may be dated prior to the report date
D. It should be addressed to the auditor

47. What would most appropriately describe the risk of incorrect rejection in terms of substantive testing?
A. The auditor concludes balance is materially correct when in actual fact it is not
B. The auditor concludes that the balance is materially misstated when in actual fact it not
C. The auditor has rejected an item for sample which was material
D. None of the above

48. Which of the following affects audit effectiveness?
A. Risk of over reliance
B. Risk of incorrect rejection
C. Risk of incorrect acceptance
D. Both A and C

49. What would most effectively describe the risk of incorrect acceptance in terms of substantive audit testing?
A. The auditor has ascertained that the balance is materially correct when in actual fact it is not
B. The auditor concludes the balance is materially misstated when in actual fact is not
C. The auditor has rejected an item from sample which was not supported by documentary evidence
D. He applies random sampling on data which is inaccurate and inconsistent

50. Which of the following Auditing Assurance Standard deals with Audit Planning?
A. AAS7
B. AAS8
C. AAS9
D. AAS3

51. Audit programme is prepared by:
A. The auditor
B. The client
C. The audit assistants
D. The auditor and his audit assistants

52. The working papers which auditor prepares for financial statements audit are:
A. Evidence for audit conclusions
B. Owned by the client
C. Owned by the auditor
D. Retained in auditor's office until a change in auditors

53. The quantity of audit working papers complied on engagement would most be affected by:
A. Management's integrity
B. Auditor's experience and professional judgment
C. Auditor's qualification
D. Control risk

54. Which of the following best describes the primary purpose of audit programme preparation?
A. To detect errors or fraud
B. To comply with GAAP
C. To gather sufficient appropriate evidence
D. To assess audit risk

55. Which of the following is not an advantage of the preparation of working paper?
A. To provide a basis for review of audit work
B. To provide a basis for subsequent audits
C. To ensure audit work is being carried out as per programme
D. To provide a guide for advising another client on similar issues

56. The auditor's permanent working paper file should not normally, include:
A. Extracts from client's bank statements
B. Past year's financial statements
C. Attorney's letters
D. Debt agreements

57. For what minimum period should audit working papers be retained by audit firm?
A. For the time period the entity remains a client of the audit firm
B. For a period of ten years
C. For a period auditor opines them to be useful in servicing the client
D. For the period the audit firm is in existence

58. Which of the following factors would least likely affect the quantity and content of an auditor's working papers?
A. The assessed level of control risk
B. The possibility of peer review
C. The nature of auditor's report
D. The content of management representation letter

59. Which of the following statement is true regarding an auditor's working papers?
A. They document the level of independence maintained by the auditor
B. They should be considered as the principle support for the auditor's report
C. They should not contain details regarding weaknesses in the internal control system
D. They help the auditor to monitor the effectiveness of the audit firm's quality control

60. Which of the following statement best describes the understanding with respect to ownership and custody of working papers prepared by an auditor?
A. The working papers may be obtained by third parties when they appear to be relevant to issues raised in litigation
B. The safe custody of working papers is the responsibility of client, if kept at his premises
C. The working papers must be retained by an audit firm for a period of 10 years
D. Successor auditors may have access to working papers of the predecessor auditors. The approval of client is not required.

61. The current file of the auditor's working papers, generally, should include:
A. A flowchart of the internal controls
B. Organisation charts
C. A copy of financial statements
D. Copies of bond and debentures

62. Knowledge of the entity's business does not help the auditor to:
A. Reduce inherent risk
B. Identify problem areas
C. Evaluate reasonableness of estimates
D. Evaluate appropriates of GAAP

63. Payment for wage should be vouched with the help of:
A. Piece work statement B. Wage sheets
C. Minutes book D. Bank pass book

64. Payment for building purchased should be vouched with the help of:
A. Title Deed
B. Correspondence with the brokers
C. Building Account
D. Cash book

65. Purchase returns should be vouched with the help of:
A. Bought notes B. Credit notes
C. Goods inward book D. Cash book

66. Receipts from sale of investments should be vouched with the help of:
A. Broker's bought notes
B. Broker's sold notes
C. Minutes book
D. Inventory of investment

67. Which of the following expenses should not be treated as capital expenditure?
A. Expenses paid on installation of a plant.
B. Cost of dismantling a building in case a new building is to be constructed on the land
C. Legal expenses incurred to defend a suit related to title of patent. The suit has been lost
D. The fees paid to engineer who constructed the plant

68. Which of the following is not a revenue expense?
A. Cost of raising a loan
B. Cost of accessories of motor vehicles spent at the time of purchase
C. Expenses incurred for laying of sewers on land purchased
D. Insurance premium paid at the time of registration of the ship

69. Depreciation does not arise form ....
A. Effluxion of time
B. Use
C. Obsolescence through technology be market changes
D. Remarket expectation

70. Which of the following Schedule of the Companies Act, 2013 deals with depreciations?
A. Schedule II B. Schedule V
C. Schedule XIII D. Schedule X

71. Schedule II of the Companies Act, 2013 has prescribed rates of depreciation for double shift and triple shift working for which one of the following assets?
A. Building B. Plant and Machinery
C. Furniture and fittings D. Ships

72. If the book value of an asset stands at .... per cent of the original cost, a company need not provide depreciation on it.
A. Two B. Fifteen
C. Five D. None of these

73. A company has bought patents. Which of the following methods is most suitable for providing depreciation on them?
A. SLM B. WDV
C. Sum of year digits D. Any of the above

74. Which of the following is a revenue reserve?
A. Capital redemption reserve
B. Security premium account
C. Debenture redemption reserve
D. Capital reserve

75. Which of the following will not lead to creation of secret reserve?
A. Undervaluation of closing stock
B. Charging capital expenditure to revenue
C. Goods sent on consignment being shown as actual sales
D. Charging higher rates of depreciation on fixed assets than actually required

76. Who is responsible for the appointment of statutory auditor of a limited company?
A. Directors of the company
B. Members of the company
C. The Central Government
D. All of the above

77. Which of the following sections of the Companies Act, 2013 deals with qualifications of the auditor?
A. Section 141
B. Section 224(1) and section 224(2)
C. Section 226(3) and section 226(4)
D. Section 224(3) and section 224

78. Which of the following statement is not true?
A. A partnership firm can be appointed as a statutory auditor of limited company
B. Appointment can be made in the name of the firm
C. Majority of the partners should be practicing in India
D. All partners should be chartered accountants

79. As per the requirements of section 141(3) a person is disqualified from being appointed as a statutory auditor if he holds:
A. Equity shares or debentures of the company
B. Equity shares carrying voting of the company
C. Shares carrying voting rights of the company
D. Security of the company

80. The board of directors shall appoint first auditor of a company:
A. Within one month of completion of capital subscription state of the company
B. Within one month of the promotion of the company
C. Within one month of the commencement of the business of the company
D. Within one month of incorporation of the company

81. The term of the auditorship of first auditor would be from the date of appointment till:
A. the conclusion of statutory meeting
B. the conclusion of first annual general meeting
C. the conclusion of next annual general meeting
D. the date of removal

82. In case the directions fail to appoint first auditor (s), the shareholders shall appoint them at .... by passing a resolution.
A. a general meeting

B. first annual general meeting
C. statutory meeting
D. annual general meeting

83. Which of the following statement is not true regarding appointment of auditor by the Central Government?
A. Such powers have been conferred upon it by section 139(7)
B. If a company fails to appoint an auditor at a general meeting
C. If an auditor refuses to accept appointment, the powers of the Central Government can be exercised
D. None of the above

84. If a casual vacancy in the office of auditor arises by his resignation it should only be filled by the company in a........
A. Board meeting
B. Extraordinary general meeting
C. General meeting
D. Annual general meeting

85. Internal check is meant for ....
A. prevention of frauds
B. detection of frauds
C. helping audit is depth
D. detection of errors

86. Purchase of machinery is a ....
A. revenue receipt B. capital receipt
C. capital expenditure D. revenue expenditure

87. Sale of land is a ....
A. revenue receipt B. capital receipt
C. capital expenditure D. revenue expenditure

88. When a transaction has not been recorded in the books of account either wholly or partially such errors are called ....
A. errors of commission B. errors of omission
C. compensating error D. error of principle

89. The auditor of a Government company is appointed by the C & AG. His remuneration is fixed by:
A. The C & AG
B. The shareholders
C. The shareholders at an annual general meeting
D. The board of directors

90. The section of the companies Act, 2013 which contains provisions regarding remuneration of the auditor is:
A. Section 139 B. Section 141
C. Section 142 D. Section 148

91. The authority to remove the first auditor before the expiry of term is with:
A. The shareholders in a general meeting
B. The shareholders in the first annual general meeting
C. The board of directors
D. The Central Government

92. Which of the following statements is not correct regarding removal of first auditor before expiry of the term?
A. He is removed at a general meeting
B. The shareholders are authorized to do so
C. The approval of the Central Government is required for such removal
D. None of these

93. The retiring auditor does not have a right to
A. make written representations
B. get his representations circulated
C. be heard at the meeting
D. speak as a member of the company

94. Who out of the following cannot be appointed as a statutory auditor of the company?
A. Erstwhile director
B. Internal auditor
C. Relative of a director
D. Only B and C

95. A statutory auditor has a right of access at all times to:
A. Books and accounts of a company
B. Books, accounts and documents of the company
C. Books, accounts and vouchers of the company
D. Notices and documents of the company

96. The auditor has a right to:
A. Obtain information and explanation
B. Obtain information and explanation from the employees and officers
C. Obtain information and explanation necessary for the purpose of audit
D. Both B and C

97. The principal auditor, as per clarification issued by the ICAI, does not have any right to:
A. Inspect working papers of the branch auditor
B. Visit branches
C. Seek information necessary for audit purposes
D. Incorporate the branch audit report in his audit report

98. Verification of the value of assets, liabilities, the balance of reserves, provision and the amount of profit earned or loss suffered a firm is called ....
A. continuous audit
B. balance sheet audit
C. interim audit
D. partial audit

99. A sale of ₹ 50000 to Mr. A was entered as a sale to Mr. B. This is an example of what?
A. Error of omission B. Error of commission
C. Compensating error D. Error of principle

100. Recording a transaction twice in the books of original entry is an error of ....
A. principle B. commission
C. duplication D. omission

ANSWERS

1	2	3	4	5	6	7	8	9	10
B	C	C	C	D	C	B	A	C	B
11	**12**	**13**	**14**	**15**	**16**	**17**	**18**	**19**	**20**
A	B	D	A	C	B	D	C	A	D
21	**22**	**23**	**24**	**25**	**26**	**27**	**28**	**29**	**30**
B	C	D	A	D	B	D	A	C	B
31	**32**	**33**	**34**	**35**	**36**	**37**	**38**	**39**	**40**
D	D	A	A	C	A	C	A	C	B
41	**42**	**43**	**44**	**45**	**46**	**47**	**48**	**49**	**50**
D	C	A	B	D	B	B	D	A	B
51	**52**	**53**	**54**	**55**	**56**	**57**	**58**	**59**	**60**
D	C	B	C	D	A	C	D	B	A
61	**62**	**63**	**64**	**65**	**66**	**67**	**68**	**69**	**70**
C	A	B	A	B	B	C	B	D	A
71	**72**	**73**	**74**	**75**	**76**	**77**	**78**	**79**	**80**
B	C	A	C	C	B	A	C	D	D
81	**82**	**83**	**84**	**85**	**86**	**87**	**88**	**89**	**90**
B	A	B	C	A	C	B	B	B	C
91	**92**	**93**	**94**	**95**	**96**	**97**	**98**	**99**	**100**
A	C	D	B	C	D	A	B	B	C

●●●

7 Business Organisation

1. According to the Principle of Subrogation
A. The insured must take all necessary steps to minimise the loss.
B. The actual amount of loss, not exceeding the amount of the policy, shall be paid.
C. The actual amount of loss should be distributed among the different insurers of the same risk.
D. On making good the loss, the insurer is entitled to succeed to all the rights of the insured regarding the subject matter of insurance.

2. The persons who agree to insure cargo, hull or freight are called
A. undertakers B. caretakers
C. underwriters D. bookkeepers

3. Partnership is a form of business organisation in which business debts can be recovered
A. the managing partners
B. all the managers and partners
C. the firm and the managers
D. the firm and all the partners

4. Of the following organisations the easiest to wind up is the
A. Public Limited Company
B. Multinational Corporation
C. Private Limited Company
D. Partnership Firm

5. Match List-I with List-II and select the correct answer using the codes given below the lists:

List-I	List-II
I. Partners and Firms	1. agent and principle relationship
II. Sole Proprietorship	2. prospectus
III. Public Limited Company	3. personal supervision
IV. Nominal Partnership	4. firm image

Codes:
A. I-1, II-2, III-3, IV-4 B. II-2, II-3, III-1, IV-4
C. I-1, II-3, III-2, IV-4 D. I-4, II-2, III-1, IV-3

6. The main object of stock exchange is to
A. Provided facilities for speculation
B Safeguard the interest of investors
C. Help in the capital formation of the country
D. Provide a ready market for securities

7. What is network form of organization called in Japan
A. Keiretsu B. Ransum
C. Deptku D. Seduku

8. 'Fishing Culture' is classified in
A. Extractive Industry B. Genetic Industry
C. Construction Industry D. None of these

9. If a partnership firm is not registered with the Registrar of firms,
A. it has to pay penalty for non-registration
B. the members can file suits against the third party
C. the members can enforce their rights among themselves
D. none of these

10. Which of the following is not an economic activity?
A. A doctor practising
B. A lawyer practising law
C. A professional cricketer playing cricket
D. A student playing cricket

11. In order an activity may be called business which of the following condition need not be satisfied?
A. There should be exchange or transfer of goods or services
B. There should be continuity of dealings
C. Dealings may be either in goods or services
D. There should be certainty of profit

12. Which among the following is a central problem of an economy
A. What to produce B. How to produce
C. Both A and B D. None of these

13. In a private business enterprise profit should be regarded as
A. the legitimate reward for honest end labour
B. the supreme objective of business
C. the sole objective of business
D. subsidiary to service motive

14. Which of the following should be regarded as the most important factor for deciding the form of business organisation?
A. Types of business, trading manufacturing, etc
B. Expected volume of business
C. Financial requirements
D. Area of operations

15. The liability of a sole proprietor is
A. limited to the extent of his capital invested in the business
B. limited to the extent of the value of business assets
C. limited to the extent of the value of business assets and his all private assets
D. none of these

16. The agreement of partnership
A. must be in oral
B. must be in writing
C. can be either oral or in writing
D. must be in writing on a stamp paper

17. Liability of partners in respect of the firm's debts is
A. limited up to the amount of his capital in the business
B. unlimited
C. limited up to the amount of gurantee given by the partner
D. limited up to the amount of his capital and loan to the firm if any

18. Partnership may come into existence
A. by the operation of law
B. by an express agreement only
C. by an express or implied agreement only
D. by inheritance of property

19. A partner has an implied authority to
A. acquire immovable property on behalf of the firm
B. enter into a partnership on behalf of the firm
C. to borrow money on behalf of the firm
D. to compromise or relinquish any claim or portion of a claim by the firm.

20. If a firm is not registered with the registrar of firms
A. it has to pay penalty for non-registration
B. it introduces certain disabilities which make registration necessary at one time or the other
C. the members of the unregistered firm can enforce their rights between themselves
D. the members of the unregistered firm can file suit against third parties.

21. Dissolution of firm takes place
A. by the death or insolvency of anyone partner
B. the retirement of any one partner
C. by the expiry of the term
D. by the insolvency of all but one partner

22. Registration of joint stock company is
A. compulsory
B. optional
C. compulsory for public companies and optional for private company
D. compulsory for companies with liabilities limited by shares and optional for companies with liabilities limited by guarantee

23. The minimum number of member require for registration of a co-operative society is
A. two B. seven
C. ten D. twenty

24. Co-operative and public companies are similar in respect of
A. the liability of members
B. the minimum number of members required for registration
C. the maximum number of members
D. none of these

25. Profits earned by a co-operative society are distributed.
A. to members in the ratio of capital held by them
B. to member in the ratio of purchases made by them
C. by providing a nominal rate of interest on capital contribution by members and remaining in the ratio of purchases made by members
D. by declaring dividend at a specific rate and remaining transfering to general reserves.

26. Management of a co-operative organisation is in the hands of
A. persons nominated by the Registrar of co-operative societies
B. an elected body by the members
C. some persons nominated by Registrar of co-operative societies and other selected by the member
D. the promoters of the co-operative organisation

27. Which of the following is an example of a company incorporated by a special act of parliament?
A. Delhi Cloth Mills Ltd.
B. Tata Iron and Steel Co. Ltd.
C. Industrial Finance Corporation.
D. Swadeshi Cotton Mills Ltd.

28. Which of the following documents need not be prepared and Registered with the Registrar of companies in public limited companies.
A. Memorandum of Association
B. Articles of Association
C. Statutory Declaration
D. Directors of undertaking to take up and pay for qualification shares.

29. The term, 'capitalisation' is used in relation to
A. sole-proprietorship
B. partnership
C. joint stock companies
D. co-operative societies

30. Which of the following methods provide a better basis of capitalisation for an establised concern?
A. Add up the cost of fixed assets and working capital required
B. Add up the cost of fixed assets, working capital and cost of promotion etc.
C. Capitalise the profits to be earned.
D. Estimate on the basis of financial position of other similar companies.

31. Watered capital means
A. over capitalistation
B. under capitalistation
C. excessive capital
D. part of the capital not reprensented by assets

32. Over capitalisation may be remedied by
A. increasing the number of equity shares
B. increasing the per value of shares
C. issuing additional preference shares
D. redemption of debentures

33. Under Capitalisat.on can be remedied by
A. isssue of bonus shares
B. redemption of preference shares
C. redemption of debentures
D. reduction of interest of debentures

34. Capital gearing means
A. proper capitalisation
B. watered capital
C. fixation of a proper ratio between two or more types of securities
D. trading on equity

35. A company is said to be low geared when the proportion of
A. equ.ty capital to the total capital is small
B. preference capital to the total capital is small
C. debentures capital to the total capital is small
D. both preference and debentures capital to the total is small

36. Working capital can be used for the purchase of
A. machinery B. goodwill
C. land and building D. raw material

37. Which of the following sources is not used for medium term financing?
A. Issue of equity shares
B. Issue of preference shares
C. Issue of debentures
D. Terms loan from banks

38. Working capital is represented by
A. current liabilities
B. current assets minus current liabilities
C. total assets minus current liabilities
D. cash-in-hand plus stock-in-trade.

39. Participating preference shares are those which participate
A. in the voting
B. in the general meeting of the company.
C. in the management of the company.
D. in the profits over and above their fixed dividend.

40. In which of the following, rate of interest/dividends is not fixed?
A. equity capital B. debentures
C. preference capital D. public deposits

41. To which of the following types of companies, debentures suit as a source of finance?
A. companies with fluctuating earnings
B. companies with stable earnings
C. companies which cannot earn a rate of profit higher than the rate of interest, payable on debentures
D. all of these

42. First debentures are those
A. which are issued before share capital
B. which are repayable before other debentures
C. which are secured by a floating charges
D. which are secured by a fixed charges

43. Underwriters are persons who
A. purchase the shares and debentures of a company
B. work as agents of the company for the sale of shares and debentures
C. manage the issue of shares and debentures
D. undertake to buy those shares and debentures not subscribed for by the public

44. Which of the following institutions undertake underwriting of shares and debentures of companies?
A. Unit Trust of India
B. Industrial Development Bank of India
C. State Finance Corporations
D. All of these

45. Which of the following sources of finance do not pose a burden on the company?
A. Public deposits
B. Debentures
C. Loans from financial institutions
D. Retained earnings

46. Which of the following is not a component of the new issue market?
A. Stock exchanges
B. Unit Trust of India
C. Financial Institution of India like IFC, IDBI
D. LIC

47. When an existing company offers its shares for sale to the existing shareholders, it is known as
A. private placing B. bonus issue
C. rights issue D. offer for sale

48. The first stock exchange was set up in India in
A. Kolkata B. Mumbai
C. Delhi D. Chennai

49. The first stock exchange was set up in India in
A. 1887 B. 1905
C. 1908 D. 1923

50. Which of the speculators expects the price of securities to rise in the near future?
A. bull B. bear
C. stag D. lame duck

51. Which of the following speculative activities is based on disparity in quote prices in different markets?
A. Option dealings B. Arbitrage
C. Margin trading D. Blank transfers

52. Cantango charge is paid by a
A. bull speculator to bear speculator
B. bear speculator to bull speculator
C. lame duck to bull speculator
D. bull to lame duck speculator

53. Listing of securities in a stock exchange for the purpose of trading indicates that
A. at the time of listing, the company is financially sound
B. at the time of listing, the company is legally organised

C. the stock exchange guarantees about the financial soundness of the company
D. all of these

54. An existing company raising additional capital
A. must offer the new shares to the existing shareholders
B. need not offer the new shares to the existing shareholders
C. issues share to debenture holders
D. issue shares to preference share holders

55. Stock exchange deals with the
A. second hand securities
B. issues of equity shares
C. issue of preference shares
D. issue of debentures

56. One of the impelling causes of business combination is
A. desire for bigness B. wasteful competition
C. influence of tariffs D. rationalisation

57. When a cement mill, a steel mill and a chemical company combine, it is a case of
A. horizontal combination B. vertical combination
C. diagonal combination D. circular combination

58. Which of the following is an example of vertical integration?
A. One small steel mill combines with a big steel mill
B. Two steel mills of the same combine
C. Iron ore firm combines with iron melting firm
D. Paper mill combines with a publishing company

59. Combination of plants at the same stage of production or in the same trade or commerce is called a
A. horizontal combination B. vertical combination
C. diagonal combination D. allied combination

60. One of the main advantages of vertical combination is that
A. it helps in avoiding competition
B. it helps in controlling the market
C. it helps in controlling the quality of raw material and finished output
D. it brings about coordination between activities of combining units

61. Pools are a type of
A. horizontal combinations
B. vertical combinations
C. allied combinations
D. none of these

62. Cartel is a type of
A. horizontal combination B. vertical combination
C. allied combination D. mixed combination

63. FICCI was formed in the year
A. 1920 B. 1925
C. 1927 D. 1951

64. Business combinations are formed to derive the advantages of
A. enabling the units to join hands and establish a monopoly
B. avoiding wasteful competition
C. enabling business units to withstand the rigours of a depression
D. all of these

65. Match the following.

List-I	List-II
I. Trust	1. Company A holds more than 51% share capital of the company B
II. Merger	3. Existing companies A and B are merged into company C
III. Holding Company	3. Business of number of firms is entrusted to the care of Board of Trustees
IV. Amalgamation	4. Company A takes over Company B

Select the correct answer from the code given below :
Codes:
A. I-2, II-3, III-1, IV-4 B. I-1, II-2, III-3, IV-4
C. I-3, II-4, III-1, IV-2 D. I-2, II-1, III-4, IV-3

66. MRTP Act came into force in
A. 1969 B. 1970
C. 1971 D. 1980

67. Resale price maintenance is a
A. restrictive trade practice
B. monopolistic trade practice
C. both of these
D. none of these

68. When custom duty is levied according to the value of the goods, it is known as
A. revenue duty B. excise duty
C. specific duty D. ad-valorem duty

69. When custom duty is levied according to the weight of good, it is known as
A. revenue duty B. excise duty
C. specific duty D. ad-valorem duty

70. Import procedure begins with
A. mate's reciept B. marine insurance
C. indent D. shipping bill

71. Shipping order is issued by the owner of the ship when
A. whole of the ship is hired
B. major part of the ship is hired
C. freight is reserved for the exporter
D. ship starts its journey

72. A shipping bill is prepared when
A. goods are damaged in the ship
B. goods reach their destination in satisfactory condition
C. goods are not cleared by the custom authorities
D. none of these

73. Entrepot trade means
A. import trade
B. export trade
C. foreign trade
D. goods imported for re-export

74. A letter of credit means
A. a letter sent by importer to exporter sanctioning credit deal
B. a letter sent by exporter to importer sanctioning credit deal
C. a letter containing conditions of credit purchase or sale
D. a bank agreeing to accept and pay on due date

75. A bill of loading transferable to another person by
A. mere delivery
B. endorsement and delivery
C. any of the above
D. this one is not transferable

76. Charter party means
A. an agreement by which the ship owner agrees to place the entire or part of the ship at the disposal of the merchant.
B. the party who works as a middleman between shipper and shipping company.
C. the party who performs loading or unloading operations on the ship.
D. the party working as a middleman between importer and exporter.

77. State Trading Corporation of India was established
A. by a special Act of Parliament
B. under the companies Act, 1956 as a private limited company
C. under the companies Act, 1956 as a public limited company
D. as departmental undertaking

78. Which of the following is not a subsidiary of the State Trading Corporation of India?
A. Indian Motion Picture Export Corporation of India
B. Handicraft and a Handlooms Export Corporation of India Ltd.
C. Project and Equipment Corporation of India Ltd.
D. All of these

79. Mate's receipt is issued by
A. the exporter
B. the importer
C. the captain of the ship or his assistant
D. the bank

80. Under which of the following principles of insurance, parties to the contract must disclose the material facts known to them?
A. Indemnity
B. Utmost good faith
C. Subrogation
D. Insurable interest

81. A person can insure
A. any body's property
B. only his own property
C. only that property in which he is interested
D. only that property in which he has financial interest

82. In the case of fire insurance, the insured must have insurable interest in the thing insured at the time
A. when policy is taken
B. when loss is incurred
C. throughout the period of contract of insurance
D. both when policy is taken and when loss is incurred

83. In marine insurance, the insured must have insurable interest at the time
A. when policy is taken
B. when the event happens
C. when policy is taken as well as event happens
D. when throughout the period of contract of insurance

84. According to the principle of cause proxima the assured can recover the loss from the insurer
A. if it is proximatry caused by any of the perils insured against
B. if it is caused by any of the remote cause
C. if it is caused by any reason, whatsoever
D. all of these

85. The principle of subrogation applies to
A. all types of insurance
B. fire insurance only
C. marine insurance only
D. fire and marine insurance

86. The principle of contribution applies when
A. there are two or more insurance on one risk
B. the insured does not take necessary steps to mitigate the loss
C. the insured insures the same risk partly with other insurers
D. the premium is not paid by the insured

87. Surrender value of a life policy is the amount payable by Life Insurance Corporation when
A. the life policy matures by death
B. the life policy matures after the expiry of the policy period
C. the life policy is withdrawn before its maturity
D. the payment of premiums is discontinued and the amount is payable at the maturity of the policy

88. Principle of subrogation states that
A. the actual amount of loss should be distributed among the differented insurers of the same risk
B. on making good the loss, the insurers is entitled to succeed to all the rights of the insured regarding the subject matter of insurance
C. the insured must take all necessary steps to minimise the loss
D. the actual amount of loss, exceeding the amount of the policy, shall be paid

89. Average clause in a fire policy is inserted in order to check mainly
A. under-insurance
B. over-insurance
C. both over-insurance and under-insurance
D. all of these

90. X mortgages certain property with Y who has insurable interest in property
A. only X
B. only Y
C. both X and Y
D. none of these

91. Principle of insurable interest applies to
A. life insurance only
B. fire insurance only
C. fire and marine insurance only
D. all types of insurance

92. In which of the following kinds of insurance, insurable interest should be present only at the time of loss subject-matter
A. life insurance B. fire insurance
C. marine insurance D. all of these

93. Unless the marine policy otherwise provides, insurer is liable
A. if the loss is caused by ordinary wear and tear
B. if the loss is caused by peril insured against.
C. if the loss is caused by ordinary leakage and breakage
D. if the loss is caused by inherent nature of the subject-matter

94. The life of a co-operative society is
A. affected by the death of a member
B. affected by the insolvency of a member
C. affected by the withdrawal by a member from membership
D. not affected by death, insolvency etc. of members

95. Non-registration of a partnership does not affect
A. the right of a partner to sue the firm
B. the right of the firm to sue third parties
C. the right of the third party to proceed against the firm or its partners
D. any of these

96. If a minor choose to continue as a partner on attaining the age of majority, he will be liable to the debts of the firm from the date of this
A. attaining majority
B. admission to profits of the firm
C. choosing to become a partner at subsequent date
D. guardian giving the option

97. The liability of the Karta in a joint Hindu family is
A. limited to his interest in the joint family
B. unlimited
C. limited to the entire property of the family
D. limited to the private properties of all the member

98. Match List-I with List-II and select the correct answer using the codes given below the lists:

List-I *(Organisation)*	**List-II** *(Associated with)*
I. Joint stock company	1. Memorandum of Association (M/A)
II. Co-operative society	2. Special Act
III. Statutory corporation	3. Mutual contract
IV. Partnership	4. Bye-laws

Codes:
A. I-1, II-2, III-3, IV-4 B. I-1, II-3, III-4, IV-2
C. I-2, II-3, III-1, IV-4 D. I-1, II-4, III-2, IV-3

99. Which one of the following is not the distinctive feature of the co-operative form of the business organisation?
A. Service before self
B. Democratic management
C. Corporate status
D. One-share one-vote system

100. Which one of the following does not constitute the purpose of setting up SEBI?
A. To protect the interest of the investors in securities
B. To promote the development of the securities markets
C. To regulate the global securities markets
D. To deal with matters connected with fraudulent and unfair trade practices relating to securities market

101. Which one of the following best supports the theory that the stock exchange is a secondary market?
In a stock exchange
A. Securities are bought and sold by way of transfer
B. An existing holder of securities can dispose of the holding to another invest or who intends to buy them
C. No new investment is created
D. Securities are dealt in for dual purposes investment and speculation

102. Combination of printing and dyeing companies is a type of
A. vertical combination B. horizontal combination
C. circular combination D. allied combination.

103. In addition to consumer forums which one of the following looks after the interest of consumers?
A. High Court
B. Company Law Board
C. M.R.T.P.
D. Bureau of Industrial Costs and Prices

104. Which one of the following is not a commercial risk
A. Insolvency of the buyer
B. New restrictions placed on import export trade
C. Damage to goods in transit
D. Change in the exchange rate

105. The average clause in a fire policy states that the insured can get back.
A. only that portion of the actual loss suffered as the sum insured bears to total value

B. the entire amount of the total loss suffered
C. the entire amount of partial loss suffered
D. a fixed percentage of loss suffered

106. Consider the following statements :
The social responsibility of business is to:
I. Do a business as per the public policy.
II. Obey all the rules and regulations of the Government.
III. Make payment of the taxes imposed by the Government.
IV. Provide not necessarily adequate but good quality of goods.
Of these statements:
A. II and III are correct
B. I and IV are correct
C. I, II and III are correct.
D. I, II, III and IV are correct.

107. One of the consequences of non-registration of a partnership firm is that
A. a partner cannot sue the other partner to enforce a right arising from a contract
B. the partner of such a firm cannot sue third parties
C. third parties cannot sue the firm for claims exceeding ₹ 100
D. the official Assignee or Receiver will have no power on the property of the dissolved firm

108. Consider the following rights:
I. Right to take part in the business.
II. Right to share profits.
III. Right to interest on advances in excess of capital
IV. Right to expel a non-cooperative partner
Codes:
A. I and II B. II and IV
C. I, II and III D. I, III and IV

109. Steps to be taken in a selling system include:
I. Receipt of order
II. Processing order
III. Shipment of merchandise
IV. Accounting for sale
The correct chronological sequence of these steps is
A. I, IV, III, II B. I, IV, II, III
C. I, II, IV, III D. I, II, III, IV

110. Match List-I with List-II and select the correct answer using the codes given below the lists:

List-I *(Type of combinations)*	List-II *(Illustrations)*
I. Association	1. Cartel
II. Federation	2. Chamber of commerce and industry
III. Partial	3. Holding Company
IV. Complete consolidation	4. Amalgamation

Codes:
A. I-2, II-1, III-3, IV-4 B. I-1, II-2, III-3, IV-4
C. I-2, II-1, III-4, IV-3 D. I-1, II-2, III-4, IV-3

111. Which one of the following is an example of a company incorporated by a special Act of Parliament?
A. Life Insurance Corporation of India.
B. Indian Oil Corporation.
C. State Trading Corporation of India.
D. Bharat Heavy Electricals Limited.

112. Match List-I with List-II and select the correct answer using the codes given below the lists:

List-I	List-II
I. Contract of uberrimal fidei	1. Public utility concern
II. Right of eminent domain	2. Co-operative society
III. Statement in lieu of prospectus	3. Partnership
IV. System of one man one vote	4. Sole trading concern
	5. Public limited company

Codes:
A. I-1, II-3, III-5, IV-4 B. I-3, II-1, III-5, IV-2
C. I-3, II-2, III-1, IV-4 D. I-1, II-2, III-5, IV-3

113. Match List-I (activity) with List-II (associated organisation) and select the correct answer by using the codes given below the lists:

List-I	List-II
I. Mutual fund	1. Stock exchange
II. Public issue of capital	2. Assets management company
III. Forward trading	3. Merchant banking
IV. Option pricing	4. Foreign market

Codes:
A. I-3, II-2, III-4, IV-1
B. I-3, II-2, III-1, IV-4
C. I-2, II-3, III-1, IV-4
D. I-2, II-3, III-4, IV-1

114. Integration of various limits of similar character producing similar products or engaged in the same sphere of business activity under a single form of management and control is called
A. vertical combination
B. horizontal combination
C. circular or mixed combination
D. lateral or allied combination

115. The scope of MRTP Act, since 1992, has been confined only to the regulation
A. consumer monopolies
B. monopolistic trade practices
C. restrictive and unfair trade practices
D. restrictive trade practices

116. EXIM bank can be described as a
A. non-banking financial company
B. commercial bank
C. non-banking non-financial company
D. schedule bank

117. Match List-I (document) with List-II (where used) and select the correct answer by using the codes given below the lists:

List-I	List-II
I. Shipping bill	1. to certify the origin of good's country
II. Bill of loading	3. for having loaded the cargo in the ship
III. Consular invoice	3. to transport cargo by ship
IV. Packing slip	4. to identify the cargo in transit

Codes:
A. I-2, II-3, III-4, IV-1 B. I-2, II-3, III-1, IV-4
C. I-3, II-2, III-1, IV-4 D. I-3, II-2, III-4, IV-1

118. In the context of foreign trade, the CIF cost may be obtained by
A. adding freight and marine insurance premium to the FOB price
B. deducting freight and marine insurance premium for the FOB price
C. adding customs duties, freight and marine insurance premium to the cost
D. deducting customs duties, freight and marine insurance premium from the price

119. Paid-up value is payable on a life insurance policy
A. on the maturity of the policy
B. when the policy lapses
C. when the policy is surrendered
D. on maturity or death which ever is earlier

120. A Co-partner partner is one who is
A. an active member of a partnership
B. a member of a joint Hindu family firm
C. a member of a joint stock company
D. a member of co-operative society

121. Every partner must account to the firm for any benefit derived by him without the consent of the other partners and thus make no secret profits. This is based on
A. the general law of contract
B. the general law of agency
C. the law of sale of goods
D. business ethics

122. In a broader sense, the activities of a co-operatives organisation are expected to ensure primarily.
A. profitability to the members
B. socialism in the economy
C. equity to the members
D. productivity to the society

123. Which of the following statements are correct?
I. A trust form of organisation cannot do business.
II. A society registered under the societies Registration Act can be formed only for non-profit purpose.
III. A partnership does not require registration.
IV. A company limited by guarantee is almost always registered for non-profit activities.

Codes:
A. II, III and IV B. I and IV
C. II and III D. I, II, III and IV

124. The basic characteristics of a partnership firm include.
A. existence of relationship, plurality of persons, contract and profit maximisation.
B. unlimited liability, contractual binding principal agent relationship and profit motive.
C. existence of business, contractual relationship group of persons, task orientation and employment conditions.
D. existence of business, plurality of persons contractual at relationship, profit motive and principle-agent relationship.

125. It is compulsory for a share broker to registered with the
A. concerned stock exchange
B. securities and exchange board of India
C. department of company affairs
D. concerned stock exchange in concurrence with the securities and exchange board of India

126. Who among the following is not a speculator in stock exchange?
A. Broker B. Bull
C. Bear D. Stag

127. The gilt edged market refers to the market for
A. industrial securities
B. Govt. and semi-govt securities
C. shares and debentures
D. public limited company securities

128. The combination of firms in successive stages of the same industry may be referred to as
A. horizontal integration B. vertical integration
C. forward integration D. backward integration

129. Which one of the following statements is true?
A. Suppliers credit and buyers credit are one and the same thing.
B. EXIM bank generally deals with export transaction above ₹ 5 crore.
C. The main focus of EXIM bank is on export and import credit for short-term.
D. ECGC provides no protection against hazards of nature.

130. Which one of the following statements are corrects?
I. Bill of loading is a document of title
II. Green shipping bill is used for export of goods entitled to duty draw back
III. An airway bill is not a document of title
IV. A consumer invoice and a proforma invoice are one and the same

Codes:
A. II and IV B. I, II and IV
C. I, II and IV D. I, II and III

131. Life insurance is a contract on the life of a man in which the insurer promises to pay a sum of money. For the consideration of a definite premium, to the insured person on his death or an attaining a particular age. Which one of the following assumptions is implicit in the above definition?

A. It is a contract of indemnity
B. It is a contract of guarantee
C. It is a contract of compensation
D. It is a contract of return on investment

132. "Causa promia" implies that the loss must arise from
A. the nearest place
B. an assertainable place source
C. the cause insured against
D. unforeseen source

133. Which one of the following risk are not covered by a marine insurance policy
I. Damage caused by delay in ships transit
II. Damage caued by unsuitable package
III. Loss due to sinking of the vessel
IV. Loss due to jettison
Select the correct answer using the codes given below:
Codes:
A. I, III and IV B. I and II
C. II and IV D. I, II, III and IV

134. Trading on equity takes place
A. when capital other than that of equity share holders is also employed
B. only when equity capital is employed
C. only when debentures funds are employed
D. when profits are ploughed back

135. Which one of the following statements is correct?
A. Co-operative organisation are based on the principle of "one vote" one share
B. A public limited company does not invite capital from the public
C. Most of the public enterprises in India are organised on the pattern of private limited companies
D. Registration of partnership is compulsory

136. Which of the following are the methods of marketing new issues of securities
I. Listing of securities
II. Jobbers and brokers
III. Private placement of securities
IV. Privileged subscriptions
Select the correct answer using the codes given below:
Codes:
A. I and II B. II and III
C. III and IV D. I, II, III and IV

137. Vertical combination helps to
A. achieve economy by combination allied activities
B. survive during the times of depression
C. fight a common enemy
D. add new product lines

138. Letter of credit is now becoming an increasingly popular method of financing
A. fixed capital needs
B. working capital needs
C. redemption of debentures
D. distribution of dividend

139. Import procedure begins with
A. indent B. marine insurance
C. mate's certificate D. shipping order

140. Which one of the following statements is correct?
A. EXIM bank promotes Indian exports through a wide variety and range of lending programmes
B. EXIM bank does not extent non-funded facility to Indian exports
C. Overseas investment finance facility is not a part of the function of EXIM bank
D. EXIM bank was established to provide assistance in raising capital in international markets

141. In which of the following types of insurance should insurable interest be present only at the time when policy is taken?
A. Fire insurance B. Life insurance
C. Marine insurance D. Life and Marine Insurance

142. Match list-I with list-II and select the correct answer using the codes given below the lists:

List-I	List-II
I. Causa proxima	1. Financial stake
II. Reinsurance	2. Main reason behind the event
III. Indemnity	3. Compensation for the loss
	4. Risking with other insurer

Codes:
A. I-2, II-4, III-3 B. I-1, II-2, III-3
C. I-2, II-3, III-1 D. I-2, II-4, III-1

143. Insurer is a person who has
A. insured his life or goods
B. helped a person to get an insurance policy
C. undertaken to make good the loss of the subject matter of insurance
D. filed a suit in a court of law to recover an insurance claim

144. In insurance contract uberimae fidie aspect is used as synonym of
A. insurable interest
B. free consent of parties
C. utmost goods faith
D. legality of consideration

145. Capital gearing ratio denotes the relationship between
A. assets and capital
B. loans and capital
C. equity share holders, funds and long term borrowed funds
D. debentures and share capital

146. Which one of the following is not applicable to a co-operative form of business organisation
A. Membership is open to all having a common interest
B. Transferability of shares is permitted among general public
C. Policy decisions are taken by the members in a general meeting
D. Major portion of profit is distributed to members by way of dividend

147. An enterprise incorporated by a special act of parliament or the state legislature intending to carry on some business of national importance is called
A. Public company
B. Statutory corporation
C. Registered company
D. Registered statutory company

148. Consider the following functions of a stock exchange
I. providing a ready market for securities.
II. helping capital formation.
III. regulating the capital structure of a company.
IV. regulating the public deposits with companies.
Of these statements
A. I, II, III and IV are correct
B. I, II, and III are correct
C. I and II are correct
D. none of these

149. Both 'securities' and 'investment' elements are available
A. only in life insurance
B. in both life and fire insurance
C. in both marine and fire insurance
D. in life, marine and fire insurance

150. Match List-I with List-II and select the correct answer using the codes given below the lists:

List-I	List-II
I. Bull	1. Buys the shares for sale but finds it difficult to meet his commitment
II. Bear	2. Buys the shares to sell them in future expecting a price rise
III. Lame duck	3. Neither buys nor sells but more applies for shares to sell at a premium
IV. Stag	4. Agree to sell on a fixed date expecting a fall in the price
	5. Buys and sells shares on the same date
	6. Agree to sell on a fixed date but finds it difficult to meet his commitment
	7. A genuine investor

Codes:
A. I-4, II-2, III-1, IV-7
B. I-4, II-2, III-3, IV-5
C. I-2, II-4, III-5, IV-1
D. I-2, II-4, III-6, IV-3

ANSWERS

1	2	3	4	5	6	7	8	9	10
D	A	D	D	C	B	A	B	D	D
11	12	13	14	15	16	17	18	19	20
D	C	D	D	C	C	B	C	C	B
21	22	23	24	25	26	27	28	29	30
D	A	C	A	D	B	C	B	C	C
31	32	33	34	35	36	37	38	39	40
D	D	A	D	D	D	A	B	D	A
41	42	43	44	45	46	47	48	49	50
B	B	D	D	D	A	C	B	A	A
51	52	53	54	55	56	57	58	59	60
B	A	B	A	A	B	D	C	A	C
61	62	63	64	65	66	67	68	69	70
A	A	C	D	C	A	A	D	C	C
71	72	73	74	75	76	77	78	79	80
C	D	D	A	C	A	B	D	C	B
81	82	83	84	85	86	87	88	89	90
D	D	B	A	D	A	C	B	A	B
91	92	93	94	95	96	97	98	99	100
D	C	B	D	C	B	B	D	D	C
101	102	103	104	105	106	107	108	109	110
B	C	C	B	A	D	B	D	D	B
111	112	113	114	115	116	117	118	119	120
A	B	D	B	C	A	B	C	D	B
121	122	123	124	125	126	127	128	129	130
B	C	D	B	D	A	B	B	C	B
131	132	133	134	135	136	137	138	139	140
B	C	B	B	A	C	A	B	A	A
141	142	143	144	145	146	147	148	149	150
B	A	C	C	C	B	B	C	A	D

●●●

8 Management Principles

1. Which one of the following defines co-ordination?
   A. Actuating force which inspires a person to put his best for the fulfilment of a task
   B. Orderly arranged of group effort to provide unity of action in the pursuit of a common purpose.
   C. Process of transmitting information from one person to another or from one unit to another.
   D. Process of determining what is to be accomplished and what has been accomplished and if necessary applying corrective measures.
2. Consider the following basic steps involved in the process of control:
   I. Identifying the strategic control points
   II. Establish the standards
   III. Measuring performance against standards.
   IV. Correcting deviations from the standards.

   The correct sequence of the above steps in the process of control is:
   A. I, IV, III, II B. IV, III, II, I
   C. II, I, IV, III D. II, III, I, IV
3. Match List-I with List-II and select the correct answer using the codes given below the lists:

List-I *(Management thinkers)*	**List-II** *(Contribution/work)*
I. Elton Mayo	1. Importance of integrating the company's and employee's goal
II. Frederic W. Taylor	2. Social problems of Industrial Civilisation
III. Henri Fayol	3. General and Industrial Management.
IV. Many Parker Follet	4. Principles of Scientific Management

   Codes:
   A. I-1, II-4, III-3, IV-2 B. I-4, II-3, III-2, IV-1
   C. I-2, II-4, III-3, IV-1 D. I-3, II-4, III-1, IV-2
4. An organisation structure is effective if it enables individuals to contribute to the objectives of the enterprise. This is known as
   A. Scalar Principle
   B. Principle of functional definition
   C. Principle of unity of objectives
   D. None of these
5. Which one of the following orders indicates the correct logical order of managerial functions?
   A. Organising, planning, directing, staffing, coordination and control
   B. Planning, organising, staffing, directing, coordination and control
   C. Planning, directing, organising, staffing, control and coordination
   D. Organising, planning, staffing, directing, control and coordination
6. Effective direction does NOT depend on the
   A. Communication process
   B. Forces at the subordinate level
   C. Ability of the manager
   D. Deployment of human resources
7. Planning refers to
   A. Looking backward
   B. Looking forward
   C. Looking forward and backward
   D. Looking and actual performance to decide action to be taken
8. Leadership is a function of all the following factors except
   A. Workgroup B. Product or service
   C. Leader D. Situation
9. The main difference between delegation and decentralisation is that
   A. delegation refers primarily to transfer of authority from one individual to another while decentralisation refers to systematic delegation of authority to all units in an organisation.
   B. delegation of authority can take place without decentralisation where as there cannot be decentralisation without delegation of authority.
   C. delegation represents sharing of excessiv burden of key managerial personnel while decentralisation refers to division of top managerial operations.
   D. delegation may take place due to administrative, technical and routine reasons while decentralisation involves deliberate action for the smooth functioning of the organisation.
10. Management by exception introduces
    A. selective, responsibility oriented reporting
    B. reporting of significant variances

C. requirement of full reports on performance
D. computation of actuals in different spheres of performance

11. Consider the following office equipments used in various offices:

I. Fax II. Typewriter
III. Dictaphone IV. Letter opener

The correct order in which they are used is

A. I, II, III, IV B. IV, III, II, I
C. II, IV, III, I D. III, II, IV, I

12. Control refers to

I. Establishment of standards
II. Measurement of actual performance against the set standards
III. Correction for deviation from standards

Of these statements:

A. I alone is correct B. III alone is correct
C. I and II are correct B. I, II, and III are correct

13. Which one of the following is not related to the trait theory of leadership?

A. Physical factors such as height
B. Intelligence and extroversion
C. Self confidence and ambition
D. Training and experience of employees

14. Match List-I with List-II and select the correct answer from the codes given below the lists:

List-I	List-II
I. Planning	1. Training
II. Staffing	2. Forecasting
III. Directing	3. Evaluating
IV. Controlling	4. Motivating
	5. Grouping

Codes :

A. I-3, II-1, III-4, IV-5 B. I-3, II-5, III-1, IV-2
C. I-2, II-1, III-4, IV-3 D. I-2, II-5, III-1, IV-3

15. Decentralisation of an organisation is commended on account of which of the following advantages?

I. Reduced burden on top executives
II. Executive development
III. Improvement of morale
IV. Solves problems of coordination

Select the correct answer from the codes given below and mark your answer sheet accordingly

Codes:

A. II and III B. I, II and IV
C. I, II and III D. III and IV

16. In a functional organisation

A. There are no advisors, the executives alone having the authority and competence
B. There are specialist advisors having no authority
C. The entire organisation is divided into functions with specific role for specialists
D. the organisation is divided into functions with specialists having authority

17. The process of grouping activities into units for the purpose of administration may be referred to as

A. Departmentalisation B. Decentralisation
C. Co-ordination D. Specialisation

18. Span of control means that

A. an organisation consists of various departments
B. each person's authority is clearly defined
C. every subordinate has one superior
D. a manager can supervise only a limited number of subordinates

19. If a general manager asks the sales manager to recruit some sales men on his behalf, it is an instance of

A. division of authority
B. decentralisation of authority
C. delegation of authority
D. delegation of responsibility

20. Which one of the following principles states that recurring decisions should be handled in a routine manner by lower level managers whereas problems involving unusal matters only should be referred to higher levels?

A. Principle of unity of command
B. Scalar principle
C. Principle of exception
D. Principle of commitment

21. MBO is a technique which requires that the objectives of the enterprise

A. be written and defined in board terms
B. lay down the time period for achieving the results
C. include a plan of action for achieving the desired results
D. be defined in terms of measurable results

22. In the field of management some of the important techniques, relate to budgeting, cost accounting, planning and control are through

A. Operational research
B. PERT & CPM
C. Budgetary control
D. Financial Administration

23. Which of the following management functions are closely related?

A. Planning and organising
B. Staffing and control
C. Planning and control
D. Planning and staffing

24. "Human Relating Approach" to management was origined by

A. Henery Fayol B. Winslow Taylor
C. Elton Mayo D. Peter F. Drucker

25. The famous book "The Philosophy of Management" was written by

A. Henery Fayol B. Oliver Sheldon
C. F.W. Taylor D. Urwick

26. Policy making is an important part of the process of
A. Planning B. Co-ordinating
C. Organising D. Motivating

27. A firm has these characteristics : It is involved in the manufacture of custom built machinery, its products have shorter life span, the products are processed through different specialists and the products have a rigid time schedule to be met. In such a circumstance, which one of the following would be the form of organisation best suited to achieve the objectives?
A. Functional organisation
B. Line and staff organisation
C. Project (Matrix) organisation
D. Line organisation

28. The managerial function of organising is
A. To review and adjust plan in the light of changing conditions
B. To establish a programme for the accomplishment of objections
C. To create a structure of functions and duties to be performed by a group of people
D. to get things done through and with the help of people

29. Span of management means
A. A good organisation should consist of departments
B. Authority of each person must be clearly defined
C. Each subordinate should have one superior
D. A manager can supervise a limited number of executives

30. Which of the following is the oldest type of organisation?
A. Functional organisation
B. Line organisation
C. Line and staff organisation
D. Committee organisation

31. 'Unity of command' principle of effective direction means
A. Subordinates should be responsible to one superior
B. Boosting the morale of the subordinates
C. decreasing the productivity of subordinates
D. All of these

32. In line organisation
A. the organisation is divided according to the skill required to perform a work
B. the organisation is divided according to the type of work involve
C. the authority flows from the man at the top to the lowest man vertically
D. each worker serves a number of supervisors

33. The function of 'staff' in 'line and staff'organisation is to
A. take advice from the line
B. advice the line
C. hold authority and responsibility
D. fix responsibility for performance of tasks in a definite manner upon certain individuals

34. Control function of management implies
A. to bring harmony in various activities
B. to keep the work force content
C. taking corrective course of action
D. to provide sufficient finance

35. The main advantage of line and staff organisation is
A. Simplicity
B. Specialisation
C. Availability of expert advice
D. Speedy decision making

36. The terms speed boss, route clerk etc. are used in relation to
A. Line organisation
B. Line and staff organisation
C. Functional organisation
D. None of these

37. General manager has delegated authority to production manager for achieving budgeted production. Who is responsible for low production to Board of Directors?
A. Production Supervisors B. Production Manager
C. General Manager D. None of these

38. Delegation can be
A. upward B. downward
C. side ward D. all of these

39. Unity of command is violated under
A. Line organisation
B. Line and staff organisation
C. Functional organisation
D. None of these

40. 'Theory Y' states that
A. Workers prefer to be directed
B. Workers exercise self-direction and self control
C. Workers have inherent disliking for work and will avoid it if they can
D. None of these

41. 'Theory X' and 'Theory Y' is given by
A. Maslow B. Herzberg
C. Mc Gregor D. Norman

42. The Need-Hierarchy Theory of Motivation is given by
A. Maslow B. Herzberg
C. Vroom D. Mc Gregor

43. Under the Need-Hierarchy Theory, When UDC designation is changed into 'Assistant', it is an example of
A. Social needs
B. Esteem needs
C. Self-actualisation needs
D. All of these

44. Maslow's Need-Hierarchy Theory of Motivation has classified the human needs into five categories as follows :
I. Safety needs
II. Esteem needs
III. Social needs
IV. Physiological needs
V. Self-actualisation needs
What is the sequence of domination of these needs?
A. I, IV, III, II, V B. IV, I, III, II, V
C. V, III, II, IV, I D. IV, I, III, II, V

45. Under Expectancy Theory of Motivation, increase in motivation results when
A. Valence increases B. Valence decreases
C. No effect on valence D. None of these

46. Which one of the following is a motivating factor as per Herzberg's Theory?
A. Salary and allowances B. Job design
C. Working conditions D. None of these

47. Which of the following functions of management are more closely related?
I. Planning II. Co-ordination
III. Motivation IV. Control
A. I and II B. II and III
C. II, III, and IV D. I, II, and IV

48. Staffing includes
I. Training II. Appraisal
III. Placement IV. Directing
A. I and III B. I, II and III
C. II and III D. I, II, III and IV

49. Match the following:

List-I	List-II
I. Need-Hierarchy Theory of Motivation	1. Taylor
II. M.B.O.	2. Maslow
III. Scientific Management	3. Herzberg
IV. Hygience Theory	4. Peter F. Drucker

Codes:
A. I-2, II-1, III-4, IV-3 B. I-3, II-2, III-4, IV-1
C. I-1, II-2, III-3, IV-4 D. I-2, II-4, III-1, IV-3

50. Decentralisation
A. increases the importance of superiors
B. decreases the importance of superiors
C. increases the importance of subordinates
D. decreases the importance of subordinates

51. When management pays attention to more important areas and when day today routine problems are looked after by lower level of management, this is known as:
A. MBO
B. Management by exception
C. Unity of command
D. Critical path method

52. A leader uses the following methods.
I. Uses criticism
II. Encourages growth
III. Sets objectives
IV. Gives orders and directions
Which of these methods are used by a democratic leader
A. I and II B. III and IV
C. II and III D. I, II and IV

53. Span of control is narrow when the
A. posts in the top management increases
B. posts in the middle management increases
C. posts in lower management increases
D. all of these

54. The delegation of authority results in
I. Decentralisation of branches at places
II. Avoiding responsibility by top management
III. Delegation of authority by top management without avoiding responsibility
Codes:
A. I and III B. I, II and III
C. III only D. I and II

55. In Taylor's functional organisation there are eight foremen
I. Time and cost clerk II. Route clerk
III. Speed boss IV. Gang boss
V. Shop disciplinarian VI. Instruction card clerk
VII. Repair boss VIII. Inspector
Which of these foremen operate at the shop level?
A. I, II, III and IV B. V, VI, VII and VIII
C. III, IV, VII and VIII D. IV, V, VI and VII

56. Match the following

List-I	List-II
I. Staff executives	1. Advisory function
II. Directing	2. Manpower development
III. Line executives	3. Guiding function
IV. Staffing	4. Management authority

Codes:
A. I-1, II-4, III-3, IV-2 B. I-1, II-3, III-3, IV-2
C. I-2, II-3, III-4, IV-1 D. I-2, II-1, III-3, IV-4

57. "Grapevine" is a term used in relation to
A. formal communication
B. informal communication
C. both formal and informal communications
D. this term is not used in relation to communication

58. Which of the following pairs are correctly matched?

List-I	List-II
I. Henri Fayol	Administration Industrial Generate
II. F.W. Taylor	The functions of the Executive
III. Douglas Mc Gregor	The Human side of Enterprise
IV. Peter Drucker	Management: Tasks, Responsibilities and Practices

Select the correct answer using the codes given below:

Codes:

A. I, II, III and IV B. III and IV
C. II and IV D. I and III

59. According to the Peter Principle, managers tend to

A. Work late as they go higher up the hierarchy
B. Work even beyond their retirement age
C. Get promoted to the level of their incompetence
D. Lose their competence with successive promotions

60. Which of the following constitute manpower planning?

I. Determining human resource requirements both quantitatively and qualitatively.
II. Finding the sources of talented individuals.
III. Planning for the human resource needs of an organisation.
IV. Reaching out to the right source for procuring the right people.

Select the correct answer using the codes given below:

Codes:

A. I, II and IV B. II and III
C. I and III D. I, II, III and IV

61. Which one of the following may not necessarily be an advantage of co-ordination?

A. Effective supervision
B. Unity of direction
C. Creative force
D. Summarisation of all management functions

62. Understanding control does not signify under standing

A. How one controls
B. What is meant by control
C. Who controls
D. What is controlled

63. Consider the following statements :

Strategic management process comprises

I. Goal setting, strategy formulation, administration and strategic control.
II. Setting courses of action attaining objective, process of seeking key areas and strategy formulation.
III. Integrating the organisation with culture.
IV. Strategic planning and acting on these plans.

Of these statements :

A. I, II and III are correct
B. II, III and IV are correct
C. I, II and IV are correct
D. I, III and IV are correct

64. Match List-I with List-II and select the correct answer using the codes given below the Lists:

List-I	List-II
I. Line authority	1. Some People in an organisation are vested with primary sources of authority
II. Staff authority	2. Some people in an organisation have legitimate right to expert influence on others.
III. Functional authority	3. Some people in an organisation lack independent.
IV. Formal authority	4. Some people have right to control activities of other departments as they relate to specific staff.

Codes :

A. I-1, II-2, III-3, IV-4 B. I-2, II-4, III-3, IV-1
C. I-1, II-3, III-4, IV-1 D. I-2, II-3, III-4, IV-1

65. Which is the most fundamental function of Management

A. Planning B. Organising
C. Staffing D. Controlling

66. Match List-I with List-II and select the correct answer using the codes given below the lists:

List-I	List-II
I. Span of control	1. The superior helps, through continuous guidance, the subordinate to reach his goals.
II. M.B.O.	2. Numerical limit of subordinates to be supervised by an executive
III. M.B.E.	3. Subordinate remains accountable to his superior and the superior has the authority to demand accountability from his subordinate
IV. Delegation of authority	4. The management will concern itself and confine its activities to those areas and operations where the actual performance is short of the target

Codes:

A. I-1, II-2, III-3, IV-4 B. I-1, II-2, III-4, IV-3
C. I-2, II-1, III-3, IV-4 D. I-2, II-1, III-4, IV-3

67. Consider the following statements:

I. MBO is a control technique in which managers devote time only on the areas of deviation.
II. MBO integrates the individual with the organisation and the organisation with the environment.
III. In MBO the control over people is Shifted to control over operations
IV. The MBO Principle must be accompanied in practice by the principle of critical-point control

Of these statements:

A. I and II are correct B. II and III are correct
C. III and IV are correct D. I and IV are correct

68. Which one of the following statements is correct?

A. Planning and controlling are essentially one and the same.
B. Controlling is a part of the planning process.
C. Controlling is a substitute for planning.
D. A control process is meaningless without pre-set goals.

69. When jobs are broadened in scope and complexity so that the person's over all area of job responsibility increases, it is a case of

A. Job rotation B. Job enrichment
C. Job specification D. Job enlargement

70. Consider the following statements :
Planning involves
I. forecasting
II. choice among alternative courses of action
III. wishful thinking
IV. decision only by production manager
Of these statements
A. I, II, III and IV are correct
B. I, III and IV are correct
C. I and II are correct
D. II and III are correct

71. Techniques of managerial control are useful in
A. Selection of plant location
B. Identifying appropriate technology.
C. Profit planning
D. Conducting share holder's meetings.

72. Motivational process and not the motivators as such is associated with the
A. Need hierarchy theory
B. Two-factor theory
C. ERG theory
D. Expectancy theory

73. "Perceived equity in reward results in satisfaction". Which one of the following motivation theories take this into account?
A. Porter and Lowler model
B. Victor Vroom's Expectancy model.
C. F.W. Taylor's incentive scheme
D. Herzberg's Two-factor theory.

74. One of the steps that may be required for achieving effective coordination is
A. reporting on performance and taking remedial measures
B. training in leadership and supervisory abilities of controllers of activity.
C. transmission of messages in a full line communication channel.
D. making an honest appraisal and initiating rewards/ punishments.

75. An important aspect of control is that the
A. manager motivates his subordinates to give better performance
B. manager sets as effective management in formation system
C. plans are checked before implementation against predetermined measures of performance
D. performance is checked against predetermined standards

76. Delegation of authority takes place when a manager thinks that
A. the job is too difficult and hazardous
B. the job requires the high skill that he does not possess
C. he cannot look after all the demanding tasks by him self
D. He needs to punish his subordinate

77. According to the principle of "Span of control", there is
A. A tendency to overload supervisors with too much of work
B. A limit to the number of subordinates a supervisor can effectively supervise
C. No limit to the number of subordinates a supervisor can supervise
D. A limit to delegation of authority to the subordinate

78. Establishment of management by objectives pre-supposes
A. That limits of authority are not defined
B. That the employees are provided with result expected
C. Unlimited freedom to operate in the assigned task
D. Unlimited freedom to set goals

79. Each subordinate should have only one superior whose command he has to obey. This is known as
A. Scalar principle
B. Exception principle
C. Unity of command principle
D. Authority responsibility principle

80. Which one of the following is the oldest form of organisation?
A. Functional organisation
B. Line organisation
C. Line and staff organisation
D. Departmentation

81. Which of the following pairs are correctly matched?

List-I	List-II
I. Planning	Sets out the objectives and complete set of policies
II. Organisation	Enables the owner or top executive of a business to arrange, money, materials and methods.
III. Co-ordination	Orderly arrangement of group effort to provide unity of action.
IV. Control	Verifying whether everything occurs in conformity with the plan adopted, the instructions issued and principles established.

Select the correct answer using the codes given below:
Codes:
A. II, III and IV B. II and IV
C. I, III and IV D. I, II and III

82. A written statement of the main duties and responsibilities which a particular job entails is called?
A. Job analysis B. Job specification
C. Job description D. Job evaluation

83. Selection process in any organisation is usually proceeded by the preparation of
A. human resources audit
B. operations audit
C. human resources inventory
D. human resources accounting

84. Which one of the following monitors critical inputs and suggests preventive measures in the form of corrective action to correct inputs and processes?
A. Feed back control B. Feed forward control
C. Budgetory control D. Operational control

85. If the span of control is narrow, a number of managers would be required in each unit of the organisation and there would be many managerial levels or layers. Such an organisational structure is referred to as
A. Flat structure B. Tall structure
C. Matrix structure D. Project structure

86. The following steps are involved in the process of organising:
I. Forming supportive objectives
II. Delegating to the head of each group the authority necessary to perform the activities
III. Establishing enterprise objectives
IV. Identifying and classifying activities
The correct sequence of these steps is
A. III, I, II, IV B. III, I, IV, II
C. I, III, IV, II D. I, III, II, IV

87. When management pays attention to more important areas and when the day-to-day routine problems are looked after by lower level management, it is known as
A. Management by Objectives
B. Management by Exception
C. Participative Management
D. Critical Path Method

88. The following steps are involved in managing by objectives:
I. Preliminary setting of objectives at the top
II. Setting subordinates objectives
III. Tying resources with the goals
IV. Clarifying the organisational steps is
A. I, II, III, IV B. I, II, IV, III
C. I, III, II, IV D. I, IV, II, III

89. Match List-I (types of securities) with List-II (Special features) and select the correct answer using the codes given below the lists:

List-I	List-II
I. Blue Chip	1. Issued by a private limited company
II. Deep Discount Bonds	2. Highly Profitable investments in a stock exchange
III. Commercial paper	3. Issued by finally sound companies
IV. Debentures	4. Small investments and big yielding.
	5. Issued by companies having large reserves
	6. Issued in lieu of loans

Codes:
A. I-2, II-1, III-3, IV-6 B. I-1, II-4, III-6, IV-5
C. I-2, II-3, III-1, IV-5 D. I-2, II-4, III-3, IV-6

90. Match List-I (Management experts) with List-II (sequence of functions advocated by them) and select the correct answer using the codes given below the lists:

List-I	List-II
I. Newman and Summer	A. Organising, planning, leading and controlling
II. Henry Fayol	B. Planning, organising, commanding, coordinating and controlling
III. Luther Gulick	C. Planning, organizing, staffing, directing and controlling
IV. Koontz and O' Donnel	D. POSDCORB

Codes:
A. I-1, II-2, III-4, IV-3 B. I-2, II-1, III-3, IV-4
C. I-1, II-2, III-3, IV-4 D. I-2, II-1, III-4, IV-3

91. Which among the following are sub-systems of business firms
A. Production system
B. Finance system
C. Research a development system
D. All of the above

92. An economy which comprises the combination of capitalism and communism with a state ownership and control of business along with private enterprises is called
A. Mixed Economy B. Financial Economy
C. Dual Economy D. Organized Economy

93. Match List-I (Motivation theory) with List-II (Management Expert) and select the correct answer using the codes given below the lists:

List-I *(Motivation Theory)*	List-II *(Management Expert)*
I. Hygiene Theory	1. Abraham H. Maslow
II. Theory 'X' and theory 'Y'	2. Victor Vroom
III. Expectancy theory	3. Fredrick Herzberg
	4. Douglas Mc Gregor

Codes:
A. I-3, II-4, III-2 B. I-1, II-4, III-2
C. I-3, II-2, III-4 D. I-1, II-2, III-4

94. In management principles, grid refers to
A. Diverse managerial styles
B. Coordination
C. Communication
D. Motivation

95. The process of determining how to pursue long term goals with the expected resources available to the organisation is called
A. Operational planning
B. Strategic planning
C. Intermediate planning
D. Tactical planning

96. Which one of the following is the most appropriate management control technique for timely completion of a project?
A. Organisation chart
B. Management by objectives
C. PERT
D. Span of control

97. Which of the following pairs are correctly matched?

I. Frederick Herzberg	Scientific management
II. Henry Fayol	Modern management
III. Max Weber	Bureaucracy
IV. Philip Kotler	Marketing

Select the correct answer using the codes given below:
A. I and II　　B. II and III
C. I and III　　D. II, III and IV

98. Hawthorne studies have underlined the significance of which of the following?
A. System approach to management
B. Contingency approach to management
C. Modern approach to management
D. Human relations approach to management

99. Is management by exception, one of the important principles of control?
A. Yes; because only the unusual deviations from standards should be brought to the notice of the management
B. No; because less significant deviations and the actual performance according to the standards are not brought to the notice of the management
C. Yes; because exception principle saves time of the subordinates staff
D. No; because the manager can attend too operative decisions, and the strategic problems can be left to the technocrats

100. Job evaluation is used for
A. study of progress of production
B. study of job composition
C. determining wage-rate differentials
D. rating the merit of an employee

101. The first step of the control process actually gets initiated in the managerial function of
A. Staffing　　B. Planning
C. Communication　　D. Coordination

102. Which one of the following statements is correct?
A. Business policy is another name for long range planning
B. Strategic planning is the function of middle management
C. Operational planning is the function of top management
D. Strategic planning is largely influenced by external environment

103. The concept 'Management by Exception' implies
A. exceptional contributions by the top management
B. achievement of objectives by participation of all concerned
C. that the immediate superior has to deal with deviations only and not with details of the work assigned to the subordinate
D. that the highest officer need not worry about the results if he/she has delegated his/her authority

104. The most complex and widely used method of job evaluation is
A. the job ranking method
B. the job classification method
C. the market pricing method
D. the points method

105. Consider the following
I. Measurement
II. Projection
III. Selection
IV. Observation
V. Comparison
VI. Decision making

The correct sequence of the above ingredients of management by exceptions is
A. I, II, III, IV, V, VI　　B. I, II, III, V, IV, VI
C. I, II, III, VI, IV, V　　D. I, II, III, IV, VI, V

106. The Psychologist A.H. Maslow has developed a widely acclaimed conceptual frame work for understanding human motivation. Human needs, according to Maslow, tend to follow the classification of five categories of needs given as under:
I. Egoistic needs　　II. Safety needs
III. Social needs　　IV. Physiological needs
V. Self-fulfillment needs

These needs, according to Maslow, follow a basic hierarchical pattern from the most basic to the highest level needs as follows:
A. I, II, III, IV, V　　B. IV, II, III, I, V
C. V, IV, III, II, I　　D. I, III, II, IV, V

107. Douglas Mc Gregor made five basic assumptions about people in his theorv Y. First four assumptions are:
I. People are ambitious.
II. They seek responsibility
III. They are dynamic
IV. They recognize and accept organisational goals
The fifth assumption is
A. People are always cooperative and cheerful at their work
B. People are not self-centred
C. People are by nature resistant to change
D. People are intelligent and possess creative potential

108. Kurt Lewins' three phases of organizational change consist of
A. Unfreezing, changing, feedback
B. Changing, refreezing, feedback
C. Unfreezing, evaluation, refreezing
D. Unfreezing, changing, refreezing

109. Which one of the following statements is not correct?
A. Management by objectives is a philosophy of management
B. Management by objectives is an approach of management
C. Management by objectives is a process of participative management
D. Management by objectives is a control technique

110. Consider the following two statements and select the correct answer using the codes given below:
I. The office supervisor is concerned with the overall managerial functions of the office activities.
II. The office manager is concerned with guiding and directing the routine work assigned to his subordinates.
Codes:
A. Only I is correct
B. Only II is correct
C. Both I and II are correct
D. Neither I nor II is correct

111. Which one of the following functions does not relate to O & M Division?
A. To enlarge the organisation
B. To improve organisation
C. To simplify methods
D. To create and maintain an efficient administrative machinery

112. The traditional concept is that authority flows from top to bottom. But a new concept of authority has been developed. This is known as acceptance theory. Who is the exponent of this view?
A. Herbert A. Simon
B. Douglas Mc Gregor
C. Chester Barnard
D. Keith Davis

113. Contingency school of management says that management is
A. Practice-oriented
B. Principle-oriented
C. Result-oriented
D. Profit and loss-oriented

114. Which among the following is the oldest and simplest device for achieving coordination?
A. Hierarchy B. Planning
C. Incentives D. Rules

115. Which one among the following is an instance of participative management?
A. Board of Directors B. Trade Unions
C. Work committees D. Task force

116. Which one of the following is the correct sequence in terms of the four management functions, first identified by Henry Fayol?
A. Planning, organising, staffing and coordinating
B. Planning, organising, leading and controlling
C. Planning, motivating, directing and reporting
D. Planning, staffing, communicating and leading

117. According to behavioural scientists, organi-sation means the structure of
A. Physical facilities
B. Tasks and relationships
C. Behaviour of the management with the working force
D. Attitude of workers with the management

118. Which one of the following styles of leadership is the most effective for a job order firm?
A. Participative leadership
B. Authoritarian leadership
C. Transformational leadership
D. Free-rein leadership

119. Match List-I with List-II and select the correct answer using the codes given below the lists:

List-I	List-II
I. F.W. Taylor	1. Principles of Management
II. Maslow	2. Team work
III. Esprit decorps	3. Scientific Management
IV. Henry Fayol	4. Theory of Human Motivation

Codes :
A. I-1, II-4, III-2, IV-3 B. I-3, II-2, III-4, IV-1
C. I-1, II-2, III-4, IV-3 D. I-3, II-4, III-2, IV-1

120. The managerial function of organising involves
A. Reviewing and adjusting plan in the list of changing conditions
B. Establishing programme for the accomplishment of objectives
C. Creating a structure of functions and duties to be performed by a group
D. Getting things done through others

121. Which one of the following is the most important function of a manager?
A. Communication B. Directing
C. Supervising D. Decision making

122. Organisations require narrow span of control if there are
A. mature subordinates within
B. competent and trained managers
C. unclear plans for non-repetitive operations
D. well-defined plans for repetitive operations

123. Which among the following is the most popular approach for accomplishing the results?
A. Management by exception
B. Reward system
C. Management by objectives
D. Mentor system

124. A systematic and orderly process of determining the worth of a job in relation to other jobs is known as
A. Job analysis
B. Job evaluation
C. Job specification
D. Job description

125. Which among the following is a direct advantage of incentive compensation?
A. Mutual cooperation among the workers
B. Decrease in absenteeism
C. Increase in productivity
D. Better industrial relations

126. Among the following 'change management' methods, which one is the most appropriate when the employees are unwilling to accept change?
A. Participative method
B. Directive method
C. Leading by example
D. Negative reinforcement

127. People resist change in organisation because of
A. fear of unemployment
B. increase in responsibility
C. need for new social adjustments
D. all the above

128. The term "organisational climate" best represents
A. human environment prevailing in an organisation
B. union-management relations with an organization
C. problems introduced by faulty organisational structure
D. Socio-cultural environment in an organization

129. Which one of the following is NOT a useful tool in decision making?
A. Annual return
B. Linear programming
C. Sales forecasts
D. Operation research

130. Which one of the following indicates the correct chronological order of management approaches in the History of management thoughts?
A. Classical, Human Relations, Behavioural, Systems, Contingency
B. Contingency, Systems, Behavioural, Human Relations, Classical
C. Classical, Behavioural, Human Relations, Systems, Contingency
D. Classical, Human Relations, Behavioural, Contingency, Systems

131. David C. Mc Clelland's motivating needs are
A. Needs for power, affiliation and growth
B. Needs for affiliation, achievement and security
C. Needs for power, achievement and relatedness
D. Needs for power, affiliation and achievement

132. Which one of the following gives the correct sequence with respect to communication process?
A. Sender, Message, Encoding, Receiver, Channel, Decoding and Feedback
B. Message, Sender, Encoding, Receiver, Channel, Decoding and Feedback
C. Encoding, Message, Sender, Decoding, Feedback, Receiver and Channel
D. Sender, Message, Encoding, Channel, Receiver, Decoding and Feedback

133. Wider span of control is effective in organi-sations where
A. authority delegation is inadequate
B. tasks are complex
C. through subordinate training scheme exists
D. the leadership style is authoritarian

134. Management by Exception is to improve
A. Control over personnel
B. Strategic management
C. Steady flow of information
D. High morale

135. Job evaluation is carried on mainly for
A. identifying geographical locational factors of business enterprise
B. promoting job satisfaction
C. simplifying wage administration
D. meeting competition effectively

136. Consider the following stages of planned change:
I. Moving
II. Refreezing
III. Unfreezing

According to Kurt Lewin, the correct sequence of these is
A. I, II, III B. II, III, I
C. III, I, II D. I, III, II

137. In which one of the following, crisis management is reflected?
A. Future expansion plans of business
B. Organisation Development programme
C. Short-term manpower planning
D. Prudent managerial leadership.

138. The most important advantage of centralisation of office services is
A. specialisation
B. higher departmental loyalty
C. no delay in providing services
D. less burden of work

139. Consider the following elements:
I. Policies
II. Objectives
III. Programmes
IV. Procedures

The correct sequence of these elements in the planning process is
A. I, II, III, IV B. I, II, IV, III
C. II, I, IV, III D. II, I, III, IV

140. TQM's major emphasis is on
A. product quality
B. company profitability
C. customer delight
D. employee training

141. The approach that considers an organisation to be in a dynamic relationship with its environment, is called
A. Contingency approach
B. Scientific approach
C. Societal approach
D. Systems approach

142. Consider the following stages in Management by Exception:
I. Setting criteria that the management will use to follow progress towards organistional objectives.
II. Measurement of current performance in the organisation.
III. Making comparison of actual and planned performance and identifying the exceptions.
IV. Decision making prescribing the action to be taken
The correct sequence of these stages is
A. II, III, IV, I B. II, I, III, IV
C. I, III, II, IV D. I, II, III, IV

143. In an organisation, performance appraisal is not expected to
A. integrate and coordinate the endeavour of individuals.
B. monitor the effects of individuals
C. provide a means of correcting or commending the efforts of individuals
D. calculate the living wage of the worker

144. A collection of duties, tasks and responsibilities assigned to a single individual is
A. Occupation
B. Position
C. Job
D. Grade

145. Computerised communication system existing within an organisation is called
A. Internet
B. Extranet
C. Local Area Network
D. Intranet

146. Scalar principle of organisation implies that
A. all subordinates have only one supervisor.
B. line of authority is defined clearly.
C. manager can directly supervise only a limited number of persons.
D. the subordinates need not necessarily have a supervisor.

147. To indicate the functions of management, the catch word POSDCORB was coined by
A. Luther Gulik
B. Henry Fayol
C. Ernest Dale
D. None of the above

148. Consider the following statements.
The social responsibility of business is to:
I. do a business as per the public policy
II. obey all the rules and regulations of the Governement
III. make payment of the taxes imposed by the Governement
IV. provide not necessarily adequate but good quality of goods
Of these statements
A. II and III are correct
B. I and IV are correct
C. I, II and III are correct
D. I, II, III and IV are correct

149. The integration of different economies of the world leading to emergence of global economy is called
A. Globalization
B. Privatisation
C. Liberalisation
D. None of these

150. The process of carrying out business transaction through internet for buying and selling of products through electronic means is known as
A. Service
B. E-commerce
C. Trade
D. Core Banking

ANSWERS

1	2	3	4	5	6	7	8	9	10
B	B	D	C	B	C	D	B	A	B
11	**12**	**13**	**14**	**15**	**16**	**17**	**18**	**19**	**20**
B	D	D	C	C	D	A	D	C	C
21	**22**	**23**	**24**	**25**	**26**	**27**	**28**	**29**	**30**
D	B	C	C	B	A	C	C	D	B
31	**32**	**33**	**34**	**35**	**36**	**37**	**38**	**39**	**40**
A	C	B	A	C	D	C	B	C	A
41	**42**	**43**	**44**	**45**	**46**	**47**	**48**	**49**	**50**
C	A	B	D	A	C	D	B	D	C
51	**52**	**53**	**54**	**55**	**56**	**57**	**58**	**59**	**60**
B	C	B	C	C	B	B	D	A	C
61	**62**	**63**	**64**	**65**	**66**	**67**	**68**	**69**	**70**
A	A	C	C	A	C	B	D	D	C
71	**72**	**73**	**74**	**75**	**76**	**77**	**78**	**79**	**80**
C	D	A	C	D	C	B	B	C	B
81	**82**	**83**	**84**	**85**	**86**	**87**	**88**	**89**	**90**
C	C	C	B	B	B	B	A	D	A
91	**92**	**93**	**94**	**95**	**96**	**97**	**98**	**99**	**100**
D	A	B	C	A	C	D	D	A	C
101	**102**	**103**	**104**	**105**	**106**	**107**	**108**	**109**	**110**
B	D	A	C	A	C	D	D	C	D
111	**112**	**113**	**114**	**115**	**116**	**117**	**118**	**119**	**120**
A	D	C	B	C	A	B	A	D	C
121	**122**	**123**	**124**	**125**	**126**	**127**	**128**	**129**	**130**
B	C	C	B	C	A	D	A	A	D
131	**132**	**133**	**134**	**135**	**136**	**137**	**138**	**139**	**140**
A	D	C	B	C	C	D	A	C	A
141	**142**	**143**	**144**	**145**	**146**	**147**	**148**	**149**	**150**
D	D	A	B	D	B	A	D	A	B

●●●

9 Marketing

1. Sending an e-mail is similar to—
A. Picturing an event B. Narrating a story
C. Writing a letter D. Creating a drawing

2. Promotion in marketing means—
A. Passing an examination
B. Elevation from are grade to another
C. Selling the products through various means
D. Selling the product in specific areas

3. Sources of sales leads area—
A. Data Mining B. Market Research
C. Media Outlets D. All of these

4. One of the methods for market monitoring is—
A. To watch TV serials
B. To discuss with other sales persons
C. To monitor media outlets
D. All of these

5. Market expansion means—
A. Hiring more staff B. Buying more products
C. Buying more companies D. None of these

6. Effective marketing helps in—
A. Developing new products
B. Creating a competitive environment
C. Building demand for products
D. All of these

7. A call in marketing means—
A. To phone the customers
B. To visit the customers
C. To visit the marketing site
D. To call on prospective customers

8. Delivery channel means—
A. Maternity wards
B. Handing over the products to the buyers
C. Places where products are made available to the buyers
D. All of these

9. One of the following is a target group for the marketing of Internet Banking—
A. All the customers
B. All the educated customers
C. All the computer educated customers
D. Only creditors

10. Innovation means—
A. Product Designing B. New ideas
C. Impulse D. Both A and B

11. One of the following is a target group for the marketing of educational loan—
A. All the customers
B. Students
C. Only poor students
D. Students having promising educational tract record

12. Service after sale is not the function of—
A. Marketing staff
B. Seller
C. Director of the company
D. Employees of the company

13. Market Survey means—
A. Market planning B. Market Research
C. Marketing strategies D. Market monitoring

14. .... can be done through digital Banking.
A. Mobile Phone B. Internet
C. Telephone D. Above all

15. A good seller should have the following quality/qualities
A. Devotion to the work B. Submissive
C. Sympathy D. All of these

16. The rural marketing is not required because—
A. Rural people do not understand marketing
B. It is not practical from the cost point of view
C. It is sheer wastage of time
D. All are wrong

17. Planned-cost service means—
A. Costly products
B. Extra profit on the same cost
C. Extra work by seller
D. All of these

18. Internet marketing means—
A. Self-marketing B. Core groups monitoring
C. Employees marketing D. None of these

19. The aim of successful marketing is—
A. To increase the sale
B. To increase the profit
C. To increase the output sellers
D. Above all

20. The International Bank for Reconstruction and Development (IBRD) is better known as—
A. World Bank B. IMF
C. ADB D. It is known by its name

21. The Bank of Calcutta, Bank of Bombay and Bank of Madras were merged in 1921 to form—
A. Imperial Bank of India B. Reserve Bank of India
C. Bank of India D. Union Bank of India

22. Which of the following is known as plastic money?
A. Credit Cards B. Bearer Cheque
C. Demand Drafts D. Above all

23. Which of the following statements best describes the concept of involvement in the context of buyer behaviour?
A. The length of time involved in the buying process
B. The potential impact of a product on an individual's self-identity
C. The number of people involved in the decision-making unit
D. The complexity of an order

24. An individual is considering buying a new microwave cooker and is faced with the possibility of several models. Which of the following describes the widest range of microwave cookers, which the buyer considers in some form?
A. The choice set B. The awareness set
C. The total set D. The pre-evaluation set

25. Which of the following labels is not associated with a role in a buying Decision making unit?
A. Supplier B. Gatekeeper
C. Decision maker D. User

26. Which of the following is not an element of a marketing Information system?
A. Marketing research
B. Decision support system
C. Production monitoring system
D. None of these

27. A name, term, sign, symbol or design used to identify the products of one firm and to differentiate them from competitive offering is commonly called as—
A. Trademark B. Brand
C. Class D. None of these

28. A name, term, sign, symbol or design used to identify the products of one firm and to differentiate them from competitive offerings and also has been given legal protection and has been granted solely to its owner is called...
A. Brand B. Trademark
C. Agmark D. None of these

29. Nike is the first thing which comes to a customer's mind in Running shoe product category. This is because of—
A. Quality B. Cost
C. Brand awareness D. None of these

30. Buying decisions generally follow a pattern of over lapping stages. Which of the following best describes the typical stages of the buying process?
A. Need recognition > Information search > Evaluation > Decision > Post purchase evaluation
B. Need recognition > Evaluation > Information Search > Decision > Post purchase evaluation
C. Information search > Need recognition > Evaluation > Decision > Post purchase evaluation
D. Need recognition > Information search > Decision > Evaluation > Post purchase evaluation

31. Which among the following is true about packaging of a product?
A. Packaging helps in branding and promoting brand loyalty
B. Packaging is a major expense in marketing
C. Packaging increases marketing costs thus reducing the profits
D. None of these

32. Which among the following are most essential aspects of labelling?
A. Statutory Obligations B. Aesthetics
C. Product Promotion D. None of these

33. Which among the following affect pricing strategy of a firm?
A. Profit and Volume
B. Profit Volume and Competition
C. Profit, Volume, Competition & Prestige
D. None of these

34. Markup pricing is an example of—
A. Cost based approach
B. Buyer based approach
C. Competition based approach
D. None of these

35. Which among the following is an example of competition based pricing?
A. Firm bidding for a particular project
B. Higher price of a highly popular brand of shoe
C. 9% mark up on cost ex-factory
D. None of these

36. Which pricing approach is used to avoid the problem of overpricing and under pricing?
A. Cost based approach
B. Buyer based approach
C. Competition based approach
D. None of these

37. In the case of prestige goods the demand is—
A. Price sensitive
B. Not price sensitive
C. Not price sensitive till a level
D. None of these

38. If you are a marketing manager of a firm you would prefer the customers who are—
A. Less price sensitive
B. More price sensitive
C. Depends upon the marketing mix
D. Above all

39. Negotiation Flow in the marketing channel does not involve—
A. Wholesaler B. Transporting Company
C. Retailer D. None of these

40. Actual physical movement of the product from the manufacturers through all the parties who take physical possessions of the product from the point of production to the final consume is called as—
A. Transportation B. Product Flow
C. Marketing Channel D. None of these

41. Some people will be happy to pay a high price for anything that is new and unique. Companies use what kind of pricing strategy for this?
A. Skimming pricing B. Penetration pricing
C. Cost plus pricing D. None of these

42. Technical complexity, relatively fewer buyers and involvement of cross functional teams in both buyer and supplier firm is a characteristic of which of the following markets?
A. B2B Market (Business to Business)
B. B2C Market (Business to Consumer)
C. Both A and B
D. None of these

43. Production and consumption takes place at about the same time. This is a characteristic of—
A. Manufacturing sector B. Agriculture sector
C. Service sector D. None of these

44. Selling iron ore to a steel manufacturer comes under which of the following category?
A. Product Marketing B. Industrial Marketing
C. Consumer Marketing D. None of these

45. The tertiary sector of economy is called as—
A. Manufacturing Industry
B. Service Industry
C. Agro and Fishing Industry
D. None of these

46. Which among the following can be an example of Non-profit marketing?
A. AIDS awareness campaign
B. Setting up an ayurvedic massage center
C. Disney setting up a park in Hong Kong
D. None of these

47. Buying and selling in the marketing functions are categorized as—
A. Exchange Functions B. Facilitating Functions
C. Distribution Functions D. None of these

48. Transporting of storing come under which category of marketing functions?
A. Facilitating Functions
B. Physical Distribution Functions
C. Both A and B
D. None of these

49. FDR is—
A. Fix Date Rate B. Fixed Deposit Receipt
C. Full Date Rate D. None of these

50. NBA stands for—
A. Net Banking Assets
B. Net Book Act
C. National Banking Act
D. National Banking Association

51. Which among the following come under 'facilitating' category of marketing functions?
A. Standardising and grading
B. Standardising and grading, Finance and Risk taking
C. Standardising and grading, Financing, Risk taking, Securing Marketing Information
D. None of these

52. Which among the following is the most basic concept underlying marketing?
A. Product
B. Market
C. Needs, Wants and Demand
D. None of these

53. The need or want for a particular product becomes a demand, when—
A. The product is available
B. It is backed by buying power
C. When a product represents that particular need
D. None of these

54. A transaction that involves trading of a good with a service will come under which category?
A. Monetary Transaction B. Barter Transaction
C. Both A and B D. None of these

55. The correct 4P's of marketing are—
A. Product, Place, Promotion, Profit
B. Product, Price, Promotion, Profit
C. Product, Place, Promotion, Pricing
D. None of these

56. The place in the 4P's of marketing describes—
A. Shops and Showrooms
B. Channels of Marketing
C. The location of customers clusters
D. None of these

57. In the transportation industry, the no-frills, low-cost airlines compete with train and luxury bus services. This is an example of—
A. Direct competition among similar products
B. Direct competition among substitute products
C. Indirect competition among similar products
D. None of these

58. Which among the following terms describe the 'universal banking'?
A. Branches of Bank in all major form of the world
B. A bank providing services in all geographical territories of its country
C. A bank providing combination of commercial banking and investment banking
D. None of these

59. Which among the following is called life blood of Business?
A. Marketing B. Product
C. Finance D. None of these

60. Which among the following is not the objective of a capital budgeting?
A. Maximise profitability
B. Optimum rationing of the available funds
C. Increase sales
D. None of these

61. In the financial market, which among the following has provided the investors profitable and safe debt capital?
A. Globalisation
B. Credit Rating
C. Financial Sector Reform
D. None of these

62. Which among the following is included in marketing decisions?
A. Promotion Decisions B. Project Cost Decision
C. Finance Decision D. None of these

63. Among which of the following is related to Bank Risks?
A. Deposits B. Bank Funds
C. NPA D. None of these

64. Which among the following is a customer oriented concept?
A. Selling Concept B. Marketing Concept
C. Production Concept D. None of these

65. Social marketing concept is based upon following—
A. Large target market with active buyers
B. Customer satisfaction and customer welfare
C. Realisation of maximum profit through service of society
D. None of these

66. Opening of maximum number of ATMs is an example of—
A. Indirect Marketing B. Direct Marketing
C. Social Marketing D. None of these

67. After sales service adds to which of the following?
A. Product Utility B. Extra Sales
C. Production D. None of these

68. Maximise profits and minimize costs is a—
A. Marketing Function B. Finance Function
C. Production Function D. None of these

69. Who among the following is not a part of place in the marketing mix?
A. Wholesalers B. Retailers
C. Customers D. None of these

70. Which among the following may be called a pillar of marketing concept?
A. Customer Orientation B. Product Planning
C. Cost Budgeting D. None of these

71. Which among the following is a component of customer satisfaction?
A. Fair Price B. Profitability
C. Brand D. None of these

72. In which era of marketing history the goal was to build a better mouse trap and it was assumed that buyers will flock the seller who does it?
A. Product Era B. Production Era
C. Sales Era D. None of these

73. Which among the following is not a direct factor of marketing environment?
A. Policy of the firm
B. Marketing Distribution Channel
C. Labour Policy of the Government
D. None of these

74. Which among the following does not come under social environment of marketing?
A. Life Style B. Caste System
C. Size of Population D. None of these

75. Which among the following are called final accounts of a Bank?
A. Trading Account, Profit and Loss Account and Balance Sheet
B. Profit and Loss Account and Balance Sheet
C. Balance Sheet Only
D. None of these

ANSWERS

1	2	3	4	5	6	7	8	9	10
C	C	D	C	D	D	D	C	C	D
11	**12**	**13**	**14**	**15**	**16**	**17**	**18**	**19**	**20**
B	A	B	D	D	D	B	D	D	A
21	**22**	**23**	**24**	**25**	**26**	**27**	**28**	**29**	**30**
A	A	A	A	B	D	B	B	C	A
31	**32**	**33**	**34**	**35**	**36**	**37**	**38**	**39**	**40**
A	A	C	A	A	C	C	A	B	B
41	**42**	**43**	**44**	**45**	**46**	**47**	**48**	**49**	**50**
A	A	C	B	B	A	A	A	B	A
51	**52**	**53**	**54**	**55**	**56**	**57**	**58**	**59**	**60**
C	C	B	B	C	B	B	C	C	D
61	**62**	**63**	**64**	**65**	**66**	**67**	**68**	**69**	**70**
B	A	C	B	B	B	A	B	C	A
71	**72**	**73**	**74**	**75**					
A	A	C	C	B					

●●●

10 Computer

1. UNIVAC is:
A. Universal Automatic Computer
B. Universal Array Computer
C. Unique Automatic Computer
D. Unvalued Automatic Computer

2. CD-ROM stands for:
A. Compactable Read Only Memory
B. Compact Data Read Only Memory
C. Compactable Disk Read Only Memory
D. Compact Disk Read Only Memory

3. ALU is:
A. Arithmetic Logic Unit
B. Array Logic Unit
C. Application Logic Unit
D. None of above

4. WAN stands for:
A. Wrap Area Network
B. Wide Area Network
C. Wide Array Network
D. Wireless Area Network

5. MICR stands for:
A. Magnetic Ink Character Reader
B. Magnetic Ink Code Reader
C. Magnetic Ink Cases Reader
D. None of these

6. The ALU of a computer responds to the commands coming from:
A. Primary memory B. Control section
C. External memory D. Cache memory

7. Which printer is very commonly used for desktop publishing?
A. Laser printer B. Inkjet printer
C. Daisywheel printer D. Dot matrix printer

8. An output device that uses words or messages recorded on a magnetic medium to produce audio response is:
A. Magnetic tape
B. Voice response unit
C. Voice recognition unit
D. Voice band

9. A storage area used to store data to a compensate for the difference in speed at which the different units can handle data is:
A. Memory B. Buffer
C. Accumulator D. Address

10. Application of information technology to the typical clerical and secretarial tasks such as communication, correspondence, documenting, and filing is called:
A. Documentation B. Document generation
C. Information retrieval D. Automation

11. ………… is a method of recording and editing the spoken word in real-time for transcription and maximum intelligibility in a digital audio format:
A. Digital transcription B. Digital dictation
C. Dictation system D. Digital editing

12. VPN means:
A. Vital Private Network
B. Virtual Private Network
C. Visual Projection Node
D. None of these

13. The technique and process of searching, recovering, and interpreting information from large amounts of stored data is called:
A. Browsing B. Chatting
C. Information Retrieval D. Desktop Publishing

14. ISDN stands for:
A. Integrated Services Digital Network
B. Integrated Security Data Network
C. Information Search and Data Nesting
D. Intelligent Serving of Data Need

15. In network terminology, MAN stands for:
A. Multi Area Network
B. Main Area Network
C. Multi Application Network
D. Metropolitan Area Network

16. Which of the following is not valid version of MS Office?
A. Office XP B. Office Vista
C. Office 2007 D. None of above

17. Portrait and Landscape are:
A. Page Orientation B. Paper Size
C. Page Layout D. All of above

18. Which of the following is not a font style?
A. Bold B. Italics
C. Regular D. Superscript

19. Which of the following is graphics solution for Word Processors?
A. Clipart B. WordArt
C. Drop Cap D. All of above

20. A character that is raised and smaller above the baseline is known as:
A. Outlined
B. Raised
C. Superscript
D. Subscript

21. Thesaurus tool in MS Word is used for:
A. Spelling suggestions
B. Grammar options
C. Synonyms and Antonyms words
D. All of above

22. In word mailing list is known as:
A. Data sheet
B. Data source
C. Mail Address
D. Data list

23. Which of the following button will allow you to add, delete, or change records in your Data Source?
A. 'Data Source' button
B. 'Edit' button
C. 'Edit Data Source' button
D. 'Data editing' button

24. It is possible to ______ a data source before performing a merge.
A. Create B. Modify
C. Sort D. all of the above

25. You can merge the main document with data source in Excel. In mail merge operation, Word is usually:
A. Server B. Source
C. Client D. None

26. Each file in a MS Excel is known as:
A. Work sheet B. Data sheet
C. EX Book D. Work Book

27. In Excel Financial function, NPER is:
A. Net Permanent Earning Rate
B. Net Past Earning
C. Net Present Earning rate
D. Number of Periods

28. In Excel Financial function, PMT means:
A. Past Monitory Transaction
B. Present Money Transaction
C. Payment
D. None of these

29. .... function is used to calculate the amount paid as interest on a loan during a period of the lifetime of a loan or an investment:
A. IPMT B. ISPMT
C. NPV D. PMT

30. .... calculates the interest paid during a specific period of an investment:
A. IPMT B. ISPMT
C. NPV D. PMT

ANSWERS

1	2	3	4	5	6	7	8	9	10
A	D	A	B	A	B	A	C	B	D
11	**12**	**13**	**14**	**15**	**16**	**17**	**18**	**19**	**20**
B	B	C	A	D	B	A	D	A	C
21	**22**	**23**	**24**	**25**	**26**	**27**	**28**	**29**	**30**
C	B	C	D	C	B	C	D	C	A

●●●

11 Indian Economy

1. Which of the following is correct?
A. Reserve Bank of India Act, 1935
B. Reserve Bank of India Act, 1934
C. Reserve Bank of India Act, 1930
D. Reserve Bank of India Act, 1937

2. The Central Office of the Reserve Bank was initially established in ....
A. Indore B. Delhi
C. Calcutta D. Mumbai

3. The Central Office of the Reserve Bank of India is now located at:
A. Mumbai B. Hyderabad
C. New Delhi D. Goa

4. The Central Office of the Reserve Bank was permanently moved to Mumbai in ....
A. 1934 B. 1937
C. 1935 D. 1938

5. When RBI came into existence on April 1, 1935, it was:
A. Privately Owned
B. Governmental Owned
C. Privately + Governmental Owned
D. All are correct

6. Reserve Bank is fully owned by the Government of India since nationalization in:
A. 1950 B. 1949
C. 1965 D. 1947

7. BFS stands for:
A. Bureau of Financial Supervision
B. Board for Financial Supervision
C. Bi-lateral Financial System
D. All of these

8. Which among the following is correct about objectives of BFS?
A. To undertake cosolidated supervision of the financial sector
B. Financial Sector comprising of commercial banks, financial institutions and non-banking finance companies
C. Both of above
D. Can't Say

9. RBI does not issue:
A. One Rupee Note B. Hundred Rupee Note
C. Twenty Rupee Note D. Fifty Rupee Note

10. Which image is on back of ₹ 20 note of Mahatma Gandhi (New) series?
A. Red Fort B. Ellora Cave
C. Sanchi Stupa D. Rani Ki Vav

11. Loans provided by banks to farmers and small traders come under the category of:
A. Priority Sector Lending B. Non-profitable Loans
C. Commercial Loans D. Zero Interest Loans

12. When RBI desires to restrict expansion of credit it raises the:
A. Bank Rate
B. SLR
C. Both SLR and Bank Rate
D. Remain Constant

13. Sub Section 12AB of section 17 of RBI Act defines the term:
A. Repo Rate B. Reverse Repo Rate
C. SLR D. Bank Rate

14. Where are four regional centres of RBI located?
A. Mumbai, Kolkata, Chennai and Delhi
B. Kolkata, Chennai, Mumbai, Gujarat
C. Gujarat, Mumbai, Kolkata, Delhi
D. Either B or C

15. "INDIA's Central Bank" is a slogan of:
A. Reserve Bank of India B. State Bank of India
C. IDBI D. Bank of India

16. SLR stands for:
A. Special Liquidity Ratio
B. Special Lending Rate
C. Statutory Liquidity Ratio
D. Either A or B

17. .... is the rate of interest which is levied on long-term loans and advances taken by commercial banks from RBI.
A. Reverse Repo Rate B. Fixed Interest Rate
C. Bank Rate D. Repo Rate

18. Reserve Bank of India was nationalized in:
A. 1948 B. 1949
C. 1947 D. 1945

19. RBI is lender of last resort which reveals:
A. RBI advances money to public whenever there is any emergency
B. Commercial banks give fund to the RBI
C. RBI advances necessary credit against eligible securities to financial institutions
D. All of the above

20. Reserve Bank of India was set up on the recommendations of which of the following commission/committee?
A. D.R. Mehta Commission
B. Basel Committee
C. Royal Commission on Indian Currency and Finance
D. K. Santhanam Committee

21. The designer of Indian Rupee Sign is:
A. Hitendra Swami
B. Udaya Kumar Dharmalingam
C. Panduranga Kumarlingam
D. Either A or C

22. Financial Inclusion is:
A. Delivery of banking services at an affordable cost to weaker sections
B. Delivery of financial services at an affordable cost to weaker sections
C. Social responsibility of banking and government system
D. All of above

23. The highest denomination note of ₹ 10,000 was printed first time by RBI in:
A. 1945 B. 1938
C. 1954 D. 1952

24. Number of Language appearing on Bank notes are:
A. 18 B. 15
C. 19 D. 27

25. Where the RBI has no branch the bank which can act as its agent is?
A. Any commercial bank B. Any nationalised bank
C. SBI D. Indian bank

26. RBI issues currency notes on the basis of........... .
A. Minimum reserve B. General reserve
C. Proportional reserve D. Gold reserve

27. Which of the following is quantitative measure of credit control of RBI?
A. Direct action B. Moral suasion
C. Open market operation D. Margin requirement

28. The rate at which RBI lends short term funds to bank is:
A. Reverse repo rate B. Repo rate
C. Interest rate D. Liquidity repo rate

29. The proportion of deposits that banks have to keep with RBI is:
A. CRR B. SLR
C. PLR D. LRR

30. .... control(s) the money supply in a country
A. RBI or Central Bank B. SEBI
C. Government D. All of these

31. .... policy is taken by RBI.
A. Monetary B. Fiscal
C. Both of them D. All of these

32. Repo rate means:
A. rate at which Govt. borrows money
B. rate at which RBI lends to banks
C. rate at which RBI borrows money
D. rate at which SBI borrows money

33. Whose signature appears on Indian ₹ 500 note?
A. Finance Minister
B. RBI Governor
C. Finance Secretary
D. Chairman, Planning Commission

34. Reverse Repo Rate has the following characteristic:
A. Borrowing by RBI from banks
B. Borrowing with government security as collateral
C. Short Term Borrowing
D. All the above

35. The following is a mechanism for injecting liquidity by RBI to the financial system:
A. Reverse Repo B. Hike in CRR
C. Hike in interest rate D. Repo

36. Increasing Cash Reserve Ratio from time to time by Reserve Bank of India leads to:
A. Decrease in deposit
B. Increasing in deposit
C. Increase in lendable resources
D. Decrease in lendable resources

37. Who was the first governor of RBI?
A. Osborne Smith B. James Taylor
C. C. Deshmukh D. B.R. Rao

38. RBI was established in 1935 pursuant to recommendation of:
A. The Hilton Young Commission
B. All India Rural Credit Survey Committee
C. Gorawala Committee
D. Talwar Committee

39. One rupee note and all coins are issued by:
A. Reserve Bank of India
B. Central Government
C. Central and State Governments collectively
D. None of the above

40. Who will sign One Rupee Note?
A. Governor—RBI
B. Governors of concerned state governments
C. Finance Secretary, Ministry of Finance
D. Finance Minister

41. The term 'moral suasion' refers to:
A. The moral duty of a borrower to deal with only one bank
B. The advice given by the Reserve Bank of India to banks/financial institutions in the matter of their lending and other operations with the objective that they might implement or follow it
C. The banker's duty of secrecy as regards the affairs and accounts of his customers
D. All of the above

42. When the Reserve Bank of India (RBI) is the lender of last resort, what does it mean?
A. RBI advances money to public whenever there is any emergency
B. Commercial banks give fund to the RBI
C. RBI advances necessary credit against eligible securities
D. All of the above

43. In periods of boom, which leads to economic instability, the Reserve Bank of India (RBI) resorts to?
A. Hike in the Bank Rate as a measure of open market operations
B. Buying of approved securities in the market as a measure of open market operations
C. Sale in the market of first class securities in its possession to reduce the supply of money as a measure of open market operations
D. All of the above

44. Which of the following instruments of credit control adopted by the Reserve Bank of India (RBI) does not fall within 'general' or 'quantitative' methods of credit control?
A. Bank rate
B. Open market operations
C. Stipulation of certain minimum margin in respect of advance against specified commodities
D. Variable reserve requirements

45. The Reserve Bank of India was originally constituted as a share holder's Bank with a share capital of
A. ₹ 50 lakh B. ₹ 100 lakh
C. ₹ 10 crores D. ₹ 5 crores

46. Credit rationing is a ……….. method of credit control.
A. quantitative credit control
B. qualitative credit control
C. direct credit control
D. continuous credit control

47. The primary function of Central Bank is to……….. of the country.
A. control the system
B. regulate the monetary system
C. plan the monetary system
D. check and balance the money flow

48. Open market operation is another important …….. weapon of credit control?
A. qualitative B. normal
C. quantitative D. self kill

49. …….. is a method of credit control adopted by the modern central banks?
A. Consumer credit B. Margin requirements
C. Variable reserve ratio D. Rationing of credit

50. What is CRR?
A. Cash Reserve Ratio B. Current Ratio Rate
C. Review Report D. Credit Rating Record

51. The rate of which discounting the bills of first class banks is done by RBI is called:
A. Bank Rate B. Prime Lending Rate
C. Loan Rate D. Discounting Rate

52. Gilt edged securities refer to:
A. Government Securities
B. Securities issued by Municipal Corporations
C. Securities issued by first class companies
D. Both B and C

53. Full form of SLR:
A. Statutory Liquidity Ratio
B. State Level Recovery
C. Sundry Leverage Ratio
D. State Liquidity Reserve

54. Which one is the banker's bank?
A. RBI B. Federal Bank
C. Union Bank D. Bank of India

55. Which one is the custodian of foreign balances of country?
A. RBI B. Federal Bank
C. Union Bank D. Bank of India

56. Which one is the controller of credit?
A. RBI B. Federal Bank
C. Union Bank D. Bank of India

57. Treasury bills are issued by:
A. RBI B. IMF
C. IBRD D. IFCI

58. REPO rate was introduced in:
A. 1990 B. 1992
C. 1982 D. 1980

59. Reverse repo is introduced in:
A. January 1996 B. April 1996
C. November 1996 D. December 1996

60. India's largest commercial Bank is:
A. Bank of Baroda B. State Bank of India
C. ICICI D. Punjab National Bank

61. 'You can Always Bank on Us' is the slogan of:
A. State Bank of Mysore
B. State Bank of Hyderabad
C. State Bank of Travancore
D. State Bank of Patiala

62. Head Office of SBI is situated at:
A. Mumbai, Maharashtra B. Kolkata, West Bengal
C. New Delhi D. Chennai, Tamil Nadu

63. Original name of the State Bank of India was:
A. Bank of Calcutta B. Bank of Bengal
C. Both the Above D. Bank of Madras

64. State Bank of India comes in to existence in the year:
A. 1947 B. 1955
C. 1959 D. 1949

65. State Bank of India was formulated under:
A. SBI Act, 1957 B. SBI Act, 1959
C. SBI Act, 1955 D. SBI Act, 1949

66. PIN stands for:
A. Portable Identification Number
B. Permanent Identification Number
C. Personal Identification Number
D. Private Identification Number

67. 'Drawer' in the bank cheques is:
A. Who receives the cheques
B. Who encash the cheques
C. Who issues the cheques
D. All of these

68. 'Drawee in the bank cheque is:
A. Who rejects the payment of cheques
B. Who encash the cheques
C. Always the Banker
D. Who doesn't encase the cheques

69. "Overdrafts" covered under which of following function?
A. Accepting Deposits B. Advancing of Loans
C. Both of Above D. Rejecting Deposits

70. For the overdraft facility, customer have to pay:
A. Interest
B. Commission
C. Normal Charges
D. Compound Interest + Commission

71. The account that allows you to buy, sell as well as transact without the need of any paperwork is:
A. Simple Account B. Demat Account
C. Current Account D. Saving Account

72. KYC is:
A. Know Your Customer B. Know Your Cheque
C. Keep Your Cash D. Know Your Balance

73. A cheque which is payable to any person who presents it for payment at the bank counter is called:
A. Cross Cheque B. Bearer Cheque
C. Open Cheque D. Account Payee Cheque

74. IFSC denotes:
A. Branch Location of any Bank
B. Branch Code of any Bank
C. District Code of any Bank
D. State Code of any Bank

75. IFSC consists of:
A. 11 digits B. 14 digits
C. 12 digits D. 15 digits

76. When a Bank returns a cheque unpaid, it is called:
A. Dishonor of the Cheque
B. Cheque Bounce
C. Both Dishonor and Bounce of the Cheque
D. All of these

77. NEFT means:
A. National Electronic Funds Transfer
B. National Electronically Financial Transfer
C. Non-Electronic Fund Transfer
D. All of these

78. Interest on savings bank account now calculated by the banks on:
A. Daily Product Basis
B. Monthly Product Basis
C. Weekly Basis
D. Yearly Product Basis

79. What is White Label ATM?
A. Owned by Bank B. Owned by RBI
C. Owned by State D. None of these

80. A bank account which does not require any minimum balance is termed as:
A. Nil balance account B. Zero balance account
C. Frill account D. No Frill account

81. Bank deposits that can be withdrawn without notice are called :
A. Demand Deposits
B. Fixed Deposits
C. On Demand and Time Deposits
D. Basic Savings Deposits

82. "DD" in banking term stands for:
A. Demand Cheque B. Doordarshan
C. Demand Draft D. Daily Delivery

83. In MICR cheque, first six numbers indicates:
A. Branch Code and Location
B. City Location
C. Cheque Number
D. Account Number

84. Which of the following is a retail banking product?
A. Home Loans
B. Working capital finance
C. Corporation term loans
D. Either B or C

85. NBFCs are an important part of the Indian financial system. What is meant by this term?
A. New Banking Financial Companies
B. Non Banking Financial Companies
C. Neo Banking Financial Confederation
D. Non Banking Fiscal Companies

86. Interest payable on savings bank accounts is?
A. De-regulated by RBI
B. Regulated by State Governments
C. Regulated by Central Govt.
D. Regulated by RBI

87. AML Stands for:
A. Anti Monitory Limit
B. Anti Money Laundering
C. Always Money Laundering
D. Anytime Money Laundering

88. Expand NPA:
A. No Provision Account
B. Non Performing Asset (An asset which ceases to generate income)
C. No Profit Account
D. Non-Personal Accounts

89. The Cash Reserve Ratio is to be maintained by Commercial Banks in the form of:
A. Cash in hand at branches
B. Balance with other banks
C. Balance in a special account with RBI
D. Funds in the currency chest

90. The paid-up capital of Non-Schedule Bank is less than:
A. ₹ 5 lakh B. ₹ 10 lakh
C. ₹ 12 lakh D. ₹ 15 lakh

91. The headquarter of Bank of India is located in which of the following city?
A. Kolkata B. New Delhi
C. Mumbai D. Manipal

92. Which of the following is NOT a Nationalized Bank in India?
A. Union Bank of India B. Central Bank of India
C. Yes Bank D. Canara Bank

93. Pay order is issued by the banks for:
A. Local payments
B. Inter-state payments
C. Foreign payments
D. Bank's employee payment

94. C.R.A. in banking parlance stands for:
A. Credit Rating Association
B. Credit Rating Agency
C. Credit Risk Assessment
D. Critical Risk Assessment

95. The full form of RBS is:
A. Risk Based Supervision
B. Rating by System
C. Role Based Supervision
D. Rating Bank Security

96. Which of the following Banks are not Commercial Banks?
A. Foreign Banks B. State Cooperative Banks
C. Private Banks D. Regional Rural Banks

97. The validity of a cheque is .... months from the date of cheque.
A. 3 months B. 6 months
C. 1 month D. 12 months

98. The power of banks to create credit depends on:
A. Deposit available with them and safe ratio
B. Safe ratio only
C. Deposit available with them only
D. All the above

99. Banking Ombudsman is appointed by ....
A. Central Finance Minister
B. Reserve Bank of India
C. SEBI
D. President

100. CBS stands for:
A. Central Banking Solutions
B. Core Banking Solution
C. Code Banking Solutions
D. Cross Banking System

101. NRI deposits are called as:
A. Hot Money B. Foreign Deposits
C. NRI Funds D. Overseas Money

102. "Microcredit" refers to:
A. Installments given by farmers against loans
B. Small credit given to poor
C. Credit given by government to improve industrialization
D. Credit given by bank to NRIs

103. RRB Act was enacted in the year:
A. 1974 B. 1979
C. 1975 D. 1976

104. Regional Rural Banks have been set up with the basic objective of:
A. Providing credit to semi-urban and urban population
B. Providing deposits facilities to farmers
C. Providing credit and deposit facilities to rural areas
D. Providing credit, deposit and other banking facilities to people in rural areas

105. Regional Rural Banks are regulated by:
A. a board of directors B. the State Government
C. the sponsor bank D. Reserve Bank of India

106. Grameen Bank and Micro Credit are associated with:
A. Manmohan Singh B. Bill Gates
C. Md. Yunus D. Aung San Su Ki

107. NABARD stands for:
A. National Bank for Agriculture and Research Development
B. National Bank for Analysis of Rural Development
C. National Bank for Agriculture and Rural Development
D. National Bank for Affordable Research and Development

108. 'NABARD' came into existence on:
A. 8th July, 1982 B. 19th July, 1982
C. 12th July, 1982 D. 15 July, 1984

109. ARDC stands for:
A. Agriculture Refinance and Development Corporation
B. Agriculture Research and Development Commission
C. Agriculture Research and Development Corporation
D. Agriculture Refinance and Development Commission

110. NABARD was set up with an initial capital of ....
A. ₹ 50 Crore B. ₹ 100 Crore
C. ₹ 200 Crore D. ₹ 500 Crore

111. Headquarter of 'NABARD' is located at:
A. Mangalore, Karnataka
B. Mumbai, Maharashtra
C. New Delhi
D. Hyderabad, Andhra Pradesh

112. NABARD was established on the recommendations of:
A. Shivaraman Committee
B. Malhotra Committee
C. Kumarmangalam Committee
D. Nambiar Committee

113. NABARD was set up essentially as a development bank for promoting:
A. Agriculture Development only
B. Rural Development only
C. Urban Development only
D. Both A and B

114. Which of the following statement(s) is/are TRUE about the activities of the NABARD?
1. NABARD has the responsibility to inspect RRBs and Co-operative Banks.
2. NABARD maintains Research and Development Fund to promote research in agriculture and rural development.
3. NABARD is a wing of Planning Commission of India.

A. Only 1 B. Only 2
C. Both 1 and 2 only D. All of these

115. Which of the following statements about the NABARD is/are TRUE?
1. NABARD has a dual role to play as it is an apex body and a refinance institution.
2. NABARD services as a refinance institution for all kinds of production and investment credit to agriculture and cottage and village industries.
3. NABARD accepts short term deposits from the public like any other bank to improve its capital base.

A. Only 1 B. Only 2
C. Only 3 D. Only 1 and 2

116. NABARD is a:
A. Department of RBI
B. Wholly owned subsidiary of RBI
C. Subsidiary of SBI
D One of the above

117. When was 'Small Industries Development Bank of India' (SIDBI) established?
A. 1st April 1986 B. 1st April 1990
C. 1st April 1994 D. 1st April 1998

118. Where is the Headquarter of SIDBI?
A. New Delhi B. Mumbai
C. Kolkata D. Lucknow

119. What is the Authorised Capital of SIDBI?
A. ₹ 250 crore B. ₹ 500 crore
C. ₹ 1000 crore D. ₹ 1200 crore

120. Which of the following is a function of SIDBI?
1. Discounting and re-discounting of bills of exchange drawn on the basis of sale of machines manufactured by small industrial units.
2. Direct loan arrangement for export financing with ragard to export of goods manufactured by small industrial units.
3. Technical, legal and administrative assistance to small and large industries.

A. Only 1 B. Only 1 and 2
C. Only 1 and 3 D. 1, 2 and 3

121. Which of the following is not, by definition, equal to National Income?
A. National output B. National expenditure
C. National product D. National wealth

122. Which of the following is a transfer payment?
A. Payment made to housewife
B. Pocket allowance to children
C. Maintenance allowance to old parents
D. All of the above

123. The difference between gross domestic product and net domestic product equals:
A. Transfer payments B. Depreciation cost
C. Indirect taxes D. Subsidies

124. The best method of computing national income is
A. Product Method
B. Income Method
C. Expenditure Method
D. Combination of Income and Production Method

125. Which of the following will directly increase the GNP?
A. A rise in the market price
B. A surplus in budget
C. An increase in investment
D. A deficit in budget

126. "National dividend is that part of objective income of the community, including of course the income derived from abroad which can be measured in money." This is the remark of:
A. Marshall B. J.R. Hicks
C. David Ricardo D. A.C. Pigou

127. While calculating personal income, we have to deduct the following from private income:
A. Saving of private corporate sector and corporation tax
B. Consumption of fixed capital
C. Direct taxes paid by households
D. All of the above

128. The National income is equal to:
A. GNP – Subsides – Taxes
B. NNP – Indirect Taxes + Subsidies
C. NNP – Direct Taxes + Subsides
D. GNP – Subsidies + Taxes

129. "National income as the aggregate net product of, and the sole source of, payment for all the agents of production" has been defined by:
A. A.C. Pigou B. Alfred Marshall
C. Robbins D. Dusenbery

130. "The labour and capital of a country acting upon its natural resources produce annually a certain net aggregate of commodities, material and immaterial including services of all kinds." This definition of National Income is given by:
A. Adam Smith B. Lionel Robbins
C. John Stuart Mill D. Alfred Marshall

131 The total income earned in any given year by the owners of productive resources is measured by:
A. Personal Income B. Disposable Income
C. Gross National Product D. National Income

132. In calculating a country's GNP at market prices one of the following is not included:
A. Wages and salaries before tax
B. Indirect taxes
C. Bonds to the employees
D. Depreciation allowances

133. An example of double counting in national income would be:
A. Wages of bus and train drivers
B. Cotton output and cotton cloth output
C. Electricity output and water output
D. Tax receipts and earnings of inland revenue officials

134. Double counting must be avoided when calculating national income. This means that there must be a deduction of the value of:
A. Food subsidies
B. Personal consumption of alcoholic drinks
C. Transfer payments
D. Net interest from abroad

135. Which of the following is counted in determining GNP?
A. A do it yourself roof repair job
B. A housewife's work at home
C. An operation performed in a hospital
D. Vegetables grown by a farmer for his own use

136. Among these statements which one clearly explains the meaning of "Subsidies"?
A. Payment by Government for purchase of goods and services
B. Payment by business enterprises to factors of production
C. Payment by companies to shareholders
D. Payment by Government to business enterprises without buying any goods and services

137. The difference between Gross National Product and Gross Domestic Product is equal to:
A. Gross Domestic investment
B. Net Foreign investment
C. Net imports
D. Net factor income from abroad

138. Net domestic product at factor cost equals net domestic product at market prices:
A. Plus subsidies – indirect taxes
B. Minus subsidies + indirect taxes
C. Minus subsidies
D. Plus indirect taxes

139. When gross investment is positive, net investment:
A. is the highest
B. is zero
C. is positive
D. can be either positive or negative

140. National product is not affected by which of the following?
A. Sale of a second hand automobile by A to B
B. Sale of a new car by an automobile dealer
C. Sale of a new car by an automobile company
D. Sale of a new car on hire purchase

141. Net foreign investment is equal to:
A. Total amount of foreign investment in a country
B. Investment by foreigners during a particular year
C. Investment by local resident in a foreign country
D. Investment by the foreigners in this country minus investment by residents of this country in foreign countries during a given time period

142. "Disposable income" does not include:
A. Business transfer payments
B. Social security benefits
C. Corporate dividends
D. Personal income taxes

143. Circular flow of income in a two sector sector model implies:
A. Payments from households to firms and back again
B. Payments from firms to firms
C. Payments from households to house-holds
D. Payments from households to firms

144. Which one of the following is not a Transfer Payment in National Income accounting?
A. Interest on government bonds held by indians
B. Drought relief payments
C. Unemployment benefits
D. Salaries of supreme court judges

145. Which one of the following is a transfer income?
A. The salary of an M.P.
B. Company dividends to shareholders
C. Rents from house property
D. Unemployment allowance

146. The smallest national income accounting aggregte is usually:
A. PI B. GNP
C. DPI D. NI

147. Which one of the following is not induded in calculating gross national product of an economy?
A. Wages and salaries before tax
B. Depreciation allowances
C. Indirect taxes
D. Subsidies

148. Interest on the national debt is included in:
A. NNP B. GNP
C. Personal income D. National income

149. Double counting has the effect of:
A. Underestimating national product
B. Overestimating national product
C. Distorting national product
D. Misleading conclusions about national income

150. The Government sector's contribution to GNP is measured by:
A. Government purchases of goods and services
B. Wages and salaries paid by the government
C. Inter-governmental surplus
D. The size of the government surplus

151. Depreciation means:
A. Destruction of a plant in a fire accident
B. Loss of equipment over time due to wear and tear
C. Closure of the plant due to raw material problem
D. Closure of the plant due to lockout

152. Depreciation is the loss of value of:
A. Capital assets B. Stocks
C. Intermediate goods D. Final goods

153. GNP is ₹ 600 crores and NNP is ₹ 475 crores: therefore depreciation is:
A. ₹ 100 B. ₹ 175
C. ₹ 50 D. ₹ 125

154. Which of the following is not true?
A. GNP – Depreciation = NNP
B. GNP = GDP + Net income from abroad
C. NNP_{FC} = NNP_{MP} + Subsidies – Indirect taxes
D. GNP = NNP – Depreciation

155. NNP at market prices and NNP at factor costs will be equal when there is:
A. No direct tax
B. No indirect tax
C. No subsidy
D. No indirect tax and no subsidy

156. Gross domestic product at factor cost plus net income from abroad minus capital consumption is equal to:
A. Gross domestic product at market prices
B. Gross national product at factor cost
C. Net national product at market prices
D. Net national product at factor cost

157. In a closed economy model one of the sectors below is not to be considered which?
A. Households B. Firms
C. Government D. Foreign trade

158. National product at market prices is higher then national product at factor cost by the amount of:
A. Subsidies
B. Indirect taxes
C. Indirect taxes plus subsides
D. Indirect taxes minus subsidies

159. Net exports are negative when:
A. Net investment is positive
B. Exports are exceeded by imports
C. Exports exceed private transfer to foreignous
D. Imports are exceeded by exports

160. Which of the following formula could be used for calculating the per capita income of a country?
A. $\frac{\text{Total family income}}{\text{Number of family members}}$
B. $\frac{\text{National Income}}{\text{Total Population}}$
C. $\frac{\text{Total income of various industries}}{\text{Total number of industrial workers}}$
D. $\frac{\text{Total government revenue}}{\text{Total population}}$

161. Per capita income increases when:
A. GNP increases at the same rate as population
B. GNP increases slower than population
C. GNP increases faster than population
D. GNP does not increase and population increases slowly

162. This year, if national product at factor cost is ₹ 600 crores, indirect taxes ₹ 200 crores and subsidies ₹ 75 crores, national product at market prices is:
A. ₹ 750 crores B. ₹ 725 crores
C. ₹ 500 crores D. ₹ 250 crores

163. Which one of the following measures does not include final goods and services?
A. GNP B. NNP
C. Disposable income D. National income

164. National product at current prices is higher than national product at constant prices during a period of:
A. Rising prices B. Falling prices
C. Stable prices D. Changing costs

165. Which of the following items are not included in estimating National income or NNP_{FC}?
A. Salary income of artists, dancers and singers
B. Income of smugglers
C. Payments to form workers in foodgrains
D. Payments of bank interest for capital borrowed

166. The purchase of a new home is included in the GNP as a part of:
A. Capital consumption allowance
B. Personal consumption expenditures
C. Investment
D. Personal saving

167. Expenditure on defence is an item of:
A. Private investment B. Public investment
C. Private consumption D. Public consumption

168. National income at constant prices can be found out by
A. $\frac{\text{Price index number}}{\text{N.I. at current prices}} \times 100$
B. $\frac{\text{N.I. at current prices}}{\text{Price index number}} \times 100$

C. $\frac{\text{N.I. at market prices}}{\text{Price index number}} \times 100$

D. $\frac{\text{N.I. at factor cost}}{\text{Price index number}} \times 100$

169. For a closed economy having no foreign trade which one of the following is correct?
A. GDP = GNP B. GDP > GNP
C. GDP < GNP D. GDP $\gtrless$ GNP

170. Which of the following statements explain the difference between NNP (Net National Product) and NMP (Net Material Product)?
1. NNP includes services 2. NNP excludes services.
3. NMP includes services 4. NMP excludes services.
Select the correct answer using the codes given below.
Codes :
A. 1 and 4 B. 2 and 4
C. 1 and 3 D. 2 and 3

171. The GNP gap is the gap between:
A. GNP and NNP
B. GNP and depreciation
C. GNP and GDP
D. Potential and actual GNP

172. National income at market price is equal to:
A. the sum of wages, interest, rent and profits earned
B. national income at factor cost *plus* indirect taxes minus subsidies
C. the sum of earnings of all the factors *plus* direct tax *minus* subsidies
D. total quantity of goods and services produced

173. Which of the following prevents national income from falling to zero when gross investment falls to zero?
A. consumption B. multiplier
C. accelerator D. none of the above

174. In India, the main source of national income is:
A. Primary sector B. Secondary sector
C. Tertiary sector D. Foreign sector

175. Consider the following statemets:
1. At the time of rising prices, NNP at current prices is less than NNP at constant prices.
2. At the time of rising prices, NNP at current prices is higher than NNP at constant prices.
3. NNP at current prices and NNP at constant prices are always same irrespective of changes in prices.
4. NNP at current prices is equal to NNP at constant prices at the time of stable prices.
Which of these statements are correct?
A. 1 and 2 B. 1 and 3
C. 2 and 3 D. 2 and 4

176. Gross Domestic Product is the monetary value of:
A. stock of goods and services
B. all final goods and services produced in a year
C. goods produced for the market only
D. goods produced for the market and for self consumption

177. National Income estimates in India is prepared by:
A. Planning Commission B. RBI
C. Finance Ministry D. C.S.O.

178. Which one of the following committees was set up to review the concept of poverty line?
A. S. Chakravarty Committee
B. K.N. Wanchoo Committee
C. D.T. Lakdawala Committee
D. R.C. Dutt Committee

179. According to 2011 census the state having highest urban population is:
A. U.P. B. Maharashtra
C. Tamil Nadu D. Kerala

180. The book 'Politics with Charkha' is written by:
A. Ashok Mehta B. J.B. Kriplani
C. K.G. Mashruwala D. Morarji Desai

181. The base year of the present Wholesale Price Index (WPI) is:
A. 2011-12 B. 1971-72
C. 1980-81 D. 1981-82

182. The base year of present Consumer Price Index (CPI) for industrial labourers is:
A. 1980 B. 1981
C. 1982 D. 1985

183. CAPART is related with:
A. Assisting and evaluating rural welfare programmes
B. Computer hardware
C. Consultant service of export promotion
D. Controlling pollution in big industries

184. SEBI was established in:
A. 1993 B. 1992
C. 1988 D. 1990

185. The working of SEBI includes:
A. To regulate the dealings of share market
B. To check the foul dealings in share market
C. To control the inside trading of shares
D. All of these

186. Rural women can avail the benefit of Mahila Samriddhi Yojana if they open their account in:
A. Rural Post Offices
B. Commercial Banks
C. Rural Development Bank
D. Any of the above

187. Pradhan Mantri Gram Sadak Yojana (PMGSY) was launched in:
A. 2000 B. 1999
C. 2001 D. 2004

188. The Headquarter of CAPART is situated at:
A. Mumbai B. Kolkata
C. New Delhi D. Bangalore

189. Which one of the following method is not used by N.S.S.O. for the measurement of unemployment in India?
A. Current Monthly Status B. Current Weekly Status
C. Current Daily Status D. Usual Principal Status

190. National Rural Development Institute is situated at:
A. Shimla B. Hyderabad
C. Patna D. New Delhi

191. Which statement of the following is false (according to literacy data of 2011 census)?
A. Literacy rate was calculated among people having age 6 years or above
B. During 2001-2011, the number of literate population increased
C. Indian literacy rate was estimated to be 73%
D. Kerala was cent-per cent literate state

192. Which pair is not correct?
A. EXIM Bank—Financing for export-import
B. RBI—Banker's bank
C. IDBI—Industrial finance
D. FCI—Financial assistance to commercial institutions

193. Which sector has the maximum quantum of disguised unemployment in India?
A. Agriculture B. Industry
C. Trade D. Transport

194. 'Food for work programme' was renamed as:
A. RLEGP B. IRDP
C. NREP D. MNP

195. Employees State Insurance Scheme in India was introduced in:
A. 1947 B. 1952
C. 1955 D. 1972

196. The CSO has changed the base year for national income estimates. The new base year is:
A. 1990-91 B. 2011-2012
C. 1994-95 D. 1995-96

197. Which state possesses the maximum percentage of SC population?
A. U.P. B. M.P.
C. Kerala D. Punjab

198. Kutir Jyoti Scheme is associated with:
A. Promoting cottage industry in villages
B. Promoting employment among rural unemployed youth
C. Providing electricity to rural families living below the poverty line
D. All of these

199. Which of the following represents the correct combination of sex-ratio in India in 1951 and 2011?
A. 941, 933 B. 946, 943
C. 946, 927 D. 972, 933

200. TRYSEM was:
A. a modern technique of agriculture production
B. a code used in space science
C. a programme to train rural youth for self employment
D. None of these

201. When development in economy takes place the share of tertiary sector in National Income?
A. Declines B. Increases
C. Remains constant D. First rises and then falls

202. National Income in India is estimated by:
A. NITI Aayog
B. Finance Commission
C. Indian Statistical Institute
D. Central Statistical Organisation

203. Population Density means:
A. No. of persons living per sq. km.
B. No. of persons living per kilometre
C. Ratio of population living below poverty line to total population
D. No. of persons in a village

204. Which sector got high rate of growth in its co-operative units?
A. Sugar B. Cotton Textile
C. Jute D. Cement

205. The first fully literate district outside the Kerala State is:
A. Wardhaman (West Bengal)
B. Chingelpattu (Tamil Nadu)
C. Nasik (Maharashtra)
D. Merkata (Karnataka)

206. Indian State having the lowest Infant Mortality Rate is:
A. Maharashtra B. Goa
C. Gujarat D. Kerala

207. The main objective of TRYSEM was:
A. To train rural youth for self employment
B. To train urban youth for self employment
C. Both of the above
D. None of these

208. The largest source of National Income in India is:
A. Service Sector B. Agriculture
C. Industrial Sector D. Trade Sector

209. Which state has the lowest women literary rate in India (2011 census)?
A. Bihar B. Jharkhand
C. U.P. D. Rajasthan

210. The State having the highest literacy rate among woman in India is:
A. Tamil Nadu B. Kerala
C. West Bengal D. Maharashtra

211. Which state has the highest per capita income?
A. Punjab B. Goa
C. Maharashtra D. Gujarat

212. According to 2011 census, per 1000 male female number is:
A. 939 B. 959
C. 943 D. 927

213. Under Prime Minister's Integrated Urban Poverty Eradication Programme (PMI-UPEP) those urban areas were included which had a population:
A. Upto 50,000
B. Between 50,000 and 1 Lakh
C. Between 50,000 to 5 Lakh
D. None of these

214. Name a Poverty Eradication Programme in which Banks played the dominant role:
A. IRDP B. MNP
C. Rojgar Bima Yojana D. Jawahar Rojgar Yojana

215. SJSRY belongs to:
A. Urban areas B. Rural areas
C. Semi-urban areas D. All of these

216. According to 2011 census, Indian Population was:
A. 98.7 crore B. 100.0 crore
C. 121.08 crore D. 105.7 crore

217. Which Union Territory ensured Lowest Population in 2011 census?
A. Delhi B. Chandigarh
C. Puducherry D. Lakshadweep

218. The Headquarter of Asian Development Bank (ADB) is at:
A. Singapore B. Manila
C. Hong Kong D. Tokyo

219. Which Indian plan ensured high growth rate as compared with targetted growth rate?
A. Fifth Plan B. Fourth Plan
C. Second Plan D. Eighth Plan

220. **Assertion (A):** Fiscal deficit is greater than budgetary deficit.
Reason (R): Fiscal deficit is the borrowing from the Reserve Bank of India plus other liabilities of the government to meet its expenditure.
A. Both A and R are true and R is the correct explanation of A
B. Both A and R are true, but R is not a correct explanation of A
C. A is true, but R is false
D. A is false, but R is true

221. One major proposal of New Industrial Policy was:
A. NRIs will not be allowed for capital investment in India
B. All types of industries have been made licence free
C. Import restrictions of technical knowhow for one year
D. Facility of direct foreign investment upto 51% in high priority industries.

222. The field given to Rangarajan Committee was:
A. Modernisation of Cloth Industry
B. To probe Share scam
C. To probe Sugar scam
D. To suggest measures for controlling BOP deficit

223. NITI Aayog was constituted in:
A. 1948 B. 1949
C. 2015 D. 1951

224. Kelkar Committee report is related on:
A. Tax Reforms B. Financial Sector Reforms
C. Trade Reforms D. Administrative Reforms

225. Which committee recommended tax on Agriculture Holdings?
A. Bhootlingam Committee
B. Wanchoo Committee
C. Raj Committee
D. None of these

226. MRTP is related to:
A. Monopoly and trade restrictions
B. Inflation control
C. Transport control
D. Foreign Exchange Regulations

227. The industry having the largest investment in Indian Economy is:
A. Tea B. Cement
C. Steel D. Jute

228. R.N. Malhotra Committee gave recommendations on the field of:
A. Sick Industries B. Tax Reforms
C. Insurance Sector D. Banking Sector

229. What is 'Hawala'?
A. Full details of a subject
B. Illegal transactions of foreign exchange
C. Illegal trading of shares
D. Tax evasion

230. MRTP Act was implemented since:
A. 1970 B. 1968
C. 1969 D. 1967

231. Which of the following statements is correct?
A. The public sector was given a dominant position in the newly Independent India
B. The foreign trade policy post Independence allowed free trade of all goods and services
C. Monetary policy post Independence sought to keep the CRR at a very low level.
D. None of the above

232. All of the following developments were noticed during 1991 (when economic reforms were enforced) except one. Identify it.
A. National debt was nearly 60 per cent of the GNP of India
B. Inflation crossed double digits
C. Foreign reserves were maintained at a very high level
D. None of the above

233. Which of the following statement is correct about the New Industrial Policy, 1991?
A. It made it compulsory for the industry to obtain license for all projects

B. It abolished licensing for all projects except 18 industries of strategic and security importance
C. It gave dominant position to the public sector
D. None of the above

234. At present only ______ industries are reserved for the public sector.
A. 5 B. 7
C. 8 D. 2

235. At present there are only _____ industries for which licensing is compulsory.
A. 18 B. 5
C. 10 D. 9

236. At present, 100 per cent FDI is allowed in ______.
A. defence
B. drugs and pharmaceuticals
C. banks
D. None of these

237. In private banking ____ per cent FDI is allowed now.
A. 100 B. 49
C. 74 D. 26

238. As a result of the New Industrial Policy, 1991:
A. Prior approval of central government is required for establishing new undertakings, and expanding the present undertaking
B. An industry intending to have more than 100 crore of assets is required to obtain the permission of the central government
C. Prior approval of central government for establishing new undertakings and expanding existing undertaking is not required
D. Two or more companies deciding to amalgamate are required to take the prior approval of the central government

239. Which of the following is also known as International Bank for Reconstruction and Development?
A. IMF B. RBI
C. WTO D. World Bank

240. As a result of the New Industrial Policy, 1991:
A. The public sector has been stripped off all its power
B. The public sector has been given the commanding heights of the economy
C. The public sector's portfolio will be reviewed with greater realism. The focus will be on strategic high tech and essential infrastructure industries
D. The public sector's management has been passed over to the private sector

241. In the pre-reform period, the banking sector:
A. Functioned in a highly regulated environment
B. Functioned in a manner detrimental to the general public
C. Concentrated on making huge profits
D. None of the above

242. Which of the following is correct in relation to banks in the post-reform period?
A. Bank rate has been increased to 20 per cent
B. CRR has been increased to 20 per cent
C. Public sector banks have been asked to raise their funds from their private resources only
D. None of the above

243. Which of the following statements is correct with regard to external sector in the prereform period?
A. The foreign trade policy was very liberal; it allowed import of all types of goods
B. Import of foodgrains was strictly prohibited
C. The balance of payments situation was quite comfortable
D. None of the above

244. Which of the following statements is correct with regard to external sector in the post reform period?
A. Quantitative restrictions have been imposed on a number of tradable items
B. Quantitative restrictions have been removed on most of the items except a few goods
C. The tariff walls have been further raised
D. Foreign investment is now being discouraged

245. FERA stands for:
A. Foreign Export Revaluation Act
B. Funds Exchange Resources Act
C. Finance and Export Regulation Association
D. Foreign Exchange Regulation Act

246. FEMA stands for:
A. Foreign Exchange Management Act
B. Funds Exchange Management Act
C. Finance Enhancement Monetary Act
D. Future Exchange Management Act

247. As a result of the foreign trade reforms:
A. The number of import licenses has increased
B. Only a few types of goods and services can now be exchanged freely
C. EPCG scheme has been abolished
D. The average tariff rates have been reduced

248. All of the following statements except one are correct about the Foreign Trade Policy, 2004-09. Identify the incorrect statement:
A. Certain thrust areas like agriculture, handlooms, handicrafts etc. were identified
B. Vishesh Krishiupaj Yojana was started
C. 'Served from India' scheme was started
D. The entry of FDI in India was restricted

249. DFEC stands for:
A. Direct Foreign Exchange Control
B. Direct Finance Exchange Control
C. Duty Free Export Credit
D. Duty Free Exchange Credit

250. EPCG stands for:
A. Export Promotion Capital Goods
B. Expert Programme for Credit Generation
C. Exchange Programme for Consumer Goods
D. Export Promotion Consumer Goods

251. FIEO stands for:
A. Foreign Import Export Organisation
B. Federation of Import Export Organisation
C. Forum of Indian Export Organisations
D. Federation of Indian Export Organisations

252. Fiscal policy means:
A. Policy relating to money and banking in a country
B. Policy relating to public revenue and public expenditure
C. Policy relating to non-banking financial institutions
D. None of the above

253. The unsustainable levels of government deficits in the late 80's can be attributed to:
A. High levels of government expenditures
B. Insufficient revenues
C. Poor returns on government investments
D. All of the above

254. CENVAT stands for:
A. Common Entity Value Added Tax
B. Corporate Entities Value Added Tax
C. Central Value Added Tax
D. None of the above

255. The FRBMA stands for:
A. Foreign Regulation and Budget Management Act
B. Fiscal Responsibility and Budget Management Act
C. Finance Regulations and Bonds Management Association
D. Funds Reallocation and Budget Management Act

256. The FRBMA, 2003 emphasises on:
A. Revenue-led fiscal consolidation
B. Better expenditure outcomes
C. Rationalisation of tax regime
D. All of the above

257. The economic reforms have failed to:
A. Keep fiscal deficits to the targeted levels
B. Fully implement industrial deregulation
C. Fully open the economy to trade
D. All of the above

258. Obtaining of Industrial License is compulsory for all of the below sector except:
A. Clothes
B. Specified Hazardous chemicals
C. Electronic aerospace
D. Cigarettes of tobacco

259. Before financials reforms, the banking system was characterised by all of the following except:
A. Administered interest rates structure
B. Quantitative restrictions on credit flow
C. High revenue requirements
D. Keeping very less lendable resources for the priority sector

260. WTO stands for:
A. World Trade Organisation
B. World Transport Organisation
C. World Tariff Organisation
D. Women Teachers Organisation

261. _____________ refers to relaxation of previous government restrictions.
A. Privatisation B. Globalisation
C. Disinvestment D. Liberalisation

262. ________ refers to the transfer of assets or services functions from public to private ownership.
A. Globalisation B. Privatisation
C. Disinvestment D. Liberalisation

263. ________ refers to disposal of public sector's units in equity in the market.
A. Globalisation B. Privatisation
C. Disinvestment D. Liberalisation

264. The pre-condition for privatisation to be successful requires
A. Liberalisation and de-regulation of the economy
B. Capital markets should be sufficiently developed
C. None of the above
D. A & B Both

265. Which of the following statements regarding privatisation is correct?
A. Privatisation is panacea for all economic problems
B. Privatisation always leads to attaining social and economic efficiency
C. Privatisation may result in lopsided development of industries in the country
D. None of the above

266. Privatisation in India has taken place in all of the cases except:
A. CMC B. BALCO
C. VSNL D. None of the above

267. Which of the following statements is correct?
A. The disinvestment programme has been successfully carried out in India
B. Privatisation up to 100 per cent has been carried out in all the PSUs in India
C. Under majority disinvestment approach, the government sells a major share to a strategic buyer
D. None of the above

268. _____________ means integrating the domestic economy with the world economy.
A. Globalisation B. Privatisation
C. Liberalisation D. Disinvestment

269. Which committee was constituted for reforms in tax-structure?
A. Narsimhan Committee B. Chelliah Committee
C. Gadgil Committee D. Kelkar Committee

270. Which of the following pairs is not correctly matched?
A. WTO—Generally forbids the use of quantitative restrictions on trade
B. IMF—Provides finance to correct disequilibrium in balance of payments
C. RBI—Promotes trade among South Asian countries
D. IBRD—Gives long term loans for development

ANSWERS

1	2	3	4	5	6	7	8	9	10
B	C	A	B	A	B	B	B	A	B
11	**12**	**13**	**14**	**15**	**16**	**17**	**18**	**19**	**20**
A	A	B	A	A	C	C	B	C	C
21	**22**	**23**	**24**	**25**	**26**	**27**	**28**	**29**	**30**
B	D	B	B	C	A	C	B	A	A
31	**32**	**33**	**34**	**35**	**36**	**37**	**38**	**39**	**40**
A	B	B	D	D	D	A	A	B	C
41	**42**	**43**	**44**	**45**	**46**	**47**	**48**	**49**	**50**
B	C	B	C	D	B	B	C	C	A
51	**52**	**53**	**54**	**55**	**56**	**57**	**58**	**59**	**60**
A	A	A	C	A	A	A	B	C	B
61	**62**	**63**	**64**	**65**	**66**	**67**	**68**	**69**	**70**
B	A	C	B	C	C	C	C	B	A
71	**72**	**73**	**74**	**75**	**76**	**77**	**78**	**79**	**80**
B	A	B	B	A	A	A	A	D	B
81	**82**	**83**	**84**	**85**	**86**	**87**	**88**	**89**	**90**
A	C	C	A	B	A	B	B	C	A
91	**92**	**93**	**94**	**95**	**96**	**97**	**98**	**99**	**100**
C	C	A	A	A	B	A	A	C	B
101	**102**	**103**	**104**	**105**	**106**	**107**	**108**	**109**	**110**
A	B	D	D	D	C	C	C	A	B
111	**112**	**113**	**114**	**115**	**116**	**117**	**118**	**119**	**120**
B	A	D	D	D	D	B	D	C	B
121	**122**	**123**	**124**	**125**	**126**	**127**	**128**	**129**	**130**
D	D	B	D	C	D	A	B	B	D
131	**132**	**133**	**134**	**135**	**136**	**137**	**138**	**139**	**140**
D	D	B	C	C	D	D	A	D	A
141	**142**	**143**	**144**	**145**	**146**	**147**	**148**	**149**	**150**
D	D	A	D	D	C	B	C	B	A
151	**152**	**153**	**154**	**155**	**156**	**157**	**158**	**159**	**160**
B	A	B	D	D	D	D	D	D	B
161	**162**	**163**	**164**	**165**	**166**	**167**	**168**	**169**	**170**
C	B	C	A	B	C	D	B	A	A
171	**172**	**173**	**174**	**175**	**176**	**177**	**178**	**179**	**180**
D	B	A	C	D	B	D	C	B	B
181	**182**	**183**	**184**	**185**	**186**	**187**	**188**	**189**	**190**
A	A	A	C	D	A	A	C	D	B
191	**192**	**193**	**194**	**195**	**196**	**197**	**198**	**199**	**200**
D	D	A	C	B	B	D	C	B	C
201	**202**	**203**	**204**	**205**	**206**	**207**	**208**	**209**	**210**
B	D	A	C	A	D	A	A	A	B
211	**212**	**213**	**214**	**215**	**216**	**217**	**218**	**219**	**220**
B	D	B	A	A	C	D	B	D	A
221	**222**	**223**	**224**	**225**	**226**	**227**	**228**	**229**	**230**
D	C	C	A	C	A	C	C	B	A
231	**232**	**233**	**234**	**235**	**236**	**237**	**238**	**239**	**240**
A	C	B	D	C	B	C	C	C	C
241	**242**	**243**	**244**	**245**	**246**	**247**	**248**	**249**	**250**
A	D	D	B	D	A	D	D	C	A
251	**252**	**253**	**254**	**255**	**256**	**257**	**258**	**259**	**260**
D	B	D	C	B	D	D	A	D	A
261	**262**	**263**	**264**	**265**	**266**	**267**	**268**	**269**	**270**
D	B	C	C	C	D	C	A	B	C

●●●

हिंदी

व्याकरण

व्याकरण वह शास्त्र है जिसके द्वारा किसी भी भाषा के शब्दों और वाक्यों के शुद्ध स्वरूपों एवं शुद्ध प्रयोगों का ज्ञान कराया जाता है।

व्याकरण के चार अंग हैं : (i) वर्ण विचार (ii) शब्द विचार (iii) पद विचार और (iv) वाक्य विचार

भाषा : भाषा अभिव्यक्ति का एक ऐसा साधन है जिसके द्वारा मनुष्य अपने विचारों को दूसरों पर प्रकट कर सकता है और दूसरों के विचार जान सकता है। भाषा के दो रूप हैं–(i) मौखिक और (ii) लिखित।

बोली : भाषा का क्षेत्रीय रूप बोली कहलाता है।

लिपि : किसी भी भाषा के लिखने की विधि को लिपि कहते हैं।

वर्ण : हिन्दी भाषा में प्रयुक्त सबसे छोटी ध्वनि वर्ण कहलाती है। जैसे–अ, आ, ई, क्, ख्, आदि

वर्णमाला : वर्णों के समुदाय को वर्णमाला कहते हैं। हिन्दी वर्णमाला में 44 वर्ण हैं। जिनमें 11 स्वर तथा 33 व्यंजन हैं।

स्वरवर्ण : उन वर्णों को कहते हैं, जिनका उच्चारण बिना किसी दूसरे वर्ण की सहायता से होता है। हिन्दी में 11 स्वर हैं–अ, आ, इ, ई, उ, ऊ, ए, ऐ, ओ, औ, ऋ।

व्यंजन वर्ण : उन वर्णों को कहते हैं, जिनका उच्चारण स्वर वर्णों की सहायता के बिना नहीं हो सकता है। इनकी संख्या 33 है–

क ख ग घ ड़ च छ ज झ ञ ट ठ

ड ढ़ ण त थ द ध न प फ ब भ

म य र ल व श ष स ह।

वर्ण : एक या अधिक वर्णों से बनी हुई स्वतन्त्र सार्थक ध्वनि शब्द कहलाती है।

शब्दों को तत्सम, तद्भव, देशज और विदेशी भागों में बाँटा जाता है।

तत्सम : जो शब्द संस्कृत भाषा से हिन्दी में बिना किसी परिवर्तन के लिए जाते हैं वे तत्सम कहलाते हैं, जैसे– अग्नि, क्षेत्र, मित्र, नासिका आदि।

तद्भव : उन शब्दों को कहते हैं, जो संस्कृत से ही लिए गए हैं, परन्तु हिन्दी में आने पर जिनका रूप बदल गया है। जैसे–आग, खेत, रात आदि।

देशज : उन शब्दों को कहते हैं, जो बोलचाल तथा देश की अन्य भाषाओं से लिए गए हैं। जैसे–कटोरा, झंझत, डिबिया, लोटा आदि।

विदेशज या विदेशी : उन शब्दों को कहते हैं, जो किसी विदेशी भाषा से आए हैं। जैसे–स्कूल, कार, कमरा, खुदा, जोश, सरकार आदि।

शब्द सम्पदा

तत्सम शब्दों के तद्भव रूप

तत्सम	तद्भव	तत्सम	तद्भव
अग्नि	आग	अद्य	आज
अष्ट	आठ	अक्षि	आँख
अर्ध	आधा	अस्थि	हड्डी
अश्रु	आँसू	आम्र	आम
ग्राम	गाँव	गर्दभ	गधा
गृध्र	गीध	गौर	गोरा
गृह	घर	घट	घड़ा
धातु	धात	धृत	घी
लक्ष	लाख	सप्त	सात
त्वम्	तुम	दुग्ध	दूध
रत्न	रतन	वर्ष	बरस
भक्त	भगत	मर्कट	बन्दर
रात्रि	रात	उलूक	उल्लू
अन्धकार	अन्धेरा	क्षीर	खीर
निद्रा	नींद	पृष्ठ	पीठ
ज्येष्ठ	जेठ	स्वर्ण	सोना
श्वास	साँस	काक	काग
कार्य	काज	कर्ण	कान

तत्सम	तद्भव	तत्सम	तद्भव
पाद	पाँव	हस्त	हाथ
नासिका	नाक	कंटक	काँटा
दश	दस	दधि	दही
दीप	दीया	निद्रा	नींद
नव	नौ	पत्र	पत्ता
प्रस्तर	पत्थर	जिह्वा	जीभ
हस्ती	हाथी	दन्त	दाँत
क्षेत्र	खेत	नृत्य	नाच
सूचिका	सूई	स्वर्णकार	सुनार
लोक	लोग	पर्यड़्क	पलंग
स्वप्न	सपना	कातर	कायर
पुत्र	पूत	मानव	मनुष्य
शत	सौ	पुष्प	फूल
पक्व	पक्का	कृषक	किसान
कर्म	कार्य	आम्र	आम
कर्ण	कान	अष्ट	आठ
घंटिका	घंटी	चन्द्र	चन्द
यव	जौ	धूम्र	धुआँ

विराम चिह्न

विराम का अर्थ रुकना। अपने विचारों को ठीक ढंग से प्रकट करने के पढ़ते अथवा लिखते समय हमें कुछ रुकना पड़ता है। इस प्रकार के रुकने को विराम कहते हैं।

प्रत्येक-विराम के लिए अलग-अलग चिह्न हैं–

पूर्ण विराम	[।]
अल्प विराम	[,]
अर्ध विराम	[;]
प्रश्न बोधक	[?]
विस्मयादि बोधक	[!]
योजक	[–]
उद्धरण	[" "]

कारक

कारक शब्द उस रूप को कहते हैं, जिससे संज्ञा या सर्वनाम वाक्य के साथ सम्बन्ध जाना जाता है। जैसे–शीला कलम **से** लिखती है।

यह सीमा **की** पुस्तक है।

कारक के भेद विभक्ति चिह्नों सहित

कारक	**विभक्ति**
कर्त्ता	ने
कर्म	को
करण	से
सम्प्रदान	के लिए
अपादान	से
सम्बन्ध	का, के, की
अधिकरण	में, पर
सम्बोधन	हे, अरे!

पर्यायवाची शब्द

जिन शब्दों से एक समान अर्थ का बोध होता है, उन्हें पर्यायवाची या समानार्थी शब्द कहते हैं।

कुछ पर्यायवाची शब्दों के उदाहरण निम्नलिखित हैं–

आग – अग्नि, अनल, पावक, हुताशन, ज्वाला।
आकाश – नभ, आसमान, गगन, लोभ।
असुर – राक्षस, दानव, निशाचर, दैत्य।
अमृत – अभिय, पीयूष, सुधा, सोम।
अन्धकार – अन्धेरा, तिमिर, तम, तमिस्त्र।
आँख – नेत्र, नयन, लोचन, चक्षु, दृग।
कमल – जलज, पंकज, नीरज, राजीव।
इन्द्र – सुरपति, देवेन्द्र, सुरेन्द्र, देवेश।
ईश्वर – प्रभु, भगवान, जगदीश, दीनबन्धु।
पक्षी – खग, विहग, चिड़िया, नभचर।
बादल – घन, जलधर, वारिद, नीरद।
गंगा – सुरसरि, जाह्नवी, त्रिपथगा, देवनदी, विष्णुपदी।
चन्द्रमा – शशि, मयंक, निशाकर, सुधाकर, सुधांशु, सोम हिमांशु, राकेश।
जल – पानी, नीर, लोभ, अम्बु, सलिल, क्षीर, वारि।
फूल – पुष्प, कुसुम, सुमन, प्रसून, सारंग।
पृथ्वी – भू, भूमि, धरा, वसुन्धरा, वसुधा, धरती क्षमा, लोक।
कपड़ा – पट, वस्त्र, चीर, अम्बर, दुकूल।
घर – गृह, गेह, निकेतन, आलय, निलय, भवन, शाला, धाम, सदन।
जंगल – वन, कानन, अरण्य, विपिन।
तालाब – सरोवर, ताल, जलाशय, तड़ाग।
दिन – दिवस, वासर, वार।
पहाड़ – गिरि, पर्वत, गूधर, नग, महीधर, मेरू।
पत्थर – पहाड़, प्रस्तर, पाहन।
पवन – वायु, समीर, हवा, मारुत, अनिल।
पुत्र – सुत, तनय, पूत, आत्मज।
बिजली – तड़ित, चपला, दामिनी।
वृक्ष – तरू, रूख, विटप, पेड़।
मनुष्य – नर, मानव, मनुज, आदमी।
हाथी – करि, हस्ती, गज।
मित्र – सखा, मीत, सहचर, दोस्त।
राजा – नरेश, नृप, महीप, भूप।
समुद्र – सागर, सिन्धु, जलधि, नीरधि।
सरस्वती – शारदा, वागेश्वरी, भारती, महाश्वेता।
साँप – पन्नग, सर्प, विषधर, अहि, व्याल।
सूर्य – दिनकर, दिवाकर, रवि, भानु, भास्कर।
स्त्री – नारी, महिला, दारा, वामा।
शरीर – देह, तन, काया, गात, बदन।
गणेश – गजानन, गणपति, विनायक, एकदन्त, गजवदन लम्बोदर, विघ्न नाशक।
घोड़ा – तुरंग, बाजि, हय, अश्व, घोटक।
युद्ध – समर, रण, संग्राम।
सिंह – केसरी, मृगराज, केहरी।
शत्रु – अरि, रिपु, बैरी।
विष्णु – हरि, कमलेश, रमापति, चक्रपाणि, केशव, माधव, पीताम्बर।
कोष – खजाना, भण्डार, निधि।
धन – दौलत, द्रव्य, मुद्रा।

तलवार – कृपाण, असि, खड्ग।
अंग – भाग, हिस्सा, अवयव।
चोर – तस्कर, दस्यु, रजनीचर।
पत्नी – भार्या, दारा, गृहिणी।
पुत्र – तनय, सुत, लड़का, बेटा।
पुत्री – तनया, सुता, लड़की, बेटी।
माता – जननी, अम्बा, अम्बिका, अम्मा, माँ, धात्री।
मोर – शिखी, नीलकण्ठ, मयूर।
मृत्यु – मौत, काल, देहान्त।
रक्त – रुधिर, शोणित, खून, लहू।
विष – जहर, हलाहल, गरल।
सोना – कंचन, स्वर्ण, कनक।
हृदय – उर, छाती, वक्ष, वक्षस्थल, हिय, हिया।
सभा – अधिवेशन, परिषद्, बैठक, महासभा, समागम, समिति, सम्मेलन।
यमुना – कालिन्दी, कृष्णा, जमुना, रविसुता तरणि-तनुजा।

विलोम-शब्द

शब्दों के अपने निश्चित अर्थ होते हैं। उन अर्थों के विपरीत अर्थ देने वाले शब्द को विलोम-शब्द कहते हैं।

शब्द	विलोम	शब्द	विलोम
अमृत	विष	उदार	संकीर्ण
अनुकूल	प्रतिकूल	अनुराग	विराग
आदि	अन्त	उत्थान	पतन
इच्छा	अनिच्छा	उचित	अनुचित
अल्पायु	दीर्घायु	अनुज	अग्रज
उन्नति	अवनति	आकाश	पाताल
अधिक	न्यून	आयात	निर्यात
एक	अनेक	अन्धकार	प्रकाश
अर्थ	अनर्थ	उदय	अस्त
परकीया	स्वकीया	जड़	चेतन
जय	पराजय	अनिवार्य	वैकल्पिक
नकद	उधार	अपेक्षा	उपेक्षा
उपस्थित	अनुपस्थित	आदर	अनादर
अन्धेरा	उजाला	अपना	पराया
उत्तम	अधम	आय	व्यय
सुपुत्र	कुपुत्र	स्वाधीन	पराधीन
आहार	निराहार	कठोर	कोमल
दाता	याचक	दोषी	निर्दोषि
खेद	प्रसन्नता	धनी	निर्धन
निकट	दूर	चर	अचर
देव	दानव	खरा	खोटा
गरीब	अमीर	प्रेम	घृणा
जीवन	मृत्यु	बुरा	भला
सजीव	निर्जीव	मित्र	शत्रु
सुगन्ध	दुर्गन्ध	मौखिक	लिखित
संक्षेप	विस्तार	कटु	मधुर
आरम्भ	अन्त	कड़वा	मीठा
कृतज्ञ	कृतघ्न	दिन	रात
साक्षर	निरक्षर	पवित्र	अपवित्र
पाप	पुण्य	जल	थल
धीर	अधीर	निर्मल	मलिन

शब्द	विलोम	शब्द	विलोम
गुण	अवगुण	नश्वर	अनश्वर
निन्दा	स्तुति	भारी	हल्का
मनुष्यता	पशुता	सरस	नीरस
मान	अपमान	क्रय	विक्रय
धर्म	अधर्म	गहरा	उथला
गुरु	शिष्य	पक्ष	विपक्ष
जन्म	मृत्यु	बन्धन	मुक्ति
यश	अपयश	ज्ञान	अज्ञान
आदर	अनादर	पूर्ण	अपूर्ण
सफल	असफल	शान्त	अशान्त
कीर्ति	अपकीर्ति	वादी	प्रतिवादी
आस्तिक	नास्तिक	स्वदेश	परदेश
सज्जन	दुर्जन	राग	द्वेष
ऊसर	उर्वर	उदार	कृपण
अगला	पिछला	अगम	सुगम
अग्नि	जल	अति	अल्प
अर्थ	अनर्थ	अतल	वितल
अत्यधिक	स्वल्प	अद्यः	उपरि
अधिकतम	न्यूनतम	अतिवृष्टि	अनावृष्टि
अनाथ	सनाथ	ईश्वर	जीव
अनुलोम	विलोम	अर्पण	ग्रहण
अवनि	अम्बर	अस्त	उदय
आकर्षण	विकर्षण	आगे	पीछे
आजाद	गुलाम	आदान	प्रदान
आधुनिक	प्राचीन	आना	जाना
आय	व्यय	आयात	निर्यात
आवश्यक	अनावश्यक	आशा	निराशा
आस्था	अनास्था	इहलोक	परलोक
उच्च	निम्न	उत्थान	पतन
उपकार	अपकार	उपयोग	दुरुपयोग
एकता	अनेकता	कल	आज
कृत्रिम	प्राकृत	कृष्ण	शुक्ल
कपूत	सपूत	कोमल	कठोर
गगन	धरा	ज्ञान	अज्ञान

लिंग

लिंग का अर्थ है 'चिह्न'। लिंग शब्द उस चिह्न को कहते हैं जिससे वस्तु के पुरुष या स्त्री होने की कल्पना हो। लिंग दो प्रकार के होते हैं—(1) पुल्लिंग (2) स्त्रीलिंग

पुल्लिंग—पुल्लिंग संज्ञा के उस रूप को कहते हैं जिससे उसके पुरुष होने का ज्ञान होता है। जैसे—राम, श्याम, घोड़ा, हाथी, कुत्ता आदि। **स्त्रीलिंग**—स्त्रीलिंग संज्ञा के उस रूप को कहते हैं जिससे उसके स्त्री होने का ज्ञान हो। जैसे—भैंस, गाय, बकरी, सीता, रमा इत्यादि।

पुल्लिंग	स्त्रीलिंग	पुल्लिंग	स्त्रीलिंग
इन्द्र	इन्द्राणी	मेहतर	मेहतरानी
नौकर	नौकरानी	जेठ	जेठानी
देवर	देवरानी	सेठ	सेठानी
पण्डित	पण्डिताइन	ओझा	ओझाइन
बनिया	बनियाइन	दुबे	दुबाइन
हलवाई	हलवाइन	चौबे	चौबाइन
गुरु	गुरुआइन	लड़का	लड़की
दास	दासी	कबूतर	कबूतरी
हिरण	हिरणी	क्षत्रिय	क्षत्राणी
मुगल	मुगलानी	हिन्दू	हिन्दुआनी
चौधरी	चौधरानी	भव	भवानी
लाला	ललाइन	पण्डा	पण्डाइन
ठाकुर	ठकुराइन	बाबू	बबुआइन
घोड़ा	घोड़ी	गूँगा	गूँगी
बच्चा	बच्ची	चाचा	चाची
बकरा	बकरी	मामा	मामी
मुर्गा	मुर्गी	साला	साली
चींटा	चींटी	रस्सा	रस्सी
देव	देवी	ब्राह्मण	ब्राह्मणी
बेटा	बेटी	बूढ़ा	बुढ़िया
चूहा	चुहिया	डिब्बा	डिबिया
गुड्डा	गुड़िया	कुम्हार	कुम्हारिन
सुनार	सुनारिन	नाती	नातिन
जुलाहा	जुलाहिन	दर्जी	दर्जिन
पापी	पापिन	हाथी	हथिनी

पुल्लिंग	स्त्रीलिंग	पुल्लिंग	स्त्रीलिंग
पिता	माता	बैल	गाय
कवि	कवयित्री	विधुर	विधवा
बाप	माँ	बादशाह	बेगम
नर	मादा	मर्द	औरत
युवक	युवती	वर	वधू
सम्राट्	सम्राज्ञी	साढू	साली
फूफा	बुआ	पुत्र	पुत्री
पहाड़	पहाड़ी	गोप	गोपी
गधा	गधी	तरुण	तरुणी
नर्तक	नर्तकी	बेटा	बिटिया
बछड़ा	बछिया	चिड़ा	चिड़िया
बन्दर	बन्दरिया	कुत्ता	कुतिया
नाई	नाइन	धोबी	धोबिन
ग्वाला	ग्वालिन	भंगी	भंगिन
स्वामी	स्वामिनी	विद्वान्	विदुषी
साधु	साध्वी	पुरुष	स्त्री
पति	पत्नी	वीर	वीरांगना
साहब	मेम	सास	ससुर
मियाँ	बीबी	राजा	रानी
बिलाड़	बिल्ली	अनुज	अनुजा
छात्र	छात्रा	महोदय	महोदया
प्रिय	प्रिया	मामा	मामी
लोटा	लुटिया	मोर	मोरनी
शेर	शेरनी	जाट	जाटिन
डाक्टर	डाक्टरनी	मालिक	मालकिन
माली	मालिन	बाघ	बाघिन
हाथी	हथिनी	स्वामी	स्वामिनी
बालक	बालिका	धनवान	धनवती
धावक	धाविका	नेता	नेत्री
गुणवान	गुणवती	नर	मादा
अभिनेता	अभिनेत्री	प्राचार्य	प्राचार्या
प्रबन्धकर्ता	प्रबन्धकर्ती	दाता	दात्री
ननदोई	ननद	अध्यापक	अध्यापिका

वचन

शब्द के जिस रूप से उसके एक अथवा अनेक होने का बोध हो, उसे वचन कहते हैं।

हिन्दी में दो वचन होते हैं—

(1) एकवचन और (2) बहुवचन

एकवचन—शब्द के जिस रूप से एक ही वस्तु का बोध हो, उसे एकवचन कहते हैं। जैसे—लड़का, गाय, बकरी, घोड़ा, राम, सीता आदि।

बहुवचन—शब्द के जिस रूप से अनेकता का बोध हो उसे बहुवचन कहते हैं। जैसे—लड़के, कपड़े, गायें आदि।

एकवचन	बहुवचन	एकवचन	बहुवचन
लड़का	लड़के	कौवा	कौवे
बेटा	बेटे	कमरा	कमरे
कपड़ा	कपड़े	बहन	बहनें
चीज	चीजें	गधा	गधे
रुपया	रुपये	घोड़ा	घोड़े
नहर	नहरें	रात	रातें
बात	बातें	सड़क	सड़कें
दाना	दाने	लोटा	लोटे
पैसा	पैसे	पुस्तक	पुस्तकें
कन्या	कन्याएँ	वधू	वधुएँ
नारी	नारियाँ	लड़की	लड़कियाँ
मुर्गा	मुर्गे	घण्टा	घण्टे
गद्दा	गद्दे	हीरा	हीरे
बच्चा	बच्चे	प्याला	प्याले
छाता	छाते	गाय	गायें
कथा	कथाएँ	कविता	कविताएँ
बहू	बहुएँ	टोपी	टोपियाँ
नाली	नालियाँ	बेटा	बेटे
ताला	ताले	जूता	जूते

एकवचन	बहुवचन	एकवचन	बहुवचन
डिबिया	डिबियाँ	नाक	नाकें
पूँछ	पूँछें	मूँछ	मूँछें
चिड़िया	चिड़ियाँ	सरिता	सरिताएँ
बालिका	बालिकाएँ	चाभी	चाभियाँ
कहानी	कहानियाँ	दरवाजा	दरवाजे
कलम	कलमें	कुटिया	कुटियाँ
रानी	रानियाँ	नाई	नाइयों
माता	माताएँ	बाल	बालों
हाथ	हाथों	मुख	मुख
कोट	कोट	दाँत	दाँतों
नाखून	नाखूनों	पैर	पैरों
बैल	बैलों	माली	मालियों
राजा	राजाओं	पिता	पिता
चन्द्रमा	चन्द्रमा	कवि	कवियों
मुनि	मुनियों	कौआ	कौए
छात्रा	छात्राएँ	सेना	सेनाएँ
दिशा	दिशाएँ	गुड़िया	गुड़ियाँ
मेज	मेजें	भैंस	भैंसें
अंगूर	अंगूरों	समुद्र	समुद्र

अनेक शब्दों के लिए एक शब्द

जिसकी कोई उपमा न हो : **अनुपम**
तेज बुद्धि वाला : **कुशाग्रबुद्धि**
कल्पना से परे हो : **कल्पनातीत**
जो उपकार नहीं मानता है : **कृतघ्न**
जो उपकार मानता है : **कृतज्ञ**
किसी की हँसी उड़ाना : **उपहास**
ऊपर कहा हुआ : **उपर्युक्त**
ऊपर लिखा हुआ : **उपरलिखित**
जिस पर उपकार किया गया हो : **उपकृत**
इतिहास का ज्ञाता : **इतिहासज्ञ**
आलोचना करने वाला : **आलोचक**
ईश्वर में आस्था रखने वाला : **आस्तिक**
बिना वेतन का : **अवैतनिक**
जो कहा न जा सके : **अकथनीय**
जो गिना न जा सके : **अगणित**
जिसका कोई शत्रु ही न जन्मा हो : **अजातशत्रु**
जिसके समान कोई दूसरा न हो : **अद्वितीय**
जो परिचित न हो : **अपरिचित**
आकाश में उड़ने वाला : **नभचर**
जो टुकड़े-टुकड़े हो गया हो : **खण्डित**

मछली की तरह आँखों वाली : **मीनाक्षी**
मयूर की तरह आँखों वाली : **मयूराक्षी**
बच्चों के लिए काम की वस्तु : **बालोपयोगी**
जिसकी बहुत अधिक चर्चा हो : **बहुचर्चित**
जिस स्त्री को कभी सन्तान न हुई हो : **बन्ध्या (बाँझ)**
फेन से भरा हुआ : **फेनिल**
प्रिय बोलने वाली स्त्री : **प्रियम्वदा**
जिसकी उपमा न हो : **निरुपम**
जो थोड़ी देर पहले पैदा हुआ हो : **नवजात**
जिसका कोई आधार न हो : **निराधार**
नगर में वास करने वाला : **नागरिक**
रात में घूमने वाला : **निशाचर**
ईश्वर में विश्वास न रखने वाला : **नास्तिक**
माँस न खाने वाला : **निरामिष**
बिल्कुल बर्बाद हो गया : **ध्वस्त**
जिसकी धर्म में निष्ठा हो : **धर्मनिष्ठ**
देखने योग्य : **दर्शनीय**
बहुत तेज चलने वाला : **द्रुतगामी**
जो किसी पक्ष में न रहे : **तटस्थ**
तत्त्व को जानने वाला : **तत्त्वज्ञ**

तप करने वाला	: **तपस्वी**
जिसे देखकर डर लगे	: **डरावना**
जो जन्म से अन्ध हो	: **जन्मान्ध**
जीने की प्रबल इच्छा	: **जिजीविषा**
जिसने इन्द्रियों को जीत लिया हो	: **जितेन्द्रिय**
चिन्ता में डूबा हुआ	: **चिन्तित**
जो बहुत समय तक ठहरे	: **चिरस्थायी**
जिसकी चार भुजाएँ हों	: **चतुर्भुज**
जिसके हाथ में चक्र हों	: **चक्रपाणि**
जिससे घृणा की जाए	: **घृणित**
जिसे गुप्त रखा जाए	: **गोपनीय**
गणित ज्ञाता	: **गणितज्ञ**
आकाश को चूमने वाला	: **गगनचुम्बी**
जिसका आदि न हो	: **अनादि**
जो कुछ न जानता हो	: **अज्ञ**
जो अनुकरण करने योग्य हो	: **अनुकरणीय**
जिसका अन्त न हो	: **अनन्त**
जो कभी न मरे	: **अमर**
जो कम बोलता हो	: **अल्पभाषी**
जिसका इलाज न हो	: **लाइलाज**
जिसका कोई नाथ न हो	: **अनाथ**
कम जानने वाला	: **अल्पज्ञ**
जहाँ जाना सम्भव न हो	: **अगम**
बड़ा भाई	: **अग्रज**
कम खाने वाला	: **अल्पाहारी**
जो बात पहले कभी न हुई हो	: **अभूतपूर्व**
दूसरों के पीछे चलने वाला	: **अनुचर**
जो पहले न पढ़ा हो	: **अपठित**
जिसके आर-पार दिखाई देता हो	: **पारदर्शी**
आज्ञा पालन करने वाला	: **आज्ञाकारी**
काम से जी चुराने वाला	: **कामचोर**
प्रतिदिन होने वाला	: **दैनिक**
जिसका कोई अर्थ न हो	: **निरर्थक**
हाथ से लिखा हुआ	: **हस्तलिखित**
आँखों के सामने होने वाला	: **प्रत्यक्ष**
जिसका आचरण अच्छा हो	: **सदाचारी**
वह पुरुष जिसकी पत्नी मर गई हो	: **विधुर**
वह स्त्री जिसका पति मर गया हो	: **विधवा**
जिसका रूप अच्छा न हो	: **कुरूप**
सदा सत्य बोलने वाला	: **सत्यवादी**
बड़ी इमारत के टूटे-फूटे भाग	: **खण्डहर**
प्रशंसा के योग्य	: **प्रशंसनीय**
जहाँ अनाथ रहते हों	: **अनाथालय**
प्रत्येक मास होने वाला	: **मासिक**
जहाँ पानी के जहाज आकर रुकते हैं	: **बन्दरगाह**
प्रत्येक सप्ताह होने वाला	: **साप्ताहिक**
प्रत्येक वर्ष होने वाला	: **वार्षिक**
जो कठिनाई से मिले	: **दुर्लभ**
जिसका आकार हो	: **साकार**
जिसका आकार न हो	: **निराकार**
जो कभी बूढ़ा न हो	: **अजर**
बहुत बोलने वाला	: **वाचाल**
पृथ्वी पर रहने वाला	: **थलचर**
जल में रहने वाला	: **जलचर**
नभ में विचरण करने वाला	: **नभचर**
जल-थल दोनों में रहने वाला	: **उभयचर**
जिसमें रस न हो	: **नीरस**
पढ़ने वाला	: **पाठक**
जो भाषण देता हो	: **वक्ता**
जो साथ में पढ़ता हो	: **सहपाठी**
जिसके नीचे रेखा खींची हो	: **रेखांकित**
जानने की इच्छा रखने वाला	: **जिज्ञासु**
जिसकी कोई सन्तान न हो	: **निःसन्तान**
जिसका कोई मूल्य न हो	: **अमूल्य**
जो वन में घूमता हो	: **वनचर**
जो इस लोक के बाहर की बात हो	: **अलौकिक**
जो इस लोक की बात हो	: **लौकिक**
जिसका सम्बन्ध पश्चिम से हो	: **पाश्चात्य**
जो स्थिर रहे	: **स्थावर**
दुःखान्त नाटक	: **त्रासदी**
ज्ञान देने वाली	: **ज्ञानदा**
भूत, वर्तमान भविष्य को देखने वाला	: **त्रिकालदर्शी**
जो क्षमा के योग्य हो	: **क्षम्य**
हिंसा करने वाला	: **हिंसक**
हित चाहने वाला	: **हितैषी**
सब कुछ जानने वाला	: **सर्वज्ञ**
जो स्वयं पैदा हुआ हो	: **स्वयंभू**
जो शरण में आया हो	: **शरणागत**
जिसका वर्णन न किया जा सके	: **वर्णनातीत**
व्याकरण जानने वाला	: **वैयाकरण**
रचना करने वाला	: **रचयिता**
खून से रंगा हुआ	: **रक्तरंजित**
अत्यन्त सुन्दर स्त्री	: **रूपसी**
कीर्तिमान पुरुष	: **यशस्वी**

महत्त्वपूर्ण शब्दों की भाववाचक संज्ञा

शब्द	भाववाचक संज्ञा	शब्द	भाववाचक संज्ञा	शब्द	भाववाचक संज्ञा	शब्द	भाववाचक संज्ञा
दास	दासता	क्षत्रिय	क्षत्रियत्व	अहं	अहंकार	अपना	अपनापन
पशु	पशुता	बालक	बालकपन	व्यक्ति	व्यक्तित्व	मीठा	मिठास
बन्धु	बन्धुत्व	मित्र	मित्रता	गरीब	गरीबी	सफल	सफलता
बूढ़ा	बुढ़ापा	सती	सतीत्व	बुरा	बुराई	स्वस्थ	स्वास्थ्य
सेवक	सेवा	शिशु	शैशव	सरल	सरलता	कंजुस	कंजुसी
अपना	अपनत्व	पराया	परायापन	कमजोर	कमजोरी	हरा	हरियाली
पण्डित	पाण्डित्य	पुरुष	पुरुषत्व	गर्म	गर्मी	मोटा	मोटाई
ब्राह्मण	ब्राह्मणत्व	बच्चा	बचपन	चालाक	चालाकी	गम्भीर	गम्भीरता
प्रभु	प्रभुता	नारी	नारीत्व	पढ़ना	पढ़ाई	लिखना	लिखाई
देव	देवत्व	लड़का	लड़कपन	थकना	थकावट	लिखना	लिखावट
मनुष्य	मनुष्यता	दानव	दानवता	लूटना	लूट	लड़ना	लड़ाई
निज	निजता	स्व	स्वत्व	हँसना	हँसी	आप	अपनत्व

महत्त्वपूर्ण शब्दों के विशेषण

शब्द	विशेषण	शब्द	विशेषण	शब्द	विशेषण	शब्द	विशेषण
अंक	अंकित	अर्थ	आर्थिक	वन	वन्य	विष्णु	वैष्णव
इतिहास	ऐतिहासिक	उदासी	उदास	शहर	शहरी	तप	तपस्वी
कलंक	कलंकित	कुसुम	कुसुमित	जापान	जापानी	तेज	तेजस्वी
जटा	जटिल	भार	भारी	तत्त्व	तात्त्विक	दया	दयालु
बनारस	बनारसी	बाजार	बाजारू	देव	दैविक	निंदा	निंदक
प्यास	प्यासा	पुराण	पौराणिक	नव	नवीन	पोषण	पोषक
पंक	पंकित	पक्ष	पाक्षिक	पेट	पेटू	पाप	पापी
धन	धनी	दो	दूसरा	पूजा	पूज्य	भूख	भूखा
तीन	तीसरा	झगड़ा	झगड़ालू	फेन	फेनिल	भारत	भारतीय
ठण्ड	ठण्डा	जाति	जातीय	माया	मायावी	रंग	रंगीन
काँटा	कँटीला	विदेश	विदेशी	विष	विषैला	श्री	श्रीमान
रोज	रोजाना	भूगोल	भौगोलिक	सुर	सुरीला	विवाह	वैवाहिक
पीड़ा	पीड़ित	पुत्र	पुत्रवान	आदर	आदरणीय	ऋण	ऋणी
आलस्य	आलसी	अंतर	आंतरिक	किताब	किताबी	क्रम	क्रमिक
ईर्ष्या	ईर्ष्यालु	कर्म	कर्मठ	ग्राम	ग्रामीण	घर	घरेलू
करुणा	कारुणिक	कृपा	कृपालु	चतुर	चतुरता	जँहर	जहरीला
गुण	गुणी	जल	जलमय	सप्ताह	साप्ताहिक	अनुभव	अनुभवी
जीव	जैविक	तट	तटस्थ	ओज	ओजस्वी	कल्पना	काल्पनिक
तर्क	तार्किक	धर्म	धार्मिक	कुल	कुलीन	गाँव	गँवार
नमक	नमकीन	पत्थर	पथरीला	चमक	चमकीला	चाचा	चचेरा
पल्लव	पल्लवित	पान	पनवाड़ी	दीन	दीनता	नगर	नागरिक
मुख	मुखर	मिठास	मीठा	नागपुर	नागपुरी	परिवार	पारिवारिक
मास	मासिक	मद	मादक	पुष्प	पुष्पित	पिता	पैतृक
रक्त	रक्तिम	रस	रसीला	फ्रांस	फ्रांसीसी	बाहर	बाहरी

शब्द	विशेषण	शब्द	विशेषण
भय	भयभीत	मधु	मधुर
मौन	मौनी	मन	मानसिक
मानव	मानवीय	रक्षा	रक्षक
रघु	राघव	रोग	रोगी
वर्ष	वार्षिक	शक्ति	शक्तिशाली
श्रम	श्रमिक	अंत	अंतिम
कागज	कागजी	मर्म	मार्मिक
शब्द	शाब्दिक	अज्ञान	अज्ञानी
गुलाब	गुलाबी	प्रकृति	प्राकृतिक
परिचय	परिचित	पूजा	पुजारी
रोग	रोगी	ग्राम	ग्रामीण
सुगंध	सुगंधित	मैं	मेरा
जो	जैसा	आप	आप-सा
तुम	तुम्हारा	कौन	कैसा
वह	वैसा	पढ़ना	पढ़ाकू

शब्द	विशेषण	शब्द	विशेषण
गाना	गायक	बेचना	बिकाऊ
भागना	भगोड़ा	वन्द	वन्दनीय
चलना	चलती	घूमना	घुमक्कड़
चलना	चालू	मरना	मरियल
भूलना	भुलक्कड़	पीछे	पिछला
भीतर	भीतरी	नीचे	निम्न
अणु	आणविक	अधिकार	आधिकारिक
अनुभव	अनुभवी	अन्याय	अन्यायी
अपमान	अपमानित	अभ्यास	अभ्यासी
अवश्य	आवश्यक	आदि	आदिम
आयु	आयुष्मान्	उदय	उदित
उपज	उपजाऊ	एकता	एक
अंत	अंतिम	कुल	कुलीन
खर्च	खर्चीला	खून	खूनी
गुण	गुणी		

श्रुतिसम भिन्नार्थक शब्द

शब्द	अर्थ	शब्द	अर्थ
आदि	आरम्भ	आदी	अभ्यस्त
कुल	वंश	कूल	किनारा
अरि	शत्रु	अरी	सम्बोधन
अगम	दुर्गम	आगम	शास्त्र
अयश	अपकीर्ति	अयस्क	लोहा
अपेक्षा	चाहना, तुलना में	उपेक्षा	निरादर
अनिल	हवा	अनल	आग
अवधि	काल, समय	अवधी	अवध की भाषा
आयात	बाहर से आना	आयत	एक आकृति
चिर	पुराना	चीर	कपड़ा
तनु	पतला	तनू	पुत्र, गाय
तरंग	लहर	तुरंग	घोड़ा
दारा	स्त्री	द्वार	दरवाजा
दूत	संदेशवाहक	द्यूत	जुआ
जलद	बादल	जलज	कमल
प्रदीप	दीपक	प्रतीप	उल्टा
प्रसाद	कृपा	प्रासाद	महल
पास	निकट	पाश	बन्धन
द्विप	हाथी	द्वीप	टापू
देव	देवता	दैव	भाग्य
नीर	जल	नीड़	घोंसला
पवन	वायु	पावन	पवित्र

शब्द	अर्थ	शब्द	अर्थ
बन्द	खुला नहीं	बद	बुरा
पथ	रास्ता	पथ्य	रोगी का भोजन
पुर	नगर	पूर	बाढ़
भवन	महल	भुवन	संसार
लक्ष्य	उद्देश्य	लक्ष	लाख
सर	तालाब	शर	बाण
सर्ग	अध्याय	स्वर्ग	एक लोक
कर्म	कार्य	क्रम	सिलसिला
चिता	शव जलाने के लिए लकड़ियों का ढेर	चीता	बाघ
शव	लाश	शब	रात
शस्त्र	हथियार	शास्त्र	ग्रन्थ
श्रवण	सुनना	श्रमण	बौद्ध संन्यासी
मत	विचार	मत्त	मस्त
शोक	दुःख	शौक	चाव
ग्रह	नक्षत्र	गृह	घर
कपट	धोखा	कपाट	दरवाजा
उपयुक्त	ठीक	उपर्युक्त	ऊपर कहा गया
सुत	बेटा	सूत	धागा
शूर	वीर	सूर	अंधा
श्याम	कृष्ण	शाम	संध्या
दिन	वार	दीन	गरीब
कटिबद्ध	तैयार रहना	करबद्ध	हाथ जोड़ना

अनेकार्थक शब्द

शब्द	विभिन्न अर्थ	शब्द	विभिन्न अर्थ
अंक	संख्या, गोद	द्विज	पक्षी, ब्राह्मण
अक्षर	वर्ण, ईश्वर	तीर	किनारा, बाण
पानी	जल, प्रतिष्ठा	प्रकृति	स्वभाव, कुदरत
अचल	पवर्त, स्थिर	पत्र	चिट्ठी, पत्र
आम	फल, सामान्य	पद	पैर, उपाधि
अंबर	वस्त्र, आकाश	फल	परिणाम, फल
अवस्था	आयु, दशा	तनु	पतला, कोमल
उत्तर	दिशा, जबाव	वर्ण	रंग, जाति
विधि	तरीका, भाग्य	हल	समाधान, खेत जोतने का साधन
कर	हाथ, टैक्स	अशोक	राजा, वृक्ष
कनक	सोना, धतुरा	आभीर	अहीर, एक राग
गुरु	श्रेष्ठ, शिक्षक	एकाक्ष	काना, कौआ
हान	भारी हथौड़ा, बादल	खल	दुष्ट, खलिहान
जड़	मूर्ख, मूल	घट	घड़ा, हृदय
कल	मशीन, आनेवाला कल, चैन	जलज	कमल, मछली
सुर	देवता, स्वर	हेम	सोना, जल

सामान्य अशुद्धियाँ

अशुद्ध	शुद्ध	अशुद्ध	शुद्ध	अशुद्ध	शुद्ध	अशुद्ध	शुद्ध
दुनियां	दुनिया	श्रीमति	श्रीमती	अनुग्रहीत	अनुगृहीत	बृज	ब्रज
सामिग्री	सामग्री	वापिस	वापस	बनस्पति	वनस्पति	श्राप	शाप
प्रदर्शिनी	प्रदर्शनी	द्वारिका	द्वारका	सैना	सेना	सेनिक	सैनिक
ऊत्थान	उत्थान	दुसरा	दूसरा	इतिहासिक	ऐतिहासिक	प्रथक	पृथक
प्रशाद	प्रसाद	अमावश्या	अमावस्या	सम्पति	सम्पत्ति	कृतघन	कृतघ्न
बसंत	वसंत	बर्ष	वर्ष	बिमारी	बीमारी	व्यक्तिक	वैयक्तिक
विना	बिना	बन	वन	वितीत	व्यतीत	निस्वार्थ	निःस्वार्थ
दाइत्व	दायित्व	सम्वाद	संवाद	परिस्थित	परिस्थिति	रचियंता	रचयिता
कुन्डली	कुण्डली	मॉसिक	मानसिक	मैथिलिशरण	मैथिलीशरण	आर्शिवाद	आशीर्वाद
कन्ठ	कण्ठ	अगामी	आगामी	निरिक्षण	निरीक्षण	पत्नि	पत्नी
सप्ताहिक	साप्ताहिक	संसारिक	सांसारिक	शताब्दि	शताब्दी	लड़ायी	लड़ाई
आधीन	अधीन	हस्ताक्षेप	हस्तक्षेप	स्थाई	स्थायी	लिखायी	लिखाई
बरात	बारात	क्षत्रीय	क्षत्रिय	अलोकिक	अलौकिक	कृप्या	कृपया
तिथी	तिथि	कालीदास	कालिदास	गंवार	गँवार	असोक	अशोक
पुर्ती	पूर्ति	अतिथी	अतिथि	दुस्कर	दुष्कर	मूल्यावान	मूल्यवान्
नीती	नीति	ग्रहणी	गृहिणी	नवम्	नवम	क्षात्र	छात्र
क्यूँ	क्यों	साधू	साधु	छमा	क्षमा	प्रन्तु	परन्तु
वधु	वधू	रेणू	रेणु	प्रीक्षा	परीक्षा	मरयादा	मर्यादा
नुपुर	नूपुर	निर्वान	निर्वाण	दुदर्शा	दुर्दशा	विषेश	विशेष
जादु	जादू	द्रश्य	दृश्य	उज्वल	उज्ज्वल	आल्हाद	आहलाद्

अशुद्ध	शुद्ध	अशुद्ध	शुद्ध
महत्व	महत्त्व	उपलक्ष	उपलक्ष्य
लीये	लिये	पिओ	पियो
हुये	हुए	कवित्री	कवयित्री
प्रमात्मा	परमात्मा	घनिष्ट	घनिष्ठ
यथेष्ठ	यथेष्ट	पियास	प्यास
व्यस्क	वयस्क	त्यौहार	त्योहार
मुसलिम	मुस्लिम	ऐनक	ऐनक
नोकरी	नौकरी	कल्यान	कल्याण
पाणी	पानी	आसा	आशा
हृदय	हृदय	घ्रणा	घृणा
श्रंगार	शृंगार	हिन्दुस्थान	हिन्दुस्तान
प्रशन	प्रश्न	ग्यान	ज्ञान
अन्धेरा	अँधेरा	पेड	पेड़
महयान्ह्न	मध्यान्ह	मेंहदी	मेहंदी
शमशान	श्मशान	चिन्ह	चिह्न
कुंज	कुञ्ज	ग्रहस्थ	गृहस्थ
अजोध्या	अयोध्या	अनधिकार	अनाधिकार
अनिष्ठा	अनिष्ट	अनुकुल	अनुकूल
अनुसंगिक	आनुषंगिक	अनुशरण	अनुसरण
अभिसेक	अभिषेक	अरमाण	अरमान
अहिल्या	अहल्या	आदरनीय	आदरणीय
आविस्कार	आविष्कार	उँचाई	ऊँचाई
उत्तरदाई	उत्तरदायी	उपर	ऊपर
उपरोक्त	उपर्युक्त	उश्रृंखल	उच्छृंखल
कलस	कलश	कल्यान	कल्याण
गनित	गणित	जबाब	जवाब
तत्व	तत्त्व	तलाब	तालाब
तिरष्कार	तिरस्कार	त्रिवार्षिक	त्रैवार्षिक
दिपिका	दीपिका	देहिक	दैहिक
द्वन्द	द्वन्द्व	नरायन	नारायण
निरव	नीरव	निरोग	नीरोग
पुष्टी	पुष्टि	पुस्प	पुष्प
पेत्रिक	पैतृक	प्रनय	प्रणय

अशुद्ध	शुद्ध	अशुद्ध	शुद्ध
प्रनाम	प्रणाम	प्रयाप्त	पर्याप्त
प्रसंशा	प्रशंसा	प्रांगन	प्रांगण
प्रान	प्राण	पृष्ट	पृष्ठ
ब्रत	व्रत	भगीरथी	भागीरथी
भरथ	भरत	भष्म	भस्म
मंत्रीमंडल	मंत्रिमण्डल	रसायण	रसायन
राज्यमहल	राजमहल	रामायन	रामायण
वनोवास	वनवास	वानी	वाणी
वाल्मीकी	वाल्मीकि	वास्प	वाष्प
व्योहार	व्यवहार	सन्यासी	संन्यासी
सम्राज	साम्राज्य	सविनयपूर्वक	सविनय
सिंदुर	सिंदूर	स्त्रवण	श्रवण
हरीश्चन्द्र	हरिश्चन्द्र	हिन्दु	हिन्दू
हिन्दूस्तान	हिन्दुस्तान	बुद्धिवान	बुद्धिमान्
भाग्यमान	भाग्यवान	विद्वान	विद्वान्
श्रीमान	श्रीमान्	आंख	आँख
ऊंट	ऊँट	कंगना	कँगना
गँगा	गंगा	गांधी	गाँधी
जांच	जाँच	तांगा	ताँगा
दांत	दाँत	मंहगा	महँगा
मांस	माँस	मुंह	मुँह
सांप	साँप	सांस	साँस
हुँकार	हुंकार	निर्पेक्ष	निरपेक्ष
भाष्कर	भास्कर	सन्मुख	सम्मुख
माताहीन	मातृहीन	विद्यार्थि	विद्यार्थी
गुणि	गुणी	द्वैवाषिक	द्विवार्षिक
पूज्यनीय	पूजनीय	अकाश	आकाश
इद	ईद	इसलाम	इस्लाम
ऐसा	ऐसा	दोसरा	दूसरा
पुत्रि	पुत्री	प्रस्तूत	प्रस्तुत
हरयाली	हरियाली	दिवाली	दीवाली
राष्ट्रिय	राष्ट्रीय	एकहरा	इकहरा
एतबार	इतबार		

वाक्यगत अशुद्धियाँ

अशुद्ध	शुद्ध
हम अच्छी भाषण दिए थे।	हमने अच्छा भाषण दिया था।
आप खाए कि नहीं?	आपने खाया कि नहीं?
वह मुझे देखा तो घबरा गया।	उसने मुझे देखा तो घबरा गया।
मैं किताब पढ़ा हूँ।	मैंने किताब पढ़ी है।
मैं सारी पुस्तक पढ़ डाली।	मैंने सारी पुस्तक पढ़ डाली।
सीता भात खायी।	सीता ने भात खाया।

अशुद्ध	शुद्ध
राम रोटी खाया।	राम ने रोटी खायी।
लड़की ने दही गिरा दी।	लड़की ने दही गिरा दिया।
शुद्ध गाय की घी दो।	गाय का शुद्ध घी दो।
तुम, मैं और वह चलेगा।	तुम, वह और मैं चलूँगा।
राम और सीता आयी थी।	राम और सीता आए थे।
भाई-बहन जा रही हैं।	भाई-बहन जा रहे हैं।

अशुद्ध	शुद्ध
वह लड़की को बुलाओ।	उस लड़की को बुलाओ।
मेरे लिए पढ़ता हूँ।	अपने लिए पढ़ता हूँ।
सीता राम की आज्ञाकारी पत्नी थी।	सीता राम की आज्ञाकारिणी पत्नी थीं।
देरी न करना।	देर न करना।
उसे मृत्युदण्ड की सजा मिली।	उसे मृत्युदण्ड मिला।
हमारे शिक्षक प्रश्न पूछते हैं।	हमारे शिक्षक प्रश्न करते हैं।
कै बजे? तीन बजा।	कितना बजा? तीन बजे।
उसका प्राण उड़ गया।	उसके प्राण उड़ गये।
मैंने आँख से देखा।	मैंने आँखों से देखा।
अपन को पढ़ना है।	मुझे पढ़ना है।
पुस्तक फट गया।	पुस्तक फट गई है।
घोड़ी तेज दौड़ता है।	घोड़ी तेज दौड़ती है।
मेरा प्रणम स्वीकार करो।	मेरा प्रणाम स्वीकार करो।
दो बालक खेलता है।	दो बालक खेलते हैं।

अशुद्ध	शुद्ध
ये सब मेरा पुस्तक है।	ये सब मेरी पुस्तकें हैं।
सूरज पूरब में उगते हैं।	सूरज पूर्व में उगता है।
वह लौट आए।	वे लौट आए।
वहाँ अनेकों लोग थे।	वहाँ अनेक लोग थे।
मेरे को मत मारो।	मुझे मत मारो।
मोहन ने पत्र को पढ़ा।	मोहन ने पत्र पढ़ा।
पुस्तक पर नहीं लिखो।	पुस्तक पर मत लिखो।
वह सज्जन पुरुष है।	वह सज्जन है।
आप हमारे घर आओ।	आप हमारे घर आइए।
हम आपसे कुछ कहे थे।	हमने आपसे कुछ कहा था।
मकान की दायीं ओर सड़क है।	मकान के दायीं ओर सड़क है।
पिताजी घर नहीं हैं।	पिताजी घर पर नहीं हैं।
घर पर सब कुशल हैं।	घर में सब कुशल हैं।
उसे भारी दुःख हुआ।	उसे बहुत दुःख हुआ।
सड़क में मत खेलो।	सड़क पर मत खेलो।

मुहावरे तथा लोकोक्तियाँ

- अँगूठी का नगीना–अत्यन्त महत्त्वपूर्ण।
- अंधा दरबार–न्यायहीन स्थान।
- अंधेर नगरी–न्याय का अभाव।
- अक्ल का दुश्मन–मूर्ख।
- अक्ल का दुम–मूर्ख।
- आँख का तारा–अतिप्रिय।
- ईद का चाँद–बहुत दिनों के बाद दिखाई देना।
- कछुआ चाल–धीमी गति।
- काला नाग–दुष्ट आदमी।
- किताबी कीड़ा–सदैव कुछ-न-कुछ पढ़ना।
- किस्मत का मारा–भाग्य का मन्द।
- कोल्हू का बैल–बहुत कठिन परिश्रम करनेवाला।
- कोड़ी का तीन–तुच्छ।
- खाली हाथ–पैसे का अभाव।
- गाजर-मूली–अशक्त।
- गुलर का फूल–दुर्लभ वस्तु।
- गोबर-गणेश–निरामूर्ख।
- घर का उजाला–कुल-दीपक।
- घड़ियाली आँसू–बनावटी शोक।
- चलता-पुरजा–चालाक।
- चाँद का टुकड़ा–परम सुन्दर वस्तु या व्यक्ति।
- चाँदी का जूता–रिश्वत।
- चार दिन की चाँदनी–थोड़े समय का सुख।
- जलती आँख–क्रोधाभिभूत।
- जीभ का पतला–लालची।
- टेढ़ी खीर–विकट काम।
- ठिकाने की बात–न्यायसंगत बात।
- अढ़ाई दिन की हुकूमत–थोड़े समय का ऐश्वर्य।
- तकदीर का सिकन्दर–भाग्य का बलवान्।
- थाली का बैंगन–मत बदलते रहना।
- दाँत कटी रोटी–घनिष्ठता।
- दाहिना हाथ–सहायक।
- दिल का बादशाह–बहुत बड़ा उदार।
- दूध का दूध और पानी का पानी–उचित न्याय।
- दूध का धोआ–निर्दोष।
- दो दिन का मेहमान–बहुत थोड़े समय ठहरने वाला।
- धरती का फूल–ऐसा व्यक्ति जो हाल में अमीर हुआ है।
- धोबी का कुत्ता–निकम्मा।
- नसीब का मारा–बुरे दिन देखनेवाला।
- निन्यानबे का फेरा–धन बढ़ाने की चिन्ता।
- पत्थर का कलेजा–हर दुःख सहने की शक्ति।
- पत्थर की लकीर–चिरस्थायी सदा सत्य।
- फूलों की सेज–आनन्ददायक कार्य।
- बगुला-भगत–कपटी व्यक्ति।

- बच्चों का खेल–साधारण काम।
- बलि का बकरा–निःसहाय व्यक्ति।
- बरसाती बादल–अस्थायी।
- बात का पक्का–सत्यवादी।
- बायें हाथ का खेल–सरल काम।
- बिन बादल बरसात–असमय लाभ।
- बे-पेंदी का लोटा–बे ठिकाने का आदमी।
- भागीरथ प्रयत्न–अत्यधिक परिश्रम।
- भीष्म प्रतिज्ञा–दृढ़ संकल्प।
- मक्खी चूस–कंजूस।
- मिट्टी के मोल–बहुत सस्ता।
- मोटा असामी–मूर्ख मालदार।
- राम कहानी–आत्मवृतान्त।
- लँगोटिया यार– बचपन का मित्र।
- हवाई महल–कोरी कल्पना।
- आँख लगना–नींद आना।
- आँख खुलना–होश में आना।
- आँखें दिखाना–क्रोध से घूरना।
- आँसू पोंछना–धैर्य बँधाना।
- अन्धे की लकड़ी–एकमात्र सहारा।
- कान भरना–चुगली करना।
- कान पर जूँ न रेंगना–कोई असर न होना।
- नाक कटना–प्रतिष्ठा खत्म होना।
- नाक रगड़ना–दीनता दिखाना।
- नाकों चने चबवाना–खूब सताना।
- मुँह की खाना–बुरी तरह हारना।
- आस्तीन का साँप–विश्वासघाती मित्र।
- कन्धे से कन्धा मिलाना–पूरा सहयोग करना।
- ईंट से ईंट बजाना–पूरी तरह नष्ट कर देना।
- नौ दो ग्यारह होना–भाग जाना।
- दाँत खट्टे करना–बुरी तरह हराना।
- हाथ मलना–पछताना।
- खून का प्यासा–जानी दुश्मन।
- घी के दिए जलाना–खुशी मनाना।
- चार चाँद लगाना–प्रतिष्ठा बढ़ाना।
- तीन तेरह होना–अलग-अलग होना।
- पानी फेर देना–नाश कर देना।
- गाल बजाना–डींगे मारना।
- जान से हाथ धो बैठना–मारा जाना।
- पानी-पानी होना–बहुत लज्जित होना।
- फूला न समाना–बहुत प्रसन्न होना।
- अपना उल्लू सीधा करना–अपना मतलब निकालना।
- आँखें चुरा लेना–अनदेखा कर देना।
- अन्धे की लाठी–एकमात्र सहारा।
- आसमान पर चढ़ना–बहुत अभिमान करना।
- आँखें खुलना–होश आना।
- चोरी और सीना जोरी–दोषी होकर धमकाना।
- आग में घी डालना–क्रोध को भड़काना।
- अँगुली पर नचाना– अच्छी तरह वश में करना।
- एक आँख से देखना–समान दृष्टि से देखना।
- एक ही थैले के चट्टे-बट्टे–एक जैसे।
- ओखली में सिर देना–जान-बूझकर आपत्ति मोल लेना।
- कलेजा मुँह को आना–बहुत दुःखी होना।
- कफन बाँधकर चलना–मौत से न घबराना।
- काँटे बिछाना–बाधा डालना।
- कलेजा ठण्डा होना–सन्तोष होना।
- कमर कसना–तैयार होना।
- खून खौलना–जोश में आना।
- खाक छानना–मारे-मारे फिरना।
- गागर में सागर भरना–थोड़े शब्दों में बहुत कुछ कह देना।
- घाव पर नमक छिड़कना–दुखी को अधिक दुखी करना।
- घी के दिए जलाना–खुशी मनाना।
- घोड़े बेचकर सोना–गहरी नींद में सोना।
- चल बसना–परलोक सिधारना।
- छठी का दूध याद आना–भारी संकट में पड़ना।
- छाती पर साँप लोटना–बहुत ईर्ष्या होना।
- जमीन पर पैर न रखना–अधिक घमण्ड होना।
- झक मारना–व्यर्थ समय खोना।
- टेढ़ी खीर–कठिन काम।
- डींग मारना–अपनी झूठी प्रशंसा करना।
- डूब मरना–बहुत लज्जित होना।
- तलवे चाटना–चापलूसी करना।
- ताक में रहना–मौका ढूँढ़ते रहना।
- दंग रह जाना–आश्चर्य में पड़ जाना।
- दाल न गलना–वश न चलना।
- दाल में काला होना–संदेह होना।
- पीठ दिखाना–हारकर भागना।
- मुँह तोड़ उत्तर देना–खरा उत्तर देना।

वस्तुनिष्ठ प्रश्न

अभ्यास-1

निर्देशः *नीचे प्रत्येक शुद्ध शब्द की वर्तनी के लिए चार विकल्प दिए गए हैं। आपको सही विकल्प का चयन करना है।*

1. A. ऋषि B. ऋषी C. रिषी D. ऋसि

2. A. विषेसन B. विशेषण C. विसेशन D. विशेशन

3. A. दुशासन B. दुसाशन C. दूशाषण D. दुःशासन

4. A. संस्कृति B. संसकृति C. संष्कृति D. संस्कृती

5. A. दूनियां B. दुनियां C. दुनिया D. दूनिआ

6. A. टिपनी B. टिप्पणि C. टिप्पणी D. टिप्पनी

7. A. शाषण B. साशन C. शासन D. शाशन

8. A. किसमस B. किरसमस C. क्रिसमूस D. कृसमस

9. A. अनुग्रहित B. अनुग्रहीत C. अनुगृहीत D. अनुग्रहित

10. A. पराकम B. प्राक्रम C. पराक्रम D. प्राकर्म

11. A. नायका B. नाइका C. नाइक D. नायिका

12. A. समरिधी B. समद्धी C. समृद्धि D. समरिद्धि

13. A. युधिष्ठर B. यूधिष्ठर C. युधिष्ठिर D. युधिष्टर

14. A. वाल्मीकि B. बाल्मीकि C. बालमीकि D. बाल्मिक

15. A. परलोकिक B. प्रलौकिक C. पारलौकिक D. परलौकिक

16. A. त्रितीय B. तर्तीय C. तृतीय D. तिरतीय

17. A. व्योहार B. व्यौहार C. व्यवहार D. ब्यवहार

18. A. अहिल्या B. अहल्या C. अहिलया D. अहीलया

19. A. आदरनीय B. आदरणीय C. आदरनीया D. आदरणीया

20. A. आर्द B. आद्र C. आर्द्र D. आर्दृ

21. A. आधीन B. अधिन C. अधीन D. अधीम

22. A. आविस्कार B. आविष्कार C. आवीस्कार D. आविश्कार

23. A. आसा B. आषा C. आशा D. अशा

24. A. उज्वल B. उजज्ज्वल C. उजज्वल D. उज्ज्वल

25. A. उन्नती B. उन्नित C. उन्नति D. उन्नती

26. A. कलस B. कलष C. कलश D. कलशा

27. A. गनीत B. गनित C. गणीत D. गणित

28. A. तलाव B. तालाव C. तलाब D. तालाब

29. A. दुष्ट B. दूष्ट C. दुस्त D. दुश्त

30. A. निरोग B. निररोग C. नीरोग D. नीरोगी

उत्तरमाला

1. A	**2.** B	**3.** D	**4.** A	**5.** C
6. C	**7.** C	**8.** C	**9.** C	**10.** C
11. D	**12.** C	**13.** C	**14.** A	**15.** C
16. C	**17.** C	**18.** B	**19.** B	**20.** C
21. C	**22.** B	**23.** C	**24.** D	**25.** C
26. C	**27.** D	**28.** D	**29.** A	**30.** C

अभ्यास-2

निर्देशः *नीचे कुछ शब्द दिए गए हैं। प्रत्येक के पर्यायवाची के चार विकल्प दिए गए हैं। इनमें से एक विकल्प सही पर्यायवाची है, उसका चयन कीजिए :*

1. अग्नि
A. अनिल B. अनल C. गर्म D. ताप

2. अमृत
A. पीयूष B. गरल C. सरस D. जीवनदायनी

3. आँख
A. लोचन B. आस्थि
C. वदन D. जलज

4. आकाश
A. अनन्त B. पाताल
C. वितल D. तल

5. कपड़ा
A. परिधान B. पटिका
C. पीताम्बर D. लँहगा

6. कमल
A. सरोज B. सरोवर
C. पंक D. पुष्प

7. गंगा
A. पाताल नदी B. हिमनदी
C. भागीरथ D. त्रिपथगा

8. चाँद
A. मयंक B. भानु
C. दिनकर D. रवि

9. नदी
A. सरिता B. प्रवाह
C. धारा D. जलधर

10. पर्वत
A. पत्थर B. चट्टान
C. शिखर D. मेरू

11. पवन
A. अनिल B. अनल
C. अग D. विहग

12. पति
A. साजन B. प्रिया
C. भार्या D. दारा

13. पानी
A. मही B. मेदिनी
C. अम्बु D. तरणी

14. पुत्र
A. आत्मज B. तनया
C. सुता D. आत्मजा

15. पुत्री
A. सुता B. सुत
C. आत्मज D. नन्दन

16. फूल
A. बहार B. मधु
C. माधव D. सुमन

17. वृक्ष
A. विटप B. अभ्र
C. प्रसून D. रसा

18. बादल
A. अज B. व्यामोह
C. नीरद D. मधुप

19. बिजली
A. चंचला B. खटका
C. त्रास D. संत्रास

20. माता
A. धात्री B. धरणी
C. धरित्री D. श्यामा

21. घोषणा
A. आवाज B. पुकारना
C. ऐलान D. ललकारना

22. उत्कर्ष
A. आकर्षण B. विकर्षण
C. उन्नति D. निष्कर्ष

23. उदय
A. अन्त B. विकास
C. प्रगट D. व्यस्त

24. दक्ष
A. निपुण B. समर्थ
C. कर्मठ D. मेहनती

25. संवाद
A. विवाद B. झगड़ा
C. सम्बोधन D. वार्तालाप

उत्तरमाला

1. B	**2.** A	**3.** A	**4.** A	**5.** A
6. A	**7.** D	**8.** A	**9.** A	**10.** D
11. A	**12.** A	**13.** C	**14.** A	**15.** A
16. D	**17.** A	**18.** C	**19.** A	**20.** A
21. C	**22.** C	**23.** C	**24.** A	**25.** D

अभ्यास-3

निर्देशः *नीचे चार-चार शब्दों के समूह दिए गए हैं। प्रत्येक समूह में एक शब्द बेमेल है तथा शेष तीन शब्द पर्यायवाची हैं, आपको उस शब्द का चयन करना है, जो बेमेल है :*

1. A. तम B. अंधकार
C. तिमिर D. अंश

2. A. अनल B. आग
C. दहन D. तमिस्त्रा

3. A. अतुल B. अद्वितीय
C. अनुपम D. शुष्मा

4. A. अहं B. अहंकार
C. दर्प D. निराला

5. A. पता B. खोज
C. जाँच D. शोध

6. A. गरल B. पीयूष
C. सुधा D. सोम

7. A. कानन B. जंगल
C. पादप D. वन

8. A. अश्व B. गज
C. घोड़ा D. तुरंग

9. A. दानव B. मानव
C. दैत्य D. राक्षस

10. A. आँख B. चक्षु
C. नयन D. मुख

11. A. अन्तरिक्ष B. वसुन्धरा
C. आसमान D. गगन

12. A. इच्छा B. अभिलाषा
C. कामना D. प्रयोजन

13. A. कपड़ा B. चीर
C. वसन D. पोशाक

14. A. अब्ज B. कमल
C. राजीव D. आम्र

15. A. कोयल B. पिक
C. काग D. वनप्रिय

16. A. गंगा B. देवनदी
C. गोदावरी D. भागीरथी

17. A. गणेश B. एकदन्त
C. देवराज D. गणपति

18. A. घर B. निलय
C. निकेतन D. झोपड़ी

19. A. चाँद B. हिमांशु
C. विनायक D. सुधांशु

20. A. नदी B. तरणी
C. तटिनी D. सरिता

21. A. पक्षी B. चिड़िया
C. सुमन D. विहग

22. A. पवन B. अचला
C. वात D. वायु

23. A. समीर B. पृथ्वी
C. भू D. भूमि

24. A. पानी B. समीर
C. अम्बु D. जल

25. A. पुत्र B. तनया
C. तनय D. सुत

26. A. पुत्र B. तनया
C. सुता D. कन्या

27. A. गृहिणी B. आदमी
C. पुरुष D. नर

28. A. मधु B. फूल
C. पुष्प D. सुमन

29. A. माधव B. तरु
C. पेड़ D. वृक्ष

30. A. माता B. अम्बु
C. अम्मा D. जननी

उत्तरमाला

1. D	**2.** D	**3.** D	**4.** D	**5.** A
6. A	**7.** C	**8.** B	**9.** B	**10.** D
11. B	**12.** D	**13.** D	**14.** D	**15.** C
16. C	**17.** C	**18.** D	**19.** C	**20.** B
21. C	**22.** B	**23.** A	**24.** B	**25.** B
26. A	**27.** A	**28.** A	**29.** A	**30.** B

अभ्यास-4

निर्देशः *गहरे काले शब्द के विलोम शब्द का चयन कीजिए:*

1. उसे हर काम में **सफलता** मिल रही है।
A. असफलता B. सफल
C. कुशलता D. निपुणता

2. कभी किसी की **निन्दा** नहीं करनी चाहिए।
A. गुणगान B. स्तुति
C. प्रशंसा D. यशोगान

3. आलस्य व्यक्ति का सबसे बड़ा **दुश्मन** है।
A. शत्रु B. घातक
C. मित्र D. सहायक

4. वे बुढ़ापे से **दुखी** हैं।
A. अप्रसन्न B. सुखी
C. खुश D. नाराज

5. यहाँ उसकी **चतुराई** नहीं चली।
A. चालाकी B. बहादुरी
C. निपुणता D. मूर्खता

6. शहद की **मिठास** कम नहीं होती।
A. मीठा B तीखा
C. कडुवा D. खट्टा

7. साहसी के **साहस** को देखकर मैं चकित रह गया।
A. हिम्मत B. बहादुरी
C. निडर D. भय

8. फिल्मोत्सव में सर्वश्रेष्ठ **अभिनेता** को पुरस्कार प्रदान किया गया।
A. हीरोइन B. नेत्री
C. मीनाक्षी D. अभिनेत्री

9. नाटक में नायक और **नायिका** की भूमिका महत्वपूर्ण होती है:
A. हीरो B. नायक
C. नेत्र D. नेता

10. कवि-सम्मेलन में एक कवि और एक **कवयित्री** को आमंत्रित किया गया था।
A. लेखक B. सम्पादक
C. नेता D. कवि

11. विद्यालय के वार्षिकोत्सव के लिए नेता और एक **नेत्री** को आमंत्रित किया गया।
A. अभिनेता B. विद्वान्
C. विदुषी D. नेता

12. मोहन बहुत **चतुर** है।
A. निपुण B. तेज
C. सुस्त D. मूर्ख

13. सोहन अब पूर्ण **स्वस्थ** है।
A. प्रसन्न B. खुश
C. अस्वस्थ D. अप्रसन्न

14. पक्षी **आकाश** में उड़ते हैं :
A. गगन B. नभ
C. धरती D. पाताल

15. वह विद्यालय में देर से आया और **अनुपस्थित** हो गया।
A. पूर्व B. उपस्थित
C. प्रवेश D. समयपूर्व

16. **बालक** चाँद की ओर देख रहा है।
A. बालिका B. लड़का
C. बच्चा D. बच्ची

17. मैं उसके विचार से बिल्कुल **सहमत** नहीं हूँ।
A. समर्थन B. सहमति
C. असहमत D. प्रशंसक

18. उसकी हालत **अधिक** खराब है।
A. बहुत B. कम
C. ठीक D. कुशल

19. **धर्म** की सर्वत्र विजय होती है:
A. अधर्म B. ज्ञान
C. भक्ति D. ईमानदारी

20. अच्छे चरित्र के बिना जीवन **निरर्थक** है:
A. व्यर्थ B. अर्थपूर्ण
C. सार्थक D. कुशल

21. **ईमानदारी** बड़ी दुर्लभ वस्तु है:
A. सच्चाई B. भलाई
C. बेइमानी D. परोपकारी

22. एवरेस्ट संसार का सबसे **ऊँचा** पर्वत है:
A. नीचा B. वितल
C. पाताल D. मध्यम

23. वह विश्वास के **योग्य** नहीं है:
A. काबिल B. विश्वासी
C. अयोग्य D. बेकार

24. क्या वह इतना **मूर्ख** है?
A. चालाक B. विद्वान्
C. बुद्धिमान D. धूर्त

25. कितना सुहावना **दृश्य** है!
A. अदृश्य B. दर्शनीय
C. सुन्दर D. व्यर्थ

उत्तरमाला

1. A	**2.** C	**3.** C	**4.** B	**5.** D
6. C	**7.** D	**8.** D	**9.** B	**10.** D
11. D	**12.** D	**13.** C	**14.** D	**15.** B
16. A	**17.** C	**18.** B	**19.** A	**20.** C
21. C	**22.** A	**23.** C	**24.** C	**25.** A

अभ्यास-5

निर्देशः नीचे प्रत्येक **काले गहरे शब्द** के चार विलोम दिए गए हैं। इनमें सही विलोम का चयन कीजिए :

1. अग्नि
A. आग B. अनल
C. दहन D. जल

2. अग्रज
A. अनुज B. भ्राता
C. भाई D. अम्बा

3. अच्छा
A. बुरा B. खराब
C. गंदा D. भ्रष्ट

4. अंत
A. प्रारम्भ B. समाप्त
C. शेष D. अल्प

5. अचल
A. विचल B. वितल
C. सजल D. चल

6. अति
A. अधिक B. बहुत
C. अल्प D. कम

7. अत्यधिक
A. अल्प B. अधिक
C. स्वल्प D. न्यूनतम

8. अंधकार
A. अंधेरा B. प्रकाश
C. रात्रि D. दिन

9. अतिवृष्टि
A. अनावृष्टि B. वृष्टि
C. वर्षा D. वर्षण

10. अनाथ
A. नाथ B. स्वामी
C. मासिक D. सनाथ

11. अनुकूल
A. मनोकूल B. प्रतिकूल
C. अनुकरण D. मनस्वी

12. अनुराग
A. राग B. विराग
C. विग्रह D. स्नेह

13. अन्त
A. श्री गणेश B. आदि
C. शुरुआत D. समाप्त

14. अपना
A. अपनत्व B. पराया
C. मित्र D. शत्रु

15. अपमान
A. मान B. सम्मान
C. वर्तमान D. स्वाभिमान

16. अपेक्षा
A. इच्छा B. स्वेच्छा
C. प्रविच्छा D. उपेक्षा

17. अमर
A. मर्त्य B. मृत्यु
C. सुधा D. गरल

18. अल्पायु
A. चिरायु B. उमरदराज
C. नश्वर D. सनातन

19. अस्त
A. उदय B. विकास
C. निर्माण D. सृष्टि

20. आकर्षण
A. प्रतिकर्षण B. विकर्षण
C. सम्मोहन D. विरत

21. आकाश
A. गगन B. नभ
C. वसुन्धरा D. पाताल

22. आगे
A. पीछे B. पूर्व
C. पृष्ट D. पृष्ठ

23. आजाद
A. स्वतंत्र B. स्वतंत्रतता
C. परतंत्र D. गुलाम

24. आदान
A. आयात B. निर्यात
C. प्रदान D. निदान

25. आधुनिक
A. अर्वाचीन B. नूतन
C. प्राचीन D. वर्तमान

उत्तरमाला

1. D	2. A	3. A	4. A	5. D
6. D	7. C	8. B	9. A	10. D
11. B	12. B	13. A	14. B	15. B
16. D	17. A	18. A	19. A	20. B
21. D	22. A	23. D	24. C	25. C

अभ्यास-6

निर्देशः *नीचे कुछ शब्द दिए गए हैं प्रत्येक शब्द के चार वैकल्पिक अर्थ दिए गए हैं। सही अर्थ का चयन कीजिए :*

1. सुरक्षित
A. कुशल B. घटना
C. दुर्घटना D. बचाव

2. प्रतिभाशाली
A. सज्जन B. कुशाग्र
C. विद्वान् D. वैभवशाली

3. आत्मसमर्पण
A. अपने आप को सौंपना B. समर्पण
C. अर्पण D. त्यागज

4. सिद्धहस्त
A. निपुण B. कर्मठ
C. मेहनती D. परिश्रमी

5. सुशोभित
A. मजेदार B. सुस्वागतम्
C. अच्छा D. शोभा पाना

6. स्वादिष्ट
A. मजेदार B. बेकार
C. मीठा D. तीखा

7. स्वावलम्बी
A. निर्भर B. परालंबी
C. आत्मनिर्भर D. अतिथि

8. उपकरण
A. साधन B. युक्ति
C. यंत्र D. मशीन

9. कीमत
A. क्रय B. विक्रय
C. मूल्य D. बिक्री

10. संगठन
A. एकता B. अनेकता
C. समूह D. संस्था

11. विपत्ति
A. दुख B. विपदा
C. मुसीबत D. सुख

12. तृण
A. तिनका B. धूल
C. धूप D. लकड़ी

13. आश्चर्य
A. निरीक्षण B. दृष्टिगोचर
C. हैरानी D. थकावट

14. हार्दिक
A. हृदय से B. शरीर से
C. मन से D. मस्तिष्क से

15. नियति
A. भाग्य B. किनारा
C. समय D. पवित्र

16. सुगन्धित
A. दुर्गन्ध B. खुशबू वाला
C. फूल D. कमल

17. उत्साह
A. होश B. हवास
C. जोश D. हिम्मत

18. सहयोग
A. मिलन सार B. मेहनती
C. परोपकारी D. आपसी सहायता

19. मुसीबत
A. विपत्ति B. सुशोभित
C. सहायता D. मदद

20. निरक्षर
A. साक्षर B. दर्शनीय
C. पठनीय D. अनपढ़

21. उपवन
A. वन B. तीर
C. जंगल D. बाग

22. मेघ
A. बादल B. पंकज
C. राजीव D. मेघनाद

23. आधुनिक
A. प्राचीन B. पुरातन
C. भूतकाल D. आज का

24. तीर
A. वाण B. धनुष
C. किनारा D. नदी

25. परीक्षण
A. जाँच B. पड़ताल
C. परीक्षा D. इम्तहान

26. अभिवादन
A. नमस्ते B. प्रणाम
C. बधाई D. शुभकामना

27. सर्वत्र
A. नश्वर B. सजीव
C. ईश्वर D. सभी जगह

28. हलवाहा
A. चरवाहा B. किसान
C. मजदूर D. हल चलाने वाला

29. शिखर
A. पर्वत B. पहाड़
C. टीला D. चोटी

30. भयानक
A. डरावना B. भयभीत
C. डरना D. खूँखार

उत्तरमाला

1. D	**2.** B	**3.** A	**4.** A	**5.** D
6. A	**7.** C	**8.** C	**9.** C	**10.** A
11. C	**12.** A	**13.** C	**14.** A	**15.** A
16. B	**17.** C	**18.** D	**19.** A	**20.** D
21. D	**22.** A	**23.** D	**24.** A	**25.** A
26. B	**27.** D	**28.** D	**29.** D	**30.** A

अभ्यास-7

निर्देशः *नीचे कुछ शब्द दिए जा रहे हैं। प्रत्येक शब्द के* ***उपसर्ग*** *के सन्दर्भ में चार विकल्प दिए गए हैं। आपको सही विकल्प का चयन करना है :*

1. अलबत्ता
A. अ B. अल
C. लब D. त्ता

2. अलगरज
A. अल B. लग
C. गर D. रज

3. कमसिन
A. क B. कम
C. सि D. सिन

4. अनमोल
A. अ B. अन
C. मो D. मोल

5. अनजान
A. अ B. अन
C. जा D. जान

6. अनपढ़
A. अ B. पढ़
C. प D. अन

7. अधखिला
A. अ B. अध
C. ला D. खिला

8. अधजला
A. अ B. ज
C. अध D. ला

9. अधपका
A. अ B. अध
C. पका D. का

10. अधखिला
A. अ B. अध
C. खिला D. ला

11. उन्नीस
A. उन B. उन्
C. नीस D. स

12. उनसठ
A. उ B. उन
C. सठ D. ठ

13. दुकाल
A. द B. दुक
C. दु D. काल

14. दुबला
A. दब B. दुब
C. ला D. दु

15. निकम्मा
A. नि B. निक
C. कम्मा D. मा

16. निर्लज्ज
A. निर B. निल
C. नि D. लज्ज

17. बिनब्याहा
A. बि B. बिन
C. ब्याहा D. हा

18. भरपेट
A. भर B. पेट
C. पे D. ट

19. भरपाई
A. भ B. र
C. पा D. भर

20. कुपात्र
A. कु B. कुप
C. पा D. पात्र

21. सुजान
A. सु B. सुज
C. सुजा D. जान

22. गैर कानूनी
A. गै B. गैर
C. कानु D. नुनी

23. गैरसरकारी
A. गैर B. सर
C. का D. कारी

24. अपमान
A. अ B. अप
C. मा D. मान

25. अनुशासन
A. अ B. शासन
C. सन D. अनु

26. अविनीत
A. अवि B. अ
C. नी D. नीत

27. अभिमान
A. अभि B. अ
C. मा D. मान

28. अभियान
A. अ B. मान
C. यान D. अभि

29. अध्ययन
A. अध् B. अधि
C. यन D. न

30. निश्चल
A. नि B. निर
C. निस D. चल

उत्तरमाला

1. B	2. A	3. B	4. B	5. B
6. D	7. B	8. C	9. B	10. B
11. A	12. B	13. C	14. D	15. B
16. A	17. B	18. A	19. D	20. A
21. A	22. B	23. A	24. B	25. D
26. B	27. A	28. D	29. B	30. A

अभ्यास-8

निर्देशः *निम्नलिखित शब्दों में प्रयुक्त प्रत्यय सम्बन्धी चार विकल्प दिए गए हैं, सही विकल्प का चयन कीजिए :*

1. भलाई
A. ई B. लाई
C. आई D. भला

2. चतुराई
A. चतु B. रा
C. ई D. आई

3. भूखा
A. भू B. भूख
C. खा D. आ

4. भिड़न्त
A. भिड् B. भि
C. न्त D. अन्त

5. प्यासा
A. आस B. सा
C. आसा D. सा

6. बिकाऊ
A. बिक B. काऊ
C. आऊ D. ऊ

7. तैराक
A. तै B. तैर
C. राक D. आक

8. सन्नाटा
A. सन् B. सन्ना
C. नाटा D. आटा

9. लोहार
A. लोह B. आरा
C. आरी D. आर

10. मिलान
A. आना B. आने
C. आनी D. आन

11. चढ़ाव
A. चढ़ B. चढ़ा
C. आव D. व

12. लगाव
A. लग B. अव
C. आव D. गाव

13. लिखावट
A. लिख B. लिखा
C. वट D. आवट

14. मिलावट
A. मिल B. वट
C. आवट D. ट

15. मिठास
A. मिठ B. ठास
C. आस D. स

16. चिकनाहट
A. चिक B. नाट्ट
C. हट D. आहट

17. सड़ियल
A. सड़ B. यल
C. ड़ियल D. इयल

18. मरियल
A. मर B. यल
C. मरि D. इयल

19. गड़रिया
A. गड़ B. इया
C. रिया D. या

20. सजीला
A. ईला B. इला
C. ला D. स

21. लुटेरा
A. लुट B. एरा
C. ऐरा D. रा

22. लठैत
A. ए B. ऐ
C. ऐत D. त

23. भगोड़ा
A. ओ B. ओड़ा
C. ड़ा D. भगो

24. खपत
A. ख B. प
C. त D. पत

25. जीवट
A. व B. अट
C. जीव D. जी

उत्तरमाला

1. C	**2.** D	**3.** D	**4.** D	**5.** D
6. C	**7.** D	**8.** D	**9.** D	**10.** D
11. C	**12.** C	**13.** D	**14.** C	**15.** C
16. D	**17.** D	**18.** D	**19.** B	**20.** A
21. B	**22.** C	**23.** B	**24.** C	**25.** B

अभ्यास-9

निर्देशः *नीचे कुछ मुहावरे दिए गए हैं। प्रत्येक के अर्थ के लिए चार विकल्प दिए गए हैं। आपको सही विकल्प का चयन करना है :*

1. अक्ल पर पत्थर पड़ना
A. बुद्धि काम न करना B. दुविधा होना
C. संकट में होना D. परेशान होना

2. अपना उल्लू सीधा करना
A. अवसर देखना B. काम निकालना
C. मतलब साधना D. मूर्ख बनाना

3. अपने मुँह मियाँ-मिट्ठू बनना
A. मिठाई खाना B. प्रशंसा करना
C. निंदा करना D. अपनी प्रशंसा स्वयं करना

4. अपने पाँव पर आप कुल्हाड़ी मारना
A. हानि पहुँचाना B. खेद होना
C. अपना पैर काटना D. अपनी हानि स्वयं करना

5. आँखें चुरा लेना
A. भाग जाना B. छिप जाना
C. अनदेखा करना D. मिल जाना

6. अक्ल का दुश्मन
A. मित्र होना B. शत्रु होना
C. महामूर्ख D. महाविद्वान्

7. अंधे की लाठी
A. एक मात्र सहारा B. मित्र होना
C. शत्रु होना D. दुख पहुँचाना

8. आकाश-पाताल एक करना
A. भाग-दौड़ करना B. परेशान होना
C. थक जाना D. कठिन परिश्रम करना

9. घड़ों पानी पड़ना
A. लज्जित होना B. तुच्छ समझना
C. लाभ होना D. थकावट

10. अगर-मगर करना
A. नुकसान करना B. बहाने बनाना
C. बदनाम करना D. कपट करना

11. मुँह की खाना
A. गिर जाना B. हार जाना
C. भाग जाना D. व्यर्थ होना

12. आस्तीन का साँप होना
A. शत्रु B. मित्र
C. कपटी मित्र D. दयालु

13. एक आँख से देखना
A. बुरा व्यवहार B. समान व्यवहार
C. कपट करना D. लज्जित होना

14. बाल-बाँका न होना
A. घायल होना B. साफ बच जाना
C. क्रोधित होना D. स्वस्थ होना

15. दाँतों तले उँगली दबाना
A. उँगली काटना B. चिंतित हो जाना
C. चकित रह जाना D. प्रसन्न हो जाना

16. जान के लाले पड़ना
A. मरने का खतरा होना B. भाग जाना
C. हार जाना D. मुश्किल में पड़ना

17. बोली मारना
A. ताना देना B. सताना
C. मजाक करना D. याद दिलाना

18. अंधों में काना राजा
A. मूर्खों में अल्पज्ञ को विद्वान् माना जाना
B. सबको मूर्ख समझना
C. अत्यधिक महत्त्वपूर्ण
D. काना राजा

19. अक्ल के घोड़े दौड़ाना
A. बुद्धि लड़ाना
B. कल्पना करना
C. तरह-तरह के उपाय सोचना
D. ज्ञान-प्राप्त करना

20. पानी उतर जाना
A. शर्म करना B. लज्जित न होना
C. भाग जाना D. इज्जत करना

21. तीन-पाँच करना
A. तितर-बितर करना
B. वचन देकर फिर जाना
C. घुमा-फिरा कर बातें करना
D. परेशान करना

22. हथियार डाल देना
A. हार जाना B. जीत जाना
C. धोखा देना D. विजय होना

23. आँख खुलना
A. होश में आना B. अत्यन्त प्यार होना
C. उल्टा काम करना D. क्रोध करना

24. कमर सीधी करना
A. थक जाना B. थकावट दूर करना
C. काम करना D. परिश्रम करना

25. पगड़ी रखना
A. चैन की सांस लेना B. अपमान करना
C. दया की भीख माँगना D. अपमान होना

26. लोहा मानना
A. संघर्ष करना B. विजय होना
C. श्रेष्ठता स्वीकार करना D. खुशामद करना

27. काठ मार जाना
A. दुःखी होना B. चुप होना
C. सफल होना D. मर जाना

28. चाँद पर थूकना
A. अपमान करना
B. बढ़कर बातें करना
C. महान पुरुष पर लांछन लगाना
D. महत्त्वाकांक्षी होना

29. उगल देना
A. अपराध स्वीकार कर लेना
B. सच बोलना
C. उल्टी करना
D. अनपच होना

30. हाथ मलना
A. पश्चाताप करना B. सर्दी मिटाना
C. दुख करना D. तैयार होना

उत्तरमाला

1. A	**2.** C	**3.** D	**4.** D	**5.** C
6. C	**7.** A	**8.** D	**9.** A	**10.** B
11. B	**12.** C	**13.** B	**14.** B	**15.** C
16. D	**17.** A	**18.** A	**19.** A	**20.** B
21. C	**22.** A	**23.** A	**24.** B	**25.** C
26. C	**27.** B	**28.** C	**29.** A	**30.** A

अभ्यास-10

निर्देशः *नीचे कुछ वाक्य खण्ड दिए गए हैं, पूरे वाक्य खण्ड के लिए एक शब्द का चयन कीजिए।*

1. जिसका आदि न हो
A. अनंत B. अमर
C. शाश्वत D. अनादि

2. जो कुछ न जानता हो
A. मूर्ख B. महामूर्ख
C. ज्ञानी D. अज्ञ

3. जो अनुकरण करने योग्य हो
A. अनुकरणीय B. अद्वितीय
C. आदरणीय D. अगम

4. जिसका अंत न हो
A. अनंत B. अनादि
C. आदि D. परलोक

5. जो कभी न मरे
A. मर्त्य B. मुर्त्त
C. अर्मुत्त D. अमर

6. जिसके समान दूसरा न हो
A. अनुकूल B. प्रतिकूल
C. कृतज्ञ D. अद्वितीय

7. जो कम बोलता हो
A. मृदुभाषी B. वाचाल
C. अल्पभाषी D. अल्पज्ञ

8. जिसका इलाज न हो
A. मरणशील B. अमरत्व
C. बिमारी D. लाइलाज

9. जिस का विश्वास न किया जा सके
A. विश्वसनीय B. अविश्वसनीय
C. विश्वासी D. धूर्त

10. जिसका कोई नाथ न हो
A. सनाथ B. स्वामी
C. नाथ D. अनाथ

11. कम जानने वाला
A. अल्पज्ञ B. अज्ञ
C. विद् D. विद्वान

12. जहाँ जाना संभव न हो
A. दुर्गम B. अगम
C. तल D. वितल

13. कम खाने वाला
A. बहुभोजी B. पेटु
C. कंजूस D. अल्पाहारी

14. जो बात पहले कभी न हुई हो
A. भूतपूर्व B. अभूतपूर्व
C. प्राचीन D. अर्वाचीन

15. जिस स्त्री के सन्तान न हों
A. बाँझ B. कुलटा
C. पतिता D. विधवा

16. जो कहा न जा सके
A. अकथनीय B. अकथ्य
C. करणीय D. सम्भव

17. एहसान न मानने वाला
A. कृतज्ञ B. कृतघ्न
C. आस्तिक D. विश्वासी

18. जिसने देश के साथ विश्वासघात किया हो
A. विश्वासघाती B. द्रोही
C. आतंकवादी D. देश द्रोही

19. जिसने राष्ट्र के हित में अपना जीवन बलिदान कर दिया हो
A. देशभक्त B. शहीद
C. राष्ट्रभूत D. भारतपुत्र

20. वह जमीन जिसमें कुछ भी पैदा न हो
A. ऊसर B. बंजर
C. उर्वर D. पथरीला

21. वह वस्तु जिसकी चाह हो
A. श्रेष्ठ B. आवश्यक
C. इच्छित D. अभीष्ट

22. दूसरों के पीछे चलने वाला
A. अनुयायी B. अनुज
C. अनुचर D. अनुकरणीय

23. जो पहले न पढ़ा हो
A. पठित B. अपठित
C. पठनीय D. अपठनीय

24. जिसके आर-पार दिखाई देता हो
A. अपारदर्शी B. गम्य
C. अगम्य D. पारदर्शी

25. आज्ञा पालन करने वाला
A. शिष्य B. शिष्या
C. अनुचर D. आज्ञाकारी

26. काम से जी चुराने वाला
A. कामचोर B. आलसी
C. कर्मठ D. परिश्रमी

27. प्रतिदिन होने वाला
A. दैनिक B. शाश्वत
C. सनातन D. अमर

28. जिसका कोई अर्थ न हो
A. सार्थक B. निरर्थक
C. आर्थिक D. अनार्थिक

29. उपकार मानने वाला
A. कृतज्ञ B. कृतघ्न
C. विश्वासी D. अनुयायी

30. हाथ से लिखा हुआ
A. पठनीय B. अपठनीय
C. स्पष्ट D. हस्तलिखित

उत्तरमाला

1. D	**2.** D	**3.** A	**4.** A	**5.** D
6. D	**7.** C	**8.** D	**9.** B	**10.** D
11. A	**12.** A	**13.** D	**14.** B	**15.** A
16. A	**17.** B	**18.** D	**19.** B	**20.** A
21. C	**22.** C	**23.** B	**24.** D	**25.** D
26. A	**27.** A	**28.** B	**29.** A	**30.** D

अभ्यास-11

निर्देशः *नीचे कुछ संज्ञा शब्द दिए जा रहे हैं। प्रत्येक के संज्ञा-भेद के लिए चार विकल्प दिए गये है। सही विकल्प का चयन कीजिए :*

1. तुलसीदास
A. जातिवाचक B. भाववाचक
C. व्यक्तिवाचक D. समूहवाचक

2. यमुना
A. व्यक्तिवाचक B. जातिवाचक
C. समूहवाचक D. भाववाचक

3. बच्चा
A. जातिवाचक B. समूहवाचक
C. भाववाचक D. व्यक्तिवाचक

4. मानवता
A. भाववाचक B. जातिवाचक
C. द्रव्यवाचक D. समूहवाचक

5. हिमालय
A. व्यक्तिवाचक B. जातिवाचक
C. भाववाचक D. समूहवाचक

6. भारत
A. जातिवाचक B. भाववाचक
C. व्यक्तिवाचक D. समूहवाचक

7. एशिया
A. व्यक्तिवाचक B. भाववाचक
C. द्रव्यवाचक D. समूहवाचक

8. महाराष्ट्र
A. जातिवाचक B. व्यक्तिवाचक
C. समूहवाचक D. द्रव्यवाचक

9. सूर सागर
A. व्यक्तिवाचक B. भाववाचक
C. द्रव्यवाचक D. समूहवाचक

10. सोमवार
A. जातिवाचक B. व्यक्तिवाचक
C. द्रव्यवाचक D. समूहवाचक

11. खटमल
A. जातिवाचक B. व्यक्तिवाचक
C. द्रव्यवाचक D. समूहवाचक

12. मैना
A. जातिवाचक B. व्यक्तिवाचक
C. द्रव्यवाचक D. समूहवाचक

13. चाँदी
A. द्रव्यवाचक B. समूहवाचक
C. भाववाचक D. व्यक्तिवाचक

14. अच्छाई
A. भाववाचक B. समूहवाचक
C. जातिवाचक D. व्यक्तिवाचक

15. पीतल
A. द्रव्यवाचक B. भाववाचक
C. व्यक्तिवाचक D. जातिवाचक

16. वीरता
A. भाववाचक B. जातिवाचक
C. द्रव्यवाचक D. समूहवाचक

17. रूस
A. जातिवाचक B. व्यक्तिवाचक
C. भाववाचक D. द्रव्यवाचक

18. लम्बाई
A. भाववाचक B. समूहवाचक
C. द्रव्यवाचक D. व्यक्तिवाचक

19. दल
A. जातिवाचक B. व्यक्तिवाचक
C. समूहवाचक D. द्रव्यवाचक

20. मार्च
A. समूहवाचक B. व्यक्तिवाचक
C. द्रव्यवाचक D. जातिवाचक

21. झुण्ड
A. समूहवाचक B. जातिवाचक
C. व्यक्तिवाचक D. द्रव्यवाचक

22. टोली
A. जातिवाचक B. व्यक्तिवाचक
C. समूहवाचक D. द्रव्यवाचक

23. सुभाष चौक
A. जातिवाचक B. समूहवाचक
C. व्यक्तिवाचक D. भाववाचक

24. संघ
A. जातिवाचक B. द्रव्यवाचक
C. समूहवाचक D. भाववाचक

25. गिरोह
A. समूहवाचक B. द्रव्यवाचक
C. जातिवाचक D. भाववाचक

उत्तरमाला

1. C	**2.** A	**3.** A	**4.** A	**5.** A
6. C	**7.** A	**8.** B	**9.** A	**10.** B
11. A	**12.** A	**13.** A	**14.** A	**15.** A
16. A	**17.** B	**18.** A	**19.** C	**20.** B
21. A	**22.** C	**23.** C	**24.** C	**25.** A

अभ्यास-12

निर्देश: *नीचे दिए गए वाक्य में रिक्त स्थान है। प्रत्येक वाक्य के नीचे कारक चिह्न दिए गए हैं। रिक्त स्थान की पूर्ति के लिए उपयुक्त कारक चिह्न का चयन कीजिए :*

1. निम्नलिखित शब्दों........अर्थ बताइए
A. का B. के
C. से D. पर

2. सरकार मुझे नौकरी........मत निकालिए
A. पर B. में
C. से D. को

3. इस कथन........पुष्टि कीजिए
A. को B. से
C. की D. ने

4. छात्र-छात्राएँ राष्ट्र........सम्पत्ति और उसके भावी कर्णधार होते हैं
A. के B. की
C. को D. में

5. प्रत्येक प्रश्न........चार सम्भावित उत्तर दिए गए हैं
A. के लिए B. में
C. के D. से

6. माता बच्चे........पढ़ाती है
A. को B. के
C. की D. से

7. गुरुजी........सबसे छोटे लड़के को एक नारंगी दी
A. ने B. को
C. से D. के लिए

8. मोहन सोहन से मिलने........गया है
A. से B. के
C. को D. के लिए

9. उसने कलम........लिखा
A. के B. में
C. पर D. से

10. मैं ड्राइवर........गाड़ी चलवाता हूँ
A. के B. पर
C. में D. से

11. शिक्षक छात्रों........पुस्तक पढ़वाते हैं
A. के लिए B. मैं
C. पर D. से

12. मैंने दाढ़ी........उसे मुसलमान समझ लिया
A. से B. के
C. को D. के लिए

13. श्याम अपने भाई हरि........आम लाया है
A. के B. के लिए
C. का D. पर

14. मोहन घर........आता है
A. में B. पर
C. से D. का

15. उसे पाँच दिनों........मूर्च्छा आया करती है
A. पर B. से
C. के D. को

16. मेधावी छात्र परीक्षा........चोरी नहीं करते
A. में B. पर
C. से D. के लिए

उत्तरमाला

1. A	**2.** C	**3.** C	**4.** B	**5.** C
6. A	**7.** A	**8.** D	**9.** D	**10.** D
11. D	**12.** A	**13.** B	**14.** C	**15.** B
16. D				

गद्यांश (अपठित-बोध)

गद्यांश 1

यदि हम निरन्तर प्रयत्न करेंगे तो निश्चय ही अपने सभी लक्ष्यों को प्राप्त कर लेंगे, किन्तु प्रायः देखा जाता है कि अधिक आशावादी लोग थोड़ा सा प्रयत्न करके अधिक फल की कामना करने लगते हैं और मनोवांछित फल प्राप्त न होने पर निराश हो जाते हैं। अतः जीवन में सफलता प्राप्त करने के लिए परिस्थितियों के समक्ष घुटने न टेकें, बल्कि दृढ़ता से उनका मुकाबला करें। याद रखें, जितना कठोर हमारा परिश्रम होगा उसका फल भी उतना ही मीठा होगा।

उपर्युक्त गद्यांश को ध्यानपूर्वक पढ़ें और निम्न प्रश्नों के उत्तर के लिए सही विकल्प को चुनें:

1. फल न मिलने पर कौन निराश हो जाते हैं?
A. आशावादी लोग B. कम आशावादी लोग
C. अधिक आशावादी लोग D. निराशावादी लोग

2. लक्ष्य प्राप्ति के लिए क्या किया जाना चाहिए?
A. फल की कामना B. हिम्मत से मुकाबला
C. निरन्तर प्रयत्न D. परिस्थितियों से मुकाबला

3. आशावादी शब्द का विलोम शब्द है:
A. निराश B. निराशावादी
B. दुखी D. अप्रसन्न

4. मनोवांछित शब्द का क्या अर्थ है?
A. इच्छित B. परीक्षित
C. लाभदायक D. मन को खुश करने वाले

5. परिश्रम शब्द का अर्थ है:
A. साहस B. हिम्मत
C. काम D. कठिन मेहनत

गद्यांश 2

पन्द्रह अगस्त 1947 को हमारा देश स्वतंत्र हुआ। स्वतन्त्रता प्राप्ति के बाद विश्व के दूसरे देशों के साथ भारत के राजनयिक एवं सांस्कृतिक सम्बन्ध जुड़े। पर्यटकों के साथ-साथ राजनीतिज्ञों और साहित्यकारों को भी विदेश यात्रा के पर्याप्त अवसर मिले। विभिन्न प्रकार की छात्रवृत्तियों के माध्यम से बहुत से लोग विदेशों में पढ़ने गए। बहुत से लोगों ने विदेशों में उपलब्ध आजीविका के अवसरों का लाभ उठाया। इन सबके परिणामस्वरूप प्रचुर मात्रा में यात्रावृत्तांत लिखे गए। विदेश-विषयक यात्रावृतांतों में रूस और स्वदेश-विषयक यात्रावृतांतों में लेखकों की दृष्टि कश्मीर से कन्याकुमारी तक व्याप्त हुई।

उपर्युक्त गद्यांश को ध्यानपूर्वक पढ़ें और निम्नलिखित प्रश्नों के उत्तर के लिए सही विकल्प को चुनें:

1. भारत कब स्वतंत्र हुआ?
A. 15 अगस्त 1947 B. 15 अगस्त 1946
C. 15 अगस्त 1948 D. 15 अगस्त 1949

2. स्वतंत्र भारत के अन्य देशों के साथ किस प्रकार के संबंध जुड़े?
A. राजनीतिक
B. राजनयिक
C. धार्मिक
D. राजनयिक एवं सांस्कृतिक

3. आजीविका का क्या अर्थ है?
A. उपार्जन B. वेतन
C. मेहनत D. रोजगार

4. यात्रा-वृत्तांत का क्या अर्थ है?
A. भ्रमण B. पर्यटन
C. सफरनामा D. विदेशभ्रमण

5. स्वतंत्र का विलोम शब्द है:
A. परतंत्र B. आजाद
C. गुलामी D. मुक्ति

गद्यांश 3

युवा वर्ग का मस्तिष्क नई-नई बातों की ओर ज्यादा तेज दौड़ता है। उसमें अन्य वर्ग के व्यक्तियों से अधिक आवेश और शक्ति होती है। इस अवस्था में यदि सही शिक्षा और उचित मार्ग-दर्शन न मिले तो यही शक्ति प्रेरणा और निर्माण के स्थान पर विनाश की ओर ले जाती है। बिगड़ने और बनने की यही आयु होती है। दुर्भाग्य से हमारे देश में शिक्षा पद्धति केवल उपाधि बाँटने का काम ही करती है। एक सम्पूर्ण व्यक्तित्वपूर्ण मनुष्य बनाना आज की शिक्षा पद्धति के लिए मुश्किल है।

उपर्युक्त गद्यांश को ध्यानपूर्वक पढ़ें और निम्नलिखित प्रश्नों के उत्तर के लिए सही विकल्प को चुनें।

1. निर्माण का विलोम शब्द क्या हैं?
A. रचना B. बनावट
C. विनाश D. सृजन

2. मार्ग-दर्शन का क्या अर्थ है?
A. उपाधि B. रास्ता
C. उद्देश्य D. रास्ता दिखलाना

3. शक्ति विनाश की ओर कब अग्रसर होती है?
A. अधिक आवेश और शक्ति के अभाव में
B. सही शिक्षा और उचित मार्ग दर्शन के अभाव में
C. दुर्भाग्यपूर्ण शिक्षा पद्धति के कारण
D. इनमें से कोई नहीं

4. हमारे देश की शिक्षा पद्धति क्या कार्य करती है?
A. मार्ग-दर्शन B. शक्ति प्रेरणा
C. उपाधि देना D. उपर्युक्त सभी

5. दुर्भाग्य का विपरीत शब्द है:
A. भाग्य B. सौभाग्य
C. भाग्यशाली D. भाग्यवान

गद्यांश 4

भिखारी की भाँति गिड़गिड़ाना प्रेम की भाषा नहीं है। यहाँ तक कि मुक्ति के लिए भगवान् की उपासना करना भी अधम उपासना में गिना जाता है। प्रेम कोई पुरस्कार नहीं चाहता। प्रेम सर्वथा प्रेम के लिए ही होता है। भक्त इसलिए प्रेम करता है कि बिना प्रेम किए वह रह ही नहीं सकता। जब तुम किसी मनोहर प्राकृतिक दृश्य को देखकर उस पर मोहित हो जाते हो तो तुम किसी फल की याचना नहीं करते और न वह दृश्य ही तुमसे कुछ माँगता है। फिर भी उस दृश्य का दर्शन तुम्हारे मन को आनंद से भर देता है।

उपर्युक्त गद्यांश को ध्यानपूर्वक पढ़ें और निम्नलिखित प्रश्नों के उत्तर के लिए सही विकल्प का चयन करें:

1. प्रेम का उद्देश्य क्या होता है?
A. मुक्ति B. उपासना
C. भक्ति D. प्रेम

2. मुक्ति का अर्थ है:
A. आजादी B. स्वतंत्रता
C. परतंत्र D. निर्वाण

3. कैसी उपासना अधम मानी गई है?
A. प्रेम की उपासना B. भगवान की उपासना
C. मुक्ति की उपासना D. भक्ति की उपासना

4. मनोहर शब्द हैं:
A. विशेषण B. संज्ञा
C. सर्वनाम D. अव्यय

5. प्राकृतिक शब्द का अर्थ है:
A. ईश्वरीय B. मानव संबंधी
C. प्रकृति संबंधी D. प्रेम संबंधी

गद्यांश 5

कुछ लोग भाग्यवादी होते हैं और सब-कुछ भाग्य के सहारे छोड़कर कर्म से विरत हो जाते हैं। ऐसे लोग समाज के लिए बोझ हैं। वे कभी कोई बड़ा काम नहीं कर पाते। बड़ी-बड़ी खोज, बड़े-बड़े आविष्कार और बड़े-बड़े निर्माण कार्य कर्मशील लोगों के द्वारा ही संभव हो सके हैं। हम अपनी बुद्धि और प्रतिभा तथा कार्य-क्षमता के बल पर सही मार्ग पर चल सकते हैं, किन्तु बिना कठिन श्रम के अपने लक्ष्य तक नहीं पहुँच सकते। कठिन परिश्रम करने के बाद पाई गई सफलता हमारे मन को अलौकिक आनंद से भर देती है। यदि हम अपने कार्य में अपेक्षित श्रम नहीं करते तो हमारा मन ग्लानि का अनुभव करता है।

उपर्युक्त गद्यांश को ध्यानपूर्वक पढ़ें और निम्नलिखित प्रश्नों के उत्तर के लिए सही विकल्प चुनें:

1. "आविष्कार" शब्द का अर्थ है :
A. अनुसंधान B. खोज
C. निर्माण D. विनाश

2. **अलौकिक** शब्द का क्या अर्थ है?
A. संसारिक B. भौतिक
C. अमानुषी D. प्राकृतिक

3. सफलता का विलोम क्या है?
A. सफल B. असफल
C. सफलतापूर्वक D. असफलता

4. परिश्रम करने और न करने से हमारे जीवन पर क्या प्रभाव पड़ता है?
A. लोग भाग्यवादी बन जाते हैं
B. कर्म से विरत हो जाते हैं
C. मन में ग्लानि का अनुभव होता है
D. इनमें से कोई नहीं

5. किस प्रकार के लोग समाज के लिए बोझ हैं?
A. भाग्यवादी B. कर्मठ
C. परिश्रमी D. प्रतिभाशाली

गद्यांश 6

वैदिक काल से हिमालय के पहाड़ बहुत पवित्र माने जाते हैं। इसमें कोई सन्देह नहीं कि हिमालय के पहाड़ों का दृश्य अति सुन्दर है। उसकी विशालता को देखकर मन में आनन्द और कृतज्ञता की लहर उठती है। ऐसा लगता है कि यह विशाल सृष्टि प्रभु की अनुपम देन है। सारी सृष्टि के प्रति समभाव जाग्रत होता है। वस्तुतः यह दृष्टि कोरी कल्पनात्मक या आध्यात्मिक नहीं है। देखा जाए तो सारे भारत की जलवायु का समतोल करने वाले यह हिमालय के पहाड़ हैं, विशेषकर उत्तरी भारत को वर्षा और पानी देने वाले ये ही हैं। गंगोत्री, यमुनोत्री, बद्री, केदार को तीर्थ माना जाता है, जो व्यर्थ कल्पना नहीं है। उन स्थानों से निकलने वाली पवित्र नदियाँ ही वास्तव में हमारी प्राणदात्री रही हैं।

उपर्युक्त गद्यांश को ध्यानपूर्वक पढ़ें और निम्नलिखित प्रश्नों के उत्तर के लिए सही विकल्प चुनें :

1. हिमालय के पर्वत बहुत पवित्र कब से माने जाते हैं?
A. पाषाण काल से B. वैदिक काल से
C. प्राचीन काल से D. आधुनिक काल से

2. विशालता शब्द है :
A. जातिवाचक B. भाववाचक
C. विशेषण D. सर्वनाम

3. भारत की जलवायु को समतोल कौन करता है?
A. गंगोत्री B. यमुनोत्री
C. केदार D. हिमालय

4. सृष्टि का समानार्थक शब्द है :
A. सृजन B. रचना
C. प्रकृति D. संसार

5. प्राणदात्री का क्या अर्थ है?
A. गंगोत्री
B. यमुनोत्री
C. प्राणसंचार करने वाली
D. समभाव जाग्रत करने वाली

गद्यांश 7

सच्चा मित्र एक शिक्षक की भाँति होता है। जिस प्रकार शिक्षक अपने छात्र को सन्मार्ग की ही ओर अग्रसर करता है, उसी प्रकार एक सच्चा मित्र अपने मित्र को पाप के गर्त में गिरने से बचाता है। मानव-जीवन अधिक रहस्यपूर्ण है। कभी-कभी जीवन में ऐसे अवसर उपस्थित हो जाते हैं, जब मनुष्य की धर्मबुद्धि नष्ट हो जाती है और उसका मन द्रुत गति से पाप की ओर दौड़ता है। ऐसे समय में मित्र का ही उपदेश अधिक कल्याणकारी सिद्ध होता है। मित्र के उपदेश का जितना प्रभाव हृदय पर पड़ता है, उतना और किसी का नहीं पड़ता है।

उपर्युक्त गद्यांश को ध्यानपूर्वक पढ़ें और निम्नलिखित प्रश्नों के उत्तर के लिए सही विकल्प चुनें :

1. सच्चा मित्र किस प्रकार का होता है?
A. विपत्ति में सहायता देने वाला
B. गलत मार्ग पर चलने से रोकने वाला
C. शिक्षक के भाँति
D. धार्मिक गुरु की तरह

2. सन्मार्ग शब्द का विपरीत शब्द है :
A. अग्रसर B. कुमार्ग
C. सुमार्ग D. मार्गदर्शक

3. व्यक्ति को पाप के गर्त्त में गिरने से कौन बचाता है?
A. शिक्षक B. भाई
C. पिता D. सच्चा मित्र

4. मानव पाप की ओर कब दौड़ता है?
A. जब स्वार्थी बन जाता है
B. जब धर्म-बुद्धि नष्ट हो जाती है
C. जब सच्चामित्र साथ छोड़ देता है
D. जब धनवान बन जाता है

5. उपदेश में कौन-सा उपसर्ग है?
A. उ B. उप
C. दे D. देश

गद्यांश 8

सब तरह के भावों को प्रकट करने की योग्यता रखने वाली और निर्दोष होने पर भी यदि कोई भाषा अपना निज का साहित्य नहीं रखती, तो वह रूपवती भिखारिन की तरह कदापि आदरणीय नहीं हो सकती। उनकी शोभा, उसकी बड़ी सम्पन्नता, उसकी मान-मर्यादा उसके साहित्य पर ही अवलम्बित रहती है। उसके विचारों और राजनैतिक स्थितियों का प्रतिबिम्ब देखने को यदि कहीं मिल सकता है, तो उसके ग्रन्थ साहित्य में मिल सकता है। सामाजिक शक्ति या सजीवता, सामाजिक अशक्ति या निर्जीवता और सामाजिक सभ्यता तथा असभ्यता का निर्णायक एकमात्र साहित्य है।

उपर्युक्त गद्यांश को ध्यानपूर्वक पढ़ें और निम्नलिखित प्रश्नों के उत्तर के लिए सही विकल्प चुनें :

1. साहित्य विहीन भाषा किस प्रकार की होती है?
A. आदरणीय B. भिखारिन
C. रूपवती D. रूपवती भिखारिन

2. रूपवती का पुल्लिंग रूप है:
A. रूपवान B. सुन्दर
C. सुन्दरी D. रूपवत

3. भाषा की मान मर्यादा किस पर निर्भर करती है?
A. लिपि पर B. साहित्यकार पर
C. भक्ति पर D. साहित्य पर

4. ''सम्पन्नता'' शब्द का विपरीत शब्द है:
A. गरीबी B. विपन्न
C. अमीर D. विपन्नता

5. राजनैतिक, सामाजिक शक्ति का दर्शन हमें किसमें मिलता है?
A. समाज B. राज्य
C. नेता D. साहित्य

गद्यांश 9

स्वतंत्र भारत का सम्पूर्ण दायित्व आज विद्यार्थियों के ही ऊपर है, क्योंकि आज जो विद्यार्थी हैं, वे ही कल स्वतंत्र भारत के नागरिक होंगे। भारत की उन्नति, उसका उत्थान उन्हीं की उन्नति और उत्थान पर निर्भर करता है। अतः विद्यार्थियों को चाहिए कि वे अपने भावी जीवन का निर्माण बड़ी सतर्कता और सावधानी के साथ करें। उन्हें प्रत्येक क्षण अपने राष्ट्र, अपने समाज, अपने धर्म, अपनी संस्कृति को अपनी आँखों के सामने रखना चाहिए, जिससे उनके जीवन से राष्ट्र को कुछ बल प्राप्त हो सके। जो विद्यार्थी राष्ट्रीय दृष्टिकोण से अपने जीवन का निर्माण नहीं करते, वे राष्ट्र और समाज के लिए भार-स्वरूप हैं।

उपर्युक्त गद्यांश को ध्यानपूर्वक पढ़ें और निम्नलिखित प्रश्नों के उत्तर के लिए सही विकल्प चुनें :

1. भारत की उन्नति किस पर निर्भर करती है?
A. युवाओं पर B. नेताओं पर
C. साहित्यकारों पर D. विद्यार्थियों पर

2. **उन्नति** का समानार्थक शब्द है :
A. पतन B. उत्थान
C. विकास D. उदय

3. **उत्थान** का विपरीत शब्द है :
A. उदय B. पतन
C. पराजय D. हार

4. किसे अपने जीवन का निर्माण सतर्कता और सावधानी से करना चाहिए?
A. युवाओं को B. नेताओं को
C. बच्चों को D. विद्यार्थियों को

5. धर्म, संस्कृति तथा समाज का रक्षक कौन है?
A. नागरिक B. ग्रामीण
C. विद्यार्थी D. युवा

गद्यांश 10

हास्य एक ऐसा माध्यम है, जो नीरस-जीवन को भी सुखद बना देता है। हास्य का जादू इतना प्रभावशाली होता है कि वह छूत के रोग की तरह चारों ओर फैल जाता है। जिसने कभी हँसना नहीं सीखा, सचमुच उसने जीना नहीं सीखा। सामान्यतः मनुष्य को जीवन में इतनी मुसीबतें झेलनी पड़ती हैं कि वह अपने जीवन को पहाड़ समझने लगता है। ऐसे दूभर जीवन को यदि जीने योग्य बनाना हो तो उसके लिए आवश्यक है कि जीवन में हँसने की गुंजाइश हो। हँसी के सहारे मनुष्य अपने कष्टों को भुलाने का प्रयत्न करता है। संघर्ष, तनाव, व्यस्तता, घुटन यदि आज के जीवन की सहज देन हैं, तो इनसे बचने के लिए यह आवश्यक है कि हम हँसना सीखें।

उपर्युक्त गद्यांश को ध्यानपूर्वक पढ़ें और निम्नलिखित प्रश्नों के उत्तर के लिए सही विकल्प चुनें :

1. नीरस जीवन को कौन सुखद बना देता है?
A. संगीत B. गीत
C. आमोद प्रमोद D. हास्य

2. **नीरस** का संधि विच्छेद है :
A. नी + रस B. नि + रस
C. निः + रस D. नीः + रस

3. किसका जीवन व्यर्थ है?
A. जिसने रोना नहीं सीखा
B. जिसने हँसना नहीं सीखा
C. जिसने गाना नहीं सीखा
D. इनमें से कोई नहीं

4. **हँसना** शब्द है :
A. संज्ञा B. विशेषण
C. क्रिया विशेषण D. क्रिया

5. तनाव और घुटन से बचने के लिए क्या करना चाहिए?
A. रोना चाहिए B. गाना चाहिए
C. हँसना चाहिए D. काम करना चाहिए

गद्यांश 11

किसी पुस्तक को पढ़ने में जल्दी नहीं करनी चाहिए, जो कुछ लेखक कहता है, उसे समझने की चेष्टा करनी चाहिए। प्रत्येक शब्द का अर्थ समझने की चेष्टा करनी चाहिए। यदि लेखक योग्य है, तो दूसरी बार वह पुस्तक और अधिक आनन्द देगी और तीसरी बार और अधिक। प्रत्येक बार अध्ययन करने पर आपको नवीन सुन्दर और नए विचार मिलेंगे और उसे आप जितना ही पढ़ेंगे, उतना ही स्नेह करने लगेंगे। सहस्रों व्यक्तियों ने गीता और रामायण तथा कुरान और बाइबिल को बार-बार पढ़ा है। उनका अनुभव है कि प्रत्येक बार उन्हें नई सूझ और नए विचार मिलते गए। कुछ लोग तो इस बात पर गर्व करते हैं कि उन्होंने अमुक पुस्तक को अनेक बार पढ़ा है, उन्हें कंठस्थ हो गई है।

उपर्युक्त गद्यांश को ध्यानपूर्वक पढ़ें और निम्नलिखित प्रश्नों के उत्तर के लिए सही विकल्प चुनें :

1. किसे समझने की चेष्टा करनी चाहिए?
A. पुस्तक B. रामायण
C. महाभारत D. गीता

2. पुस्तक की सजीवता किस पर निर्भर करती है?
A. लेखक B. प्रकाशक
C. पाठक D. चिन्तक

3. **आनन्द** का विपरीत शब्द है :
A. शोक B. दुख
C. संताप D. खुशी

4. नवीन, सुन्दर और नए विचार हमें कहाँ से प्राप्त होता हैं?
A. पुस्तक को बार-बार पढ़कर
B. सुनकर
C. भाषण से
D. अच्छे व्यक्तियों से मिलने पर

5. **कंठस्थ** शब्द का शब्दार्थ है :
A. कंठ में स्थित B. सुंदर कंठ
C. जबानी याद D. पंडित जी

गद्यांश 12

अहिंसा परम धर्म है और हिंसा आपद् धर्म। मनुष्य बराबर अहिंसा की ओर चलना चाहता है, किन्तु परिस्थितियाँ उससे हिंसा कराती है, अर्थात् परमधर्म की रक्षा के लिए आदमी बराबर आपद्धर्म से काम लेता रहा है। भारत अपनी सेनाओं को विघटित कर दे, तब भी उसका अपमान उससे अधिक होने वाला नहीं, जितना नेफा में हुआ। किन्तु परमधर्म पर टिकने की सामर्थ्य अगर भारत में नहीं है, तो आपद्धर्म पर उसे आना चाहिए। व्यवहारतः आपद्धर्म परमधर्म का विरोधी नहीं, उसका रक्षक है।

उपर्युक्त गद्यांश को ध्यानपूर्वक पढ़ें और निम्नलिखित प्रश्नों के उत्तर के लिए सही विकल्प चुनें :

1. **परमधर्म** का विपरीत शब्द है :
A. महान धर्म B. आपद्धर्म
C. सच्चाधर्म D. इनमें से कोई नहीं

2. आपद्धर्म किसे कहा जाता है?
A. अहिंसा B. सत्याग्रह
C. विपत्ति D. हिंसा

3. मानव से हिंसा कौन करवाती है?
A. लोभ B. स्वार्थ
C. द्वेष D. परिस्थितियाँ

4. **सामर्थ्य** का शब्दार्थ है :
A. संघर्ष B. परिश्रम
C. शक्ति D. पराक्रम

5. **परमधर्म** की रक्षा कौन करता है?
A. अहिंसा B. हिंसा
C. आपदधर्म D. युद्ध

गद्यांश 13

वर्तमान काल विज्ञापन का युग माना जाता है। समाचार-पत्रों के अतिरिक्त रेडियो और टेलीविजन भी विज्ञापन के सफल साधन हैं। विज्ञापन का मूल उद्देश्य उत्पादक और भोक्ता में सीधा सम्पर्क स्थापित करना होता है। जितना अधिक विज्ञापन किसी पदार्थ का होगा, उतनी ही उसकी लोकप्रियता बढ़ेगी। इन विज्ञापनों पर धन तो अधिक व्यय होता है, पर इनसे बिक्री बढ़ जाती है। ग्राहक जब इन आकर्षक विज्ञापनों को देखता है तो वह उस वस्तु-विशेष के प्रति आकृष्ट होकर उसे खरीदने को बाध्य हो जाता है।

उपर्युक्त गद्यांश को ध्यानपूर्वक पढ़ें और निम्नलिखित प्रश्नों के उत्तर के लिए सही विकल्प चुनें :

1. वर्तमान को किसका युग माना जाता है?

A. फैशन B. विज्ञापन
C. संगीत D. धन

2. उत्पादक तथा भोक्ता के बीच कौन संबंध स्थापित करता है?

A. टेलीविजन B. समाचार-पत्र
C. रेडियो D. विज्ञापन

3. **वर्तमान** शब्द का विपरीत शब्द है :

A. अर्वाचीन B. आधुनिक
C. आजकल D. प्राचीन

4. **आकर्षक** का शब्दार्थ है :

A. विकर्षक B. सुन्दर
C. मनमोहक D. आश्चर्यजनक

5. भोक्ता किस कारण वस्तुओं को खरीदने के लिए बाध्य हो जाता है?

A. विज्ञापन
B. आकर्षक विज्ञापन
C. लोकप्रियता के कारण
D. आसानी से उपलब्ध होना

गद्यांश 14

लगभग दो सौ वर्ष की गुलामी ने भारत के राष्ट्रीय स्वाभिमान को पैरों से रौंद डाला, हमारी संस्कृति को समाप्त कर दिया, हमारे विश्वासों को हिला दिया और हमारे आत्मविश्वास को चकनाचूर कर दिया, किन्तु अपने इस बूढ़े देश से प्यार करने वाले, इसके एक सामान्य संकेत पर प्राण न्यौछावर करने वाले दीवानों का अभाव न था। एक आवाज उठी और देखते ही देखते राष्ट्र का दबा हुआ आत्माभिमान उन्मत्त हो उठा। इतिहास साक्षी है जाने और अनजाने सहस्त्रों देशभक्त स्वतंत्रता की अनमोल निधि को पाने के लिए शहीद हो गए।

उपर्युक्त गद्यांश को ध्यानपूर्वक पढ़ें और निम्नलिखित प्रश्नों के उत्तर के लिए सही विकल्प चुनें :

1. **स्वाभिमान** का संधि विच्छेद है:

A. स्वा + भिमान B. स्वः + अभिमान
C. स्व + अभिमान D. स्वा + अभिमान

2. भारत का राष्ट्रीय स्वाभिमान किस कारण समाप्त हो गया था?

A. लम्बे गुलामी से B. निरंकुश शासक से
C. स्वार्थी मानव से D. धर्म के विनाश से

3. **आत्मविश्वास** का शब्दार्थ है

A. घमण्ड B. गर्व
C. अपने पर विश्वास D. अभिमान

4. भारत की अनमोल निधि को पाने के लिए कौन शहीद हो गए?

A. देशभक्त B. नेता
C. युवा D. युवती

5. **अनमोल निधि** का शब्दार्थ है:

A. अनन्त खजाना B. अमूल्य खजाना
C. बहुमूल्य D. स्वतंत्रता

गद्यांश 15

दुनिया के विभिन्न देशों के विकास पर विहंगम दृष्टि डालने से यह स्पष्ट हो जाता है कि आज जिस देश ने वैज्ञानिक उपलब्धियों के सहारे अपना औद्योगीकरण कर लिया, उसी को उन्नत देश कहा जाता है। जिस देश में औद्योगीकरण का स्तर नीचा है, वह पिछड़ा हुआ देश कहा जाता है। वैज्ञानिक आविष्कारों और औद्योगीकरण के आधार पर ही किसी देश की प्रगति को आँका जाता रहा है। विज्ञान ने मानव को पूरी तरह बदल दिया है।

उपर्युक्त गद्यांश को ध्यानपूर्वक पढ़ें और निम्नलिखित प्रश्नों के उत्तर के लिए सही विकल्प चुनें :

1. **विहंगम दृष्टि** का क्या अर्थ है?

A. एक झलक B. गहन दृष्टि
C. गहन चिन्तन D. इनमें से कोई नहीं

2. **विकास** का विपरीत शब्द है :

A. उत्थान B. उदय
C. पतन D. विनाश

3. **वैज्ञानिक** शब्द में कौन-सा प्रत्यय हैं?

A. निक B. वै
C. ईक D. इक

4. मानव जीवन को किसने बदल दिया है :

A. विकास B. वैज्ञानिक
C. विज्ञान D. उद्योग

5. किसी भी देश की स्तर को किससे नापा जाता है?

A. उपलब्धियों पर B. औद्योगीकरण से
C. वैज्ञानिकों से D. आविष्कारों से

गद्यांश 16

विश्व का वर्तमान उन्नत रूप मानव-श्रम की ही कहानी कह रहा है। गगन चुंबी अट्टालिकाएँ, लंबी-चौड़ी सड़कें, बड़े-बड़े विशाल नगर आकाश में उड़ते वायुयान तथा मानव-जीवन को सुखी और समृद्ध बनाने में योगदान करने वाले ज्ञान-विज्ञान के अनन्त रूप-ये सभी मनुष्य के श्रम का जयघोष करते हैं। स्पष्ट है कि मनुष्य और उसका शरीर विधाता की अनुपम रचना है जो निश्चय ही महान उद्देश्यों की संपूर्ति के

लिए दिया गया है। इस दुर्लभ तन को यदि हम आलस्य, प्रसाद अथवा घटिया कामों में गँवा देते हैं तो उस विधाता के प्रति अन्याय करते हैं।

उपर्युक्त गद्यांश को ध्यानपूर्वक पढ़ें और निम्नलिखित प्रश्नों के उत्तर के लिए सही विकल्प चुनें :

1. विश्व का वर्तमान रूप किसका उद्योतक है?
   A. चिन्तक का B. नेता का
   C. वैज्ञानिक का D. मानव श्रम
2. **गगन चुंबी अट्टालिकाएँ** का अर्थ है :
   A. आकाश में उड़ने वाला B. आकाश को छूने वाला
   C. बहुमंजिली इमारत D. इनमें से कोई नहीं
3. आकाश का समानार्थक शब्द है :
   A. वसुन्धरा B. धरा
   C. पयोद D. गगन
4. **सुखी** का विपरीत शब्द है :
   A. प्रसन्न B. अप्रसन्न
   C. दुखी D. उदासी
5. विधाता की अनुपम रचना क्या है?
   A. मानव शरीर B. समुद्र
   C. वन D. पृथ्वी

गद्यांश 17

हमारे देश में एक ऐसा भी युग था जब नैतिक और आध्यात्मिक विकास ही जीवन का वास्तविक लक्ष्य माना जाता था। अहिंसा की भावना सर्वोपरि थी। आज पूरा जीवन दर्शन ही बदल गया है। सर्वत्र पैसे की हाय-हाय तथा धन का उपार्जन ही मुख्य ध्येय हो गया है, भले ही धन-उपार्जन के तरीके गलत ही क्यों न हों? इन सबका असर मनुष्य के प्रतिदिन के जीवन पर पड़ रहा है। समाज का वातावरण दूषित हो गया है—

बाह्य वातावरण तो दूषित है ही, आज सब जानते हैं पर्यावरण की समस्याएँ कितनी चिन्तनीय हो उठी है। इन सबके कारण मानसिक और शारीरिक तनाव-खिंचाव और व्याधियाँ पैदा हो रही हैं।

उपर्युक्त गद्यांश को ध्यानपूर्वक पढ़ें और निम्नलिखित प्रश्नों के उत्तर के लिए सही विकल्प चुनें :

1. भारत का प्राचीन आदर्श था :
   A. सत्य और अहिंसा B. नैतिक और आध्यात्मिक विकास
   C. धन उपार्जन D. इनमें से कोई नहीं
2. **अहिंसा** का विपरीत शब्द है :
   A. हिंसा B. सत्याग्रह
   C. विनम्रता D. नैतिकता
3. जीवन दर्शन क्यों बदल गया है?
   A. हिंसा के कारण B. अहिंसा के कारण
   C. धन लिप्सा के कारण D. आध्यात्मिक विकास के कारण
4. समाज का वातावरण दूषित क्यों हो गया है?
   A. शारीरिक तनाव B. मानसिक व्याधियाँ
   C. पर्यावरण की समस्याएँ D. धन उपार्जन के गलत तरीके
5. **पर्यावरण** का शब्दार्थ है:
   A. जलमंडल B. स्थलमंडल
   C. वायुमंडल D. वातावरण

उत्तरमाला

गद्यांश 1
1. C 2. D 3. B 4. A 5. D

गद्यांश 2
1. A 2. D 3. D 4. C 5. A

गद्यांश 3
1. C 2. D 3. B 4. C 5. B

गद्यांश 4
1. D 2. D 3. C 4. A 5. C

गद्यांश 5
1. B 2. D 3. D 4. C 5. A

गद्यांश 6
1. B 2. B 3. D 4. A 5. C

गद्यांश 7
1. C 2. B 3. D 4. B 5. B

गद्यांश 8
1. D 2. A 3. D 4. D 5. D

गद्यांश 9
1. D 2. B 3. B 4. D 5. C

गद्यांश 10
1. D 2. C 3. B 4. D 5. C

गद्यांश 11
1. A 2. A 3. A 4. A 5. C

गद्यांश 12
1. B 2. D 3. D 4. C 5. C

गद्यांश 13
1. B 2. D 3. D 4. C 5. B

गद्यांश 14
1. C 2. A 3. C 4. A 5. B

गद्यांश 15
1. A 2. D 3. C 4. C 5. B

गद्यांश 16
1. D 2. C 3. D 4. C 5. A

गद्यांश 17
1. B 2. A 3. C 4. D 5. D

●●●

English Language

1

Comprehension Passages

ENGLISH LANGUAGE COMPREHENSION

The objective of language comprehension test is to ascertain the ability of the candidates to understand the passage properly.

Therefore candidates are required to take notice of the following points:

1. Read the full passage very attentively and intelligently.
2. Try to comprehend the gist of it.
3. Make a mental note of all the important details and points given in the passage.
4. Read the passage for the second time in case you have not been able to understand it satisfactorily.
5. Divide the time proportionately for all the passages.
6. Answer the questions on the basis of facts, as given in the paragraph.
7. Don't waste much time in answering the questions of any one passage.
8. Check all the answers once again, very carefully, to see whether any question is left unanswered by mistake.

MODEL QUESTIONS (FOR PRACTICE)

Directions: *Each of the following passages is followed by five questions. Read the passage carefully and then answer the questions that follow each. For each question, four probable answers A, B, C and D are given. Only one out of these is correct. Choose the correct answer.*

PASSAGE-1

The use of words like 'welcome', 'thank you', 'please', etc., at the right moment reflects a polite nature. The civic sense also lies within the scope of good manners. We should not shout or talk loudly in public places like hospitals and libraries and create disturbance. We should not cheat people or make fun of them. Cleanliness is also necessary. We must not throw the waste on roads and make use of dustbins. We should not harm the public property as it belongs to all of us. While in a queue, discipline should be maintained. We must give fair chance to others.

1. Expressions like 'welcome' 'thank you' and 'please' reflect
   A. happiness B. discipline
   C. civic sense D. polite nature
2. While in a library, we should
   A. respect others B. avoid arguments
   C. talk in low tone D. be courteous
3. A public property belongs to
   A. nobody B. all of us
   C. government D. one who maintains it
4. Discipline is
   A. the rule of proper conduct or action
   B. the rule of road sense
   C. making use of dustbins
   D. forming a queue
5. The most appropriate title for this passage would be
   A. Polite Nature B. Courtesy
   C. Good Manners D. Civic Sense

PASSAGE-2

There is an old proverb 'Early to bed and early to rise makes a man healthy and wise.' I am in the habit of getting up early in the morning and have formed the habit of taking long morning walks in the past two years. It is a light exercise and best for physical fitness. The morning air which is fresh and pure is beneficial for the lungs. The early rays of the rising sun are good for healthy skin. 'Health is wealth' and doctors also recommend morning walk to their patients for gaining sound health and freshness of energy.

1. What is good for lungs?
   A. Sunrays B. Fresh air
   C. Sound sleep D. Light exercise
2. What is a light exercise?
   A. Early to bed B. Early to rise
   C. Morning walk D. Gaining sound health
3. What is good for skin?
   A. Fresh air B. Morning air
   C. Morning walk D. Rising sun's rays
4. What is best for physical fitness?
   A. Light exercise B. Long morning walk
   C. Early to rise D. Fresh and pure air
5. Long morning walk
   A. bring sound sleep
   B. ensures physical fitness
   C. ensures healthy skin
   D. keeps healthy, wealthy and wise

PASSAGE-3

Mahatma Gandhi lived a splendid long life and has set great moral standards before us. He showed to the world the true way to peace. He wished to see India prosper but he became a martyr for the noble cause of Hindu-Muslim unity at the time of partition when a religious fanatic, Nathuram Godse, shot him dead on January 30, 1948. His last words were 'Hey Ram'. He lived and died for his country and countryman.

1. Mahatma Gandhi showed the world the true way to
A. prosperity B. love
C. truth D. peace

2. Mahatma Gandhi became a martyr for the noble cause of
A. truth B. non-violence
C. freedom of India D. Hindu-Muslim unity

3. Mahatma Gandhi was shot dead
A. before India achieved independence
B. by a mad man
C. by an intolerant religious person
D. by a non-religious person

4. Mahatma Gandhi set great moral standards. It means
A. he was a great religious teacher
B. he was a great moralist
C. he made India morally stronger
D. moral was everything to him

5. Gandhiji lived and died for his country and countryman. It means
A. he was born in India and died in India
B. he was a patriot
C. he was a great moralist
D. he sacrified his life for India and her people

PASSAGE-4

On one hot day a crow felt very thirsty. He flew from one place to another in search of water. After long hours of labour he found a pitcher. Eagerly, he perched on the mouth of the pitcher. He found that the water was at the bottom of the vessel. He tried his best to dip his beak but did not succeed. He did not know what to do. Suddenly some pebbles lying nearby gave him an idea. One by one he dropped the pebbles with his beak into the pitcher. The level of water slowly came up to the mouth of the pitcher. The crow then drank the water and quenched his thirst.

1. The crow found a pitcher
A. as it flew
B. after many hours of labour
C. full of water
D. which was empty

2. What is the moral of the passage?
A. No pains, no gains
B. God helps those who help themselves
C. Necessity is the mother of invention
D. Try and try again, you will succeed at last

3. The crow flew from place to place
A. in search of pitcher B. in search of pebbles
C. in search of water D. in search of a vessel

4. The pitcher, the crow found
A. was full of water
B. was dry
C. had little water in the bottom
D. had water up to its mouth

5. As the crow dropped pebbles into the pitcher, what happend?
A. The pitcher broke down
B. The water leaked one of the pitcher
C. The level of water into the pitcher rose up slowly
D. Water level immediately rose to the mouth of the pitcher

PASSAGE-5

Once upon a time a crane and a fox lived in a forest. They were good friend. One day the fox invited the crane to a feast. He made a tasty food and served it before the crane on a plate. The crane could not eat anything because of the long beak. But the fox licked all his food. The crane felt insulted. He decided to teach the fox a lesson. Next day he invited the fox. He prepared the same tasty food and placed it in front of the fox inside a narrow glass. The crane ate easily while the fox looked on. Now, it was the fox's turn to remain hungry.

1. What is the moral of the passage?
A. Beware of the wicked
B. One good turn deserves another
C. Be contented with what you have
D. Tit for tat

2. The crane could not eat tasty food because the
A. food was served in a shallow plate
B. food was very hot
C. food was served in a long jar
D. crane was not hungry

3. The fox had to remain hungry because
A. the food served was not enough in quantity
B. the food was served inside a narrow glass
C. the food served was not tasty
D. the food was all liquid

4. Why did the crane feel insulted?
A. Because he was invited to feast but he could not eat anything
B. Because the food was served in a shallow plate and he could not eat
C. Because the food was too hot
D. Because the fox gulped all the food quickly

5. The crane successfully taught a lesson to the fox when he invited the fox to a feast and served the food
A. in a narrow glass B. in a large plate
C. in a broken plate D. in a long jar

PASSAGE-6

The family set down at the table and began to talk about the summer holidays. They had to decide a place to visit during the vacation. Should they go to their village or to a hill station? The parents preferred the village while the children wished to go the hill station. After few moments of discussion the elders decided to visit both the places. First they shall go to the village for a week and then stay at the hill station for the remaining days. For the first time the family shall be together during the holidays. The children were happy with the holiday plan.

1. The purpose for which the family set down at the table was
 A. to decide a place to visit during the vacation
 B. to educate the children how to carry articles during a visit to a hill station
 C. to decide the date when they should start their journey
 D. to tell the children that they will visit a hill station during this vacation

2. The final plan was to visit
 A. their village
 B. a hill station
 C. their village as well as a hill station
 D. their home town

3. The final decision was made by
 A. the boys B. the girls
 C. the women D. the elders

4. They decided first to go to their village and stay there for
 A. a day B. a week
 C. ten days D. a fortnight

5. Why were children happy?
 A. Because a hill station was included in their holiday plan
 B. Because a visit to their village was excluded from their holiday plan
 C. Because their choice prevailed
 D. Because they were going all alone to the hill station

PASSAGE-7

Once Govind intended to go on pilgrimage with his family. He asked Mirind to accompany. But for his trade's reason, he did not go with him. So Govind thought it safe to leave the box of his jewellery with him, as it was dangerous to leave it in a lone house or take it on the journey. So he went to him with the box. He took him to a lonely place under a tree and handed it over to him. He told Mirind, "Keep it safe with you. I shall return from the journey after six month then I shall take it back from you." Mirind said, "Don't worry, I shall keep it as safe as own."

1. Govind intended to go
 A. for a business trip
 B. to a hill station
 C. on a long journey to a sacred place
 D. to his home town for a long period

2. Why did Govind leave his box of jewellery with Mirind?
 A. Because it was not safe to take the box with him on a long journey
 B. Because Mirind was his fast friend
 C. Because the box was very heavy
 D. Because his house was unsafe

3. Why did Govind take Mirind to a lonely place?
 A. To tell him that the box contained valuable jewellery
 B. So that no third person could see box
 C. To show him what was within the box
 D. To tell him that the box will remain with him

4. Where did Govind hand over the box of jewellery to Mirind?
 A. At Mirind's house
 B. At his own house
 C. In a lonely place
 D. In a lonely place under a tree

5. It was not safe to leave the box in a lone house. Here the word 'lone house' means
 A. a house in a deserted place
 B. a house where none lives
 C. a house without door and lock
 D. a house near the forest

PASSAGE-8

Zahir-ud-din Babar was the first Mughal emperor of India. A descendent of Timur on father's side and Changez Khan on his mother's side, Babar was a brave warrior. After defeating Ibrahim Lodhi in the First Battle of Panipat in 1526 he entered Delhi and soon gained control over Agra. After many more battles with Rajputs he extended his empire over Punjab, Uttar Pradesh and north Bihar. He died at a young age of 48 years in 1530 at his capital Agra without getting much time to consolidate his victories.

1. Zahir-ud-din Babar was the first
 A. Muslim ruler of India B. Mughal ruler of India
 C. Afghan ruler of India D. Turk ruler of India

2. Babar was born in the years
 A. 1480 B. 1482
 C. 1492 D. 1962

3. Babar first occupied
 A. Punjab B. Agra
 C. Delhi D. Panipat

4. Babar was a brave warrior. Here brave warrior means
 A. courageous soldier B. a kind hearted soldier
 C. a clever fighter D. a victorious general

5. Babar extended his empire over Punjab and Uttar Pradesh after many more battles with the
 A. Afghans B. Rajputs
 C. Mughals D. Lodhies

PASSAGE-9

Our National Flag is tricolour. It has three equal horizontal strips. The strip at the top is saffron, in the middle is white and at the bottom is green. The ratio of width to length of the flag is 2 : 3. In the centre of the white strip is a wheel in navy blue. The wheel represents the *chakra*. Its design is similar to the wheel which appears on the abacus of the Sarnath Lion Capital of Ashoka. Its diameter approximates to the width of the white strip. The wheel has 24 spokes. It was adopted by Constituent Assembly on July 22, 1947. We love our national flag. We respect it. We are ready to sacrifice our life to protect its honour. It represents the nation. So it is a symbol of national honour.

1. In our national flag the wheel is located in the centre of
A. saffron strip B. white strip
C. green strip D. blue strip

2. In our national flag which of the strips is at the bottom in our national flag
A. blue C. saffron
B. white D. green

3. Why do we love our national flag?
A. Because it is tricolour
B. Because it has three strips
C. Because it has a wheel at the centre
D. Because it is a symbol of national honour

4. Our national flag was approved by
A. President
B. Lok Sabha
C. Parliament
D. Constituent Assembly

5. The diameter approximates to the width of the white strip. Here the word 'approximates' means
A. is more or less equal
B. is exactly equal
C. is not equal
D. is related

PASSAGE-10

Distance in large cities are long. All the people do not have their own means of transport. They have to depend upon the state or private buses. The number of bus users is very large. Every bus stop is, therefore, crowded. The number of buses is not adequate. Thus people suffer the torture of long wait at the bus stop. Some bus stops are quite orderly. People form queues and get into the buses turn by turn. However, often this order is forgotten and confusion spreads when the bus comes and the law of jungle prevails.

1. Why are the bus stops crowded?
A. Because they are small is size
B. Because the number of passengers is very large
C. Because they are situated at some busy centre
D. Because people do not form queues

2. Long wait at the bus stop is the result of
A. over-crowding in the buses
B. late running of buses
C. shortage of buses
D. slow speed of buses

3. Some bus stops are quite orderly where
A. there is no crowd
B. the number of buses is adequate
C. people do not have to wait for long
D. people form queues and enter the buses one by one

4. Most of the people who travel by buses are
A. non-working
B. do not have their own vehicles
C. have to go a long distance
D. live in large cities

5. What happens when people do not have their own transport?
A. They have to wait for a bus at a bus stop
B. They have to depend upon the state or private buses
C. They have to travel long distances
D. They form queues and get into buses one by one

ANSWERS

	1	2	3	4	5
Passage 1.	D	C	B	A	C
Passage 2.	B	C	D	B	B
Passage 3.	D	D	C	B	D
Passage 4.	B	C	C	C	C
Passage 5.	D	A	B	B	A
Passage 6.	A	C	D	B	A
Passage 7.	C	A	B	D	B
Passage 8.	B	B	C	A	B
Passage 9.	B	D	D	D	A
Passage 10.	B	C	D	B	B

●●●

2

English Grammar

PARTS OF SPEECH

Part of speech	Definition or Function	Examples
Noun	Name of a person, place, animal, quality or thing	Ram, boy, dog pen, sun, Delhi, truth, honesty
Pronoun	Used in place of a noun	I, you, he she, they
Articles & Determiners	Points out indefinite and definite nouns	a, an, the, few, some
Adjective	Describes a noun or pronoun	big, honest, wooden valuable, quiet, deep, soft, narrow
Adverb	Describes a verb, an adjective or another adverb	silently, widely, softly, quietly, very, carefully
Verb	Tells about action or state of something or someone	is, am, was, have, do, like, walk, work, make, throw, tell
Conjuction	Joins words, clauses or sentences	and, but, when, yet, while, else
Preposition	Links a noun or pronoun to another word	at, to, after, on for, under, over, with
Interjection	Expresses sudden feelings or emotions	Ah!, Alas!, oh!, ouch!, hi!, well!, Hurrah!

NOUNS

A word which denotes a person, a thing, an animal or a place is said to be a noun.

There are two noun numbers in English — the *Singular* and the *Plural*.

Singular Numbers : A noun that denotes one person or one thing, is said to be in the Singular number. For example — book, pencil, bird, dog, hen etc. are in singular number.

Plural Number : A noun that denotes more than one person or one thing is said to be in plural number. For example — boys, pens, lions, girls, men etc. are in plural number.

REMEMBER

Singular	*Plural*	*Singular*	*Plural*
Cat	Cats	Book	Books
Pen	Pens	Room	Rooms
Tree	Trees	Bus	Buses
Bush	Bushes	Box	Boxes
Glass	Glasses	Dish	Dishes
Judge	Judges	Tax	Taxes
Watch	Watches	Calf	Calves
Thief	Thieves	Knife	Knives
Scarf	Scarves	Wife	Wives
Leaf	Leaves	Wolf	Wolves
Half	Halves	Monarch	Monarchs
Roof	Roofs	Hoof	Hoofs
Gulf	Gulfs	Staff	Staffs
Radio	Radios	Bamboo	Bamboos
Folio	Folios	Hero	Heroes
Volcano	Volcanoes	Mango	Mangoes
Potato	Potatoes	Photo	Photos
Piano	Pianos	Baby	Babies
Fly	Flies	Country	Countries
Lady	Ladies	Boy	Boys
Monkey	Monkeys	Ox	Oxen
Child	Children	Man	Men
Woman	Women	Tooth	Teeth
Axis	Axes	Basis	Bases
Foot	Feet	Goose	Geese
Englishman	Englishmen	Radius	Radii
Vertex	Vertices	Stimulus	Stimuli

1. Note the plurals of the following nouns:

Singular	*Plural*	*Singular*	*Plural*
copy	copies	cry	cries
baby	babies	duty	duties
body	bodies	country	countries
family	families	diary	diaries
fly	flies	fairy	fairies
city	cities	spy	spies
army	armies	storey	storeys
bay	bays	monkey	monkeys

2. The following nouns do not undergo any change in plural form, in general.

Singular	*Plural*	*Singular*	*Plural*
deer	deer	sheep	sheep
thousand	thousand	pair	pair
hundred	hundred	score	score
dozen	dozen	gross	gross

Note: We can write—
(*a*) thousands of men; (*b*) two pairs of shoes; (*c*) dozens of mangoes; (*d*) scores of people etc. But—
(*a*) two thousand rupees; (*b*) three hundred men; (*c*) five dozen eggs, etc.

3. The following nouns are usually used in plural forms. They take a plural verb after them—

eatables	fetters	surroundings
riches	alms	spectacles
trousers	pants	scissors
premises	thanks	annals
congratulations	goods	shorts
tongs	pains	arms
breeches	(for troubles)	

4. The following are the nouns which are plural in appearance but are usually used in singular number. They are followed by a singular verb—

news	politics	physics
mathematics	economics	ethics
politics	classics	gallows
statistics	athletics	innings
mechanics	summons	mumps

5. Collective nouns often used as plurals—

public	police	cattle
audience	clergy	folk
people	poultry	nation
elite	gentry	glitterati

6. The nouns that are usually used in singular forms—

advice	hair	rice
fuel	alphabet	machinery
offspring	issue	furniture
mischief	stationery	luggage
bedding	information	abuse

7. Material nouns are always used in singular number—

gold	copper	milk
water	silk	wool

Note: They may be used in plural with a different meaning. copper coins (coppers), chains or fetters (irons), cans made of tin (tins).

GENDERS

The difference in sex is denoted by Gender in grammar. The various genders are as follows :

1. **Masculine Gender :** A noun that denotes a male is said to be of the masculine gender, as man, uncle, ox, boy etc.
2. **Feminine Gender :** A noun that denotes a female is said to be of feminine gender, as woman, aunt, princess, cow etc.
3. **Common Gender :** Nouns which denote both males and females are said to be of the common gender, as friend, cousin, person, parent, baby etc.
4. **Neuter Gender :** A noun that denotes the name of object without life is said to be of neuter gender, as file, table, pencil.

REMEMBER

Masculine	*Feminine*
Boy	Girl
Son	Daughter
Brother	Sister
Murderer	Murderess
Sorcerer	Sorceress
Son-in-law	Daughter-in-law
Father-in-law	Mother-in-law
Man-servant	Maid-servant
Land-lord	Land-lady
Bachelor	Maid
Gentleman	Lady
Monk	Nun
Earl	Countess
Lad	Lass
Sir	Madam
Duke	Dutchess
Emperor	Empress
Milk-man	Milk-maid
Pea-cock	Pea-hen
Step-father	Step-mother
Hero	Heroine
Viceroy	Vicerine
Mr.	Mrs.
Governor	Governess
Master	Mistress
Wizard	Witch
Heir	Heiress
Host	Hostess
Lion	Lioness
Mayor	Mayoress
Actor	Actress
Buck	Doe
Colt	Filly
Dog	Bitch
Horse	Mare
Count	Countess
Hunter	Huntress
Prince	Princess
Abbot	Abbess
God	Goddess
Author	Authoress
Ox	Cow
Widower	Widow
Grand-father	Grand-mother
He-goat	She-goat
Milk-man	Milk-woman
Bridegroom	Bride
Tiger	Tigress
Priest	Priestess
Poet	Poetess
Shepherd	Shepherdess
Nephew	Niece
Stag	Hind

PRONOUNS

The repetition of a noun in a sentence or a set of sentences is really boring. So, instead of repeating the noun, we can use a word (for that noun) called the pronoun.
"A pronoun is a word that we use instead of a noun".

Example:
This is *Sachin. He* plays cricket.
Note: *He* is the pronoun used in place of *Sachin.*

Kinds of Pronouns

1. **Personal pronouns :** A pronoun which is used instead of the name of a person is known as a 'Personal Pronoun'. A list of the 'Personal pronouns' is listed below :
   I, my, mine, me, we (First Person)
   You, your, yours (Second Person)
   He, his, him, she, her, hers, it,
   its, they, their, theirs, them (Third Person)

2. **Demonstrative, Indefinite and Distributive Pronouns :**
   (a) Demonstrative Pronouns : Pronouns used to point out the objects to which they refer are called Demonstrative Pronouns.
   Examples :
   (i) *This* is a present from my uncle.
   (ii) *These* are merely excuses.
   (iii) Bembay mangoes are better than *those* of Bangaluru.
   (b) Indefinite Pronouns : All pronouns which refer to persons or things in a general way and do not refer to any particular person or thing are called Indefinite Pronouns.
   Examples :
   (i) *Somebody* has stolen my watch.
   (ii) *Few* escaped unhurt.
   (iii) Did you ask *anybody* to come?
   (c) Distributive Pronouns : Each, either, neither are called distributive pronouns because they refer to persons or things one at a time. For this reason they are always singular and followed by the verb in singular.
   Examples :
   (i) *Each* of the men received a reward.
   (ii) *These* men received *each* a reward.
   (iii) *Either* of you can go.

3. **Relative Pronouns :** A relative pronoun refers or relates to some noun going before, which is called its Antecedent.
   Examples :
   (i) I met Hari *who* used to live here.
   (ii) I have found the pen *which* I had lost.
   (iii) Here is the book *that* you lent me.

4. **Interrogative Pronouns :** These pronouns, are used for asking questions.
   Examples :
   (i) *Whose* book is this?
   (ii) *What* will all the neighbours say?
   (iii) *Which* do you prefer, tea or coffee?

Note : Interrogative pronouns can also be used in asking indirect questions. Consider the following examples :
(i) I asked *who* was speaking.
(ii) Tell me *what* you have done.
(iii) Say *which* you would like best.

Behaviour of the Pronouns

1. If three pronouns are used together in the same sentence they are arranged in the following order :
   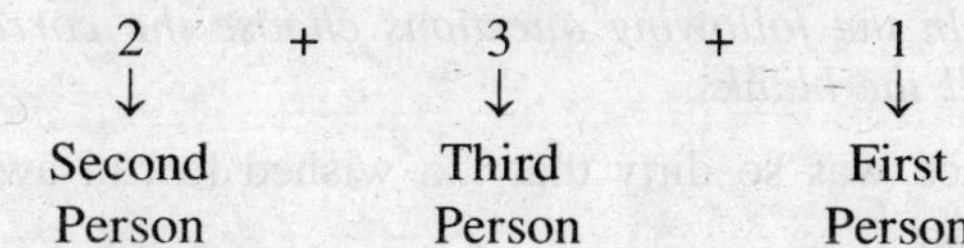

   Examples :
   I, you and he must help *that* poor man. (Incorrect)
   You, he and I must help *that* poor man. Correct)
2. When two or more singular nouns are joined by and, the pronoun used for them should be plural.
   Examples :
   Mohan and Sohan are friends. *They* play football. *They* live at Lajpat Nagar.
3. But if these nouns joined by and refer to the same person or thing, the pronoun used should be singular.
   Examples :
   (i) Delhi, the beautiful city and the capital of India, is famous for *its* historical monuments.
   (ii) The manager and owner of the firm expressed *his* views on the demands of the workers.
4. When two nouns are used with as well as, the pronoun agrees with the first subject.
   Examples :
   (a) Mohan as well as his friends is doing *his* work.
   (b) The students as well as their teachers are doing *their* work.
5. When two singular nouns joined by 'and' are preceded by *each* or *every,* the pronoun used must be singular and should agree in gender with the second noun.
   Examples :
   (a) Every man and every woman will do *her* best for the nation.
   (b) Each boy and each girl went to *her* house.
6. When two nouns are joined by using 'with', the pronoun agrees with the noun coming before 'with'.
   Examples :
   (a) The boy with *his* parents has gone to see a movie.
   (b) The children with *their* parents have gone to picnic.
7. When two different nouns are joined by either......... or; neither .... nor, the pronoun is used according to the number and gender of the second noun.

Examples :
(a) Either your sister or you have done *your* work.
(b) Neither the students nor the teacher was in *his* class.

8. The pronoun coming after '*than*' must be in the same case as that coming before '*than*'.
Examples :
(a) She plays better than *me*. (Incorrect)
She plays better than *I*. (Correct)
(b) His elder brother is more intelligent than *him*. (Incorrect)
His elder brother is more intelligent than *he*. (Correct)

9. 'Many a' always takes a singular pronoun and singular verb.
Example :
Many a soldier has met *his* death in the battle field.

10. 'Who', 'Whose', 'Whom' are used only for persons.
Examples :
(a) *Who* is knocking at the door?
(b) *Whose* pen is this?
(c) *What* do you want?

11. 'Which' is used for things.
Example : *Which* game do you like?

MULTIPLE CHOICE QUESTIONS

Directions: *In the following questions choose the correct options to fill the blanks.*

1. The place was so dirty that ..... wished to run away from there.
A. everybody B. anybody
C. few D. some

2. ..... was there to help me.
A. Somebody B. Anything
C. Anybody D. Nobody

3. Is there .... to eat?
A. some B. something
C. any D. few

4. ..... of the students were making a great noise.
A. Anyone B. Somebody
C. Many D. Nobody

5. ..... of the students can solve this sum.
A. Someone B. Anybody
C. Somebody D. None

6. ...... of us should try our best to make India a heaven.
A. Any B. Somebody
C. Anybody D. All

7. ...... of us do not know the real meaning of our lives.
A. Any B. Something
C. Several D. Many

8. My .... black.
A. hairs are B. hair is
C. hairs shall D. hair will

9. She saw two .... on the last Sunday.
A. thiefs B. theifs
C. thieves D. theives

10. My sister is a ....
A. bacheloress B. bachelor
C. unmaried D. spinster

11. One is supposed to do ....
A. our duty B. their duty
C. one's duty D. his duty

12. Take anything .... you want.
A. that B. which
C. than D. then

13. I cannot tolerate ....
A. separated you B. your separation
C. separation from you D. you separated

14. He is .... faithful partner.
A. Yours B. You
C. Your D. Your's

15. Ajay is more smart than ....
A. her B. hers
C. herself D. she

16. Vivek works harder than ....
A. me B. I
C. her D. his

17. They should help ....
A. the poor people B. the poor
C. the poor persons D. the poor peoples

18. .... are mad.
A. All his sons B. His all sons
C. Sons all his D. All sons his

19. The poor fellow .... to fate.
A. resigned B. resigned himself
C. resigned itself D. resigned themselves

20. Nobody will help you but ....
A. I B. me
C. ours D. his

21. It is a good chance, You must avail ...... this opportunity.
A. of B. yourself of
C. for D. from

22. The person who is elected .... my relative.
A. is B. he is
C. his D. him

23. He made ....
A. yours mention B. mention of you
C. mention for you D. mention about you

24. .... I know, he is quite faithful.
A. As far as B. So far as
C. So far this D. So far so

25. It is a duty of a person to take .... for his family.

A. pain B. pains
C. pain-killers D. pained

26. She does not love .... husband.

A. his B. her
C. its D. their

27. Let .... work together.

A. him and me B. he and I
C. he and him D. I and me

28. Copper, Silver and Gold ....

A. each will do B. either will do
C. any one will do D. any will do

29. Jessica and Roma are very irregular .... habits.

A. in her B. in their
C. in its D. in every

30. One likes to enjoy .... who was a great poet.

A. The sonnets of Shakespeare
B. Shakespeare's sonnets
C. Sonnets
D. Shakespeare

ANSWERS

1	2	3	4	5	6	7	8	9	10
A	D	B	C	D	D	D	B	C	D
11	**12**	**13**	**14**	**15**	**16**	**17**	**18**	**19**	**20**
C	A	C	C	D	B	B	A	B	B
21	**22**	**23**	**24**	**25**	**26**	**27**	**28**	**29**	**30**
B	A	B	A	B	B	A	C	B	A

ARTICLES

The family of the articles has only three members. They are : A, An and The. However, they fall under two groups :

(a) Definite Article *(b)* Indefinite Article

'The' is known as definite article whereas 'a' and 'an' are known as indefinite articles.

Use of the Definite Article 'The'

'The' is used before

1. The superlative degree :
   He is the ablest man of the town.
   (ablest is a superlative degree)
2. The name of states, countries etc. having a descriptive name :
   (i) The J & K is a small state. (J & K is a descriptive name)
   (ii) He lives in the U.S.A. (U.S.A. is a descriptive name)
   (But the Delhi and the America are wrong because neither Delhi nor America is a descriptive name)
3. The names of the scriptures :
   The Gita is a holy book. (Gita is a scripture)
4. Name of newspapers :
   The Tribune is published from Chandigarh.
5. Name of rivers, canals, seas, oceans, bays, gulfs, groups of islands etc. :
   (i) The Ganga is a holy river.
   (ii) The Indian Ocean is the deepest ocean.
   (iii) The Persian Gulf is a narrow gulf.
6. The name of famous buildings :
   The Taj is one of the best buildings in India.
7. The names of nationals, sects and communities:
   (i) The English defeated the Germans in the World War.
   (ii) The rich should help the poor.
   (iii) The Hindus believe in the caste system.
8. Proper nouns used as common nouns :
   (i) Kalidas is the Shakespeare of India.
   (ii) Delhi is the London of India.
9. Famous historical events :
   The Industrial Revolution changed the face of England.
10. The directions and the celestial bodies:
    The sun rises in the east.
11. Titles : Akbar, the Great was loved by his subjects.

Do not use 'the'

1. Before languages :
   The English is an international language. (Incorrect)
   English is an international language. (Correct)
2. Before the names of games :
   The hockey is a popular game. (Incorrect)
   Hockey is a popular game. (Correct)

Use of the Indefinite Articles 'A' and 'An'

'A' is used before :

1. All singular common nouns beginning with a consonant :
   (i) A boy sings a song.
   (ii) A black and a white cow were grazing in the field.
2. If a word begins with a vowel but gives the sound of a consonant, 'a' should be used before it :
   (i) He was helped in his work by a European.
   (ii) He is a one-eyed man.
   (iii) It is a useful work.

'An' is used as follows :

1. All singular common nouns beginning with a vowel (*i.e.*, a, e, i, o, u) :
   (i) He is an artist. (ii) He is an old man. (iii) I intend to buy an umbrella.
2. If a word starts with a consonant but gives the sound of a vowel, "an" should be used before it :
   (i) Brutus is an honourable man.
   (ii) He is an honour to his profession.
   (iii) He is an L.L.B.

Demonstratives, that, these and those

1. The demonstrative adjectives and pronouns are for objects nearby the speaker:
   this (singular) those (plural)
   and for objects far away from the speaker.
   That (singular) those (plural)
2. Demonstratives are the only adjectives that agree in number with their nouns.
   That hat is nice.
   Those hats are nice.
3. When there is the idea of selection, the pronoun "one" (or "ones") often follows the demonstrative.
   I want a book. I'll get this (one).
   If the demonstrative is followed by an adjective, "one"(or "ones") must be used.
   I want a book. I'll get this big one.

MULTIPLE CHOICE QUESTIONS

Directions: *In the following questions choose the correct options to fill the blanks.*

1. .... will have to be paid for this material.
A. Half rupee B. Half a rupee
C. A half rupee D. An half rupee

2. .... is taking keen interest in India.
A. The USA B. USA
C. An USA D. A USA

3. Only .... can save our country.
A. the Hitler B. a Hitler
C. Hitler D. an Hitler

4. I can run for ....
A. hundred miles B. the hundred miles
C. a hundred miles D. an hundred miles.

5. .... man-eater has been killed.
A. The B. A
C. An D. Either A or B

6. What .... fine idea!
A. the B. an
C. a D. No article

7. .... earth is moving around the sun.
A. An B. A
C. The D. No article

8. This is .... first example while I got.
A. the B. a
C. an D. No article

9. This is .... house which was built during earthquake.
A. a B. an
C. the D. No article

10. .... America is a rich country.
A. The B. An
C. A D. No article

11. .... U.S.A. is a developed country.
A. A B. An
C. The D. No article

12. .... Bible is a holy book.
A. A B. The
C. An D. No article

13. .... rich should help the poor.
A. The B. A
C. An D. No article

14. .... Gold is a costly metal.
A. The B. A
C. An D. No article

15. Kalidas is .... Shakespeare of India.
A. a B. an
C. the D. No article

16. I cannot do .... difficult work.
A. a such B. the such
C. such the D. such a

17. How foolish .... plan it is!
A. a B. an
C. the D. No article

18. An ink is .... useful article.
A. an B. a
C. the D. No article

19. There are .... husband and wife.
A. a B. an
C. the D. No article

20. He is learning .... French
A. the B. a
C. an D. No article

ANSWERS

1	2	3	4	5	6	7	8	9	10
B	A	B	C	D	C	C	A	C	D
11	**12**	**13**	**14**	**15**	**16**	**17**	**18**	**19**	**20**
C	B	A	D	C	D	A	B	D	D

ADJECTIVES & ADVERBS

An Adjective is a word which adds something to the meaning of a noun or a pronoun.

Mridula is an *intelligent* girl. He has a *black* goat.
He is a *brilliant* student. She is a *clever* girl.
It is a *beautiful* picture.

In the sentences given above, the words in italics are adjectives.

An Adverb is a word which qualifies the meaning of a Verb, an Adjective or another Adverb.

(*i*) He talks *slowly*.
(*ii*) He is a *very* good student.
(*iii*) He talks *very* slowly.

In sentence (*i*), *slowly* qualifies the verb *talks*.
In sentence (*ii*), *very* qualifies the adjective *good*.
In sentence (*iii*), *very* qualifies the adverb *slowly*.

Adjectives have three degrees of comparison :

1. **Positive Degree :** It expresses the common form of an adjective.
   Example :
   Ram is a *tall* boy.
   In the above sentence *tall* is an adjective and expresses the common form.
2. **Comparative Degree :** It expresses the more of the same form.
   Example :
   Ram is *taller* than Mahesh.
   In the above sentence *taller* is an adjective that expresses the more of the common form of the adjective *tall*.

"When and How to Use" Comparative Degree?

(a) Comparative Degree is used when two persons or two groups of persons or things are compared.
Examples :
(a)He is *wiser* than his younger brother.
(b)This glass is *cleaner* than the other.

(b) When two different qualities in the same person are compared, more is used instead of 'er' to form the comparative. The formula used in this case should be :
More + Positive Degree
She is *fairer* than polite. (Incorrect)
She is *more fair* than polite. (Correct)

(c) When selection of one out of two persons or things is meant, the degree of comparison is followed by of and *the* is used before it.
Example :
Zia is abler of *the* two sisters.

(d) If two comparatives are used in the same sentence to impress upon an idea, both should be preceded by the definite article.
Examples :
(i) The higher you go, the cooler it is.
(ii) The more we get, the more we desire.

(e) When one person or thing is compared with another of the same kind, other is used after the comparative degree. In such sentences other is normally preceded by any or all.
Examples :
(i) Kalidas is greater than any dramatist. (Incorrect)
Kalidas is greater than any other dramatist. (Correct)
(ii) Lead is heavier than all metals. (Incorrect)
Lead is heavier than all other metals. (Correct)

(f) Senior, junior, superior, inferior, prior, anterior (earlier than) and posterior (later than) are always followed by 'to'.

Examples :
(i) Ram is senior *to* Mohan by three years.
(ii) That pen is inferior *to* that.
(iii) He is junior *to* me in rank.
(iv) This event was posterior *to* that.

Note: Never use *than* after the above mentioned adjectives.

Important Information

(a) 'Preferable' is also used as an adjective of the comparative degree. As such, it is always followed by *to* and not *a*.
Death is preferable than dishonour. (Incorrect)
Death is preferable *to* dishonour. (Correct)

(b) To intensify the Degree of comparison, we use *far* or *much* before the comparative.
Examples :
(i) This book is *far* better than that.
(ii) His performance was *much* better than Mohan's.
Warning : Always avoid the use of double comparatives.
Don't say : Ram is more cleverer than his younger brother.
Say: Ram is cleverer than his younger brother.

3. **Superlative Degree :** It expresses the most of the common form of an adjective.
   Example :
   He is the ablest man of the town.

How and when to use the Superlative Degree?

(a) The Superlative Degree is used when more than two persons or things are compared.

(b) The Superlative Degree is generally preceded by 'the' and followed by 'of' in most of the cases or otherwise.

(c) When an adjective of the superlative degree is preceded by a Possessive Adjective or a Noun in the Possessive case, 'the' should not be used before it.
Example :
Which is Kalidas' best play?

It will be a blunder to use 'the' before the Superlative Degree in such cases.

Don't say : Which is Kalidas' the best play.

(d) To intensify the degree of comparison, *by far* is used before the superlative degree.

Example :

India is *by far* the most beautiful country of the world.

Note: Always avoid the use of double superlatives.

Don't say : He is the most strongest boy in the class.

Say : He is the strongest boy in the class.

Use of some Important Adjectives

1. (a) '**Some**' is used as follows :

(i) With countable nouns where it means— a little, a small quantity.

(ii) In a question which shows some request.

Examples :

(i) There is some water in the bottle.

(ii) Some of the students were absent yesterday.

(iii) Will you have some milk?

(iv) Will you buy some fruit for me?

(b) **'Any'** is used as follows :

(i) In negative sentences.

(ii) In interrogative sentences.

(iii) After 'Hardly', 'Scarcely' and 'Barely'.

(iv) After 'If'.

Examples :

(i) There is not any sugar in the pot.

(ii) We haven't any rice in the house.

(iii) I have hardly any money.

(iv) There are scarcely any plants in this field.

(v) If there is any danger, blow the whistle.

2. (a) **Older :** Older (and oldest) are used for persons animals and things. But 'Older' and 'Oldest' refer to the persons who do not belong to the same family.

Examples :

(i) Radha is older than Shyama.

(ii) John is the oldest member of the staff. 'Older' and 'Oldest' refer to the persons who do not belong to the same family.

(b) **Elder** (and **eldest**) are used in respect of the members of the same family like sons, daughters, brothers, sisters.

Examples :

(i) My elder sister is a lecturer.

(ii) Meenakshi is the eldest of the three sisters.

Note :

(i) 'Elder' is not followed by 'than'.

(ii) 'Elder' and 'Eldest' cannot be used for things.

3. (a) **'Few'** is negative and is the opposite of 'Many'. It means 'not many'.

(b) **'A few'** is positive and means 'some at least'. It is the opposite of 'None'.

(c) **'The few'** means 'minority' and suggests 'whether there is'.

Examples :

(i) We have few holidays in school.

(ii) Only a few boys will fail in the examination.

(iii) The few poems that he wrote are very popular.

4. (a) **Further** means 'something additional'.

(b) **Farther** means 'a greater distance'.

Examples :

(i) Further discussion will be held in the office of the principal.

(ii) Amritsar is farther from Delhi than Ambala.

5. (a) **Little** is negative. It means, 'not much', or 'hardly any'.

(b) **A little** is positive. It means 'some quantity'.

(c) **The little** denotes quantity. It means, 'not much but all that is, or whatever quantity there is'.

Examples :

(i) There is little hope of his success.

(ii) He knows a little of everything.

(iii) I have spent the little money I had.

(iv) The little knowledge of shoe-making proved very useful to me.

6. (a) '**Much**' expresses 'quantity'.

(b) '**Many**' expresses 'number'.

(c) **'Many a'**—'Singular noun' and 'Singular verb' are used with 'many a'.

Examples :

(i) There is not *much* water in the jug.

(ii) *Many* boys are absent today.

(iii) *Many* a battle has been fought on the soil of India.

7. (a) '**Less**' denotes 'in a small degree'.

(b) '**Fewer**' denotes 'number'.

Examples :

(i) He devotes less time to his studies.

(ii) There are no fewer than ten chairs in this room.

8. (a) '**Each**' is used for a single number of 'two persons' or 'things'.

(b) '**Every**' is used for a single number of 'many persons' or 'things'.

Examples :

(i) Each boy must take part in games.

(ii) There are only two poets. Each poet recited his poem.

(iii) Every man dies in this world.

(iv) Every man is expected to do his duty.

9. (a) '**Either**' means one of the two or both.

(b) '**Neither**' is negative of the either.

Examples :

(i) You may buy either of these two chairs.

(ii) Neither of them could speak on the stage.

10. (a) '**Later**' expresses 'late in time'.

(b) '**Latter**' means 'second in position or order'.

Examples :

(i) My father reached later than I expected.

(ii) The latter position was better than the former.

Use of some Important Adverbs

1. (a) Also, too, enough:
   (i) He taught English. Also, he edited the school magazine
   (ii) He is a writer and also he is a painter.
   (iii) He is too obstinate to listen to any reason.
   (iv) This is too difficult a piece for the junior students.
   (v) Sarla was kind enough to help the poor.
   (vi) He is brave enough to help the truth.
   Note: 'Too' is used in a negative sense, but enough is used in a positive sense.

   (b) Fairly and rather: Both suggest the meaning 'moderately'. But, mainly 'fairly' is used with the words that denote a positive meaning and rather is used with the words that denote a negative meaning:
   (i) Rita did fairly well in that competition, but her performance was rather poor in sports.
   (ii) Mona is fairly rich, but she is rather stingy.
   Note: 'Rather' can also be used in a positive sense.
   (i) This is a rather interesting job.
   (ii) That boy is rather smart.

   (c) Hardly, barely, scarcely: These words mostly convey the negative suggestions and are almost similar.
   (i) I have hardly any strength now.
   (ii) There was barely any supply to the township,
   (iii) There were scarcely a hundred guests present.
   Note: With slight variance in the meaning, the words given above convey the idea of 'very little', 'not enough', 'lack of quantity and number'.

   (d) Yet, Still: These adverbs can often be used to connect the sentence units:
   (i) He has been defeated many times in the contest; still he wants to be a competitor.
   (ii) Mona was sick; yet she went on doing her work.

   (e) Alone:
   (i) He alone (none else) is capable of handling that fire,
   (ii) He hunted all alone in the forest. (not in any company)

Special Note:

(a) Apart from their conventional positions the adverbs might be used in different positions with different meanings and angles.
   (i) He had only four books.
   (ii) John only contacted his friend in need.
   (iii) He greeted me only.
   (iv) Only he greeted me there.

(b) Inversion: Some adverbs can be inverted *i.e.* placed in the beginning of the sentence and then be followed by an interrogative form. The most common of these adverb are: so, seldom, never, nowhere, under no circumstances, hardly, scarcely etc.
   (i) So big was the bus that it could not enter the narrow lane.
   (ii) Hardly had he reached the station when he received the message.

MULTIPLE CHOICE QUESTIONS

Directions: *In the following questions choose the correct options to fill the blanks.*

1. The girl whom you met is the .... sister of Ravi.
A. eldest B. elder
C. older D. oldest

2. The historical place is ....
A. seeing worth B. worthy of seeing
C. worth seeing D. worthy seeing

3. These flowers smell ....
A. sweet B. sweetly
C. more sweetly D. sweetest

4. .... aspirant cannot pass the entrance examination.
A. Each B. Every
C. All D. No

5. Harivansh Rai .... second Shakespeare.
A. is a B. is
C. is the D. is an

6. .... student in the class got prizes.
A. Each and every B. Every and each
C. Every D. Never

7. It is .... picture than the one we saw last Monday.
A. interesting B. much interesting
C. more interesting D. most interesting

8. She is clever ....
A. that her mother is B. as her mother is
C. to her mother is D. than her mother is

9. They will get ....
A. Red, green and black paper
B. Red, green black paper
C. Red and green and black paper
D. Red green black paper

10. Health is .... wealth.
A. preferable to B. more preferable than
C. more preferable to D. most preferable then

11. .... water that was in the jug evaporated.
A. Little B. The little
C. Small D. A small

12. He has not sung .... songs.
A. much B. most
C. more D. many

13. Srishti has searched .... office.
A. whole the B. the whole
C. a whole D. some whole

14. Premchand was .... best and .... famous writer.
A. a, the most B. the, a most
C. the, more D. the, the most

15. William Shakespeare is famous as ....
A. a poet and a dramatist
B. a poet and dramatist
C. the poet and the dramatist
D. a poet and the dramatist

16. What does .... leader suggest?
A. other B. another
C. others D. anothers

17. He .... money.
A. has few B. have few
C. has little D. have little

18. The .... boys are rewarded.
A. first two B. two first
C. firsts two D. two's first

19. He is .... brave.
A. stronger than
B. stronger then
C. more strong then
D. more strong than

20. No sooner said ....
A. so done B. and done
C. then done D. but done

21. She returned .... than I had thought.
A. quickly B. more quicker
C. more quickly D. quicker

22. He is .... foolish person.
A. rather the B. a rather
C. rather a D. rather

23. This pen .... rupees.
A. costs twenty B. twenty costs only
C. costs only twenty D. only costs twenty

24. It is .... pride.
A. nothing else but B. nothing else than
C. else nothing than D. but

25. This tea is .... to drink.
A. too hot B. very hot
C. enough hot D. much hot

ANSWERS

1	2	3	4	5	6	7	8	9	10
A	C	A	B	A	C	C	C	A	A
11	**12**	**13**	**14**	**15**	**16**	**17**	**18**	**19**	**20**
B	D	B	D	B	B	C	A	D	C
21	**22**	**23**	**24**	**25**					
C	C	C	A	A					

DETERMINERS

Determiners are actually Adjectives. They are always followed by nouns.

Determiners are of the following kinds:

1. **Demonstrative Determiners :** this, that, these, those
2. **Possessive Determiners :** my, our, your, his, her, its, their
3. **Quantitative Determiners :** some, any, much, enough, sufficient, whole, a little, the little, little, all, both
4. **Numerical Determiners:** a few, some, few, the few, any, several, many, no, etc.
   One, two, three ... (Cardinals)
   First, second, third ... (Ordinals)
5. **Distributive Determiners:** either, neither
6. **Articles: Indefinite:** a, an, **Definite:** the

MULTIPLE CHOICE QUESTIONS

Directions: *In the following questions choose the correct options to fill the blanks.*

1. Give me .... rice.
A. some B. few
C. a few D. any

2. ...... sheep grazing on the slope of the hill had gone away.
A. Any B. The few
C. This D. Much

3. Have you got .... magazines to read?
A. all B. much
C. some D. little

4. I have .... money that I want to spend on shares.
A. any B. much
C. less D. some

5. There is .... owl on the branch of the tree.
A. a B. the
C. an D. some

6. My brother is .... MBA.
A. a B. an
C. the D. any

7. Have you got .... cheese?
A. some B. many
C. a few D. few

8. No, I have not got .... cheese.
A. many B. few
C. any D. some

9. There is only .... milk left in the bottle.
A. enough B. few
C. much D. a little

10. There is .... hope of his recovery.
A. any B. little
C. many D. few

11. .... dogs were barking at the strangers.
A. Some B. Any
C. Much D. Less

12. The girl bought her father .... juice.
A. few B. some
C. any D. many

13. You should take .... honey everyday.
A. any B. many
C. a little D. a few

14. .... boy was punished by the teacher.
A. Either B. All
C. Any D. Many

15. .... girl was asked to join the army.
A. None B. Neither
C. All D. Any

16. .... water in the jug has been drunk by Mohan.
A. The little B. The few
C. A few D. Few

17. I shall play .... piano at the party.
A. some B. any
C. the D. few

18. .... labourers were found dead in the mine.
A. Any B. Fewer
C. Many D. Less

19. Could I borrow .... umbrella?
A. our B. your
C. yours D. my

20. My brother is standing in the .... row.
A. any B. many
C. some D. first

ANSWERS

1	2	3	4	5	6	7	8	9	10
A	B	C	D	C	B	A	C	D	B
11	**12**	**13**	**14**	**15**	**16**	**17**	**18**	**19**	**20**
A	B	C	A	B	A	C	C	B	D

THE VERB

A Verb is a word that tells something about the action or state of or happenning to a person or thing.

A Verb tells the following:

1. What a person or thing does.
Sachin goes to school daily.
The bell *rang* loudly.
Many birds fly in the sky.
She *sang* a song.

2. What a person or thing is.
India *is* the biggest democracy in the world.
Ram Mehar *is* very rich.
They *are* happy.

3. What is done to a person or thing.
You *are liked* by all.
Two thieves *were arrested.*
Four students *were punished* by the teacher.

4. What happens to a person or thing.
His maternal uncle *died* last week.
Two ships *sank* yesterday.
Leaves *turn* yellow in autumn.

5. What a person or thing has, had, and so on.
I *have* a new car.
He *had* a scooter last year.
He *has* several cows and goats.

It goes without saying that a verb is the most important part of a sentence. No sentence is complete without a Verb.

Important Information

1. **If two or more singular nouns are joined by 'and' the verb used will be plural.**
   Example:
   (i) He and I were going to the market.
   (ii) Ram and Mohan are friends.

2. **If two singular nouns joined by 'and' points out to the same thing or person, the verb used must be singular.**
   Example:
   (i) Rice and curry is the favourite food of the Punjabis.
   (ii) The Collector and District Magistrate is away.

3. In case two subjects are joined by 'as well as' the verb agrees with the first subject.
   Example :
   (i) Kanta as well as her children is playing.
   (ii) Children as well as their mother are playing.
   In the case of first sentence the verb (is) agrees with Kanta and in the case of second sentence the verb (are) agrees with the children.

4. 'Neither', 'Either', 'Every', 'Each', 'Everyone', and 'Many a' are followed by a singular verb.
   Example :
   (i) Either of the plans is to be adopted.
   (ii) Neither of the two brothers is sure to pass.
   (iii) Every student is expected to be obedient.
   (iv) Everyone of them desires this.
   (v) Many a person is drowned in the sea.

5. If two subjects are joined by 'Either .... or' / 'Neither .... nor', the verb agrees with the subject near to it.

Example :

(i) Either my brother or I am to do this work.

(ii) Neither he nor they are prepared to do this work.

6. 'A great many' is always followed by a 'plural noun' and a 'plural verb'. For example :

A great many students have been declared successful.

7. Similarly if two subjects are joined by 'with', 'together with', 'no less than', in addition to 'and not', etc. the verb agrees with the first subject.

Example :

(i) The boy with his parents has arrived.

(ii) He, no less than I, is to blame.

8. Nouns, plural in form, but singular in meaning, take a singular verb.

Example :

This news was broadcast from television yesterday.

MULTIPLE CHOICE QUESTIONS

Directions: *In the following questions choose the correct options to fill the blanks.*

1. The bus with all its passengers .... lost.
A. were B. was
C. are D. would

2. You as well as I .... responsible for this work.
A. am B. are
C. was D. is

3. Raghava like all his companions .... a spoiled child.
A. are B. were
C. is D. will be

4. Pen and ink .... required for me.
A. are B. were
C. is D. has required

5. Every girl and every boy .... attended the seminar.
A. have B. has
C. is D. are

6. Not only she but all her sisters ...... been married.
A. has B. have
C. is D. are

7. There .... nothing but miseries in life.
A. is B. are
C. were D. will be

8. Neither prose nor poem .... given.
A. were B. was
C. has D. have

9. Either he or I .... wrong.
A. is B. are
C. am D. were

10. Either Sulekha or Rekha .... coming here.
A. are B. is
C. were D. have

11. .... the child or his parents to blame?
A. Is B. Are
C. Were D. Has

12. You and I .... neighbours.
A. am B. are
C. was D. has

13. The house with all its belongings ..... sold away.
A. were B. are
C. was D. must

14. Either water or juice .... required.
A. is B. are
C. were D. has

15. There were not as many tables as .... required.
A. was B. were
C. is D. are

16. They each .... a book.
A. have B. are
C. has D. is

17. He and I .... class friends.
A. is B. am
C. was D. are

18. She as well as I .... guilty.
A. is B. are
C. am D. must be

19. Purushottam .... not read more on this chapter.
A. needs
B. has been need
C. need
D. had been need

20. He came .... to his aunt.
A. run B. running
C. to run D. in run

ANSWERS

1	2	3	4	5	6	7	8	9	10
B	B	C	C	B	B	A	B	C	B
11	**12**	**13**	**14**	**15**	**16**	**17**	**18**	**19**	**20**
A	B	C	A	B	A	D	A	C	B

CONJUNCTIONS

A conjunction is a word which connects words, clauses or sentences.

Look at the following sentences.

(i) He bought apples *and* mangoes.

(ii) God made the country *and* man made the town.

(iii) The door was open *but* there was no one in the house.

(iv) He knows that I am here *and* that I want to see him.

In the sentence (i), *and* connects two words—*apples* and *mangoes.*

In the sentence (ii), *and* connects two sentences—*God made the country* and *man made the town.*

In the sentence (iii), *but* connects two sentences— *The door was open* and *there was no one in the house.*

In the sentence (iv), *and* connects two clauses—*that I am here* and *that I want to see him.*

The main coordinating conjunctions are:

and, but, for, or, nor, also, either ..... or, neither ..... nor.

There are some conjunctions which are used in pairs. They are:

either .... or, ... neither .... nor, both .... and, though .... yet, whether .... or, not only .... but also.

Example: *Either* take it *or* leave it.

It is *neither* useful *nor* ornamental.

They *both* like *and* respect me.

Though he is suffering from high fever, *yet* he does not cry.

He does not care *whether* you go *or* stay.

He is *not only* doltish, *but also* obstinate.

The conjunctions which are used in pairs in this way, are called correlative conjunctions, or merely correlatives.

Use of Important Conjunctions

1. **As soon as :** As soon as denotes simultaneous time.
   Example : As soon as he saw his enemy, he took to his heels.
2. **No sooner .... than :**
   (a) 'No sooner' is always followed by 'than'.
   (b) Please remember that 'No sooner' is always followed by do/does/did. As such only first form of the verb should be used after the subject.
   Example :
   No sooner did he see his enemy than he took to his heels.
3. **Hardly :** Hardly is followed by when.
   Examples :
   (i) Hardly had I left the house when it started raining.
   (ii) We had hardly come into the room when his father began chastising him.
   Note :
   A. Hardly is never followed by than.
   B. 'Scarcely' can also be used in the sense and manner of 'Hardly'.
4. **Lest :** Lest is used in the sense of so that .... not. It is always followed by should. Lest is negative in sense. Hence 'not' should never be used with it.
   Example :
   Work hard lest you should fail.
   Note : 'Lest' is always followed by 'should' and not 'may'.
5. **Unless :** Unless expresses condition. It is also used in the negative sense. Use of 'not' is not allowed with unless because unless is already in the negative sense.
   Example :
   Unless you labour hard you will not pass.
6. **Until :** 'Until' expresses time. It means 'till not'.
   Example : Wait here until I return.
   Note : Until is in the negative sense. So 'not' should not be used with it. Example :
   Wait here until I do not return. (Incorrect)
   Wait here until I return. (Correct)
7. **As well as :** When two subjects are joined by 'as well as', the verb always agrees with the first subject.
   Examples :
   (i) The teacher as well as students is playing.
   (ii) Students as well as the teacher are playing.
   Note : 'Both' and 'as well as' cannot be used together in the same sentence.
   Examples :
   Both Sita as well as Kanta are beautiful. (Incorrect)
   Sita as well as Kanta is beautiful. (Correct)
   Both Sita and Kanta are beautiful. (Correct)
8. **As if :** 'As if' is used in the sense of pretension. While using 'as if' in a sentence, we should see that even the third person singular subject gets 'were'.
   Example : He talks as if he were mad.
9. **Till :** Till expresses time. Till is always used in the affirmative.
   Example :
   We did not come back till sunset.
10. **Rather than :** 'Rather than' is used in the sense of 'preference'. 'Rather' is always followed by 'than'.
    Example :
    I would rather die than submit.
11. **As long as/so long as :** Both express time during which an action or event takes place.
    Example :
    As long as there is life, there is hope.
12. **However :** It is both a subordinate and co-ordinate clause.
    Examples :
    (a) Mala worked hard, she however, failed.
    (b) However hard he may work, he cannot pass.
13. **Such as :** 'Such as' gives us the sense of 'like'. Such is always followed by 'as'.
    Example :
    Life is such a puzzle as cannot be solved.

MULTIPLE CHOICE QUESTIONS

Directions: *In the following questions choose the correct options to fill the blanks.*

1. Neither he .... his friend is good.
A. or B. and
C. but D. nor

2. The officer asked the peon .... why he was late.
A. that B. if
C. but D. No word needed

3. Both Ajay .... Vijay are intelligent.
A. or B. nor
C. and D. No word needed

4. No Sooner did the thief see the public .... he ran away.
A. then B. and
C. but D. than

5. Abhinav .... his brothers was going to Mumbai.
A. but
B. yet
C. No word needed
D. together with

6. He behaves .... he were the captain of the team.
A. as if B. as
C. No word needed D. that

7. Either Rupali .... Sonali is going to attend the meeting.
A. and B. but
C. nor D. or

8. Neither Nirmal .... Ashwinee is going to listen the speech.
A. and B. but
C. nor D. or

9. Ravi .... Prakash are going to Kolkata.
A. or B. nor
C. but D. and

10. Rice .... curry is my usual breakfast.
A. and B. but
C. then D. than

11. Hardly had he left .... his brother came.
A. then B. than
C. when D. that

12. I would rather have a copy .... a book.
A. then B. than
C. when D. that

13. He is no other .... my friend.
A. then B. than
C. when D. but

14. He saw a snake ....he awoke.
A. then B. when
C. than D. No word needed

15. Ten years have passed .... my grandmother died.
A. since B. when
C. then D. than

16. She is .... good .... bad.
A. either, not B. neither, or
C. neither, nor D. neither, than

17. The cellphone is both cheap .... best.
A. than B. and
C. then D. or

18. No sooner did the rogue see the police .... he disappeared.
A. then B. than
C. so D. because

19. Srishti will go .... Sanju goes.
A. if B. than
C. then D. although

20. She is wise .... timid.
A. and B. yet
C. but D. however

21. Make hay .... the sun shines.
A. though B. while
C. after D. before

22. He is so weak .... he cannot walk.
A. but B. that
C. then D. so

23. Although he is rich, ... he is unhappy.
A. but B. yet
C. so D. still

24. Wait here .... I come back.
A. till B. until
C. before D. after

25. He is my friend .... I shall help him.
A. so B. hence
C. that is why D. therefore

26. He must go away .... he will be beaten.
A. otherwise B. and
C. or D. else

27. God loves good men .... good men love God.
A. and B. or
C. that D. those

28. He was late .... he was not punished.
A. but B. yet
C. still D. therefore

29. Walk slowly ...., you may fall.
A. and B. or
C. so D. otherwise

30. Work hard, ... you will fail.
A. and B. or
C. otherwise D. else

ANSWERS

1	2	3	4	5	6	7	8	9	10
D	D	C	D	D	A	D	C	D	A
11	**12**	**13**	**14**	**15**	**16**	**17**	**18**	**19**	**20**
C	B	B	B	A	C	B	B	A	C
21	**22**	**23**	**24**	**25**	**26**	**27**	**28**	**29**	**30**
B	B	B	A	B	C	A	C	D	D

PREPOSITIONS

A *Preposition* is a word which is placed before a noun or a pronoun to show its relation to some other word in the sentence.

1. I saw a goat *in* the field.
2. I am fond *of* hot coffee.

In sentence 1, the word *in* shows the relation between two things—*goat* and *field.*

In sentence 2, the word *of* shows the relation between the attribute expressed by the adjective *found* and *tea.*

The words *in* and *of* are here used as prepositions.

The noun or pronoun which is used with a preposition is called its object. The noun or pronoun is in the objective case. It is governed by the preposition. Now it is absolutely clear that in sentence 1, the noun *field* is in the objective case. The word *field* is governed by the preposition *in.*

A preposition may have two or more objects.

The road runs over *hill* and *plain.*

Here, the words *hill* and *plain* are used as objects.

Use of Important Prepositions

1. Among, Between

'**Among**' is used for more than two persons or things; '**Between**' is used only for two.

Examples :

(i) Distribute these sweets *among* the poor students of the class.

(ii) Distribute these books *between* Ram and Shyam.

2. Among, In

'**Among**' is used before collective plural nouns. '**In**' is used before collective singular nouns.

Examples :

(i) I found him standing *among* the crowd.

(ii) I saw him in the crowd.

3. Beside, Besides

'**Beside**' means 'by the side of'. '**Besides**' means 'in addition to'.

Examples :

(i) The daughter was sitting *beside* her mother.

(ii) *Besides* his relatives, he invited his friends also.

4. In, Within

'**In**' means at the expiry of a period of time in future, '**Within**' means before the expiry of a period of time in any tense.

Examples :

(i) She will return *in* a week.

(ii) I shall finish my work *within* a weak.

5. On, Upon

'**On**' is used for things at rest; '**Upon**' is used for things in motion.

Examples :

(i) He is sitting *on* the floor.

(ii) The dog sprang *upon* the table.

6. By, With

'**By**' denotes the agent or doer, '**With**' denotes the instrument with which anything is done.

Examples :

(i) The bird was killed *by* the hunter with an arrow.

(ii) He beat the dog *with* a stick.

(iii) I shall reach here *by* five o'clock.

7. After, In

'**After**' means at the end of a period of time in the past. '**In**' means at the end of a period of time in future.

Examples :

(i) I shall return your book *in* a week.

(ii) He returned the book *after* a week.

8. For, From, Since

'**For**' is used before a noun denoting a period of time with all the tenses. '**From**' is used before a noun or phrase denoting a point of time, it is used in all the tenses. '**Since**' is used before a noun or phrase denoting some point of time and is always produced by a verb in the perfect continuous tense or third form of a verb.

Examples :

(i) We have been playing cards *for* two hours.

(ii) She stayed with her uncle *from* the 15th of March to the 15th of May.

(iii) I have been reading this book *since* morning.

9. Above, Over

'**Above**' means 'higher from', **Over** is used in the following four senses :

(i) In the sense of 'above' :
At noon, the sun is *over* our heads.

(ii) In the sense of 'beyond' :
I cannot get *over* my disappointment.

(iii) In the sense of 'Superiority' :
God *over* all blesses for ever more.

(iv) In the sense of 'Conclusion' :
It is all *over* with me.

10. At, Towards

'**At**' denotes the idea of aim, '**Towards**' denotes the idea of destination.

Examples :

(i) He threw the stone *at* the cat.

(ii) He went *towards* the house.

11. At, In, On

'At' is used as follows :

(i) '**At**' is used with small towns and villages. **Examples:**

(a) He was born *at* Sonepat.

(b) He lives *at* village Bangra. (Bangra is a village)

(ii) '**At**' is used before a noun denoting a definite point of time.

Example :

He called on me *at* 9 p.m. yesterday.

'In' is used as follows :

(iii) '**In**' is used with the names of big cities, provinces and countries.

Examples :

(a) His father lives *in* England.

(b) His younger brother lives *in* Calcutta.

(iv) '**In**' is used before the names of months and years.

Example :

His elder sister was born *in* 1972 *in* the month of May.

'**On**' is used with dates and names of days. **Examples:**

(a) I joined college *on* the 26th April.

(b) He will leave for Kolkata *on* Wednesday next.

Important Information

1. '**In**' is also used in the following phrases :
   In the morning; In the evening, In winter, In summer.
2. '**In**' also denotes a place inside anything.
   He travelled *in* a crowded bus.
3. '**At**' is used in the following phrases :
   At home, *At* the station, *At* work, *At* play.

12. Below, Beneath

Below means 'of lower level in position, dignity and expectation' etc. *Beneath* means 'under'.

Examples :

(i) It is *below* my dignity to talk to her.

(ii) They rested *beneath* the shade of a tree.

13. In, Into, To

'**In**' expresses Rest or Motion inside anything. '**Into**' expresses Motion towards the inside of anything or change from one medium to another. '**To**' denotes motion from one place to another.

Examples :

(i) The boys are *in* the room.

(ii) Translate this passage from English *into* Hindi.

(iii) Every morning he goes *to* the temple.

14. Till, By, Of, Off

- 'Till' means upto or not earlier than.
- 'By' means not later than.
- 'Of' shows cause, source, separation, quality, contents, possession, apposition, point of reference, space in time etc.
- 'Off' shows separation at a near distance, and detached condition.

Consider the following examples:

(i) I shall work *till* 5 a.m.

(ii) Madhu died *of* cancer.

(iii) The nib *of* the pen is made *of* gold.

(iv) He presented me a bottle *of* perfume.

(v) Our principal is a man *of* principle.

(vi) He lived in the house *of* his friend.

(vii) *By* this time tomorrow, I'll have finished my job.

(viii) My house is *off* the road.

(ix) The book fell *off* the table.

MULTIPLE CHOICE QUESTIONS

Directions: *Tick the correct preposition for the blank in each of the following sentences.*

1. He applied ...... the manager.
A. for B. to
C. with D. by

2. Trust ...... God and do the right.
A. in B. for
C. to D. with

3. She is worthy ...... a prize.
A. with B. for
C. to D. of

4. Mr. Gomes has no taste ...... music.
A. of B. for
C. with D. to

5. You are hard ...... hearing.
A. at B. of
C. with D. for

6. He is sure ...... his success
A. for B. with
C. on D. of

7. Preeti was warned ...... the danger ahead.
A. for B. at
C. of D. about

8. I am thankful ...... you for a good advice.
A. for B. with
C. to D. of

9. Deepak would not surrender ...... the police.
A. with B. to
C. for D. on

10. The small plant in your lawn is very sensitive ...... touch.
A. on B. with
C. to D. about

11. Divya was sure to succeed ..... the examination.
A. for B. in
C. to D. with

12. Geeta was jealous ...... Ravina's beauty.
A. to B. with
C. for D. of

13. He was ignorant ..... what was happening there.
A. for B. of
C. to D. with

14. Your pen is inferior ...... mine.
A. than B. with
C. from D. to

15. Reenu is no match ...... Meenu.
A. to B. for
C. with D. upon

16. It is necessary ...... you to apply for this job.
A. on B. with
C. for D. to

17. Be loyal ...... your country.
A. for B. to
C. on D. with

18. Mukesh is junior ...... me.
A. than B. to
C. from D. of

19. Deepika was innocent ...... the crime.
A. of B. with
C. from D. to

20. I am desirous.... joining the Indian cricket team.
A. for B. of
C. to D. on

ANSWERS

1	2	3	4	5	6	7	8	9	10
B	A	D	B	B	D	D	D	B	D
11	12	13	14	15	16	17	18	19	20
B	D	B	D	B	D	B	B	A	B

SYNONYMS

A synonym is a word which conveys a meaning similar to the given word.

REMEMBER

Words	***Synonyms***
Add	Increase
Adequate	Enough
Adjust	Adapt
All	Aggregate
Allow	Permit
Abode	Dwelling
Apt	Proper
Assess	Appraise
Accuse	Calumniate
Abashed	Timid
Annoy	Displease
Ample	Enough, Sufficient
Amplify	Increase
Apathetic	Unenthusiastic
Accost	Address
Authentic	True
Adjust	Fit
Approve	Assent, Allow, Accept
Adapt	Conform
Adversary	Opponent, Rival, Competitor
Beat	Whack
Benign	Kind
Breeze	Zephyr
Baffle	Puzzle
Booty	Spoil

Words	***Synonyms***
Beauty	Charm
Beast	Animal
Bandit	Robber
Blaze	Shine
Bond	Tie
Bend	Twist
Bate	Diminish
Beg	Plead
Barbaric	Wild, Savage
Bashful	Shy, Reserved
Begin	Start
Blend	Mix, Mingle
Bizarre	Funny
Below	Under
Bedevil	Confuse
Bemoan	Lament
Babble	Nonsense
Blame	Fault
Behaviour	Demeanour
Call	Accost
Copy	Imitate
Close	Shut
Caress	Love
Camp	Stay
Connect	Attach
Cut	Injure, Curtail
Cling	Stick
Conical	Funny
Convey	Carry
Conspicuous	Prominent
Cheerful	Happy, Pleasant

Words	Synonyms
Curtail	Decrease
Cheerless	Sad, Dejected
Curious	Strange
Circumstance	Factor, Situation, Condition
Competent	Capable
Congruent	Overlapping
Cope	Deal, Endure
Confident	Sure
Complex	Intricate
Cajole	Coax, Flatter
Cunning	Crafty
Delectable	Joyful, Delightful
Devilish	Diabolical
Delicate	Soft
Devil	Fiend
Delay	Postpone
Dislike	Repugnance
Destroy	Ruin
Dwell	Live, Dilate
Declare	Pronounce
Drunk	Flushed
Deficient	Lacking
Damn	Condemn, Curse
Decrease	Diminish
Destruction	Devastation
Efficient	Competent
Ethnic	Racial
Enthral	Enslave
Earnest	Serious
Envious	Jealous
Ending	Final
Egg	Incite
Extempore	At once
Extensive	Far-ranging
Extra	Surplus
Existence	Life
Exceed	Overstep
Enormous	Vast
Excessive	Superfluous
Free	Unhindered
Frigid	Cold
Feed	Cater
Fame	Reputation
Frame	Make
First	Initial
Frighten	Terrorise, Intimidate
Fervent	Fervid
Fall	Decline
Feeble	Frail
Fickle	Changeable
Finish	Conclude
Fraud	Deception
Forgiving	Placable

Words	Synonyms
Grow	Develop
Greed	Avidity
Greet	Welcome
Grave	Serious
Group	Constellation
Given	Bestowed
Gratitude	Thankfulness
Have	Possess
Hire	Rent
Hit	Strike
Handsome	Beautiful
Hinder	Prevent
Heap	Pile
Hope	Expect
Hard	Harsh
Help	Aid
Hymn	Song
Henpecked	Enslaved
Hoodwink	Mystify, Cheat
Humble	Polite, Urbane, Modest
Harass	Vex, Trouble
Impart	Instil
Intact	Untouched
Instal	Establish
Indict	Impeach
Imitate	Ape
Instigate	Incite
Initiate	Start, Introduce
Inimical	Unfriendly
Insufferable	Intolerable
Impartiality	Justice
Jolly	Merry
Joyful	Delectable
Join	Conjoin
Kind	Benign
Kill	Murder
Kindred	Similar
Kinship	Relationship
Keen	Sharp
Knowledge	Scholarship
Lazy	Slothful
Large	Substantial, Gargantuan
Listless	Careless, Lackadaisical
Lax	Loose
Little	Small
Lifelike	Realistic
Lofty	High
Lenient	Soft, Gentle
Lacking	Deficient, Wanting
Lessen	Decrease
Middleclass	Bourgeois
Mitigate	Lessen, Abate
Modesty	Humility, Lowliness

Words	Synonyms
Mix	Mingle, Blend
Mixture	Mingling
Mixed	Assorted
Modify	Decrease
Mean	Imply
Multifarious	Varied
Miscarry	Abort
Note	Notice
Noble	Stately
Native	Indigenous
Needful	Necessary
Notify	Declare
Nervous	Shaky, Tremulous, Timid
Natural	Spontaneous
Near	Close
Normal	Natural
Offend	Displease
Oppress	Persecute, Tyrannize
Opponent	Adversary
Obstruct	Hinder, Check
Offence	Fault
Offender	Villain
Overstep	Exceed
Overlapping	Congruent
Occult	Mystic
Profane	Unholy
Patience	Forbearance
Pornographic	Obscene
Plenitude	Abundance
Prominent	Important
Prodigal	Spender
Procrastinate	Postpone
Promote	Develop, Honour
Persecute	Tyrannise
Profess	Claim
Pliant	Flexible
Plebian	Common
Polished	Sophisticated
Quake	Shake
Quit	Leave
Queer	Eccentric
Quell	Suppress
Quantify	Allot
Reply	Answer
Relinquish	Retire
Read	Peruse
Relation	Reference
Render	Do
Remainder	Residuals
Repeat	Reiterate
Repentant	Contrite
Retaliative	Retaliatory
Rumour	Hearsay
Reveal	Divulge

Words	Synonyms
Ritualistic	Ceremonious
Soft	Delicate
Sort	Kind, Choose, Select
Selfish	Egoistic
Sensual	Earthly
Suppress	Quell, Check
Stimulate	Provoke
Tasteless	Insipid
Travel	Journey
True	Authentic, Faithful, Truthful
Turbulence	Turmoil
Tragedy	Calamity
Tasteful	Tasty, Delicious
Touching	Painful
Thankful	Grateful
Tremendous	Great, Huge
Tough	Strong
Terminate	Conclude, End
Theory	Doctrine
Tell	Relate
Tremble	Shake, Shiver
Urge	Spur
Unbeaten	Unsubdued
Use	Utilize, Practise
Underhand	Unfair, Undue
Unfair	Unjust
Unravel	Reveal, Divulge
Unimportant	Common
Unconcerned	Apathetic
Unimitated	Inimitable
Unfortunate	Unlucky
Understand	Perceive, Comprehend
Vain	Proud, Haughty, Conceited, Shameless
Vale	Valley, Dale, Dell
Vice	Fault
Virtue	Quality
Veracity	Reality
Value	Price, Prize
Vex	Tease
Vibrate	Quiver, Shake
Violent	Excessive
Vivid	Clear, Lucid
Victory	Triumph
Vulgar	Indecent
Virtuous	Honest
Variegated	Varied, Multifarious
Well	Good
Yell	Cry, Shout
Yonder	There
Yearn	Wish, Desire
Yoke	Slavery
Zest	Earnestness, Enthusiasm
Zealous	Earnest

ANTONYMS

A antonym is a word which conveys a meaning opposite to the given word.

REMEMBER

Words	*Antonyms*
Abhor	Love
Abnormal	Normal
Able	Unable
Acceptable	Unacceptable
Adequate	Inadequate
Amusing	Boring
Angry	Calm
Apex	Bottom
Attract	Repel
Bad	Good
Barren	Fertile
Beautiful	Ugly
Bitter	Sweet
Brave	Cowardly
Brief	Lengthy
Bright	Dull
Calm	Violent
Careful	Careless
Clear	Vague, Cloudy
Cold	Hot
Cruel	Kind
Dear	Cheap
Deep	Shallow
Difficult	Easy
Direct	Indirect
Dishonest	Honest
Disobey	Obey
Encourage	Discourage
Enormous	Tiny
Excellent	Bad
Expensive	Cheap
Eat	Fast
Fair	Unfair
Fake	Authentic
False	True
Famous	Notorious
Fool	Genius
Generous	Miserly
Genius	Fool
Genuine	Unauthentic
Gigantic	Tiny
Glad	Depressed
Good	Bad
Great	Little
Happy	Sad
Hard	Soft
Hate	Love
Honest	Dishonest
Idle	Busy

Words	*Antonyms*
Immoral	Moral
Include	Exclude
Incorrect	Correct
Intelligent	Unintelligent
Kind	Cruel
Like	Dislike
Long	Short
Lucid	Vague
Major	Minor
Naive	Experienced
Nadir	Apex
Neat	Clumsy
Obedient	Disobedient
Obscure	Clear
Oppose	Support
Optimistic	Pessimistic
Out	In
Patience	Impatience
Peaceful	Belligerent
Pious	Impious
Polite	Impolite
Potent	Impotent
Prominent	Unimportant
Proper	Improper
Pure	Impure
Quick	Slow
Quiet	Disturbance
Real	False, Unreal
Reject	Select, Choose
Reliable	Unreliable
Respect	Disrespect
Right	Wrong
Robust	Feeble, Weak
Sad	Happy
Secret	Open
Sensible	Insensible
Severe	Mild
Sharp	Blunt
Simple	Complex
Sociable	Unsociable
Tall	Short
Tidy	Untidy
Uncanny	Canny
Violent	Calm
Vivid	Vague
Strong	Weak
Big	Small
Easy	Difficult
Fast	Slow
High	Low
Catchy	Unattractive
Ugly	Handsome, Beautiful, Tidy
Tasty	Insipid
Sonorous	Harsh

MULTIPLE CHOICE QUESTIONS

Directions (Qs. 1 to 20): *In the following questions choose the word which best expresses the meaning of the given word.*

1. ABSURD
A. Foolish B. Simple
C. Courageous D. Silly

2. ABANDON
A. Lose B. Profit
C. Vacate D. Foil

3. CAJOLE
A. Pause B. Lenient
C. Blast D. Lure

4. COMBAT
A. Fight B. Conflict
C. Shoot D. Quarrel

5. LAMENT
A. Condone B. Console
C. Complain D. Contribution

6. DEBACLE
A. Disgrace B. Defeat
C. Collapse D. Decline

7. SHIVER
A. Fear B. Tremble
C. Shake D. Ache

8. TORTURE
A. Terror B. Harassment
C. Torment D. Tranquility

9. LAUDABLE
A. Lovable B. Commendable
C. Profitable D. Oblivious

10. FIXED
A. Sterile B. Static
C. Stubborn D. Parennial

11. QUEER
A. Unfamiliar B. Cute
C. Curious D. Strange

12. SUFFICIENT
A. Fit B. Proper
C. Adequate D. Vast

13. GLOSS
A. Brightness B. Soothing
C. Rubbing D. Miracle

14. LONGING
A. Prune B. Apathy
C. Curtail D. Craving

15. JEER
A. Applaud B. Magnanimity
C. Avoid D. Scoff

16. ZENITH
A. Minimum B. Nadir
C. Plant D. Peak

17. GARB
A. Distort B. Dress
C. Trivial D. Rage

18. ABHOR
A. Rude B. Reconcile
C. Crave D. Detest

19. YIELD
A. Shum B. Incisive
C. Retain D. Surrender

20. YOKE
A. Twist B. Release
C. Link D. Extra

Directions (Qs. 21 to 26): *In the following questions choose the word which best expresses the opposite of the given word.*

21. TRAGIC
A. Dramatic B. Strong
C. Gentle D. Comic

22. ORAL
A. Verbal B. Sane
C. Minor D. Written

23. ADMIRE
A. Hate B. Unlike
C. Dislike D. Enough

24. VIOLENT
A. Gentle B. Savage
C. Haughty D. Decline

25. ADVERSITY
A. Windfall B. Inprosperity
C. Prosperity D. Slave

26. GENUINE
A. Spurious B. Obscure
C. Countless D. Apathetic

ANSWERS

1	2	3	4	5	6	7	8	9	10
D	C	D	A	C	C	B	C	B	B
11	**12**	**13**	**14**	**15**	**16**	**17**	**18**	**19**	**20**
D	C	A	D	D	D	B	D	D	C
21	**22**	**23**	**24**	**25**	**26**				
D	D	C	A	C	A				

●●●

3

Sentence Completion

It is such an exercise which starts with the primary schools and continues in the highest level of competitive examinations. One must practise it regularly to score well.

Directions (Qs. 1 to 15): *Pick out the most effective word(s) from the given words to fill in the blanks to make the sentence meaningfully complete.*

1. The student ...... that book from the library to study at home.
A. issued B. borrowed
C. hired D. lent

2. I wish I ...... a king.
A. was B. am
C. should be D. were

3. He ...... to listen to my arguments and walked away.
A. denied B. disliked
C. objected D. refused

4. The flow of blood was so ...... that the patient died.
A. intense B. adequate
C. profuse D. extensive

5. When I met her yesterday, it was the first time I ...... her since Christmas.
A. saw B. have seen
C. had seen D. have been seing

6. Can you pay ...... all these articles?
A. for B. of
C. off D. out

7. I ...... you to be at the party this evening.
A. expect B. hope
C. look forward to D. desire

8. ...... being a handicapped person, he is very cooperative and self-reliant.
A. Because B. Although
C. Since D. Despite

9. The child broke ...... from his mother and ran towards the painting.
A. away B. after
C. down D. with

10. With his ...... income, he finds it difficult to live a comfortable life.
A. brief
B. sufficient
C. meagre
D. huge

11. He could ...... a lot of money in such a short time by using his intelligence and working hard.
A. spend
B. spoil
C. exchange
D. accumulate

12. Though the brothers are twins, they look ......
A. alike B. handsome
C. indifferent D. different

13. Unfavourable weather conditions can ..... illness.
A. cure B. detect
C. treat D. enhance

14. No sooner did the bell ring, ... the actor started singing.
A. when B. than
C. after D. before

15. If I ...... realised it, I would not have acted on his advice.
A. was B. had
C. were D. have

Directions (Qs. 16 to 25): *In each question, an incomplete statement (Stem) followed by four fillers is given. Pick out the best one which can complete the incomplete stem correctly and meaningfully.*

16. Unless you work harder you will fail, means .....
A. if you fail you will work harder.
B. you must at least plan well than you will not fail.
C. hardly you will fail if you do not desire so.
D. if you do not put more efforts, then you will fail.

17. Even if it rains I shall come, means .....
A. if I come it will not rain.
B. if it rains I shall not come.
C. I will certainly come whether it rains or not.
D. whenever there is rain I shall come.

18. Dinesh is as stupid as he is lazy means .....
A. Dinesh is stupid because he is lazy.
B. Dinesh is lazy because he is stupid.
C. Dinesh is either stupid or lazy.
D. Dinesh is equally stupid and lazy.

19. He is so lazy that he .....
A. cannot depend on others for getting his work done.
B. cannot delay the schedule of completing the work.
C. can seldom complete his work on time.
D. dislike to postpone the work that he undertakes to do.

20. He always stammers in public meetings, but his today's speech .....
A. was fairly audible to everyone present in the hall.
B. was not received satisfactorily.
C. could not be understood properly.
D. was free from that defect.

21. In order to raise the company's profit, the employees.....
A. demanded two additional increments.
B. decided to go on paid holidays.
C. requested the management to implement new welfare schemes.
D. offered to work overtime without any compensation.

22. Although, he is reputed for making very candid statements, ...
A. his today's speech was not fairly audible.
B. his promises had always been realistic.
C. his speech was very interesting.
D. his today's statements were very ambiguous.

23. I felt somewhat more relaxed .....
A. but tense as compared to earlier.
B. and tense as compared to earlier.
C. as there was already no tension at all.
D. and tension-free as compared to earlier.

24. With great efforts his son succeeded in convincing him not to donate his entire wealth to an orphanage ....
A. and lead the life of a wealthy merchant.
B. but to a home for the forsaken children.
C. and make an orphan of himself.
D. as the orphanage needed a lot of donations.

25. Even though it is a very large house, ...
A. there is a lot of space available in it for children.
B. there is hardly any space available for children.
C. there is no dearth of space for children.
D. the servants take a long time to clean it.

ANSWERS

1	2	3	4	5	6	7	8	9	10
B	D	D	C	C	A	A	D	A	C
11	**12**	**13**	**14**	**15**	**16**	**17**	**18**	**19**	**20**
D	D	D	B	B	D	C	D	C	D
21	**22**	**23**	**24**	**25**					
D	D	D	C	B					

●●●

4

Spotting Errors

The most common errors in English are of spellings, grammar and usage of words. By regular practice, the errors can be easily spotted and minimised.

MULTIPLE CHOICE QUESTIONS

Directions: *In the following questions some of the sentences have errors and some are correct. Find out which part of a sentence has an error, the number of that part is your answer. If a sentence is free from errors, then your answer is D i.e., No error.*

1. (A) Either Ram or/(B) you is responsible/(C) for this action./(D) No error.

2. (A) The student flatly denied/(B) that he had copied/ (C) in the examination hall./(D) No error.

3. (A) By the time you arrive tomorrow/(B) I have finished/ (C) my work./(D) No error.

4. (A) The captain with the members of his team/(B) are returning/(C) after a fortnight./(D) No error.

5. (A) After returning from/(B) an all-India tour/(C) I had to describe about it./(D) No error.

6. (A) The teacher asked his students/(B) if they had gone through/(C) either of the three chapters included in the prescribed text./(D) No error.

7. (A) Do you know/(B) how old were you/(C) when you came here?/(D) No error.

8. (A) Beware of/(B) a fair-weather friend/(C) who is neither a friend in need nor a friend indeed./(D) No error.

9. (A) Copernicus proved/(B) that Earth/(C) moves round the Sun./(D) No error.

10. (A) The property/(B) was divided/(C) among the two brothers./(D) No error.

11. (A) I am quite certain/(B) that the lady is not only greedy/(C) but miserly./(D) No error.

12. (A) The brilliant success in the examination/(B) as well as his record in sports/(C) deserves high praise./(D) No error.

13. (A) I cannot find/(B) where has he gone/(C) though I have tried may best./(D) No error.

14. (A) If I was/(B) the Prime Minister of India/(C) I would work wonders/(D) No error.

15. (A) If it weren't/(B) for you,/(C) I wouldn't be alive today./(D) No error.

16. (A) He looked like a lion/(B) baulked from/(C) its prey./ (D) No error.

17. (A) Widespread flooding/(B) is affecting/(C) large areas of the villages./(D) No error.

18. (A) If we really set to/(B) we can get the whole house/ (C) cleaned in an afternoon./(D) No error.

ANSWERS

1	2	3	4	5	6	7	8	9	10
B	D	B	B	C	C	D	D	B	C
11	**12**	**13**	**14**	**15**	**16**	**17**	**18**	**19**	**20**
C	D	B	A	C	C	C	A	A	C

EXPLANATORY ANSWERS

1. Replace 'is' by 'are'.

2. No error.

3. Replace 'have' by 'would have'.

4. Replace 'are' by 'is'.

5. Replace 'had to describe' by 'described'.

6. Replace 'either' by 'any'.

7. No error.

8. No error.

9. Omit 'that'.

10. Replace 'among' by 'between'.

11. Add 'also'.

12. No error.

13. Replace 'has he' by 'he has'.

14. Replace 'was' by 'were'.

15. Replace 'wouldn't be' by 'would not have been'.

16. Replace 'its' by 'his'.

17. Replace 'areas' by 'area'.

18. Replace 'set to' by 'set on'.

●●●

5

One Word Substitution

There are many single words in English language which can be perfectly used for a number of words. These words help in expressing ideas in a short and correct manner for the right occasion. Such words not only increase the vocabulary but also enable you to economise in the use of words to a great extent.

Multiple Word Expression	*Substitution*
One who always looks towards the bright side of things	Optimist
One who always looks towards the dark side of things	Pessimist
The time when one develops from a child into an adult	Adolescence
The process of growing more plants in order to form a forest.	Afforestation
The science which deals with farming	Agriculture
From some other country or place etc.	Alien
A term, etc. giving more than one meaning	Ambiguous
A vehicle which is used to carry sick persons	Ambulance
An animal which can live both in water and on land	Amphibian
A lawless situation when there is no government	Anarchy
Belonging to the history of thousands of years old	Ancient
Once a year	Annual
A very old object but still valuable	Antique
Words of opposite meanings	Antonyms
Words of similar meanings	Synonyms
Signatures of a famous person	Autograph
A government led by one person with absolute authority	Autocracy
A written work of one's own life history	Autobiography
A person who has never been married	Bachelor
A person usually having no hair on his head	Bald
A place where one can deposit money and get interest	Bank
A person who cuts our hair	Barber
A building/group of buildings where soldiers live	Barracks
A person who makes buns and biscuits	Baker
A person who lives by asking people for food and money without doing any useful job	Beggar
The crime of having married to two persons at the same time	Bigamy
The branch of science which deals with the study of plants	Botany
Able to speak two languages	Bilingual
Able to speak more than two languages	Polyglot
The branch of science which deals with the living organisms	Biology
A powerful snow storm	Blizzard
A great successful book or movie	Blockbuster
A short news on the radio or TV	Bulletin
A system in which the most important works are organised by the government officials	Bureaucracy
A person who has no vision in his eyes	Blind
A page or a series of pages on which the information of days, weeks, months, etc. is given	Calendar
A person who eats human flesh	Cannibal
A complete list of items often arranged alphabetically	Catalogue
A sudden disaster	Catastrophe
A period of 100 years	Century

Multiple Word Expression	*Substitution*
A branch of science which deals with chemicals	Chemistry
A printed leaf usually issued by banks that we sign to carry certain financial deal	Cheque
A person who makes or mends shoes	Cobbler
A group of people who has been chosen by others to make decisions on their own	Committee
A building in which nuns live	Convent
An animal which feeds on other animals	Carnivorous
A person who does criticism	Critic
A person who cannot hear	Deaf
A condition in which one loses a lot of water from one's body because of vomiting, etc.	Dehydration
A system of government in which the people cast their votes to elect their leaders	Democracy
The study of skin problems	Dermatology
A long piece of land covered with sand	Desert
The art of managing relationships between countries	Diplomacy
A piece of information about the words in a book form	Dictionary
A piece of information about the telephone numbers of the people in a book from	Directory
A person in charge of a newspapers, magazine etc.	Editor
A person who thinks he is better than the others	Egoist
To leave your country and settle in some other country	Emigrate
A book or series of books giving almost all knowledge about an area or some persons etc.	Encyclopaedia
Study of insects	Entomology
Time when day and night are of the same duration	Equinox
To sell things out of the country	Export
To purchase things from some other country	Import
A plant or animal no longer in existence	Extinct
A situation when there is a shortage of food for a long period of time	Famine
An amount of money that we pay for some action or services	Fee
Related to women	Feminine
An animal strong and aggressive	Ferocious
A piece of land where plants grow easily from the soil that is favourable to them	Fertile
A work of literature having some imaginary events	Fiction
A large amount of water covering certain area	Flood
A person who sells flowers	Florist
A religious ceremony for burying or cremating a dead person	Funeral
A substance which kills fungus	Fungicide
A person studying or having studied the diseases and the related things of female reproductory system	Gynaecologist
The murder of the person of the same group race or country	Genocide
A substance which kills germs	Germicide
A situation in which many people die because of fire during war	Holocaust
The act of killing a person deliberately	Homicide
A word having the pronunciation as the other one does but it differs in meaning	Homophone
A word having the same spelling as the other one does but it is pronounced in some other way	Homonym
A person who is attracted towards the person of the same sex	Homosexual
Go across and parallel to the ground	Horizontal
A substance which kills the insects	Insecticide
That cannot be corrected	Incorrigible
That cannot be defeated	Invincible
That cannot be eaten	Inedible
That cannot be seen	Invisible
A place in a school or college where books are kept for the benefit of students, teachers etc.	Library
A place in a school or college where scientific experiments are performed	Laboratory

Multiple Word Expression	*Substitution*
An official who is a judge in the lowest court	Magistrate
A piece of music or a book before it is printed	Manuscript
Related to men	Masculine
One who believes in the existence of God	A theist
One who does not believe in the existence of good	An atheist
That can be believed	Credible
That cannot be believed	Incredible
That which dissolves in a solvent	Soluble
That which does not dissolves in a solvent	Insoluble
Hard writing that can be read	Legible
Hard writing that cannot be read	Illegible
A person who does jobs beneficial to mankind	Philanthropist
A person who goes on foot	Pedestrian
A person who fights for his own country	Patriot
An act of killing oneself	Suicide
A woman whose husband is dead	Widow
A man whose wife is dead	Widower
A person who eats vegetarian and non-vegetarian diets	Omnivorous
Something which is everywhere at the same time	Omnipresent
One who knows everything	Omniscient
A child who does not have parents	Orphan
An award etc. given after the death of the person	Posthumous
The place where animals are kept for amusement and to increase the knowledge of the public	Zoo
The science which deals with the study of animals	Zoology

MULTIPLE CHOICE QUESTIONS

Directions: *In questions given below, out of the four alternatives, choose the one which can be substituted for the given words/sentences.*

1. Something that relates to everyone in the world
A. General B. Common
C. Usual D. Universal

2. An expression of mild disapproval
A. Warning B. Denigration
C. Impertinence D. Reproof

3. One who is not easily pleased by anything
A. Maiden B. Medieval
C. Precarious D. Fastidious

4. Murder of a king
A. Infanticide B. Matricide
C. Genocide D. Regicide

5. A remedy for all diseases
A. Stoic B. Marvel
C. Panacea D. Recompense

6. A dramatic performance
A. Mask B. Mosque
C. Masque D. Mascot

7. Study of birds
A. Orology B. Optology
C. Ophthalmology D. Ornithology

8. Ready to believe
A. Credulous B. Credible
C. Creditable D. Incredible

9. Incapable of being seen through
A. Ductile B. Opaque
C. Obsolete D. Potable

10. One who eats everything
A. Omnivorous B. Omniscient
C. Irresistible D. Insolvent

11. A place where bees are kept is called
A. An apiary B. A mole
C. A hive D. A sanctuary

12. One who cannot be corrected
A. Incurable B. Incorrigible
C. Hardened D. Invulnerable

13. One who is in charge of a museum
A. Curator B. Supervisor
C. Caretaker D. Warden

14. Continuing fight between parties, families, clans, etc.
A. Enmity B. Feud
C. Quarrel D. Skirmish

15. A voice loud enough to be heard
A. Audible B. Applaudable
C. Laudable D. Oral

16. A paper written by hand
A. Handicraft B. Manuscript
C. Handiwork D. Thesis

17. Habitually silent or talking little
A. Serville B. Unequivocal
C. Taciturn D. Synoptic

18. To slap with a flat object
A. Chop B. Hew
C. Gnaw D. Swat

19. A person who speaks many languages
A. Linguist B. Monolingual
C. Polyglot D. Bilingual

20. A light sailing-boat built specially for racing
A. Canoe B. Yacht
C. Frigate D. Dinghy

21. A fixed orbit in space in relation to earth
A. Geological B. Geo-synchronous
C. Geo-centric D. Geo-stationary

22. A style in which a writer makes a display of his knowledge
A. Pedantic B. Verbose
C. Pompous D. Ornate

23. A religious discourse
A. Preach B. Stanza
C. Sanctorum D. Sermon

24. A place that provides refuge
A. Asylum B. Sanatorium
C. Shelter D. Orphanage

25. Detailed plan of a journey
A. Travelogue B. Travelkit
C. Schedule D. Itinerary

26. A person who insists on something
A. Disciplinarian B. Stickler
C. Instantaneous D. Boaster

27. A drawing on transparent paper
A. Red print B. Blue print
C. Negative D. Transparency

28. One who believes that all things and events in life are predetermined is a
A. Fatalist B. Puritan
C. Egoist D. Tyrant

29. A school boy who cuts classes frequently is a
A. Defeatist B. Sycophant
C. Truant D. Martinet

30. The act of violating the sanctity of the church is
A. Blasphemy B. Heresy
C. Sacrilege D. Desecration

31. A place where monks live as a secluded community
A. Cathedral B. Diocese
C. Convent D. Monastery

32. One who is fond of fighting
A. Bellicose B. Aggressive
C. Belligerent D. Militant

33. Tending to move away from the centre or axis
A. Centrifugal B. Centripetal
C. Axiomatic D. Awry

34. Words inscribed on tomb
A. Epitome B. Epistle
C. Epilogue D. Epitaph

35. Leave or remove from a place considered dangerous
A. Evade B. Evacuate
C. Avoid D. Exterminate

36. Original inhabitants of a country
A. Abroge B. Aborger
C. Aborgory D. Aborigins

37. Government by the officials
A. Theocracy B. Plutocracy
C. Bureaucracy D. Democracy

38. Incapable of being exhausted
A. Inexhaustible B. Inaexhaustible
C. Exhaustable D. Non-tired

39. A person of good understanding, knowledge and reasoning power
A. Expert B. Intellectual
C. Snob D. Literate

40. One absorbed in his own thoughts and feelings rather than in things outside
A. Scholar B. Recluse
C. Introvert D. Intellectual

ANSWERS

1	2	3	4	5	6	7	8	9	10
D	D	D	D	C	C	D	A	B	A
11	12	13	14	15	16	17	18	19	20
A	B	A	B	A	B	C	D	A	B
21	22	23	24	25	26	27	28	29	30
D	A	D	A	D	B	D	A	C	C
31	32	33	34	35	36	37	38	39	40
D	A	A	D	B	B	C	A	B	C

●●●

6

Spelling Errors

There are thousands of words in English language. It is difficult to remember the spellings and meanings of all at once. Try to learn as many as you can. Use a dictionary regularly.

Directions: *Find the correctly spelt words.*

1. A. Damage B. Dammage C. Damaige D. Dammege
2. A. Efficiant B. Effecient C. Efficient D. Eficient
3. A. Schedule B. Schdule C. Schedale D. Schedeule
4. A. Occurad B. Occurred C. Ocurred D. Occured
5. A. Grieff B. Grief C. Grieef D. Grrief
6. A. Guarantee B. Garuntee C. Guaruntee D. Gaurantee
7. A. Meddicine B. Medicine C. Medicene D. Medicinne
8. A. Benefeted B. Benefitted C. Benifited D. Benefited
9. A. Acommodation B. Acomodation C. Accomodation D. Accommodation
10. A. Querrelsome B. Quarrelsame C. Quarrelsome D. Querralsome
11. A. Sympathetic B. Smypathetic C. Sympothetic D. Sympethetic
12. A. Prograssive B. Progressive C. Progresive D. Prograsive
13. A. Uncivilized B. Uncevilized C. Uncivillized D. Uncevelized
14. A. Extravagant B. Extreragent C. Extreregant D. Extravegent
15. A. Missunderstood B. Miesunderstood C. Misunderstood D. Misunderstod
16. A. Belligerent B. Beligirent C. Belligarant D. Belligerrent
17. A. Astonished B. Astronished C. Astoneshed D. Asstonished
18. A. Sincerely B. Sencerely C. Sincerelly D. Sincerrely
19. A. Rigourous B. Rigerous C. Rigorous D. Regerous
20. A. Satellite B. Sattellite C. Satelite D. Sattelite
21. A. Pesanger B. Passenger C. Pessenger D. Pasanger
22. A. Humurous B. Humorous C. Humoreus D. Humorrous
23. A. Exeggerate B. Exaggerate C. Exadgerate D. Exagerate
24. A. Fariegn B. Forein C. Foriegn D. Foreign
25. A. Excesive B. Excessive C. Exccessive D. Exccesive
26. A. Forcaust B. Forcast C. Forecast D. Forecaste
27. A. Paralleted B. Paralelled C. Parralleled D. Parallelled
28. A. Ocasion B. Occassion C. Occasion D. Ocassion
29. A. Boquet B. Bouquet C. Bouquete D. Bouquette
30. A. Chettering B. Chaterring C. Chattering D. Chatering
31. A. Discourage B. Disscourage C. Discourege D. Discaurage
32. A. Curageous B. Courageous C. Courrageous D. Couregeous
33. A. Abandon B. Abanddon C. Abendon D. Abbandon
34. A. Embarassment B. Emberrassement C. Embarrassment D. Embbaresment
35. A. Eccintric B. Eccentrie C. Eccentric D. Eccintrie
36. A. Occasional B. Occassional C. Occesional D. Occessional
37. A. Querrel B. Querral C. Quarrel D. Quarel
38. A. Contrebution B. Contribution C. Contributtion D. Conterbution

39. A. Desgrace B. Disgrece
C. Disgrice D. Disgrace

40. A. Harassment B. Herassment
C. Harasment D. Harassmient

41. A. Imaginative B. Imeginative
C. Imagenative D. Imaginetive

42. A. Suficient B. Suficiant
C. Sufficient D. Sufficiant

43. A. Adequate B. Edequate
C. Adaquete D. Edaquete

44. A. Exparienced B. Experianced
C. Experienced D. Experrienced

45. A. Flatering B. Fletering
C. Flattering D. Fletaring

46. A. Cuttiveted B. Culltrivated
C. Cultivated D. Caltivated

47. A. Praiceworthy B. Peiseworthy
C. Praiseworthy D. Praisaworthy

48. A. Profesional B. Professionel
C. Professional D. Profissional

49. A. Ameteur B. Amateur
C. Amataur D. Amateor

50. A. Unfevourable B. Unfevaurable
C. Unfavourable D. Unfivourable

ANSWERS

1	2	3	4	5	6	7	8	9	10
A	C	A	B	B	A	B	B	D	C
11	**12**	**13**	**14**	**15**	**16**	**17**	**18**	**19**	**20**
A	B	A	A	C	A	A	A	C	A
21	**22**	**23**	**24**	**25**	**26**	**27**	**28**	**29**	**30**
B	B	B	D	B	C	A	C	B	C
31	**32**	**33**	**34**	**35**	**36**	**37**	**38**	**39**	**40**
A	B	A	C	C	A	C	B	D	A
41	**42**	**43**	**44**	**45**	**46**	**47**	**48**	**49**	**50**
A	C	A	C	A	C	C	C	B	C

●●●

QUANTITATIVE APTITUDE

NUMBER SYSTEM

1. There are four numbers A, B, C and D. Average of the first three *i.e.*, A, B and C is 15 and that of B, C and D is 16. If the last number, *i.e.*, D is 19, then the first number is—
A. 15 B. 16
C. 17 D. 18

2. Of the three numbers, the first is twice the second and thrice the third. If the average of three is 22, the three numbers are—
A. 12, 18, 36
B. 18, 12, 36
C. 36, 12, 18
D. 36, 18, 12

3. If a person is standing on the sixth number in the queue from both the ends, the total persons in the queue are—
A. 9 B. 11
C. 12 D. 13

4. A number '*x*' when multiplied by 5 and added to three times its own gives 64, the number is—
A. 8 B. 12
C. 14 D. 18

5. A number which when multiplied by 11 is as much above 180 as it was originally below it. The number is—
A. 25 B. 30
C. 40 D. 45

6. The sum of a number and its reciprocal is thrice the difference of the number and its reciprocal. Find the number.
A. $\sqrt{2}$ B. $\sqrt{3}$
C. $\sqrt{5}$ D. $\sqrt{7}$

7. A boy was asked to find $\frac{7}{9}$ of a fraction. He made a mistake of dividing the fraction by $\frac{7}{9}$ and so got an answer which exceeded the correct answer by $\frac{8}{21}$. Find the correct answer.
A. $\frac{2}{3}$ B. $\frac{5}{7}$
C. $\frac{7}{12}$ D. $\frac{7}{15}$

8. There are 408 boys and 312 girls in a school, which are to be divided into equal sections of either boys or girls alone. Find the maximum number of boys or girls that can be placed in a section. Also find the total number of sections thus formed.
A. 10, 20 B. 24, 30
C. 24, 40 D. 30, 30

9. The sum of all possible two-digit number formed from three different one-digit natural numbers, when divided by the sum of the original three numbers is equal to—
A. 11 B. 18
C. 22 D. 36

10. There are four prime numbers written in ascending order. The product of the first three is 385 and that of the last three is 1001. The last number is—
A. 19 B. 17
C. 13 D. 11

11. If the number 357 ★ 25 ★ is divisible by both 3 and 5, then the missing digits in the unit's place and thousandth place respectively are—
A. 0, 4 B. 5, 4
C. 5, 6 D. 0, 6

12. The difference between two numbers is 1365. When the larger number is divided by the smaller one, the quotient is 6 and the remainder is 15. The smaller number is:
A. 360 B. 295
C. 270 D. 240

13. When a number is divided by 31, the remainder is 29. When the same number is divided by 16, what will be the remainder?
A. 15 B. 13
C. 11 D. Data inadequate

14. In dividing a number by 585, a student applied the method of short division. He divided the number successively by 5, 9 and 13 (factor of 585) and got the remainders 4, 8 and 12. If he had divided the number by 585, the remainder would have been:
A. 584 B. 292
C. 144 D. 24

15. When a number divided by 6 leaves a remainder 3. When the square of the same number is divided by 6, the remainder is:
A. 3 B. 2
C. 1 D. zero

ANSWERS

1	2	3	4	5	6	7	8	9	10
B	D	B	A	B	A	C	B	C	C
11	**12**	**13**	**14**	**15**					
C	C	D	A	A					

EXPLANATORY ANSWERS

1. $\frac{A+B+C}{3} = 15,$

or, $A + B + C = 15 \times 3 = 45$ ... (*i*)

$\frac{B+C+D}{3} = 16,$

or $B + C + D = 48$ ... (*ii*)

$D = 19$

$\therefore\ B + C + 19 = 48$ or, B +

$C = 48 - 19 = 29$

But, $A + B + C = 45$

Putting the value of B + C = 29 in the above equation (*i*), we get $A + 29 = 45$

$\therefore\ A = 45 - 29 = 16.$

2. Let the third number $= x$

$\therefore$ First number $= 3x$

Second number $= \frac{3x}{2}$

$\therefore\ \frac{1}{3}\left[x+3x+\frac{3x}{2}\right] = 22 \Rightarrow \frac{11}{2}x = 66$

$\Rightarrow x = \frac{66\times 2}{11} = 12$ = Third number,

$12 \times 3 = 36$ = First number,

$\frac{12\times 3}{2} = 18$ = Second number.

3. If the person is standing at sixth number in the queue from both sides, that means there are five persons ahead and five persons behind him. Hence, total number of persons in the queue is $5 + 1 + 5 = 11$.

4. $5 \times x + 3x = 64 \Rightarrow 8x = 64$

$\therefore\ x = \frac{64}{8} = 8.$

5. Let the number is x

$\therefore\ 180 - x = 11x - 180$

$\Rightarrow\ 180 + 180 = 11x + x$

$\Rightarrow\ 360 = 12x,$

$\Rightarrow\ x = \frac{360}{12} = 30.$

6. Let the no. $= x$ then its reciprocal $= \frac{1}{x}$

By the question, $\left(x+\frac{1}{x}\right) = 3\left(x-\frac{1}{x}\right)$

$\Rightarrow\ \frac{x^2+1}{x} = \frac{3\left(x^2-1\right)}{x}$

$\Rightarrow\ x^2 + 1 = 3x^2 - 3$

$\Rightarrow\ 3x^2 - x^2 = 3 + 1$

$\therefore\ x = \sqrt{2}.$

7. Let the required fraction $= x$

then, by the question $x \div \frac{7}{9} - x \times \frac{7}{9} = \frac{8}{21}$

$\Rightarrow\ x \times \frac{9}{7} - \frac{7x}{9} = \frac{8}{21}$

$\Rightarrow\ \frac{32x}{63} = \frac{8}{21}$

$\Rightarrow\ x = \frac{8}{21} \times \frac{63}{32} = \frac{3}{4}$

Hence, the correct answer $= \frac{3}{4} \times \frac{7}{9} = \frac{7}{12}.$

8.
```
312) 408(1
     312
      96) 312 (3
          288
           24) 96 (4
               96
               ×
```

$\therefore$ Maximum number of girls or boys that can be placed in a section = 24 and total number of such

section $= \frac{408}{24} + \frac{312}{24}$

$= 17 + 13 = 30$

9. Let three different one digit natural numbers be x, y and z.

Then, sum of all possible two digits numbers

$= (10x + y) + (10y + x) + (10x + z) + (10z + x) + (10y + z) + (10z + y)$

$= 22x + 22y + 22z = 22\ (x + y + z)$

Hence, required number = 22.

10. Let four prime numbers be a, b, c and d respectively.

Now, $\frac{abc}{bcd} = \frac{385}{1001}$

$\Rightarrow \frac{c}{d} = \frac{5}{13}$

Hence, $a = 5$ and $d = 13$

11. 357 ★ 25 ★

For divisible by 5, the last digit must be either 0 or 5.

If last digit is 0, then other required digit will be 2 or 5 or 8

Hence, the numbers are (0, 2) or (0, 5) or (0, 8)

If last digit is 5, then other required digit will be 0 or 3 or 6 or 9

Hence, the numbers are (5, 0) or (5, 3) or (5, 6) or (5, 9)

So, correct option is (c).

12. Here, $(x + 1365) = 6x + 15$

$\Rightarrow 5x = 1350$

$\therefore x = \frac{1350}{5} = 270$

Hence, the smaller number = 270.

13. The number = $31x + 29$.

Here, given data is inadequate.

14.

5	a
9	$b - 4$
13	$c - 8$
	$1 - 12$

Now, $c = 13 \times 1 + 12 = 25$

$b = 9c + 8 = 9 \times 25 + 8 = 233$

$a = 5b + 4 = 5 \times 233 + 4$

$= 1165 + 4 = 1169$

$1169 = 585 \times 1 + 584$

Hence, required remainder = 584.

15. The number = $6x + 3$

Now, $(6x + 3)^2 = 36x^2 + 36x + 9$

$= (36x^2 + 36x + 6) + 3$

$= 6(6x^2 + 6x + 1) + 3$

Hence, required remainder = 3.

LCM AND HCF

1. The L.C.M. and H.C.F. of two numbers are 4284 and 32 respectively. If one of the numbers is 204, the other is

A. 672 B. 576
C. 676 D. 572

2. Two numbers are in the ratio of 8 : 15. If their H.C.F. is 4, the numbers are

A. 32 and 60 B. 16 and 30
C. 80 and 150 D. 64 and 120

3. The greatest number that will divide 366, 513 and 324 leaving the same remainder in each case is

A. 21 B. 18
C. 27 D. 42

4. The L.C.M. of two numbers is 45 times their H.C.F. If the sum of the L.C.M. and the H.C.F. of these two numbers is 1150 and one of the numbers is 125, then the other number is

A. 256 B. 225
C. 250 D. 255

5. The H.C.F. and the L.C.M. of two numbers are 50 and 250 respectively. On dividing one of these numbers by 2, 50 is obtained as quotient. The numbrs are

A. 100, 125 B. 80, 100
C. 125, 100 D. 200, 250

6. Three bells ring respectively at an interval of 15 seconds, 20 seconds and 24 seconds. If they ring continuously for 12 minutes then how many times, during this period, will they ring together?

A. 2 times B. 6 times
C. 5 times D. 3 times

7. If the sum of two numbers is 55 and the H.C.F. and L.C.M. of these numbers are 5 and 120 respectively. Find the sum of their reciprocals.

A. $\frac{120}{11}$ B. $\frac{11}{120}$
C. $\frac{601}{55}$ D. $\frac{55}{601}$

8. The LCM of two numbers is 48. The numbers are in the ratio of 2 : 3. The sum of the numbers is

A. 64 B. 40
C. 32 D. 28

9. Find the greatest number that will divide 43, 91 and 183 so as to leave the same remainder in each case.

A. 13 B. 9
C. 7 D. 4

10. The greatest possible length which can be used to measure exactly the length 7m, 3m 85cm, 12m 95 cm is

A. 42 cm B. 35 cm
C. 25 cm D. 15 cm

11. A, B and C start at the same time in the same direction to run around a circular park. A completes a round in 252 seconds, B in 308 seconds and C in 198 seconds, all starting at the same point. After what time will they meet again at the starting point?
A. 46 minutes 12 seconds
B. 45 minutes
C. 42 minutes 36 seconds
D. 26 minutes 18 seconds

12. Which of the following has most numbers of divisors?
A. 182 B. 176
C. 101 D. 99

13. Which is of the following is a co-primes?
A. (23, 92) B. (21, 35)
C. (18, 25) D. (16, 62)

14. Let N be the greatest number that will divide 1305, 4665 and 6905, leaving the same remainder in each case. Then find the sum of the digits in N.
A. 8 B. 6
C. 5 D. 4

15. The greatest number which one dividing 1657 and 2037 leaves remainder 6 and 5 respectively, is:
A. 305 B. 235
C. 127 D. 123

ANSWERS

1	2	3	4	5	6	7	8	9	10
A	A	A	B	A	B	B	B	D	B
11	**12**	**13**	**14**	**15**					
A	B	C	D	C					

EXPLANATORY ANSWERS

1. 1st number × 2nd number = LCM × HCF
$\therefore$ 204 × 2nd number = 4284 × 32
$\therefore$ 2nd number $= \dfrac{4284 \times 32}{204} = 672$
$\therefore$ 2nd number = 672

2. Let the numbers be $8x$ and $15x$
$8x = 2 \times 2 \times 2 \times x$
$15x = 3 \times 5 \times x$
$\therefore$ LCM of $8x$ and $15x = 2 \times 2 \times 2 \times x \times 3 \times 5$, $= 120x$
Now, 1st number × 2nd number = HCF × LCM
$\Rightarrow 8x \times 15x = 4 \times 120x$
$\Rightarrow 120x^2 = 4 \times 120x$
$\Rightarrow x = 4$
$\therefore$ Numbers are 8 × 4 = 32 and 15 × 4 = 60

3. Difference between 366 and 513 = 513 – 366 = 147
and difference between 513 and 324 = 513 – 324 = 189
$\therefore$ HCF of 147 and 189

```
147) 189 (1
     147
     ----
      42) 147 (3
          126
          ---
           21) 42 (2
               42
               --
                ×
```

$\therefore$ The required largest number is 21.

4. LCM of the two numbers = 45 × HCF
and LCM + HCF = 1150
$\Rightarrow$ 45 × HCF + HCF = 1150
$\Rightarrow$ HCF(45 + 1) = 1150
$\Rightarrow$ HCF $= \dfrac{1150}{46} = 25$
$\therefore$ LCM = 45 × 25 = 1125
$\because$ 1st number × 2nd number = LCM × HCF
$\therefore$ 125 × 2nd number = 1125 × 25
$\therefore$ 2nd number $= \dfrac{1125 \times 25}{125} = 225.$

5. According to the condition of the problem, 50 is obtained on dividing one of the numbers by 2
$\therefore$ One of the numbers = 50 × 2 = 100
Now, 1st number × 2nd number = LCM × HCF
100 × 2nd number = 250 × 50
$\therefore$ 2nd number $= \dfrac{250 \times 50}{100} = 125$
Hence, numbers are 100 and 125.

6. LCM of 15, 20 and 24

5	15, 20, 24
4	3, 4, 24
3	3, 1, 6
	1, 1, 2

LCM = 5 × 4 × 3 × 2 = 120
$\because$ 12 minutes = 12 × 60 = 720 seconds
$\therefore$ Number of times the bells will ring together during 12 minutes
$= \dfrac{720}{120} = 6$ times.

7. Let the number be x and y.
Then, $x + y = 55$;
$xy = \text{HCF} \times \text{LCM} = 5 \times 120$
$\therefore$ Sum of their reciprocals
$$= \frac{1}{x} + \frac{1}{y} = \frac{x+y}{xy} = \frac{55}{5 \times 120} = \frac{11}{120}.$$

8. Let the two numbers be $2x$ and $3x$;
their LCM = $6x$
Now, $6x = 48$ $\therefore$ $x = 8$
Hence, the numbers are 2×8, $3 \times 8 = 16, 24$
Their sum = 16 + 24 = 40.

9.
```
2240) 3360 (1
      2240
      1120 ) 2240 (2
             2240
              ×

1120) 5600 (5
      5600
       ×
```
Hence, N = HCF of 3360, 2240 and 5600 = 1120
Sum of digits in N = 1 + 1 + 2 + 0 = 4.

10. 7m = 700 cm;
3m 85 = 385 cm;
12m 95cm = 1295 cm
```
385) 700 (1
     385
     315) 385 (1
          315
           70) 315 (4
               280
                35 ) 70 (2
                     70
                      ×

35) 1295 (37
    105
     245
     245
      ×
```
Hence, required length = HCF of 700 cm, 385 cm, 1295 cm = 35 cm.

11.

2	252, 308, 198
2	126, 154, 99
3	63, 77, 99
3	21, 77, 33
7	7, 77, 11
11	1, 11, 11
	1, 1, 1

Hence, LCM = $2 \times 2 \times 3 \times 3 \times 7 \times 11 = 2772$
Hence, A, B, C will meet again at the starting point after 2772 sec. = 46 min 12 sec.

12. ***Numbers*** ***Their divisors***
182 → 1, 2, 7, 13, 14, 26, 91 and 182
176 → 1, 2, 4, 8, 16, 22, 44, 88 and 176
101 → 1 and 101
99 → 1, 3, 9, 11, 33 and 99
Therefore, 176 has the most number of divisors.

13. HCF of 23 and 92 = 23
HCF of 21 and 35 = 7
HCF of 18 and 25 = 1
HCF of 16 and 62 = 2
Hence, 18 and 25 are co-prime numbers.

14. N = HCF of (4665 – 1305), (6905 – 4665) and (6905 – 1305)
= HCF of 3360, 2240 and 5600 = 112
Sum of digit of 1 + 1 + 2 = 4.

15. Required number = HCF of (1657 – 6) and (2037 – 5)
= HCF of 1651 and 2032 = 127.
```
1651) 2032 (1
      1651
       381) 1651 (4
            1524
             127) 381 (3
                  381
                   ×
```

AVERAGE

1. One-third of a certain journey was covered at the rate of 25 km per hour, one-fourth at the rate of 30 km per hour and the rest at the 50 km per hour. What is the average speed per hour for whole journey?
A. $33\frac{1}{3}$ kmph B. $44\frac{1}{4}$ kmph
C. $22\frac{1}{2}$ kmph D. 33 kmph

2. A batsman has a certain average of runs for 16 innings. In the 17th innings, he makes a score of 85 runs thereby increasing his average by 3. What is the average after the 17th inning?
A. 33 runs B. 34 runs
C. 37 runs D. 36 runs

3. The average of 6 observations is 12. A new seventh observation is included and the new average is decreased by 1. The seventh observation is

A. 1 B. 3
C. 5 D. 6

4. The average age of 30 students in a class is 12 years. The average age of a group of 5 of the students is 10 years and that of another group of 5 of them is 14 years. The average age of the remaining students is
A. 8 years B. 10 years
C. 12 years D. 14 years

5. Out of the three given numbers, the first number is twice the second and thrice the third. If the average of three numbers is 121, what is the difference between the first and third number?
A. 144 B. 77
C. 99 D. 132

6. If the average marks of three batches of 55, 60 and 45 students is 50, 55 and 60, then average marks of all the students is:
A. 55 B. 54
C. 54.68 D. 55.68

7. The average of 8 numbers is 20. The average of first two numbers is $15\frac{1}{2}$ and that of the next three is $21\frac{1}{3}$. If the sixth number is less than the seventh and eighth numbers by 4 and 7 respectively, then the eighth number is:
A. 27 B. 25
C. 22 D. 18

8. A pupil's marks were wrongly entered as 83 instead of 63. Due to that the average marks for the class got increased by half. What is the number of pupils in the class?
A. 73 B. 40
C. 40 D. 10

9. A cricketer whose bowling average is 12.4 runs per wicket takes 5 wickets for 26 runs and thereby decreases his average by 0.4. The number of wickets taken by him till the last match was:
A. 85 B. 80
C. 72 D. 64

10. The average weight of a class of 24 students is 35 kg. If the weight of the teacher is included, the average rises by 400 g. What is the weight of the teacher?
A. 55 kg B. 53 kg
C. 50 kg D. 45 kg

11. Nine men went to a hotel. Eight of them spent Rs. 3 for each over their meals and the ninth spent Rs. 2 more than the average expenditure of all the nine. What is the total money spent by them?
A. Rs. 29.25 B. Rs. 29.50
C. Rs. 29 D. Rs. 30

12. The average age of 24 students in a class is 10. If the teacher's age is included, the average increases by one. The age of the teacher is
A. 25 B. 30
C. 35 D. 40

13. The average of 5 consecutive even numbers A, B, C, D and E is 34. What is the product of B and D?
A. 1152 B. 1368
C. 1224 D. 1088

14. The average of 50 numbers is 30. If two numbers, 35 and 40 are discarded, then the average of the remaining numbers is nearly:
A. 29.68 B. 29.27
C. 28.78 D. 28.32

15. The average monthly salary of 20 employees of an organisation is Rs. 1500. If the manager's salary is added, then the average salary increases by Rs. 100. Find the manager's monthly salary?
A. Rs. 4800 B. Rs. 3600
C. Rs. 2400 D. Rs. 2000

ANSWERS

1	2	3	4	5	6	7	8	9	10
A	C	C	C	D	C	B	B	A	D
11	**12**	**13**	**14**	**15**					
A	C	A	A	B					

EXPLANATORY ANSWERS

1. Let the total distance covered during journey = 60 km

$\frac{1}{3}$ of the distance covered during journey

$$= 60 \times \frac{1}{3} = 20 \text{ km}$$

$\frac{1}{4}$ of the distance covered during journey

$$= \frac{1}{4} \times 60 = 15 \text{ km}$$

$\therefore$ The distance covered during the rest of journey = 60 – (20 + 15) = 25 km

Time taken to cover 20 km at 25 km/h

$= \frac{20}{25}$ hours $= \frac{4}{5}$ hour

Time taken to cover 15 km at 30 km/h

$= \frac{15}{30}$ hours $= \frac{1}{2}$ hour

Time taken to cover 25 km at 50 km/h

$= \frac{25}{50}$ hours $= \frac{1}{2}$ hour

Total time taken $= \frac{4}{5} + \frac{1}{2} + \frac{1}{2}$

$= \frac{9}{5}$ hours

Hence average speed per hour $= 60 \div \frac{9}{5}$

$= \frac{60 \times 5}{9} = \frac{100}{3}$ km/h

$= 33\frac{1}{3}$ km/h

2. Average increase in the score of 17 innings

= 3 runs

Total increase in the score of 17 innings

= 3 × 17 = 51 runs

∴ His average of 16 innings = 85 – 51

= 34 runs

Hence, average after the 17th innings

= 34 + 3 = 37 runs

3. Seventh observation = (7 × 11 – 6 × 12) = 5

4. Let, the required average age be x

Then, $5 \times 10 + 5 \times 14 + 20 \times x = 30 \times 12$

$\Rightarrow \quad 20x = 360 - 120$

$\Rightarrow \quad 20x = 240$

$\Rightarrow \quad x = 12$

5. Let the three numbers be x, $\frac{x}{2}$ and $\frac{x}{3}$ respectively,

Now, $\frac{1}{3}\left(x + \frac{x}{2} + \frac{x}{3}\right) = 121$

$\Rightarrow \frac{11x}{6} = 121 \times 3$

$\therefore\ x = \frac{121 \times 3 \times 6}{11} = 198$

Hence, required difference $= x - \frac{x}{3} = \frac{2x}{3}$

$= \frac{2}{3} \times 198 = 132$

6. Required average Marks

$= \frac{55 \times 50 + 60 \times 55 + 45 \times 60}{55 + 60 + 45} = \frac{8750}{160} = 54.68$

7. Let the sixth, seventh and eighth numbers are x, x + 4 and x + 7.

Sum of last three numbers

$= 8 \times 20 - (2 \times \frac{31}{2} + 3 \times \frac{64}{3})$

$\Rightarrow x + x + 4 + x + 7 = 160 - 95$

$\Rightarrow 3x + 11 = 65$

$\Rightarrow 3x = 54 \quad \therefore x = 18$

New eighth number = x + 7 = 18 + 7 = 25

8. Let the total number of pupils in the class be x; then,

$\frac{83 - 63}{x} = \frac{1}{2} \quad \Rightarrow \quad \frac{20}{x} = \frac{1}{2} \quad \therefore x = 40$

9. Let the number of wickets taken by him be x till the last match.

Then, $\frac{x \times 12.4 + 26}{x + 5} = 12$

$\Rightarrow \quad 12.4x + 26 = 12x + 60$

$\Rightarrow 0.4x = 34 \quad \therefore \quad x = \frac{340}{4} = 85$

10. Let the weight of the teacher be x kgs, then

$\frac{24 \times 35 + x}{25} = 35.4$

$\Rightarrow \quad 840 + x = 885 \quad \therefore \quad x = 45$ kgs

12. Age of the teacher = (25 × 11 – 24 × 10) years

= 35 years

13. Let 5 consecutive even numbers A, B, C, D and E be x, x + 2, x + 4, x + 6 and x + 8 respectively.

Now, $\frac{x + x + 2 + x + 4 + x + 6 + x + 8}{5} = 34$

$\Rightarrow 5x + 20 = 170$

$\Rightarrow 5x = 150 \quad \therefore x = 30$

Then, B = x + 2 = 30 + 2 = 32;

D = x + 6 = 30 + 6 = 36

Hence, their product = 32 × 36 = 1152

14. The average of remaining 48 numbers

$= \frac{50 \times 30 - (35 + 40)}{48} = \frac{1500 - 75}{48}$

$= \frac{1425}{48} = 29.68$

15. Let manager's salary be Rs. x, then

$\frac{20 \times 1500 + x}{21} = 1600$

$\Rightarrow \quad 30{,}000 + x = 33600$

$\therefore \quad x$ = Rs. 3600

PROBLEMS BASED ON AGES

1. The ratio of ages of A and B is 3 : 11. After 3 years the ratio becomes 1 : 3. What are the ages of A and B?
   A. 9 years, 33 years
   B. 10 years, 40 years
   C. 9 years, 27 years
   D. None of these
2. Two years ago, the ratio of Ram's and Mohan's age was 3 : 2 and at present 7 : 5. What are their present ages?
   A. 14 years, 10 years B. 15 years, 10 years
   C. 13 years, 9 years D. None of these
3. The ages of Samir and Saurabh are in the ratio of 8 : 15 respectively. After 9 years the ratio of their ages will be 11 : 18. What is the difference between their ages in years?
   A. 20 years B. 21 years
   C. 22 years D. 24 years
4. The present age of father is 34 years more than that of his son. 12 years ago, father's age was 18 times the age of his son. The present age of son in years is:
   A. 12 B. 14
   C. 16 D. 18
5. A mother is 25 years older than her daughter. Five years ago, the age of the mother was 6 times the age of the daughter. What is the present age of mother?
   A. 25 years B. 29 years
   C. 32 years D. 35 years
6. The difference between the present ages of P and Q is 4 years. The ratio of their ages after 5 years will be 9 : 8. The present age of P is:
   A. 24 years B. 30 years
   C. 32 years D. None of these
7. Ten years ago, the age of Divya was half of the age of Namrata. If the ratio of present ages of both is 3 : 4, the sum of their present ages is:
   A. 35 years B. 30 years
   C. 25 years D. 18 years
8. The ratio between the present ages of A and B is 5 : 3 respectively. The ratio between A's age 4 years ago and B's age 4 years hence is 1 : 1. The ratio between A's age 4 years hence and B's age 4 years ago is:
   A. 4 : 1 B. 3 : 1
   C. 2 : 1 D. 1 : 3
9. Ram got married 8 years ago. His present age is $\frac{6}{5}$ times his age at the time of marriage. Ram's sister was 10 years younger to him at the time of his marriage. What is the present age of Ram's sister?
   A. 40 years B. 38 years
   C. 36 years D. 32 years
10. A father said to his son, "I was as old as you are at present at the time of your birth." If the father's age is 38 years now. Five years ago the age of son was:
    A. 38 years B. 33 years
    C. 19 years D. 14 years

ANSWERS

1	2	3	4	5	6	7	8	9	10
A	A	B	B	D	D	A	B	B	D

EXPLANATORY ANSWERS

1. Let the ages of A and B be $3x$ and $11x$ years; then

$$\frac{3x+3}{11x+3} = \frac{1}{3} \quad \Rightarrow \quad 9x + 9 = 11x + 3$$

$\Rightarrow 2x = 6 \quad \therefore \quad x = 3$

Hence, their present age, $3x = 3 \times 3 = 9$ years; $11x = 11 \times 3 = 33$ years

2. Let the present ages of Ram and Mohan are $7x$ and $5x$ years; then

$$\frac{7x-2}{5x-2} = \frac{3}{2} \quad \Rightarrow \quad 14x - 4 = 15x - 6 \quad \therefore x = 2$$

Hence, their present ages : $7 \times 2 = 14$ years and $5 \times 2 = 10$ years

3. Let the present ages of Samir and Saurabh are $8x$ and $15x$ years respectively; then

$$\frac{8x+9}{15x+9} = \frac{11}{18} \quad \Rightarrow \quad 144x + 162 = 165x + 99$$

$\Rightarrow 21x = 63 \quad \therefore \quad x = 3$

Hence, difference of their ages $= 15x - 8x = 7x = 7 \times 3 = 21$ years

4. Let the present ages of father and his son be $x + 34$ and x years respectively; then

$18(x - 12) = x + 34 - 12$

$\Rightarrow 18x - 216 = x + 22$

$\Rightarrow 17x = 238 \quad \therefore x = 14$

Hence, present age of his son = 14 years

5. Let the present ages of mother and her daughter are $(x + 25)$ and x years respectively; then

$6(x - 5) = x + 25 - 5$

$\Rightarrow 6x - 30 = x + 20$

$\Rightarrow 5x = 50 \quad \therefore x = 10$

Hence, the age of the mother = 10 + 25 = 35 years

6. Let the present ages of P and Q be $(x + 4)$ and x years;

then, $\frac{x+4+5}{x+5} = \frac{9}{8} \Rightarrow 8x + 72 = 9x + 45 \quad \therefore x = 27$

Hence, present age of P = 27 + 4 = 31 years

7. Let the present ages of Divya and Namrata are $3x$ and $4x$ years respectively; then

$\frac{3x-10}{4x-10} = \frac{1}{2}$

$\Rightarrow 6x - 20 = 4x - 10$

$\Rightarrow 2x = 10 \quad \therefore x = 5$

Hence, sum of their ages = $3x + 4x = 7x$ = 7×5 = 35 years

8. Let the present ages of A and B are $5x$ and $3x$ years respectively; then,

$\frac{5x-4}{3x+4} = 1 \Rightarrow 5x - 4 = 3x + 4$

$\Rightarrow 2x = 8 \quad \therefore x = 4$

Hence, their present ages are 20 years and 12 years.

So, required ratio = $(20 + 4) : (12 - 4)$ = $24 : 8 = 3 : 1$

9. Let the present age of Ram be x years; then

$\frac{x}{x-8} = \frac{6}{5} \Rightarrow 5x = 6x - 48$

$\therefore x = 48$

Hence, present age of Ram's sister = 48 – 10 = 38 years.

10. Let the age of father was x years at the time of his son's birth, then present age of father and his son will be $2x$ and x years,

Now, $2x = 38 \quad \therefore x = 19$ years

Hence, 5 years ago the age of son was 19 – 5 = 14 years

CHAIN RULE

1. A fort has provision for 50 days. After 15 days a reinforcement of 150 men arrives and the provision now lasts 25 days. How many men were there in the fort?

A. 300 B. 225
C. 275 D. 200

2. In a fort there is provisions for 40 days for 275 persons. If after 16 days 125 persons leave the fort for how many more days the provisions will last?

A. 35 days B. 44 days
C. 45 days D. 53 days

3. 60 men could complete a work in 250 days. They worked together for 200 days. After that the work had to be stopped for 10 days due to bad weather. How many more men should be engaged to complete the work in time?

A. 20 B. 18
C. 15 D. 10

4. A contractor undertook to complete a project in 90 days and employed 60 men on it. After 60 days, he found that $\frac{3}{4}$ of the work has already been completed. How many men can he discharge so that the project may completed exactly on time?

A. 15 B. 20
C. 30 D. 40

5. A flagstaff 17.5 m high casts a shadow of length 40.25 m. The height of the building, which casts a shadow of length 28.75m under similar condition will be:

A. 21.25 m B. 17.5 m
C. 12.5 m D. 10 m

6. If 5 men or 9 women can do a piece of work in 19 days, then 3 men and 6 women will do the same work in how many days?

A. 21 B. 18
C. 15 D. 12

7. A certain number of men can finish a piece of work in 100 days. If there were 10 men less, it will take 10 days more for the work to be finished. How many men were there originally?

A. 110 B. 100
C. 82 D. 75

8. Some persons can do a piece of work in 12 days. Two times the number of such persons will do half of that work in:

A. 12 days B. 3 days
C. 6 days D. 4 days

9. 2 men and 7 boys can do a piece of work in 14 days; 3 men and 8 boys can do the same in 11 days. Then 8 men and 6 boys can do three times of this work in
A. 30 days B. 4 days
C. 21 days D. 18 days

10. If 3 men or 6 boys, working 7 hours a day can do a piece of work in 10 days; how many days will it take to complete a piece of work twice as large with 6 men and 2 boys working together for 8 hours a day?
A. 9 B. $8\frac{1}{2}$
C. $7\frac{1}{2}$ D. $6\frac{1}{2}$

11. If 15 men can do a certain amount of work in 20 days working 8 hours a day, in how many days will 10 men do three times the work working 6 hours a day?
A. 120 days B. 70 days
C. 100 days D. None of these

12. 40 men consume 60 kgs of rice in 15 days, then in how many days will 30 men consume 12 kgs of rice?
A. 9 days B. $6\frac{1}{4}$ days
C. 4 days D. $3\frac{1}{4}$ days

13. 56 men can complete a piece of work in 24 days. In how many days can 42 men complete the same piece of work?
A. 48 B. 32
C. 20 D. 16

14. Running at the same constant rate, 6 identical machines can produce a total of 270 bottles per minute. At this rate, how many bottles could 10 such machines produce in 4 minutes?
A. 1400 B. 1600
C. 1800 D. 2000

15. 400 persons, working 9 hours a day complete $\frac{1}{4}$*th* of the work in 10 days. The number of additional persons, working 8 hours a day, required to complete the remaining work in 20 days, is:
A. 275 B. 250
C. 675 D. 200

ANSWERS

1	2	3	4	5	6	7	8	9	10
B	B	C	B	C	C	A	B	C	C
11	**12**	**13**	**14**	**15**					
A	C	B	C	C					

EXPLANATORY ANSWERS

1.

Days	Men
35 ↑	x
25	$x + 150$ ↓

$$\Rightarrow \frac{x+150}{x} = \frac{35}{25} \quad \Rightarrow 1 + \frac{150}{x} = \frac{35}{25}$$

$$\Rightarrow \frac{150}{x} = \frac{10}{25}$$

$$\therefore x = \frac{25}{10} \times 150 = 375$$

Required number of men = 375 – 150 = 225

2.

Persons	Days
275 ↑	24
150	x ↓

$$\Rightarrow \frac{x}{24} = \frac{275}{150} \quad \therefore \quad x = \frac{275}{150} \times 24 = 44 \text{ days}$$

3.

Days	Men
50 ↑	60
40	x ↓

$$\Rightarrow \frac{x}{60} = \frac{50}{40} \quad \therefore \quad x = \frac{50}{40} \times 60 = 75 \text{ men}$$

Hence, number of additional men = 75 – 60
= 15

4.

Work	Days	Men
$\frac{3}{4}$	60 ↑	60
$\frac{1}{4}$ ↓	30	x ↓

$$\Rightarrow \frac{x}{60} = \frac{60}{30} \times \frac{1/4}{3/4}$$

$$\therefore \quad x = \frac{60}{30} \times \frac{1}{3} \times 60 = 40 \text{ days}$$

Hence, number of men to be discharged

$= 60 - 40 = 20$

5. Shadow (m) Object (m)

40.25 ↓ 17.5 ↓

28.75 x

$$\Rightarrow \frac{x}{17.5} = \frac{28.75}{40.25}$$

$$\therefore\ x = \frac{28.75 \times 17.5}{40.25} = 12.5 \text{ m}$$

6. 5 men ≡ 9 women

$$\therefore\ 3 \text{ men} = \frac{9}{5} \times 3 = \frac{27}{5} \text{ women}$$

$$\text{Hence, 3 men and 6 women} = \frac{27}{5} + 6$$

$$= \frac{57}{5} \text{ women}$$

Women Days

9 ↑ 19 ↓

$\frac{57}{5}$ x

$$\Rightarrow \frac{x}{19} = \frac{9 \times 5}{57}$$

$$\therefore\ x = \frac{9 \times 5}{57} \times 19$$

$= 15$ days

7. Days Men

100 ↑ x ↓

110 $x - 10$

$$\Rightarrow \frac{x-10}{x} = \frac{100}{110}$$

$\Rightarrow\ 110x - 1100 = 100x$

$\Rightarrow 10x = 1100 \quad \therefore\ x = 110$

Hence, initially the number of men = 110

8. Work Persons Days

1 ↓ x ↑ 12 ↓

$\frac{1}{2}$ $2x$ a

$$\Rightarrow \frac{a}{12} = \frac{x}{2x} \times \frac{1}{2} \qquad \therefore\ a = \frac{1}{4} \times 12 = 3 \text{ days}$$

9. Here, 14×2 men + 14×7 boys ≡ 11×3 men + 11×8 boys

$\Rightarrow$ 28 men + 98 boys ≡ 33 men + 88 boys

$\Rightarrow$ 5 men = 10 boys

$\therefore$ 1 man = 2 boys

Then, 2 men and 7 boys ≡ 4 boys + 7 boys

= 11 boys

& also, 8 men and 6 boys ≡ 16 boys + 6 boys

= 22 boys

Work Boys Days

1 ↓ 11 ↑ 14 ↓

3 22 x

$$\Rightarrow \frac{x}{14} = \frac{11}{22} \times \frac{3}{1}$$

$$\therefore\ x = \frac{1}{2} \times 3 \times 14$$

= 21 days

12. Men Rice (kgs) Days

40 ↑ 60 ↓ 15 ↓

30 12 x

$$\Rightarrow \frac{x}{15} = \frac{12}{60} \times \frac{40}{30}$$

$$\therefore\ x = \frac{12}{60} \times \frac{40}{30} \times 15 = 4 \text{ days}$$

14. Machines Time (minutes) Bottles

6 ↓ 1 ↓ 270 ↓

10 4 x

$$\Rightarrow \frac{x}{270} = \frac{4}{1} \times \frac{10}{6}$$

$$\therefore\ x = \frac{4 \times 10}{6} \times 270$$

= 1800 bottles

15. Work Hours Days Persons

$\frac{1}{4}$ ↓ 9 ↑ 10 ↑ 400 ↓

$\frac{3}{4}$ 8 20 x

$$\Rightarrow \frac{x}{400} = \frac{10}{20} \times \frac{9}{8} \times \frac{3/4}{1/4}$$

$$\therefore\ x = \frac{1}{2} \times \frac{9}{8} \times 3 \times 400 = 675$$

Hence, number of additional persons

$= 675 - 400 = 275$

TIME AND DISTANCE

1. Starting from a point at a speed of 4 km/hr a man reaches at a cerain place and returns back to the point from where he had started journey on bicycle at the speed of 16 km/hr. His average speed during the entire journey will be :

A. 6.4 km/h B. 8.4 km/h
C. 5.4 km/h D. 10 km/h

2. A motorist covers a certain distance at a average speed of 48 km/h in 45 minutes. What speed in km/h he must maintain to cover the same distance in 30 minutes?

A. 66 km/h B. 79 km/h
C. 80 km/h D. 72 km/h

3. A policeman saw a thief at a distance of 200 m. The policeman and the thief started running at the same time. If the policeman runs at a speed of $4\frac{1}{6}$ m per second and the thief at a speed of $3\frac{1}{3}$ m per second, after what time the policeman will catch the thief?

A. 12 min B. 10 min
C. 9 min D. 4 min

4. A monkey wants to climb up a glazed pole. He climbs 12 metres in 1 minute and then he slips back 3 metres in the next minute. If the pole is 63 metre high, how long does he take to climb at the top of the pole?

A. $11\frac{1}{4}$ min B. $12\frac{1}{2}$ min
C. $12\frac{3}{4}$ min D. $14\frac{3}{4}$ min

5. The distance between two stations A and B is 300 km. A train leaves the station A with a speed of 40 km/hr. At the same time another train departs from the station B with a speed of 50 km/hr. How much time will these two trains take to cross each other?

A. 3 hrs 40 min B. 3 hrs 20 min
C. 2 hrs 20 min D. 3 hrs 45 min

6. Nilesh goes to school from his village at the speed of 4 km/hr and returns from school to village at the speed of 2 km/hr. If he takes 6 hours in all, then what is the distance between the village and the school?

A. 8 km B. 6 km
C. 5 km D. 4 km

7. By increasing the speed of the bus by 10 km/hr the time of journey for 72 km is reduced by 36 minutes. What was the original speed of the bus?

A. 30 km/hr B. 35 km/hr
C. 40 km/hr D. 45 km/hr

8. A train covers a distance in 50 minutes, if it runs at a speed of 48 km/hr on an average. The speed at which the train must run to reduce the time of journey to 40 minutes will be:

A. 70 km/hr B. 60 km/hr
C. 55 km/hr D. 50 km/hr

9. A certain distance is covered by a vehicle at a certain speed. If half of this distance is covered by another vehicle in double the time, the ratio of the speeds of the two vehicles is:

A. 4 : 1 B. 1 : 4
C. 2 : 1 D. 1 : 2

10. A is faster than B. A and B each walk 24 km. The sum of their speeds is 7 km/hr and sum of times taken by them is 14 hours. What is the speed of A?

A. 7 km/hr B. 5 km/hr
C. 4 km/hr D. 3 km/hr

ANSWERS

1	2	3	4	5	6	7	8	9	10
A	D	D	C	B	A	A	B	A	C

EXPLANATORY ANSWERS

1. Average speed during the entire journey

$$= \frac{2xy}{x+y} = \frac{2 \times 4 \times 16}{4+16} = \frac{8 \times 16}{20} = 6.4 \text{ km/hr.}$$

2. Let required speed be x km/hr; then

$$x \times \frac{1}{2} = 48 \times \frac{3}{4} \quad \therefore \quad x = 48 \times \frac{3}{4} \times 2$$

$$= 72 \text{ km/hr}$$

3. Suppose the policeman will catch the thief after t seconds

then, $\left(\frac{25}{6}-\frac{10}{3}\right)t = 200 \Rightarrow \frac{5}{6}t = 200$

$\therefore t = \frac{200 \times 6}{5} = 240$ sec = 4 min.

4. The monkey climbs 12 metres in 1 minute and then he slips back 3 metres in the next minute
∴ The monkey climbs in the first 2 minutes
= 12 – 3 = 9 metres
∴ In the first 12 minutes the monkey climbs
= 9 × 6 = 54 metres
Remaining height of the pole to be covered by the monkey = 63 – 54 = 9 metre
∴ The monkey will climb the height of 9 metres in the 13th minute
∵ The monkey climbs 12 metres in 1 minute

∴ The monkey will climb 9 metres in $\frac{1}{12} \times 9$

$= \frac{3}{4}$ minute

∴ Time spent in climbing at the top of the pole

$= \left(12+\frac{3}{4}\right)$ minutes $= 12\frac{3}{4}$ minutes

5. The two trains are moving in the opposite directions
∴ Relative speed = 40 + 50 = 90 km/hr.

∴ Time taken to cross each other $= \frac{300}{90} = 3\frac{1}{3}$ hours

or, 3 hours 20 minutes.

6. Let x km be the distance between village and the school; then

$\frac{x}{4}+\frac{x}{2}=6 \quad \Rightarrow \frac{3x}{4}=6$

$\therefore x = \frac{6 \times 4}{3} = 8$ km

8. Let x km/hr be the required speed of the train; then

$x \times \frac{40}{60} = 48 \times \frac{50}{60}$

$\therefore x = \frac{48 \times 50}{40} = 60$ km/hr

9. Let x km/hr and t hr be the certain speed and certain time.

Then, ratio of their speeds $= \frac{x}{t} : \frac{x}{2 \times 2t} = 1 : \frac{1}{4} = 4 : 1$

10. Let speeds of A and B are x_1 and x_2 km/hr and times taken by them are t_1 and t_2 hrs, then

$x_1 + x_2 = 7$ km/hr ...(i)

$t_1 + t_2 = 14$ hrs ...(ii)

Now, $\frac{24}{x_1}+\frac{24}{x_2} = 14 \Rightarrow \frac{24(x_1+x_2)}{x_1 x_2} = 14$

$\therefore x_1 x_2 = \frac{24 \times 7}{14} = 12$

Then, $x_1 - x_2 = \sqrt{(x_1+x_2)^2 - 4x_1x_2}$

$= \sqrt{(7)^2 - 4 \times 12} = 1$ ...(iii)

Solving *(i)* and *(iii)* we get $x_1 = 4$ km/hr

TIME AND WORK

1. A and B working together complete a work in 35 days. If A takes 60 days to complete it, how long would B alone take to complete it?
A. 64 days B. 72 days
C. 81 days D. 84 days

2. A few children working together can do a piece of work in 18 days. If the number of children employed on the work is made double, how long would they take to complete half of the work?
A. $4\frac{1}{2}$ days B. $2\frac{1}{3}$ days
C. $8\frac{3}{4}$ days D. $6\frac{1}{2}$ days

3. 10 men or 18 boys can do a piece of work in 15 days. In how many days would 25 men and 15 boys complete the same work working together?
A. $5\frac{1}{2}$ days B. $4\frac{1}{2}$ days
C. $6\frac{2}{3}$ days D. $2\frac{1}{3}$ days

4. A cistern is filled by a tap in $3\frac{1}{2}$ hours. Due to a leak in the bottom of the cistern, it takes half an hour longer to fill the cistern. If the cistern is full, how long will it take the leak to empty it?
A. 28 hours B. 29 hours
C. $31\frac{1}{3}$ hours D. 38 hours

5. A is twice as good a workman as B and thrice as good a workman as C. If C alone can do a piece of work in 24 days, how long would the three persons take to finish the work working together?

A. $3\frac{3}{11}$ days B. $4\frac{4}{7}$ days

C. $4\frac{4}{11}$ days D. $3\frac{4}{11}$ days

6. If 3 men and 5 women can do a piece of work in 8 days and 2 men and 7 boys can do the same work in 12 days. Find the number of boys, the work done by whom can equate the work done by 10 women.
A. 19 boys B. 21 boys
C. 23 boys D. 15 boys

7. 8 men alone can complete a piece of work in 12 days. 4 women alone can complete the same piece of work in 48 days and 10 children alone can complete the piece of work in 24 days. In how many days can 10 men, 4 women and 10 children together complete the piece of work?
A. 6 B. 8
C. 10 D. 15

8. A works twice as fast as B. If B can complete a piece of work independently in 12 days. Find in how many days A and B together can complete the work?
A. 8 days B. 6 days
C. 4 days D. 18 days

9. A contractor undertook to complete a project in 90 days and employed 60 men on it. After 60 days, he found that $\frac{3}{4}$ of the work has already been completed.

How many men can he discharge so that the project may be completed exactly on time?
A. 15 B. 20
C. 30 D. 40

10. A can do a piece of work in 25 days and B can do it in 20 days. They work together for 5 days and then A goes away. In how many days will B finish the remaining work?
A. 33 days B. 20 days
C. 11 days D. 10 days

ANSWERS

1	2	3	4	5	6	7	8	9	10
D	A	B	A	C	B	A	C	B	C

EXPLANATORY ANSWERS

1. (A + B)'s 1 day's work = $\frac{1}{35}$

and also, A's 1 day's work = $\frac{1}{60}$

Hence, B's 1 day's work = $\frac{1}{35}-\frac{1}{60}=\frac{5}{420}=\frac{1}{84}$

So, B will do the whole work in 84 days.

3. 10 men ≡ 18 boys

25 men ≡ $\frac{18}{10}\times 25 = 45$ boys

Hence, 25 men + 15 boys = 45 + 15 = 60 boys

Now, 18 boys can do a piece of work in 15 days.

Hence, 60 boys will do a piece of work in $\frac{15\times 18}{60}=\frac{9}{2}$ days = $4\frac{1}{2}$ days.

4. In 1 hour $\frac{2}{7}$ cistern is filled by the tap.

Hence, in $\frac{1}{2}$ hour $\frac{2}{14}=\frac{1}{7}$ cistern is filled by the tap.

So, $\frac{1}{7}$ cistern is emptied by the leakage in 4 hours.

So, 1 cistern will be emptied by the leakage in 28 hours.

6. Here, (3 men + 5 women) × 8
≡ (2 men + 7 boys) × 12
⇒ 40 women ≡ 84 boys

∴ 10 women ≡ $\frac{84}{40}\times 10$ = 21 boys

Hence, work done by 10 women
= work done of 21 boys.

7. B's 1 day's work = $\frac{1}{4}-\frac{1}{12}=\frac{2}{12}=\frac{1}{6}$

Hence, B alone will complete the work in 6 days.

8. Ratio of efficiency of A and B = 2 : 1
Then, ratio of their time taking = 1 : 2
Hence, if B can complete the work in 12 days, then A in 6 days.

Now, (A + B)'s 1 day's work = $\frac{1}{6}+\frac{1}{12}=\frac{3}{12}=\frac{1}{4}$

So, A and B together can complete the work in 4 days.

9. After 60 days remaining work = $1-\frac{3}{4}=\frac{1}{4}$

In 60 days $\frac{3}{4}$ work has been done by 60 men

In 30 days $\frac{1}{4}$ work will be done by $60\times\frac{4}{3}\times\frac{1}{4}\times\frac{60}{30}$ = 40 men.

Hence, required number of men = 60 – 40 = 20 (which are to be discharged).

BOATS AND STREAMS

1. A boat goes 6 km upstream and back to the starting point in 2 hours. If the current of the stream runs at the rate of 4 km/hr, find the speed of the boat in still water.

A. 6 km/hr B. 8 km/hr
C. 10 km/hr D. 12 km/hr

2. A boat covers 24 km upstream and 36 km downstream in 6 hours, while it covers 36 km upstream and 24 km downstream in 6½ horus. Find the speed of the current.

A. 2 km/hr B. 4 km/hr
C. 6 km/hr D. 8 km/hr

3. A man can row 5 km/hr in still water and the speed of the stream is 1.5 km/hr. He takes an hour when he travels upstream to a place and back again to the starting point. How far is the place from the starting point?

A. 2.275 km B. 3.5 km
C. 1.5 km D. None of these

4. The speed of a boat in still water is 6 km/hr and the speed of the stream is 1.5 km/hr. A man rows to a place at a distance of 22.5 km and comes back to the starting point. Find the total time taken by him.

A. 8 hours B. 10 hours
C. 12 hours D. 4 hours

5. A boat covers 20 km downstream and 6 km upstream in 3 hours, while it covers 30 km downstream and 12 km upstream in 5 hours. What is the speed of boat in still water?

A. 6 km/hr B. 8 km/hr
C. 10 km/hr D. 12 km/hr.

6. Samir can travel 12 miles downstream in a certain river in 6 hours less than it takes him to travel the same distance upstream. But when he could double his rowing rate for his 24-mile round trip, the downstream 12 miles would then take only one hour less than the upstream 12 miles. Find the speed of the current in miles/hour.

A. $2\frac{2}{3}$ B. $2\frac{1}{3}$
C. $1\frac{2}{3}$ D. $1\frac{1}{3}$

7. A boat takes 6 hours to travel from place M to N downstream and back from N to M upstream. If the speed of the boat in still water is 4 km/hr; what is the distance between two places?

A. 6 kms B. 8 kms
C. 12 kms D. Data inadequate

8. A man can row upstream at 8 km/hr and downstream at 13 km/hr. The speed of the stream is:

A. 2.5 km/hr B. 4.2 km/hr
C. 5 km/hr D. 10.5 km/hr

9. A man's speed with the current is 15 km/hr and the speed of the current is 2.5 km/hr. The man's speed against the current is:

A. 12.5 km/hr B. 10 km/hr
C. 9 km/hr D. 8.5 km/hr

10. A motorboat, whose speed is 15 km/hr in still water goes 30 km downstream and comes back in a total of 4 hours 30 minutes. What is the speed of the stream (in km/hr)?

A. 10 B. 6
C. 5 D. 4

ANSWERS

1	2	3	4	5	6	7	8	9	10
B	A	A	A	B	B	D	A	B	C

EXPLANATORY ANSWERS

1. Let the speed of a boat in still water = x km/hr; then

$$\frac{6}{x-4}+\frac{6}{x+4}=2 \Rightarrow \frac{2x}{x^2-16}=\frac{1}{3}$$

$\Rightarrow x^2 - 6x - 16 = 0$

$\Rightarrow (x - 8)(x + 2) = 0$

Hence, the speed of the boat = 8 km/hr.

2. Let x km/hr and y km/hr be the speeds of the boat in still water and the speed of the current respectively, then

$$\frac{24}{x-y}+\frac{36}{x+y}=6 \Rightarrow \frac{4}{x-y}+\frac{6}{x+y}=1 \quad ...(i)$$

And, $$\frac{36}{x-y}+\frac{24}{x+y}=\frac{13}{2} \quad ...(ii)$$

Solving these two equations, we get

$x + y = 12;\ x - y = 8$

Hence, $y = \frac{1}{2}(12-8) = 2$ km/hr.

3. Let required distance be x km, then

$$\frac{x}{5-1.5}+\frac{x}{5+1.5}=1 \Rightarrow \frac{x\times 2}{7}+\frac{x\times 2}{13}=1$$

$\Rightarrow 40x = 91 \quad \therefore x = 91/40 = 2.275$ km

4. Required time period $= \frac{22.5}{6+1.5}+\frac{22.5}{6-1.5}$

$= \frac{45}{15}+\frac{45}{9} = 8$ hours.

5. Let x km/hr and y km/hr be the speed of boat in still water and speed of current respectively; then

$$\frac{20}{x+y}+\frac{6}{x-y}=3 \quad ...(i)$$

and also, $$\frac{30}{x+y}+\frac{12}{x-y}=5$$

$$\Rightarrow \frac{15}{x+y}+\frac{6}{x-y}=\frac{5}{2} \quad ...(ii)$$

Solving equations *(i)* & *(ii)*, we get $x + y = 10$ and $x - y = 6$

Since, $x = \frac{1}{2}(10 + 6) = 8$ km/hr.

6. Let x km/hr and y km/hr be the speed of rowing in still water and speed of the current respectively; then

$$\frac{12}{x-y}-\frac{12}{x+y}=6 \Rightarrow \frac{24y}{x^2-y^2}=6$$

$$\Rightarrow x^2 = y^2 + 4y \quad ...(i)$$

Again, $$\frac{12}{2x-y}-\frac{12}{2x+y}=1$$

$$\Rightarrow \frac{24y}{4x^2-y^2}=1 \Rightarrow x^2 = \frac{y^2+24y}{4} \quad ...(ii)$$

From equations (i) and (ii), we get

$$y^2 + 4y = \frac{y^2+24y}{4} \Rightarrow 3y^2 = 8y$$

$\therefore y = \frac{8}{3} = 2\frac{1}{3}$ miles/hr.

8. The speed of the stream $= \frac{1}{2}(13 - 8) = \frac{5}{2}$

$= 2.5$ km/hr.

9. The man's speed in still water

$= 15 - 2.5 = 12.5$ km/hr

Hence, the men's speed against the current

$= 12.5 - 2.5 = 10$ km/hr

10. Let speed of the stream be x km/hr, then

$$\frac{30}{15+x}+\frac{30}{15-x}=4\frac{1}{2} \Rightarrow \frac{30\times 30}{225-x^2}=\frac{9}{2}$$

$\Rightarrow \frac{200}{225-x^2}=1 \quad \Rightarrow x^2 = 225 - 200$

$\Rightarrow x^2 = 25 \quad \therefore x = 5$ km/hr.

ALLIGATION OR MIXTURE

1. A shopkeeper buys 26 kgs of milk @ Rs. 16 per kg. He also buys from another source an inferior quality of milk @ Rs. 10 per kg. How much quantity of the latter should he buy to mix it with the former so that he can sell the mixture @ Rs. 14 per kg without making any loss?

A. 13 kgs B. 12 kgs
C. 14 kgs D. 16 kgs

2. Two vessels A and B contain mixture of milk and water in the ratio 4 : 1 and 9 : 11 respectively. They are mixed in the ratio of 3 : 2. Find the ratio of milk : water in the resulting mixture.

A. 34 : 16 B. 33 : 17
C. 16 : 34 D. 17 : 33

3. A shopkeeper has 50 kgs of rice. He sells a part of it at 20% profit and the rest at 40% profit. If he gains 25% on the whole, find the quantity of each part.

A. 12.5 kgs and 37.5 kgs
B. 37.5 kgs and 12.5 kgs
C. 23.5 kgs and 21.5 kgs
D. 21.5 kgs and 23.5 kgs

4. A man bought a certain quantity of sugar for Rs. 8000. He sells one-fourth of it at 20% loss. At what per cent profit should he sell the remainder stock so as to make an overall profit of 20%?

A. 20% B. 30%
C. 35% D. 40%

5. Rs. 675 was divided among 75 boys and girls. Each boy gets Rs. 20 whereas a girl gets Rs. 5. Find the number of boys and girls.

A. 20, 55 B. 15, 60
C. 25, 50 D. 30, 45

6. A vessel contains mixture of liquids A and B in the ratio 3 : 2. When 20 litres of the mixture is taken out and replaced by 20 litres of liquid B, the ratio changes to 1 : 4. How many litres of liquid A was there initially present in the vessel?

A. 12 litres B. 18 litres
C. 24 litres D. 22 litres

7. A container is full of milk. One-third of milk is taken out of it and replaced by same quantity of water. Then again one-third of the mixture is taken out of it and replaced by the same quantity of water. The process is repeated 4 times. If 16 litres of milk is left in the container at the end of 4th operation, find the capacity of the container.

A. 76 litres B. 81 litres
C. 82 litres D. 85 litres

8. The cost of type-I rice is Rs. 15 per kg and type-II is Rs. 20 per kg. If both type I and type II are mixed in the ratio of 2 : 3, then find the price per kg of the mixed variety.

A. Rs. 19.50 B. Rs. 19
C. Rs. 18.50 D. Rs. 18

9. In what ratio must a grocer mix two varieties of tea worth Rs. 60 a kg and Rs. 65 a kg so that by selling the mixture at Rs. 68.20 a kg he may gain 10%?

A. 4 : 5 B. 3 : 5
C. 3 : 4 D. 3 : 2

10. A vessel contains 80 litres of milk. 16 litres of milk was taken out of the vessel and replaced by water. Then 16 litres of mixture was withdrawn and again replaced by water. The operation was repeated for third time. How much milk is now left in the vessel?

A. 96.40 litres
B. 50.36 litres
C. 40.96 litres
D. 32.76 litres

ANSWERS

1	2	3	4	5	6	7	8	9	10
A	B	B	B	A	B	B	D	D	C

EXPLANATORY ANSWERS

1.

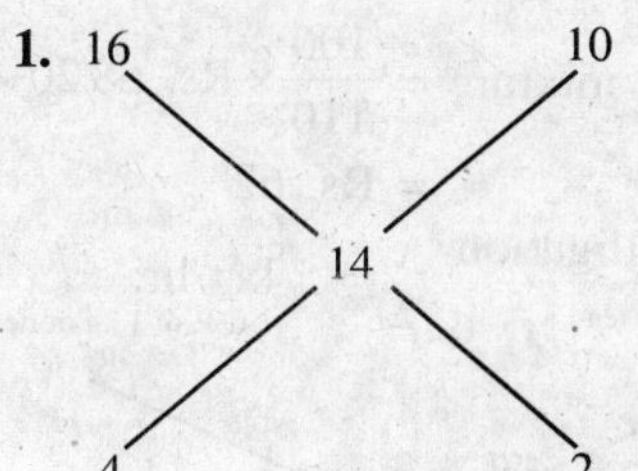

or 2 : 1 $\dfrac{\text{Quantity of milk @ Rs.10 per kg}}{\text{Quantity of milk @ Rs. 16 per kg}} = \dfrac{1}{2}$

So, quantity of milk @ Rs. 10 per kg. $= \dfrac{26}{2} = 13$ kgs.

2. Fraction is *Milk* *Water*

A : $\dfrac{4}{5}$ $\dfrac{1}{5}$

B : $\dfrac{9}{20}$ $\dfrac{11}{20}$

$(3A + 2B) = A \text{ and } B : \left(\dfrac{12}{5} + \dfrac{9}{10}\right) \left(\dfrac{3}{5} + \dfrac{11}{10}\right)$

$\dfrac{33}{10}$ $\dfrac{17}{10}$

So, Ratio of milk : water in the resulting mixture = 33 : 17.

3.

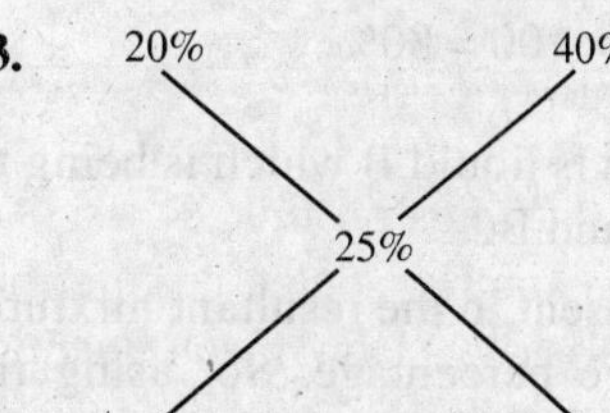

or 3 : 1

$$\text{Quantity sold at 20\% profit} = \frac{3}{3+1} \times 50$$

$$= 37.5 \text{ kgs.}$$

$$\text{Quantity sold at 40\% profit} = (50 - 37.5)$$

$$= 12.5 \text{ kgs.}$$

4. Let the remainder stock be sold at x% profit.

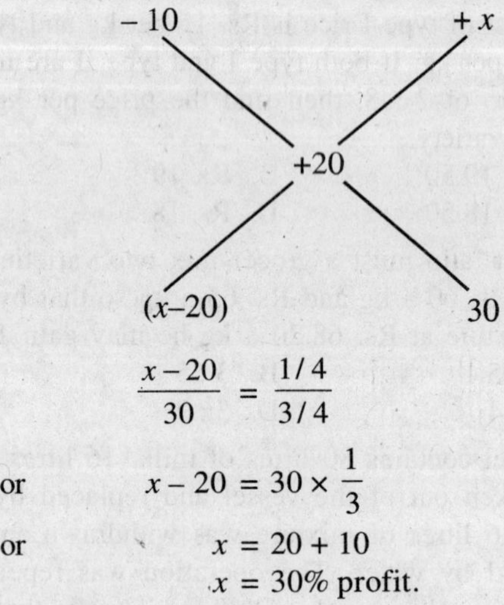

$$\frac{x-20}{30} = \frac{1/4}{3/4}$$

or $\quad x - 20 = 30 \times \frac{1}{3}$

or $\quad x = 20 + 10$

$x = 30\%$ profit.

5. Average money per head (boy or girl)

$$= \text{Rs. } \frac{675}{75} = \text{Rs. } 9$$

(Boys) Rs. 20 (Girls) Rs. 5

(Average) Rs. 9

4 11

$$\text{Number of boys} = \frac{4}{4+11} \times 75 = 20$$

$$\text{Number of girls} = \frac{11}{4+11} \times 75 = 55.$$

6. % of liquid B initially present in the vessel

$$= \frac{2}{3+2} \times 100 = 40\%$$

% of liquid B finally present in the vessel

$$= \frac{4}{1+4} \times 100 = 80\%$$

The second solution is liquid B which is being mixed and it has 100% liquid B.

80% of liquid B present in the resultant mixture may be taken as average percentage. So, using rule of alligation on liquid B per cent, we can write,

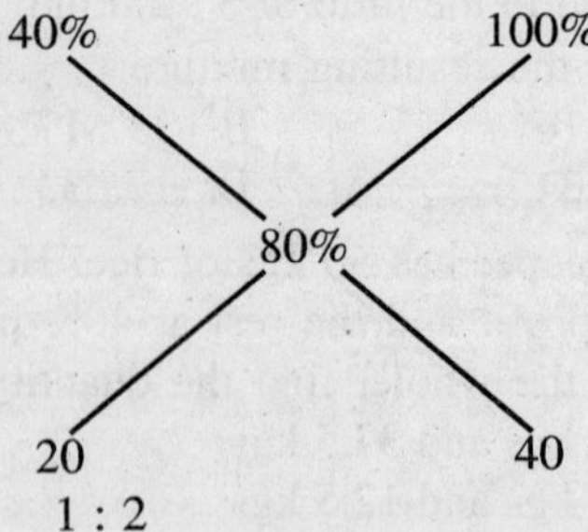

or $\quad$ 1 : 2

The ratio of liquid left in the vessel to liquid B being mixed = 1 : 2

Since the quantity of liquid B being mixed is 20 litres, the quantity of liquid left in the vessel is 10 litres. Therefore, the total quantity of liquid initially present in the vessel

$$= 10 + 20 = 30 \text{ litres}$$

$$\text{Quantity of liquid A} = \frac{3}{2+3} \times 30 = 18 \text{ litres.}$$

7. Let capacity of the container be x litre; then

$$x(1 - 1/3)^4 = 16 \quad \Rightarrow \quad x\left(\frac{2}{3}\right)^4 = 16$$

$$\Rightarrow x \times \frac{16}{81} = 16 \qquad \therefore \; x = 81 \text{ litres}$$

8. Let the price per kg of mixed variety be Rs. x; then

By the rule of alligation,

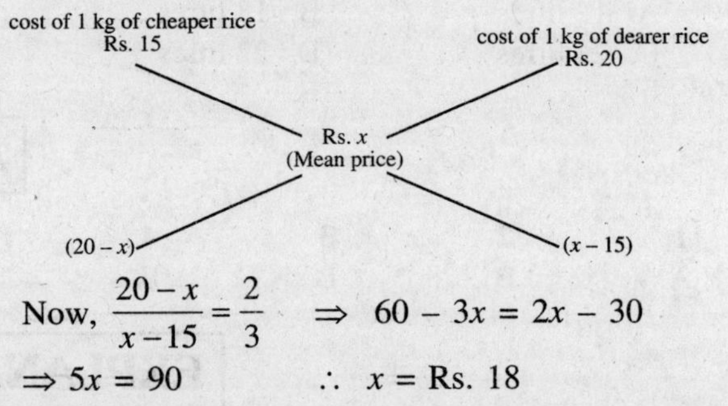

$$\text{Now, } \frac{20-x}{x-15} = \frac{2}{3} \quad \Rightarrow \quad 60 - 3x = 2x - 30$$

$$\Rightarrow 5x = 90 \qquad \therefore \; x = \text{Rs. } 18$$

9. S.P. of 1 kg mixture = Rs. 68.20, Gain % = 10%

$$\text{Hence, C.P. of 1 kg mixture} = \frac{100}{110} \times \text{Rs. } 68.20$$

$$= \text{Rs. } 62$$

By the rule of alligation

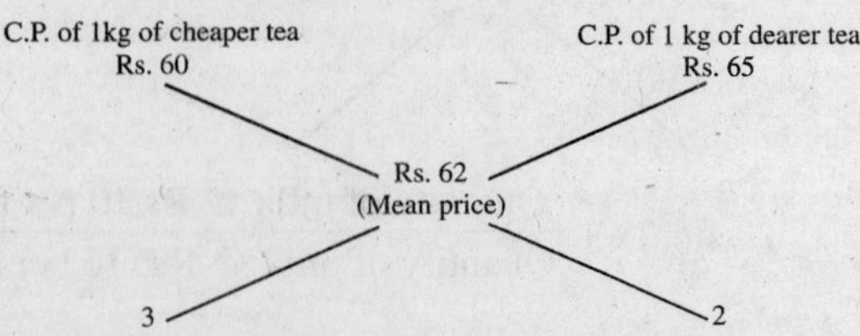

Hence, required ratio = 3 : 2

10. $\text{Amount of milk left} = 80\left(1 - \frac{16}{80}\right)^3 = 80\left(\frac{4}{5}\right)^3$

$$80 \times \frac{64}{125} = 40.96 \text{ litres.}$$

PERCENTAGE

1. A student who secures 20% marks in an examination fails by 30 marks. Another student who secures 32% gets 42 marks more than those required to pass. The percentage of marks required to pass is:
   A. 20 B. 25
   C. 28 D. 30

2. In a college election, a candidate secured 62% of the votes and is elected by a majority of 144 votes. The total number of votes polled is:
   A. 600 B. 800
   C. 925 D. 1200

3. In an organisation, 40% of the employees are matriculates, 50% of the remaining are graduates and the remaining 180 are postgraduates. How many employees are graduates?
   A. 360 B. 240
   C. 300 D. 180

4. The population of a village is 4500. $\frac{5}{9}$th of them are males and rest females. If 40% of the males are married, then the percentage of married female is :
   A. 35 B. 40
   C. 50 D. 60

5. A's income is 10% more than B's. How much per cent is B's income is less than A's?
   A. 10% B. 7%
   C. $9\frac{1}{11}$% D. $6\frac{1}{2}$%

6. If the price of a television set is increased by 25%, then by what percentage should the new price be reduced to bring the price back to original level?
   A. 15% B. 20%
   C. 25% D. 30%

7. In an election one of the two candidates gets 40% votes and loses by 100 votes. Total number of votes is :
   A. 500 B. 400
   C. 600 D. 1000

8. The gross income of a person is Rs. 20000. 10% of his income is exempted from income tax and his net income is Rs. 19100. The rate of income tax is :
   A. 3% B. 2%
   C. 4% D. 5%

9. The owner of a cell phone shop charges his customer 32% more than the cost price. If a customer paid Rs. 6600 for the cell phone, then what was the cost price of the cell phone?
   A. Rs. 5000 B. Rs. 5500
   C. Rs. 5800 D. Rs. 6100

10. If the cost of pins reduced by Rs. 4 per dozen, 12 more pins can be purchased for Rs. 48. The cost of pins per dozen after reduction is:
    A. Rs. 8 B. Rs. 12
    C. Rs. 16 D. Rs. 20

11. In an examination 80% of the students passed in Mathematics and 70% passed in English, while 10% students failed in both the subjects. If 360 students passed in both the subjects, find the total number of students who appeared in the examination.
    A. 400 B. 600
    C. 630 D. 640

12. Electric tax is increased by 20% and its consumption is decreased by 20%. The change in the expenditure is:
    A. 4% decrease B. 4% increase
    C. 5% decrease D. 5% increase

13. The selling price of certain commodity was reduced by 25%. As a result of it, the sales increased by 30%. What was the effect of it on cash collected by daily sales?
    A. 2.5% decrease B. 2.5% increase
    C. 5% decrease D. 5% increase

14. The wheat sold by a grocer contained 10% low quality wheat. What quantity of good quality wheat should be added to 150 kgs of wheat so that the percentage of low quality wheat becomes 5%?
    A. 50 kgs B. 85 kgs
    C. 135 kgs D. 150 kgs

15. Nilam spends 15% of her monthly income on household expenses. She spends 17% of the monthly income in travelling and 6% on medical expenses and saves the rest Rs. 15,500. What is her monthly income?
    A. Rs. 20,000 B. Rs. 25,000
    C. Rs. 30,000 D. Rs. 35,000

ANSWERS

1	2	3	4	5	6	7	8	9	10
B	A	D	C	C	B	A	D	A	B
11	**12**	**13**	**14**	**15**					
B	A	A	D	B					

EXPLANATORY ANSWERS

1. 20% of $x + 30 = 32\%$ of $x - 42$

$\Rightarrow$ 12% of $x = 72$

$$\Rightarrow \quad x = \frac{72 \times 100}{12} = 600$$

Pass Mark $= 20\%$ of $600 + 30 = 150$

$$\text{Pass percentage} = \left(\frac{150}{600} \times 100\right)\% = 25\%$$

2. (62% of $x - 38\%$ of x) $= 144$

$$\Rightarrow 24\% \text{ of } x = 144 \quad \Rightarrow x = \frac{144 \times 100}{24} = 600$$

3.
$$\text{Matriculates} = \frac{40}{100}x = \frac{2x}{5}$$

$$\text{Remaining} = \left(x - \frac{2x}{5}\right) = \frac{3x}{5}$$

$$\text{Graduates} = \frac{50}{100} \times \frac{3x}{5} = \frac{3x}{10}$$

$$\text{Remaining} = \frac{3x}{5} - \frac{3x}{10} = \frac{3x}{10}$$

$$\text{Now, } \frac{3x}{10} = 180 \quad \therefore x = \frac{10 \times 180}{3} = 600$$

$$\therefore \text{Graduates} = \frac{3 \times 600}{10} = 180.$$

4. $\text{Males} = \left(\frac{5}{9} \times 4500\right) = 2500$

Females $= 2000$

$$\therefore \quad \text{Married males} = \frac{40}{100} \times 2500 = 1000$$

and married females $= 1000$

$\therefore$ Percentage of married females

$$= \left(\frac{1000}{2000} \times 100\right)\% = 50\%.$$

5. $\text{Required percentage} = \left[\frac{10}{(100 + 10)} \times 100\right]\% = 9\frac{1}{11}\%.$

6. $\text{Required reduction} = \frac{25}{100 + 25} \times 100 = 20\%.$

7. Out of 100, difference in votes $= (60 - 40) = 20$

20% of $x = 100$

$$\therefore x = \frac{100 \times 100}{20} = 500.$$

8. Gross income $=$ Rs. 20000

Income exempted from income tax $= 10\%$ of gross income

$\therefore$ Income on which income tax is chargeable $= (100 - 10\%) = 90\%$ of gross income

$$= 20000 \times \frac{90}{100} = \text{Rs. } 18000$$

$\therefore$ Total income tax paid on

$=$ Rs. 20000 $-$ Rs. 19100 $=$ Rs. 900

$$\therefore \text{Rate per cent of income tax} = \frac{900}{18000} \times 100 = 5\%$$

9. Let cost price of the cell phone be Rs. x; then

$$x + \frac{32}{100} \times x = 6600 \quad \Rightarrow \frac{132x}{100} = 6600$$

$$\therefore x = \frac{100 \times 6600}{132} = \text{Rs. } 5000.$$

10. Let reduced price by Rs. x per dozen, then

$$\frac{48}{x} - \frac{48}{x+4} = 1 \quad \Rightarrow \quad \frac{48 \times 4}{x^2 + 4x} = 1$$

$\Rightarrow \quad x^2 + 4x - 192 = 0$

$\Rightarrow \quad (x + 16)(x - 12) = 0$

$\therefore \quad x =$ Rs. 12.

11. Here, percentage of students failed in Mathematics and English be 30% and 20% respectively.

Percentage of students failed either one or both subjects $= 30 + 20 - 10 = 40\%$

Hence, percentage of pass students $= 100 - 40 = 60\%$

Now, $60\% = 360$

$$\therefore 100\% = \frac{360}{60} \times 100 = 600.$$

12. Let initially electric tax is Rs. 100 and consumption $=$ 100 units

Decrease in consumption

$= 100 \times 100 - 120 \times 80 =$ Rs. 400

$$\text{Hence, decrease percentage} = \frac{400 \times 100}{100 \times 100} = 4\%.$$

13. Let the selling price of a commodity be Rs. 100 and number of sales $= 100$ units

Decrease in daily cash $= 100 \times 100 - 75 \times 130$

$=$ Rs. 250

$$\text{Hence, decrease percentage} = \frac{250 \times 100}{100 \times 100} = 2.5\%.$$

14. Let x kg of good wheat be added; then

$$\frac{10}{100} \times 150 = \frac{5}{100}(150 + x)$$

$\Rightarrow 150 + x = 300 \quad \therefore \quad x = 150$ kg.

15. Let her monthly income be Rs. x; then

$$x - \left(\frac{15}{100} \times x + \frac{17}{100} \times x + \frac{6}{100} \times x\right) = 15{,}500$$

$$\Rightarrow x - \frac{38x}{100} = 15500 \quad \Rightarrow \frac{62x}{100} = 15500$$

$$\therefore \quad x = \frac{15500 \times 100}{62} = \text{Rs. } 25000.$$

PROFIT AND LOSS

1. Ashok bought 25 kg of rice at the rate of Rs. 6 per kg and 35 kg of rice at the rate of Rs. 7 per kg. He mixed the two and sold the mixture at the rate of Rs. 6.75 per kg. What was his gain or loss in the transaction?

A. Rs. 16 gain　　B. Rs. 16 loss
C. Rs. 10 gain　　D. None of these

2. Profit after selling a commodity for Rs. 425 is same as loss after selling it for Rs. 355. The cost of the commodity is :

A. Rs. 285　　B. Rs. 390
C. Rs. 295　　D. Rs. 400

3. Ram bought 4 dozen apples at Rs. 12 per dozen and 2 dozen at Rs. 16 per dozen. He sold all of them to earn 20%. At what price per dozen did he sell the apples?

A. Rs. 14.40　　B. Rs. 16.00
C. Rs. 16.80　　D. Rs. 16.20

4. At what price must Kantilal sell a mixture of 80 kg sugar at Rs. 6.75 per kg with 120 kg at Rs. 8 per kg to gain 20%?

A. Rs. 7.50 per kg　　B. Rs. 8.20 per kg
C. Rs. 8.35 per kg　　D. Rs. 9 per kg

5. A person bought an article and sold it at a loss of 10%. If he had bought it for 20% less and sold it for Rs. 55 more, he would have had a profit of 40%. The C.P. of the article is :

A. Rs. 200　　B. Rs. 225
C. Rs. 250　　D. None of these

6. A dealer sold a machine to a shopkeeper at 20% profit. The shopkeeper sold the machine to a customer so as to get 25% profit for himself. The difference between the selling price of the dealer and that of the shopkeeper was found to be Rs. 129. What is the initial price of the machine?

A. Rs. 410　　B. Rs. 420
C. Rs. 430　　D. Rs. 440

7. A man bought a horse and cart. If he sold the horse at 10% loss and the cart at 20% gain he would not loss anything. If he sold the horse at 5% loss and the cart at 5% gain he would lose Rs. 10 in the bargain. What did he pay for each?

A. Rs. 400, Rs. 200　　B. Rs. 300, Rs. 300
C. Rs. 250, Rs. 350　　D. Rs. 350, Rs. 250

8. The marked price of a radio is 20% more than its cost price. If a discount of 10% is given on the marked price, the gain percentage is:

A. 8　　B. 10
C. 12　　D. 15

9. A dishonest dealer sells his goods at the cost price and still earns a profit of 60% by underweight. What weight does he use for a kg?

A. 625 gms　　B. 750 gms
C. 800 gms　　D. 850 gms

10. A man sells two horses for Rs. 990 each. On one he gains 10% and the other he loses 10%. What is his total percentage of gain or loss in the transaction?

A. 1% gain　　B. 1% loss
C. 2% gain　　D. 2% loss

ANSWERS

1	2	3	4	5	6	7	8	9	10
C	B	B	D	C	C	A	A	A	B

EXPLANATORY ANSWERS

1. C.P. of 60 kg mixture = Rs. $(25 \times 6 + 35 \times 7)$
= Rs. 395
S.P. of 60 kg mixtire = Rs. (60×6.75)
= Rs. 405
∴ Gain = Rs. $(405 - 395)$
= Rs. 10

2. Let C.P. = Rs. x
Then, $425 - x = x - 355 \Rightarrow 2x = 780$
∴ $x =$ Rs. 390

3. C.P. of 6 dozen apples = Rs. $(12 \times 4 + 16 \times 2)$
= Rs. 80
∴ S.P. = Rs. $\left(\frac{120}{100} \times 80\right)$
= Rs. 96
∴ S.P. per dozen = Rs. $\left(\frac{96}{6}\right)$ = Rs. 16

4. C.P. of 1 kg sugar $= \dfrac{80\times 6.75+120\times 8}{200}$

$= $ Rs. 7.50

$\therefore$ S.P. of 1 kg $=$ Rs. $\left(\dfrac{120}{100}\times 7.50\right)$

$= $ Rs. 9 per kg

5. Let, C.P. $=$ Rs. x,

then, S.P. $= \dfrac{90}{100}\times x =$ Rs. $\dfrac{9x}{10}$

Now, when C.P. $=$ Rs. $\dfrac{80x}{100} =$ Rs. $\dfrac{4x}{5}$;

then, S.P. $= \dfrac{140}{100}\times\dfrac{4x}{5} =$ Rs. $\dfrac{28x}{25}$

But, $\dfrac{28x}{25}-\dfrac{9x}{10}=55 \Rightarrow \dfrac{11x}{50}=55$

$\therefore$ $x =$ Rs. 250

6. Let the initial price $=$ Rs. x; then C.P. for dealer

$= \dfrac{120}{100}\times x =$ Rs. $\dfrac{6x}{5}$

Again, C.P. for shopkeeper $= \dfrac{125}{100}\times\dfrac{6x}{5}$

$=$ Rs. $\dfrac{3x}{2}$

Now, $\dfrac{3x}{2}-\dfrac{6x}{5}=129 \Rightarrow \dfrac{3x}{10}=129$

$\therefore\ x = \dfrac{10\times 129}{3} =$ Rs. 430

7. Here, 10% C.P. of horse $=$ 20% C.P. of cart; Hence, C.P. of horse $= 2\times$ C.P. of cart;
Let C.P. of cart and horse be Rs. x and Rs. $2x$ respectively; then,

$\dfrac{5}{100}\times 2x-\dfrac{5}{100}\times x=10 \Rightarrow \dfrac{1}{20}x=10$

$\therefore x = 200$

Hence, C.P. of a cart $=$ Rs. 200 and C.P. of a horse $= 2\times 200 =$ Rs. 400

8. Let C.P. be Rs. 100; then marked price $=$ Rs. 120

Since, S.P. $= \dfrac{90}{100}\times 120 =$ Rs. 108

$\therefore$ Profit $= 108-100 =$ Rs. 8, Hence, **gain = 8%.**

9. Required weight $= \dfrac{100}{160}\times 1000 = 625$ gms.

10. Here, loss % $= \left(\dfrac{10}{10}\right)^2 = 1\%$.

SIMPLE INTEREST

1. A lent a sum of Rs. 1250 to B at a certain rate of interest for 3 years and a sum of Rs. 1500 to C at the same rate of interest for 2 years. If he was paid total Rs. 258.75 as interest in both cases, find the rate of interest at which money was lent by him.
   A. $4\frac{1}{6}\%$ B. $6\frac{1}{4}\%$
   C. $2\frac{1}{7}\%$ D. $3\frac{5}{6}\%$

2. A invested Rs. 5000 at a certain rate of simple interest and Rs. 4000 for the same period at 1% higher rate of interest. If the interest in both cases is same, the former rate of interest is :
   A. 3% B. 4%
   C. 6% D. 5%

3. If a certain sum of money at simple interest amounts to Rs. 1900 in 3 years and to Rs. 2050 in 5 years, the rate per cent per annum is :
   A. 4½% B. 3½%
   C. 2½% D. 5¼%

4. A certain sum of money lent out on simple interest amounts to Rs. 1760 in 2 years and to Rs. 2000 in 5 years. Find the sum.
   A. Rs. 1650 B. Rs. 1500
   C. Rs. 1580 D. Rs. 1600

5. Out of the sum of Rs. 1550, a part was lent out at 5% p.a. simple interest and the remaining at 8% p.a. simple interest. If the total interest in both cases after 3 years is Rs. 300, the sum of money lent out at 8% p.a. simple interest was:
   A. Rs. 760 B. Rs. 775
   C. Rs. 750 D. Rs. 780

6. If simple interest on a certain sum of money for 4 years at 5% p.a. is same as the simple interest on Rs. 840 for 10 years at the rate of 4% p.a., the sum of money is:
   A. Rs. 1780 B. Rs. 1660
   C. Rs. 1680 D. Rs. 1620

7. What equal instalment of annual payment will discharge a debt which is due as Rs. 848 at the end of 4 years at 4% **per annum simple interest?**

A. Rs. 200 B. Rs. 212
C. Rs. 225 D. Rs. 250

8. Madhavi lent Rs. 5000 to Kamla for 5 years and Rs. 3000 to Vimla for 4 years. Find the rate of interest, if Madhavi gets an interest of Rs. 600 in the end.
A. 1.62% B. 2.5%
C. 3% D. 4%

9. A sum of money doubles itself in 7 years at simple interest. In how many years it will become four fold?
A. 10 years B. 14 years
C. 21 years D. 35 years

10. An amount doubles itself at the end of 8 years with a certain rate of simple interest. What will be the total simple interest on Rs. 8000 at that rate at the end of 4 years?
A. Rs. 2000 B. Rs. 4000
C. Rs. 6000 D. None of these

ANSWERS

1	2	3	4	5	6	7	8	9	10
D	B	A	D	C	C	A	A	C	B

EXPLANATORY ANSWERS

1. $\frac{1250 \times R \times 3}{100} + \frac{1500 \times R \times 2}{100} = 258.75$

$\Rightarrow 6750\ R = 25875$

$\therefore \quad R = \frac{25875}{6750} = \frac{23}{6} = 3\frac{5}{6}\%$

2. Here, $\frac{5000 \times R \times T}{100} = \frac{4000 \times (R+1) \times T}{100}$

$\Rightarrow 5R = 4R + 4 \quad \therefore\ R = 4\%$

3. Simple interest for 2 years
= Rs. 2050 – Rs. 1900 = Rs. 150

$\therefore$ Simple interest for 1 year = Rs. $\frac{150}{2}$ = Rs. 75

Since simple interest for 3 years = Rs. 75 × 3
= Rs. 225

$\therefore$ Principal = Rs. 1900 – Rs. 225 = Rs. 1675

Hence, Rate = $\frac{75 \times 100}{1675 \times 1} = 4\frac{1}{2}\%$

4. Interest for 3 years = Rs. 2000 – Rs. 1760
= Rs. 240

$\therefore$ Interest for 1 year = Rs. $\frac{240}{3}$ = Rs. 80

And interest for 2 years = Rs. 80 × 2 = Rs. 160
$\therefore$ Principal = Rs. 1760 – Rs. 160 = Rs. 1600

5. Let Rs. x and Rs $(1550 - x)$ were lent out at 8% and 5% respectively; then

$\frac{x \times 8 \times 3}{100} + \frac{(1550 - x) \times 5 \times 3}{100} = 300$

$\Rightarrow 24x + 23250 - 15x = 30000$

$\Rightarrow 9x = 6750 \quad \therefore\ x = \frac{6750}{9}$ = Rs. 750

6. Here, $\frac{P \times 5 \times 4}{100} = \frac{840 \times 4 \times 10}{100} \Rightarrow 5P = 8400$

$\therefore \quad P = \frac{8400}{5}$ = Rs. 1680

7. Let equal instalment be Rs. x; then

$x + \frac{x \times 4 \times 3}{100} + x + \frac{x \times 4 \times 2}{100} + x + \frac{x \times 4 \times 1}{100} + x = 848$

$\Rightarrow 4x + \frac{24x}{100} = 848 \quad \Rightarrow \frac{106x}{25} = 848$

$\therefore x = \frac{848 \times 25}{106}$ = Rs. 200

8. $\frac{5000 \times R \times 5}{100} + \frac{3000 \times R \times 4}{100} = 600$

$\Rightarrow \quad 250\ R + 120\ R = 600$

$\Rightarrow \quad 370R = 600$

$\therefore \quad R = \frac{600}{370} = 1.62\%$

9. Let principal be Rs. x; then amount = Rs. $2x$, Hence, I = $2x - x$ = Rs. x.

$R = \frac{x \times 100}{x \times 7} = \frac{100}{7}\%$ p.a.

Now, amount = Rs. $4x$; then I = $4x - x$ = Rs. $3x$

Hence, $T = \frac{3x \times 100}{x \times \frac{100}{7}} = \frac{3 \times 100 \times 7}{100}$ = 21 years

10. Let principal = Rs. x; then amount = Rs. $2x$; I = $2x - x$ = Rs. x

$R = \frac{x \times 100}{x \times 8} = \frac{25}{2}\%$

Again, $I = \frac{8000 \times 25 \times 4}{100 \times 2}$ = Rs. 4000

COMPOUND INTEREST

1. The compound interest on a certain sum of money invested for 3 years at 5% per annum is Rs. 1891.50. What will be the simple interest on the same sum at the same rate for 2 years?

A. Rs. 1700 B. Rs. 1200
C. Rs. 1500 D. Rs. 2100

2. A sum of money lent out at a certain rate of simple interest amounts to Rs. 6600 in 2 years and to Rs. 6900 in 3 years. What will be the compound interest on the same sum of money if lent out at the same rate for 2 years?

A. Rs. 605 B. Rs. 715
C. Rs. 615 D. Rs. 595

3. A man deposits Rs. 1200 in a bank on the 1st day of each year. If the bank pays 5% per annum compound interest on deposited sum of money, what will be the amount to his credit on the 10th day of the second year?

A. Rs. 2560 B. Rs. 2460
C. Rs. 2370 D. Rs. 2860

4. If the difference between compound and simple interest on a certain sum of money for 3 years at 5% per annum is Rs. 244, the sum is :

A. Rs. 40000 B. Rs. 25000
C. Rs. 30000 D. Rs. 32000

5. A man purchased a sewing machine for Rs. 5000. If due to sustained use value of this sewing machine depreciates by 6% annually, find its value after 3 years.

A. Rs. 3775.67 B. Rs. 4152.92
C. Rs. 4250.25 D. Rs. 4356.25

6. Find the sum on which the difference between compound and simple interest for 3 years at 10% per annum will be Rs. 868.

A. Rs. 29500 B. Rs. 27625
C. Rs. 28500 D. Rs. 28000

7. Samir invested Rs. 15000 at the rate of interest 10% p.a. for 1 year. If the interest compound six months. What amount will Samir get at the end of the year?

A. Rs. 16,500 B. Rs. 16525.50
C. Rs. 16537.50 D. Rs. 18,150

8. The compound interest on a certain sum for 2 years at 10% per annum is Rs. 525. The simple interest on the same sum for double the time at half the rate per cent per annum is:

A. Rs. 800 B. Rs. 600
C. Rs. 500 D. Rs. 400

9. The least number of complete years in which a sum of money put at 20% compound interest will be more than doubled is:

A. 6 B. 5
C. 4 D. 3

10. On a sum of money, the simple interest for 2 years is Rs. 660, while the compound interest is Rs. 696.30, the rate of interest being the same in both cases. Find the rate of interest.

A. Rs. 12% B. 11%
C. 10% D. 9%

ANSWERS

1	2	3	4	5	6	7	8	9	10
B	C	B	D	B	D	C	C	C	B

EXPLANATORY ANSWERS

1. Here, $1891.50 = P\left[\left(1+\frac{5}{100}\right)^3 - 1\right]$

$\Rightarrow \quad 1891.50 = P\left[\left(\frac{21}{20}\right)^3 - 1\right]$

$\Rightarrow \quad 1891.50 = P\left(\frac{1261}{8000}\right)$

$\therefore \; P = \frac{1891.50 \times 8000}{1261} = \text{Rs. } 12000$

Now, $\quad \text{S.I.} = \frac{12000 \times 5 \times 2}{100} = \text{Rs. } 1200$

2. Here, 1 year's S.I. = Rs. 6900 – Rs. 6600 = Rs. 300

$\therefore$ 2 year's S.I. = 300 × 2 = Rs. 600

$\therefore$ Principal = Rs. 6600 – Rs. 600 = Rs. 6000

Hence, $\quad \text{Rate} = \frac{600 \times 100}{6000 \times 2} = 5\%$

$\therefore$ C.I. $= 6000\left[\left(1+\frac{5}{100}\right)^2-1\right]$

$= 6000\left[\left(\frac{21}{20}\right)^2-1\right] = \frac{6000\times 41}{400}$ = Rs. 615

3. Required amount $= 1200\left(1+\frac{5}{100}\right) + 1200$

$= 1200 \times \frac{21}{20} + 1200 = 1260 + 1200 =$ Rs. 2460

4. Here, $P\left[\left(1+\frac{5}{100}\right)^3-1\right]-\frac{P\times 5\times 3}{100} = 244$

$\Rightarrow P\times\frac{1261}{8000}-\frac{3P}{20} = 244 \Rightarrow P\times\frac{61}{8000} = 244$

$\therefore\ P = \frac{244\times 8000}{61}$ = Rs. 32000

5. Here, value of the machine after 3 years

$= 5000\left(1-\frac{6}{100}\right)^3 = 5000\times\frac{47}{50}\times\frac{47}{50}\times\frac{47}{50}$

= Rs. 4152.92.

6. Here, $P\left[\left(1+\frac{10}{100}\right)^3-1\right]-\frac{P\times 10\times 3}{100} = 868$

$\Rightarrow P\times\frac{331}{1000}-\frac{3P}{10} = 868$

$\Rightarrow P\times\frac{31}{1000} = 868 \therefore P = \frac{868\times 1000}{31}$

= Rs. 28000

7. $A = 15000\left(1+\frac{5}{100}\right)^2 = 15000\times\frac{441}{400}$

= Rs. 16537.50

8. Here, $P\left[\left(1+\frac{10}{100}\right)^2-1\right] = 525$

$\Rightarrow P\left[\frac{121}{100}-1\right] = 525 \Rightarrow P\times\frac{21}{100} = 525$

$\therefore\ P = \frac{525\times 100}{21}$ = Rs. 2500

Hence, required S.I. $= \frac{2500\times 5\times 4}{100}$ = Rs. 500

9. Here, $P\left(1+\frac{20}{100}\right)^n > 2P \Rightarrow \left(\frac{6}{5}\right)^n > 2$

Hence, if $n = 4$ then, $\left(\frac{6}{5}\right)^4 = \frac{1296}{625} > 2$

So, $n = 4$ years

10. Here, S.I. for 1 year = Rs. 330
Since, simple interest of Rs. 330 for 1 year
= 696.30 – 660 = Rs. 36.30

Hence, required rate $= \frac{36.30\times 100}{330\times 1} = \frac{3630}{330} = 11\%$

AREA AND PERIMETER

1. If side of a square is reduced by 50%, its area will be reduced by

A. 50% B. 75%
C. 80% D. 60%

2. If each side of a square is doubled, its area will become

A. double B. four times
C. three times D. eight times

3. Three sides of a triangle are in the ratio of 17 : 15 : 8. If the perimeter of this triangle is 40 m, find its area

A. 50 sq. m. B. 49 sq. m.
C. 60 sq. m. D. 69 sq. m.

4. If the length of a rectangle is increased by 20% and width is decreased by 15%, then its area

A. decreases by 4% B. increases by 2%
C. decreases by 2% D. increases by 3%

5. If the length of a rectangle is increased by 20%, then by how much per cent its breadth must be decreased so as to keep its area unaltered?

A. 25% B. $8\frac{1}{3}\%$
C. $16\frac{2}{3}\%$ D. 20%

6. The ratio of length and breadth of a rectangular plot is 71 : 61 respectively. The area of the plot is 17324 m^2. What is perimeter of the plot?

A. 264 m B. 284 m
C. 528 m D. 614 m

7. If the length and breadth of a rectangular field are increased, the area increases by 50%. If the increase in length was 20%, by what percentage was the breadth increased?

A. 20% B. 25%
C. 30% D. 40%

8. The length and breadth of a varandah is 40 m and 15 m respectively. How many stone slabs of size 6 decimetre × 5 decimetre each are needed in flooring it:

A. 1000 B. 2000
C. 3000 D. 4000

9. The circumference of a circular plot is 396 m. What is the area of the circular plot?

A. 9,446 m^2 B. 9,856 m^2
C. 12,474 m^2 D. 18,634 m^2

10. If the sides of an equilateral triangle are increased by 20%, 30% and 50% respectively to form a new triangle, the increase in the perimeter of the equilateral triangle is:

A. 25% B. $33\frac{1}{3}\%$
C. 50% D. 100%

ANSWERS

1	2	3	4	5	6	7	8	9	10
B	B	C	B	C	C	B	B	C	B

EXPLANATORY ANSWERS

1. Area of the square = x^2 sq. m.

Side of the new square = $x - 50\%$ of $x = \frac{x}{2}$ m

$\therefore$ Area of the new square $= \left(\frac{x}{2}\right)^2 = \frac{x^2}{4}$ sq. m.

$\therefore$ Reduction in area of the square $= x^2 - \frac{x^2}{4}$

$= \frac{3x^2}{4}$ sq. m.

$\therefore$ Percentage reduction $= \frac{3x^2/4}{x^2} \times 100 = 75\%$

2. Area of the square = x^2 sq. m

Now, area of the new square = $(2x)^2 = 4x^2$ sq. m

Hence, it is clear that if side of a square is doubled, its area becomes four times.

3. Suppose sides of the triangle are $17x$ m, $15x$ m and $8x$ metres

$\therefore$ Perimeter $= 17x + 15x + 8x = 40x$

Now, $40x = 40$

$\Rightarrow x = 1$ m

Therefore, the sides are $17 \times 1 = 17$ m, $15 \times 1 = 15$ m and $8 \times 1 = 8$ m

$\because (17)^2 = (15)^2 + (8)^2$,

i.e., it is a right angled triangle

$\therefore$ Area of the right angled triangle

$= \frac{1}{2} \times 8 \times 15 = 60$ sq. m.

4. Area of the rectangle = xy sq. metre

Area of the new rectangle $= \frac{120}{100} x \times \frac{85}{100} y$

$= 1.020\, xy$ sq. metre

$\therefore$ Increase in the area $= 1.02\, xy - xy = .02\, xy$ sq. m.

$\therefore$ Percentage increase $= \frac{.02xy}{xy} \times 100 = 2\%$

5. Area of the rectangle = xy

On reducing the breadth by A% and increasing the length by 20%

Length of the new rectangle $= \frac{120x}{100} x = 1.2x$

Breadth of the new rectangle $= y - \text{A}\%$ of $y = y\left(1 - \frac{\text{A}}{100}\right)$

$\therefore$ Area of the new rectangle $= 1.2x \times y\left(1 - \frac{\text{A}}{100}\right)$

Now, $xy = 1.2\, xy\left(1 - \frac{\text{A}}{100}\right) \Rightarrow 1 = 1.2\frac{(100 - \text{A})}{100}$

$\Rightarrow 1.2\,\text{A} = 120 - 100$

$\therefore \text{A} = \frac{20}{1.2} = 16\frac{2}{3}\%$

6. Let length and breadth of a rectangle be $71x$ and $61x$ m; then

$71x \times 61x = 17324 \Rightarrow x^2 = \frac{17324}{71 \times 61} = 4$

$\therefore x = 2$

Hence, length $= 71 \times 2 = 142$ m; breadth $= 61 \times 2 = 122$ m

Since, perimeter $= 2(142 + 122) = 2 \times 264 = 528$ m

7. Here, $20 + x + \frac{20 \times x}{100} = 50 \Rightarrow x + \frac{x}{5} = 30$

$\Rightarrow \frac{6x}{5} = 30$ $\therefore x = \frac{5 \times 30}{6} = 25$

Hence, breadth was increased by 25%

8. Required number of stone slabs $= \frac{40 \times 15}{\frac{6}{10} \times \frac{5}{10}}$

$= \frac{40 \times 15 \times 100}{6 \times 5} = 2000$

VOLUME AND SURFACE AREA

1. If a solid sphere of 3 cm radius is melted and recast into a right circular cone whose base radius is same as that of the sphere, the height of the cone will be
A. 8 cm B. 12 cm
C. 6 cm D. 5 cm

2. Diameter of a roller is 2.4 m and it is 1.68 m long. If it takes 1000 complete revolutions once over to level a field, the area of the field is
A. 12672 sq. m B. 12671 sq. m
C. 12762 sq. m D. 11768 sq. m

3. If each edge of a cube is increased by 10%, then by how much per cent will the surface area of this cube be increased?
A. 21% B. 18%
C. 15% D. 20%

4. Height and base radius of a solid cylinder are 14 m and 4 m respectively. It is melted and recast into a solid cone of the same base radius as that of the cylinder, what will be the height of the cone?
A. 21 m B. 42 m
C. 48 m D. 54 m

5. A room is in the form of a cube of side 10 m. How many bales of cotton can be kept in it if each bale covers 5 cu m space?
A. 100 B. 175
C. 200 D. 225

6. Three cubes having side 2 cm, 3 cm and 4 cm respectively are melted together to form a new cube. The side of the new cube will be
A. 3.526 cm B. 4.628 cm
C. 4.626 cm D. 4.528 cm

7. If base diameter of a cylinder is increased by 50%, then by how much per cent its height must be decreased so as to keep its volume unaltered?
A. 45.56% B. 55.56%
C. 50.16% D. 62.33%

8. The surface area of a cube is 600 sq. m. Its diagonal is
A. $10\sqrt{3}$ cm B. $5\sqrt{3}$ cm
C. $4\sqrt{2}$ cm D. $10\sqrt{2}$ cm

9. The base diameter of a conical tomb is 28 m and its slant height is 50 m. Find the cost of white washing its curved surface at the rate of 80 paise per sq. m?
A. Rs. 1860 B. Rs. 1760
C. Rs. 1950 D. Rs. 1875

10. The volume of a cuboid is 1120 cu cm and its height is 5 cm while the length and the breadth of the cuboid are in the ratio 8 : 7. The length of this cylinder exceeds the breadth by
A. 4 cm B. 2 cm
C. 7 cm D. 5 cm

ANSWERS

1	2	3	4	5	6	7	8	9	10
B	A	A	B	C	C	B	A	B	B

EXPLANATORY ANSWERS

1. Volume of the cone = Volume of the sphere

$\therefore \quad \frac{1}{3}\pi(3)^2 \times h = \frac{4}{3}\pi \times 3^3 \Rightarrow h = 12$ cm

Hence, height of the cone = 12 cm.

2. Surface area of the roller = $2\pi rh$

$= 2 \times \frac{22}{7} \times 1.2 \times 1.68 = 12.672$ sq. m

In one complete revolution, the roller covers 12.672 sq. m.

$\therefore$ It will cover in 1000 revolutions

= 12.672 × 1000 = 12672 sq. m

Hence, area of the field = 12672 sq. m.

3. Percentage increase in the surface area of the cube

$= \left(x + y + \frac{xy}{100}\right)\%$

$= \left(10 + 10 + \frac{10 \times 10}{100}\right)\% = 21\%.$

4. Here,

volume of the cone = Volume of the cylinder

$\Rightarrow \quad \frac{1}{3}\pi r^2 \times \text{height} = \pi r^2 \times 14$

$\therefore \quad$ Height = 14 × 3 = 42 m

Thus, height of the cone = 42 m.

5. Volume of the cubical room = $(10)^3$
= 1000 cu m

Number of cotton bales which can be placed in the room

$$= \frac{\text{Volume of the room}}{\text{Volume of each cotton bale}} = \frac{1000}{5} = 200.$$

6. Volume of the new cube = $2^3 + 3^3 + 4^3$
= 8 + 27 + 64 = 99cu cm

$\therefore$ Side of the new cube = $\sqrt[3]{99}$ = 4.626 cm.

7. Change in the volume of the cylinder

$$= \left(x+y+(-z)+\frac{xy+y(-z)+(-zx)}{100}+\frac{xy(-z)}{100^2}\right)\%$$

Since volume of the cylinder remains unchanged.

$\therefore$ Change = 0%

Now, $\left(50+50+(-z)+\frac{50\times50-50z-50z}{100}+\frac{50\times50\times(-z)}{100^2}\right)=0$

$\therefore$ 100 − z + 25 − z − .25z = 0

$\Rightarrow 2.25z = 125 \Rightarrow z = \frac{125}{2.25} = 55.56$

$\therefore$ Height of the cylinder should be decreased by 55.56%.

8. Here, $6 \times (\text{side})^2 = 600$

$\Rightarrow \text{side}^2 = 100$

$\Rightarrow \text{side} = \sqrt{100} = 10$ cm

$\therefore$ Diagonal of the cube= $\sqrt{3}\times\text{side}$

$= \sqrt{3}\times 10$

$= 10\sqrt{3}$ cm.

9. Area of the curved surface of the cone

$= \frac{22}{7}\times\frac{28}{2}\times 50 = 2200$ sq. m.

$\therefore$ Cost of white washing at 80 paise per sq. m

$= 2200\times\frac{80}{100} =$ Rs. 1760.

10. Suppose the length and the breadth of the cuboid are 8x cm and 7x cm

$\therefore$ Here, $8x \times 7x \times 5 = 1120$

$\Rightarrow x^2 = \frac{1120}{280} = 4 = (2)^2 \Rightarrow x = 2$

$\therefore$ Length of the cuboid = 8 × 2 = 16 cm

Breadth of the cuboid = 7 × 2 = 14 cm

Hence, it is clear that length of the cuboid exceeds the breadth by 2 cm.

SERIES

Directions (Qs. 1 to 7) : *In the following number series, one of the numbers does not fit into the series. Find the wrong number.*

1. 2, 5, 10, 18, 26, 37, 50
A. 2 B. 5
C. 37 D. 18

2. 3 , 18, 38, 78, 123, 178, 243
A. 123 B. 178
C. 3 D. 38

3. 380, 188, 92, 48, 20, 8, 2
A. 188 B. 92
C. 48 D. 20

4. 5, 11, 23, 47, 96, 191, 383
A. 11 B. 23
C. 47 D. 96

5. 89, 78, 86, 80, 85, 82, 83
A. 78 B. 86
C. 80 D. 85

6. 58, 57, 54, 50, 42, 33, 32
A. 57 B. 54
C. 50 D. 32

7. 2, 20, 27, 44, 64
A. 27 B. 8
C. 20 D. 44

Directions (Qs. 8 to 10) : *Complete the following series.*

8. 1 4 9 16 25 36 49 ....
A. 54 B. 56
C. 64 D. 81

9. 11 13 17 19 23 29 31 37 41 ....
A. 43 B. 47
C. 53 D. 51

10. 3 7 6 5 9 3 12 1 15 ....
A. 18 B. 13
C. −1 D. 3

ANSWERS

1	2	3	4	5	6	7	8	9	10
D	C	C	D	A	C	C	C	A	C

EXPLANATORY ANSWERS

1. 2 5 10 18 26 37 50

↓ ↓ ↓ ↓ ↓ ↓ ↓

1^2+1 2^2+1 3^2+1 4^2+1 5^2+1 6^2+1 7^2+1

Wrong no. = 18, Correct no. = 17.

2. Only 3 is a prime number.

3. Wrong no. = 48, Correct no. = 44

Each term will be four more than two times the next term.

4. 5 11 23 47 96 191 383

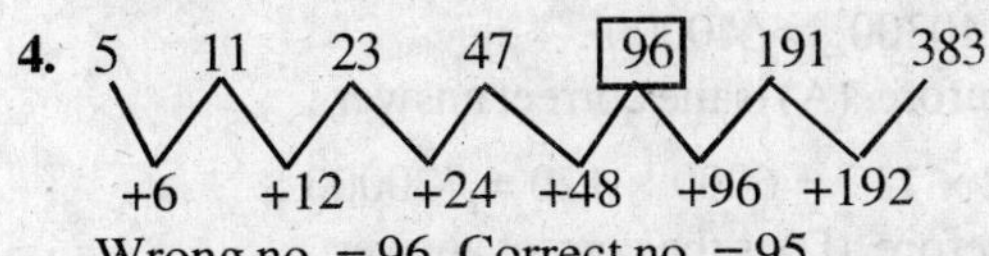

+6 +12 +24 +48 +96 +192

Wrong no. = 96, Correct no. = 95.

5. If 87 is written in place of 78 then tens digit of each term will be 8.

6. 58 57 54 50 42 33 22

−1 −3 −5 −7 −9 −11

Wrong no. = 50, Correct no. = 49.

7. 2 20 27 44 64

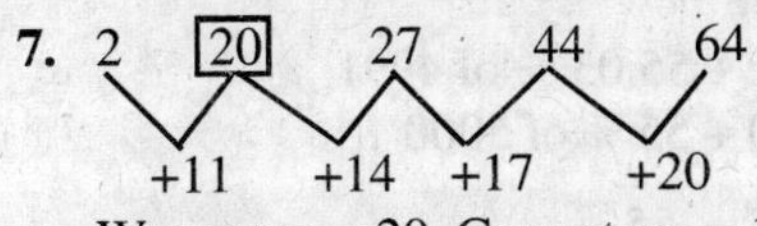

+11 +14 +17 +20

Wrong no. = 20, Correct no. = 13.

8. Numbers are $1^2, 2^2, 3^2, 4^2, 5^2, 6^2, 7^2$.

So, the next number is $8^2 = 64$.

9. Numbers are all primes. The next prime is 43.

10. There are two series, beginning respectively with 3 and 7. In one 3 is added and in another 2 is subtracted. The next number is $1 - 2 = -1$.

APPROXIMATE VALUES

1. $85432 \div 2106 + 59.5614 = ?$

(*a*) 100 (*b*) 60

(*c*) 80 (*d*) 140

2. $\sqrt{67621} = ?$

(*a*) 320 (*b*) 260

(*c*) 200 (*d*) 280

3. 9.7 % of 5011 + 55.03 % of 4991

(*a*) 5500 (*b*) 7200

(*c*) 6000 (*d*) 4200

4. $730 \times 199 = ?$

(*a*) 350000 (*b*) 335000

(*c*) 300000 (*d*) 34600

5. $.0144 \times 0.36 = ?$

(*a*) 0.5 (*b*) 0.005

(*c*) 0.05 (*d*) 0.005

6. 31% of 1508 + 26% of 2018

(*a*) 1500 (*b*) 2000

(*c*) 1000 (*d*) 1200

7. $3015 + 13594 + 3738 = ?$

(*a*) 40000 (*b*) 36000

(*c*) 42000 (*d*) 46000

8. $6012 \times 119 = ?$

(*a*) 560000 (*b*) 448000

(*c*) 900000 (*d*) 720000

9. $2712.1563 \div 1805.4018 + 3.4982 = ?$

(*a*) 9 (*b*) 8

(*c*) 4 (*d*) 5

10. $4182.365 \div 20.886 = ?$

(*a*) 300 (*b*) 200

(*c*) 150 (*d*) 250

ANSWERS

1	2	3	4	5	6	7	8	9	10
A	B	D	A	B	C	A	D	D	B

EXPLANATORY ANSWERS

1. 85432 ÷ 2106 + 60 = 40 + 60 = 100
Therefore, (B) is the correct answer.

2. $\sqrt{67621} = \sqrt{67600} = 260$
Therefore, (B) is the correct answer.

3. 29.7 % of 5011 + 55.03 % of 4991
= 30 % of 5000 + 55 % of 5000

$= \frac{30}{100} \times 5000 + \frac{55}{100} \times 5000$

= 1500 + 2750 = 4250 ⇒ 4200
Therefore, (D) is the correct answer.

4. 1730 × 199 = 1730 × 200
= 346000 ⇒ 350000
Therefore, (B) is the correct answer.

5. 0.0144 × 0.36 = 0.0140 × 0.36 = .005040
⇒ .005
Therefore, (B) is the correct answer.

6. 31% of 1508 + 26% of 2018
= 30% of 1500 + 25% × 2000

$= \frac{30}{100} \times 1500 + \frac{25}{100} \times 2000$

= 450 + 500 = 950 ⇒ 1000
Therefore, (C) is the correct answer.

7. 23015 + 13594 + 3738
= 23000 + 13600 + 3700
= 40300 ⇒ 40000
Therefore, (A) is the correct answer.

8. 6012 × 119 = 6000 × 120 = 720000
Therefore, (D) is the correct answer.

9. 2712.1563 ÷ 1805.4018 + 3.4982
= 2700 ÷ 1800 + 3.5 = 1.5 + 3.5 = 5
Therefore, (D) is the correct answer.

10. 4182. 365 ÷ 20.886 = 4200 ÷ 21 = 200
Therefore, (B) is the correct answer.

REASONING ABILITY

SERIES

Directions : *In each of the following series determine the order of the letters. Then from the given options select the one which will complete the given series.*

1. BMK, DLM, FKO, HJQ, ?
A. JIR B. JIT
C. JHS D. JIS

2. A, CD, FGH, ?
A. IJKL B. KLMN
C. JKLM D. LMNO

3. BXJ, ETL, HPN, KLP, ?
A. PHR B. NIR
C. NHR D. MHR

4. PUF, QVG, RWH, ?
A. SXI B. SYZ
C. SXJ D. SVI

5. DEF, HIJ, MNO, ?
A. RTV B. STU
C. PTU D. SRU

Directions : *Which of the following groups of letters will complete the given series?*

6. ab---b-bbaa-
A. babba B. abaab
C. abbab D. baaab

7. aa-ab--aaa-a
A. baaa B. abab
C. aaab D. aabb

8. -baa-aab-a-a
A. baab B. abab
C. aaba D. aabb

9. -a cca-ccca-acccc-aaa
A. ccaa B. acca
C. caac D. caaa

10. c-bbb--abbbb-abbb-
A. abccb B. bacbb
C. aabcb D. abacb

Directions : *In the following questions, select the number(s) from the given options for completing the given series.*

11. 3, 9, 27, 81, 243, ?
A. 486 B. 729
C. 972 D. 359

12. 1, 6, 12, 19, 27, ?
A. 38 B. 35
C. 36 D. 54

13. 2, 6, 14, 30, 62, ?
A. 126 B. 128
C. 120 D. 130

14. 8, 48, 16, 96, 32, ?
A. 192 B. 150
C. 64 D. 288

15. 2, 8, 14, 24, 34, 48, ?
A. 66 B. 62
C. 58 D. 64

Directions : *In the given series find the number which is wrong.*

16. 5, 25, 120, 625, 3125, 15625
A. 15625 B. 625
C. 120 D. 5

17. 4, 8, 11, 22, 18, 36, 24, 50
A. 8 B. 22
C. 36 D. 24

18. 2, 4, 12, 24, 72, 142, 432
A. 432 B. 12
C. 142 D. 72

19. 2, 3, 4, 4, 6, 8, 9, 12, 16
A. 3 B. 9
C. 6 D. 12

20. 97, 91, 86, 83, 79, 77, 76, 76
A. 86 B. 76
C. 91 D. 83

ANSWERS

1	2	3	4	5	6	7	8	9	10
D	C	C	A	B	D	C	B	D	A
11	**12**	**13**	**14**	**15**	**16**	**17**	**18**	**19**	**20**
B	C	A	A	B	C	D	C	B	D

EXPLANATORY ANSWERS

1. The letters in one group correspond to the letters in the next group in the manner +2, –1, +2 respectively.

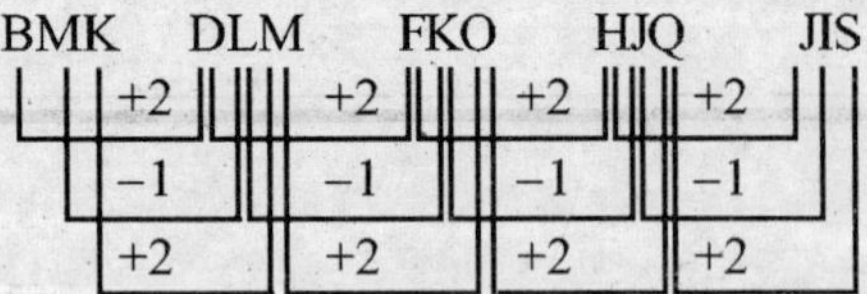

2. The letters are in natural sequence and from one group to the next one letter is dropped. Also the number of letters in groups is increased by one.

A CD FGH JKLM
↓ ↓ ↓
B E I

3. The letters in one group correspond to the letters in the next group in the manner +3, – 4, +2 respectively, *i.e.*,

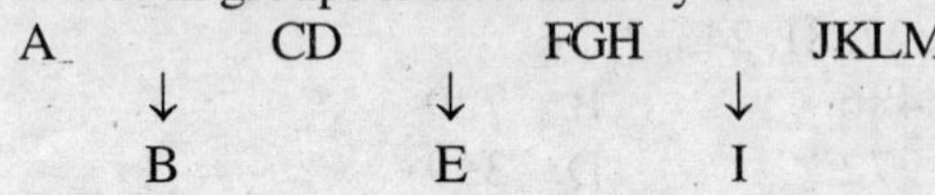

4. The three letters in each group are moved one step forward.

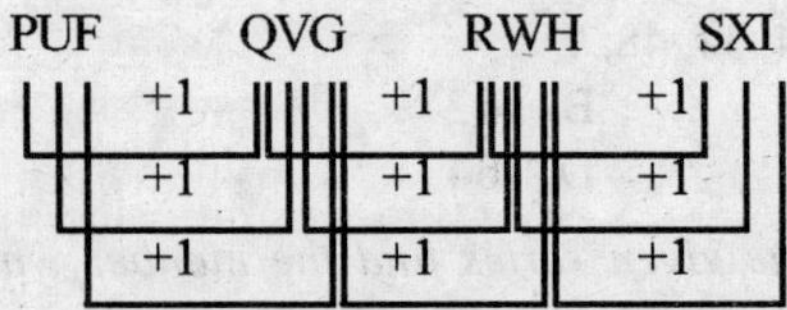

5. The letters are in natural order. The number of letters dropped in between the groups is increased by one at each step.

DEF HIJ MNO STU
↓ ↓ ↓
G KL PQR

6. The series is abbaab, abbaab

7. The series is aaaaba, aaaaba

8. The series is aba, aba, aba, aba

9. The series is c,a,cc,aa, ccc, aaa, cccc, aaaa

10. The series is cabbbb, cabbbb, cabbbb

11. The numbers in the series are multiplied by 3 to get the next numbers.

12. The difference between the numbers in the series increases by 1, after beginning from 5, *i.e.*,

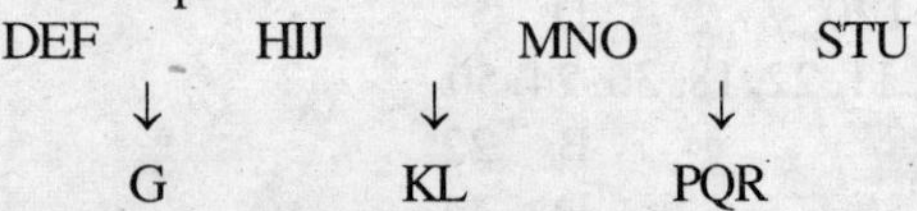

13. The difference between the numbers in the series doubles each time, after beginning from 4, *i.e.*,

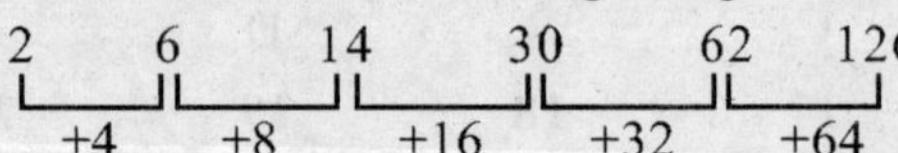

14. *Explanation I* : The sequence in the series is × 6, ÷ 3 which is repeated.

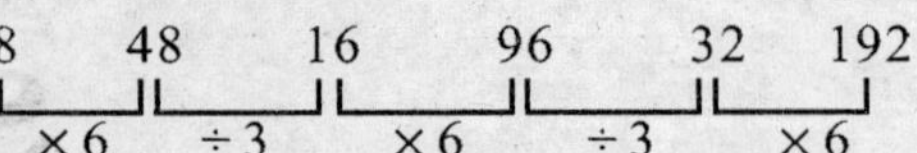

Explanation II : There are two alternate series and the numbers are multiplied by 2.

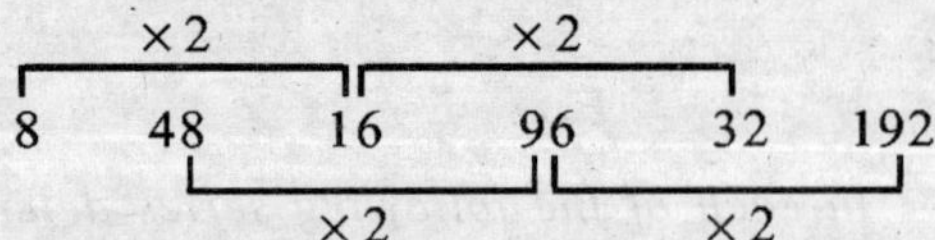

Series I : 8, 16, 32

Series II : 48, 96, 192

15. The sequence in the series is :

2 8 14 24 34 48 62
+6 +6 +10 +10 +14 +14

The difference increases by 4 at alternate step.

16. The numbers in the series are multiplied by 5 to get the next number.

∴ 125 should be in place of 120.

17. Two numbers form a pair. The first number increases by 7 for the next pair and the second number is the double of first number.

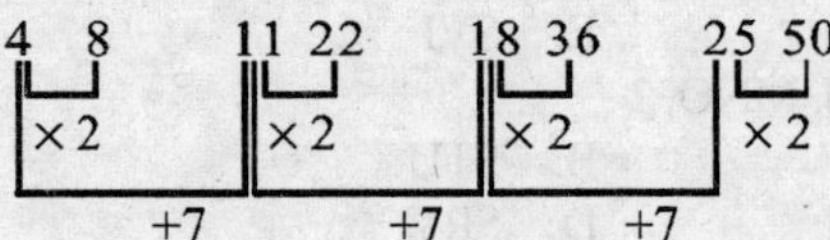

∴ 25 should be in place of 24.

18. There are two alternate series and in each series, the numbers are multiplied by 6 to get the next number.

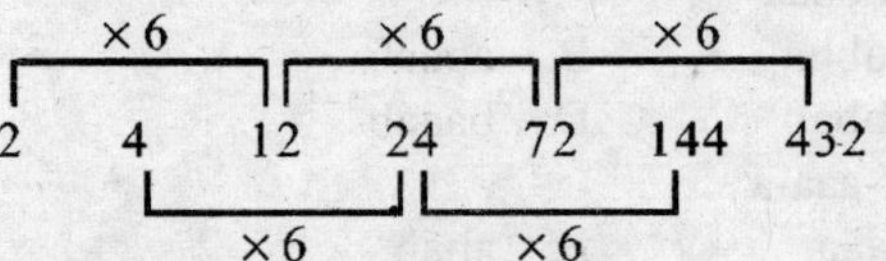

∴ 144 should be in place of 142.

19. There are three alternate series and in each series, the numbers are multiplied by 2 to get the next number.

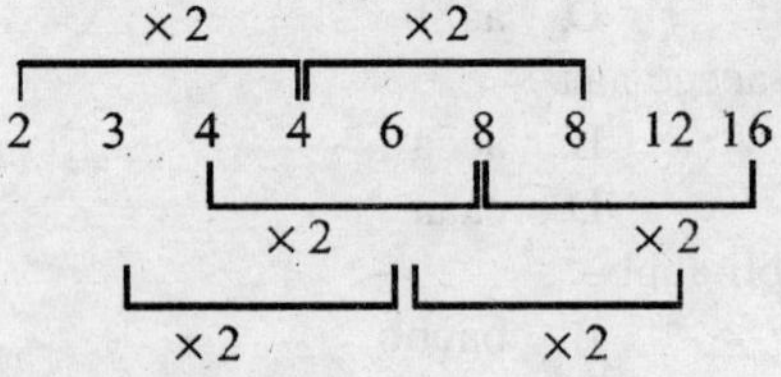

Series I : 2, 4, 8

Series II : 3, 6, 12

Series III : 4, 8, 16

∴ 8 should be in place of 9.

20. The difference between the consecutive numbers in the series decreases by 1 at each step.

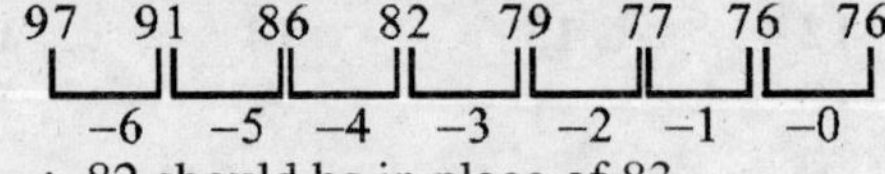

∴ 82 should be in place of 83.

ANALOGIES OR RELATIONSHIPS

Directions : *In the questions given below establish the relationship between the two words. Then from the given options select one which has the same relationship as of the given two words.*

1. ADULT : BABY : : FLOWER : ?
A. Seed B. Bud
C. Fruit D. Butterfly

2. WRITER : READER : : PRODUCER : ?
A. Creator B. Contractor
C. Creature D. Consumer

3. ENTRANCE : EXIT : : LOYALTY : ?
A. Treachery B. Patriotism
C. Fidelity D. Reward

4. MOTHER : MATERNAL : : FATHER : ?
A. Eternal B. Detrimental
C. Paternal D. Formidable

Directions : *In the questions given below one term is missing. Based on the relationship of the two given words find the missing term from the given options.*

5. GFC : CFG : : RPJ : ?
A. JRP B. JPR
C. PJR D. RJP

6. BCF : DEG : : MNQ : ?
A. OPR B. PQS
C. OPP D. QRT

7. NATION : ANITNO : : HUNGRY : ?
A. HNUGRY B. UNHGYR
C. YRNGUH D. UHGNYR

8. SSTU : MMNO : : AABC : ?
A. GGHH B. IJKK
C. XXYZ D. NOOP

ANSWERS

1	2	3	4	5	6	7	8
B	D	A	C	B	A	D	C

EXPLANATORY ANSWERS

1. The youngone of an adult is a baby and that of a flower is a bud.

2. A writer aims to please the readers by his writings, a producer aims to please the consumers by his products.

3. The related words are opposites.

4. Relations on the mother's side are maternal and on the father's side paternal.

5. The letters of the first group are reversed.

GFC : CFG : : RPJ : JPR

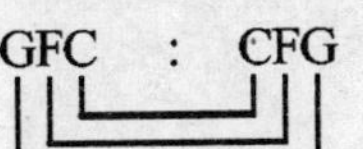

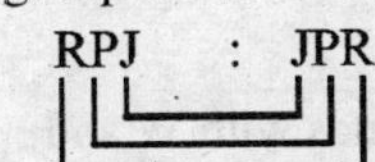

6. The three letters are moved 2, 2 and 1 steps forward respectively.

BCF : DEG : : MNQ : OPR
+2 +2 +1 +2 +2 +1

7. The word is divided in sections of two letters and the letters are reversed.

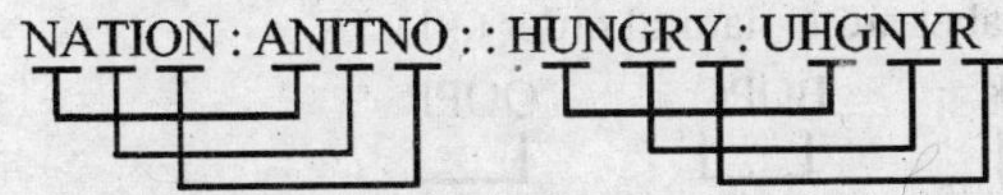

8. The first letter in each group is repeated and followed by two consecutive letters.

ODD ONE OUT

Directions : *Three of the following four in each question are alike in a certain way and so form a group. Select the group of letters that does not belong to that group.*

1. A. ACE B. LOR
C. GIK D. VXZ

2. A. TSR B. LKJ
C. PQO D. HGF

3. A. EF LM B. KJ SR
C. XW HG D. ED YX

4. A. JOPK B. BOPC
C. QOPR D. TOPS

5. A. DfH B. MoQ
C. UwY D. lnO

6. A. JKkL B. OPpQ
C. DEEf D. VWwX

7. A. BdfH B. FHJL
C. RTvX D. uVwX

8. A. DFHEG B. TWXUV
C. OQSPR D. JLNKM

9. A. FEUV B. DCXW
C. BAZY D. HGTS

10. A. UTSR B. XYZW
C. ONML D. IHGF

ANSWERS

1	2	3	4	5	6	7	8	9	10
B	C	A	D	D	C	D	B	A	B

EXPLANATORY ANSWERS

1. The sequence in each group is +2. Only option B has sequence in +3, *i.e.,*

ABCDE (+2 +2) LMNOPQR (+3 +3)

GHIJK (+2 +2) VWXYZ (+2 +2)

2. The sequence of alphabet in each group is in reverse order. Only option C has sequence in disturbed order.

3. Two consecutive alphabet in each group are in reverse sequence (–1), *i.e.,*

KJ SR; XW HG; ED YX
–1 –1 –1 –1 –1 –1

Only in option (A) the sequence is in natural order (+1), *i.e.,*

4. In each group, letters 'OP' are common. The two corner alphabet are in natural order (+1); *i.e.,*

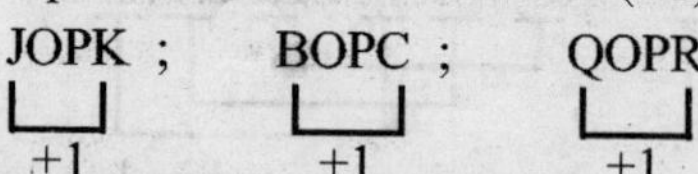

Only in option (D) they are in reverse order (–1); *i.e.,*

5. In other groups, only the alphabet in the centre is of lower case. In this option letter 'L' on the left is also in lower case.

6. In other groups, the third letter which is a repeat of the second alphabet is in lower case.

7. In each group, the sequence of the alphabet, irrespective of the case, is +2; *i.e.,*

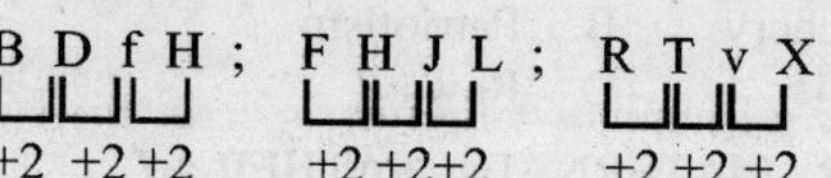

Only in option (D) the sequence is in natural order (+1), *i.e.,*

uV wX
+1 +1 +1

8. In each group; the alphabet at positions-first, fourth, second, fifth and third, form a natural sequence.

In option (B), the alphabet at positions first, fourth, fifth, second and third, form the natural sequence.

9. In each group, two alphabets in the corner and two alphabets in the centre correspond to their reverse order positioned alphabet. *i.e.,*

natural order → A B C D E F G H I J K L M
reverse order → Z Y X W V U T S R Q P O N
natural order → N O P Q R S T U V W X Y Z
reverse order → M L K J I H G F E D C B A

As such—
D corresponds with W and
C corresponds with X.
B corresponds with Y and
A corresponds with Z.
H corresponds with S and
G corresponds with T.

Similarly,
F should correspond with U and
E should correspond with V;
i.e. letters 'UV' should be written as 'VU'

10. In each group, the alphabet are in reverse order.
In option (B), the order is disturbed.

CODING AND DECODING

Directions : *In the following questions select the right option which indicates the correct code for the word or letter given in the question.*

1. If CHAIR is coded as FKDLU then RAID is coded as:

A. ULGD B. ULKG
C. ULDG D. UDLG

2. If CONDEMN is coded as CNODMEN, then TEACHER is coded as :

A. TEACHER B. TAEECHR
C. TCAEEHR D. TAECEHR

3. In a code language COME is written as XLNV and ABLE as ZYOV. How will MOLLY be written in that code?

A. NLOBO B. NLBOO
C. LNOOB D. NLOOB

4. In a certain code PROFESSION is written as EFORPNOISS. In the same code DICTIONARY will be written as :

A. YRANOITCID B. ITCIDYRANO
C. ITCIDYRNAO D. ITCDIYARNO

5. JUNE is coded as NXPF, how will STAY be coded in the same manner?

A. WWCZ B. WVCZ
C. WWDB D. VWZC

Directions : *In the following questions study the coded patterns and then select the right option from the given alternatives.*

6. In a certain language, (a) 'go ju mi' stands for 'plenty of money'; (b) pao ju go nei vu' for 'money creates lots of problems'; (c) 'kol vu nei' for 'problems create tension'; and (d) 'sol tun ju haw' for 'still money is needed'. Which of the following words stand for 'money'?

A. nei B. ju
C. haw D. go

7. In a certain language, (a) 'FOR' stands for 'old is gold'; (b) 'ROT' stands for 'gold is pure'; (c) 'ROM' stands for 'gold is costly'. How will 'pure old gold is costly' be written?

A. TFROM B. FOTRM
C. FTORM D. TOMRF

8. In a certain code '415' means 'milk is hot'; '18' means 'hot soup'; and '895' means 'soup is tasty'. What number will indicate the word 'tasty'?

A. 9 B. 8
C. 5 D. 4

9. In a certain code '643' means 'she is beautiful', '593' means 'he is handsome', and '567' means 'handsome meets beautiful'. What number will indicate the word 'meets'?

A. 5 B. 3
C. 7 D. 6

10. In a certain code language, (a) 'dugo hui mul zo' stands for 'work is very hard'; (b) 'hui dugo ba ki' for 'Bingo is very smart'; (c) 'nano mul dugo' for 'cake is hard', and (d) 'mul ki qu' for 'smart and hard'. Which of the following words stand for 'Bingo'?

A. jalu B. dugo
C. ki D. ba

ANSWERS

1	2	3	4	5	6	7	8	9	10
D	D	D	B	A	B	A	A	C	D

EXPLANATORY ANSWERS

2. In this word, the second and third letters interchange their places and the fifth and sixth letters do the same. Other letters retain their position.

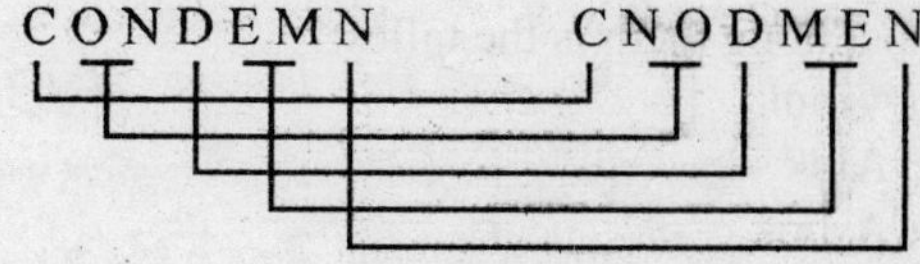

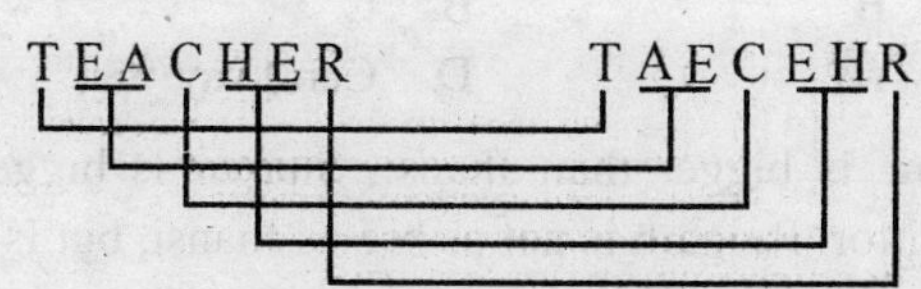

3. The letters of the word are coded by their represented letters in the reverse series.

C O M E → letters in natural series
X L N V → letters in reverse series
↓ ↓ ↓ ↓
3rd 15th 13th 5th → position of letters
A B L E → letters in natural series
Z Y O V → letters in reverse series
↓ ↓ ↓ ↓
1st 2nd 12th 5th → position of letters

Similarly,

M O L L Y → letters in natural series
N L O O B → letters in reverse series
↓ ↓ ↓ ↓ ↓
13th 15th 12th 12th 25th → position of letters

4. The word is divided into two equal parts and the letters of each part are written backwards.

Similarly,

5. The word is coded by moving the letters +4, +3, +2, and +1 steps respectively.

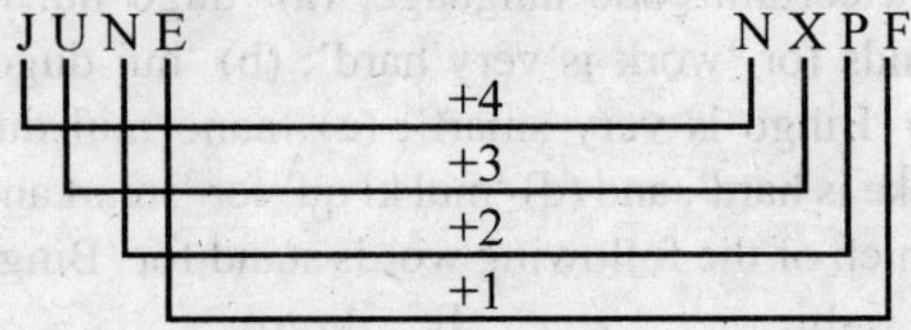

Similarly,

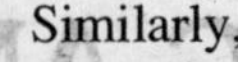

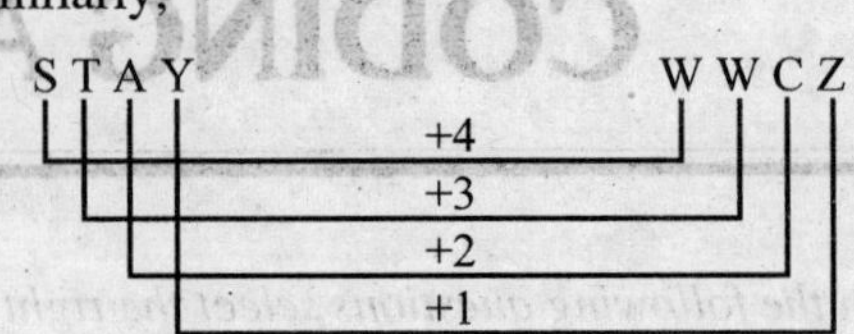

6. *Code* — *Sentence*
1. go *ju* mi — plenty of *money*
2. pao *ju* go nei vu — *money* creates lots of problems
3. kol vu nei — problems create tension
4. sol tun *ju* haw — still *money* is needed

In 1st, 2nd and 4th codes and their sentences the word 'ju' is repeated and so is 'money'.

8. *Code* — *Sentence*
1. 415 — milk is hot
2. 18 — hot soup
3. 895 — soup is *tasty*

From 3rd code and its sentence neither number '9' is repeated nor the word 'tasty'.

9. *Code* — *Sentence*
1. 643 — she is beautiful
2. 593 — he is handsome
3. 567 — handsome *meets* beautiful

From 3rd code and its sentence, neither number '7' nor the word 'meets' is repeated.

10. *Code* — *Sentence*
1. *dugo hui* mul zo — work *is very* hard
2. *hui dugo* **ba** *ki* — **Bingo** *is very smart*
3. nano mul *dugo* — cake is *hard*
4. mul *ki* qu — *smart* and hard

From 2nd code and its sentence, neither 'ba' nor 'Bingo' is repeated.
(Words repeated are in italics)

STATEMENT ANALYSIS

1. Among five friends, A is heavier than B; C is lighter than D; B is lighter than D but heavier than E. Who among them is the heaviest?
   A. B
   B. C
   C. A
   D. Can't say

2. Pune is bigger than Jhansi, Sitapur is bigger than Chittor. Raigarh is not as big as Jhansi, but is bigger than Sitapur. Chittor is not as big as Sitapur. Which is the smallest?
   A. Jhansi
   B. Pune
   C. Chittor
   D. Sitapur

3. Ajay works more than Ram. Alok works as much as Raju. Pankaj works less than Alok. Ram works more than Alok. Who works the most of all?
   A. Ajay
   B. Ram
   C. Alok
   D. Raju

4. Vipul is taller than Hans. Hans is taller than Anand. Alok is taller than Ashok. Ashok is taller than Hans. Who among them is the tallest?
   A. Vipul
   B. Alok
   C. Ashok
   D. Cannot be determined

5. Pramod is taller than Gopal. Gopal is shorter than Madhu. To find out who among them is the tallest, which of the following further informations is necessary?
   A. Madhu is taller than Gopal.
   B. Madhu is shorter than Pramod's brother
   C. Pramod is taller than Madhu.
   D. Pramod is taller than Madhu's brother.

6. Among five friends P, Q, R, S and T, who is the youngest? To arrive at the answer which of the following information given in the statements (*a*) and (*b*) is sufficient?
   (*a*) R is younger than P and T.
   (*b*) S is younger than Q.
   A. Only (*a*) alone is sufficient
   B. Either (*a*) or (*b*) is sufficient
   C. Both (*a*) and (*b*) together are needed
   D. Both (*a*) and (*b*) together are not sufficient

7. Sushma is richer than Rashmi whereas Anand is richer than Priya. Arun is as rich as Rashmi. Shoba is richer than Sushma.
   Which of the following statements is correct according to the above propositions?
   A. Rashmi is poorer than Priya.
   B. Priya is richer than Arun
   C. Arun is poorer than Sushma.
   D. Anand is richer than Rashmi

8. A is elder to B while C and D are elder to E who lies between A and B. If C be elder to B, which one of the following statements is necessarily true?
   A. E is elder to B
   B. A is elder to C
   C. C is elder to D
   D. D is elder to C

9. Vikram is taller than Rajan but shorter than Annie. Jamal is taller than Annie. Sita is taller than Vikram. Rajan is shorter than Sita. Who is the shortest of all in the group?
   A. Sita
   B. Rajan
   C. Vikram
   D. Cannot be determined

10. Suresh is as much older than Kamal as he is younger than Prabodh. Navin is as old as Kamal. Which of the following statements is wrong?
   A. Suresh is older than Navin
   B. Kamal is younger than Suresh
   C. Prabodh is not the oldest
   D. Navin is younger than Prabodh

ANSWERS

1	2	3	4	5	6	7	8	9	10
D	C	A	D	C	D	C	A	B	C

EXPLANATORY ANSWERS

1. The five friends in descending order of weight are : A/D, B/C, E or A/D, B, C/E. Either A or D is the heaviest.
2. The order of cities in descending order of size is : Pune, Jhansi, Raigarh, Sitapur, Chittor.
3. On the basis of doing work, the descending order will be : Ajay, Ram, Alok/Raju, Pankaj.
4. On the basis of height, the descending order will be Vipul/Alok, Ashok, Hans, Anand. Either Vipul or Alok is the tallest.
5. According to the information both Pramod and Madhu are taller than Gopal. Option (c) decides who is the tallest.
6. Statements are not inter-related.
7. On the basis of wealth, the descending order will be :
   1. Shobha, Sushma, Rashmi/Arun
   2. Anand, *and* Priya
   (The two statements are not inter-related.)
8. The order in descending seniority will be : A/C/D, E, B.
9. On the basis of height the descending order will be :
   Jamal/Sita, Annie, Vikram, Rajan.
   or
   Jamal, Sita/Annie, Vikram, Rajan.
10. On the basis of age the descending order will be : Prabodh, Suresh, Kamal/Navin.

PLACE ARRANGEMENT

Directions: *In the following questions, understand the arrangement pattern and then select the right answer from the given options :*

1. Five boys are sitting in a row. Raghu is not adjacent to Shyam or Amit. Ajay is not adjacent to Shyam. Raghu is adjacent to Mayank. If Mayank is at the middle in the row, then Ajay is adjacent to whom out of the following?

   A. Amit B. Raghu
   C. Mayank D. Shyam

2. Mini is to the right of Rajni but to the left of Ananta. Saya is to the right of Mini but to the left of Jaya. Who is on the extreme left if all the girls are facing North?

   A. Jaya B. Mini
   C. Rajni D. Saya

3. Kittu is in-between Mohan and Sohan. Raju is to the left of Sohan and Shyam is to the right of Mohan. If all of the friends are sitting facing South, then who is on their extreme right?

   A. Mohan B. Sohan
   C. Kittu D. Shyam

4. A, B, C, D and E are running one behind the other. C is not near E and A is not near D. B is next to A and E is not near D. Who is in the middle?

   A. B B. E
   C. A D. Cannot be said

5. O, P, Q, R, S and T are standing on a bench according to their height. P is taller than O but shorter than S. Only S is taller than T. R is shorter than P but taller than Q. Who is the shortest?

   A. O B. Q
   C. P D. Cannot be said

ANSWERS

1	2	3	4	5
B	C	D	A	D

EXPLANATORY ANSWERS

1. The order of sitting is :
   Amit, Shyam, Mayank, Ajay, Raghu
   or
   Ajay, Raghu, Mayank, Amit, Shyam

2. The order in which the girls are positioned is :
   Rajni, Mini, Ananta, Saya, Jaya
   or
   Saya, Jaya, Ananta
   or
   Saya, Ananta, Jaya

3. The order of sitting while facing South is:
   Shyam, Mohan, Kittu, Sohan, Raju.

4. The positions while running behind the other is :

   E, A, B, C, D *or* E, A, B, D, C

5. In descending order of height, the standing positions are :

   S, T, P, R, O, Q *or* S, T, P, R, Q, O

   Either O or Q is the shortest. The information given is not enough to clarify the answer.

DIRECTION SENSE

Directions : *In the following questions, select the right answer from the given options to depict the correct direction/distance.*

1. Kittu walks towards East and then towards South. After walking some distance he turns towards West and then turns to his left. In which direction is he walking now?

A. North B. South
C. East D. West

2. A person is driving towards West. What sequence of directions should he follow so that he is driving towards South?

A. left, right, right
B. right, right, left
C. left, left, left
D. right, right, right

3. Richa drives 8 km to the South, turns left and drives 5 km. Again, she turns left and drives 8 km. How far is she from her starting point?

A. 3 km B. 5 km
C. 8 km D. 13 km

4. Dingi runs 40 km towards North then turns right and runs 50 km. He turns right and runs 30 km, and once again turns right and runs 50 km. How far is he from his starting point?

A. 90 km B. 50 km
C. 10 km D. 5 km

5. Debu walks towards East then towards North and turning 45° right walks for a while and lastly turns towards left. In which direction is he walking now?

A. North B. East
C. South-East D. North-West

ANSWERS

1	2	3	4	5
B	D	B	C	D

EXPLANATORY ANSWERS

1. Kitto → E, S, left turn, W. (N, W, E, S)

2. right, right, right; W, Starting Point, S (N, W, E, S)

3. Starting Point, Finishing Point; 5 km; 8 km; 8 km; 5 km (N, W, E, S)

4. 50 km; 40 km; 30 km; 50 km; 10 km; Finishing Point; Starting Point (N, W, E, S)

5.

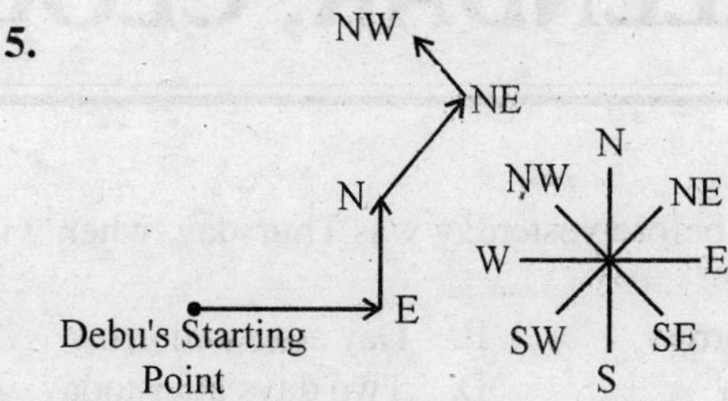

BLOOD RELATIONSHIPS

Directions : *In each of the following questions keenly study the relationship mentioned between the persons, and then from the given options select the right relationship as the answer.*

1. 'A' is the father of 'B' and 'C'. 'B' is the son of 'A' but 'C' is not the son of 'A'. What is 'C's' relation with 'A'?

A. Daughter B. Son
C. Niece D. Nephew

2. A lady said, "The person standing there is my grandfather's only son's daughter". How is the lady related to the standing person?

A. Sister B. Mother
C. Aunt D. Cousin

3. Ravi is the brother of Amit's son's son. What is Amit's relation to Ravi?

A. Cousin B. Father
C. Grandfather D. Son

4. Mayank said, "My mother is the sister of Rajat's brother." What is Rajat's relation with Mayank?
A. Cousin B. Maternal uncle
C. Uncle D. Brother-in-law

5. Introducing Lily, Raghav said, "Her father is my mother's only son". How is Lily related to Raghav?
A. Aunt B. Daughter
C. Mother D. Sister

ANSWERS

1	2	3	4	5
A	A	C	B	B

EXPLANATORY ANSWERS

1.

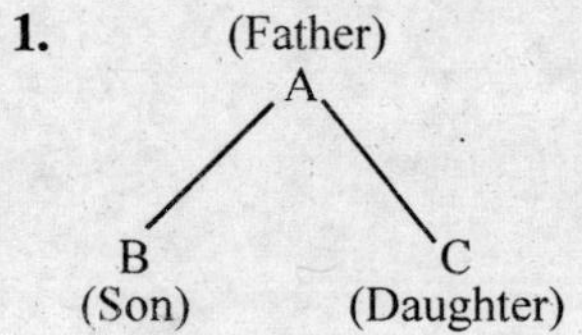

'C' is not the son of 'A', but 'A' is the father of 'C'. So, 'C' is the daughter of 'A'.

2.

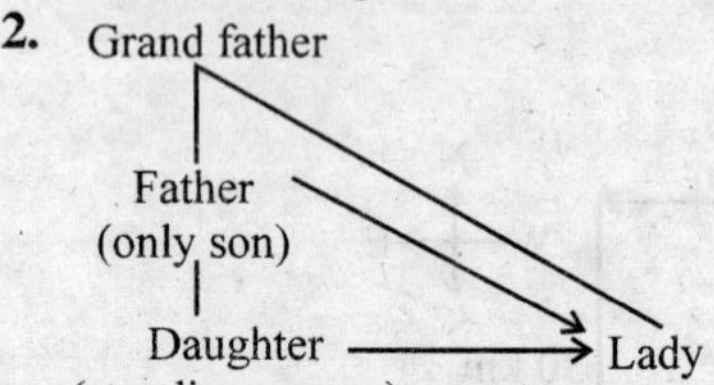

Lady's grandfather's son is lady's father and father's daughter will only be lady's sister.

4.

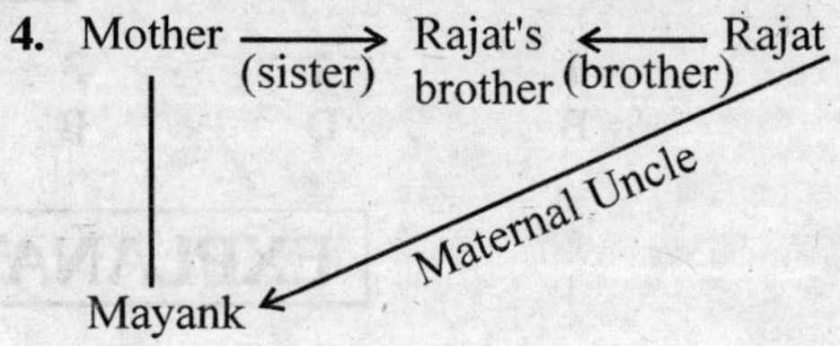

Mayank's mother is the sister of Rajat's brother. So Rajat is also the brother of Mayank's mother. Relation of the brother with his sister's child is maternal. So Rajat is Mayank's maternal uncle.

CALENDAR, CLOCK, TIME, DISTANCE

1. If the day before yesterday was Thursday, when will Sunday be?
A. Tomorrow B. Day after tomorrow
C. Today D. Two days after today

2. There are twenty people working in an office. The first group of five works between 8:00 A.M. and 2:00 PM. The second group of ten works between 10:00 AM to 4:00 PM. And the third group of five works between 12 noon to 6:00 PM. There are three computers in the office which all the employees frequently use. During which of the following hours the computers are likely to be used most?
A. 1:00 PM - 3:00 PM
B. 12 noon - 2:00 PM
C. 2:00 PM - 4:00 PM
D. 10:00 AM - 12 noon

3. If the seventh day of a month is three (3) days earlier than Friday, what day will it be on the nineteenth day of the month?
A. Sunday B. Monday
C. Wednesday D. Friday

4. Radha remembers that her father's birthday is after 16th but before 21st of March, while her brother Mangesh remembers that his father's birthday is before 22nd but after 19th of March. On which date is the birthday of their father?
A. 19th
B. 20th
C. 21st
D. Cannot be determined

5. A man is three (3) years older than his wife and four (4) times as old as his son. If the son attains an age of fifteen (15) years after three (3) years, what is the present age of the mother?
A. 45 years B. 51 years
C. 48 years D. 60 years

6. A clock is so placed that at 12 noon its minute hand points towards north-east. In which direction does its hour hand point at 1.30 P.M.?

A. East B. West

C. North D. South

7. If in the above question clock is turned through an angle of 135° in an anticlockwise direction, in which direction will its minute hand point at 8.45 P.M.?

A. East B. West

C. North D. South

8. A couple married in 1980 had two children, one in 1982 and the other in 1984. Their combined ages will equal the years of the marriage in?

A. 1986 B. 1985

C. 1987 D. 1988

9. Manoj left home for the bus stop 15 minutes earlier than the usual time. It takes 10 minutes to reach the stop. He reached the stop at 8.40 a.m. What time does he usually leave home for the bus stop?

A. 8.30 a.m. B. 8.55 a.m.

C. 8.45 p.m. D. None of these

10. Mamuni went to the movies nine days ago. She goes to the movies only on Thursday. What day of the week is today?

A. Sunday B. Tuesday

C. Thursday D. Saturday

11. If Thursday was the day after the day before yesterday five days ago, what is the least number of days ago when Sunday was three days before the day after tomorrow?

A. Two days ago B. Three days ago

C. Four days ago D. Five days ago

12. 1.12.91 is the first Sunday. Which is the fourth Tuesday of December 91?

A. 31.12.91 B. 24.12.91

C. 17.12.91 D. 26.12.91

13. If the third day of a month is Monday, which of the following will be the fifth day from 21st of that month?

A. Tuesday B. Monday

C. Wednesday D. Thursday

14. Keshav runs a factory in three shifts of eight hours each with 210 employees. In each shift minimum of 80 employees are required to run the factory effectively. No employee can be allowed to work for more than 16 hours a day. At least how many employees will be required to work for 16 hours every day?

A. 30 B. 60

C. Data inadequate D. None of these

15. If 15 horses eat 15 bags of gram in 15 days, in how many days will one horse eat one bag of grain?

A. 15 days B. 1/15 days

C. 1 day D. 30 days

16. A century leap year is divisible by :

A. 4 B. 16

C. 40 D. 400

17. If the fifth day of a month is Friday, which of the following will be the Seventh day from 10th of that month?

A. Tuesday B. Monday

C. Wednesday D. Thursday

18. Day after tomorrow is my birthday. On the same day next week falls 'Holi'. Today is Monday. What will be the day after 'Holi'?

A. Wednesday B. Thursday

C. Friday D. Saturday

19. A clock shows the time as 3 : 30 p.m. If the minute hand gains 2 minutes every hour, how many minutes will the clock gain by 4 a.m.?

A. 23 Minutes B. 24 Minutes

C. 25 Minutes D. 26 Minutes

20. Two brothers were expected to return home on the same day. Rajat returned 3 days earlier but Rohit returned 4 days later. If Rajat returned on Thursday, what was the expected day when both the brothers were to return home and when did Rohit Return?

A. Wednesday, Sunday

B. Thursday, Monday

C. Sunday, Thursday

D. Monday, Friday

ANSWERS

1	2	3	4	5	6	7	8	9	10
A	B	A	B	A	A	D	A	D	D
11	**12**	**13**	**14**	**15**	**16**	**17**	**18**	**19**	**20**
A	B	C	D	A	D	C	B	C	C

EXPLANATORY ANSWERS

1. Thursday —Day-before-yesterday

Friday —Yesterday

Saturday —Today

Sunday — Tomorrow

2. 1. 5 people work between 8 a.m. to 2 p.m.

2. 10 people work between 10 a.m. to 4 p.m.

3. 5 people work between 12 noon to 6 p.m.

So, computers are used most between 12 noon to 2 p.m.

3. 7th day is 3 days earlier than Friday so, 10th day is Friday, so also is 17th.

∴ 19th day will be 2nd day ahead of Friday, *i.e.*, Sunday.

4. Father's birthday

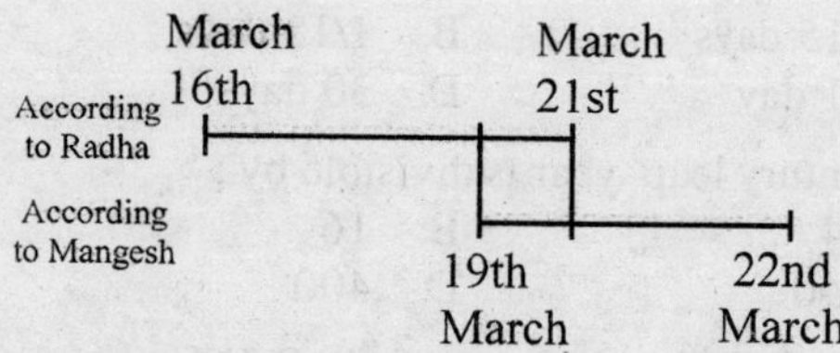

∴ Their father's birthday is on 20th March.

5. Present age of son is 15 – 3 = 12 years. Age of the man is 4 times the age of son, *i.e.*,

12 × 4 = 48 years

Man is 3 years elder to his wife/son's mother.

So Age of the mother is 48 – 3 = 45 years

6.

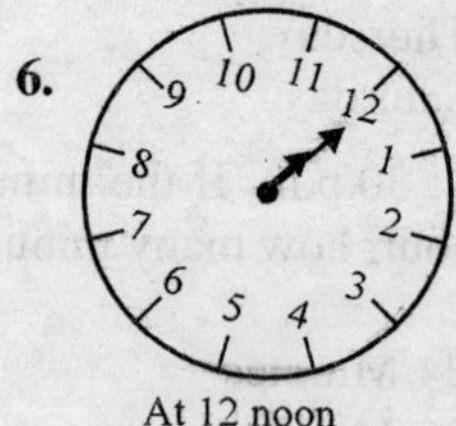

At 12 noon

At 1.30 p.m. the hour hand will point towards East.

7.

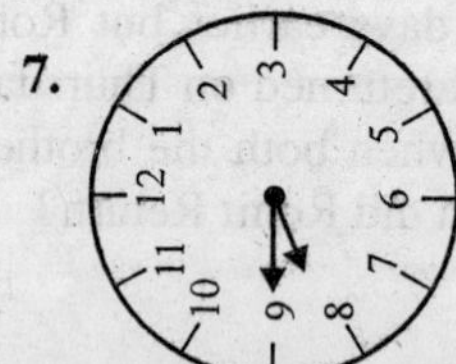

After rotating the clock in earlier question, its minute hand will point towards South at 8:45 p.m.

8. 1982 — 2 years later — 1st child

1984 — 4 years later — 2nd child

Total age of children — 2 years.

1985 — 5 years later — Total age of children: 4 years.

1986 — 6 years later — Total age of children : 6 years.

9. Manoj reached the bus stop at 8.40 a.m. He left his home at 8:40 – 10 minutes = 8:30 a.m. He left 15 minutes earlier than usual, so his actual time of leaving home is 8:30 am + 15 minutes = 8:45 a.m.

10. Mamuni goes to the movies on Thursday, so nine days ago was Thursday.

∴ Two days ago was also Thursday. So, today is Saturday.

11. Day after the day-before-yesterday five days ago is the 6th day which is Thursday. And so, the 3rd day will be Sunday. Three days before the day-after-tomorrow is Yesterday which is the 1st day of the five days. So, two days ago was Sunday.

12. First Sunday is on 1st December

First Tuesday is on 3rd December

3 weeks later, Fourth Tuesday will be on 3 + (7 × 3) = 24th December.

13. 3rd day of the month is Monday

5th day from 21st is 26th

26 – 3 = 23 days

23 days later, 23/7 leaves 2 days.

So, two days ahead of Monday will be Wednesday.

14. 80 employees are required for double shift.

15. 15 horses eat 15 bags of grain in 15 days

15 horses eat 1 bag of grain in 1 day

1 horse eats 1 bag of grain in 15 days

16. A leap year is divisible by 4 and a century leap year is divisible by 400.

17. Seventh day from 10th is 17th.

5th day is Friday. Next Friday is on 12th, 17 – 12 = 5, 5 days ahead of Friday will be Wednesday. So, 17th is Wednesday.

18. Today is Monday

Day-after-tomorrow is Wednesday

Next week 'Holi' is also on Wednesday

So, Day after Holi is Thursday.

19. Hours between 3:30 p.m. and 4 a.m. are — 12½ hours. Number of minutes gained will be 12½ × 2 = 25 minutes.

20. Rajat returned on Thursday. 3 days later was the day of expected return, *i.e.*, Sunday. Rohit returned 4 days after Sunday, *i.e.*, Thursday.

ROWS AND RANKS

1. In a row of trees, one tree is fifth from either end of the row. How many trees are in the row?
A. 11 B. 8
C. 10 D. 9

2. Jaya ranks 5th in a class of 53. What is her rank from the bottom in the class?
A. 49th B. 48th
C. 47th D. 50th

3. Mohan ranks twenty-first in a class of sixty-five students. What will be his (Mohan's) rank if the lowest candidate is assigned rank 1?
A. 44th B. 45th
C. 46th D. Data inadequate

4. If Rahul finds that he is 12th from the right in a line of boys and 4th from the left, how many boys should be added to the line such that there are 28 boys in the line?
A. 12 B. 14
C. 20 D. 13

5. In a row of boys, Rajan is tenth from the right and Suraj is tenth from the left. When Rajan and Suraj interchange their positions, Suraj will be twenty-seventh from the left. Which of the following will be Rajan's position from the right?
A. Tenth B. Twenty-sixth
C. Twenty-ninth D. None of these

6. Mahesh and Suresh are ranked 11th and 12th respectively from the top in a class of 41 students. What will be their respective ranks from the bottom?
A. 32nd and 33rd B. 29th and 30th
C. 30th and 31st D. 31st and 30th

7. Uma ranked 8th from the top and 37th from bottom in a class. How many students are there in the class?
A. 47 B. 46
C. 45 D. None of these

8. In a queue, Sadiq is 14th from the front and Joseph is 17th from the end, while Jane is in between Sadiq and Joseph. If Sadiq be ahead of Joseph and there be 48 persons in the queue, how many persons are there between Sadiq and Jane?
A. 5 B. 6
C. 7 D. 8

9. Rohan ranked eleventh from the top and twenty-seventh from the bottom among the students who passed the annual examination in a class. If the number of students who failed in the examination was 12, how many students appeared for the examination?
A. 48
B. 49
C. 50
D. Cannot be determined

10. Some boys are sitting in a row. P is sitting fourteenth from the left and Q is seventh from the right. If there are four boys between P and Q, how many boys are there in the row?
A. 19 B. 21
C. 25 D. 23

ANSWERS

1	2	3	4	5	6	7	8	9	10
D	A	B	D	D	D	D	C	B	C

EXPLANATORY ANSWERS

1.

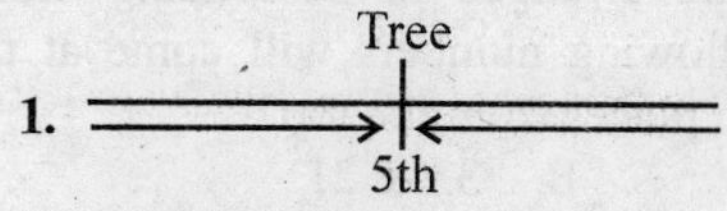

Total number of trees in the row are :
(5 + 5) –1 =9

2.

Jaya's rank from the bottom is :
(53 – 5) +1 = 49th.

3.

Note : Mohan's rank from the last or the question asked means the same.
Mohan's rank is (65 – 21) +1 = 45th

4. 

The number of boys in the line are :
(4 + 12) – 1 = 15
To make a line of 28 boys, (28 –15) *i.e.* 13 more boys are needed.

5. 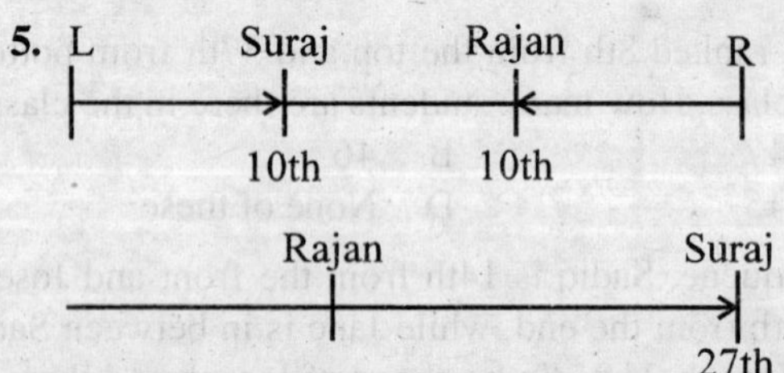

As the position of boys is equal from both ends, Rajan will also be 27th from the right after changing positions.

6. 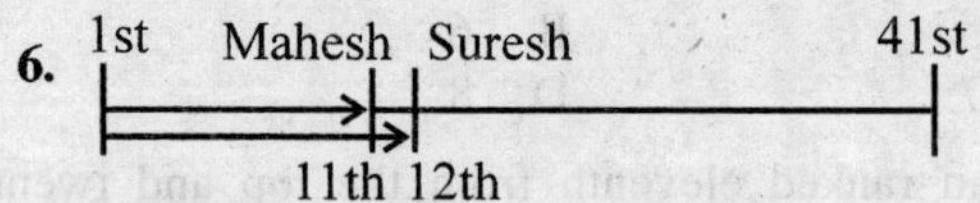

Mahesh's position from bottom is :
(41 – 11) + 1 = 31st
Suresh's position from bottom is :
(41 – 12) +1 = 30th

7. 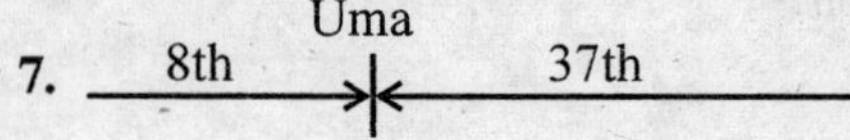

Total number of students in the class are :
(8 + 37) – 1 = 44

8. 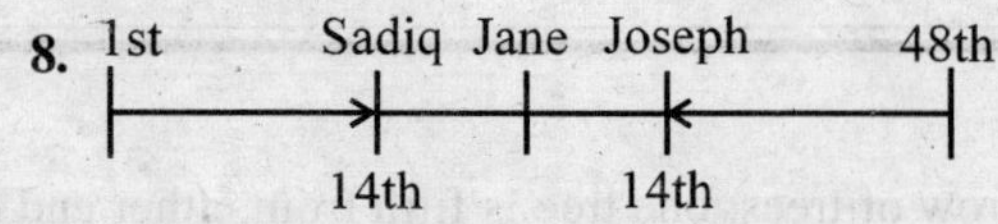

Sadiq's position from last is :
(48 – 14) + 1 = 35th
Number of persons between Sadiq and Joseph are (35 – 17) – 1 = 17
Jane is in-between Sadiq and Joseph *i.e.,* she's at 9th position from both the boys.
∴ there are 8 persons between Sadiq and Jane.
Note : (8 + 8) – 1 = 17

9. 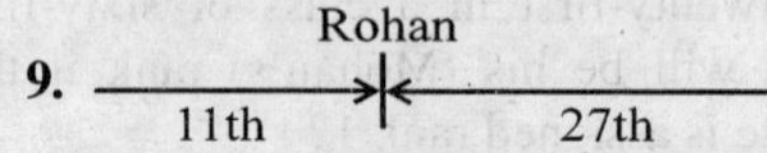

Number of students who passed the examination (11+ 27) – 1 = 37
Those who failed = 12
Total number of students who appeared in the examination = 37 + 12 = 49.

10. 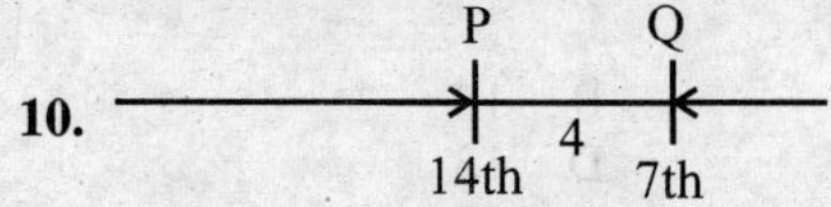

The number of boys in the row are :
(14 + 4 + 7) = 25

NUMBER PROBLEMS

1. How many 6's are there in the following series of numbers which are preceded by 7 but not immediately followed by 9?
6 7 9 5 6 9 7 6 8 7 6 7 8 6 9 4 6 7 7 6 9 5 7 6 3

A. One B. Two
C. Three D. Four

2. In a chess tournament each of six players will play every other player exactly once. How many matches will be played during the tournament?

A. 12 B. 15
C. 30 D. 36

3. How many 4's are there in the following series which are preceded by 7, but are not preceded by 8?
3 4 5 7 4 3 7 4 8 5 4 3 7 4 9 8 4 7 2 7 4 1 3 6

A. 1 B. 2
C. 3 D. 4

4. How many even numbers are there in the following series of numbers, each of which is immediately preceded by an odd number, but not immediately followed by an even number?
5 3 4 8 9 7 1 6 5 3 2 9 8 4 3 5

A. Nil B. 1
C. 2 D. 3

5. If all the numbers from 1 to 51 which are exactly divisible by 3 are arranged in descending order, which of the following numbers will come at the seventh and tenth places from the top?

A. 33 & 27 B. 33 & 21
C. 21 & 30 D. 33 & 24

ANSWERS

1	2	3	4	5
C	B	D	C	D

EXPLANATORY ANSWERS

1. 679569 $\underline{768}$ $\underline{767}$ 8694677695 $\underline{763}$
1 2 3

2. When all the players have to play with each other then the method of calculating the number of matches to be played is $\frac{n(n-1)}{2}$ where '*n*' is the number of players playing the match. So, the number of matches played will be :
$(6 \times 5) \div 2 = 30 \div 2 = 15$

3. 3457 $\underline{74}$ 37 $\underline{74}$ 854 37 $\underline{74}$ 9847 2 $\underline{74}$ 136
1 2 3 4

4. 5 3 4 8 9 7 $\underline{1\ 6\ 5}$ $\underline{3\ 2\ 9}$ 8 4 3 5
1 2

5. The numbers divisible by 3 in descending order are :
51, 48, 45, 42, 39, 36, 33, 30, 27, 24, 21,
(30 = 7th, 24 = 10th)
18, 15, 12, 9, 6, 3.

SYMBOL SUBSTITUTION

1. If "+" means "–"; "–" means "×"; "×"means "÷" and "÷" means "+", then
$15 \times 5 \div 10 + 5 - 3 = ?$

A. 9.5 B. 0
C. – 2 D. 24

2. If "+" means "–"; "–" means "×"; "×"means "÷" and "÷" means "+", then
$15 \times 3 \div 15 + 5 - 2 = ?$

A. 0 B. 10
C. 20 D. 6

3. If "+" means "÷"; "×" means "–"; "÷"means "+" and "–" means "×", then
$16 \div 8 \times 6 - 2 + 12 = ?$

A. 22 B. 24
C. 23 D. 20

4. If "+" means "×"; "–" means "÷"; "÷"means "+" and "×" means "–", then what will be the value of 20 ÷ 40 – 4 × 5 + 6 = ?

A. 60 B. 1.67
C. 150 D. 0

5. If "+" means "×"; "–" means "÷"; "×"means "–" and "÷" means "+", then
$5 + 8 - 4 \times 2 \div 9 = ?$

A. 15 B. 13
C. 17 D. 11

ANSWERS

1	2	3	4	5
C	B	C	D	C

EXPLANATORY ANSWERS

1. $15 \div 5 + 10 - 5 \times 3$
$3 + 10 - 15 = -2$

2. $15 \div 3 + 15 - 5 \times 2$
$5 + 15 - 10 = 10$

3. $16 + 8 - 6 \times 2 \div 12$
$16 + 8 - 1 = 23$

4. $20 + 40 \div 4 - 5 \times 6$
$20 + 10 - 30 = 0$

5. $5 \times 8 \div 4 - 2 + 9$
$10 - 2 + 9 = 17$

MISSING NUMBERS

Directions: *In each question given below which one number can be placed at the sign of interrogation?*

1.

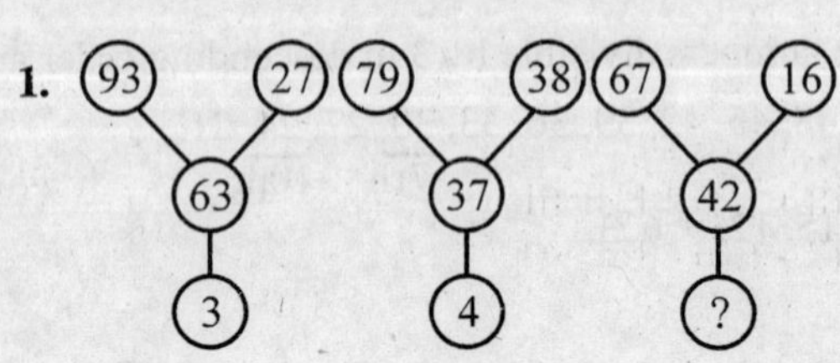

A. 5 B. 6
C. 8 D. 9

2.

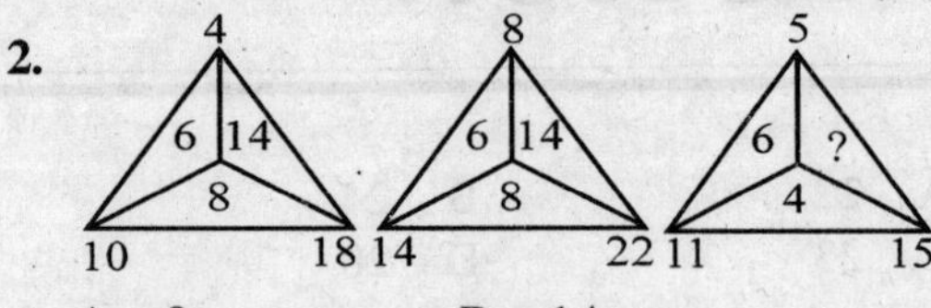

A. 8 B. 14
C. 10 D. 6

3.

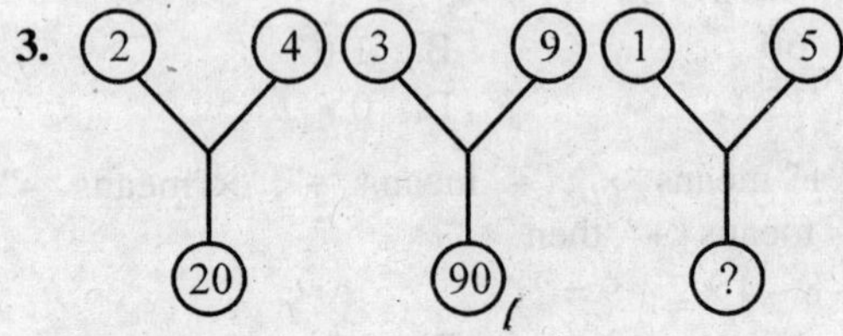

A. 20 B. 25
C. 26 D. 75

4.

27	22	50
13	12	26
9	2	?

A. 12 B. 39
C. 18 D. 24

5.

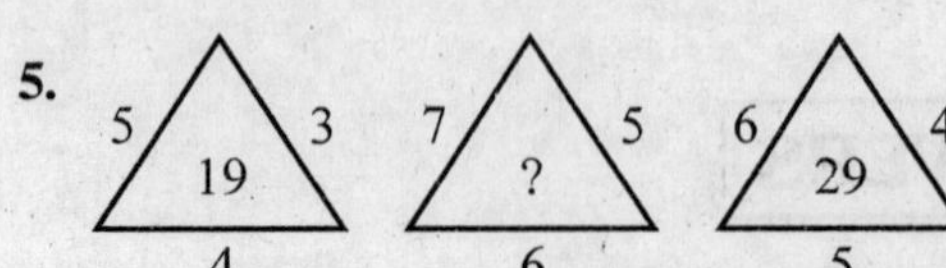

A. 25 B. 47
C. 37 D. 41

6.

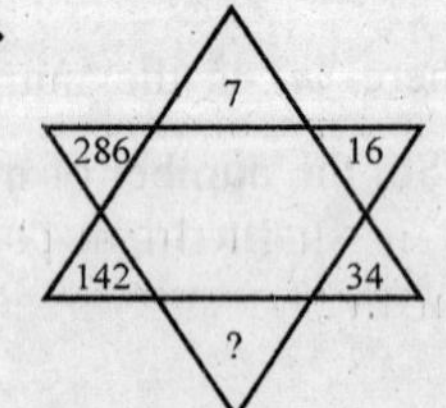

A. 70 B. 68
C. 56 D. 92

7.

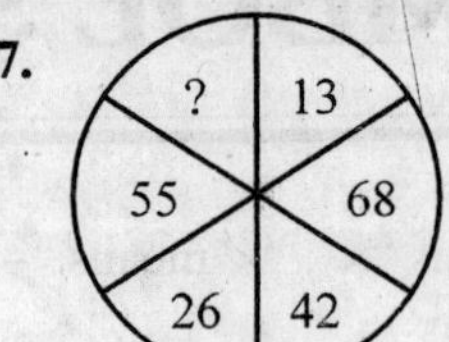

A. 41 B. 37
C. 29 D. 25

8.

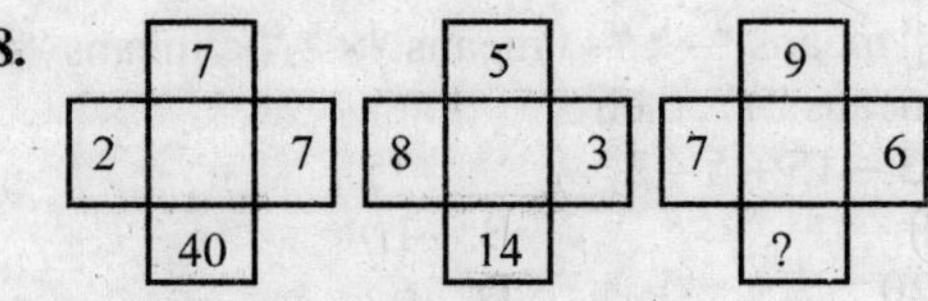

A. 72 B. 68
C. 82 D. 96

9.

42	(21)	22
78	(?)	84
162	(18)	99

A. 12 B. 13
C. 60 D. 72

10.

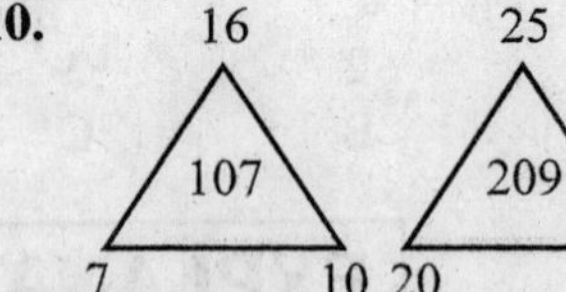

A. 68 B. 93
C. 175 D. 217

ANSWERS

1	2	3	4	5	6	7	8	9	10
D	C	C	A	D	A	C	B	B	A

EXPLANATORY ANSWERS

1. The sum of numbers on right and centre subtracted from the number on the left gives the number at the bottom, *i.e.,*

$93 - (27 + 63) = 3$
$79 - (38 + 37) = 4$

Similarly,
$67 - (16 + 42) = 9$

2. The number inside each triangle is the difference of the numbers at its base *i.e.*
$10 - 4 = 6$, $18 - 4 = 14$ and $18 - 10 = 8$
$14 - 8 = 6$, $22 - 8 = 14$ and $22 - 14 = 8$, similarly
$11 - 5 = 6$, $15 - 5 = 10$ and $15 - 11 = 4$.

3. The sum of squares of two numbers at the top gives the third number below, *i.e.*,
$2^2 + 4^2 = 20$
$3^2 + 9^2 = 90$, similarly
$1^2 + 5^2 = 26$

4. The sum of numbers in 1st and 2nd column plus 1 is the number in the 3rd column, *i.e.*,
$27 + 22 + 1 = 50$
$13 + 12 + 1 = 26$, similarly
$9 + 2 + 1 = 12$

5. The product of numbers on either side of the triangle plus the number at the base is the number inside the triangle, *i.e.*,
$(5 \times 3) + 4 = 19$
$(6 \times 4) + 5 = 29$, similarly
$(7 \times 5) + 6 = 41$

6. Clockwise starting from number 7, the next number is obtained by doubling the number and adding 2, *i.e.*,
$(7 \times 2) + 2 = 16$
$(16 \times 2) + 2 = 34 \ldots$, similarly
$(34 \times 2) + 2 = 70$
$(70 \times 2) + 2 = 142$
$(142 \times 2) + 2 = 286$

7. The difference between the numbers in opposite sectors is 13, *i.e.*,
$26 - 13 = 13$
$68 - 55 = 13$, similarly
The missing number is $42 - 13 = 29$
($42 + 13 = 55$ is not given as option)

8. The number at the bottom is obtained by subtracting the sum of two numbers in the centre grid line from the square of the number at the top, *i.e.*,
$7^2 - (2 + 7) = 40$
$5^2 - (8 + 3) = 14$, similarly
$9^2 - (7 + 6) = 68$

9. The number inside the brackets is obtained by multiplying the number on the left by 2 and then dividing the product by the sum of digits of number on the right, *i.e.*,
$(42 \times 2) \div (2 + 2) = 21$
$(162 \times 2) \div (9 + 9) = 18$, similarly
$(78 \times 2) \div (8 + 4) = 13$

10. Subtracting the sum of squares of two numbers at the base from the square of number at the apex gives the number inside the triangle, *i.e.*,
$16^2 - (7^2 + 10^2) = 107$
$25^2 - (20^2 + 4^2) = 209$, similarly
$19^2 - (2^2 + 17^2) = 68$

ALPHABET PROBLEMS

Directions : *The following questions are based on alphabet series in natural or reverse order and the combinations that can be made by changing the position of alphabet in given words.*

1. Which alphabet comes immediately before the sixth alphabet from the left extreme in alphabetical series?

A. U B. E
C. F D. V

2. Which letter is midway between G and S?

A. L B. N
C. M D. No letter

3. Which letter should be ninth letter to the left of ninth letter from the right if the first half of the alphabet is reversed?

A. I B. D
C. F D. E

4. If the alphabet is in reverse order, which letter will be eighth letter to the left of the seventh letter counting from the right end?

A. O B. P
C. N D. Q

5. What will be the fifth letter to the right of the thirteenth letter from the right?

A. R B. S
C. I D. O

ANSWERS

1	2	3	4	5
B	C	D	A	B

EXPLANATORY ANSWERS

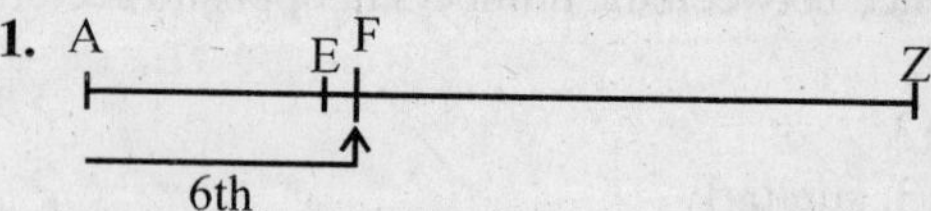

Sixth letter from left is 'F' and letter immediately before 'F' is 'E'.

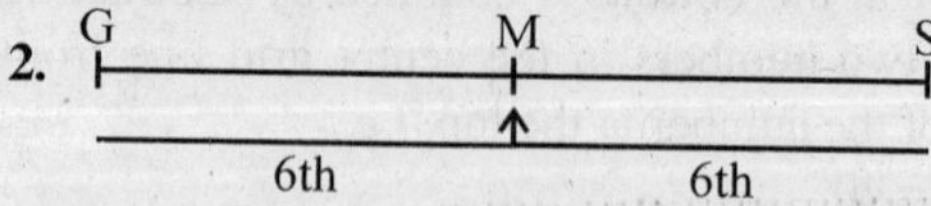

'M' is midway between G and S.

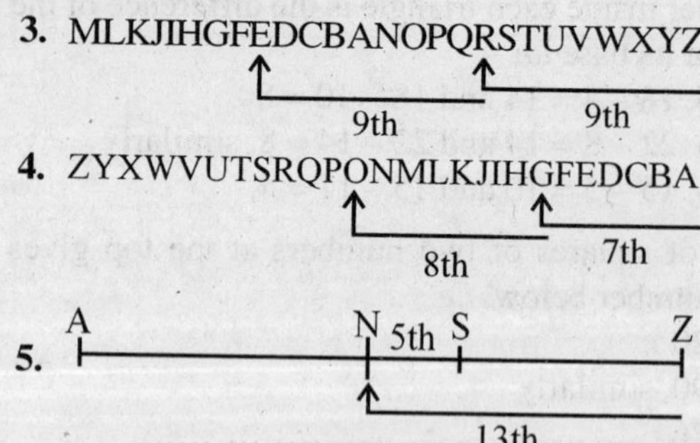

13th letter from right is 'N' and 5th letter to the right of 'N' is 'S'.

NON-VERBAL SERIES

Directions (Q. 1–10) : *In each of the following questions which one of the five answer figures given below should come after the problem figures if the sequence are continued?*

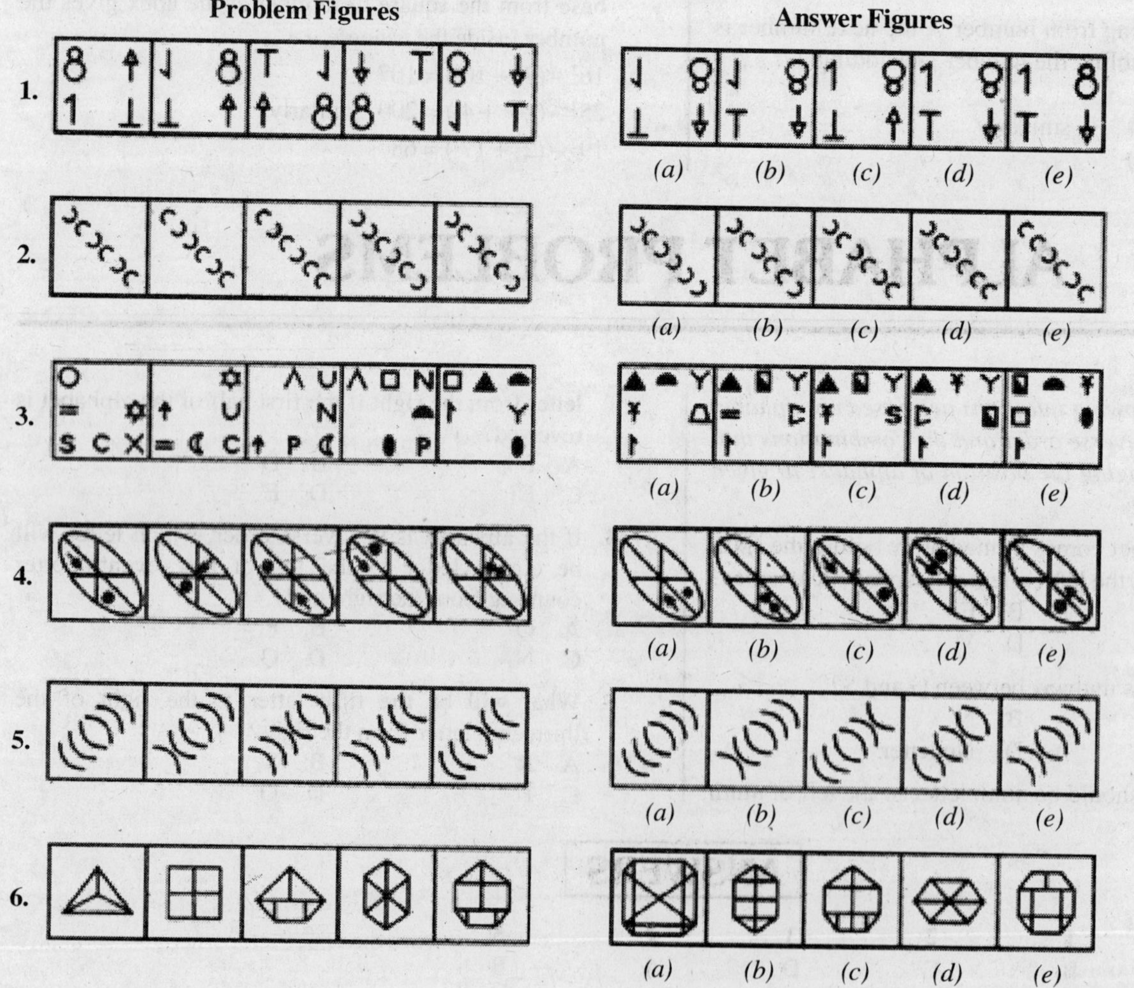

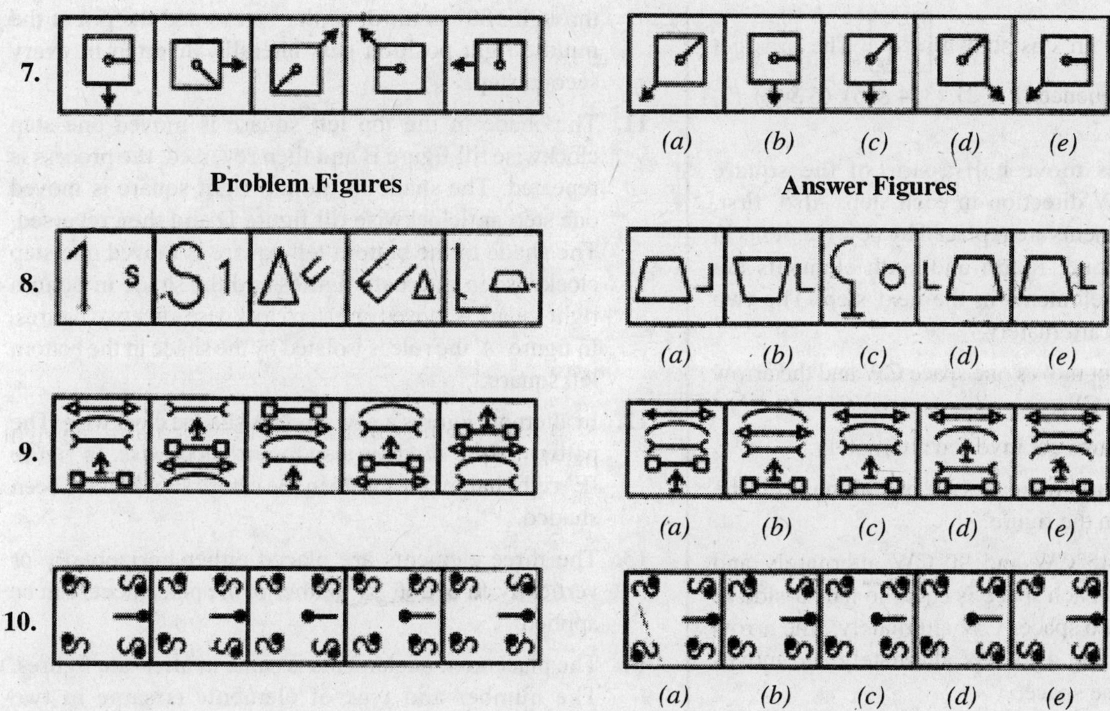

Directions (Q. 11-20) : *In each of these questions, a series begins with an unmarked figure on the extreme left in the row of figures. One and only one of the five lettered figures in the series does not fit into the series. The two unmarked figures, one on the extreme left and the other on the extreme right fit into the series. Take as many aspects into account as possible of the figures in the series and find out the one and only of the five marked figures which does not fit into the series. The letter of that figure is the answer.*

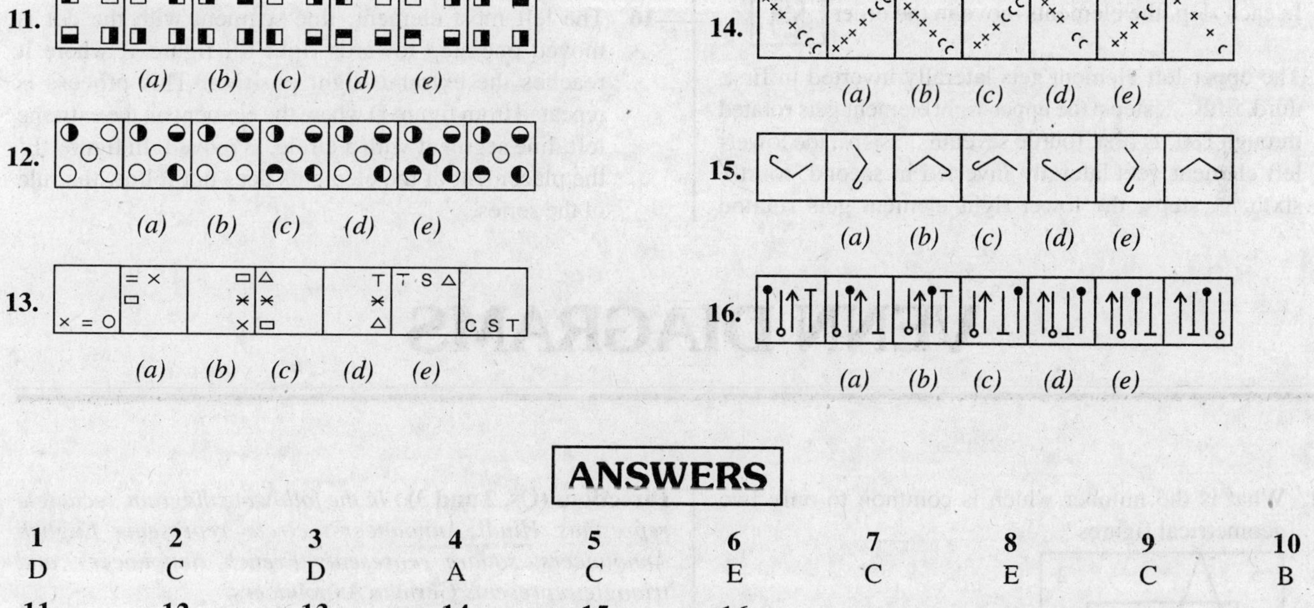

ANSWERS

1	2	3	4	5	6	7	8	9	10
D	C	D	A	C	E	C	E	C	B
11	12	13	14	15	16				
A	E	A	C	C	E				

EXPLANATORY ANSWERS

1. In each step, all the elements move to the adjacent corner (of the square boundary) in a CW direction and the element that reaches the upper-left corner gets vertically inverted.

2. We can label the arcs as shown [1, 2, 3, 4, 5, 6]. The arcs get inverted in the sequence (1 & 2), (3, 4 & 5), (6 & 1), (2, 3 & 4), (5 & 6), ...

3. All the elements move half-a-side of the square boundary in ACW direction in each step. Also, first, third and fifth elements are replaced by new elements in one step and second, fourth and sixth elements are replaced by new elements in the next step. The two steps are repeated alternately.

4. In each step, the dot moves one space CW and the arrow moves two spaces CW.

5. One arc and four arcs get inverted alternately.

6. The number of parts increases by one along with the number of sides in the figure.

7. The pin rotates 45°CW and 90°CW alternately and moves one space (each space is equal to half-a-side of the square) and two spaces CW alternately. The arrow rotates 90°ACW and 45°ACW alternately and moves two spaces and one space.

8. In one step, the two elements interchange positions and the smaller element gets enlarged while the larger element gets reduced in size. In the next step, the smaller element is replaced by a new small element and the larger element is replaced by a new large element.

9. In each step, the elements move in the order .

10. The upper-left element gets laterally inverted in first, third, fifth. .... steps; the upper-right element gets rotated through 180° is first, fourth, seventh,.... steps; the lower-left element gets laterally inverted in second, fourth, sixth, ... steps; the lower-right element gets rotated through 180° in third, sixth,... steps and the pin at the middle-right position gets laterally inverted in every second step.

11. The shade in the top left square is moved one step clockwise till figure B and then reversed, the process is repeated. The shade in the top right square is moved one step anticlockwise till figure D and then reversed. The shade in the bottom left square is moved one step clockwise in alternate figures and the shade in bottom right square is moved one step clockwise after two figures. In figure 'A' the rule is isolated by the shade in the bottom left square.

12. In alternate figures a new circle is shaded clockwise. The pattern of the shade is also moved clockwise. In figure 'E' right half of the circle in the centre should have been shaded.

13. The three elements are placed either horizontally or vertically. In option 'A' neither of the placements can be applied.

14. The placement of elements is same in alternate figures. The number and type of elements is same in two subsequent figures. In this manner, figure 'C' should have four crosses and two C shapes.

15. *(c)* : The element is moved one step anticlockwise and the arc at one end is turned outside and inside alternately. In figure 'C' the element should be on the right side with the arc turned outside on the top side.

16. The left most element, line segment with the dot is moved one step towards right till figure C where it reaches the extreme right position. This process is repeated from figure D where the element on the extreme left, line segment with a circle, is moved. In figure 'E' the placement of the elements does not follow the rule of the series.

VENN DIAGRAMS

1. What is the number which is common to only two geometrical figures?

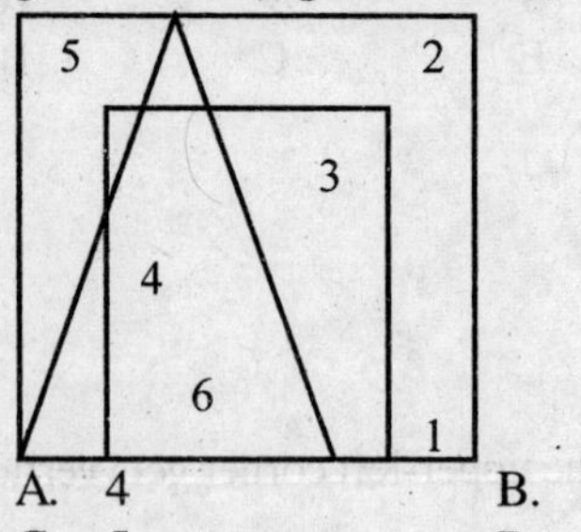

A. 4 B. 3
C. 5 D. 2

Directions (Qs. 2 and 3) : *In the following diagram, rectangle represents Hindi Announcers, circle represents English Announcers, square represents French Announcers, and triangle represents German Announcers.*

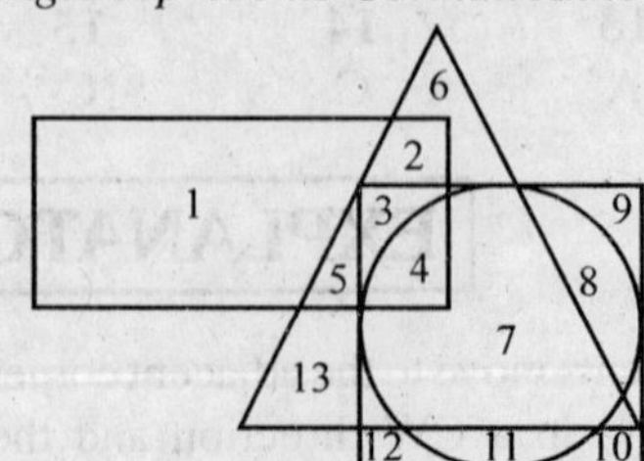

2. Which area represents those announcers who can present programmes in Hindi, French and German only?

A. 1 B. 2
C. 3 D. 4

3 Which area represents those announcers who can present programmes in French and English only?

A. 7 B. 9
C. 11 D. 13

Directions (Qs. 4 and 5) : *Study the diagram to answer these questions.*

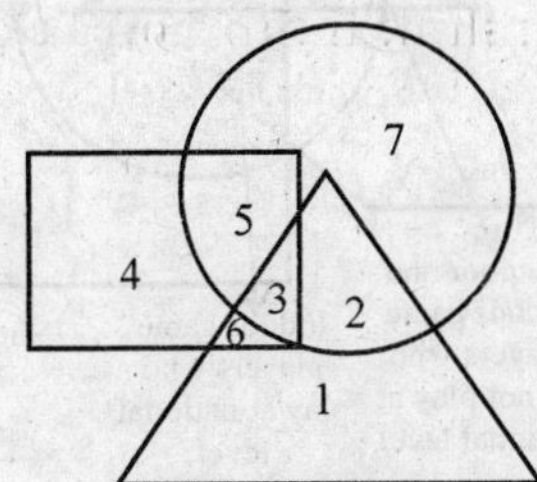

4. Which number is in all the geometrical figures?

A. 5 B. 6
C. 2 D. 3

5. Number 6 is in :

A. Rectangle and triangle
B. Circle and traingle
C. Rectangle and circle
D. Rectangle only

Directions (Qs. 6 to 9) : *In the following diagram*

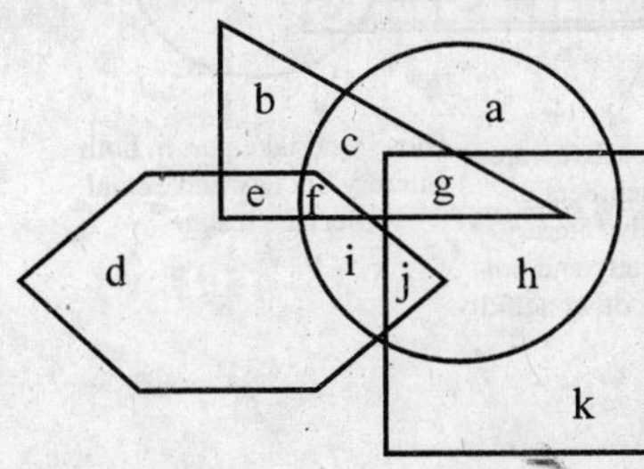

The Circle represents players
The Triangle represents outdoor games
The Hexagon represents indoor games and
The Square represents national level players
Study the diagram and answer the questions given below :

6. The letter in the section representing the players who play indoor games at national level is :

A. f B. i
C. j D. g

7. The letter representing the section of outdoor as well as indoor game players who do not play at the national level is :

A. c B. f
C. e D. i

8. The section representing national level players who do not play either outdoor or indoor games but still come under the category of players is :

A. k B. g
C. c D. h

9. Persons who play outdoor games but do not come under the category of players are represented in the section marked :

A. b B. c
C. a D. d

Directions (Qs. 10 to 13) : *Study the diagram given below.*

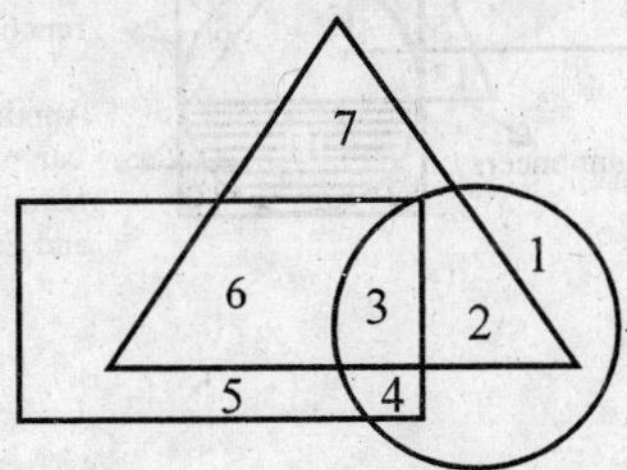

A college provides three different activities, students union represented by triangle, literary society represented by rectangle and social service league represented by circle.

10. Those who take part in both literary society and social service league but not in students union are represented by :

A. 3 & 4 B. 5 & 6
C. 5 & 1 D. 4

11. Those who take part in students union but not in social service league are represented by:

A. 2 & 7 B. 6 & 7
C. 6 D. 7

12. Those students who are members of literary society only and not of any other activity are represented by:

A. 2 B. 5
C. 3 & 4 D. 3

13. Those students who are members of all three groups are represented by :

A. 2 B. 3
C. 4 D. 6

ANSWERS

1	2	3	4	5	6	7	8	9	10
B	C	C	D	A	C	B	D	A	D
11	**12**	**13**							
B	B	B							

EXPLANATORY ANSWERS

1.

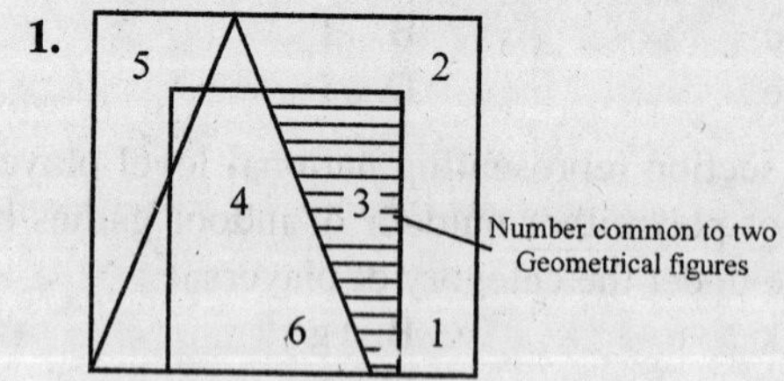

Note : Numbers 4 and 6 are common to all three geometrical figures.

Qs. 2 and 3.

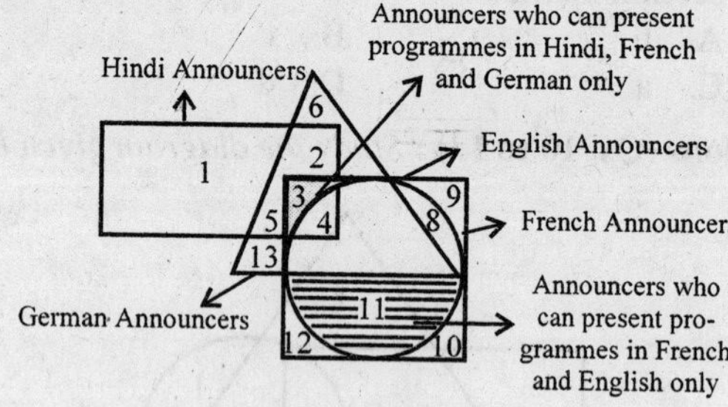

Qs. 4 and 5.

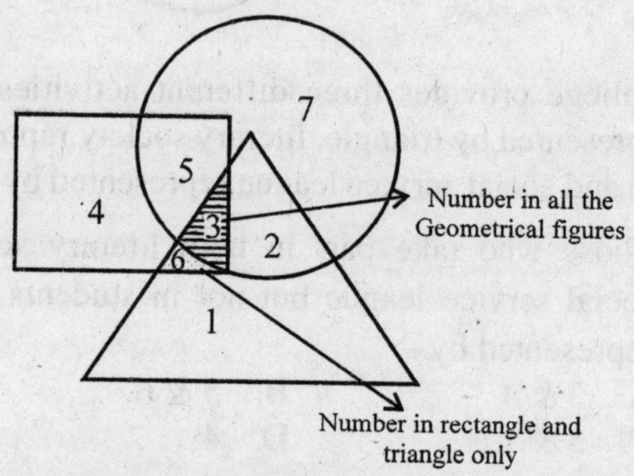

Qs. 6 to 9.

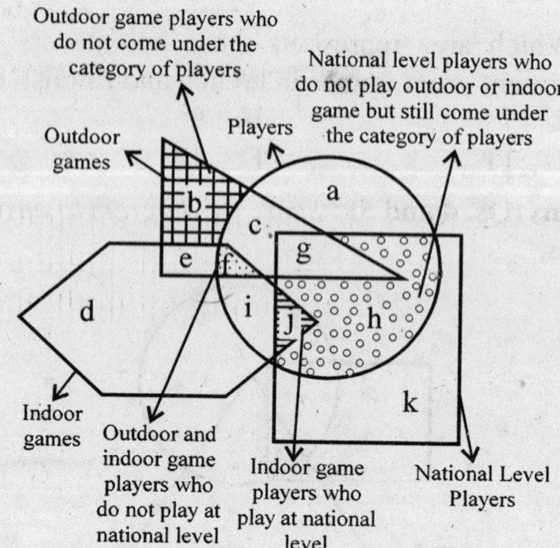

Qs. 10 to 13.

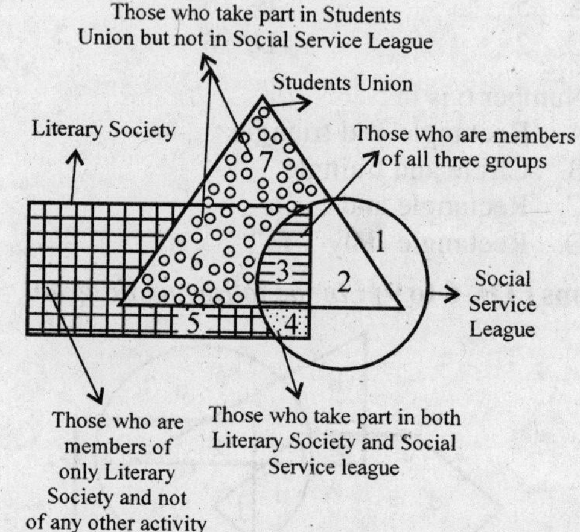

HARYANA

General Knowledge & Awareness

Multiple Choice Questions

1. During the ancient age, modern Haryana state was known as:
(*a*) Brahmavarta (*b*) Brahmarshi region
(*c*) Uttravedi of Brahma (*d*) All of the above

2. Who of the following rulers of Bharata vamsha (descendants of Bharata, according to Rigveda, who were a group of people who lived in the north-west of India) started his campaign from Haryana for establishing his authority in various other Kingdoms of the time?
(*a*) Sudas (*b*) Arjuna
(*c*) Bharata (*d*) Bhishma

3. The famous war of Mahabharata was fought at which of the following places in Haryana?
(*a*) Panipat (*b*) Kurukshetra
(*c*) Jhajjhar (*d*) Ballabh Garh

4. During Mughals, Janapadas of this state were replaced by
(*a*) Gana Sangha (*b*) Gana System
(*c*) Khaps (*d*) Panchayata

5. The territory of modern Haryana was included in which of the following Mahajanapadas of Buddha period?
(*a*) Kuru and Panchala (*b*) Kosala and Vajji
(*c*) Sursena and Avanti (*d*) Asmaka and Vatsa

6. At which of the following places in the state, capital of the Agreyagana was situated?
(*a*) Rewari (*b*) Sirsa
(*c*) Hansi (*d*) Agroha

7. Mahamud Gaznavi attacked on Thanesar in:
(*a*) 1013 AD (*b*) 1014 AD
(*c*) 1016 AD (*d*) 1017 AD

8. Thanesar (now in Haryana) was the capital of which of the following famous rulers of ancient India?
(*a*) Harsha Vardhan
(*b*) Ashoka
(*c*) Chandragupta Vikramaditya
(*d*) Kanishka

9. During the 12th century A.D. who of the following rulers of Chauhan dynasty defeated Tomars of Haryana?
(*a*) Vigraha Raja VI (*b*) Vigrah Raja II
(*c*) Arno Raja (*d*) Prithvi Raj Chauhan

10. When did Sultan Balban of Ghulam dynasty attacked on Mevas of Haryana with a view to establish his authority on Mevas?
(*a*) 1260 AD (*b*) 1265 AD
(*c*) 1266 AD (*d*) 1267 AD

11. Feroz Tughlaq of Tughlaq dynasty built which of the following cities in Haryana?
(*a*) Tohana (*b*) Hansi
(*c*) Siwani (*d*) Fatehabad

12. Timur made an attack on which of the following cities of Haryana?
(*a*) Sirsa (*b*) Fatehabad
(*c*) Hissar (*d*) All of the above

13. The famous battle of 1526 between Babur and Ibrahim Lodi was fought at which of the following places of Haryana?
(*a*) Panipat (*b*) Kurukshetra
(*c*) Tawaru (*d*) Jind

14. Who was the King of Rewari during the reign of famous Mughal Emperor Akbar?
(*a*) Tularam (*b*) Karna Singh
(*c*) Hemachandra (Hemu) (*d*) Phool Singh

15. The famous second battle of Panipat between Akbar and Hemachandra (Hemu) was fought in:
(*a*) 1550 AD (*b*) 1552 AD
(*c*) 1554 AD (*d*) 1556 AD

16. Which of the following famous battle was fought in the state of Haryana between the Marathas and Ahmadshah Abdali?
(*a*) The third battle of Panipat
(*b*) The second battle of Panipat
(*c*) The first battle of Panipat
(*d*) None of these

17. George Thomas built his capital at which of the following places of the state?
(*a*) Raniya (*b*) Tohana
(*c*) The fort of Hansi (*d*) Behram Pur

18. In 1802 AD George Thomas died at which of the following places in Haryana?
(*a*) Mahendragarh (*b*) Behram Pur
(*c*) Narnaul (*d*) Bawal

19. During 1809-10 AD, entire territories of Haryana was under the control of:
(*a*) Marathas (*b*) Satnamies
(*c*) Mughals (*d*) Britishers

20. Modern Haryana state was built on:
(*a*) 1 November, 1966 (*b*) 5 January, 1967
(*c*) 1 November, 1958 (*d*) 15 August, 1947

21. Evidences of Early-Harappan, Mature Harappan and Late Harappan culture have been found at which of the following places in Haryana?
(*a*) Banawali (*b*) Sosawal
(*c*) Mirzapur (*d*) All of the above

22. The period of Aryans of Kuru Vamsha, centuries before the Mahabharata period was marked with the beginning of which of the following ages?
(*a*) Cultivation Age (*b*) Copper Age
(*c*) Iron Age (*d*) Metal Age

23. The essence of the philosophy of Bhagvad Gita preached by Lord Krishna to Arjuna, a noted Commander of the Mahabharata War in the form of a dialogue between the two was delivered at which of the following places of Haryana?
(*a*) Rewari (*b*) Pehwa
(*c*) Kurukshetra (*d*) Panipat

24. During Youdheya period, Haryana was known as:
(*a*) Youdheya confederacy (*b*) Bahudhanyaka region
(*c*) Matsya region (*d*) Gana region

25. The famous pilgrim Hiuen Tsang in his book Si-Yo-ki, has described the prosperity of which of the following cities of Haryana?
(*a*) Sthaneshwar (Thanesmar)
(*b*) Panipat
(*c*) Rohtak
(*d*) Ambala

26. Which of the following treatise provide valuable information about the advancement of trade, art and culture in Haryana during the reign of Tomar Kings?
(*a*) Tahkik-i-Hind (*b*) Harsh Charita
(*c*) Kadambari (*d*) Yashastilak Champu

27. Who was the ruler of the Tawaroo pargana during the invasion of Babur in 1526-27?
(*a*) Hasan Khan (*b*) Mohan Singh Mandhar
(*c*) Faizal Khan (*d*) Jalal Khan

28. During the period of Babur, the Rajput King Mohan Singh Mandhar had its kingdom in Haryana at:
(*a*) Mandhar Pargana of Kaithal
(*b*) Tawaroo
(*c*) Jind
(*d*) Panipat

29. During 1756-57, Haryana was under the control of:
(*a*) Mughals (*b*) Sikhs
(*c*) Marathas (*d*) Satnamies

30. While returning back to his homeland, Ahmad Shah Abdali put the northern part of Haryana (Ambala, Jind, Kurukshetra and Karnal Districts) under the charge of:
(*a*) Mughals
(*b*) Sikhs
(*c*) Jain Khan, the Governor of Sarhind
(*d*) Gen Khan the Governor of Durrani

31. In the sepoy mutiny that broke out in 1857 at Meerut, majority of soldiers who took part in the revolt hailed from which of the following districts of Haryana?
(*a*) Gurugram (*b*) Rohtak
(*c*) Hissar (*d*) All of these

32. Who of the following great warriors of Haryana was the Naib Kotwal of Meerut at the time of Sepoy mutiny:
(*a*) Abdus Samad Khan (*b*) Vikram Singh
(*c*) Rao Krishna Gopal (*d*) Rameshwar Dayal

33. In the battle (for the freedom of India) fought at the village Naseebpur situated near Narnaul, Britishers destroyed which of the following three powers?
(*a*) Rewari, Jhajjhar and Jodhpur
(*b*) Gurugram, Rewari and Jodhpur
(*c*) Jind, Jagadari and Pehwa
(*d*) Panipat, Jhajjhar and Tawaroo

34. In the first Freedom struggle, who of the following Kings of Ballabhgarh led the revolutionary army in Delhi?
(*a*) Raja Karn Singh (*b*) Raja Nahan Singh
(*c*) Raja Suraj Bhan (*d*) Raja Satyapal

35. Which of the following provinces of Haryana extended valuable cooperation to the British army in the revolt of 1857?
(*a*) Bahadurgarh (*b*) Tawaroo
(*c*) Jhajjhar (*d*) Jind

36. In the second Calcutta session of the Indian National Congress held in the year 1886, Haryana was represented by:
(*a*) Pandit Deen Dayal Sharma
(*b*) Lala Murlidhar
(*c*) Bal Mukund Gupta
(*d*) All of these

37. Lala Lajpat Rai had selected which of the following places situated in Haryana as his political and social work-field?
(*a*) Hissar (*b*) Sonipat
(*c*) Gurugram (*d*) Nooh

38. In the fourth session of the Indian National Congress held in 1888 at Allahabad who of the following national leaders represented Hissar?
(*a*) Lala Sultan Singh (*b*) Baldeo Singh
(*c*) Lala Lajpat Rai (*d*) Baini Singh

39. On 8 April, 1919, Gandhiji was arrested from which of the following places of Haryana?
(*a*) Kaithal (*b*) Palwal
(*c*) Gohana (*d*) Ambala

40. When was a conference held at Rohtak presided by Pt. Rambhaj Dutta in which a decision was taken to implement the Non-cooperation movement launched by Gandhiji?
(*a*) January, 1919 (*b*) November, 1919
(*c*) November, 1920 (*d*) September, 1921

41. In the annual session of Congress held at Nagpur, Haryana was represented by :
(*a*) Sardar Buta Singh (*b*) Lala Ugrasen
(*c*) Babu Shyam Lal (*d*) Pt. Neki Ram Sharma

42. On the appeal of Punjab Pradesh Congress, Independence Day was celebrated in entire Haryana on:
(*a*) 12 January, 1932 (*b*) 10 December, 1932
(*c*) 15 August, 1935 (*d*) 26 January, 1932

43. On which day was the Golden Jubilee of Congress celebrated in Haryana?
(*a*) 18 August, 1930 (*b*) 30 January, 1935
(*c*) 28 December, 1935 (*d*) 10 December, 1936

44. Who of the following was the great hero of Haryana who as a member of the INA hoisted the tricoloured flag for the first time on the land of Manipur?
(*a*) Major Pratap Singh (*b*) Major Suraj Mal
(*c*) Darbara Singh (*d*) Bhajan Lal

45. Chaudhary Chhotu Ram started a vigorous campaigns to popularize the Unionist Party in Haryana. In Haryana state this Party was called as:
(*a*) Zamindara League (*b*) Zamindari System
(*c*) Hindu-Muslim (*d*) None of these

46. Publication of which of the following weekly magazine was started by Chaudhary Chhotu Ram in 1916 from Rohtak?
(*a*) Hindu Gazette (*b*) Sikh Gazette
(*c*) Jat Gazette (*d*) None of the above

47. Chaudhary Chhotu Ram alongwith Shri Fazali Hussain set up the Unionist Party in Punjab in:
(*a*) 1919 (*b*) 1921
(*c*) 1922 (*d*) 1923

48. With a view to keep a control on the political activities in Patiala, Jind and Nabha states, a law was enforced in Samvat 1988 Vikrami. What was that law termed as:
(*a*) Hidayat Samvat (*b*) Hizri Samvat
(*c*) Vikram Samvat (*d*) Saka Samvat

49. In 1938, Jind Prajamandal was set up at Sangrur, the capital of Jind by:
(*a*) Rajendra Kumar Jain (*b*) Sadhu Ram
(*c*) Hansraj Rahbar (*d*) Nand Kishore

50. Gandhji was arrested from Palwal on:
(*a*) 5 January, 1919 (*b*) 8 May, 1920
(*c*) 8 April, 1919 (*d*) 17 April, 1921

51. Pt. Deen Dayal Sharma who made a very important contribution in popularizing Sanatan Dharma in whole of the Northern India, hailed from which of the following places of Haryana?
(*a*) Jhajjhar (*b*) Kaithal
(*c*) Hissar (*d*) Jind

52. In the Lahore Session of the Congress in 1892, Hissar was represented by:
(*a*) Balmukund Gupta (*b*) Lala Murlidhar
(*c*) Lala Lajpat Rai (*d*) Pt. Deen Dayal Sharma

53. When was Lala Lajpat Rai and Sardar Ajit Singh were arrested by the British Government and sent to Mandley Jail?
(*a*) In 1907 (*b*) In 1895
(*c*) In 1902 . (*d*) In 1896

54. Mahatma Gandhi accompanied with Muhammad Ali and Shaukat Ali arrived Rohtak on:
(*a*) 10 January, 1919 (*b*) 8 October, 1920
(*c*) 1 October, 1920 (*d*) 18 March, 1920

55. The Divisional Political Conference of Ambala Division which was attended by Mahatma Gandhi alongwith Ali brothers, was held at Bhiwani in:
(*a*) March, 1918 (*b*) June, 1920
(*c*) October, 1919 (*d*) October, 1920

56. Even after India became free in 1947, Haryana remained a part of which of the following Indian Provinces?
(*a*) Delhi (*b*) Punjab
(*c*) Uttra Pradesh (*d*) Rajasthan

57. The state Restructuring Commission set up in 1955 by the Government of India had recommended to include which of the following two places in the state of Haryana?
(*a*) Mahendragarh and Jind (*b*) Patiala and Hissar
(*c*) Panipat and Kaithal (*d*) Rohtak and Gurugram

58. The tourist place called 'Tiliyar' is situated in which of the following districts of Haryana?
(*a*) Jind (*b*) Mahendragarh
(*c*) Rohtak (*d*) Kaithal

59. Who was the first Governor of Haryana?
(*a*) Shri Satyapal (*b*) Shri Dharmvir
(*c*) Shri Devilal (*d*) Shri Bansilal

60. Name of the first Non-Congress Chief Minister of Haryana who assumed this office on 24 March, 1967.
(*a*) Chaudhary Bhajan Lal (*b*) Devi Lal
(*c*) Bansi Lal (*d*) Rao Virendra Singh

61. Which of the following Rivers flow from the adjoining areas of Eastern Haryana and Uttar Pradesh?
(*a*) Ganga (*b*) Saraswati
(*c*) Ghaghghar (*d*) Yamuna

62. The main land of Haryana state stretches from 27° 39° N to 30° 55° N latitudes in the North-West of India. It stretches from .... E to .... E longitudes.
(*a*) 74° 28° E to 77° 36° E (*b*) 65° 33° E to 77° 28° E
(*c*) 50° 28° E to 64° 36° E (*d*) 84° 42° E to 89° 41° E

63. Which of the following states is located to the North of Haryana?
(*a*) Uttar Pradesh (*b*) Punjab
(*c*) Himachal Pradesh (*d*) Rajasthan

64. Which of the following states is located to the west of Haryana?
(*a*) Punjab (*b*) Rajasthan
(*c*) Uttar Pradesh (*d*) Himachal Pradesh

65. What is the area of the state of Haryana?
(*a*) 36,154 Sq. km. (*b*) 44,212 Sq. km.
(*c*) 49,105 Sq. km. (*d*) 51,206 Sq. km.

66. Which of the following state is not larger than Haryana by area?
(*a*) Meghalaya (*b*) Bihar
(*c*) Himachal Pradesh (*d*) Punjab

67. Dabwali is a subdivision of which district?
(*a*) Sirsa (*b*) Hissar
(*c*) Rohtak (*d*) Jhajjar

68. The mainland of Haryana is located at the height of .... from the sea level.
(*a*) 700 to 900 ft. (*b*) 750 to 880 ft.
(*c*) 800 to 1000 ft. (*d*) 900 to 1100 ft.

69. Shivalik range is located in which part of Haryana?
(*a*) North-West (*b*) North-East
(*c*) South-West (*d*) South-East

70. Which of the following rivers originate from Shivalik range to flow through the mainland of Haryana?
(*a*) Ghaghghar (*b*) Markanda
(*c*) Tangri (*d*) All of these

71. Which of the following natural parts of Haryana is the largest?
(*a*) the hilly region of the Shivalik
(*b*) the desert of Haryana
(*c*) the mainland of Haryana
(*d*) the dry plains of Aravali range

72. The famous Bibipur and Najafgarh lakes are located in which natural part of Haryana?
(*a*) The Plain
(*b*) The desert
(*c*) Hilly region of the Shivalik
(*d*) The dry plain of Aravali range

73. Which of the following cities of Haryana is not the part of National Capital Region?
(*a*) Sonipat (*b*) Faridabad
(*c*) Hisar (*d*) Gurugram

74. Which part of Haryana experiences maximum rainfall?
(*a*) South-Western Part (*b*) North-Eastern Part
(*c*) North-Western Part (*d*) South-Eastern Part

75. Which of the following parts of Haryana experiences minimum annual rainfall?
(*a*) North-Eastern Part (*b*) South-Eastern Part
(*c*) North-Western Part (*d*) South-Western Part

76. Which type of soil is found on Morney hills of the state?
(*a*) Sandy Soil (*b*) Brownish Soil
(*c*) Laterite Soil (*d*) Sandy Clayee Soil

77. Generally, which type of soil is found in the plains of Haryana?
(*a*) Fertile Soil of Yellow brownish colour
(*b*) Laterite Soil
(*c*) Sandy Soil
(*d*) Sandy Clayee Soil

78. In which of the following districts of Haryana, red
(*a*) Rohtak (*b*) Sirsa
(*c*) Yamuna Nagar (*d*) Bhivani

79. Which of the following rivers of the state of Haryana joins Markanda river near Mulana?
(*a*) Sahibi (*b*) Tangri
(*c*) Krishnawati (*d*) Dohan

80. Which of the following is the oldest and the most important canal of Haryana?
(*a*) Gurugram Canal (*b*) Bhiwani Canal
(*c*) Bhakra Canal (*d*) Western Yamuna Canal

81. Which of the following canals originates from the Yamuna river near Tazewala situated on the Jagadhari-Pona road?
(*a*) Bhakra Canal
(*b*) Western and Eastern Yamuna Canal
(*c*) Jawahar Lal Nehru Canal
(*d*) None of these

82. Jawahar Lal Nehru canal of Haryana originates from:
(*a*) Bhakra Canal (*b*) Bhiwani Canal
(*c*) Gurugram Canal (*d*) Yamuna Canal

83. Which of the following lakes is located in Haryana?
(*a*) Damdama Lake (*b*) Kotla Lake
(*c*) Khalilpur Lake (*d*) All of these

84. Which of the following lakes is situated in Farrukh Nagar block of the state?
(*a*) Sultanpur lake (*b*) Damdama lake
(*c*) Khalilpur lake (*d*) Kotla lake

85. The famous Badkal lake is situated in which of the following districts of Haryana?
(*a*) Gurugram (*b*) Bhivani
(*c*) Faridabad (*d*) Rohtak

86. Which of the following canals of Haryana originates from Yamuna river at Okhla in Delhi?
(*a*) Bhakra Canal (*b*) Gurugram Canal
(*c*) Eastern Yamuna Canal (*d*) None of these

87. Bhakra Canal provides water for irrigation in which of the following districts of Haryana?
(*a*) Sirsa (*b*) Hissar
(*c*) Rohtak (*d*) All of these

88. Which of the following districts of the state gets water for irrigation from Jawahar Lal Nehru Canal?
(*a*) Sirsa (*b*) Rohtak
(*c*) Mahendragarh (*d*) Jind

89. Bhiwani canal originates from which of the following canals?
(*a*) Bhakra Canal (*b*) Gurugram Canal
(*c*) Western Yamuna Canal (*d*) Eastern Yamuna Canal

90. When was the famous Badkal lake of Haryana built?
(*a*) In 1940 (*b*) In 1950
(*c*) In 1974 (*d*) In 1947

91. The famous tourist place 'Tajewala Headworks' is situated in which of the following districts of Haryana?
(*a*) Rohtak (*b*) Faridabad
(*c*) Gurugram (*d*) Yamuna Nagar

92. Haryana has been divided into:
(*a*) 6 Divisions (*b*) 5 Sub Divisions
(*c*) 4 Divisions (*d*) 8 Divisions

93. How many total sub-divisions exist in Haryana state till January, 2025?
(*a*) 60 Sub-Divisions (*b*) 65 Sub-Divisions
(*c*) 68 Sub-Divisions (*d*) 80 Sub-Divisions

94. How many total Tehsils exist in Haryana till January, 2025?
(*a*) 94 (*b*) 68
(*c*) 70 (*d*) 85

95. How many total sub-Tehsils exist in Haryana till January, 2025?
(*a*) 30 (*b*) 31
(*c*) 49 (*d*) 40

96. How many total Blocks exist in Haryana till January, 2025?
(*a*) 95 (*b*) 143
(*c*) 115 (*d*) 119

97. Total number of populated villages in Haryana is:
(*a*) 4,390 (*b*) 4,950
(*c*) 5,845 (*d*) 6,841

98. According to the Census of 2011, the total population of Haryana is:
(*a*) 2,53,51,462 (*b*) 2,40,55,400
(*c*) 2,25,83,912 (*d*) 2,20,45,657

99. Salarganj Gate is situated near which of the following town of Haryana?
(*a*) Rohtak (*b*) Hissar
(*c*) Panipat (*d*) Ambala

100. In terms of area the largest district of Haryana is:
(*a*) Rohtak (*b*) Sirsa
(*c*) Panipat (*d*) Ambala

101. Which of the following minerals is found in abundance in Mahendragarh district of Haryana?
(*a*) Lime stone (*b*) China clay
(*c*) Copper (*d*) All of these

102. At which of the following places in district Rewari, Slate-stone is found in abundance?
(*a*) Kund (*b*) Baval
(*c*) Kusal (*d*) Khol

103. Consider the following statements:
1. Nada Sahib Gurudwara is situated in Ambala.
2. Nada Sahib Gurudwara is situated on the bank of river Ghaggar.

Which of the above statements is/are correct?
(*a*) 2 only (*b*) Both 1 and 2
(*c*) Neither 1 nor 2 (*d*) 1 only

104. At which of the following places in district Bhiwani Granite stones are found?
(*a*) Village Nigana Kalan (*b*) Delheri
(*c*) Riwasa (*d*) All of these

105. When was Shri Krishna Museum established in Kurukshetra?
(*a*) 1987 (*b*) 1970
(*c*) 1989 (*d*) 1995

106. What is the area of the total forest land in Haryana?
(*a*) 1,428 Sq. km. (*b*) 1,614.26 Sq. km.
(*c*) 1,852 Sq. km. (*d*) 1,812 Sq. km.

107. During which of the following years, a comprehensive afforestation scheme 'Greening of Haryana' was started?
(*a*) 1982 - 83 (*b*) 1983 - 86
(*c*) 1989 - 90 (*d*) 1994 - 95

108. Haryana has announced its new Industrial Policy in ....
(*a*) 1995 (*b*) 2011
(*c*) 2005 (*d*) 2002

109. With the aid of the European Union "Haryana Community Development Scheme" (Haryana Samudayiki) was introduced in Haryana in:
(*a*) 1992 - 93 (*b*) 1994 - 95
(*c*) 1996 - 97 (*d*) 1998 - 99

110. Basai wetland is located in which district of Haryana?
(*a*) Gurugram (*b*) Jhajjar
(*c*) Faridabad (*d*) Kurukshetra

111. As per census 2011, literacy of Haryana is:
(*a*) 80.40% (*b*) 65.72%
(*c*) 75.6% (*d*) 68.85%

112. Which of the following tourist place is situated on Samauli Road Panipat?
(*a*) Jyotisar (*b*) Kala Amb
(*c*) Damdama Lake (*d*) King Fisher

113. Which of the following minerals is found in districts Hissar and Karnal?
(*a*) Pig Iron (*b*) Mica
(*c*) Nitre (*d*) Marble

114. Which of the following minerals is found in Rohtak district?
(*a*) Lime (*b*) Copper
(*c*) Manganese (*d*) Mica

115. Which of the following trees are found in abundance in Jind district of Haryana?
(*a*) Rosewood tree (Sesam) (*b*) Acacia tree (Kikar)
(*c*) Safeda (*d*) All of these

116. In the Agricultural University, Hissar 'research on Paddy' was started in:
(*a*) 1966 (*b*) 1970
(*c*) 1974 (*d*) 1989

117. Where is National Cancer Institute situated?
(*a*) Sampla (*b*) Meham
(*c*) Kalanaur (*d*) Badsa

118. Which of the following districts of Haryana is pre-eminent in the production of mushroom (Khumbhi) in India?
(*a*) Ambala (*b*) Sirsa
(*c*) Sonepat (*d*) Yamuna Nagar

119. Which of the following is a major crop produced in Rohtak district of Haryana?
(*a*) Pearl Millet (*b*) Great Millet
(*c*) Sugar cane (*d*) All of these

120. Sugar Mill is located at which of the following places in Kurukshetra?
(*a*) Pehwa (*b*) Shahabad Markanda
(*c*) Ladawa (*d*) Babain

121. Which of the following districts of Haryana is called "a big bowl of paddy" as it has gained world fame in the production of Basmati rice?
(*a*) Hissar (*b*) Kurukshetra
(*c*) Karnal (*d*) Jind

122. Navagrah temple in Haryana is located at ....
(*a*) Kurukshetra (*b*) Kaithal
(*c*) Gurugram (*d*) Faridabad

123. The total installed capacity of energy available to the state till 2023-24 is ....
(*a*) 8,575 MW (*b*) 8,200 MW
(*c*) 14,026.68 MW (*d*) 9,510 MW

124. What was the quantum of production of horticulture crops in Haryana during 2023-24?
(*a*) 41.20 Lakh M.T. (*b*) 85.63 Lakh M.T.
(*c*) 62.15 Lakh M.T. (*d*) 52.25 Lakh M.T.

125. In which of the following districts of Haryana, with a view to check the soil erosion in Shivalik areas, coordinated water flow Development Project is being implemented?
(*a*) Ambala (*b*) Panchkula
(*c*) Yamuna Nagar (*d*) All of these

126. Indira Gandhi Super Thermal Power Project is situated in which district of Haryana?
(*a*) Sirsa (*b*) Hisar
(*c*) Jind (*d*) Jhajjar

127. In the Ambala district of Haryana, canal irrigation system was made available after completion of which of the following irrigation project?
(*a*) Nangal Lift Irrigation Project
(*b*) Hathni Reservoir Barrage Project
(*c*) Jawahar Lal Nehru Irrigation Project
(*d*) Sewani Lift Irrigation Project

128. Which of the following system of irrigation is used in the sandy plains of Haryana?
(*a*) Canal
(*b*) Well
(*c*) With the help of Tubewell-Fountain irrigation
(*d*) Rain water

129. Water from western Yamuna Canal is used for irrigation in which of the following districts of Haryana?
(*a*) Karnal (*b*) Sonepat
(*c*) Rohtak (*d*) All of these

130. Besides Gurugram, in which of the following districts of Haryana water from Gurgaon canal is used for irrigation?
(*a*) Panipat (*b*) Faridabad
(*c*) Sonepat (*d*) Kaithal

131. Hathni Reservoir Barrage Project is related with which of the following districts of Haryana?
(*a*) Yamuna Nagar (*b*) Gurugram
(*c*) Rohtak (*d*) Faridabad

132. Which of the following irrigation projects was launched in Mahendragarh district of Haryana with a view to bring improvement in the field of agriculture?
(*a*) Loharu Lift Irrigation Project
(*b*) Western Yamuna Nagar Scheme
(*c*) J.L.N. Lift Irrigation Project
(*d*) Hathni Reservoir Barrage Project

133. When water was released for the first time from J.L.N. Lift Irrigation Project launched in Mahendragarh district of Haryana?
(*a*) In 1976 (*b*) In 1980
(*c*) In 1982 (*d*) In 1995

134. Which of the following irrigation projects provided irrigation facilities in Swarup Kalauda, Khurl Kalan, Bhikhewala, Kharadwala, Nehra, Fuliya kalan etc. villages of the state?
(*a*) Jhajjhar Lift Irrigation Project
(*b*) Nakhana Irrigation Project
(*c*) Nangal Lift Irrigation Project
(*d*) Jawahar Lal Nehru Lift Irrigation Project

135. Which of the following irrigation schemes was launched for providing irrigation facility in Ahriwal region of Haryana?
(*a*) Rewari Lift Irrigation Scheme
(*b*) Hathni Reservoir Barrage Irrigation Scheme
(*c*) Mewat Lift Irrigation Scheme
(*d*) Bhakra Canal Irrigation Scheme

136. The largest Animal Farm of Haryana is situated at which of the following places?
(*a*) Rohtak (*b*) Hissar
(*c*) Panch Kula (*d*) Jind

137. Which of the following breeds of the Buffalo of Haryana is famous in entire India?
(*a*) Murra (*b*) Tura
(*c*) Puspa (*d*) Chassa

138. At which of the following places of Haryana cooperative milk plant has been set up?
(*a*) Ambala (*b*) Bhivani
(*c*) Jind (*d*) All of the above

139. In the Thanesar town of district Kurukshetra, the building for Pouttry disease diagnosis Laboratory was built in:
(*a*) 1980 – 81 (*b*) 1984 – 85
(*c*) 1988 – 89 (*d*) 1995 – 96

140. Besides Nilokheri in Haryana, at which of the following places of the state, training in poultry is imparted?
(*a*) Ambala (*b*) Karnal
(*c*) Hissar (*d*) Kaithal

141. Consider the following statements:
1. Rohtak has a Police Commissionerate located there.
2. Sonipat has a Police Commissionerate located there.

Which of the above statements is/are correct?
(*a*) 2 only (*b*) Both 1 and 2
(*c*) Neither 1 nor 2 (*d*) 1 only

142. Intensive Animal Development project in district Bhivani was launched in:
(*a*) 1966 (*b*) 1970
(*c*) 1972 (*d*) 1978

143. At which place in district Mahendragarh a Semen Bank is located and a liquid Nitrogen Plant has been set-up?
(*a*) Ateli (*b*) Narnaul
(*c*) Nangal Chaudhary (*d*) Mahendragarh

144. In district Bhiwani of Haryana, for diagnosing the diseases in animals the District Village Development Body set up the "Animal Disease Diagnosis Laboratory" in:
(*a*) 1978 (*b*) 1980
(*c*) 1984 (*d*) 1990

145. Haryana gets an average rainfall of ....
(*a*) 100 cms. (*b*) 85 cms.
(*c*) 75 cms. (*d*) 45 cms.

146. The ancient town 'Bery' is situated in which of the following districts of Haryana?
(*a*) Jhajjar (*b*) Yamuna Nagar
(*c*) Karnal (*d*) Kurukshetra

147. Where in Haryana, the National Institute of Fashion Technology is located?
(*a*) Panipat (*b*) Ambala
(*c*) Panchkula (*d*) Kurukshetra

148. The products manufactured by the industrial units of district Yamuna Nagar are exported to which of the following countries?
(*a*) Dubai (*b*) Germany
(*c*) South Africa (*d*) All of the above

149. Saraswati Sugar Mill is located in which of the following districts of Haryana?
(*a*) Rohtak (*b*) Panipat
(*c*) Yamuna Nagar (*d*) Faridabad

150. In Yamuna Nagar, Yanuma Gases Limited was set up in:
(*a*) 1973 (*b*) 1975
(*c*) 1980 (*d*) 1981

51. Yamuna Gases Limited operating in Yamuna Nagar attained a leading position in the production of gases in the year:
(*a*) 1969 (*b*) 1973
(*c*) 1972 (*d*) 1975

52. Bharat Starch Chemical Ltd. was established in Yamuna Nagar in:
(*a*) 1929 (*b*) 1932
(*c*) 1938 (*d*) 1948

153. Before 1947, the Timber Market of Yamuna Nagar was known as:
(*a*) Abdullapur Mandi
(*b*) Sadapur Mandi
(*c*) Yamuna Nagar Mandi
(*d*) Yamuna Pur Mandi

154. Charkhi Dadri was carved out from which district?
(*a*) Bhiwani (*b*) Hissar
(*c*) Sirsa (*d*) Rewari

155. "Bhiwani Textile Mill" in Haryana was established in:
(*a*) 1930 (*b*) 1937
(*c*) 1942 (*d*) 1950

156. In Haryana, where the Vulture Conservation Centre is located?
(*a*) Pinjore (*b*) Jind
(*c*) Mahendragarh (*d*) Ambala

157. The Sahibi river does not flow in which of the following district?
(*a*) Rewari (*b*) Jhajjar
(*c*) Gurugram (*d*) Rohtak

158. Consider the following statements in respect of National Security Guards (NSG):
1. Operational Headquarter of NSG is in Manesar.
2. NSG comes under the control of Union Ministry of Home Affairs.

Which of the above statements is/are correct?
(*a*) 2 only (*b*) Both 1 and 2
(*c*) Neither 1 nor 2 (*d*) 1 only

159. Indian Cement Corporation, A Government of India undertaking, took possession of the factory located at Charkhi-Dadri of Haryana on:
(*a*) 5 April, 1980 (*b*) 23 June, 1981
(*c*) 10 June, 1984 (*d*) 23 June, 1988

160. National Beekeeping and Honey Mission (NBHM) Scheme was started in which year in Haryana?
(*a*) 2017 (*b*) 2018
(*c*) 2019 (*d*) 2020

161. Captive Electricity Plant has been set up in which of the following districts of Haryana?
(*a*) Panipat (*b*) Hissar
(*c*) Rohtak (*d*) Karnal

162. At Baholi of district Panipat which of the following factories has been set up?
(*a*) Cloth Factory
(*b*) Agricultural Implements Factory
(*c*) Oil Refinery
(*d*) Slippers Factory

163. 'Ammonia Plant' has been installed in which of the following districts of Haryana?
(*a*) Panipat (*b*) Kaithal
(*c*) Gurugram (*d*) Karnal

164. District Mahanderagarh ranks first in the state of Haryana in the production of:
(*a*) Rice (*b*) Utensils
(*c*) Mustard (*d*) Bicycle

165. According to the 2011 census sex ratio in the state is ....

(*a*) 787 (*b*) 879
(*c*) 987 (*d*) 973

166. Which of the following industries in Rewari district of Haryana is famous all over India?

(*a*) Shoe Sole Industry
(*b*) Brass Utensil Industry
(*c*) Hero Honda Motor Cycle Factory
(*d*) All of these

167. In addition to Bicycle Factory, which of the following other factories are located in Jind district of Haryana?

(*a*) Utensil Factory (*b*) Textile Factory
(*c*) Sugar Factory (*d*) Leather Shoe Factory

168. According to the 2011 census population density in the state is ....

(*a*) 573 (*b*) 752
(*c*) 482 (*d*) 531

169. Total covered area of the Shri Krishna Museum is:

(*a*) 8764 sq.m. (*b*) 8885 sq.m.
(*c*) 8129 sq.m. (*d*) 8649 sq.m.

170. Which of the following articles manufactured in Karnal district are exported to foreign countries also?

(*a*) Liberty Shoes (*b*) Paint
(*c*) Wooden Furnitures (*d*) Steel Furniture

171. Shahabad Cooperative Sugar Mill in district Kurukshetra was established in:

(*a*) 1976 – 77 (*b*) 1984 – 85
(*c*) 1991 – 92 (*d*) 1994 – 95

172. Which of the following factories have been set up in Faridabad District of Haryana?

(*a*) Tractor Factory (*b*) Refrigerator Factory
(*c*) Rubber Tyre Factory (*d*) All of these

173. In which year the strength of Haryana Assembly was raised to 90?

(*a*) 1977 (*b*) 1967
(*c*) 1971 (*d*) 1985

174. At which of the following places in Haryana Maruti Cars are manufactured?

(*a*) Gurugram (*b*) Ambala
(*c*) Faridabad (*d*) Hissar

175. Which among the following is the highly populated district, as per the 2011 census?

(*a*) Rohtak (*b*) Karnal
(*c*) Gurugram (*d*) Faridabad

176. During which of the following years Government of Haryana decided to confer honour on Freedom Fighters?

(*a*) 1980 (*b*) 1981
(*c*) 1985 (*d*) 1997

177. Which of the following districts of Haryana does not share its boundary with any other state of India?

(*a*) Charkhi Dadri (*b*) Palwal
(*c*) Gurugram (*d*) Jind

178. Skylark Tourist Complex is located at ....

(*a*) Faridabad (*b*) Panipat
(*c*) Karnal (*d*) Rohtak

179. Scheme of granting cash amount, amount payable annually and cash in lieu of land to the soldiers awarded with 'Yuddha Sewa Medal' was discontinued in 1988. This scheme was launched again by the Government of Bansi Lal in:

(*a*) April 1995 (*b*) April 1997
(*c*) April 1996 (*d*) April 1998

180. Chaudhary Devi Lal University in Haryana is located at:

(*a*) Hissar (*b*) Karnal
(*c*) Sirsa (*d*) Panipat

181. Who among the following was not the chief minister of Haryana?

(*a*) Babu Parmanand (*b*) B.D. Gupta
(*c*) Devi Lal (*d*) Hukum Singh

182. National Dairy Research Institute is located at ....

(*a*) Karnal (*b*) Hissar
(*c*) Sirsa (*d*) Rohtak

183. Who was the first governor of Haryana?

(*a*) R.S. Narula (*b*) G.D. Tapse
(*c*) Dharamvir (*d*) B.D. Sharma

184. Hostel for the boys of Scheduled Castes who are engaged in unclean occupation is located at:

(*a*) Karnal (*b*) Faridabad
(*c*) Ambala (*d*) All of these

185. Hostel for the boys of exempted castes is located at :

(*a*) Rohtak (*b*) Jind
(*c*) Faridabad (*d*) Gurugram

186. Legal provisions for ban on liquor were enforced in Haryana on:

(*a*) 1 December, 1991 (*b*) 1 June, 1993
(*c*) 1 July, 1996 (*d*) 1 May, 1997

187. Ban on the sale of liquor was lifted by the state government on:

(*a*) 1 May, 1996 (*b*) 1 May, 1997
(*c*) 1 February, 1996 (*d*) 1 April, 1998

188. Which of the following Child Development Projects is related with the State of Haryana?

(*a*) Coordinated Child Development Project
(*b*) Child Health Project
(*c*) Infant Nutrition Programme
(*d*) Helpless Child Development Project

189. Which of the following schemes are being run for the welfare of the girls belonging to poor families?

(*a*) Paraya Dhan Parayee Beti
(*b*) Apni Beti Paraya Dhan
(*c*) Apni Beti Apna Dhan
(*d*) None of these

190. The total length of National Highway in Haryana till November, 2024 is:
(*a*) 1900 kms. (*b*) 1503 kms.
(*c*) 1800 kms. (*d*) 3391 kms.

191. Each and every village of the State of Haryana became electrified on:
(*a*) 10 June, 1966 (*b*) 25 March, 1971
(*c*) 15 April, 1968 (*d*) 29 November, 1970

192. Aruna is the ancient name of which river?
(*a*) Markanda (*b*) Sahibi
(*c*) Ghaggar (*d*) Yamuna

193. Red Soil is found in ....
(*a*) Rohtak (*b*) Sirsa
(*c*) Karnal (*d*) Bihwani

194. With a view to bring improvement in the availability of electricity in Southern Haryana, a new 50 km long single circuit line has been laid from :
(*a*) Gurugram to Badshahpur
(*b*) Badshahpur to Rewari
(*c*) Faridabad to Rewari
(*d*) Jind to Kaithal

195. Which one of the following pairs is not correctly matched?
(*a*) Surajkund Lake – Kurukshetra
(*b*) Tilyaar Lake – Rohtak
(*c*) Damdama Lake – Gurugram
(*d*) Badkhal Lake – Faridabad

196. Sultanpur Lake is located in which district?
(*a*) Bhiwani (*b*) Mahendragarh
(*c*) Gurugram (*d*) Rewari

197. According to the demands made by farmers, which of the following systems for electricity on the basis of the depth of tubewells has been adopted in the entire state?
(*a*) Stove System
(*b*) Electricity Measurement System
(*c*) Test System
(*d*) None of these

198. Thermal Power Station is located at which of the following places in Haryana?
(*a*) Hissar (*b*) Kaithal
(*c*) Jind (*d*) Faridabad

199. At which of the following places, the Power Plant of 432 MW based on Gas has been installed by NTPC in Haryana?
(*a*) Gurugram (*b*) Faridabad
(*c*) Panipat (*d*) Karnal

200. What is the total length of road in Haryana till November, 2024?
(*a*) 33,453 km (*b*) 24,065 km
(*c*) 25,074 km (*d*) 40,760 km

201. The strength of Legislative Assembly of Haryana is ....
(*a*) 102 (*b*) 110
(*c*) 75 (*d*) 90

202. Where is Nahar Wildlife Sanctuary is situated?
(*a*) Ambala (*b*) Sonipat
(*c*) Rewari (*d*) Yamunanagar

203. When the Public Transport in Haryana was brought under the possession of the Government?
(*a*) In 1972 (*b*) In 1976
(*c*) In 1980 (*d*) In 1985

204. 'Rao Tej Singh Pond' is located in:
(*a*) Panipat (*b*) Sonipat
(*c*) Palwal (*d*) Rewari

205. The Magazine of Haryana Sahitya Academy is:
(*a*) Harigandha (*b*) Haryana Samvad
(*c*) Haryana Sandesh (*d*) Panchajanya

206. While travelling on the National Highway from Delhi to Ferozepur, which of the following important town of Haryana comes on the way:
(*a*) Rohtak (*b*) Sirsa
(*c*) Hissar (*d*) All of these

207. Manu Bhaker of Haryana is related with which sports?
(*a*) Badminton (*b*) Boxing
(*c*) Shooting (*d*) Wrestling

208. Which of the following tourist places is situated at Bahadurgarh in Haryana?
(*a*) Dairango Tourist Place (*b*) Gureya
(*c*) Jal Tarang (*d*) Tiliyar

209. In Haryana, in addition to Hissar, Karnal, Bhiwani, Narnaul and Jind, at which of the following airports metalled run-way has been built?
(*a*) Panipat (*b*) Pinjore
(*c*) Faridabad (*d*) Rewari

210. Where is Tilyar lake is situated?
(*a*) Rohtak (*b*) Gurugram
(*c*) Jind (*d*) Faridabad

211. At which of the following places in Haryana, Heavy Vehicle Driving Training Institute is located?
(*a*) Murthal (*b*) Charkhi-Dadri
(*c*) Ambala (*d*) Tawaroo

212. In Shivalik hills near Pinjore-Kalka in Haryana, utensils have been found which pertain to which of the following ages?
(*a*) Stone Age (*b*) Later Vedic Age
(*c*) Harappan Age (*d*) Early Vedic Age

213. In the treatise named "Avanti Sunderi Katha" Vaivast Manu who is known as the father of human beings is said to be the resident of which of the following places?
(*a*) Panipat (*b*) Rohtak
(*c*) Sthaneshwar (*d*) Panchkula

214. Evidences found from the excavations done at Banwali, Siswal, Kunal, Mirzapur, Daulatpur and Bhagawanpura in the state of Haryana revealed links dating back to:

(a) Early Harappan Culture
(b) Mature Harappan Culture
(c) Late Harappan Culture
(d) All of the above phases

215. Who of the following started archaeological survey in Haryana for the first time?
(a) Sir John (b) Alexander Kaningham
(c) Lord Munro (d) John Marshall

216. Archaeological Survey in Haryana started in:
(a) 1862 (b) 1892
(c) 1900 (d) 1905

217. Under the supervision of Dr. Suraj Bhan, excavations at which of the following places of Haryana brought out very valuable historical evidences?
(a) Mithathal (b) Dadri
(c) Ailanabad (d) Safidon

218. From which of the following sites of Haryana, evidences have been found for the first time regarding co-existence of the people of Late Harappan culture and Painted Grey Ware (PGW) culture?
(a) Narnaul (b) Bhagwanpura
(c) Sirsa (d) Mahendragarh

219. A great mound pertaining to Harappan culture is situated at which of the following places in district Jind of Haryana?
(a) Safidon (b) Uchana
(c) Narwana (d) Rakhigarhi

220. Remains of a Stupa have been found at Chaneti which is situated three kilometers east of Jagadhari. Height of this Stupa is 8 m. Its periphery is:
(a) 20 m (b) 30 m
(c) 45 m (d) 50 m

221. Consider the following statements:
1. Sonipat and Jhajjar share border with Delhi.
2. Rohtak does not share border with Delhi.
Which of the above statements is/are correct?
(a) 2 only (b) Both 1 and 2
(c) Neither 1 nor 2 (d) 1 only

222. A battle axe type Gold Coin which pertains to the age of Samudra Gupta has been found at which of the following places in Haryana?
(a) Kosali (b) Rohana
(c) Mithathal (d) Raniya

223. Which of the following areas of Haryana was under the control of Yudheyas during the 3rd century A.D.?
(a) Panipat (b) Rohtak
(c) Hissar (d) Ambala

224. The Gold Coin obtained from Jagadhari pertains to which of the following emperors of the ancient India?
(a) Kanishka (b) Kumar Gupta
(c) Pushyamitra Sunga (d) Samudragupta

225. From which of the following places in Haryana, copper coin of the age of Harsha Vardhan has been found which contains an account of Pushyabhuti dynasty of Thanesar?
(a) Sonepat (b) Sirsa
(c) Gurugram (d) Kaithal

226. At which of the following places located in district Hissar of Haryana excavations was done by Shri H.L. Srivastava of Archaeo-logical Survey of India?
(a) Uklana (b) Fatehabad
(c) Agroha (d) Adampur

227. What is the total number of Primary and Pre Primary Schools in Haryana till 2023-24?
(a) 9,872 (b) 9,399
(c) 11,582 (d) 8,780

228. What is the total number of Middle Schools in Haryana till 2023-24?
(a) 6,215 (b) 2,312
(c) 5,640 (d) 3,850

229. In Haryana 'Brahma Sarovar' is located in:
(a) Palwal (b) Kurukshetra
(c) Panipat (d) Sonipat

230. 'Uchana' is located in:
(a) Jind (b) Karnal
(c) Rohtak (d) Faridabad

231. The tenure of nagarpalika, municipality or municipal corporation in Haryana is ....
(a) 3 years (b) 1 year
(c) 4 years (d) 5 years

232. What is the area of Sirsa district?
(a) 4,277 sq.km (b) 5,780 sq.km
(c) 3,760 sq.km (d) 2,765 sq.km

233. What is the total number of literate people in Haryana?
(a) 1,66,25,728 (b) 1,65,98,988
(c) 1,78,10,882 (d) 1,32,58,652

234. The historical monument known as the corridor Chhatta of Rai Mukund Das (Birbal Ka Chhatta) is in:
(a) Panipat (b) Karnal
(c) Kaithal (d) Narnaul

235. Navodaya Vidyalaya is situated at which of the following places in the state?
(a) Titaram (Kurukshetra) (b) Odha (Sirsa)
(c) Deorala (Bhiwani) (d) All of these

236. During which of the following years Government of Haryana introduced 10+2+3 system of Education in Haryana?
(a) 1980 - 81 (b) 1976 - 77
(c) 1988 - 89 (d) 1985 - 86

237. M.D. University is located in which of the following towns of Haryana?
(a) Rohtak (b) Hissar
(c) Faridabad (d) Rewari

238. Chaudhary Charan Singh Agricultural University is located in which of the following towns of the state?
(*a*) Jind (*b*) Gurugram
(*c*) Hissar (*d*) Kurukshetra

239. In order to promote Punjabi language in Haryana it has been made the .... language of the state.
(*a*) First (*b*) Second
(*c*) Third (*d*) Fourth

240. Chaudhary Devilal University is located in which of the following towns of Haryana?
(*a*) Kurukshetra (*b*) Hissar
(*c*) Rohtak (*d*) Sirsa

241. In order to give promotion to sports in Haryana, the State Government has launched which of the following important schemes?
(*a*) Providing Grant in aid to the Sports Institutions
(*b*) Training Scheme
(*c*) Sports Stadium
(*d*) All of the above

242. In order to impart training to the players through modern and scientific methods, at which of the following places of Haryana a sports hostel has been set up?
(*a*) Gurugram (*b*) Rohtak
(*c*) Faridabad (*d*) Panipat

243. A sports school is situated at Rai in Sonepat district of Haryana. What is the name of this sports school?
(*a*) Jawahar Lal Nehru Sports School
(*b*) Indira Gandhi Sports School
(*c*) Moti Lal Nehru Sports School
(*d*) Rajiv Gandhi Sports School

244. Kamla Nehru School situated in the premises of Moti Lal Nehru Sports School at Rai in Sonepat district was established in
(*a*) 1970 (*b*) 1974
(*c*) 1982 (*d*) 1986

245. Haryana Shehari Vikas Pradhikaran (HSVP), formerly Haryana Urban Development Authority (HUDA) was constituted in ....
(*a*) 1977 (*b*) 1972
(*c*) 1970 (*d*) 1966

246. Who has variously been described as Plato of Jat Tribes?
(*a*) Suraj Mal (*b*) Churaman
(*c*) Raja Ram Bhajja (*d*) None of these

247. Khoria dance is famous in ....
(*a*) Eastern Haryana (*b*) Western Haryana
(*c*) Central Haryana (*d*) Northern Haryana

248. Which player of Haryana won gold medal in Tokyo Olympics 2020?
(*a*) Bajarang Punia (*b*) Neeraj Chopra
(*c*) Ravi Kumar (*d*) Vijendra Singh

249. The Haryana Shawl is known as ....
(*a*) Phulkari (*b*) Ghagra
(*c*) Iungis (*d*) Bagh

250. The famous story writer of Hindi Shri Vishvambhar Nath Kaushik was born in Haryana at
(*a*) Ambala Cantt (*b*) Sirsa
(*c*) Panchkula (*d*) Rohtak

251. Famous writer of Haryana Pt. Neki Ram Sharma had brought out which of the following papers from Bhiwani?
(*a*) Samvahak (*b*) Sandesh
(*c*) Nivaran (*d*) Vani

252. Who of the following players of Indian Cricket hails from Haryana?
(*a*) Kapil Dev (*b*) Sunil Gavaskar
(*c*) Ajay Jadeja (*d*) Azharuddin

253. The Cricket Test Match in which Kapil Dev of Haryana took 432nd wicket to make a record of taking maximum number of wickets was held on
(*a*) 10 January, 1992 (*b*) 8 December, 1996
(*c*) 8 February, 1994 (*d*) 12 August, 1997

254. Kapil Dev announced to abandon the international cricket on
(*a*) 6 November, 1993 (*b*) 2 November, 1994
(*c*) 18 November, 1997 (*d*) 15 November, 1998

255. Who of the following players of Haryana is not related with Gymnastic?
(*a*) Sunita Sharma (*b*) Sandhya
(*c*) Nirmala Guliya (*d*) Geeta Jutshi

256. Who of the following first ever poet is considered a native poet of Haryana?
(*a*) Goswami Tulsi Das (*b*) Kabir Das
(*c*) Kavi Chandbardai (*d*) Rahim Das

257. Who of the following Muslim Saints of Haryana had made significant contributions in the development of Hindi literature?
(*a*) Shekh-U-Alishaha Kalander
(*b*) Saint Sadullah
(*c*) Shekh Bahauddin Chishti
(*d*) All of these

258. Who of the following first ever poet is not related with Haryana?
(*a*) Virbhan (*b*) Mahatma Haridas
(*c*) Banarsi Das (*d*) Narottam Das

259. Haryana got the status of a full state on
(*a*) 1 November, 1964 (*b*) 10 December, 1965
(*c*) 1 November, 1966 (*d*) 15 June, 1968

260. The capital city of Haryana is
(*a*) Chandigarh (*b*) Rohtak
(*c*) Karnal (*d*) Yamuna Nagar

261. With a view to administrative convenience, Haryana has been divided into
(*a*) Three Divisions (*b*) Six Divisions
(*c*) Five Divisions (*d*) Four Divisions

262. The number of Districts in Haryana is
(*a*) 16 (*b*) 17
(*c*) 18 (*d*) 22

263. The tourist place called Oasis is situated at which of the following places in Haryana?
(*a*) Faridabad (*b*) Bhiwani
(*c*) Uchchhana (*d*) Rewari

264. Which of the following famous tourist place of Haryana is located at a distance of about 20 kms from Delhi?
(*a*) Suraj Kund (*b*) Red Robin
(*c*) Paracot (*d*) Damdama Lake

265. In vast rocky areas extended to the west of Faridabad by the Delhi-Mathura National Highway which of the following tourist place is situated?
(*a*) Damdama Lake (*b*) Badkhal Lake
(*c*) King Fisher (*d*) Dabchik

266. Between the hills of Arawali on Delhi-Alwar road which of the following famous tourist place of Haryana is located?
(*a*) Shama (*b*) Blue-ze
(*c*) Sohana (*d*) Dairangon

267. Who had discovered the Sultanpur Bird Sanctuary of Haryana situated on Gurugram Farrukh Nagar road?
(*a*) Peter Jackson (*b*) Thomar Roe
(*c*) Sir John Marshall (*d*) Robin Hood

268. On the Gurugram-Farrukhabad road which of the following tourist places of Haryana is situated?
(*a*) Dab-bich
(*b*) Sultanpur Bird Sanctuary
(*c*) Oasis
(*d*) Red Robin

269. The Turban worn by male in Haryana is called
(*a*) Khandwa (*b*) Paggada
(*c*) Toda (*d*) Pagari

270. The tourist centre called 'Shama' is situated at which of the following towns of Haryana?
(*a*) Faridabad (*b*) Kaithal
(*c*) Gurugram (*d*) Jind

271. In Haryana, the skirt worn by females from waist to ankle which is without any gusset and made of hand-spun coarse cloth knitted by using four blue and four red threads is called
(*a*) Dharna (*b*) Khara
(*c*) Thara (*d*) Kachara

272. Which of the following ornaments used in the state is not worn around neck?
(*a*) Hansla (*b*) Fool
(*c*) Galshree (*d*) Batan

273. Which of the following ornaments is worn on face and head on the ladies of the state?
(*a*) Singar Patti (*b*) Tagga
(*c*) Bessar (*d*) All of these

274. Which of the following ornaments used in the state is not worn on nose?
(*a*) Nath (*b*) Purli
(*c*) Dhede (*d*) Kokka

275. Which of the following ornaments used in the state is not worn on hands?
(*a*) Pauhchi (*b*) Kandulla
(*c*) Pachhelli (*d*) Bankri

276. According to the augury, which of the following is considered a good omen in the state of Haryana?
(*a*) A pitcher full of water
(*b*) To have a view of a deer
(*c*) A sweeper with a broom in hand
(*d*) All of the above

277. According to the augury, which of the following is considered a bad omen in the state of the Haryana?
(*a*) Empty pitcher
(*b*) To have a view of grass
(*c*) To experience an itching sensation in feet
(*d*) Meeting with a water carrier carrying water.

278. Which of the traditional ornaments is worn by males in Haryana?
(*a*) Goph (*b*) Tagari
(*c*) Nada (*d*) Kadi

279. At which of the following places of religious importance, lakhs of people from all over India go for a religious ritual on the occurrence of solar eclipse?
(*a*) Gurugram (*b*) Kurukshetra
(*c*) Jagadhari (*d*) None of these

280. At Islampur in the district Gurugram, which of the following festivals (Mela) is organised on the ninth day of Bhado (the sixth month of the year according to the Hindu calendar)?
(*a*) Guga Naumi (*b*) Nag Pooja
(*c*) Yamuna Snan (*d*) Shiv Mela

281. In the months of Chait and Aashadh (respectively the opening and the fourth month of the year according to the Hindu caldendar) in district Gurugram of Haryana on every Monday and Tuesday which of the following famous festivals (Melas) is organised?
(*a*) Buddho Mata Ka Mela
(*b*) Shivji Ka Mela
(*c*) Shitla Mata Ka Mela
(*d*) Baba Buddha Ka Mela

282. In which of the following districts of Haryana famous festivals of Ramṣarai and Bhuteshwar are organised?
(*a*) Faridabad (*b*) Jind
(*c*) Rohtak (*d*) Jhajjhar

283. In the monastery at Asthal Bohar in Rohtak district of Haryana which of the following festivals (Melas) is organised during the months of February and March?
(*a*) Baba Mastnath Ka Mela
(*b*) Kapal Mochan Ka Mela
(*c*) Devi Mela
(*d*) Pathari Mata Ka Mela

284. Which of the following festivals (Melas) is organised on Kartik-Purnima at Bilaspur situated near Jagadhari?
(*a*) Aadi Badri Mela (*b*) Mela Kali Mai
(*c*) Kapal Mochan Mela (*d*) Panchmukhi Mela

285. At Lakhan Majra in Rohtak district "Gurudwara of Manji Sahib" is situated. Here which of the following festivals (Melas) is organised?
(*a*) Festival of Satya Teej
(*b*) Festival of Mohola Halla
(*c*) Bawan Dwadashi
(*d*) Maanu Mela

286. At Pathri in district Sonepat, on every Wednesday in the months of Chait and Aashadh, which of the following festivals (Melas) is organised?
(*a*) Mata Ka Mela (*b*) Shiva Mela
(*c*) Dehati Mela (*d*) Pathri Mata Ka Mela

287. At Kharak Ramji situated in district Jind, which of the following festivals (Melas) is organised on the day of Holi?
(*a*) Mata Ka Mela
(*b*) Nag Devata Ka Mela
(*c*) Baba Bhalu Nath Ka Mela
(*d*) Mela Sachcha Sauda

288. At Dubaldhan Majra in Rohtak district which of the following festivals (Melas) is organised in the months of February-March?
(*a*) Mela Mata (*b*) Mela Devi
(*c*) Mela Shyamji (*d*) Mela Baba Buddha

289. At Khori in the Gurugram district which of the following festivals (Melas) is organised during the months of April-May?
(*a*) Shah Chokha Khori Mela
(*b*) Shiva Ka Mela
(*c*) Nagpooja Ka Mela
(*d*) Baba Mast Nath Ka Mela

290. At which of the following places in district Sonepat, festival (Mela) of Dera Nagn Balaknath is organised during the months of February-March?
(*a*) Bega (Tehsil Sonepat)
(*b*) Mehripur (Tehsil Sonepat)
(*c*) Rabhara (Tehsil Gohana)
(*d*) Chulkana (Tehsil Sonepat)

291. Which of the following festivals (Melas) is oraganised at Khubadu situated in district Sonepat during the months of February-March?
(*a*) Satakumbha Mela (*b*) Mela Baba Shamakshah
(*c*) Mela Sanjhi (*d*) Devi Mela

292. Which amongst the following is the State Tree of Haryana?
(*a*) Sacred Fig (*b*) Mango Tree
(*c*) Sal Tree (*d*) Banyan Tree

293. At which of the following places in Haryana festival (Mela) of Baba Khedewala is organised on the day of Raksha Bandhan?
(*a*) Naurangabad (*b*) Kaharak Kalan
(*c*) Riwasa (*d*) Tosham

294. On which of the following occasions in the state of Haryana auspicious "Piliya" folk song is sung?
(*a*) In the months of July-August
(*b*) On the occasion of the birth of a male child in the family
(*c*) On the occasion of marriage ceremony
(*d*) In the months of February-March

295. On which of the following occasions, in the state of Haryana folk songs are sung?
(*a*) On the occasion of the birth of a male child in the family
(*b*) In the months of July-August
(*c*) On the occasion of a festival
(*d*) On all of the above occasions

296. In the state, males perform which of the following dances in open field at moon-lit night on flute, scooped gourd (Tumbi), etc.?
(*a*) Dhamal Dance (*b*) Manjeera Dance
(*c*) Loor Dance (*d*) Damru Dance

297. Which of the following dance performances is famous in Mewat area of Haryana which is accompanied with beating huge kettle drum, tambourine and cymbals?
(*a*) Ghora Dance (*b*) Dhamal Dance
(*c*) Manjeera Dance (*d*) Chhathi Dance

298. In Bagar area of Haryana which of the following dance performances is famous that is performed during the festival of Holi?
(*a*) Damru Dance (*b*) Manjeera Dance
(*c*) Ghora Dance (*d*) Loor Dance

299. The Ghora folk dance popular in Haryana is generally performed on which of the following occasions?
(*a*) On the occasion of marriage
(*b*) In the month of February-March
(*c*) On the occasion of birth of a male child in the family
(*d*) In the Month of July-August

300. In Haryana, which of the following dances is performed after the worship of Guggapir in the month of August-September?
(*a*) Dhamal Dance (*b*) Chchari Dance
(*c*) Loor Dance (*d*) Damru Dance

301. Which of the following folk dances is performed by women in the state?
(*a*) Teej Dance (*b*) Dhamal Dance
(*c*) Damru Dance (*d*) Khodiya Dance

302. Which dance is performed by males among the following folk dances practised in the state?
(*a*) Chhatthi dance (*b*) Teej dance
(*c*) Damru dance (*d*) Khodia dance

303. Which of the following folk dances is performed by men and women both in the state?
(*a*) Teej Dance (*b*) Loor Dance
(*c*) Khodiya Dance (*d*) Fag Dance

304. Which of the following Gurudwaras is situated near Pratap Gate in Kaithal town of Haryana?
(*a*) Gurudwara Neem Sahib
(*b*) Gurudwara Nauvi Patshahi
(*c*) Ragdhaar Gurudwara
(*d*) Gurudwara Chhathi Patshahi

305. Gurudwara Manji Sahib is situated in which of the following towns of Haryana?
(*a*) Karnal (*b*) Panipat
(*c*) Kaithal (*d*) Ambala

306. Which place in Haryana is called as "Chhoti Kashi" due to presence of "Navagraha Kunds"?
(*a*) Narnaul (*b*) Kaithal
(*c*) Gurugram (*d*) Kurukshetra

307. At a few distance from Kaithal in Haryana the grave of which of the following great men is situated where every year next dayof Dushera a large festival is organised?
(*a*) Baba Kali Kamli Wale
(*b*) Baba Haridas
(*c*) Baba Ladana
(*d*) Baba Ramdas

308. Which of the following famous places of pilgrimage is situated near Thanesar City Station in district Kurukshetra of Haryana?
(*a*) Brahma Sarovar (*b*) Hatakeshwar
(*c*) Dhosi (*d*) Pundarik Sarovar

309. Which of the following places of pilgrimage is situated on the Kurukshetra-Pehwa road near Kurukshetra Railway Station which is considered as the permanent abode of Lord Vishnu?
(*a*) Brahma Sarovar (*b*) Kaleshwar Tirth
(*c*) Sannihit Sarovar (*d*) Markanday Tirth

310. At which place of piligrimage in Kurukshetra district Shri Krishna had preached Arjuna?
(*a*) Brahm Sarovar (*b*) Kamal Nabh Tirth
(*c*) Prachi Tirth (*d*) Jyotishwar Sarovar

311. When did Maharaja Darbhanga build metalled platform around the Akshya Vat located near the Jyotishwar Sarovar situated in district Kurukshetra?
(*a*) In 1924 (*b*) In 1930
(*c*) In 1932 (*d*) In 1949

312. Who had built the Krishna-Arjuna Rath (Chariot) and the temple of Shankaracharya near the Jyotishwar Sarovar situated in district Kurukshetra?
(*a*) Maharaja Darbhanga
(*b*) Shankaracharya of Kam Koti Peeth
(*c*) King of Kashmir
(*d*) Swami Vishuddhananda Maharaj

313. What is the total length of Jyotishwar Sarovar situated in district Kurukshetra?
(*a*) 1000 ft. (*b*) 1500 ft.
(*c*) 2000 ft. (*d*) 2500 ft.

314. Who was the founder of "Baba Kali Kamli Wale Ka Dera" situated in district Kurukshetra?
(*a*) Swami Ram Tirth
(*b*) Shri Swami Vishuddhananda Maharaja
(*c*) Shankaracharya of Kamkoti Peeth
(*d*) Swami Parmananda Maharaj

315. Gaudiya Math (monastery) related with the period of Bhakti movement in India, is situated in which of the following districts of Haryana?
(*a*) Ambala (*b*) Jind
(*c*) Kurukshetra (*d*) Mahendragarh

316. At which of the following places in district Kurukshetra Baba Laxman Giri Maharaj went into eternal trance?
(*a*) Ban Ganga (*b*) Prachi Tirth
(*c*) Gaudiya Math (*d*) Balmiki Aashram

317. Raj Ghat Gurudwara is situated at which of the following places in Haryana?
(*a*) Kurukshetra (*b*) Yamuna Nagar
(*c*) Kaithal (*d*) Bhiwani

318. Which of the following places of pilgrimage is not situated in district Kurukshetra of Haryana?
(*a*) Kalkeshwar Tirth
(*b*) Prachi Tirth
(*c*) Dhosi Tirth
(*d*) Kuber Tirth

319. Which of the following places of pilgrimage is situated at a distance of 1 km. to the North-West of Kurukshetra University in district Kurukshetra of Haryana?
(*a*) Markandya Tirth
(*b*) Narakatari (Anrak Tirth)
(*c*) Prachi Tirth
(*d*) Kuber Tirth

320. Which of the following important places of pilgrimage is situated at a distance of 25 km to the west of Thanesar in Haryana that is given the same importance by the people of Haryana and adjoining areas as is given to Gaya by the people of Eastern region of India?
(*a*) Pehova (*b*) Panchavati
(*c*) Safeedon (*d*) Pandu-Pindara

321. In which district of Haryana the 'National Institute of Animal Genetics' is located?
(*a*) Hisar (*b*) Yamunanagar
(*c*) Karnal (*d*) Rohtak

322. A place of pilgrimage known as "Panchavati" is situated at which of the following districts of Haryana?
(*a*) Ambala (*b*) Jind
(*c*) Kurukshetra (*d*) Palwal

323. Which of the following is an ancient place of pilgrimage located by Jind-Gohana Road near Jind where a fair is organised every year on Somawati Amavasya?
(*a*) Pandu-Pindara
(*b*) Safeedon
(*c*) Hans Daihar
(*d*) None of the above

324. Temple of Sthaneshwar Mahadeva situated at a distance of a few kilometres from Thanesar was built by which of the following kings prior to Harshavardhan?
(*a*) Pushyabhuti (*b*) Adityavardhan
(*c*) Narvardhan (*d*) Prabhakarvardhan

325. Mahmud Ghaznavi during his return course to Ghazni took away with him from Haryana to Ghazni, statue of which of the ancient temple located in Haryana?
(*a*) Dukh Bhanjaneshwar Temple (Kuruk-shetra)
(*b*) Lord Shiva Temple (Narnaul)
(*c*) Sarveshwar Mahadeva Temple (Kuruk-shetra)
(*d*) Sthaneshwar Mahadeva Temple (Thanesar)

326. Sthaneshwar Temple of Haryana was reconstructed by
(*a*) Maratha Sadashiva Rao
(*b*) Chandra Gupta Vikramaditya
(*c*) Harshavardhan
(*d*) Narvardhan

327. Devikoop (Bhadra Kali Temple) is one of the 51 Shakti Peeths (Seats of goddess personifying divine power) of India. This temple is located at which of the following places in the state?
(*a*) Rohtak (*b*) Kurukshetra
(*c*) Panipat (*d*) Thanesar

328. Which of the following temples is situated near Sannihit Sarovar in Kurukshetra?
(*a*) Narayana Temple
(*b*) Laxmi Narayan Temple
(*c*) Dukh Bhanjaneshwar Temple
(*d*) Birla Mandir

329. Which of the following temples of Kurukshetra was built by the perfect Saint of Giri Sect Baba Shiv Giri Maharaj?
(*a*) Sarveshwar Mahadeva Temple
(*b*) Narayana Temple
(*c*) Laxmi Narayan Temple
(*d*) Dukh Bhanajaneshwar Temple

330. Who had built the famous 'Sarveshwar Mahadeva Temple' of Kurukshetra?
(*a*) Baba Shravan Nath (*b*) Baba Shiva Giri
(*c*) Baba Tarak Nath (*d*) Shri Jugal Kishore Birla

331. Birla Temple situated by the Kurukshetra-Pehova road was built by Shri Jugal Kishore Birla in
(*a*) 1950 (*b*) 1955
(*c*) 1965 (*d*) 1978

332. "Gyarah Rudri Shiva Temple" is situated in which of the following towns of Haryana?
(*a*) Jind (*b*) Panipat
(*c*) Hissar (*d*) Kaithal

333. Maratha General Mangal Raghu Nath Ji had built which of the following temples after the third battle of Panipat?
(*a*) Shiva Temple of Devi Pond
(*b*) Hanuman Temple
(*c*) Devi Temple
(*d*) Rudra Temple

334. In Amin village of Kurukshetra district which one of the following ancient temples is situated?
(*a*) Panchvati Temple
(*b*) Shiva Temple
(*c*) Temple of Aditi
(*d*) Temple of Dauji

335. In Vanchari village situated at a distance of 55 km. from Faridabad, which of the following ancient temples is situated?
(*a*) Temple of Dauji
(*b*) Temple of Aditi
(*c*) Panchvati Temple
(*d*) Temple of Chamunda Devi

336. The famous ancient temple of Mata Sheetala Devi is situated at which of the following places in Haryana?
(*a*) Rewari (*b*) Gurugram
(*c*) Narnaul (*d*) Jind

337. Temple of Mata Sheetala Devi situated at Gurugram was built by Maharaja of Bharatpur in
(*a*) 1620 (*b*) 1645
(*c*) 1648 (*d*) 1650

338. The ancient Shiva temple where the grave of Baba Thandipuri is also located, is situated at which of the following places?
(*a*) Pundrik Tirth (*b*) Gurugram
(*c*) Hissar (*d*) Rohtak

339. Which of the following ancient temples is situated at village Beri of district Jhajjar in Haryana?
(*a*) Old Shiva-Parvati Temple
(*b*) Temple of Mata Sheetala Devi
(*c*) Lal Rudhmal Temple
(*d*) Temple of Dauji

340. The height of the Shivalaya located in Rudhmal temple at village Beri in district Jhajjar of Haryana is
(*a*) 116 ft. (*b*) 122 ft.
(*c*) 132 ft. (*d*) 140 ft.

341. The Shivalaya located in Rudhmal temple at village Beri in district Jhajjar of Haryana was built in
(*a*) 1842 (*b*) 1850
(*c*) 1892 (*d*) 1899

342. The Shivalaya located in Rudhmal temple at village Beri in district Jhajjar was resurrected for the first time in
(*a*) 1943 (*b*) 1945
(*c*) 1950 (*d*) 1953

343. The temple of Chamunda Devi situated at Narnaul was built and resurrected by
(*a*) Raja Parikshit (*b*) Raja Dilip
(*c*) Raja Noorkaran (*d*) Pandavas

344. Chisti sect was established in Haryana by
(*a*) Boo Alishah Kalandar
(*b*) Shekh Farid (Farid-ud-din-Shakarganj)
(*c*) Altaf Hussain
(*d*) Ibrahim Abidullah

345. The eminent saint of Chisti sect Boo Alishah Kalandar made which of the following places the centre of his meditation?
(*a*) Panipat (*b*) Rohtak
(*c*) Sonepat (*d*) Gurugram

346. Dargah of Sufi Saint Altaf Hussain Hali is situated at which of the following places in Haryana?
(*a*) Jhajjhar (*b*) Rewari
(*c*) Panipat (*d*) Rohtak

347. Regarding which of the following Dargahs (tombs of saints which are pilgrimage spots and places of worship) situated at Panipat is believed that bowing heads by believers accomplishes their attending in celebration of Urs of Khwaza of Ajmer?
(*a*) Dargah of Khwaza Shamshuddin Makhdoom Zalaluddin
(*b*) Dargah of Shekh Usman Jindapeer
(*c*) Dargah of Gauss Alishah
(*d*) Dargah of Boo Alishah Kalandar

348. Dargah of which of the following famous saints is situated at village Dharsun which is at a distance of about 10 kms from Narnaul?
(*a*) Hazarat Shah Kalmuddin Hamzapeer Hussain
(*b*) Meer Shah (Baba Shah Khan)
(*c*) Sheikh Nijamuddin
(*d*) Sheikh Junaid

349. At Fatehabad in the courtyard of the tomb of which of the following Sufi saints inscription of Mughal emperor Humayun is engraved on a stone?
(*a*) Mir Taki Khan
(*b*) Mir Junaidi
(*c*) Sheikh Nizamuddin
(*d*) Mir Shah (Baba Shah Khan)

350. Which of the following tombs situated in Haryana has been declared a monument of National importance under the Archaeological Site and Remnant Act, 1958?
(*a*) Sheikh Chehli
(*b*) Boo Alishah Kalandar
(*c*) Sheikh Farid (Farid-ud-din-Shakarganj)
(*d*) Peer Jamal

351. Tomb of Baba Shah Kamal is situated at which of the following places in Haryana?
(*a*) Gohan (*b*) Fatehabad
(*c*) Kaithal (*d*) Rohtak

352. At which one of the following places in the state, tombs of four Sufi-saints (Kutub Sheikh Jamaluddin Ahmad, Kutub Maulana, Basohddin Sufi Qutubuddin Mannawar, Qutub Nuruddin) are located?
(*a*) Karnal (*b*) Hissar
(*c*) Palwal (*d*) Hansi

353. The tomb of who of the following Sufi-saints is situated between Shahabad and Ambala where watch is offered after a desire is fulfilled?
(*a*) Peer Nagauji (*b*) Hamja Peer
(*c*) Peer Naugaja (*d*) Ibrahim Abidullah

354. Which of the following mosques in Rohtak which was previously a temple was turned into a mosque during the reign of Aurangzeb?
(*a*) Qazi Ki Masjid (*b*) Dini Masjid
(*c*) Lal Masjid (*d*) None of these

355. The Lal Masjid situated in Rohtak was built by famous trader Haji Aashiq Ali in
(*a*) 1930 (*b*) 1931
(*c*) 1935 (*d*) 1939

356. Mosque at Sarai Alawardi village in district Gurugram was built during the reign of
(*a*) Babur (*b*) Jahangir
(*c*) Shahjahan (*d*) Alauddin Khilji

357. Which of the following ancient historical Mosques is situated at village Dujana, situated at a distance of 22 km by Jhajjhar road from Rohtak?
(*a*) Lal Masjid (*b*) Qaji Ki Masjid
(*c*) Karim Ji Ki Masjid (*d*) Jama Masjid

358. The famous historic Lal Masjid at Rewari was built during the reign of which of the following Mughal Emperors?
(*a*) Babur (*b*) Humayun
(*c*) Akbar (*d*) Jahangir

359. In addition to Narnaul, Panipat and Ambala, Sufi-saints made which of the following towns of Haryana as a centre of Sufi-sect?
(*a*) Kaithal (*b*) Thanesar
(*c*) Karnal (*d*) Sonepat

360. The majority of Sufi-saints who lived in Haryana for propagating sufi cult belonged to which of the following sects?
(*a*) Chisti (*b*) Nakshbandi
(*c*) Kadari (*d*) All of the above

361. Tomb of famous Sufi-saint Sheikh Chehli which is called as the Tajmahal of Haryana is situated at
(*a*) Hissar (*b*) Fatehabad
(*c*) Thanesar (*d*) Panipat

362. Tomb of which of the following saints is situated at Kalyana village of Charkhi Dadri district where fair is organised on every Wednesday?
(*a*) Peer Mubarak Shah
(*b*) Sheikh Usman Jindapeer
(*c*) Sheikh Nizamuddin
(*d*) Muhammad Afzal

363. Tomb of Meeran Sahib is situated in which of the following towns of Haryana?
(*a*) Ambala (*b*) Panipat
(*c*) Karnal (*d*) Kaithal

364. Where did Lord Krishna delivered his inspirational messages to Arjuna which have been described in "Gita" as a dialogue between the two?
(*a*) Panipat (*b*) Kurukshetra
(*c*) Hodal (*d*) Thanesar

365. Which of the following towns of Haryana was the capital of Shrikantha Janapada during ancient times?
(*a*) Thanesar (*b*) Chandigarh
(*c*) Rohtak (*d*) Gurugram

366. The detailed description of which of the following ancient cities of Haryana is given in the account presented by Chinese pilgrim Huen Tsang?
(*a*) Rohtak (*b*) Ambala
(*c*) Thaneshwar (*d*) Bhiwani

367. Thaneshwar City of this state was at the pinnacle of its glory during
(*a*) Vardhan period (*b*) Gupta period
(*c*) Sunga period (*d*) Maurya period

368. The famous battle between the armies of Babur and Ibrahim Lodi in 1526 was fought at which of the following places in Haryana?
(*a*) Jhajjhar (*b*) Kurukshetra
(*c*) Rohtak (*d*) Panipat

369. Panipat town was given the status of District on
(*a*) 1 January, 1988 (*b*) 1 November, 1989
(*c*) 1 December, 1990 (*d*) 17 June, 1980

370. Rewari district was formed on
(*a*) 10 June, 1977 (*b*) 5 February, 1979
(*c*) 1 November, 1989 (*d*) 17 June, 1980

371. Hissar is the birth place of which of the following famous kings?
(*a*) Shershah Suri (*b*) Akbar
(*c*) Muhammad Tughlaq (*d*) Feroz Tughlaq

372. In which of the following towns has the largest cattle farm of Haryana?
(*a*) Narnaul (*b*) Hissar
(*c*) Panipat (*d*) Karnal

373. In 1354, who of the following famous ruler of the medieval India built the town of Hissar as a fort?
(*a*) Muhammad Tughlaq (*b*) Balban
(*c*) Feroz Tughlaq (*d*) Alauddin Khilji

374. During ancient times, Mahendragarh town of this state was known as
(*a*) Janauva (*b*) Karnpur
(*c*) Mahipgarh (*d*) Kanaud

375. Name the last king of Ballabhgarh who died as a martyr during freedom struggle of 1857.
(*a*) Nahar Singh (*b*) Vijay Singh
(*c*) Pratap Singh (*d*) Mahar Singh

376. Ballabhgarh town is included in which of the following districts of Haryana?
(*a*) Rohtak (*b*) Faridabad
(*c*) Gurugram (*d*) Karnal

377. Narwana Tehsil is situated in which of the following Districts of the state?
(*a*) Sirsa (*b*) Bhiwani
(*c*) Jind (*d*) Fatehabad

378. Grave of the famous Sultana Raziya of Ghulam dynasty is located in which of the following districts of the state?
(*a*) Kaithal (*b*) Gurugram
(*c*) Ambala (*d*) Faridabad

379. Which of the following towns of Haryana is termed as 'a big bowl of paddy' and 'Paris of Haryana'?
(*a*) Rohtak (*b*) Sonepat
(*c*) Faridabad (*d*) Karnal

380. In 1607, Faridabad town was built by
(*a*) Feroz Shah (*b*) Mubarakshah
(*c*) Baba Farid (*d*) Mansub Ali

381. During the Mahabharata period Sirsa was known as
(*a*) Shishira (*b*) Shairishkam
(*c*) Saurish (*d*) Sirisa

382. During ancient times, Gohana town of the state was known as
(*a*) Gawabh Bhawana (*b*) Gadhana
(*c*) Gapat Zamana (*d*) None of these

383. During ancient times, Bahadurgarh town of the state was known as
(*a*) Bahawalgarh (*b*) Shafirabad
(*c*) Sharfabad (*d*) Balramgarh

384. Britishers confiscated Bahadurgarh from Scindia King and handed it as a Jaghir to the brother of Nawab of Jhajjhar in
(*a*) 1800 AD (*b*) 1801 AD
(*c*) 1805 AD (*d*) 1803 AD

385. Which of the following towns of the state was built by a Rajput named Amba in the 14th century?
(*a*) Jhajjhar (*b*) Rohtak
(*c*) Ambala (*d*) Bhiwani

386. Abdur Rahman Khan who sacrificed his life during freedom struggle, hailed from which of the following towns of Haryana?
(*a*) Kurukshetra (*b*) Jhajjhar
(*c*) Farrukh Nagar (*d*) Rewari

387. Farrukh Nagar was built by which of the following Biloch rulers?
(*a*) Dalel Khan (Faujdar Khan)
(*b*) Shaffuddin Khan
(*c*) Badar Khan
(*d*) Jamaluddin Khan

388. Biloch ruler Dalel Khan (Faujdar Khan) built the town of Farrukh Nagar in the name of which of the following Emperors?
(*a*) Fakhruddin Ahmad (*b*) Farukh Ali
(*c*) Ferozshah Tughlaq (*d*) Farrukh Siyar

389. Great epic Mahabharata was composed by Maharshi Ved Vyas in which of the following towns of Haryana?
(*a*) Panipat (*b*) Rewari
(*c*) Kurukshetra (*d*) Hissar

390. Rise of Vardhan dynasty took place in which of the following towns of Haryana?
(*a*) Thanesar (Sthaneshwar)
(*b*) Rohtak
(*c*) Panipat
(*d*) Kurukshetra

391. In 1556, the famous battle between the forces of Akbar and Hemchandra (Hemu) of Rewari was fought at which of the following places in Haryana?
(*a*) Rewari (*b*) Jind
(*c*) Kurukshetra (*d*) Panipat

392. In 1761 the third battle of Panipat was fought between the forces of
(*a*) Babur and Ibrahim Lodi
(*b*) Akbar and Hemchandra (Hemu)
(*c*) Afghans and Marathas
(*d*) Britishers and Sikhs

393. The town of Panipat was under which of the following districts of Haryana till 31 October, 1989?
(*a*) Rewari (*b*) Ambala
(*c*) Karnal (*d*) Hissar

394. Which of the following districts of the state was included under Gurugram and Mahendragarh districts before 1989?
(*a*) Mahendragarh (*b*) Faridabad
(*c*) Jind (*d*) Rewari

395. Jind was given the status of district in
(*a*) 1966 (*b*) 1972
(*c*) 1968 (*d*) 1975

396. Which of the following districts of Haryana has its headquarters at Narnaul?
(*a*) Hissar (*b*) Faridabad
(*c*) Mahendragarh (*d*) Karnal

397. Who amongst the following did not play for Haryana in Ranji Trophy?
(*a*) Kapil Dev (*b*) Rajinder Goel
(*c*) Sarkar Talwar (*d*) Maninder Singh

398. When Palwal came into existence as the 21st districts of Haryana?
(*a*) 2006 (*b*) 2005
(*c*) 2008 (*d*) 2007

399. During Mahabharat period, which of the following places was given by Raja Yudhishthir to his Guru Dronacharya as a gift?
(*a*) Gurugram village (*b*) Kaithal
(*c*) Hodal (*d*) Sirsa

400. Who was the Collector of Gurugram during the freedom struggle of 1857?
(*a*) Henry (*b*) Sir Helley
(*c*) John Marshall (*d*) Shri Ford

401. In 1858, which of the following districts of Haryana was included in Punjab?
(*a*) Faridabad (*b*) Gurugram
(*c*) Hissar (*d*) Mahendragarh

402. When Faridabad came into existence as the 12th district of Haryana?
(*a*) 15 August, 1970 (*b*) 02 August, 1979
(*c*) 26 January, 1979 (*d*) 8 March, 1982

403. Bahadurgarh town is included in which of the following districts of Haryana?
(*a*) Jhajjar (*b*) Karnal
(*c*) Yamun Nagar (*d*) Faridabad

404. The historical town Gohana is included in which of the following districts of Haryana?
(*a*) Panipat (*b*) Sirsa
(*c*) Sonepat (*d*) Rewari

405. In which year 'Sirsa' became a district?
(*a*) 1980 (*b*) 1975
(*c*) 1990 (*d*) 1995

406. Hodal Sub-division is located in which district of Haryana?
(*a*) Rohtak (*b*) Sonepat
(*c*) Palwal (*d*) Panipat

407. Tosham town of district. Bhiwani was given the status of Sub-Division on
(*a*) 27 April, 1993 (*b*) 10 June, 1995
(*c*) 5 March, 1997 (*d*) 27 April, 1998

408. Which of the following famous temples is situated at historical town "Sadhaura"of district Yamuna Nagar?
(*a*) Manokamna Temple (*b*) Gagarwala Temple
(*c*) Toranwala Temple (*d*) All of these

409. In which of the following historical towns of Yamuna Nagar district, the Gurudwara of Buddhushah is situated which had helped Guru Govind Singh in the battle of Bhagani?
(*a*) Sadhaura (*b*) Radaur
(*c*) Bilaspur (*d*) Chhachhrauli

410. In ancient times Bahadurgarh town of Haryana was called as
(*a*) Charkhabad (*b*) Hasinpur
(*c*) Sharfabad (*d*) Betawabad

411. The historical town of Maham is situated in which of the following districts of the state?
(*a*) Bhiwani (*b*) Rohtak
(*c*) Yamuna Nagar (*d*) Jhajjhar

412. Maham town situated in district Rohtak was rebuilt by a person called Peshora of Kayastha (Baniya) Community in
(*a*) 1266 (*b*) 1295
(*c*) 1298 (*d*) 1299

413. Ailanabad town situated in district Sirsa was earlier known as
(*a*) Ailisabad (*b*) Chavipur
(*c*) Kalisabad (*d*) Khariyal

414. What was the earlier name of the historical town 'Raniyan' situated in district Sirsa?
(*a*) Rajabpur (*b*) Sajupur
(*c*) Rajipur (*d*) Ratipur

415. Which of the following towns situated in district Ambala was built by the King of Sirmour (Himachal Pradesh) Raja Laxmi Narayan?
(*a*) Barara (*b*) Mulana
(*c*) Narayangarh (*d*) Raipur Rani

416. By excavations done in which of the following historical towns of Sonepat district, earthen utensils belonging to Mahabharata period have been found?
(*a*) Rai (*b*) Kheri Gujjar
(*c*) Gankaur (*d*) Gohana

417. Mythological village Aadi Badri is situated in which of the following districts of Haryana?
(*a*) Yamuna Nagar (*b*) Bhiwani
(*c*) Sirsa (*d*) Rewari

418. Which of the following historical villages situated in district Yamuna Nagar is associated with King Santanu of the Mahabharata period?
(*a*) Chhachhrauli (*b*) Aadi Badri
(*c*) Basantar (*d*) None of these

419. At which of the following places Mazaar of Altaf Hussain Hali is located?
(*a*) Sonepat (*b*) Gurugram
(*c*) Panipat (*d*) Jind

420. Which of the following places was made a powerful centre of Afghan chiefs by Ahmadshah Abdali before the third battle of Panipat?
(*a*) Gharauda (*b*) Nilpe Khedi
(*c*) Asangh (*d*) Kunjpura

ANSWERS

1	**2**	**3**	**4**	**5**	**6**	**7**	**8**	**9**	**10**
(*d*)	(*a*)	(*b*)	(*c*)	(*a*)	(*d*)	(*b*)	(*a*)	(*c*)	(*b*)
11	**12**	**13**	**14**	**15**	**16**	**17**	**18**	**19**	**20**
(*d*)	(*d*)	(*a*)	(*c*)	(*d*)	(*a*)	(*c*)	(*b*)	(*d*)	(*a*)
21	**22**	**23**	**24**	**25**	**26**	**27**	**28**	**29**	**30**
(*d*)	(*a*)	(*c*)	(*b*)	(*a*)	(*d*)	(*d*)	(*a*)	(*c*)	(*c*)
31	**32**	**33**	**34**	**35**	**36**	**37**	**38**	**39**	**40**
(*d*)	(*c*)	(*a*)	(*b*)	(*d*)	(*d*)	(*a*)	(*c*)	(*b*)	(*c*)
41	**42**	**43**	**44**	**45**	**46**	**47**	**48**	**49**	**50**
(*d*)	(*a*)	(*c*)	(*b*)	(*a*)	(*c*)	(*d*)	(*a*)	(*c*)	(*c*)
51	**52**	**53**	**54**	**55**	**56**	**57**	**58**	**59**	**60**
(*a*)	(*c*)	(*a*)	(*b*)	(*d*)	(*b*)	(*a*)	(*c*)	(*b*)	(*d*)
61	**62**	**63**	**64**	**65**	**66**	**67**	**68**	**69**	**70**
(*d*)	(*a*)	(*c*)	(*a*)	(*b*)	(*a*)	(*a*)	(*a*)	(*b*)	(*d*)
71	**72**	**73**	**74**	**75**	**76**	**77**	**78**	**79**	**80**
(*c*)	(*a*)	(*c*)	(*b*)	(*d*)	(*c*)	(*a*)	(*c*)	(*b*)	(*d*)
81	**82**	**83**	**84**	**85**	**86**	**87**	**88**	**89**	**90**
(*b*)	(*a*)	(*d*)	(*a*)	(*c*)	(*b*)	(*d*)	(*c*)	(*a*)	(*d*)
91	**92**	**93**	**94**	**95**	**96**	**97**	**98**	**99**	**100**
(*d*)	(*a*)	(*d*)	(*a*)	(*c*)	(*b*)	(*d*)	(*a*)	(*c*)	(*b*)
101	**102**	**103**	**104**	**105**	**106**	**107**	**108**	**109**	**110**
(*d*)	(*a*)	(*a*)	(*d*)	(*a*)	(*b*)	(*c*)	(*b*)	(*d*)	(*a*)
111	**112**	**113**	**114**	**115**	**116**	**117**	**118**	**119**	**120**
(*c*)	(*b*)	(*c*)	(*a*)	(*d*)	(*b*)	(*d*)	(*c*)	(*a*)	(*b*)
121	**122**	**123**	**124**	**125**	**126**	**127**	**128**	**129**	**130**
(*c*)	(*b*)	(*c*)	(*b*)	(*d*)	(*d*)	(*a*)	(*c*)	(*d*)	(*b*)
131	**132**	**133**	**134**	**135**	**136**	**137**	**138**	**139**	**140**
(*a*)	(*c*)	(*a*)	(*b*)	(*a*)	(*b*)	(*a*)	(*d*)	(*c*)	(*b*)
141	**142**	**143**	**144**	**145**	**146**	**147**	**148**	**149**	**150**
(*a*)	(*c*)	(*b*)	(*a*)	(*d*)	(*a*)	(*c*)	(*d*)	(*c*)	(*a*)
151	**152**	**153**	**154**	**155**	**156**	**157**	**158**	**159**	**160**
(*d*)	(*c*)	(*a*)	(*a*)	(*b*)	(*a*)	(*d*)	(*b*)	(*b*)	(*d*)
161	**162**	**163**	**164**	**165**	**166**	**167**	**168**	**169**	**170**
(*a*)	(*c*)	(*a*)	(*c*)	(*b*)	(*d*)	(*c*)	(*a*)	(*b*)	(*a*)

171	**172**	**173**	**174**	**175**	**176**	**177**	**178**	**179**	**180**
(*b*)	(*d*)	(*a*)	(*a*)	(*d*)	(*b*)	(*a*)	(*b*)	(*b*)	(*c*)
181	**182**	**183**	**184**	**185**	**186**	**187**	**188**	**189**	**190**
(*a*)	(*a*)	(*c*)	(*d*)	(*b*)	(*c*)	(*d*)	(*a*)	(*c*)	(*d*)
191	**192**	**193**	**194**	**195**	**196**	**197**	**198**	**199**	**200**
(*d*)	(*a*)	(*b*)	(*b*)	(*a*)	(*c*)	(*a*)	(*d*)	(*b*)	(*c*)
201	**202**	**203**	**204**	**205**	**206**	**207**	**208**	**209**	**210**
(*d*)	(*c*)	(*a*)	(*d*)	(*a*)	(*d*)	(*c*)	(*b*)	(*b*)	(*a*)
211	**212**	**213**	**214**	**215**	**216**	**217**	**218**	**219**	**220**
(*a*)	(*a*)	(*c*)	(*d*)	(*b*)	(*a*)	(*a*)	(*b*)	(*d*)	(*a*)
221	**222**	**223**	**224**	**225**	**226**	**227**	**228**	**229**	**230**
(*b*)	(*c*)	(*b*)	(*d*)	(*a*)	(*c*)	(*a*)	(*c*)	(*b*)	(*a*)
231	**232**	**233**	**234**	**235**	**236**	**237**	**238**	**239**	**240**
(*d*)	(*a*)	(*b*)	(*a*)	(*d*)	(*d*)	(*a*)	(*c*)	(*b*)	(*d*)
241	**242**	**243**	**244**	**245**	**246**	**247**	**248**	**249**	**250**
(*d*)	(*a*)	(*c*)	(*b*)	(*a*)	(*a*)	(*c*)	(*b*)	(*a*)	(*a*)
251	**252**	**253**	**254**	**255**	**256**	**257**	**258**	**259**	**260**
(*b*)	(*a*)	(*c*)	(*b*)	(*d*)	(*c*)	(*d*)	(*d*)	(*c*)	(*a*)
261	**262**	**263**	**264**	**265**	**266**	**267**	**268**	**269**	**270**
(*b*)	(*d*)	(*c*)	(*a*)	(*b*)	(*c*)	(*a*)	(*b*)	(*a*)	(*c*)
271	**272**	**273**	**274**	**275**	**276**	**277**	**278**	**279**	**280**
(*b*)	(*b*)	(*d*)	(*c*)	(*d*)	(*d*)	(*a*)	(*a*)	(*b*)	(*a*)
281	**282**	**283**	**284**	**285**	**286**	**287**	**288**	**289**	**290**
(*c*)	(*b*)	(*a*)	(*c*)	(*b*)	(*d*)	(*c*)	(*c*)	(*a*)	(*c*)
291	**292**	**293**	**294**	**295**	**296**	**297**	**298**	**299**	**300**
(*b*)	(*a*)	(*a*)	(*b*)	(*d*)	(*a*)	(*c*)	(*d*)	(*a*)	(*b*)
301	**302**	**303**	**304**	**305**	**306**	**307**	**308**	**309**	**310**
(*a*)	(*c*)	(*d*)	(*a*)	(*c*)	(*b*)	(*c*)	(*a*)	(*c*)	(*d*)
311	**312**	**313**	**314**	**315**	**316**	**317**	**318**	**319**	**320**
(*a*)	(*b*)	(*a*)	(*b*)	(*c*)	(*d*)	(*a*)	(*c*)	(*b*)	(*a*)
321	**322**	**323**	**324**	**325**	**326**	**327**	**328**	**329**	**330**
(*c*)	(*d*)	(*a*)	(*a*)	(*d*)	(*a*)	(*b*)	(*d*)	(*c*)	(*a*)
331	**332**	**333**	**334**	**335**	**336**	**337**	**338**	**339**	**340**
(*b*)	(*d*)	(*a*)	(*c*)	(*a*)	(*b*)	(*d*)	(*a*)	(*c*)	(*a*)
341	**342**	**343**	**344**	**345**	**346**	**347**	**348**	**349**	**350**
(*c*)	(*d*)	(*c*)	(*b*)	(*a*)	(*c*)	(*d*)	(*a*)	(*d*)	(*a*)
351	**352**	**353**	**354**	**355**	**356**	**357**	**358**	**359**	**360**
(*c*)	(*d*)	(*c*)	(*b*)	(*d*)	(*d*)	(*b*)	(*c*)	(*b*)	(*d*)
361	**362**	**363**	**364**	**365**	**366**	**367**	**368**	**369**	**370**
(*c*)	(*a*)	(*c*)	(*b*)	(*a*)	(*c*)	(*a*)	(*d*)	(*b*)	(*c*)
371	**372**	**373**	**374**	**375**	**376**	**377**	**378**	**379**	**380**
(*a*)	(*b*)	(*c*)	(*d*)	(*a*)	(*b*)	(*c*)	(*a*)	(*d*)	(*c*)
381	**382**	**383**	**384**	**385**	**386**	**387**	**388**	**389**	**390**
(*b*)	(*a*)	(*c*)	(*d*)	(*c*)	(*b*)	(*a*)	(*d*)	(*c*)	(*a*)
391	**392**	**393**	**394**	**395**	**396**	**397**	**398**	**399**	**400**
(*d*)	(*c*)	(*c*)	(*d*)	(*a*)	(*c*)	(*d*)	(*c*)	(*a*)	(*a*)
401	**402**	**403**	**404**	**405**	**406**	**407**	**408**	**409**	**410**
(*b*)	(*b*)	(*a*)	(*c*)	(*b*)	(*c*)	(*a*)	(*d*)	(*a*)	(*c*)
411	**412**	**413**	**414**	**415**	**416**	**417**	**418**	**419**	**420**
(*b*)	(*a*)	(*d*)	(*a*)	(*c*)	(*b*)	(*a*)	(*c*)	(*c*)	(*d*)

❑ ❑ ❑